FROM JACK JOHNSON TO LEBRON JAMES

From **JACK JOHNSON** to **LEBRON JAMES**

SPORTS, MEDIA, AND THE COLOR LINE

Edited by Chris Lamb

UNIVERSITY OF NEBRASKA PRESS | LINCOLN AND LONDON

Source acknowledgments for the use of copyrighted
material appear on pages 603–6, which
constitute an extension of the copyright page.

Library of Congress Cataloging-in-Publication Data

From Jack Johnson to Lebron James: sports, media,
and the color line / edited by Chris Lamb.
pages   cm
Includes bibliographical references and index.
ISBN 978-0-8032-7680-2 (paperback: alk. paper)
ISBN 978-0-8032-8524-8 (epub)
ISBN 978-0-8032-8525-5 (mobi)
ISBN 978-0-8032-8526-2 (pdf)
1. Mass media and sports—United States. 2. Sports—
Social aspects—United States. 3. African American
athletes. 4. Discrimination in sports—United States.
5. Racism in sports—United States. 6. Racism in
mass media—United States. I. Lamb, Chris, 1958–
GV742.F76 2016
070.4'49796—dc23
2015028762

Set in Lyon by M. Scheer.
Designed by N. Putens.

CONTENTS

List of Tables.. ix

Introduction 1
CHRIS LAMB

1. Framing White Hopes: The Press, Social Drama,
   and the Era of Jack Johnson, 1908–1915 19
   PHILLIP J. HUTCHISON

2. Jesse Owens, a Black Pearl amidst an Ocean of Fury: A Case
   Study of Press Coverage of the 1936 Berlin Olympic Games........52
   PAMELA C. LAUCELLA

3. Multifarious Hero: Joe Louis, American Society, and
   Race Relations during World Crisis, 1935–1945 86
   DOMINIC J. CAPECI JR. AND MARTHA WILKERSON

4. Outside the Pale: The Exclusion of Blacks from the
   National Football League, 1934–1946 117
   THOMAS G. SMITH

5. Democracy on the Field: The Black Press
   Takes On White Baseball 148
   CHRIS LAMB AND GLEN L. BLESKE

6. A Nod from Destiny: How Sportswriters for White and
   African American Newspapers Covered Kenny Washington's
   Entry into the National Football League 170
   RONALD BISHOP

7. Jackie Robinson and the American Mind:
   Journalistic Perceptions of the Reintegration of Baseball 199
   WILLIAM SIMONS

8. "This Is It!" The Public Relations Campaign Waged by
   Wendell Smith and Jackie Robinson to Cast Robinson's
   First Season as an Unqualified Success............................237
   BRIAN CARROLL

9. Integrating New Year's Day: The Racial Politics of
   College Bowl Games in the American South 267
   CHARLES H. MARTIN

10. Main Bout, Inc., Black Economic Power, and Professional
    Boxing: The Canceled Muhammad Ali–Ernie Terrell Fight........293
    MICHAEL EZRA

11. A "Race" for Equality: Print Media Coverage of the 1968
    Olympic Protest by Tommie Smith and John Carlos...............332
    JASON PETERSON

12. *Sports Illustrated*'s African American Athlete
    Series as Socially Responsible Journalism 357
    REED SMITH

13. Rebellion in the Kingdom of Swat: Sportswriters,
    African American Athletes, and Coverage of Curt Flood's
    Lawsuit against Major League Baseball...........................383
    WILLIAM GILLIS

14. Chasing Babe Ruth: An Analysis of Newspaper Coverage of
    Hank Aaron's Pursuit of the Career Home Run Record 417
    MAUREEN SMITH

15. Arthur Ashe: An Analysis of Newspaper Journalists'
    Coverage of USA *Today*'s Outing..................................442
    PAMELA C. LAUCELLA

16. Michael Jordan's Family Values: Marketing, Meaning, and Post-Reagan America...468
  MARY G. MCDONALD

17. Rush Limbaugh, Donovan McNabb, and "a Little Social Concern": Reflections on the Problems of Whiteness in Contemporary American Sport 501
  DOUGLAS HARTMANN

18. I'm the King of the World: Barry Bonds and the Race for the Record...522
  LISA DORIS ALEXANDER

19. Redemption on the Field: Framing, Narrative, and Race in Media Coverage of Michael Vick...........................534
  BRYAN CARR

20. Weighing In on the Coaching Decision: Discussing Sports and Race Online 555
  JIMMY SANDERSON

21. The LeBron James Decision in the Age of Obama 582
  JAMAL L. RATCHFORD

Source Acknowledgments...603

Contributors 607

Index..613

TABLES

1. Positive, Negative, and Neutral Frames in Vick Coverage 544

2. Narrative Frame Types in Media Coverage of Michael Vick 545

3. Sources of Redemption in Vick Coverage 545

4. Positive and Negative Frames across Time 546

5. Narrative Frames across Time 547

6. Sources of Redemption in Vick Coverage 547

7. Commentary Frequencies in Participants
   Responding to espn.com 563

8. Coding Elements for Participant Themes 566

FROM JACK JOHNSON TO LEBRON JAMES

INTRODUCTION

CHRIS LAMB

Jack Johnson wanted to be the heavyweight champion of the world so much that he stalked the reigning champion, Tommy Burns, to England. Johnson taunted Burns in the press. But Burns still refused to fight Johnson. Burns told reporters that he did not like blacks, in general, and Johnson in particular. "All coons are yellow," Burns told reporters and left England for Australia. Johnson followed him. Burns finally agreed to fight Johnson for the then-lordly sum of thirty thousand dollars. When Johnson entered the ring on Christmas night in Sydney, 1908, the crowd met him with calls of "nigger" and "coon." Johnson laughed, bowed, and threw kisses at those who yelled the loudest. Johnson smiled as he waited for Burns to enter the ring. Johnson knew he would not have to wait much longer to claim the title that should have been his long ago. Twenty thousand spectators were in the stands, including novelist Jack London, who reported on the fight for the *New York Herald*. In his story about the fight, London said, "There was no fight." Johnson dominated Burns. It was not enough for Johnson to defeat Burns; he humiliated him. "Poor, poor, Tommy," Johnson mocked the champion in the ring, "Who taught you to hit? Your mother? You a woman?"

In his biography of Johnson, *Papa Jack: Jack Johnson and the Era of White Hopes*, Randy Roberts wrote that the boxer may have become heavyweight champion, but he was still a black man—and, as such, was expected to be deferential to whites, even to those who were his inferiors, in and out of the ring. In his defense of his title, Johnson humiliated his white challengers and then sneered contemptuously at their battered bodies as they lay crumpled on the canvas. He laughed at the white spectators who—from their safety of their seats—called him "nigger" and "coon." It gave him joy to know how white sportswriters hated having to write that he had won another fight against another white hope. "Undoubtedly he believed the title of world champion set him apart from others of his race. And in this he was right. He would never be viewed as just another black boxer," Roberts wrote. "But he was wrong in his assumption that the crown carried with it some immunity against the dictates of whites and traditions of white society. Now more than ever Johnson was expected to conform. And now more than ever Johnson felt he did not have to. The collision course was set."

Nothing is more threatening to white supremacy than blacks who do not accept "their place." And Jack Johnson did not accept his place. Johnson was, as Muhammad Ali once said of himself, "a bad man." Johnson was, in the language of his day, "a bad nigger," someone who cared nothing about what white America thought about him. He flamboyantly confronted the social mores of the day by humiliating white opponents, by driving expensive cars, by wearing expensive clothes, and by dating white women, and, in particular, white prostitutes. With his victory, he mocked the principle of white supremacy and the notion of "separate but equal," which had been sanctioned by the U.S. Supreme Court in *Plessy v. Ferguson* a little more than a decade before he won the heavyweight championship.

Johnson's victory over Burns struck fear among American whites—in no small part because he had defeated a white man in the manliest of sports. But Johnson's victory had not been his alone. Black Americans saw it as their victory. A growing number of blacks refused to accept their place. They walked taller among whites and refused to accept inferior status. In Chicago, the Manassas Club, an organization of wealthy blacks with white wives, hired white waiters to serve them food and drinks at a banquet to celebrate Johnson's triumph. "Johnson's victory demonstrates the physical superiority of the black over the Caucasian," one of the club's members said. "The basis of mental superiority in most men is physical superiority. If the negro can raise his mental standard to his physical eminence, some day he will be a leader among men."

Johnson's victory over Burns was unacceptable to white America—because Johnson refused to demonstrate the proper respect for the law and the custom of American society and because he believed he was equal to (or perhaps superior to) whites. What would happen to America and its democracy if enough other blacks began to believe that they, too, were equal? Johnson needed to be taught a lesson. He needed to be put in his place. Only then would the natural order of things be preserved. White newspapers begged former heavyweight champion James Jeffries to come out of retirement to put Johnson—and, by implication, all other blacks—in their place. By agreeing to fight Johnson, Jeffries became, according to newspapers, the "Hope of the White Race."

Both races understood that the stakes were high for the fight. The *Chicago Defender*, a black newspaper, said Jeffries and Johnson would "settle the mooted question of supremacy." The *Omaha Daily News*, a white newspaper, said that a Jeffries victory would restore superiority to the white race. "If the black man wins," the *New York Times* editorialized before the fight on July 4, 1910, "thousands and thousands of his ignorant brothers will misinterpret his victory." After Johnson defeated Jeffries, the *Los Angeles Times* warned blacks to accept their place in white society or face the consequences. "Do not point your nose too high. Do not swell your chest too much. Do not boast too loudly. Do not be puffed up. Let not your ambitions be inordinate or take a wrong direction. Let no treasured resentments rise up and spill over," the newspaper said. "Remember you have done nothing at all. You are just the same member of society today you were last week. Your place in the world is just what it was. You are on no higher plane, deserve no new consideration, and will get none."

Johnson's triumph ignited a series of bloody confrontations between blacks and whites. When black construction workers celebrated Johnson's victory near the town of Uvaldo, Georgia, whites responded by firing their guns at the blacks. Three were killed and five were injured. As Roberts chronicles in *Papa Jack*, such scenes were repeated throughout the United States. When a black man in Houston celebrated Johnson's win over Jeffries, a white man "slashed his throat from ear to ear." Six blacks were critically injured by a white mob in Roanoke, Virginia; dozens of blacks were attacked by whites in Norfolk, Virginia; and one black was killed and scores injured in New York City. "Johnson was seen as the prototype of the independent black who acted as he pleased and accepted no bar to his conduct," Roberts said. "As such, Johnson was transcended into a racial symbol that threatened America's social order."

If Johnson could triumph over whites, what about other blacks? White America could see the impact that Johnson had on others of his race. Every time Johnson won, he laughed louder and he strutted more arrogantly. Every time he won, other blacks walked taller and demanded to be treated with more respect. It was, therefore, necessary for Johnson to be destroyed. America's whites sought to destroy Johnson with other "white hopes," but Johnson defeated every challenger. He could not be defeated inside the ring so he would have to be destroyed outside the ring. This required the federal government, law enforcement agencies, the court system, the white press, and Johnson himself. He was charged with violating the White Slave Traffic Act—or the Mann Act as it was known—for transporting women across states with the "purpose of prostitution or debauchery, or any other immoral purpose." Johnson's arrest and ultimate conviction were enthusiastically applauded in white newspapers. Black newspapers, however, saw the conviction for what it was: Johnson had committed the grievous sin of triumphing in a white society, of beating the house in a rigged game.

White America's perception of the self-assured black man as uppity remained throughout the decades that followed Jack Johnson. Joe Louis, who would be heavyweight champion in the 1930s and 1940s, would be acceptable toward whites because, according to white America, he knew his place. He could be heavyweight champion without giving any indication he thought he was superior—or even equal—to the white boxer outside the ring. He did not question the social order. Muhammad Ali, by contrast, who won the heavyweight championship in the 1960s, challenged racial attitudes and confronted social injustices in white-dominated

America. Joe Louis was the "right type" of black. He did not challenge racial discrimination—whether as a boxer, as a man, or as an officer in the U.S. Army. Ali, like Johnson, was the "wrong type" of black and paid the price for his insubordination with unrelenting criticism in mainstream newspapers. When Ali refused induction into the armed services, he was stripped of his heavyweight crown and put in his place.

This book, *From Jack Johnson to LeBron James: Sports, Media, and the Color Line*, includes, as the title suggests, a collection of essays on sports, race, and the media from the early twentieth century to the present. Some of the most publicized stories in the campaign for racial equality in the twentieth century happened in sports: the Jack Johnson–James Jeffries fight; Jesse Owens's four gold medals at the 1936 Olympic Games in Berlin; Jackie Robinson and the breaking of baseball's color barrier; the integration of college athletics in the South; Tommie Smith and John Carlos raising their fists on the medal podium at the 1968 Olympics in Mexico City; Curt Flood's legal challenge against Major League Baseball. The essays in this book examine the aforementioned stories and a number of other stories involving athletes who forced the United States and its media to look differently at sports—Joe Louis and Muhammad Ali in boxing; Hank Aaron and Barry Bonds in baseball; Kenny Washington and Michael Vick in football; Michael Jordan and LeBron James in basketball; and Arthur Ashe in tennis.

As the editor of this book, I am interested in examining how these stories were covered (or not covered) in the nation's newspapers. I am interested in identifying the threads common in the reporting of these stories. And finally, I am interested in how these stories reflected what was happening in civil rights elsewhere in the country. The essays in this book are linked by these and other questions: How did the black and white press differ in their reporting of these stories in content and context? Did the press recognize these stories as historically significant? How did sports journalists acknowledge race in their stories? Was integration in sports treated as a part of or as separate from the campaign for racial equality in U.S. society? At what point did the white press modify its approach to covering race in sports and how did it do so?

The essays in this book are organized chronologically to demonstrate how evolving racial attitudes in sports reflected—and often foreshadowed—evolving racial attitudes in the rest of U.S. society. Our understanding of the civil rights movement is often told in terms of bus boycotts, lunch counter sit-ins, freedom riders, and racist southern demagogues. It is told in terms of U.S. Supreme Court decisions, congressional legislation, and emotional speeches outside the Lincoln Memorial.

But one cannot truly appreciate or truly comprehend the story of civil rights in the United States without an appreciation of what was happening in sports in the United States. Sports influenced the racial attitudes of Americans who came to believe that not only should blacks have equality on the playing fields of baseball and football but they should also have equality in jobs, housing, and education. The campaign for racial equality in sports often inspired and foreshadowed the campaign for racial equality in society. Martin Luther King Jr. recognized this. "Back in the days when integration wasn't fashionable," King said of Jackie Robinson, "he underwent the trauma and the humiliation and the loneliness which comes with being a pilgrim walking the lonesome byways toward the high road of Freedom. He was a sit-inner before sit-ins, a freedom rider before freedom rides." In historian Jules Tygiel's landmark book *Baseball's Great Experiment*, which was published in 1983, he wrote that the integration of baseball reflected America as it moved from acceptance of racial bigotry to rejection of it, as it moved from espousing equality to practicing it, and as it moved from legal segregation to integration. "The integration of baseball represented both a symbol of imminent racial challenge and a direct agent of social change," Tygiel wrote.

Tygiel's work had an immediate and profound impact on other writers and scholars. Historian William Simons, in his essay in this book, "Jackie Robinson and the American Mind," called the story of Jackie Robinson and the breaking of baseball's color barrier "the most commented on episode in American race relations of its time." In his 1985 essay, which is reprinted here, Simons captured the importance of the integration of baseball in the struggle for racial equality by casting the story within the context of the American press. The October 23, 1945, signing of Robinson to a contract with the Brooklyn Dodgers received attention in white newspapers but little explanation of its historical, sociological, or cultural value. Simons wrote that the United States—and perhaps, most importantly, the mainstream press, "had little awareness of the extent and severity of racism in the nation's social fabric." Jackie Robinson changed this. "Robinson's campaign against the color line in 1946–1947," Tygiel said, "captured the imagination of millions of Americans who had previously ignored the nation's racial dilemma."

This book includes two other essays about Jackie Robinson. In one of them, Glen Bleske and I examine Robinson's first spring training as a Minor League prospect with the Montreal Royals in 1946. The press coverage of Robinson's spring training represents the very different perspectives of black and white journalists. The reporting in white newspapers, we wrote, "was limited, both in content and context, by a mindset that kept white reporters, their newspapers, and their readers from appreciating the historical significance and meaning of the story." To black sportswriters, however, we added, "the story symbolized the hopes and dreams of integration, not merely on a ballfield but in society."

Brian Carroll contributes the other essay on Robinson, which examines the involvement of Wendell Smith, the influential sports editor of the black newspaper the *Pittsburgh Courier*, who, beginning in the late 1930s, became the journalist most associated with the campaign to integrate baseball. Smith became Robinson's friend, confidant, ghostwriter, and biographer. Smith described himself as "Robinson's Boswell." Carroll's essay analyzes the columns that Robinson wrote for the *Courier* during his rookie year with the Dodgers in 1947. The columns, which were ghostwritten by Smith, purposely constructed an image of Robinson that revealed little of the unrelenting pressure faced by the ballplayer. Instead, Robinson's column perpetuated the image created by white sportswriters that he was the "right type" of black man: humble, nonconfrontational. "In Smith's and Robinson's columns," Carroll wrote, "the famously proud player comes off as unfazed by his victimization, the insults and isolation bouncing off like bullets shot at Superman. . . . Robinson's 'aw shucks, everything is swell' serenity proved merely an illusion, however, or a carefully crafted façade to reduce potential causes—real or perceived—of failure, foment, or bad publicity."

Black sportswriters, including Smith, Sam Lacy, Joe Bostic, and others, framed the campaign to end segregation in baseball in terms of democracy and equal opportunity. World War II revealed the racial hypocrisy in the United States, where the country went to war to fight racism in Europe while practicing racial discrimination against its black soldiers and civilians and did nothing to end the racism on U.S. soil. The story of the desegregation of baseball became an important part of the larger narrative of the campaign for racial equality following World War II. To black America, if there could be racial equality in baseball, there could be racial equality elsewhere in society. To black America, the signing of Robinson reached far beyond the white lines of baseball to the white lines of American society. "Coming at the end of a war that encouraged Americans to define themselves by a liberalism not found in Germany," William Simons wrote, "the announcement that Robinson would become the first black to participate in Organized Baseball since the late nineteenth century generated extensive public discussion about consensus, conflict, equality, liberty, opportunity, prejudice, democracy, and national character."

Black journalists and their readers had engaged in these discussions for more than a century before the signing of Robinson—ever since the first issue of *Freedom's Journal*, the first black newspaper, was published in 1827. Black newspapers chronicled the acts of injustice, discrimination, and intimidation faced by black Americans. But little of this found its way into the white newspapers nor, thus, into white society. In their Pulitzer Prize–winning book, *The Race Beat*, Eugene Roberts and Hank Klibanoff said that calls for that racial equality among black civil rights figures and their white supporters failed to generate traction in the decades before 1950 because the white, mainstream newspapers paid little attention to what sociologist Gunnar Myrdal called America's "racial dilemma." As long as white newspapers ignored the "racial dilemma," so would legislators, judges, and law enforcement agencies. In my book *Conspiracy of Silence: Sportswriters and the Long Campaign to Desegregate Baseball*, I wrote that the color line could not have existed as long as it did in baseball without the aid and comfort of the nation's white mainstream press, specifically white mainstream sportswriters, who participated in what black sportswriter Joe Bostic of the *People's Voice* called a "conspiracy of silence."

White Americans accepted what they heard about the inferiority of blacks, in part because of what Myrdal called "the convenience of ignorance." They knew little about most of black America and its doctors, lawyers, musicians, politicians, and business leaders because white newspapers ignored what happened in black communities. White sports fans, however, knew the names of great black athletes because in sports such as boxing, college football, and track and field, blacks competed against whites, and, thus, white sportswriters witnessed how blacks were the equals of—and often superior to—white athletes. White sportswriters extolled the successes of black athletes—providing they were the right type—without mentioning race or the existence of a color line that prohibited most blacks from competing in professional sports.

When white sportswriters wrote about black athletes, they often described the athletes in terms of racial epithets and racist stereotypes. For instance, Westbrook Pegler referred to black sprinters as "African savages" and called Joe Louis "the colored boy" and "a cotton-field Negro." Paul Gallico wrote that Louis "lives like an animal, fights like an animal, has all the cruelty and ferocity of a wild thing." Bill Corum wrote the following about Louis: "He's a big, superbly built Negro youth who was born to listen to jazz music, eat a lot of fried chicken, play ball with the gang on the corner, and never do a lick of heavy work he could escape." The southern-born Grantland Rice called boxer Jack Johnson "The Smoke" and "The Chocolate Champ" and in private conversations referred to Owens and later Jackie Robinson as "niggers." Furthermore, Rice, like other sportswriters, denigrated the success of black athletes by saying that their skill was "a matter of instinct" and not of hard work, as was the case with white athletes.

Brian Carroll, in his book *When to Stop the Cheering? The Black Press, the Black Community, and the Integration of Professional Baseball,* wrote that the story of the color line in sports "offers an opportunity to examine the ways in which the issues of race, segregation, and racial equality were covered by the press, as well as how they were not covered." The objective of this book is to chronicle the story of race and sports from Jack Johnson to the present by examining how racial issues were covered in the nation's newspapers. The essays in this book, as I have mentioned earlier, demonstrate how evolving racial attitudes in sports reflected—and often foreshadowed—evolving racial attitudes in the rest of U.S. society. The essays chronicle the decades of whites excluding blacks in most sports. This is followed by a few decades of grudging inclusion, and then, finally, by acceptance. A century after the *Los Angeles Times* warned blacks to know and accept their place, racism no longer presents an impenetrable barrier for black athletes on the playing fields of athletic competition—though racism remains an issue for any minority interested in owning a team, serving in a front-office position, or broadcasting for a team.

A century ago, white America ruined Jack Johnson for practicing self-determination. A half-century ago, white America sent Muhammad Ali to prison for practicing self-determination. In recent years, black athletes, including Michael Jordan and LeBron James, who are subjects of essays in this book, practiced self-determination without being ruined, imprisoned, or ostracized. They became among the best, the highest paid, and the most recognized athletes in the world—in part because of white journalists, white fans, and white society, the same forces that had destroyed Johnson, Ali, and countless other black athletes. While the racism may not be as overt as it once was, we are kidding ourselves if we think it no longer exists. It does. There are still white lines in sports.

This book begins with Phillip Hutchison's essay "Framing White Hopes: The Press, Social Drama, and the Era of Jack Johnson, 1908-1915," which analyzes how the white press reflected and advanced the prevailing racist ideology of white supremacy in its coverage of Johnson by framing Jeffries as a "white hope" and by condemning Johnson as a social deviant and then as a criminal, with the intent of not only destroying the fighter but also marginalizing any black who, as the *Los Angeles Times* said, did not accept his or her inferior status.

In the next essay, "Jesse Owens, a Black Pearl amidst an Ocean of Fury," Pamela Laucella writes that white sportswriters praised Owens for his historic performance at the 1936 Berlin Olympics and how he demonstrated the superiority of American democracy to German fascism. Owens may have been a first-rate athlete and a shining example of American greatness, but this did not mean he was anything better than a third-class athlete once he returned to the United States. As long as Owens understood this, he was accepted. Sportswriters wrote about Owens's skin color but not his race. For instance, Grantland Rice described Owens's performance at the Berlin Olympics as that of "a wild Zulu running amuck."

Joe Louis, who held the heavyweight title longer than anyone else, learned from Jack Johnson's example that he could win all his fights in the ring but still lose his title if he was, in the opinion of mainstream America, the "wrong type" of black. In their essay "Multifarious Hero: Joe Louis, American Society, and Race Relations during World Crisis, 1935–1945," Dominic Capeci Jr. and Martha Wilkerson describe how Louis was warned by his handlers to act humble and avoid politics. "If I ever do anything to disgrace my race," Louis said. "I hope to die."

During the period when Louis held the heavyweight title, he knew that other blacks were denied the opportunity to play professional sports. Organized professional baseball had allowed blacks to play for a brief time in the 1870s and 1880s before owners agreed that no more blacks would be allowed. Professional football also had tolerated blacks during its early years of existence in the 1920s and early 1930s. The National Football League drew its color line after the 1933 season. Thomas Smith's essay "Outside the Pale: The Exclusion of Blacks from the National Football League, 1934–1946" chronicles this period and acknowledges how most white sportswriters went along with racial segregation in professional football. But as Smith importantly points out, not all white sportswriters did. In addition, black sportswriters became increasingly critical of the color ban in professional sports. William Brower wrote that there were "no arresting or rational excuses for professional football to follow the dubious precedent set by professional baseball."

This period reflected the growing sense of protest among blacks—and a number of whites—in the United States that racism ran contradictory to the country's democratic principles.

While Branch Rickey broke baseball's color barrier motivated by both faith and economics, the color line in professional football ended when black journalists objected to the use of the Los Angeles coliseum if the city's team, the Rams, discriminated against black players. On March 21, 1946, the Rams signed Kenny Washington, who had been an All-American halfback in the same UCLA backfield as Jackie Robinson.

Ron Bishop's essay "A Nod from Destiny: How Sportswriters for White and African American Newspapers Covered Kenny Washington's Entry into the National Football League" examines the desegregation of professional football. The signing of Washington received far less publicity than the Brooklyn Dodgers' announcement that it had signed Robinson, which came five months earlier. Baseball also was far more popular than football. "Convincing the Rams to sign Washington was part of a well-orchestrated campaign by these journalists to reintegrate professional football," Bishop writes. "They were just as zealous in their efforts to push Washington's signing as they and their colleagues were in pushing Branch Rickey to sign Jackie Robinson."

Jackie Robinson and Kenny Washington were among the many blacks who played college football. Although tolerated, they faced bigotry from opposing players and fans. In the segregated South, colleges and universities often refused to play against other schools with black players. Charles Martin's essay "Integrating New Year's Day: The Racial Politics of College Bowl Games in the American South" reveals how southern schools modified their segregationist policies to play in or host financially profitable New Year's Day bowl games. It is worth noting that integration often became acceptable in sports before it was acceptable for the rest of society. "Integrated bowl contests provided an important precedent for additional desegregation and reflected a modest liberalization in southern race relations," Martin writes.

The next essays are characterized by the convergence of television, radical politics, and self-empowerment. In his essay "Main Bout, Inc., Black Economic Power, and Professional Boxing: The Canceled Muhammad Ali–Ernie Terrell Fight" Michael Ezra examines how Ali and his corporation, Main Bout, drew the enmity of white sportswriters for wanting to control the promotional rights to the heavyweight champion's fights. According to Ezra, Ali and Main Bout embraced the strategy of black economic empowerment endorsed by Booker T. Washington, Marcus Garvey, and Malcolm X. White sportswriters saw Ali and Main Bout—and their involvement in the Nation of Islam—as a threat to the white power structure. This suspicion intensified when Ali refused induction into the U.S. Army because of his opposition to the Vietnam War on religious and political grounds. In 1967, Ali was forced to surrender his heavyweight title and Main Bout went out of business.

During the 1968 Olympic Games in Mexico City, U.S. sprinters Tommie Smith and John Carlos, having won the gold and bronze medals, respectively, in the 200-meter dash, stood on the winners' podium at the medal awards ceremony. Each then raised a fist, covered in a black glove, as a symbol of protest against the treatment of blacks in the United States. White sportswriters and sportscasters responded to the protest with disgust, Jason Peterson writes in his essay "A 'Race' for Equality: Print Media Coverage of the 1968 Olympic Protest by Tommie Smith and John Carlos." Brett Musburger, who was then a sportswriter for the *Chicago American,* said that Smith and Carlos acted like "a pair of dark-skinned storm troopers." Peterson writes that the media response to the protest by Smith and Carlos focused purely on the raising of the fists and "failed to contextualize the political statement behind their act."

William Gillis's essay "Rebellion in the Kingdom of Swat: Sportswriters, African American Athletes, and Coverage of Curt Flood's Lawsuit against Major League Baseball" found that white journalists who condemned the ballplayer also missed the point of the ballplayer's lawsuit. Flood's 1970 court challenge against baseball's player reserve clause was neither the act of an uppity black man nor an act of selfish greed; it had to do with challenging a rule that bound ballplayers to a single team, which could release them, trade them, or pay them whatever they wanted. Flood believed that the reserve clause was tantamount to slavery. Unlike Ali, Smith, and Carlos, Flood received the support of a number of white sportswriters, who, in the matter of a few years, had grown more sensitive to issues of race.

If white sportswriters were any more progressive on racial issues than most of America, perhaps this was a result of both the integration of sports but also the publication of a series of articles in *Sports Illustrated* called "The Black Athlete: A Shameful Story," which is the subject of Reed Smith's essay "*Sports Illustrated*'s African American Athlete Series as Socially Responsible Journalism." As Smith writes, the series was the first of its kind to investigate racial discrimination in sports and criticize the sports establishment for its treatment of black athletes. The series motivated other sports journalists to take a closer look at social issues that had previously been ignored.

Maureen Smith's essay "Chasing Babe Ruth: An Analysis of Newspaper Coverage of Hank Aaron's Pursuit of the Career Home Run Record" presents a striking contrast to the previous essays that compared the press coverage of black and white newspapers on issues of race in sports. First of all, black newspapers were far less effusive in their praise of Aaron's feat than they had been of the signing of Robinson. Second, white sportswriters were more vocal about Aaron's feat than they had been of the signing of Robinson. The breaking of Babe Ruth's record was rightly seen as less racially significant than the breaking of baseball's color line. But this is not to suggest that Aaron was playing in a postracial world. Black newspapers recognized how far baseball had come since Jackie Robinson but that the shadow of Jim Crow still hung over the sport. An editorial in the *Washington Afro-American* acknowledged that Aaron received death threats. Aaron's "crime" was not that "he threatens to destroy a white legend. Rather, it is that he is black and threatens to destroy a white legend."

In her essay, Smith recommends that scholars compare the coverage of Aaron's pursuit of Ruth's career home run record with that of Barry Bonds's pursuit of Aaron's home run record in 2007. Lisa Alexander does this in her essay "I'm the King of the World: Barry Bonds and the Race for the Record," which examines the presence of race in the media coverage of Bonds's attempt to surpass Aaron's record. What could have been a period of celebration for Bonds was instead a period of invective because of the widely held—but not proven—suspicion that the player used performance-enhancing drugs. In addition, Bonds was widely viewed by sports journalists as, in the words of one sportswriter, "cold, angry, condescending." Bonds was not the humble Aaron. Alexander raises the possibility that Bonds's race played a part in how he was covered during his pursuit of the record. Sportswriters and fans must be willing to admit the possibility that race plays a part in how athletes are perceived. Race permeates every aspect of U.S. history, institutions, politics, economy, and culture, she says.

Like Muhammad Ali, tennis great Arthur Ashe became involved in civil rights, challenging apartheid in South Africa and advocating for racial equality in the United States. To white America, Ali was loud, brash, and arrogant while Ashe was quiet, thoughtful, and dignified. In April 1992, the newspaper USA Today reported that Ashe had HIV (human immuno-deficiency virus), a disease he contracted through a blood transfusion and not through drug use or unprotected sexual contact, as was often the case. Because of the sensitive nature of the disease, Ashe had not gone public with his diagnosis until USA Today reported it. In her essay "Arthur Ashe: An Analysis of Newspaper Journalists' Coverage of USA Today's's Outing," Pamela Laucella wrote that the nation's sportswriters vilified USA Today and portrayed Ashe as a sympathetic victim of media excess. Ashe's race was not emphasized in the coverage. But, according to Laucella, this does not mean that race was not a factor in the coverage.

Early in the 2003 NFL season, conservative commentator Rush Limbaugh, while appearing on ESPN's NFL Countdown, said that Philadelphia Eagles quarterback Donovan McNabb had thus far underperformed but had not been criticized because the league as well as the media believed that a successful black quarterback was in their best interests. Sports journalists condemned Limbaugh and his comments as racist. In "Rush Limbaugh, Donovan McNabb, and 'a Little Social Concern,'" Douglas Hartmann writes that the response from the NFL and from sports journalists gave the impression that they were racially progressive. But this obscured the fact that Limbaugh was primarily criticizing the league and the media, and only secondarily McNabb. To understand the Limbaugh-McNabb episode, one must understand that the polarizing Limbaugh, who had a reputation for making racist comments, was hired to increase ratings for ESPN.

In 2007, Atlanta Falcons quarterback Michael Vick was arrested after police discovered he was running a dogfighting business. After Vick's indictment, he was suspended by NFL commissioner Roger Goodell. Vick was later sentenced to prison. In his essay "Redemption on the Field: Framing, Narrative, and Race in Media Coverage of Michael Vick," Bryan Carr uses framing theory to examine media coverage of Vick's return to the NFL with the Philadelphia Eagles in 2009. Carr found that upon Vick's return he was seen as a redemptive figure, in part because he was perceived in the media as a talented quarterback and not as a talented black quarterback.

Mary McDonald's essay "Michael Jordan's Family Values: Marketing, Meaning, and Post-Reagan America" examines how Jordan transformed greatness on the basketball court into status as a marketing icon. To do this, McDonald writes, Jordan presented himself as masculine and athletic but also as apolitical and as nonthreatening to whites. This required that he be perceived as a family man. The "portrait of Jordan apparently counters and challenges the socially constructed representations of African American men as dangerous, incompetent, and overtly hypersexualized," she writes.

New technologies allow us to express ourselves to large numbers of people without having to go through the filter of traditional media. Because of this, as Jimmy Sanderson writes in his essay "Weighing In on the Coaching Decision: Discussing Sports and Race Online," sports fans can now engage in discussions about race and racism on online discussion forums. In his study of discussions of racism in Division 1 college football hiring practices, Sanderson found that those participating anonymously in online discussions are apt to use more racially charged language than those using traditional media, where commentators understand the risks involved. Such risks are less relevant for those on social media. "In this study, it appeared that discursive anonymity certainly emboldened audience members to voice controversial and problematic beliefs and opinions about the role of racism in sports," Sanderson writes, "and—though sometimes troubling—they nonetheless demonstrated that racism still surfaces throughout sports."

Jamal Ratchford's essay "The LeBron James Decision in the Age of Obama" serves as a fitting work to end this book because it demonstrates the distance we have come since Jack Johnson reigned as heavyweight champion more than a century ago. The essay looks specifically at the "dynamics of race and sport" from Tommie Smith's and John Carlos's silent protest at the 1968 Olympic Games to basketball great LeBron James's decision to leave the Cleveland Cavaliers for the Miami Heat in 2010. By determining his own fate, James no longer had to obey the constructs of the white establishment. But James's decision to leave Cleveland—and, particularly, the way he did so, in an hour-long program on ESPN—resulted in intense criticism of him as a self-obsessed celebrity. Much has happened between Jack Johnson and LeBron James. "In conclusion," Ratchford writes, "the relationship between black athletes and self-determination remains contested in American culture."

1
....

Framing White Hopes
The Press, Social Drama, and the Era
of Jack Johnson, 1908–1915

PHILLIP J. HUTCHISON

The story of African American boxing champion Jack Johnson and white America's seven-year struggle to repudiate him represents an epic American narrative. As the subject of numerous books, research articles, a Broadway play, a major motion picture, and several documentaries, the historical subject matter informs diverse social and historical concerns.[1] Correspondingly, in addressing Johnson's famous 1910 fight with James J. Jeffries, a particularly intense episode within the larger controversy, historian and journalist Lerone Bennett paraphrases veteran *Chicago Tribune* editor Henry Wales by observing, "No other single event dug so deep into world consciousness until the Lindbergh flight seventeen years later. . . . This was the first great modern happening; it was the first great media morality play."[2] Yet despite the far-reaching nature of the subject matter, and despite acknowledgment that the press played a key role in the epic controversy, scholars have yet to truly focus on the situation from the perspective of journalism history.

This situation is mitigated somewhat by the fact that most Johnson histories draw heavily on press reportage as primary source material, and they cite this material liberally. Yet even as these accounts are thorough in many respects, they fail to fully address the centrality of the press in constructing the lengthy controversy involving the boxer.[3] Most notably,

Johnson histories tend to fixate on the boxer in ways that reflect hagiographic qualities; in many ways, they position the boxer as a heroic figure whose epic acts of defiance shaped history as it played out on a social stage.[4] This orientation reflects two problematic trends: It tends to conflate events into a retrospective narrative, an account that loses sight of the open-ended qualities of the situation as it was lived in real time. Moreover, this orientation tacitly portrays the press as a cog that functions within a mechanistic whole, rather than as a historical force in and of itself.[5]

These existing historical narratives, although valuable, need to be complemented by research that more explicitly addresses the manner in which the white press of that era constructed the entire situation as an overarching narrative, one that unfolded in real time for nearly seven years. This essay seeks to better account for the nature of this latter narrative, the vital framing strategy the press employed to render diverse, sometimes discordant, events as socially coherent news for the duration of the controversy. By better accounting for how and why such symbolic strategies cohered socially, this orientation better depicts the ironic and contradictory nature of press reportage of this situation. When events are viewed through the lens of journalism history in this manner, the press more readily appears as an agent of history, a national institution that shaped the episode by defining situations though its reportage and editorial practices.

The Era of White Hopes and Journalism History

The Johnson controversy represents a topically rich and revealing episode in journalism history, one that informs several lines of scholarship that address the form and social impact of the American press at the turn of the twentieth century. Some of these key issues include the construction of race in the press, the transition from the eras of yellow journalism and muckraking to contemporary conceptions of objective journalism, the relationship between the press and the nascent commercial leisure industry, the use of celebrity reporters, the emergence of literary journalism, the affiliations among the press and promotional interests, and assorted institutional insights into reportage and editorial practices during the period.

Naturally, a thorough analysis of press reportage that involves seven years of twists and turns, absurdities and outrages, and paradoxes and contradictions requires a far larger work than a single essay. Yet as a useful entry point for associating these broader issues with journalism history, this essay provides missing perspective that can help historians better interpret the relationship between the press and Johnson. This approach draws heavily on the theories of James W. Carey, who emphasizes the close relationship among journalism, communication technology, and culture. Carey contends that periods of transition, particularly those that reflect seams or ruptures in social systems, are particularly revealing periods for historical inquiry.[6] During such periods, repressed or taken-for-granted issues tend to be contested in the open in ways that provide historians with better access to the consciousness of particular eras.

Assorted scholars have documented that the turn of the twentieth century represents a key transitional period in journalism history. During this period the basic structures of journalism, ranging from approaches to journalistic management to forms of journalistic presentation, evolved significantly. Michael Schudson addresses journalism's marked shift from the sensationalism of the late nineteenth century to a growing sense of professionalism that began to reshape the profession in the early twentieth century.[7] Other scholars, as exemplified by John Hartsock's work, demonstrate that the early twentieth century was marked by tension between what some characterize as "traditional," fact-based conceptions of news and emergent literary (or narrative) conceptions of journalism.[8] Charles Ponce De Leon documents how such factors led to the growth of human interest reporting and its attendant emphasis on celebrity as a news value during this period. Related to this trend, as Robert McChesney documents, newspapers created sports pages and specialized sports reporting beats to accommodate the public's growing interest in sports as part of the nascent commercial leisure industry.[9]

By the time Jack Johnson emerged as a national figure, each of these trends was shaping how journalists engaged audiences and structured reality as news. The present critical-historical study seeks to better synthesize such issues by providing an overview of how the early twentieth-century white press constructed the Johnson episode as a continuing news story.[10] In this regard, as Carey emphasizes, journalism needs to be examined and understood as a corpus, an overarching perspective that includes "multiple treatments of the same story" and "other forms of journalism that surround, correct, and complete the daily newspaper."[11] This orientation helps us better understand how the Johnson controversy reflects Carey's conception of journalism: "News is not information, but drama. It does not describe the world but portrays dramatic forces and action."[12]

Toward this objective, Victor Turner's theory of processual social drama offers an instrumental framework for interpreting how the press structured its reportage of Johnson as a lived narrative, one that oriented—and in many ways animated—the individual news stories associated with Johnson.[13] Turner contends that social dramas are enacted when regular, norm-governed social relations are breached in some manner, and that, if left unsealed, such a breach would undermine the symbolic foundations of a culture. It thus becomes necessary for diverse social interests to coalesce temporarily and engage in redressive actions to seal the breach. In some important ways, Johnson reportage during this period reflected these dynamics: the press defined the fundamental breach and quickly created a basic narrative trajectory toward redress. Because this trajectory implicitly structured news over time, it represented a powerful force that conjoined diverse social forces, shaped the interpretation of unfolding events, and defined news values throughout the controversy.[14]

The Press, Narrative, and Jack Johnson

This approach advances a multifaceted body of literature that examines the narrative construction of news in both historical and contemporary settings. Among the most significant works that address these dynamics is Schudson's discussion of the relationship between narrative and news conventions over time.[15] Further, in a widely cited work, Elizabeth Bird and Robert Dardenne explain how forms of narrative provide order and normality to news.[16] They portray narrative as a symbolic process that delineates news by placing boundaries on happenings and transforming them into events. This orientation has informed diverse journalism history research such as Jack Lule's study of the use of myth to structure reportage in various historical settings.[17] Similarly, Jeffrey Bridger and David Maines demonstrate how specific narrative structures create master frames that both shape and restrict public understanding of significant news events.[18]

The Johnson situation sheds further light on such perspectives, by explaining how America's white press used such narrative strategies to construct what media critic Stuart Hall terms "a preferred reading" of events, a dominant account that effectively marginalized many divergent voices, including those of boxing detractors and the African American press.[19] This theory-informed interpretive framework challenges prevailing historical narratives about the Johnson situation, particularly personality-oriented portrayals that, by their nature, ignore some significant events and conflate others. In the latter respect, most histories portray the controversies surrounding Jack Johnson as a two-act morality play: Johnson inflames white America, and then he defiantly remains "his own man" in spite of unjust persecution. Although valid in some ways, this de facto conventional wisdom is problematic in two key respects: First, it fixates on Johnson at the expense of other social actors and institutions; second, it collapses time and compresses events in ways that lose some vital nuances reflective of the social action as it was lived.

The present study demonstrates that the white press, with little variance, spontaneously framed the open-ended events involving Jack Johnson in terms of an overarching breach-to-redress (or pollution-to-sanctification) narrative trajectory that spanned nearly seven years. In contrast to the previously cited two-act narrative that dominates most Johnson histories, this study explains how the press-driven Jack Johnson social drama played out in three acts, with a substantial complication involving the Mann Act (white slavery laws) during the third act.[20] As explained in noted journalist John Lardner's 1951 account of the era of white hopes, the press constructed the Johnson controversy more around white hopes than around Johnson himself.[21] The first two acts reflected, respectively, journalists' efforts to goad former champion Jeffries out of retirement and the press-fueled buildup to his ill-fated July 4, 1910, fight with Johnson. The third act involves a five-year maudlin period that followed Johnson's victory over Jeffries.

For its textual material, the analysis focuses on the daily reportage of three influential metropolitan newspapers: the *New York Times*, the *Chicago Tribune*, and the *San Francisco Examiner*.[22] Each reflects its strategic geographic location in relation to most key events, and each reflects its distinctive perspective of news values, news coverage, and newsroom management. In terms of geography, much of the action occurred in three cities: New York, the national center of media and sports action; Chicago, Johnson's adopted hometown; and San Francisco, the cultural center of the West and the original site of the Johnson-Jeffries fight.[23] Each newspaper also reflects widely recognized, and clearly distinctive, journalistic practices and philosophies during this era. By 1908, Adolph Ochs's *New York Times* was quickly establishing a paradigm for contemporary conceptions of objective, professional journalism.[24] Robert R. McCormick's newly acquired *Chicago Tribune* stood out as one of the most influential Midwest newspapers, an outlet that both generated news coverage and received common perspectives of geographically distant issues through freelancers who provided "specials" to newspapers.[25] The *San Francisco Examiner*, in its role as the flagship newspaper in William Randolph Hearst's expanding chain of publications, dominated West Coast reportage. Hearst's well-documented ties between his *Examiner* and his influential *New York Journal* also represent a transcontinental linkage in news coverage and news management.[26] In each case the analysis addresses Johnson reportage as a collective body of work—versus the product of individual reporters or columnists.

Jack Johnson as Social Drama

The Breach

At the dawn of the twentieth century the world's heavyweight championship had been imbued with great symbolic significance. Since the 1880s the title had evolved into a vital, and profitable, popular culture ritual that helped construct America in terms of whiteness, masculinity, and nationalism.[27] Yet by 1905, heavyweight championship boxing faced significant troubles on two counts: first, the sport itself was under fire from the era's influential progressive movement; second, the top four challengers to Jeffries's title were black.[28] Faced with this reality, Jeffries retired in 1905 and presided over the orderly transfer of his title to the best of the era's paltry lot of white contenders.[29] By 1908, after the title had languished in the hands of two uninspiring white champions for three years, the paucity of this strategy became apparent. In hopes of a lucrative payday then-champion Tommy Burns broke the championship's longstanding color barrier and agreed to fight Johnson on December 26, 1908, in Sydney, Australia. For Burns, the decision represented a big mistake. Johnson thrashed him so thoroughly that the police had to stop the fight in the fourteenth round. Although many members of the ringside press initially missed the significance of this situation, Jack London provided a now-infamous assessment for the readers of the *New York Herald*:

> The fight! There was no fight. No Armenian massacre could compare with the hopeless slaughter that took place to-day.... "Hit here Tahmy" he would say exposing the side of his unprotected stomach ... then would receive the blow with a happy, carefree smile.... But one thing now remains, Jeffries must emerge from his alfalfa farm and remove that golden smile from Johnson's face. Jeff, it's up to you![30]

Johnson's victory, indeed, represented a critical rupture in the symbolic relationship between the heavyweight championship and the social interests it had come to represent over the preceding two decades. This reality was manifest in journalists' rapid reassessment of the fight and its participants. Before the fight, newspapers reflected an indifferent—if not occasionally complimentary—attitude toward Johnson, an attitude that was consistent with purely sporting considerations.[31] After the fight, however, the media seamlessly positioned Johnson at the center of a national morality play, while, over the course of just one hour, Burns became a nonentity.[32] In short, the situation represented a far-reaching social breach that required redressive action.

Act I: Jeffries Must Commit

Although most histories focus on Johnson during this period, the actions and status of Jeffries, not Johnson, animated the social drama for its first seventeen months. Press reportage demonstrates that the badly out-of-shape Jeffries's willingness to come out of retirement was not a foregone conclusion.[33] Thus, white America's fixation with goading Jeffries out of retirement played out as a dramatic act of its own, one involving enough suspense that it shaped news values in ways that overshadowed Johnson's actions—to include his five boxing matches against white opponents—throughout 1909. Even as Jack London's account of the Johnson-Burns fight concisely characterizes this strategic shift, this reaction was not as instantaneous among the press as most histories imply. Initially, some newspapers, including the *New York Times* and Hearst's newspapers, were somewhat complimentary of the new champion. The *San Francisco Examiner*, for example, opened its primary coverage of the fight in Sydney by observing, "Perhaps never before in the history of pugilism was such an ovation tendered a new-born champion as that afforded the giant Negro."[34]

Yet within days, most of the white press came to realize what London sensed instantly: the situation was intractable and troubling. A black man rightly laid claim to a cherished title that over decades had been crafted—largely in the press—as the epitome of masculinity and civilization. As it acknowledged this quandary, the press also quickly realized that Jeffries represented the only white boxer capable of beating Johnson; thus, the press positioned Jeffries—and Jeffries alone—as a heroic agent of redemption.[35] Within two days of Johnson's victory, stories shifted from lamenting Burns's shortcomings to emphasizing various promoters' inducements to lure Jeffries out of retirement.[36] With news values now structured around Jeffries's actions, reportage during early 1909 shifted from gossiping about Jeffries's intentions (e.g., dropping hints or secretly visiting a training gym) to constructing a full-fledged heroic frame related to the "adoring throngs" who greeted Jeffries wherever he appeared. The latter news angle is nicely reflected by a *New York Times* story of March 3, 1909, that featured the headline "Riotous Welcome for J. J. Jeffries." The story addresses a "clamoring mob" and "tumultuous uproar" that greeted Jeffries upon his arrival in New York.[37]

In contrast to what most Johnson histories imply, once the press established Jeffries as the heroic agent of redemption, Johnson assumed secondary news value for several reasons.[38] Most notably, because he was dependent upon surface transportation to return from Australia to North America, Johnson was largely outside of the view of the American press until March 1909. Further, even as the press reported the champion's conspicuous peccadilloes—particularly his white wife—after March 1909, Johnson's controversial persona remained subordinate to the Jeffries-centric trajectory that shaped news values.[39] Consequently, press concern with Johnson's controversial persona was not as constant over time as many histories suggest.

Therefore, it is important to acknowledge that Johnson's actions complemented, more so than they precipitated, the master narratives the press created earlier that year. This reality was manifest in the relatively prosaic early reportage (particularly as compared to the reportage of late 1912) of Johnson's personal life. During this period these factors included prominently displaying his white wives, conspicuously philandering with white prostitutes, indulging in public drunkenness and fights outside of the ring, and driving recklessly in major cities across the nation.[40] Additionally, this reaction extended to the light—almost disinterested—coverage of Johnson's five 1909 bouts against mediocre white opponents.[41]

With the situation festering in the spring months of 1909, Jeffries faced increasing public pressure from both fans and editorialists.[42] This pressure reached a peak in late March and early April 1909 when reportage and editorial commentary targeted Jeffries personally. During March, the *San Francisco Examiner*, for example, addressed the "When will Jeffries commit?" question nearly every day.[43] This sort of pressure descended to a nadir on April 4, when the *Chicago Tribune* prominently featured a photo illustration depicting a young white girl (three or four years old) pointing at Jeffries with an "Uncle Sam Wants You" pose. The caption below reads, "Please Mr. Jeffries, are you going to fight Mr. Johnson?"[44]

Jeffries succumbed to the pressure on April 20, 1909, when he announced publicly that he was "willing" to fight Johnson.[45] Accordingly, with questions of "whether?" superseded by questions of "when?" the press intensified its focus on Jeffries's physical condition.[46] Although newspapers had reported on Jeffries's weight since Johnson won the title, by the summer of 1909 journalists became active weight watchers. In contrast to earlier "it appears he has lost a lot of weight" reports, by the summer months, newspaper headlines had established a public baseline of approximately 220–225 pounds for Jeffries's weight.[47] During the early fall of 1909, press accounts reflected the palpable sense of excitement related to Jeffries's steadily improving physical status. The public and press were so fixated on Jeffries's health in the fall of 1909 that even while returning from a trip to Europe on an ocean liner, he had to send wireless updates on a cold he caught in Europe.[48]

As the *New York Times* put it, the reason for the concern was clear: "Jeffries is the man who is expected to regain individual physical supremacy for the white race."[49] Thus, even as Johnson was preparing to defend his title against middleweight champion Stanley Ketchel, October headlines emphasized, "Jeff is Ready."[50] This situation finally culminated on October 30 when months of speculation and anticipation reached its climax in the form of a major story headlined "Jeffries Matched to Fight Negro."[51] Thus with only the formal signing remaining to formally conclude act I, in November 1909, the press shifted its attention to act II.

Act II: A Journey to the Center of the Universe

Historian and biographer Finis Farr observed that "students of human absurdity would have to go far before discovering a richer mine than the periodical files from December 1909 until July 4 the following year."[52] Farr is referring to the notorious second act of the press-fueled Jack Johnson social drama, an act that formally began on December 4, 1909, when Johnson and Jeffries signed the contract to fight in July 1910.[53] With the press no longer focusing on Jeffries's decision, act II reoriented the reportage on an act of sanctification in the boxing ring. This strategic shift restructured key news values to emphasize material details associated with the pending fight.[54] As Farr suggests, this period was marked by intense news coverage that in retrospect often appears bizarre, outrageous, and contradictory. Yet despite the social discord that the looming Johnson-Jeffries fight unleashed, in the eyes of the public of 1910, events were performed with reasonable coherence. In this regard, the social drama's fundamental breach-to-sanctification framing strategy enabled the press to accommodate a cacophony of voices and an array of plot complications that would emerge over the next seven months.

Accordingly, the press now began to address each fighter as a key social actor who would have to perform his respective role in the boxing ring. In this regard, not much was expected of Johnson because he was viewed as the end product of inferior racial attributes.[55] Jeffries, on the other hand, now was tasked with carrying the historical constructions of masculinity, whiteness, and civilization on his shoulders—a burden that would become increasingly heavy over time. Thus, even as few significant events occurred in the months immediately after the signing, the press maintained the momentum of its coverage by emphasizing this line of affective character contrast. Much of this momentum can be attributed to former heavyweight champion James J. Corbett, who was vital in articulating the affective dimensions of the broader press narrative. During this generally underemphasized fallow period, Corbett used his nationally syndicated column and longstanding affiliations with reporters to release a stream of specious analyses to a credulous national audience.[56] In early 1910 Corbett regularly assailed Johnson's character (e.g., his purported "yellow streak") and at the same time fortified Jeffries's already inflated status as a hero. As Corbett explained in one such analysis, just one of Jeffries's blows would cause Johnson to lose "25 percent of his speed, 50 percent of his nerve, and 75 percent of his strength."[57]

By April 1910, events progressed to a point that the sheer material reality of the fight came to dominate press reportage. When Jeffries opened his training camp in early April, accounts of his progress—no matter how trivial—emerged as dominant national news stories. Even seemingly mundane daily reports such as "Stiff Punches for Jeff" now generated headlines across the nation.[58] As awareness of these factors became more widespread during April, voices of dissent began to emerge into the center of the unfolding action. These voices represented complex, somewhat-discordant interests (e.g., gamblers, clergy, promoters, government officials, and social activists), yet despite their potential to diverge from the central action, the press seamlessly positioned these developments as plot complications within its trajectory-driven narrative frame. Thus, to manage the potential cacophony, the reportage delineated the action thematically and employed narrative counterpoint to maintain coherence.

For example, the press seamlessly organized a good deal of news around a dialectic between those seeking to arrange the details of the fight and those who wanted to prohibit the fight altogether.[59] After this issue was resolved in June, when organizers moved the fight from San Francisco to Reno, the press managed a complex dialectic between the interest of gamblers, whose wallets were basically colorblind, and the advocates of racial essentialism.[60] This interplay took the form of pervasive reporting of Jeffries mythology (e.g., he once killed a lion with one blow) as it contrasted with more clear-minded observations that the balding and moody Jeffries did not appear impressive in training.[61] Similarly, myriad racist depictions of Johnson in the press conflicted with gamblers' acknowledgements that the articulate Johnson looked very impressive in training.[62] Finally, the reportage featured an amusing mélange of expert prognostications and reflections of egotism that the press generally portrayed dialectically as individual personality conflicts.[63]

As the action shifted to Reno the full spectrum of the era's news outlets struggled to keep up with both the frantic pace of events and the public's voracious appetite for news about the upcoming fight. Rex Beach, the famous novelist and playwright who was one of many celebrity reporters covering the fight, observed in the *Chicago Tribune* that Reno had become "the magnetic center of the civilized world."[64] In addition to flooding Reno with correspondents, virtually every major newspaper in the nation devoted vast editorial space to fight-related coverage. Leading most of its competitors in this respect, Hearst newspapers each day devoted a special section to fight-related coverage. In contrast, other newspapers, as exemplified by the *Chicago Tribune* and *New York Times*, greatly expanded their sports pages and spilled extensive Reno-related reportage onto their news pages. By early July 1910, newspapers across the nation were replete with stories from Reno that featured assorted rumors and last-minute prognostication.

On the afternoon of July 4, as massive crowds gathered in front of newspaper offices across the nation, a boisterous crowd in Reno greeted

Johnson by singing the then-popular song "All Coons Look Alike to Me." Unfazed, a supremely confident Johnson entered the ring and systematically dismantled Jeffries. Even as newspapers across the world recounted Johnson's fifteenth-round knockout victory in detail, few words were necessary. A *San Francisco Examiner* headline for Alfred Henry Lewis's account concisely summarized the action: "Black is Faster and Cleverer; Hits Harder, Cleaner, Oftener."[65] In figurative terms, far more than just Jeffries crashed to the canvas in Reno that afternoon. The entire structure of a vital national narrative collapsed alongside the former champion—and white America was stunned. For nearly eighteen months, much of the American public had coalesced around a press-constructed social drama only to watch it implode within an hour. As a once-boisterous crowd silently shuffled out of the arena in Reno, the remnants of the media's redressive strategy still smoldered in the now-empty boxing ring. Given the symbolic issues involved, the repercussions would be profound.

Act III: The Maudlin Period

Existing histories have documented how an array of emotions ranging from shock to anger to resignation swept across the nation in the aftermath of Johnson's one-sided victory. Yet from an interpretive perspective, it is useful to look beyond suggestions that this reaction merely represented dissatisfaction with the results of a discrete event. As Lardner suggests, Jeffries's resounding defeat threw white America into a Johnson-related funk that lasted nearly five years. The nature of this reaction, as a close reading of the press reportage indicates, can be understood in terms of collective grief, a process that occurs in multiple stages.[66] An array of psychologists portray grief as a natural, phased response to any major loss in life—and, without question, white America lost a great deal on July 4, 1910. Not only did it witness the collapse of its far-reaching symbolic strategy to construct social identity, but the debacle was performed in front of what was, perhaps, the largest worldwide media audience to that date.

Given these realities, and commensurate with the stages of grief, white America's reaction over time appears consistent—both in terms of what transpired and how it played out in the press. Rex Beach's first postfight dispatch to the *Chicago Tribune* exemplifies this reaction: "Today we saw a tragedy. A tremendous, crushing anti-climax and we are dazed."[67] Similarly, the *New York Times* reported the scene outside its offices:

> The bulletin boards showed nothing for a moment or two, then came the flash from Reno: "Johnson wins in the fifteenth." In silence the 30,000 men, women and children read the words. It was a terrible blow and they began to move away sadly.[68]

The silence, however, did not last long. Across the nation, by the time the dinner hour passed, foul moods had festered and the shock steadily turned to anger. Then, as the sun went down, a spasm of emotion exploded across the nation. With almost choreographed consistency, as Hearst chain newspapers reported, "there was rioting in virtually every city and town in the United States, and in many places, the police were powerless to quell the excited throngs."[69] Existing histories have addressed this (largely white on black) violence in detail, and in the context of this critical analysis, the reportage of these incidents—as well as the violence itself—seems repetitive and banal. The sheer uniformity of the violence across geography, as a reflector of collective grief, stands out as its most distinctive feature.

Even as the violence was short-lived, the anger phase of the grieving process lingered for several weeks. Ironically, during the height of this phase, much of the anger was directed at the erstwhile hope of the white race: James J. Jeffries. For example, J. Lawrence Toole charged in the *San Francisco Examiner* that fans should "show no sorrow" for Jeffries because he "betrayed his friends" with his dismal performance.[70] Hugh E. Keough similarly chastised Jeffries in the pages of the *Chicago Tribune*: "Jeff was shown only pity for his folly and his egotism."[71] Yet after several cycles of Jeffries-bashing, the reportage shifted to emphasize more thoughtful attempts at rationalization and renegotiation. Some accounts stressed—particularly to African American audiences—that the results of a boxing match meant nothing.[72] Other accounts directed anger at the fight's relationship to forces of moral decay.[73]

These latter concerns became manifest as a spontaneous national movement that sought to ban the display of motion pictures of the fight.

The movement comprised a de facto coalition of journalists, clergy, intellectuals, political leaders, and economic leaders, and it is noteworthy that, like the spontaneous postfight violence, the movement was not formally organized across geography.[74] Although this movement represented a topic of sustained press interest during much of the summer of 1910, by early fall, public concern about the issue began to dissipate as interest in the Reno fight waned.[75] After the films were shown without incident in some cities and banned in others, eventually the issue went dormant—largely because Johnson did not fight again for two years.

By September 1910 the splenetic tone of much of the postfight analysis and reportage shifted to reflect a palpable sense of resignation. In contrast to the focused movement along a trajectory that characterized the media reportage from December 1908 until July 1910, reportage in the fall of 1910 appears drifting and unsubstantial.[76] As white America emerged from its post-Reno hangover with no plausible redressive strategies in sight, various social and economic interests recognized the need for some sense of hope at both a symbolic and a promotional level. In early 1911, building upon an impulse that emerged soon after the fight in Reno, the press and promoters organized a formal strategy to address this quandary: the white hope phenomenon.[77]

White Hopes: An Etymology

The moniker "white hope" represents perhaps the most enduring artifact to emerge from the era of Jack Johnson.[78] Yet a search of media indexes and databases reveals that if the specific term "white hope" (i.e., a generic designator for any Caucasian challenger to Johnson) was used prior to late 1910, its use was rare and obscure.[79] That noted, relatively early in the Johnson social drama various members of the press referred to Jeffries as "the hope of the white race" or "the white man's hope."[80] Consequently, it is useful for historians to acknowledge that the social drama produced two parallel, but different, versions of the term. The first variations were reserved for addressing Jeffries's focused and specific role within the context of the first two acts of the social drama. Other white fighters during this period did not warrant these designations.[81] After Jeffries's downfall, the "hope" moniker became generic and should be understood as a product of journalists and promoters during the maudlin period of 1911–1915.

By early 1911, the label "white hope" proved to be a useful strategy for the press and promoters to conjoin key symbolic and economic interests. In contrast to the trajectory-driven efforts to promote Jeffries's comeback, the concept of "white hopes" allowed promoters and the press to feed off the energy and momentum of the Johnson situation without addressing him directly.[82] These efforts were manifest in urban strategies such as white hope tournaments, which invariably were unsuccessful at producing anything but scores of novice fighters of no promise.[83] Correspondingly, promoters and the press exploited then-pervasive American mythology about frontier demigods and the purity of rural America. During this period, newspapers were replete with stories of Bunyonesque giants rising from America's western states to solve the Jack Johnson problem. Two factors stand as noteworthy: equating size with "hope" status, and an unspoken rule that only Northern European names qualified as "white."[84]

Rumors of white hopes—although they were not yet called that—began appearing in the press immediately following Jeffries's defeat. On July 5, 1910, morning newspapers across the nation reported that Bill McGowan, a six-foot, seven-inch "giant" from Olympia, Washington, suddenly stepped forward to challenge Johnson. According to Hearst newspapers, McGowan not only was huge, "he is a clever boxer and can hit a terrific blow."[85] A few weeks later, Corbett joined the fray by announcing he had discovered a "mystery giant" who would challenge Johnson. In contrast to what turned out to be unfounded hype regarding McGowan, Corbett supported his claims with five thousand dollars in backing from promoter H. D. McIntyre. The pair then employed former heavyweight contender Joe Choynski to train their six-foot, six-inch protégé, a Missouri farmer named Miles McLeod.[86] In 1912 a Chicago sports columnist recounted the promotion:

> Joe slipped a pair of mitts on the farmer's fists and showed him how to pose. The reporters got flashlight photos of him; Joe told 'em how Miles nearly killed him with a punch while they were sparring. . . . On the strength of it Joe secured a nice vaudeville engagement for himself

and his giant pal. He managed to teach McLeod how to put up his hands and go through a sort of denatured boxing exhibition. Of course McLeod never meant to go into the ring, and he didn't either.[87]

Many white hopes actually entered the boxing ring, but none lived up to expectations. The most widely cited misfire involved Carl Morris, a six-foot, four-inch railroad engineer from Oklahoma. Morris's much-hyped September 1911 debut in New York failed miserably as the *New York Times* reported: "It is doubtful that any pugilist was ever battered out of shape more than was Morris last night. He bled continually from the second round to the finish as if an artery had been severed."[88] Morris represented the pattern that characterized the post-Jeffries white hope phenomenon: high hopes to no hope. Yet faced with a nagging social breach and a dearth of redressive strategies, the white press and its readers seemed anxious for any sort of news item that could turn an impulse toward redemption into a full-fledged trajectory. Consequently, the public and press subjected themselves to repeat cycles of eagerness to disillusionment. So many white hopes would emerge between 1911 and 1915 that, over time, this pattern of relentless promotion and letdown became a news template of the age.[89]

As of the summer of 1912 the white-hope strategy had failed to turn out a single suitable white challenger for Johnson, who was growing desperate for a significant payday. The best that all parties could arrange was a bizarre parody of the fight in Reno: a July 4, 1912, title defense in Las Vegas, New Mexico, against undersized journeyman Jim Flynn, whom Johnson had knocked out five years earlier. The foul-filled travesty, in which Flynn was disqualified in the ninth round, represented a depressing spectacle on multiple counts.[90] Most notably, the mismatch reinvigorated the anti-fight film movement, this time resulting in Congress quickly and quietly passing legislation that banned the interstate transportation of boxing motion pictures.[91] Further, press reaction to the farce underscored the extent to which the white press had totally soured on Johnson. Influential *San Francisco Examiner* sports editor W. W. Naughton's reportage exemplifies this trend. Before the Jeffries fight, Naughton presented Johnson as a colorful, rather than as a threatening character.[92] By the summer of 1912, however, Naughton expressed little more than scornful assessments of Johnson's "idiotic smile" and his "lack of stamina."[93]

A Major Plot Complication

Johnson was familiar with being unpopular among white Americans, and for the previous four years he had been able to buy himself out of many legal predicaments.[94] Thus, as fall of 1912 neared, Johnson exhibited an unwarranted sense of invulnerability. In August 1912 he opened a new saloon in Chicago, and he anticipated lucrative paydays from fights with some of the emerging white hopes.[95] However, on September 12, 1912, the situation changed dramatically when front pages of newspapers throughout the nation were filled with variants of the headline "Jack Johnson's Wife Shoots Self."[96] When Johnson's deeply depressed white wife, Etta Duryea, died later that day, the reportage was mixed. The *New York Times* offered some sympathy: "His venture in miscegenation has come to an end (only) a little more dreadful than was confidently to be expected of the social proprieties, still his apparently sincere grief . . . shows that he is not the entirely callous animal that a Negro prize-fighter is supposed by most to be."[97] Conversely, the *Chicago Tribune* placed the blame directly on Johnson:

> She told friends her husband was paying attentions to other women. One day about a year ago she was taken to the Washington Park hospital, her face beaten until it was hardly recognizable. It was said Johnson had grabbed her by the throat and used his pugilistic fists upon her until she had lost consciousness.[98]

Recognizing the volatile nature of the situation, Johnson quickly refuted the (true) accusations of abuse by weeping openly in front of reporters. "I thought the world of her and she thought the world of me," he sobbed.[99] Johnson's instinctive damage-control strategy might have worked had he changed his ways at that point. However, just two weeks after the coroner officially ruled Duryea's death a suicide, the champion appeared in public with Lucille Cameron, a fawning nineteen-year-old blonde, on his arm. When accounts quickly spread through Chicago's gossip channels,

Cameron's mother allied with a notorious Chicago divorce attorney and charged through the press that Johnson had abducted her daughter.[100] Johnson's world then imploded. The boxer did not help his case when he responded to initial inquiries by flippantly telling Chicago reporters, "How can I help it if the girl is crazy about me?"[101] He further inflamed his critics by pointing to his sports car and observing, "Some of the best white women in Chicago ride in this car" and saying that he could "get any white woman he wanted."[102]

In stark contrast to the comparatively restrained press reaction to the white-women issue in 1909 and 1910, the Cameron charges resulted in national hysteria. Lurid headlines, which featured words such as "white girl" and "abduction," ran prominently on the front pages of newspapers throughout the nation.[103] Within two days, Chicago mobs hanged Johnson in effigy in front of the full gaze of the national press. Letters poured into Chicago, particularly from southern states, explaining that they "knew how to deal with niggers" like Johnson.[104] Three weeks later, Johnson found himself sitting in an eight-by-four-and-a-half-foot jail cell facing federal charges that he abducted Cameron in violation of recent white slavery laws.[105]

Johnson's Mann Act prosecution of 1913 has been discussed in detail in each of his biographies. These histories explain that Johnson, at worst, was guilty only of violating the letter, but certainly not the spirit, of the era's white slavery laws, which prohibited the interstate transportation of women for prostitution. Of significance in the context of this analysis, despite the incendiary nature of the issues involved, the controversy generally did not alter the social drama's basic narrative frame. In similar fashion to the divergent issues that emerged before the fight in Reno, the press managed the issue as a plot complication. Thus, once Johnson's perfunctory prosecution and conviction ran its course in the spring of 1913, the Mann Act furor rapidly subsided in the press.[106] After receiving his sentence in June, the financially strapped Johnson jumped bail and accepted several title defenses in Europe over the next eighteen months. His poor performances in those fights seamlessly shifted interest back to the boxing ring as the site of symbolic redemption.[107] In the fall of 1914, as war erupted across Europe, the press continued to reflect awareness that some white hope eventually would vanquish the fading Johnson.[108]

On April 5, 1915, age and lack of training finally caught up with Johnson in Havana, Cuba. That day, after twenty-six grueling rounds in the Havana sun, he succumbed to white hope Jess Willard, a six-foot, six-inch "giant" from Kansas. Given the white-hope disappointments in the past, the pre-fight promotion was guarded. As the *San Francisco Examiner* observed, Willard had lost to some mediocre opposition in the past and "the good-natured giant with a particularly tender heart" possibly lacked the temperament to prevail under adversity.[109] However, when Willard triumphed, newspapers across America heralded the news with banner headlines. America's seven-year ordeal had ended; Willard instantly became a national hero.[110]

To most white Americans, Willard's achievement represented a satisfactory conclusion to their vexation; in a very real sense, the reluctant Kansas farmer had performed, finally, the symbolic atonement in the boxing ring. Press accounts, particularly the widely circulated Associated Press report of the fight, portrayed the contest as a victory of character over skill. The AP gushed about how Willard "took twenty rounds of severe punishment, but laughed the blows aside and kept standing up against the rushes of the Negro."[111] In ways not seen since the social drama's first act, the press and fans portrayed Willard as a hero in every sense; his victory was a cause for great celebration in white America.[112] Much as in the reaction to Jeffries in act I, headlines enthusiastically documented each instance of the "riotous greetings" that welcomed the new champion as he traveled from Havana to New York via the Florida Keys and Georgia.[113] As a *New York Times* dispatch noted, "not since the days of John L. Sullivan . . . have similar scenes and excitement been created by the advent of a fighter."[114]

Yet after greeting Willard "like a Roman general returning from the Gallic wars," the public quickly lost interest in the new champion.[115] Willard's victory may have ended a social drama, but it was not able to resurrect the heroic era of Sullivan, Corbett, and Jeffries. Ultimately, Willard's prominence was the product of press-generated heroic characterizations that addressed a now-resolved social drama. As for Johnson, the initial press accounts of his defeat appealed to some residual vicarious interest in his vanquished status.[116] Despite Johnson's fading visibility after his loss to Willard, the plot complication related to the Mann Act conviction continued unresolved. That issue, too, ultimately was resolved in July 1920, when after living in unhappy exile in Mexico, Johnson surrendered to federal officials and returned to serve his one-year sentence in Fort Leavenworth, Kansas. Even as the news was greeted with headlines, Johnson-related reportage waned within days.[117] Newspaper databases indicate that after 1920, the white press paid little attention to Johnson. From that point on, Johnson would be defined by the past through narratives that were recounted but which no longer were lived in the press as open-ended. By then relegated to the realm of epic American narratives, for the rest of his life and beyond, Johnson and the social drama he inspired would exist only in the domain of history.

Conclusion

Despite the complexity of the Johnson situation, the white press was able to construct the boxer's social presence in terms of an overarching narrative framework that structured—and in effect contained—news reportage for nearly seven years. This essay, by examining these processes at a macro level, has offered a sense of proportion and perspective that has been missing from existing histories. This account also provides a historically situated case study that challenges the notion of objective reporting and, accordingly, challenges historians to better conceptualize the transition from journalistic partisanship to objectivity during this period.

The case study illustrates the extent to which journalists wrote their episodic accounts of the Johnson situation to fit a broader social narrative of the time. Journalistic agendas were shaped by the sort of implicit breach-to-sanctification trajectory that Turner describes, even if these symbolic dynamics were outside of the conscious awareness of individual journalists. Such insights inform journalism history in several significant ways. At the broadest level, this viewpoint demonstrates the scope and power of the early twentieth-century white press as a national institution, one that constructed news as a value-laden commodity to fortify particular interests. Further, in accordance with Lardner's observation, this perspective highlights the extent to which, for the first eighteen months of the Johnson situation, press reportage revolved around Jeffries, not Johnson. Acknowledging this key factor represents an important step in establishing a more complete and accurate etymology of the term "white hope," a historically significant moniker that has been misused in many contemporary studies of Johnson. Further, these insights underscore the extent to which the white press perpetuated a narrative that effectively marginalized the voice of the African American press. Finally, this perspective provides a clearer sense of how events transpired at the time, and, as such, it better accounts for the historical consciousness implicit in the situation.

As this essay's findings suggest, the broader issues related to the press and Johnson represents rich subject matter for additional research. For example, journalism historians would benefit from better understanding the specific ways in which the press constructed race (to include whiteness) during the Johnson controversy. This strand of research should address the nature of racial representation in the press and explore the manner in which the African American press was marginalized and forced to react to the overarching narratives that the white press established. Additionally, the high visibility of the Johnson controversy represents a valuable platform for more detailed explorations of journalism practices during the period. These topics include comparative studies of editorial practices, the use of celebrities as journalists, the relationship between sports and news, and the manner in which early wire services and special reports linked news outlets in ways that created a de facto national news media in the years preceding the advent of broadcasting. In each of these cases, as this essay has demonstrated, the subject matter represents one of the more revealing episodes in early twentieth-century journalism.

NOTES

1. Research has addressed this topic in terms of issues including race, masculinity, nationalism, social Darwinism, early twentieth-century progressivism, and popular culture.

2. Lerone Bennett, "Jack Johnson and the Great White Hope," *Ebony* 49 (April 1994): 86–98.

3. These studies draw so heavily upon press coverage of Johnson that the studies serve as a basic index of reportage and events. Yet despite this thoroughness, existing research does not assimilate and interpret reportage in terms of its place in journalism history. Given that none of these descriptive studies was informed by communication theory, the present study provides needed perspective to prevailing Johnson histories.

4. *Unforgivable Blackness: The Rise and Fall of Jack Johnson*, directed by Ken Burns (Washington: PBS, 2005). If most accounts of Johnson represent these attributes to some degree, Burns's documentary explicitly presents this situation.

5. Exemplars of such perspectives of Johnson include Bennett, "Jack Johnson"; Thomas R. Hietala, *The Fight of the Century: Jack Johnson, Joe Louis, and the Struggle for Racial Equality* (Armonk NY: M.E. Sharpe, 2002); Kevin J. Mumford, *Interzones: Black/White Sex Districts in Chicago and New York in the Early Twentieth Century* (New York: Columbia University Press, 1997), 3–18; Martin Ritt, "The Great White Hope" (USA: Twentieth Century Fox Film Corp., 1970). The fictionalized motion picture closely parallels the life of Johnson. For a functional portrayal of Johnson see Al-Tony Gilmore, *Bad Nigger! The National Impact of Jack Johnson* (Port Washington NY: Kennikat Press, 1975). Gilmore offers a functionalist sociological assessment of Johnson's "impact" on social systems.

6. James W. Carey, "The Chicago School and the History of Mass Communication Research," in *James Carey: A Critical Reader*, edited by Eve Stryker Munson and Catherine A. Warren (Minneapolis: University of Minnesota Press, 1997), 24–25.

7. Michael Schudson, "The Objectivity Norm in American Journalism," *Journalism* 2, no. 2 (2001): 149–70.

8. John C. Hartsock, *A History of American Literary Journalism: The Emergence of a Modern Narrative Form*. Amherst: University of Massachusetts, 2000.

9. Robert McChesney, "Media Made Sport: A History of Sports Coverage in the United States," in *Media, Sports, & Society*, edited by Lawrence A. Wenner, 49–69 (Newbury Park CA: Sage, 1989).

10. These widely noted issues include the early years of Jim Crow America, the need to assimilate a massive wave of immigrants, emerging communication technology, and the growth of the commercial leisure industry as it accommodated urbanization and industrialization.

11. James W. Carey, "The Dark Continent of American Journalism," In *James Carey: A Critical Reader*, edited by E. S. Munson and C. Warren (Minneapolis: University of Minnesota Press, 1997), 148.

12. James W. Carey, "A Cultural Approach to Communication," *Communication* 2 (1975): 21.

13. Victor Turner, *From Ritual to Theatre: The Human Seriousness of Play* (New York: Performing Arts Journal Publications, 1982).

14. Specific strategies represent both temporal and affective qualities. At the most basic level they define unfolding events in terms of an end state that naturally reflects a news value hierarchy (i.e., emphasizing occurrences that move events toward the end state). See Frank Kermode, *The Sense of an Ending: Studies in the Theory of Fiction* (New York: Oxford University Press, 1967). Simultaneously, these narratives also ascribe affective qualities to particular characters and situations (e.g., heroic, tragic, foolish). See Kenneth Burke, *Attitudes toward History*, 3rd ed. (Berkeley: University of California Press, 1984): 124–34.

15. Michael Schudson, "The Politics of Narrative Form: The Emergence of News Conventions in Print and Television," *Print Culture and Video Culture* 111, no. 4 (Fall 1982): 97–112; Michael Schudson, "News as Stories," in *Media Anthropology*, edited by Eric W. Rothenbuhler and Mihai Coman, 121–28 (Thousand Oaks CA: Sage, 2005).

16. Elizabeth Bird and Robert W. Dardenne, "Myth, Chronicle and Story: Exploring the Narrative Qualities of News," in *Social Meanings of News: A Text Reader*, edited by Dan Berkowitz (Thousand Oaks CA: Sage, 1997), 333–50.

17. Jack Lule, *Daily News, Eternal Stories: The Mythological Role of Journalism* (New York: Guilford Press, 2001).

18. Jeffrey C. Bridger and David R. Maines. "Narrative Structures and the Catholic Church Closings in Detroit," *Qualitative Sociology* 21, no. 3 (1998): 319–40.

19. Stuart Hall, *Culture, Media, Language: Working Papers in Cultural Studies, 1972–1979* (Birmingham UK: Centre for Contemporary Cultural Studies, 1980): 128–38.

20. The observation should be understood in accordance with the dramatic axiom that plot complications underscore (versus undermine) a work's overarching narrative framework.

21. For this reason, this study focuses exclusively on the white press. Existing histories demonstrate that although the African American press actively commented on the situation over time, it had little, if any, voice in constructing the larger narrative structure of events. As a marginalized entity, its voice largely was limited to reacting to the narrative frame the white press established and perpetuated.

22. In addition to examining nearly seven years of daily reportage from these three newspapers, the analysis also surveyed—although not on a daily basis—an assortment of major metropolitan and local newspapers across the nation.

Some of these newspapers include the *Los Angeles Times, Oakland Tribune, Washington Post, Salt Lake Tribune, Boston Globe, Atlanta Journal,* and *San Antonio Light*. Insights gained from this reportage help validate the observations gleaned from the analysis of the primary newspapers.

23. In addition to representing the original site for the Johnson-Jeffries fight, San Francisco was physically close to Jeffries's Burbank, California, home. For these reasons, a good deal of white hope–related press coverage emanated from San Francisco.

24. Will Irwin, Clifford F. Weigle, and David G. Clark, *The American Newspaper*, 1st ed. (Ames: Iowa State University Press, 1969), 18. Irwin acknowledges this point in his noted 1911 essay.

25. Lloyd Wendt, *Chicago Tribune: The Rise of a Great American Newspaper* (Chicago: Rand McNally, 1979).

26. John Winkler, *William Randolph Hearst: A New Appraisal* (New York: Hastings House, 1955).

27. Gail Bederman, *Manliness & Civilization: A Cultural History of Gender and Race in the United States, 1880-1917* (Chicago: University of Chicago Press, 1995): 1–45.

28. Rex Lardner and Alan Bodian, *The Legendary Champions* (New York: American Heritage Press, 1972), 39–60.

29. "Marvin Hart Is Champion," *New York Times*, July 4, 1905, 3.

30. An image of the complete article can be found in Lardner and Bodian, *Legendary Champions*, 195.

31. This reality has not always been adequately emphasized in previous writings. Most prefight reportage reflects only limited interest in the Sydney fight and it generally portrays Johnson as a formidable athlete.

32. After the dust settled, Burns warranted little press coverage. He nearly disappeared from the pages of the *New York Times*, and although the *San Francisco Examiner* and *Chicago Tribune*, as part of each newspaper's more robust sports coverage, mentioned him occasionally, it usually was in negative terms, as demonstrated, for instance, by the mocking article "Burns Now a Humorist" (*Chicago Tribune*, March 29, 1909, 12).

33. Even as previous writings document Jeffries's reticence, their retrospective orientation fails to adequately emphasize just how open-ended this issue was in 1909. See "Jeffries Won't Fight," *New York Times*, December 28, 1908, 5; and "'No Fight for Me,' Says 'Jeff,'" *Chicago Tribune*, December 28, 1908, 1. Such reports, which alternated with reports of various financial inducements, were common in the weeks following the Johnson-Burns fight.

34. "Johnson Vanquishes Burns in Bitter Fight."

35. James J. Corbett, "Negro Fighters in Front Rank," *Chicago Tribune*, January 10, 1909, B1. As a matter of practical reality, no white heavyweight boxer had not already been defeated by one of the era's four major black heavyweights, Johnson, Sam Langford, Joe Jeannette, and Sam McVey. In fact, Johnson alone had beaten most of the leading white heavyweights of 1909.

36. "Offer to Jeffries Purse of $50,000," *New York Times*, December 28, 1908, 5; "Sullivan Offers $75,000," *New York Times*, January 31, 1909, 7.

37. "Riotous Welcome for J. J. Jeffries," *New York Times*, March 4, 1909, 7.

38. Most histories structure their narratives in ways that miss this key point.

39. "Bar Johnson's White Wife," *New York Times*, March 16, 1909, 7; "Johnson Is Back, Talks of Fight," *Chicago Tribune*, March 10, 1909, 8. In the latter article, the *Tribune* raises the white wife issue in the opening paragraph. Such references, which were not uncommon in the reportage during this period, generally appeared only as one- or two-paragraph news items. These articles stand in stark contrast to the sensational reportage of Johnson's Mann Act controversy in 1912.

40. Even as Johnson's controversial persona remained subordinate to the building sense of anticipation related to Jeffries's actions, growing public awareness of Johnson's controversies intensified the stakes implicit in Jeffries's decision. These factors laid the groundwork for the hero-villain/virtue-vice morality play that would characterize the affective nature of the news frame over time.

41. These insignificant fights are overemphasized in most accounts of Johnson. In fact, many accounts incorrectly identify these fighters as "white hopes." Except for the October 1909 bout with middleweight Stanley Ketchel, none of these fights was billed as a championship contest per se. However, had any of these undersized or under-talented opponents accidentally knocked out Johnson, the victor probably would have been deemed the new champion and the social drama would have concluded at that point. However, as virtually everyone in both the press and general public understood, there was little chance of such an eventuality. See "Johnson and O'Brien Fight to a Draw," *New York Times*, May 20, 1909, 7; and "Johnson Beats Ross in Ring," *New York Times*, July 1, 1909, 7. These two-paragraph summary stories exemplify the brief coverage of such fights.

42. "Jeffries in City Is Non-Committal," *Chicago Tribune*, March 2, 1909, 6.

43. W. W. Naughton, "Now Time for Jeffries to Declare Intentions," *San Francisco Examiner*, March 14, 1909, S1; Tad Dorgan, "Nobody Will Flirt with the Colored Dude," *San Francisco Examiner*, March 17, 1909, 10. Naughton's editorial supplemented Dorgan's cartoon, which depicted a portly, grinning Jeffries

saying, "Ask me no questions, I'll tell you no lies." Three days later, Dorgan depicted Jeffries as an old maid sitting on the park bench and rebuffing the overtures of a Sambo-caricatured "Artha" Johnson.

44. "Please Mr. Jeffries, Are You Going to Fight Mr. Johnson?" *Chicago Tribune*, April 4, 1909, 3:4.

45. "Jeffries Willing to Fight Johnson," *New York Times*, April 21, 1909, 8. As he explained, apparently in an effort to negate some of the mounting criticism, "I wanted to be sure I was absolutely the same Jeffries." By clearly confirming his intentions to a national media audience, Jeffries allowed the press to shift its coverage from focusing on speculation to focusing on the end state.

46. "Jeffries Shows He Means Fight," *Chicago Tribune*, May 15, 1909, 9.

47. "'Jeff' Will Fight Johnson Sure," *New York Times*, July 15, 1909, 8; "Jeffries Meets Gov. Johnson," *New York Times*, July 23, 1909, 2; "Jeffries in Fine Shape," *New York Times*, September 30, 1909. During this period Jeffries's fitness was so closely aligned with the projected climax and resolution of the social drama's first act that even anecdotal accounts of his fitness could become nationally featured news items. For example, when the governor of Minnesota told Jeffries, "You look fit enough to fight right now and kill almost anybody," newspapers across the nation reported the observation.

48. "Jeff, in Wireless, Expects to Fight," *Chicago Tribune*, October 21, 1909, 8.

49. "Jeffries Ready to Fight Johnson," *New York Times*, October 23, 1909, 12.

50. "Jeffries Ready to Fight Johnson."

51. "Jeffries Matched to Fight Negro," *New York Times*, October 30, 1909, 11. As a reflection of the racism implicit in that period, early headlines frequently referred to Johnson only as "Negro."

52. Finis Farr, *Black Champion: The Life and Times of Jack Johnson* (New York: Scribner, 1964), 77.

53. "Fight Fans Line Up in Hoboken To-day," *New York Times*, December 1, 1909, 12.

54. "Frisco Welcomes Jeffries," *New York Times*, February 21, 1910, 7; "Jeffries Nearly Starts Run on Bank," *New York Times*, February 24, 1910, 11.

55. "Arm of Law Grabs Jack Johnson," *Chicago Tribune*, January 21, 1910, 12; "Jack Johnson Fined in Boston," *New York Times*, 11; "Ocean View Site for the Big Fight," *New York Times*, January 18, 1910, 9; "Detroit's Ban on Johnson," *New York Times*, February 6, 1910, S3; "Jack Johnson Arrested," *New York Times*, February 9, 1910, 9.

56. James J. Corbett, "Jeff's Mule Kick to Jar Johnson," *Chicago Tribune*, January 23, 1910, C1.

57. "Big Fight Figured Mathematically," *New York Times*, January 25, 1910, 10. Although such specious analyses foreshadowed a form of racial essentialism that would serve to delineate and justify the action in later months, in early 1910, such characterizations still tended to underscore the heroic portrayal of Jeffries.

58. "Stiff Punches for 'Jeff' in Training," *New York Times*, April 9, 1910, 12; "Jeffries Puts on Full Steam," *Chicago Tribune*, May 8, 1910, 3:2.

59. "Pastors Condemn Big Fight," *New York Times*, April 26, 1910, 20; "More Opposition to Fight," *Chicago Tribune*, May 4, 1910, 13; "Reno Gets the Big Battle and Jeffries Is on His Way," *San Francisco Examiner*, June 22, 1910, 11.

60. "Betting Waits for Better Odds," *San Francisco Examiner*, July 1, 1910, 16; "Betting in San Francisco," *New York Times*, June 29, 1910, 3.

61. James J. Corbett, "Jeff Is Sure to Win," *Chicago Tribune*, July 4, 1910, 1; "The Psychology of the Prize Fight," *Current Literature*, July 1910, 57–58; William Muldoon, "Jeff Needs More Sparring Is Judgment of Muldoon," *San Francisco Examiner*, July 1, 1910, 15; Douglas Erskine, "Jeffries' Muscles Showing Signs of Age," *San Francisco Examiner*, July 3, 1910, 50.

62. "Sambo Remus Rastus Brown on His Way from Reno Town," *Chicago Tribune*, July 5, 1910, 24; "Lil' Artha in Politics," *San Francisco Examiner*, July 6, 1910, 8; Alfred H. Lewis, "Johnson Waits with Stolid Unconcern," *San Francisco Examiner*, July 1, 1910, 11; Douglas Erskine, "Here's the Johnson Dope, Athletes Never Come Back," *San Francisco Examiner*, July 4, 1910, 12; Tad Dorgan, "Johnson More Clever; Should Win Easily," *San Francisco Examiner*, July 4, 1910, 14.

63. "12 World-Famous Experts Cover the Fight for Examiner," *San Francisco Examiner*, June 19, 1910, 66; John L. Sullivan, "Jeffries Refuses to See Sullivan," *New York Times*, June 24, 1910, 10; "Jeffries Bars Sullivan from Camp: Rickard Defends John L," *San Francisco Examiner*, June 24, 1910, 11; "Sullivan Dignified," *New York Times*, June 24, 1910, 10. The most newsworthy row to emerge from these clashes of egos involved a squabble between erstwhile ring opponents James J. Corbett and John L. Sullivan. Sullivan, who served as a celebrity reporter for the *New York Times*, allegedly commented about the fight's integrity in ways that roiled Corbett, who aligned himself with the Jeffries camp.

64. Alfred H. Lewis, "Reno Is Filled with Fight Fans Who Argue and Argue," *San Francisco Examiner*, July 2, 1910, 48; Rex Beach, "Reno Now Center of Universe," *Chicago Tribune*, July 2, 1910, 1; Farr, *Black Champion*, 19. Across town, the *Chicago Daily News* offered similar sentiments when it ran a cartoon depicting the world as a wheel, with Reno positioned as "the hub of the universe."

65. Alfred H. Lewis, "Black Is Faster and Cleverer; Hits Harder, Cleaner, Oftener," *San Francisco Examiner*, July 5, 1910, 1.

66. Elisabeth Keubler-Ross, *On Death and Dying*, 1st Hudson River ed. (New York: Macmillan, 1991). This seminal work, originally published in 1969, has influenced myriad widely accepted theories about the stages of grief.

67. Rex Beach, "Johnson and Age Defeat Jeffries," *Chicago Tribune*, July 5, 1910, 1.

68. "Crowd Is Saddened When Johnson Wins," *New York Times*, July 5, 1910, 4.

69. "Riots Follow Victory of Jack Johnson," *San Francisco Examiner*, July 5, 1910, 17–18.

70. J. Lawrence Toole, "No Sorrow for Jeff; None to Salve His Defeat," *San Francisco Examiner*, July 5, 1910, 9; William Muldoon, "Jeffries on the Verge of Nervous Collapse; in a Stupor before He Entered Ring," *San Francisco Examiner*, July 17, 1910, 11. The story appeared as one of a series beneath the broader banner headline. See W. W. Naughton, "Hope of White Race Now Gibe of White Race," *San Francisco Examiner*, July 17, 1910, 11.

71. Hugh E. Keough, "King Is Dead, Long Live the King; Even Though He Is a Negro," *Chicago Tribune*, July 5, 1910, 24.

72. "A Word to the Black Man," *Los Angeles Times*, July 6, 1910, 6. This widely cited editorial cautions blacks that "nobody will think a bit higher of you because your complexion is the same as that of the victor at Reno."

73. "The Race Question," *New York Times*, July 6, 1910, 6; "The Wonderful Refining Influence of the Prize Fight," *Current Literature*, August 1910, 128.

74. This is not to imply that there was no coordination at any level, since some groups appealed to established social channels (e.g., church or political organizations). Rather, it is worth acknowledging that diverse social interests converged quickly and spontaneously through largely decentralized efforts.

75. Despite fears that the public display of the motion pictures would result in riots, in the instances where the films were displayed, few problems ensued. Ironically, fans rioted in New York when a theater, unable to get the real fight films, displayed still photographs instead of motion pictures. See "Theatre Wrecked in Fight Pictures Row," *New York Times*, July 12, 1910, 14.

76. Examples of the sorts of unrelated topics that garnered brief news reportage in the fall of 1910 include hints of challenges from Johnson's black contenders and a briefly hyped road race between Johnson and leading white race car driver Barney Oldfield, an event Oldfield won easily. See "Jack Johnson Beaten," *New York Times*, October 26, 1910, 6.

77. Immediately following Jeffries's defeat, even while the former champion was still icing his swollen face, stories and rumors of nascent white saviors appeared spontaneously in the media reportage. In each case, the reports represented unsubstantiated hype. See "Washington Giant Challenges Jack Johnson," *San Francisco Examiner*, July 6, 1910, 11; "Corbett's 'Unknown' Revealed," *New York Times*, August 3, 1910, 9; "Giant Will Box Choynski," *Chicago Tribune*, September 28, 1910, 11.

78. The term "hope" is used widely in contemporary popular culture to portray underdog status within the context of race. The term has been used in popular music, politics, and sports. It even has been expanded to include the designator "black hope" in this context.

79. As a point of perspective, searches of databases for prior to 1911 generally do not turn up the exact term "white hope." However, for after January 1911, the same search terms will return hundreds of results.

80. "Scientists are Making Study of Upcoming Big Fight," *Washington Post*, February 27, 1910, M8; Hugh E. Keough, "Jeff Convinces His Critics," *Chicago Tribune*, June 11, 1910, 13. Both represent several articles that refer to Jeffries with these terms.

81. None of Johnson's white challengers in 1909 were hyped in terms of "white hope" status; however, most contemporary research refers to these fighters as white hopes.

82. Although these efforts to compartmentalize the Johnson quandary could not generate clear narrative trajectories, they did feature hopeful impulses toward redress. This impulse proved to be enough to frame the Johnson situation through much of the post-Reno maudlin period.

83. "Johnson and White Hopes Fraternize," *New York Times*, May 27, 1911, 8. Johnson attended one of the larger tournaments, and as the *New York Times* reported, the ineptitude of the participants caused him to laugh throughout the event.

84. Despite representing various Caucasian ethnicities, virtually all of the white hopes boasted anglicized names, a factor that demonstrates the tenuous nature of whiteness during that era.

85. "Washington Giant Challenges Jack Johnson," *San Francisco Examiner*, July 6, 1910, 11.

86. "Corbett's 'Unknown' Revealed," 9. Similarly, Corbett and others were also quick to tout a promising British fighter named "Bombardier" Billy Wells. Unlike the bogus "unknown" challenger and the faux hope from Washington, Wells was a real fighter who would emerge into the white hope fray in later months. During the summer of 1910, however, Wells did not captivate the American

media, partially because of his unfamiliar competition and his distance from major American media markets.

87. "Another 'White Hope' Exposed," *Washington Post*, December 1, 1912, S2.

88. "Fireman Jim Flynn Whips Carl Morris," *New York Times*, September 16, 1911, 8.

89. Headline databases are filled with words such as "fizzles" and "flops" during this period.

90. "Johnson-Flynn Bout Regarded as a Joke," *New York Times*, June 23, 1912, C9; "The Las Vegas Incident," *New York Times*, July 5, 1912, 12.

91. Gilmore, *Bad Nigger!* 89. The notorious legislation received very little attention from the press at the time. For example, none of the sampled newspapers highlighted the issue.

92. W. W. Naughton, "I'll Fight Jeffries without a Moment's Hesitation," *San Francisco Examiner*, March 10, 1909, 13. This feature interview covered nearly the top half of the sports page. It included a huge photograph of a dapper Johnson posing in an expensive suit and a derby. Obviously more concerned with sporting issues than social issues, Naughton mentioned Johnson's wife (a role then filled by a prostitute to whom Johnson was not legally married) without mentioning her race. Consistent with this account, Naughton's reports—although not necessarily pro-Johnson—consistently reflected the keen sense of the excitement Johnson brought to the sporting world.

93. W. W. Naughton, "Police Stop Johnson-Flynn Fight in Ninth Round," *San Francisco Examiner*, July 5, 1912, 10. Not only did the tone of this article differ dramatically from the tone of Naughton's portrayals of Johnson in 1909 and 1910, but all reports on the fight were smaller and relegated to a less-prominent corner of the sports page.

94. "Fines Jack Johnson $9,600," *New York Times*, April 4, 1912, 1. While many of these offenses were not significant, during this period some federal officials tried to convict Johnson of smuggling a necklace into the nation. However, the case did not gain much traction since it basically involved paying customs duties and Johnson was able to buy his way out of the problem fairly easily.

95. "Café De Champion? Sure Is!" *Chicago Tribune*, July 9, 1912, 3. The *Tribune* portrays the soon-to-open saloon as an ostentatious undertaking that features fifteen thousand dollars in paintings—mostly of Johnson.

96. "Jack Johnson's Wife Self-Shot," *Chicago Tribune*, September 12, 1912, 1. Because Duryea shot herself late on the evening of September 11 and did not die until after morning newspapers had gone to press, initial stories and headlines did not mention her death. Duryea and Johnson legally married in early 1911. Prior

to that, Johnson informally rotated his white-wife role between two prostitutes, Hattie McClay and Belle Schreiber. After Duryea's death he legally married two more white women.

97. "Reflections on a Suicide," *New York Times*, September 14, 1912, 12; "Mrs. Johnson Tries Suicide," *New York Times*, September 12, 1912, 6.

98. "Jack Johnson's Wife Self-Shot."

99. "Johnson Says He Too Attempted Suicide," *New York Times*, September 13, 1912, 6; "Johnson Denies Beating Up Wife," *Chicago Tribune*, September 13, 1912, 10.

100. Johnson's biographers establish that she went to the press after the police balked because Cameron was older than eighteen.

101. "Jail Girl to Foil Pugilist Johnson," *Chicago Tribune*, October 18, 1912, 3.

102. "Jail Girl to Foil Pugilist Johnson."

103. Gilmore, *Bad Nigger!* 98. In the initial reports from Chicago, a family friend of Cameron's called Johnson "the scum of the earth." The *Police Gazette*, a pro-boxing national sporting magazine, joined the fray, calling Johnson "the vilest, most despicable creature that lives."

104. "Pugilist Johnson Hanged in Effigy," *Chicago Tribune*, October 20, 1910, 20. In a less crass action, hundreds of mothers in Chicago signed a petition of solidarity with Cameron's mother.

105. In the photograph section of his book, Ward provides a photograph of a widely reproduced *Chicago American* headline that says as much.

106. On June 5, 1913, a federal judge sentenced Johnson to a thousand-dollar fine and a year in prison. Given the intensity of emotion leading to the Mann Act charges, the media response to this development appears surprisingly subdued. Outside of Chicago, news reports tended to be short and prosaic (e.g., the *San Francisco Examiner* and *New York Times* announced the news with two- and four-inch stories, respectively).

107. "Jack Johnson Close to Defeat," *New York Times*, December 20, 1913, 1. Johnson's poor showing in a title defense against "Battling" Jim Johnson, a second-rate African American boxer, underscored observations reporters had been making since Johnson's poor showing against Jim Flynn. See W. W. Naughton, "Las Vegas Fight Demonstrated That Jack Johnson Is Not the Powerful Man He Was," *San Francisco Examiner*, July 9, 1912, 12.

108. "Johnson Retains His Championship," *New York Times*, June 28, 1914, 1. In the aftermath of an unimpressive showing against white hope Frank Moran, it is noteworthy that even the world war did not erase concern with the social breach Johnson represented.

109. "Johnson Fans Are Confident," *San Francisco Examiner*, April 2, 1915, 13.

110. "Cowboy Willard Regains World's Fistic Supremacy for the White Race," *San Francisco Examiner*, April 6, 1915, 11.

111. "Story of the Battle," *New York Times*, April 6, 1915, 8.

112. "Pelted with Flowers by Fans after His Victory," *San Francisco Examiner*, April 6, 1915, 11.

113. "Riotous Crowds Greet Willard," *New York Times*, April 8, 1915, 11; "New York Welcomes Big Jess Willard," *New York Times*, April 11, 1915, 15.

114. "Thousands Cheer Willard in South," *New York Times*, April 12, 1915, 12.

115. "Willard Makes His First Speech," *New York Times*, April 13, 1915, 8. Coverage of Willard decreased significantly in the weeks following the fight. Over time, the uncharismatic champion became downright unpopular with fans.

116. "Sans Country, Sans Title; It Is Farewell," *San Francisco Examiner*, April 6, 1915, 11.

117. "Seize Jack Johnson at Mexican Border," *New York Times*, July 21, 1920, 13.

2

Jesse Owens, a Black Pearl amidst an Ocean of Fury
A Case Study of Press Coverage of the 1936 Berlin Olympic Games

PAMELA C. LAUCELLA

Jesse Owens, the son of a sharecropper and grandson of a slave, achieved what no Olympian before him had accomplished. His stunning victories and achievement of four gold medals at the 1936 Olympic Games in Berlin have made him the best-remembered of all Olympic athletes. His outstanding performance during the 1936 Olympic games not only discredited Adolf Hitler's heinous claims, it also affirmed that individual excellence, rather than race or national origin, distinguishes one man or woman from another.[1] While Olympic track star Jesse Owens received accolades and praise later in life, W. E. B. Dubois's notion that "the problem of the twentieth century is the problem of the color line"[2] proved apropos to many black Americans and specifically to Jesse Owens during this epoch.[3] According to sociologist Douglas Kellner, "the extent to which the spectacles of sports have promoted the interests of African Americans and people of color has not yet been adequately understood," but one thing is certain: the confluence of race and sports in America has long dominated sports discourse and deserves attention.[4]

This exploration seeks to disclose that sports texts' meanings expand beyond "archetypal heroic myths" of the sports arena to provide insight into cultural values.[5] Cultural historian James Carey suggests that when examining a journalistic account as a cultural form it should be viewed as a "creative and imaginative work, a symbolic strategy."[6] By studying journalism history we study the diverse ways individuals "have grasped reality" and the actors within.[7]

Communication and cultural historian Marion Marzolf emphasized past media content, the journalists who produced discourse, and the "fit between these and the cultural context and society in which they existed."[8] Through content assessment, or the "extensive reading of great quantities of newspapers, using the historian's method of reading, sifting, weighing, comparing and analyzing the evidence in order to tell the story," scholars can gain a glimpse into culture, its complexities, and intimate stories of life.[9] According to Marzolf, "journalists' writings can be analyzed for literary style and form, and can be considered for the values and choices presented."[10] This essay will examine the Berlin Olympic Games, its depictions of race, and specifically of Jesse Owens, and how the story was covered in terms of "information, values and opinions."[11]

The purpose of this essay is to explore legendary sports journalist Grantland Rice's coverage of Jesse Owens and to compare and contrast his writings with those of sports journalists from the black press. Owens won four gold medals in track and field events at the 1936 Berlin Olympic Games, including the 100-meter dash, the 200-meter dash, the long jump, and the 400-meter relay.[12] In total, Owens surpassed nine Olympic records and tied two.[13] Since Grantland Rice has been touted as the "the first important American sportswriter,"[14] having written more than sixty-seven million words, twenty-two thousand columns, seven thousand sets of verse, and one thousand magazine articles[15] in fifty-three years, an analysis of his discourse on Owens will not only explore the significance of his texts but will also reveal one prominent mainstream sports journalist's perceptions of athletes and race in pre–World War II America.[16]

To delve into the longstanding issues of race, sports, and Jesse Owens, the following questions warrant analysis:

> How did sports journalists use language to create, attribute, or sustain the persona of Jesse Owens during the 1936 Olympic Games?

Specifically, what characterizations did Grantland Rice and journalists from the black newspaper the *New York Amsterdam News* use to describe a prominent athletic event like the Olympic Games and athlete Jesse Owens?

And finally, how did Grantland Rice's depictions of Jesse Owens differ from those of his colleagues at the *New York Amsterdam News*?

Jesse Owens: The Person, the Athlete, and the Hero

While many know Owens only from his Olympic feats, he overcame much adversity to attain athletic and personal success. James Cleveland Owens was born in Oakville, Alabama, in 1913 to Henry Cleveland and Mary Emma Owens.[17] The couple raised nine children in a "sharecropper's shanty" and worked in the cotton fields of this poverty-stricken town.[18] After World War I when Owens was eight, the family migrated north like many black Americans and headed for Cleveland, Ohio.[19]

At Fairmount Junior High School Owens met Charles Riley,[20] a white coach and physical education teacher of Irish descent.[21] He taught Owens to run like his feet "were moving over the cinders[,] . . . like the ground was a burning fire" he "didn't want to touch, a full stride in front of all the runners."[22] Owens then attended Cleveland East Technical High School and there became a full-fledged "track star."[23] Under the guidance of Edgar Weil, Owens tied the world record of 9.4 seconds in the 100-yard dash and set a new world record of 20.7 seconds in the 220-yard dash his senior year at the National Interscholastic Championships.[24]

After graduating high school Owens entered Ohio State University, where he endured segregated conditions and worked part-time jobs to pay for his education.[25] Larry Snyder, another "white man who was color blind,"[26] coached him to a "break out" Saturday in Michigan at the Big Ten Championships.[27] According to Owens, "all the books say my 'best' days were those days in Berlin. It isn't so. By far my finest one was May 25, 1935."[28] Despite a back injury, Owens broke three world records and tied one in less than an hour.[29] In all, he surpassed records in the 220-yard sprint, long jump, and 220-yard hurdles and tied the record in the

100-yard dash.[30] His broad jump record lasted twenty-four years and was nearly two inches longer than his jump at the Berlin Olympic Games.[31]

Owens compared the uniqueness of his life to a "patchwork quilt," saying his life was "wrapped up, summed up—and stopped up by a single incident," the "clash with Adolf Hitler in the 1936 Olympics."[32] He wrote, "The lines were drawn then as they had never been drawn before, or since. The Germans were hosting the Games and, with each passing day, were coming to represent everything that free people have always feared."[33] After Owens won the broad jump, he exclaimed,

> I really thought it all *had* come true. *He* [Hitler] wasn't even in his box glaring at the end. He couldn't take it and had left. It was as if I'd destroyed Hitler and his Aryan-supremacy, anti-Negro, anti-Jew viciousness. The good guys had won. In fact, not just "the good guys," but the best possible "guy"—an American Negro.[34]

After Owens's spectacular Olympic accomplishments while a sophomore at Ohio State University, the Associated Press awarded him their Athlete of the Year award in 1936.[35] Nevertheless, his post-Olympic experience proved disheartening. Owens could not support himself and "was just one more black man trying to make it in a white man's country."[36] He left Ohio State before his senior year and signed a contract with Consolidated Radio Artists of New York City in 1937.[37] Here he toured with a black twelve-piece band, tap-danced, and later raced horses and trains, quickly fading into obscurity.[38]

However, in the early 1950s Owens moved to Chicago and once again "catapulted to eminence in the American mainstream."[39] He served as executive director of the South Side Boys Club in Chicago and secretary of the Illinois State Athletic Commission, appeared on radio and television shows, directed his own public relations firm, and served on the Eisenhower administration's "People-to-People" Program, which promoted understanding between Americans and individuals worldwide.[40]

Owens's financial woes and indebtedness plagued him for years,[41] and in 1965 Owens pled nolo contendere to the government's indictment for not filing tax returns from 1959–1962.[42] Nevertheless in 1976, President

Ford awarded him the highest civilian honor in the United States, the Medal of Freedom. This accolade recognized his feats in overcoming adversity in his fight for racial equity in sports.

While W. E. B. Dubois responded to prejudice with aggression, Owens instead reacted with acceptance and accommodation like his hero Booker T. Washington.[43] As Donald Spivey professed, "when Owens finally became economically secure in the late 1960s, he became an ardent supporter of the status quo and a foe of the Black Athletic Revolution."[44] Owens died of lung cancer on March 31, 1980.[45]

Social Darwinism, Nazi Logic, and Native Modernism in the Early Twentieth Century

This research expands upon literature written about race, sports, and particularly Jesse Owens and the Berlin Olympic Games and delves into perceptions and media portrayals of black athletes. It especially draws on work from William J. Baker, Edward Caudill, Jon Entine, William Benn Michaels, Laurel Davis and Othello Harris, Ben Carrington, Richard Mandell, Charles Fountain, and Norman Katkov.

Many white individuals proclaimed the social Darwinian theory of evolution as a justification for discrimination against blacks.[46] "The evolutionary process was characterized by a struggle and conflict in which the stronger, more advanced . . . would naturally triumph over the inferior weaker . . . peoples."[47] According to Caudill, Germans made the legitimization of racism an important research goal, and their "racial science" became part of the nationalist ideology.[48] Nazi logic had the following philosophy: "Nations struggle for space, just as animals struggle for survival. . . . The stronger nations, like the stronger animals, survive, while the weaker ones die. Alien or non-Aryan races . . . threaten German vitality by making the race weaker; Germans are obligated to eradicate inferior races in order to assure survival of the superior race. These natural laws are also the laws of God."[49]

Here in the United States, the "utopian myth of racial purity" rarely appeared in mainstream publications.[50] However, individuals supported disparate ideas from Nazism's junction of "race, science, and society."[51]

The *Catholic World* stated that Hitler's "actions were not and are not the actions of an irresponsible wild man.... Rather, Herr Hitler is ruthlessly and quite logically following out the Nazi theory of race and blood.... Hitler is quite reasonable and logical in so far as he sticks to his program of racial purification."[52]

Michaels studied the changing notions of identity and Americanization, primarily focusing on post–World War I America. He claimed that the social movement of nativism and the aesthetic movement of modernism united during the 1920s to unravel "linguistic, national, cultural, and racial" identities.[53] During this era of cultural pluralism, America experienced a "rewriting of race and nation,"[54] and culture was a means of rethinking and protecting the fundamental outlines of racial identity.[55] According to Michaels, "what makes blacks black is ... the shared experience of being visually or cognitively identified as black by a white racist society, and the punitive and damaging effects of that identification."[56]

The media contributed to this "racial logic," presenting negative portrayals of blackness in American culture and debasing even the greatest of black athletes.[57] In the 1920s and 1930s black men were often portrayed as "Uncle Tom" or "Sambo" and black women as "Mammies."[58] Despite the successes of black athletes like Owens and Joe Louis, sports journalists' coverage reflected the times and reinforced prejudices.[59] The media often fortified the stereotype of African Americans as "natural athletes" possessing a "superior physiology."[60] Davis and Harris defined a stereotype as "a generalization about a category of people that is negative or misleading."[61] The researchers contended that "for much of the history of the United States, people openly stereotyped people of African descent as ignorant, lazy, happy-go-lucky, savage and animal-like."[62] This signified deeper cultural meanings.

According to Carrington,

> racial signification of sport means that sports contests are more than just significant events.... They act as a key signifier for wider questions about identity within racially demarcated societies in which racial narratives about the self and society are read both into and from sporting contests that are imbued with racial meanings.[63]

Jesse Owens and the 1936 Berlin Olympic Games

Overall, American black athletes secured six individual gold medals and eight total in track and field, accounting for 83 of the Americans' total 167 points.[64] According to Entine, Owens and other black athletes of the 1936 Olympic Games "had made a statement with their victories that no one could ignore."[65] Following eighteen lynchings in 1935 and eight in 1936, Mandell concurred by writing, "All of these individuals, but Jesse Owens particularly, made two contributions to the world in 1936. They made the general, abstract one of gnawing away at the frontiers of human accomplishment. . . . The Olympics and sporting competitions exist partly for this purpose. Another contribution was that they all lifted their race a little from imposed obscurity and degradation."[66]

Fountain also discussed the importance of the 1936 Berlin Olympic Games and Rice's coverage of Owens briefly in his biography of Rice. He wrote,

> Americans found themselves confronted with the uncomfortable choice between two prejudices—their longstanding racial bias and their continued dislike and distrust of the Germans. . . . For the most part nationalism prevailed over racism. . . . Even those Americans who suffered from a less-virulent strain of his poisonous notion of Aryan superiority found themselves in the unlikely position of cheering for a black man.[67]

Nevertheless, Fountain wrote, "the race of Jesse Owens and his black teammates was a factor in every story American journalists wrote, and when the black runners emerged as dominant athletes of the games, writers felt compelled to mention race whenever a white American athlete won a medal."[68] Fountain noted Rice's reinforcement of stereotypes while also stating his belief that "this glibness was offset in part by other comments."[69] While Rice seemed uncomfortable with race, he believed the positive reactions to Owens reinforced the "unifying power of sport."[70] Fountain concluded,

> Jesse Owens' place in this could not be denied. His accommodating nature . . . allowed him to be accepted, by his teammates, by the press,

by white America. In a competition staged to showcase a society built upon racism, Jesse Owens' inspiring gifts as an athlete, and his humble yet noble bearing as a man, prompted white America to confront their shame.[71]

Mandell further expounded on Owens's demeanor, writing, "As a superior individual who was a self-effacing gentleman, Jesse Owens was both a paragon and a refutation" and a "credit to his race."[72] Katkov's intimate interview with Owens for *Sport* magazine also reinforced the perception of a "shy" man with a "humble smile."[73] He resounded the importance of Owens's feats when he wrote,

> You have to think of the 1936 Olympics as Jesse Owens's. . . . Jesse Owens emerged as the only superman in the Olympic Stadium. Even the huge German crowds applauded in wonder as Owens flew across the finish line with a burst of speed that no human being could equal.[74]

A Sample of Stories on Owens and the 1936 Olympic Games

While many scholars have offered insight on the 1936 Olympic Games and Jesse Owens, a detailed analysis of sports journalists' articles in their entirety will expand upon their research and further clarify the importance of their stories. Word choice, language, tone, and content were specifically targeted, following Marzolf's model of content assessment and the fit between content, culture, and society.

This investigation addresses the complexities of race and athlete Jesse Owens as described in ten of Grantland Rice's nationally syndicated columns on August 2–6 and August 8–12, 1936. These represent all of Rice's newspaper columns pertaining to Owens during the 1936 Berlin Olympic Games. Additionally, Rice's article on August 27, 1936, "Germans Study Makeup of Negro," though retrospective, will supplement the sample due to its relevance in describing Jesse Owens and race.

In addition, seven articles from the third-largest black newspaper, the *New York Amsterdam News*,[75] will complete the sample. Using stories from a New York newspaper promotes uniformity since Rice worked as a New

York journalist for forty years at such newspapers as the *New York Tribune* and *New York Herald Tribune*[76] and enjoyed a thirty-five year relationship with *Colliers*,[77] where he wrote more than five hundred articles and his "All-America" football selections from 1925 to 1947.[78]

Additionally, the Harlem weekly publicized its "firsthand" information from correspondent William Charles Chase.[79] The specific selection of articles by Chase, and of all cited columns pertaining to Owens, was chosen to coincide with the time frame of the cited columns by Rice in order to allow for the most meaningful comparison.

Jesse Owens as Portrayed by Rice, Chase, Taylor, and Ottley

Owens ascended to the pinnacle of success at the Berlin Olympic Games[80] as the first track and field competitor since 1900 to win three gold medals in one Olympics.[81] While newspapers reported on his athletic prowess and extraordinary feats, did they concede to racial stereotypes and marked language, and if so, did this signify cultural attitudes and perspectives?

Rice began his August 2 article by referencing the broader implications of the Olympic Games.

> Contrary to Kipling, the tumult and the shouting never die, the captains never depart. Just 22 years ago this day the world went to war. On this 22nd anniversary of the outbreak of that great conflict I passed through more than 700,000 uniforms on my way to the Olympic Stadium—brown shirts, black guards, gray-green waves of regular army men and marines—seven massed military miles rivaling the mobilization of August 1, 1914.[82]

Rice alluded to Kipling and progressed into an intimate description and comparative analysis between the Olympic Games' Opening Ceremony and World War I.[83] He tried to recreate the scenes of World War I through imagery and stylistic devices like alliteration with his use of "men," "marines," "massed military miles," and "mobilization."[84]

Rice embellished with more stylistic devices by expounding on the audience's receptions of nations. First he wrote, "The nations giving the Nazi salute received a thundering welcome from the 110,000 spectators massed in the stadium."[85] Rice substituted "nations" for the individual athletes with metonymy and followed with hyperbole in the exaggerated "thundering welcome."[86] Using hyperbole, Rice contrasted the fans' "ear-crashing roar" and "local loyalty" exhibited for those federations with the meager applause for Great Britain and the United States.[87]

Rice wrote, "The British team marched stolidly past Hitler's box . . . and their reception by the crowd was fainter than a southern zephyr. Later the United States team, 357 strong[,] . . . received an even fainter demonstration from the crowd than did Britain."[88] In these instances, Rice used the metaphor of "zephyr" to animate his piece and lure readers through imagery and description.

Rice detailed everything from Hitler's 4:00 entry and the "gray" and "threatening" weather to the incoming march of "50 nations presenting all the colors of the rainbow from Germany's 427 entries to Haiti and Costa Rica with one each."[89] He touted the event as "one of the most impressive sights of sport or war."[90]

While the article mainly addressed the games' political implications, it referenced race in its final paragraph, which read, "Anyway, the big test starts Sunday on track and field, where the answer will be given in what looks to be the greatest Olympics ever held, so far as color and competition go. I still believe the United States will dominate the military-athletic pageant."[91] Rice established ethos by granting insider information and foretelling the American athletes' successes and domination.

In Rice's August 3 article, he used persuasive appeals to invent and bolster his argument. He began by hyping the German fans' ardent passion in an "uproarious opening day" of "well over a hundred thousand persons."[92] He introduced Owens in the third paragraph, relying on personification when he wrote, "The real opening day finished at top speed."[93] Rice continued, "Jesse Owens broke the world's record for the 100-meter run in the second heat at 10.2, though it was subsequently ruled unofficial on account of favoring winds and merely counted as equaling the 1932 Olympic record of 10.3 made by Eddie Tolan."[94]

While Rice offered a detached perspective toward the issue, he still praised Owens's "marvelous running" as the "day's big feature," adding his prediction that "it was the forerunner of coming triumph."[95] Rice established credibility by offering his opinions in an authoritative and ceremonial manner. After he reported the results of other track and field events, he concluded by reinforcing his premise and ending on a high note when he wrote,

> Germany's opening day, showing two Olympic first place flags, has Berlin at the highest pitch, with the greatest gayety, since pre-war days.... The outbreak of national feeling is beyond belief. The days ahead presage even more excitement and color in view of the opening day's results. The winning of the home team is always a big event, but Owens, Towns and Hardin, plus the pole vaulters will soon be heard from.[96]

Throughout the article, Rice maintained a detached stance towards Owens and race by exhibiting cautious optimism in future competitions. Conversely, the August 4 article began,

> The heritage of the cotton fields and canebrakes of the South and the foothills of the Ozark mountains of Missouri dominated the second day of the Olympic show. Herr Hitler was alternately elated and depressed at the changing tides of Nordic supremacy. On the male side it was a darktown parade as Jesse Owens equaled the Olympic record by winning the finals in the 100-meter run on a slow track after a day of rain and cold wind with Metcalfe second and Ossendarp of Holland third.[97]

Rice added, "Hitler was rooting for the Germans like a Yale sophomore at a Harvard game."[98] His lead stressed race, with cotton fields and canebreaks composing the first sentence and "darktown" the second.[99] The similes and analogies supplemented the descriptive language. Rice then dismissed the American shot putters and hammer throwers by calling them "third grade and outclassed."[100] Rice called Owens "African" and then called a Canadian runner "Negro."[101]

In Rice's August 5 column he asserted that "Glenn Hardin, the Mississippi hurdler, startled the German multitude by proving that the United States had a white man who could win."[102] The lead paragraph read,

"Tuesday was a dark, raw day of rain and wind, but it looked even darker to the fifty other nations participating in the Olympic games as our Ethiopian troops continued their deadly fire."[103] Later in the article Rice wrote,

Owens had been like a wild Zulu running amock [*sic*]. He has started six times, in the 100-meters, the 200-meter heats and the broad jump, and has broken the Olympic record four times and has equaled the record in his other two starts. He has been deadly poison to Nordic supremacy, not only by his victories but by the best form and smoothest style that coaches from all over the world have ever seen.[104]

Rice then complimented Owens, stating, "He will be remembered among the outstanding Olympic artists of all time. He stopped to applaud Don Lash, qualifying in the 5,000-meter run, a few seconds before making his record jump."[105] In this instance, Rice elevated Owens by considering him one of the best Olympic athletes of all time and praised his sportsmanship, rather than using a racial reference.

Rice also nicknamed and stereotyped other Olympic competitors, calling Woodruff a "Pittsburgh Negro," Helen Stephens the "Ozark flash," and Gisela Mauermayer the "German girl."[106] In the latter part of the article Rice wrote, "The Negroes are just better runners and jumpers, with more to come later on. The collapse of the American whites has been terrific. Towns, the Georgia hurdler, promises he will come to the white rescue."[107]

Rice continued, "Apparently the race here is to the swift, and the black and sepia are too strong. The white man's burden has broken the white man's back as far as America is concerned. The United States would be outclassed except for our black skinned frontal and flanking fire."[108] Rice never once assimilated black athletes as Americans and the "frontal and flanking fire's" alliteration focused attention on Rice's racial reference here.[109] His comments also implied biological differences between white and black athletes.

On August 6, 1936, Rice began his column with an exaggerated hyperbole, "Jesse Owens, the Buckeye Blizzard, will take back to Buckeye soil enough Olympic oak trees to start a new oak forest," describing his performance in the 200-meter dash under adverse weather conditions.[110] He explained his "record-shattering path" by explaining how the "Ohio Negro's flying feet ate up time and turf."[111]

Rice continued with his dramatic narrative, writing, "Dark clouds were hovering over the field above the shivering 100,000 spectators as Owens left the starter's mark like a shot from a gun. Off to the lead, he looked like a dark streak of lightning. Still traveling his effortless style, he pulled steadily away to finish in 20.7 seconds, three-tenths of a second faster than the race had ever been run before."[112] In this section, Rice compared Owens's speed to a gun and lightning and complimented his graceful movements. Additionally, he imbued "dark clouds" with the human attribute of "hovering," an example of personification.[113]

The August 8, 1936, column included the following racially marked language in the first paragraph. "Brown is Germany's national color, and brown remains the official color of the Olympic Games. The only change is from brown shirts to brown skins."[114] The second paragraph added, "You can call them all-browns or the sepia fusileers. At any rate, they have turned Berlin's magnificent Olympic spectacle into darktown on parade."[115]

Rice called Archie Williams a "California Negro" and "dark lightning" and implied stereotypical attributes for the black athletes in the following passage:

> Easily, almost lazily, and minus any show of extra effort, they have turned sport's greatest spectacle into the "Black Birds of 1936." All week, crowds of 110,000 must have had black spots dancing before their bewildered eyes. However you may feel about it, the four American Negroes, Owens, Johnson, Woodruff and Williams, have won six main firsts, leading the United States to a smashing victory in the eleventh Olympiad, as far too many American whites fell down badly.[116]

On August 9, 1936, Rice led with information on American decathlete Glenn Morris's world record followed by Americans Bob Clark and Jack Parker's sweep of the medals, lauding it as the "greatest showing the United States has ever made."[117] He followed with the United States' relay team and its performance. Wrote Rice, "In one of the biggest days for the United States, the relay team led by Jesse Owens ran the 400 meters in 40 seconds flat, outclassing the field. Lawson Robertson, the United States Olympic track and field coach, picked the best United States team regardless of race and color, thereby using wise judgment despite any criticism. Owens delighted the biggest crowd of the week, which packed and jammed the Stadium, with Chancellor Hitler remaining for the finish around 9 p.m."[118]

Rice minimized the use of stylistic devices and electrically charged language in this article and instead presented a fairly blasé commentary. While Rice detailed Hitler's attendance and the enthusiasm displayed for Owens, the piece's explicit persuasive appeals waned in comparison to those of articles earlier in the week.

In the August 10, 1936, column Rice expressed a more positive and objective tone by writing, "United States athletes Owens, Towns, Morris and the relay team accounted for five of the eight world records and most of the Olympic marks that were shattered as the athletes and spectators of fifty rival nations looked on in wonderment as the Stars and Stripes clung almost continuously to the Olympic masthead."[119]

The United States won twelve of twenty-three events. Rice used two coaches' quotes, instilling credibility and promoting official perspectives. Dean Cromwell presented a sugarcoated view by contending, "The performances of Owens and Glenn Morris . . . were incredible. The crowds were extremely fair, unusually so considering the preponderance of United States victories. No other Olympic has been even close in crowds, records, color and fairness."[120]

Lawson Robertson, the coach of the U.S. track and field team, added, "This is the all-time top,"[121] and in a subsequent article said that "Owens is a complete standout. . . . Not only is he a perfect athlete, but a fine boy and a 100 percent sportsman."[122] Rice praised Owens's sportsmanship when he "shoved Metcalfe forward in his place for the Olympic crowning in the 400-meter event."[123]

On August 12, 1936, Rice quoted Ernest Hanfstaengl, a "Harvard man and one of the German heads."[124] Hanfstaengl asserted,

There is not the slightest objection here to the Negroes. . . . We are looking for the best. But in our own case we would enter them from the colonies, not from Germany. It was Africa that dominated the Olympic track and field, not the United States. Why not give the home nation the credit due?[125]

While this may not directly reveal Rice's opinion, his use of this comment reiterated and reinforced the segregation between nation and race and black from white. The rhetorical question at the end invited readers to contemplate the issue and opinions presented in the article.

In Rice's post-Olympic column on August 27, 1936, he compared the Olympic Games to a party. Wrote Rice, "The large Olympic party put on by American Negroes will have Germany's savants, philosophers and research experts busy for some time. Being a pretty thorough set of people along whatever line they follow, the Germans want to know how it happened and why it happened—especially why."[126] Rice used hyperbole and stereotyped the German people in their attention to detail. Regarding the success of "Owens, Johnson, Metcalfe, Woodruff, Williams, Lu Valle" and other black American athletes, Rice quoted an anonymous but alleged "expert":

It is the Negro's ability to relax and keep relaxed, plus his inborn sense of rhythm. . . . I watched them at rest around the Olympic village and it seemed to me that most of the time they were dozing or yawning. They were not worn down by too many jumpy nerves.[127]

Rice clearly affirmed the idea that black athletes were genetically predisposed to excelling in sport due to their physical and emotional composition. He additionally bolstered the stereotype that black individuals are lazier than members of other races. While he credited Owens as being able to "put on full pressure without breaking perfect form" and his "ability to look completely at ease and relaxed even in the midst of a record breaking race," the article's tone appeared curious yet uninformed.[128]

Rice then quoted an anonymous U.S. coach who reinforced the notion of blacks' "greater natural rhythm" by saying, "The average Negro of 18 or 19 is as much developed physically as the average white of 22 or 23.... This makes a difference. On a general average, they are also more agile as a race."[129]

Rice concluded on a lighter note with the coach saying, "Certainly it will be a long time before we get another Owens. He is one of those rarities who happen along every other lifetime."[130] While the last sentence praised Owens, most of the article focused on the alleged genetic and psychological differences between the races and his choice of quotations and stylistic devices reinforced this premise.

General Observations on Rice's Articles

During the 1920s and continuing into the 1930s, significant sports events often graced newspapers' front-page headlines with descriptive and florid language. Writers sought to instill excitement in their readers through vivid imagery and stylistic devices. Rice's writing unquestionably possessed unity, lyricism, and eloquence. He informed and commented with elaborate yet mellifluous prose and excelled at scene-setting techniques, instilling a feeling of immersion and participation in his readers. His writings enabled American fans to experience the excitement of the Berlin Olympic Games through his intimate commentary.

As the analysis indicated, Rice's articles rarely included detailed analyses of Jesse Owens's talents, character, or ability to overcome adversity and racial prejudices. They focused instead on detailed accounts of the surrounding scenes, biological explanations of the black athletes' dominance of the Olympic Games, and the audiences' reactions to the athletes' victories. The conversational yet authoritative tone gained intimacy with readers while establishing credibility. Rice compared sports to war and drama, reverting back to his military experiences from World War I. The columns reflected the fun, the fancy, the frivolity of sports in an escapist way yet hinted at deeper implications like race relations and politics. As cultural historian Warren Susman wrote regarding the era's sports journalists, "They invented along the way an often brilliantly different and always special kind of rhetoric and style. Their unique prose delighted readers, sold more copies, appealed to more advertising agencies with products to sell."[131]

Journalists' Writings from the *New York Amsterdam News*

William Charles Chase's first article appeared on August 8 and began with a war metaphor:

> When the good ship Manhattan left its berth with the United States Olympic team for its foreign invasion, the experts claimed that it bore the strongest track and field teams to have ever left the American shores. Ten Negro boys were on that boat as track and field Olympic entries, and these ten boys, so the critics said, were the strongest part of the American forces in that division.[132]

Chase noted the "black contingent" and detailed Owens's three gold medals; Johnson and Woodruff's one gold medal, respectively; and the silver medals won by Albritton and Robinson.[133] He called Owens an "individual star" who "truly earned the title of the world's fastest human by his triple victory."[134] Chase stressed that Owens matched Paavo Nurmi of Finland, who won three gold medals in 1924.[135] He wrote, "He streaked down the track to establish a new world's record in the amazing time of 0:10.2 seconds."[136] However, "the International Amateur Athletic Federation would not allow the record to stand, as there was a favoring wind at the back of Owens."[137] While Chase reported the incident, he did not criticize the ruling nor allege it was unfair.

Chase next described the 100-meter finals, where Owens equaled the world record of 0:10.3 seconds, the broad jump competition, and Owens's battle with German Lutz Long, whom he later befriended.[138] Wrote Chase, "Owens came thundering down the runway and drove into space a moment later. He had taken the play away at 7.94 meters and then drove beyond Long's reach with his final jump of 8.06 meters. That cemented the distinction of his becoming the first 26-footer in Olympic history. Score No. 2 for Owens."[139] Chase's use of metaphor and hyperbole reinforced the distinction he intended to draw between Owens and his competitors.

Chase then described the 200-meter race and the rivalry between Owens and American Mack Robinson, regarding them as "American hopes in the final of this event."[140] In the final fifty meters of the race, "Robinson unleashed a killing burst, but was unable to catch the flying Owens, who won the race by four feet over Robinson. The United States had made another 'small slam' with its black contingent playing the honor role."[141] Both Americans broke existing world records, and Chase described the Germans' response in the following manner:

> The 110,000 people in the huge stadium rose to the man to give Owens one of the grandest ovations ever accorded an athlete. Cries of "Owens!" rang throughout the arena as the greatest living athlete strode casually back to where he had left his warm-ups.[142]

Chase elaborated on Woodruff by saying he was "inspired by the feats of Owens and the rest of his dark-skinned brothers."[143] To conclude, he offered an overview of the Americans' victories and dominance by writing, "The American team is conceded to be the strongest ever sent to these Olympic wars, with ten gallant Negro boys counted upon to literally win the track and field championship for the United States."[144] In the last paragraph he wrote, "These victories bring the point total of the Negro stars up to 80. . . . The boys can pick up around 20 more points if the form charts continue to hold out."[145]

Chase's celebratory tone stressed American patriotism as well as the brotherhood that existed between the black track and field athletes. Like Rice, he used war metaphors, but overall his use of stylistic devices and embellished language waned in comparison and his columns lacked the lyricism of Rice's work.

In Randy Taylor's August 8 "Sportopics" column, he commended the athletes' feats. He first noted that he's "pinch-hitting for Roi Ottley" and began by writing,

> All I can think about is the Olympic Games at Berlin and America's "Black Gang." . . . The dusky-hued stars are certainly stealing the show from Herr Hitler. . . . Hitler promised the world that there would be no show of racial bias or prejudice at the games. . . . I guess Hitler suffered a lapse of memory when he failed to greet the winners of the high jump.[146]

He next stressed his point by writing, "If Hitler is trying to dodge the Afro-Americans he'll have a hard time, for Owens, Metcalfe, Johnson, Albritton, Woodruff, Williams et al. are going to make it tough for him."[147] He called Owens "the tops" and then wrote, "This boy is a record-breaking fool: he broke the world's record in the 100 meters."[148]

After discussing Johnson, Albritton, and Woodruff, Taylor returned to Owens and called him the "World's Greatest Athlete."[149] He set Owens apart from all athletes in writing,

> Jesse Owens, the pride of Ohio, stands out in bold relief as the greatest athlete in the world today. When he won three Olympic championships, he moved into the favored class occupied only by the peerless Paavo Nurmi. However, the feats of Owens overshadow those of Nurmi, primarily because the Finn was a track man and won all of his honors in the flat races in 1924. Owens is the first athlete to combine both track and field activities and win Olympic championships in all of them.[150]

After Taylor discussed Owens's high school achievements and records, he expounded on Hitler's reaction to Owens at the Olympic Games:

> Der Fuehrer forgot that Owens had won the broad jump and he congratulated Lutz Long, the German, who placed second.... What would have happened if the Negroes of the United States had protested against colored stars competing in the Berlin games? ... Methinks the German Chancellor would have felt a lot better.[151]

Chase ended conversationally by saying, "Well, folks, these colored boys are so good that their performances make goose pimples break out all over my flesh."[152]

On August 15 Chase's article entitled "Hitler's Aide in Talk to Chase Denies Insult," referred to his interview with Reich Minister of Propaganda Goebbels, who said that Hitler maintained a "definite schedule" and was therefore unable to meet Jesse Owens.[153] Chase countered by saying Hitler waited two hours to greet German victors. He then indicated that the propaganda minister showed respect for Owens but not for other black athletes. Wrote Chase, "If any Negroe was excepted, it was Jesse

Owens only, who is treated as a special pet in the midst of much antagonistic feeling."[154]

Chase noted the "continual surveillance" of "all non-Aryans, notably Jews and Negroes" and revealed that "only the fact that some Negroes vote in America and, therefore, have some voice in international affairs, seem to have won over the functionaries of the Propaganda Office to calendar the interview, which, incidentally, is the only one granted to any Negro weekly by so close an adviser and representative of Hitler."[155]

Taylor's "Sportopics" on August 15, 1936, termed Owens "the Unbeatable" and "the greatest sprinter."[156] He wrote, "This commentator has been beefing loud and long from the housetops that it's 'Owens'—can't be anybody else. . . . You can't beat figures."[157] Taylor selected Owens over athletes Howard Drew, Charley Paddock, Eddie Tolan, and Ralph Metcalfe, explaining, "He runs with all the ease and grace of a piece of oiled machinery. He is mechanical to say the least, but still he possesses the true heart of a champion."[158]

Taylor next emphasized his records by writing, "But when it comes to being a record holder, he's the tops; he holds the world's records in the 100 meters, 200 meters, 100 yards, 220 yards, 220 yard low hurdles and the broad jump. I don't suppose there are any more records he can gather in."[159] He then reiterated effusive praise by writing, "He won four gold medals, thus becoming the third individual to accomplish this feat in the Olympic Games, joining A. E. Kraenzlein, U.S.A., and Paavo Nurmi, Finland, in this favored group. The triumphs of Owens stamp him as the outstanding athlete to have performed in the eleventh Olympiad."[160]

Taylor commented on the Nazi reaction in writing, "Der Feuhrer had quite a difficult time getting around the congratulatory ceremonies for the colored lads. . . . The Nazi press took up the war cry, claiming that the U.S. had to use its 'black auxiliary forces' to win the track and field title. . . . Someone suggested that the U.S. ought to send its dark brothers as a separate team."[161]

Taylor addressed the German papers' assertion that Owens might turn professional after the Olympic Games, admitting it was an ideal time for such a move. He wrote, "The fact that he is at the peak of his prominence makes it possible for him to land lucrative contracts. . . . And in these times of stress and strain, one can't overlook any opportunities to cash in on his abilities. . . . We wish Jesse luck in any decision he makes."[162]

In Chase's other August 15 article, entitled, "Germans Look for Savage Negro, Chase Says, Citing Nazi Slander,"[163] he began by writing,

The Germans were insistent that America cleaned up in the track and field games because they brought over their "alien" Negro athletes. No argument could convince them that Negroes are real Americans, for they have classified them like the Jews who were persecuted religiously by the Nazis until Olympic party manners were instituted.

The hospitality shown toward Negroes at the beginning of the games was overdone, and little incidents kept cropping up at times to convince one that the National Socialist spirit of antagonism toward non-Aryan races is beginning to permeate the people.[164]

He noted that German papers incorrectly reported that several Negro track and field victors "got drunk to celebrate" and another newspaper showed a picture of Owens and Metcalfe shivering and said, "Germany with its cold breezes is no place for a black man."[165]

Chase suggested that many Germans had never seen Negroes, and one German allegedly explained that he expected the black athletes to eat with fingers rather than utensils.[166] For balance, Chase noted, "no racial segregation or discrimination existed at the Olympic Village" even among "white Southerners."[167] He concluded by stressing the Germans' intrigue and obsession with Owens. Chase wrote, "Many Germans know but two English words, and they are 'Jesse Owens.'"[168] "Almost every Negro man on the streets was approached by a German woman offering to make love for a price. I was informed that they consider their attentions worth four times as much from Negroes as from whites."[169]

On August 29, 1936, Roi Ottley wrote a front-page article entitled "Olympic Hero Returns to Weigh Proposals—No Unkind Words Even for Hitler."[170] He created a majestic and almost ethereal scene by beginning, "The magnificent ocean liner, Queen Mary, flagship of the Cunard, White Star Line, brought the magnificent Jesse Owens home Monday. He came back from his foreign triumphs to receive a stunning reception. At Quarantine his parents, delegations from Cleveland and more than 300 newspapermen welcomed the Olympic star, who had scored so brilliantly in Berlin."[171]

His article primarily reported on Owens's demeanor and perspectives towards the games. Wrote Ottley, "The fact that he had been suspended from the A.A.U. for failure to accompany the American Olympic team on its 'barnstorming' trip through Europe apparently had not made the youthful hero bitter."[172] Ottley alleged that Owens had been "coached" not to make "offensive declarations that might later impair his professional career."[173] After all, Owens admitted that he wanted "security" for himself and his family.[174]

In the article Owens is quoted as having emphatically stated, "There was absolutely no discrimination at all. Everyone was friendly to me, and our athletes were accorded the greatest ovation I ever heard when we arrived in Germany."[175] Ottley then ended with this commentary: "The international idol was expansive and warm in his praise of Lutz Long, the German broad jumper, who he declared gave him his stiffest fight in athletic competition. He thinks Long is one of the great athletes of the world."[176]

Ottley presented a heroic image of Owens despite the prejudices and adversity he faced in Nazi Germany. He appeared as a perfect and humble gentleman and athlete, a role model for all individuals alike.

General Observations on the *New York Amsterdam News*'s Journalists

Regarding specific differences between the three journalists at the *New York Amsterdam News*, Chase used more metaphors and hyperbole, stressing the unification and camaraderie between the "dark-skinned brothers."[177] Chase's articles exuded a positive perspective towards white America but derided Germans towards the end of the games. He compared the black athletes' experiences to those of Jews in Germany and his tone appeared more realistic. Taylor openly criticized Hitler from the beginning of the games, thereby separating Owens from his nemesis and the rest of the Olympic field. He placed Owens within history, claiming he was a greater athlete than predecessors Nurmi and Kraenzlein. Likewise, Taylor expressed understanding about Owens's relinquishment of his amateur status. Ottley's post-Olympic article likewise presented Owens as a hero by emphasizing his modest, mild-mannered, and gracious deportment.

Further Discussion and Racial Significance

When analyzing Rice's articles singularly or by our cultural standards, he appeared blatantly racist in his use of language and characterizations. From his cautious optimism at the beginning of the Olympic Games to his commendation later on, Rice's embellished prose obfuscated his true feelings about race. Rice never intentionally criticized Owens and other black athletes. However, despite his commendations for Owens's pursuits and character, his columns exhibited racially marked language, remarks, references, and stereotypes.

While Rice used apposition to describe where white athletes lived, as when he denoted Hardin's Mississippi background, he instead referenced black athletes' race, as in his use of "Negro runner and jumper" to describe Owens.[178] Whether Rice characterized Owens as a "noble savage," an African or Ethiopian, a Negro, or "wild Zulu," the writings used racially marked language and gave inequitable treatment to Owens.[179] He never quoted Jesse Owens and instead cited "reliable sources" and coaches for their perspectives of the events and festivities. Most articles included such racially descriptive qualifiers as black, fast, and lazy as Rice frequently focused on alleged biological differences between the races. The columns reflected what Fountain said about his treatment of black athletes: "It is certainly not enlightened.... It is, at bottom, complicated and uncomfortable—a veritable mirror of the ugly contradiction that was America in the years of segregation."[180]

Rice lauded Owens's athletic capability and remarkable victories yet failed to provide in-depth analyses and commentary on his accomplishments. He instead suggested that black athletes exerted a biological advantage and rarely attributed successes to skill or character. While Rice stereotyped German athletes and American Helen Stephens, his repetitive branding of black athletes continually reinforced racially separatist ideologies.

Nevertheless, it would be shortsighted to judge Rice and his works without understanding his Tennessee upbringing, the historical context of 1930s America, and other writers' perspectives.[181] At the least, the stories suggested that Rice possessed southern attitudes toward race, failed to criticize thoughts of the period, and either exhibited apathy or sustained stereotypes, subconsciously or consciously.

While Rice failed to change or challenge the status quo, he still praised Owens's athletic prowess and achievements, thereby reinforcing and sustaining the racial opinions and prejudices of American society during the 1930s. This suggests that black individuals who did not challenge the white man's system could gain respect on some levels. However, it chiefly included athletic skills and certain personality characteristics rather than intelligence or mental capacities.

Surprisingly, the black journalists' writings resembled Rice's in their celebratory tone and commentary, war and battle metaphors, audience reactions, and minimal quotations. However, unlike Rice, the writers stressed Owens's place in history, his gracious and humble demeanor, and the unification of the black athletes at the games. While the writers relied on fewer metaphors and hyperbole, they used more colloquial and conversational terms. They used less racially marked language; however some still appeared in their columns. Regardless, they never once questioned the black athletes' nationality and stressed their victories for America.

As the articles reveal, the black journalists' primary goal was to tout Jesse Owens and the American athletes' dominance of the Aryan-hosted Olympic Games while maintaining a fairly objective and neutral tone. Like Rice, they stressed nationalism and pride for American athletes, yet they never once called black athletes "African" or "Ethiopian." They never referred to biological variances between the races, thereby refusing to play into existing cultural perspectives toward race and Aryan supremacy. While the black journalists did not necessarily alter the status quo or present controversial columns in their treatment of events, they established equitable treatment of all athletes in their passive yet resolute tone.

Conclusion: Four Views of the Black Pearl

Like a black pearl, Owens was "beautiful, authentic, and exceptional."[182] All journalists, black and white, recognized that Owens's talent was rare and his gracious demeanor mysterious and mystical. However, unlike black pearls that are "perfect at birth,"[183] Owens overcame such physical ailments as pneumonia and bronchial problems, poverty, and racial prejudices to attain athletic perfection. His long, graceful stride, his svelte yet toned physique, and his soft-spoken deportment enabled individuals of any race to accept and embrace him.

Historian William Manchester's concept of "generational chauvinism" establishes that society cannot judge previous generations' practices by contemporary times since their actions may have been "appropriate and consistent" with society.[184] In part, this proves true here since differences between black and white journalists' depictions were not as drastically different as might be expected, signifying that journalists reinforced society's ideologies through language, tone, and content. Even though it can be difficult to decipher the thoughts and feelings behind words and phrases and though they possess different meanings depending on the individual and time period,[185] a study of this nature provides a glimpse into the drama and fury of the Berlin Olympic Games and their prize gem, Jesse Owens. After all, we need to overcome what Dr. Stephen Butler terms "historical amnesia," or failing to understand the importance of the past.[186]

This notion further emphasizes the necessity of historical sports research, both as a singular entity and in a more comparative tradition with contemporary sports studies. Potential research includes a comparative study of other mainstream sports journalists' articles on the 1936 Olympics to help further clarify whether Rice was merely a product of his time or perceived race differently from Paul Gallico and others. A comparative content analysis of the white and black presses' coverage and the content of the Communist *Daily Worker* would also prove enlightening as a companion study. To further investigate the similarities and differences between sports journalists' coverage of race, a comparative examination between coverage of Jesse Owens and that of a prominent white athlete of the day, like Olympic track and field decathlete Glenn Morris, could also prove informative.

It is also important to consider the following issues. In 1936 individuals embraced Owens's victories, but how would they have reacted if Owens had been more vocal in his fight? Would journalists and fans have rooted for him if the Olympic Games had occurred outside Berlin? Or did they view him as a catalyst for uniting America and overcoming Hitler and his ideologies?

While these questions remain, one thing remains clear. The journalists' celebratory articles sought to inform readers of the importance of Jesse Owens and other Olympic heroes through literary devices, emotion, and drama; however the impact of writing in its entirety must also be recognized. After all, neither the athletes nor writers were as perfect as they were depicted during this era of acculturation, "participation and belonging."[187]

NOTES

1. Jesse Owens Foundation, November 30, 2001.
2. W. E. B. Dubois, "To the Nations of the World," July 25, 1900, accessed March 21, 2015, http://www.blackpast.org/1900-w-e-b-du-bois-nations-world.
3. Douglas Kellner, "Sports, Media Culture, and Race—Some Reflections on Michael Jordan," *Sociology of Sport Journal* 13 (1996): 465.
4. Kellner, "Sports, Media Culture, and Race," 464; DeWayne Wickham, "Racism Persists in Pro Sports, New Media," *USA Today*, April 14, 1998, 15A.
5. Lawrence A. Wenner, "Playing the MediaSport Game," in *MediaSport*, edited by Lawrence A. Wenner (London: Routledge, 1998), 5.
6. James Carey, *James Carey: A Critical Reader* (Minneapolis: University of Minnesota Press, 1997), 91.
7. Carey, *James Carey*, 92.
8. Marion Marzolf, "American Studies—Ideas for Media Historians?" *Journalism History* 5, no. 1 (1978): 15.
9. Marzolf, "American Studies," 15. Marzolf stressed the need to "expose the old and accepted history to new viewpoints, theories, questions and methods" and offered potential questions and approaches for studying content, culture and society. Using her foundation, this approach considers the following questions

regarding content: "What *was* in the newspapers? What values, attitudes, and social norms were conveyed through the newspapers?" "What picture of society, community, and the various groups within that community was presented?" Regarding culture and society, this approach considers the following questions: "What is the significance of journalism in the presentation of information, values, and opinions to the elites and non-elites of society?" "Was the newspaper's reality the same as the social reality? What role did the newspaper play in the society of its time?"

10. Marzolf, "American Studies," 16.

11. Marzolf, 15.

12. Douglas A. Noverr and Lawrence E. Ziewacz, *The Games They Played: Sports in American History, 1865–1980* (Chicago: Nelson-Hall, 1983), 129. Please see Norman Katkov, "Jesse Owens Revisited," in *The World of Sport*, edited by Al Silverman (New York: Holt, Rinehart and Winston, 1962), 289. Here Katkov lists all of Owens's feats: the "200-meter race, setting a new Olympic record—20.7 seconds. He won the broad jump: 26 feet, 5 5/16 inches. He helped win the 400-meter relay race for the Americans. The quartet of Owens, Metcalfe, Draper and Wykoff ran the Olympic distance faster than it ever has been run—before or since. Their world record was 39.8."

13. Grantland Rice, *The Tumult and the Shouting* (New York: A.S. Barnes, 1954), 252–53.

14. Charles Fountain, *Sportswriter: The Life and Times of Grantland Rice* (New York: Oxford University Press, 1972), 4. Please also see p. 193 in the same work. In the 1920s eighty to one hundred papers published Rice's daily column, which boasted a circulation of more than ten million. Fountain also notes on p. 4 that Rice contributed to setting the agenda of "American popular culture."

15. Rice, *The Tumult and the Shouting*, xv.

16. Fountain, *Sportswriter*, 56, 85, 138. After graduating Phi Beta Kappa from Vanderbilt University in 1901, Rice also worked for the *Atlanta Journal* and *Nashville Tennessean*. See also p. 207. His popularity skyrocketed during the 1920s "Golden Age of Journalism," and in 1925, his salary of fifty-two thousand dollars as an associate editor for the *Herald Tribune* equaled Babe Ruth's (Rice, *Tumult and the Shouting*, 258). In other ventures, Rice partnered with Jack Eaton to produce one-reel films at Sportlight Films, where he received two Academy Awards for short-subject features. Please see Fountain, *Sportswriter*, 194–96, 285–86. He also provided the play-by-play for the first World Series game covered live on radio in 1922. On July 13, 1954, Rice died of a stroke at the age of seventy-three.

17. William J. Baker, *Jesse Owens: An American Life* (New York: Free Press, 1986), 6.

18. Baker, *Jesse Owens*, 7, 9.

19. Baker, *Jesse Owens*, 14–15. By 1936, Baker noted that 2.5 million black Americans inhabited northern metropolitan areas (p. 134).

20. Baker, *Jesse Owens*, 21.

21. Jesse Owens with Paul Neimark, *I Have Changed* (New York: William Morrow, 1972), 31.

22. Owens with Neimark, *I Have Changed*, 31.

23. JesseOwens.com, November 30, 2001.

24. Baker, *Jesse Owens*, 28, 32.

25. JesseOwens.com, November 30, 2001.

26. Owens with Neimark, *I Have Changed*, 27.

27. Owens with Neimark, *I Have Changed*, 32.

28. Owens with Neimark, *I Have Changed*, 27.

29. Baker, *Jesse Owens*, 50.

30. Baker, *Jesse Owens*, 50.

31. Owens with Neimark, *I Have Changed*, 32.

32. Owens with Neimark, *I Have Changed*, 17–18.

33. Owens with Neimark, *I Have Changed*, 18.

34. Owens with Neimark, *I Have Changed*, 19.

35. Baker, *Jesse Owens*, 140.

36. Baker, *Jesse Owens*, 106.

37. Baker, *Jesse Owens*, 150.

38. Baker, *Jesse Owens*, 107.

39. Baker, *Jesse Owens*, 171.

40. Baker, *Jesse Owens*, 170–81.

41. Stephen A. Riess, ed., *Major Problems in American Sports History* (Boston: Houghton Mifflin, 1997), 321.

42. Baker, *Jesse Owens*, 199–201.

43. Joseph Dorinson, lecture given in Dr. Richard Zamoff's Sociology 701 class, George Washington University, Washington DC, September 30, 1999.

44. Please see Donald Spivey, "Black Consciousness and Olympic Protest Movement, 1964–1980," in *Sport in America* (Westport: Greenwood Press, 1985), 239–62.

45. Baker, *Jesse Owens*, 225.

46. Al-Tony Gilmore, "Jack Johnson: A Magnificent Black Anachronism of the Early Twentieth Century," in *The American Sporting Experience: A Historical Anthology of Sport in America*, edited by Steven A. Riess (Champaign IL: Leisure Press, 1984), 308.

47. Gilmore, "Jack Johnson," 307-8. Please see Louis L. Knowles and Kenneth Prewitt, eds., *Institutional Racism in America* (Englewood Cliffs NJ: Prentice-Hall, 1969), 9.

48. Edward Caudill, *Darwinian Myths: The Legends and Misuses of a Theory* (Knoxville: University of Tennessee Press, 1997), 119.

49. Caudill, *Darwinian Myths*, 120.

50. Caudill, *Darwinian Myths*, 132.

51. Caudill, *Darwinian Myths*, 132.

52. Richard L-G. Ceverall, "Racism," *Catholic World* 148 (January 1939): 398-404, quoted in Caudill, *Darwinian Myths*, 128.

53. Walter Benn Michaels, *Our America: Nativism, Modernism, and Pluralism* (Durham: Duke University Press, 1995), 2-3.

54. Michaels, *Our America*, 11.

55. Michaels, *Our America*, 13.

56. Michaels, *Our America*, 133.

57. Kellner, "Sports, Media Culture, and Race," 465.

58. Joseph Dorinson, lecture given in Dr. Richard Zamoff's Sociology 701 class, George Washington University, Washington DC, September 30, 1999.

59. Fountain, *Sportswriter*, 252.

60. Laurel R. Davis and Othello Harris, "Race and Ethnicity in US Sports Media," in *MediaSport*, edited by Lawrence A. Wenner (London: Routledge, 1998), 158.

61. Davis and Harris, "Race and Ethnicity," 157.

62. Davis and Harris, "Race and Ethnicity," 157.

63. Ben Carrington, "Sport, Masculinity, and Black Cultural Resistance," *Journal of Sport and Social Issues* 22 (1998): 275-98.

64. Jon Entine, *Taboo: Why Black Athletes Dominate Sports and Why We Are Afraid to Talk about It* (New York: Public Affairs, 2000), 185.

65. Entine, *Taboo*, 187. Entine discussed the 1936 Berlin Olympic Games and the variances between Western press coverage and Nazi propaganda. The *Volkischer Beobachter* proclaimed that if black athletes were not excluded, the "sacred grandeur of the Olympiad" would be damaged (p. 183). Please see David K. Wiggins, "The 1936 Olympic Games in Berlin: The Response of America's Black Press," *Research Quarterly for Exercise and Sport* 54 (September 1983): 282; and Entine, *Taboo*, viii. The *New York Times* inaccurately wrote, "Hitler greets all medallists except Americans," since Owens competed the following day. Nevertheless, the International Olympic Committee urged Hitler to greet all or none of the gold-medal winners and he opted for the latter (p. 184). Please also see Arnd Kruger, "The 1936 Olympic Games Berlin," in *The*

Modern Olympics, edited by Peter J. Graham and Norst Veberhorst (West Point NY: Leisure Press, 1976), 173–86.

66. Richard D. Mandell, *The Nazi Olympics* (New York: Macmillan Company, 1971), 231–32.

67. Fountain, *Sportswriter*, 250.

68. Fountain, *Sportswriter*, 252.

69. Fountain, *Sportswriter*, 252.

70. Fountain, *Sportswriter*, 253.

71. Fountain, *Sportswriter*, 254.

72. Mandell, *Nazi Olympics*, 225.

73. Norman Katkov, "Jesse Owens Revisited," in *The World of Sport*, edited by Al Silverman (New York: Holt, Rinehart and Winston, 1962), 280.

74. Katkov, "Jesse Owens Revisited," 279–80.

75. Frank Luther Mott, *American Journalism A History: 1690-1960*, 3rd ed. (New York: Macmillan, 1962), 795.

76. Fountain, *Sportswriter*, 138, 206. In 1924, the *New York Herald* purchased the *New York Tribune* and the two united to form the *New York Herald Tribune*.

77. Robert Manning, "Good Sports," *Columbia Journalism Review* 33, no. 5 (1994): 52.

78. Fountain, *Sportswriter*, 129.

79. William Charles Chase, "America's Hopes Depend on These," *New York Amsterdam News*, August 1, 1936, 2. The *New York Amsterdam News* promoted his columns prior to the opening ceremonies with a quarter-page photo of Jesse Owens and teammate Ralph Metcalf, which read, "America's Hopes Depend Upon These at the Olympics in Berlin, Germany as well as the Other NEGRO STARS Competing in the Greatest Athletic Event in the World."

80. Noverr and Ziewacz, *Games They Played*, 128–29.

81. Baker, *Jesse Owens*, 101.

82. Grantland Rice, "U.S. Withholds Nazi Salute, Has Cool Olympic Reception," *Boston Globe*, August 2, 1936, 1.

83. Rice, "U.S. Withholds," 1.

84. Rice, "U.S. Withholds," 1; Edward P. J. Corbett, *Classical Rhetoric for the Modern Student* (New York: Oxford University Press, 1990), 459.

85. Rice, "U.S. Withholds," 30.

86. Corbett, *Classical Rhetoric*, 460.

87. Rice, "U.S. Withholds," 30.

88. Rice, "U.S. Withholds," 30.

89. Rice, "U.S. Withholds," 30.

90. Rice, "U.S. Withholds," 30.

91. Rice, "U.S. Withholds," 30.

92. Grantland Rice, "The Sportlight," *New York Sun*, August 3, 1936, 25.

93. Corbett, *Classical Rhetoric*, 460; Rice, "The Sportlight," *New York Sun*, August 3, 1936, 25. Personification is "investing abstractions or inanimate objects with human qualities or abilities."

94. Rice, "The Sportlight," *New York Sun*, August 3, 1936, 25.

95. Rice, "The Sportlight," *New York Sun*, August 3, 1936, 25.

96. Rice, "The Sportlight," *New York Sun*, August 3, 1936, 25.

97. Grantland Rice, "The Sportlight: Girl from the Ozark Breaks World Record," *New York Sun*, 4 August 1936, 27.

98. Rice, "Girl," 27.

99. Rice, "Girl," 27.

100. Rice, "Girl," 27.

101. Rice, "Girl," 27.

102. Grantland Rice, "The Sportlight: Owens Wins Broad Jump; Dominates Olympic Show," *New York Sun*, August 5, 1936, 29.

103. Rice, "Owens Wins," 29.

104. Rice, "Owens Wins," 29.

105. Rice, "Owens Wins," 29.

106. Rice, "Owens Wins," 29.

107. Rice, "Owens Wins," 29.

108. Rice, "Owens Wins," 29.

109. Rice, "Owens Wins," 29.

110. Grantland Rice, "Sportlight: US Team Adds to Huge Score," *Boston Globe*, August 6, 1936, 1. Per Katkov, "Jesse Owens Revisited," the Olympic Organizing Committee gave Owens a potted oak tree "as a living memorial to the victory" (p. 289).

111. Rice, "US Team," 1.

112. Rice, "US Team," 21.

113. Corbett, *Classical Rhetoric*, 459–60.

114. Grantland Rice, "The Sportlight: Williams Captures 400 for Sixth U.S. First," *New York Sun*, August 8, 1936, 30.

115. Rice, "Williams," 30.

116. Rice, "Williams," 30.

117. Grantland Rice, "Morris Victory Caps Olympics," *Boston Globe*, August 9, 1936, 1, 23.

118. Rice, "Morris," 23.

119. Grantland Rice, "Sportlight," *New York Sun*, August 10, 1936, 26.

120. Rice, "Sportlight," August 10, 1936, 26.

121. Rice, "Sportlight," August 10, 1936, 26.

122. Grantland Rice, "Sportlight: Japanese Take Lead in Swimming Events," *New York Sun*, August 11, 1936, 28.

123. Grantland Rice, "Sportlight," August 10, 1936, 36.

124. Grantland Rice, "Sportlight: Move Seen to Segregate Men's, Women's Olympics," *New York Sun*, August 12, 1936, 30.

125. Rice, "Move," 30.

126. Grantland Rice, "The Sportlight: Germans Study Makeup of Negro," *Boston Sunday Globe*, August 27, 1936, 22.

127. Rice, "Germans," 22.

128. Rice, "Germans," 22.

129. Rice, "Germans," 22.

130. Rice, "Germans," 22.

131. Warren I. Susman, *Culture as History: The Transformation of American Society in the Twentieth Century* (New York: Pantheon Books, 1984), 143.

132. William C. Chase, "Owens Captures 3 Crowns at Berlin; 2 Other in First," *New York Amsterdam News*, August 8, 1936, 1.

133. Chase, "Owens Captures," 1.

134. Chase, "Owens Captures," 1.

135. Chase, "Owens Captures," 1.

136. Chase, "Owens Captures," 1.

137. Chase, "Owens Captures," 1.

138. Chase, "Owens Captures," 1, 14.

139. Chase, "Owens Captures," 14.

140. Chase, "Owens Captures," 14.

141. Chase, "Owens Captures," 14.

142. Chase, "Owens Captures," 14.

143. Chase, "Owens Captures," 14.

144. Chase, "Owens Captures," 14.

145. Chase, "Owens Captures," 14.

146. Randy Taylor, "Sportopics," *New York Amsterdam News*, August 8, 1936, 14.

147. Taylor, "Sportopics," August 8, 1936, 14.

148. Taylor, "Sportopics," August 8, 1936, 14.

149. Taylor, "Sportopics," August 8, 1936, 14.

150. Taylor, "Sportopics," August 8, 1936, 14.

151. Taylor, "Sportopics," August 8, 1936, 14.

152. Taylor, "Sportopics," August 8, 1936, 14.

153. William Chase, "Hitler's Aide in Talk to Chase Denies Insult," *New York Amsterdam News*, August 15, 1936, 1.

154. Chase, "Hitler's Aide," 1.

155. Chase, "Hitler's Aide," 1.

156. Randy Taylor, "Sportopics," August 15, 1936, 14.

157. Taylor, "Sportopics," August 15, 1936, 14.

158. Taylor, "Sportopics," August 15, 1936, 14.

159. Taylor, "Sportopics," August 15, 1936, 14.

160. Taylor, "Sportopics," August 15, 1936, 14.

161. Taylor, "Sportopics," August 15, 1936, 14.

162. Taylor, "Sportopics," August 15, 1936, 14.

163. William C. Chase, "Germans Look for Savage Negro, Chase Says, Citing Nazi Slander," *New York Amsterdam News*, August 22, 1936, 1, 13.

164. Chase, "Germans Look," 1.

165. Chase, "Germans Look," 1.

166. Chase, "Germans Look," 13.

167. Chase, "Germans Look," 1.

168. Chase, "Germans Look," 1.

169. Chase, "Germans Look," 1.

170. Roi Ottley, "40,000 Is A Lot of Money to Pass Up, Says Owens," *New York Amsterdam News*, August 29, 1936, 1.

171. Ottley, "40,000," 1.

172. Ottley, "40,000," 1.

173. Ottley, "40,000," 1.

174. Ottley, "40,000," 13.

175. Ottley, "40,000," 13.

176. Ottley, "40,000," 13.

177. Chase, "Owens Captures," 14.

178. Please see Rice, "Owens Wins Broad Jump," August 5, 1936, 29; and Rice, "Owens Breaks World Record," August 3, 1936, 1.

179. Rice, "Owens Wins," August 5, 1936, 29.

180. Fountain, *Sportswriter*, 246.

181. Please see Fountain, *Sportswriter*, 34–35. Bolling and Beaulah Rice raised him in Murfreesboro, Tennessee, in the late nineteenth century and named him after his grandfather, Confederate major Henry Grantland Rice.

182. "Market and Community," GIE Perles de Tahiti website, accessed December 10, 2001, http://web.archive.org/web/20020210144815/http://www.tahiti-blackpearls.com/market/index.html.

183. "Market and Community."

184. Please see William Manchester's letter to *New York Times Book Review*, 1991. Quoted in Fountain, *Sportswriter*, 247.

185. Catherine Marshall and Gretchen B. Rossman, *Designing Qualitative Research* (Thousand Oaks CA: Sage, 1995), 90.

186. Stephen Butler, lecture given in Dr. Richard Zamoff's Sociology 701 class, George Washington University, Washington DC, September 16, 1999.

187. Susman, *Culture as History*, 172, 183.

3

Multifarious Hero
Joe Louis, American Society, and Race
Relations during World Crisis, 1935–1945

DOMINIC J. CAPECI JR. AND MARTHA WILKERSON

In an effort to interpret race relations during the 1930s and 1940s, historians have tussled with the interaction between the individual and society.
Some have focused on leaders, others on organizations and events; all have
demonstrated stirrings of change in the Depression decade and, especially,
the war years.[1] Yet few have studied heroes, those who cast light on how
citizens perceive "the essence of themselves" and on the social milieu in
which they live.[2] More than any other hero, heavyweight boxer Joe Louis
loomed large from 1934 to 1945, a time when African Americans encountered severe hardship, challenged racial mores, and laid foundations for
future advances. Amidst both the hostile racism and reform spirit of the
Great Depression, he exemplified black perseverance: God, wrote novelist
Ernest Gaines, sent Joe to lift "the colored people's heart."[3] More surprising, he emerged an American hero in the Second World War because of the
dramatic impact of Nazism on racial attitudes. In each period, he and his
admirers inspired, nurtured, and reinforced one another, resulting in his
playing several, sometimes contradictory—indeed, multifarious—roles. As
a black man in a racist environment, his remarkable transition from race
champion to national idol signaled the interplay of the individual, society,
and changing times; as much as any leader, organization, or event, his
experience provides insights into this watershed period of race relations.

Born May 13, 1914, the son of sharecroppers Lily Reese and Munrow Barrow, Louis grew up near Lafayette, Alabama, with his seven brothers and sisters.[4] He was happy despite his father's early separation from the family and the confines of segregation. After his family migrated to Detroit in 1926, he engaged in hijinks and street fights but never ran afoul of the law. Introduced to boxing by a friend in 1932, he fell in love with the sport, the environment, and, most of all, the thoughts of money and respect that came to those in the ghetto who hit hard and moved quickly. He turned professional by his twentieth birthday.

Louis was enormously influenced by a handful of people. Earthy and religious, his mother taught him to "trust in God, work hard, and hope for the best." She said "a good name" was "better than money" and encouraged him to be somebody.[5] The aspiring, courageous and decent lives that she and her second husband, Pat Brooks, lived impressed young Louis. Managers John Roxborough and Julien Black echoed this message of black dignity. Aware of the resentment triggered by Jack Johnson, the first black heavyweight champion (who challenged racial mores and fled conviction for violating the Mann Act), they instructed Louis in clean living and sportsmanlike conduct; Jack Blackburn, Louis's trainer and father-like confidant, constantly berated "that fool nigger with his white woman, acting like he owned the world."[6] Marva Trotter, whom Louis married in 1935, also reinforced his drive for excellence. Black and supportive, all of them assisted Louis through his early life, a time of "increased vulnerability and heightened potential."[7]

Between his initiation as a professional boxer in 1934 and his rematch with Max Schmeling in 1938, Louis captured the imagination of blacks everywhere. In a time of economic crises, when white citizens displayed racial intolerance, when white leaders approached civil rights with "political calculus," and when white liberals, North and South, ignored society's deep-seated, institutionalized anti-black attitude, Louis appeared messianic; as black leadership became more aggressive and black masses more aware, he dramatized their struggle between "good and evil."[8] After he defeated Primo Carnera in 1935, for example, Harlem residents poured through the streets "shooting, clapping, laughing, and even crying."[9]

Given black opposition to Mussolini's invasion of Ethiopia, they celebrated more than a boxing match. Louis seemed invincible in the ring, recording thirty-five wins, twenty-nine knockouts, and one loss (to Schmeling, in 1936) before becoming champion the following year.[10] Graceful, quick, and powerful at 6'1½", two hundred pounds, he annihilated all comers, permitting admirers vicarious victories, "even dreams of vengeance," over white society.[11] As significantly, he seemed both Superman and Little Man, greater than his supporters yet acceptable to them; he challenged stereotypes, instilled hope, and provided models for racial advancement.[12] Galahad-like, fighting clean and complimenting opponents, he enhanced black respectability; inarticulate and untutored, having stammered as a youth and never advancing beyond sixth grade, he appealed to those— waifs and highbrows alike—who understood action as eloquence and poise as bearing. Whether fighting in the ring or starring in *The Spirit of Youth*, a thinly veiled biographic film about himself, he portrayed "black ambition without blundering into fantasy."[13] To Maya Angelou growing up in rural Arkansas, he proved that "we were the strongest people in the world."[14]

While there is some sketchy evidence that segments of upper-class black society played down his achievements during the mid-1930s, the overwhelming majority of blacks identified with Louis.[15] Below the Mason-Dixon line sharecroppers gathered at general stores or in the yards of white neighbors to hear the broadcast of Louis's fights.[16] They honored him with letters and song, as did Florida stevedores who celebrated his defeat of James Braddock:

Joe Louis hit him so hard he tum roun and roun
He thought he was Alabama bound, Ah, Ah[17]

Slum-locked welfare recipients helped fill Comiskey Park for that championship fight, while most residents of Chicago's South Side, Detroit's Paradise Valle, and New York's Harlem huddled in small groups about their radios before reveling in the streets victoriously.[18] Elites, too, cheered Louis. Lena Horne noted that Louis "carried so many of our hopes," while Charles C. Diggs, Michigan state senator from Detroit, convinced legislative colleagues to officially congratulate the new champion for serving as "an example and inspiration to American youth."[19]

Louis genuinely related to all segments of black America. He always remembered his rural, southern roots. He ate black-eyed peas superstitiously on fight day and he gave money to Alabama "relatives" who appeared on his mother's doorstep in Detroit.[20] Northern blacks knew that Louis had roamed the streets of Detroit's eastside and worked at Ford Motor Company, just as they had done there or in similar settings. Perhaps most endearing, Louis organized jobless pals into the Brown Bomber Softball Team and donated to the community chest. Humble origins aside, Louis hobnobbed with celebrities. He became the darling of entertainers like Bill "Bo Jangles" Robinson, who introduced him to Hollywood. Louis meshed well with all blacks because they worshipped him for his feats and, as pointedly, for his divine mettle. In the poetry of Langston Hughes,

Joe has sense enough to know
He is a god
So many gods don't know.[21]

Yet Louis enamored few whites before the mid-1930s, as racism continued relatively unabated throughout the Depression. In his hometown of Detroit, for instance, whites barred blacks from jobs and housing and, through the Klan-like Black Legion, terrorized them.[22] Occasionally, writers for publications ranging from the New York Times to the Literary Digest questioned Louis's intelligence, ridiculed his speech, or stereotyped him as "kinky-haired, thick-lipped," and "shuffling."[23] If many whites "stored up" criticism "for Joe," as an NAACP official suspected, white elites embraced him.[24] Small in number, news-hungry celebrities were drawn by his fame and vote-seeking politicians by his popularity among blacks.[25] Intellectuals and liberals, who challenged white supremacy on the basis of overwhelming scientific research and fought for reform primarily along economic lines (thereby aiding blacks without confronting larger society's racist beliefs), found in Louis a powerful yet unthreatening symbol of black excellence and interracial unity: "Isn't Joe Louis wonderful?" marveled author Carl

Van Vechten.[26] Certainly a handful of the champion's personal friends thought so, including Joe DiMaggio and Ed Sullivan.

Inside the ring, racial attitudes began to shift. Louis's handlers knew that prejudice permeated boxing as white fighters and investors, ever mindful of Jack Johnson, denied black contenders a chance for the heavyweight title. Indeed, the color line that Jack Dempsey and promoter Tex Richard had drawn from 1919 to 1926 carried into the next decade.[27] By that time, however, boxing had fallen into disrepute, marred by scandal, ignoble champions, and undesirable gunmen. Roxborough and Black recognized Louis's talent and the opportunity for personal gain and social change in this atmosphere, providing they could avoid scandal and bury the memory of Johnson. They established rules of public behavior for Louis and, in 1935, contracted with white promoter Mike Jacobs. Shrewdly, he scheduled the Carnera bout in Yankee Stadium, which exposed Louis to a known opponent in all-important New York City and challenged the Madison Square Garden impresarios who ignored black fighters. The ring announcer—himself aware of the fight's social significance—reminded spectators of democratic tenets and sportsmanlike conduct.[28] For his exemplary behavior and victories over Carnera and thirteen other heavyweights that year, Louis became *Ring Magazine*'s "Boxer of the Year" and the Associated Press's "Athlete of the Year"; even rank-and-file white boxing fans and southern white journalists considered this "well-behaved" "good nigger" as "the savior of a dying sport."[29]

Publicly Louis embodied the Galahad image promoted by his handlers. He brought dignity to the race, but he did not comprehend fully the plight of black people. Before the Carnera fight, when blacks envisioned him a savior capable of humiliating the symbol of Mussolini's Ethiopian invasion, Louis heard the name of Back-to-Africa advocate Marcus Garvey for the first time.[30] Rather than serve as a race symbol, however, he desired to make money and party "with pretty girls." After devastating Carnera and four other opponents, he became cocky and out of shape, losing the first Schmeling fight by a knockout. Crestfallen and disturbed that blacks took his loss to Hitler's henchman personally, Louis returned home to nurse his pride and his wounds.

Only twenty-four when winning the title, he understandably failed to grasp his relationship with black society. Publicly the paragon, privately he played with the Brown Bombers against the approval of his managers, who feared possible injury; he engaged in numerous sexual encounters and love affairs, sometimes with white women.[31] He received double messages from Roxborough and Black, who directed him never to be photographed with white ladies but said nothing about dating them. Perhaps he emulated Roxborough, who acted legitimate publicly while operating numbers privately; success drew approval despite black awareness of shady activities.[32] Outwardly, Louis became the person his mother desired and upheld the image his handlers forged.[33]

Louis's personal growth accompanied the national shift from economic depression to war. Between 1937 and 1941, particularly as a result of the Schmeling rematch, he and African Americans gained confidence. They both smarted over the first bout, which cast doubt on his title and their manhood. In addition, the rise of Hitler abroad placed discrimination at home in bold relief and stimulated black protest for civil rights.[34] Nazism also revealed racism as "an unmitigated evil," forcing white society to question its own moral integrity.[35] In this milieu, black and white citizens alike placed the second Louis-Schmeling fight in an international, racial context: American democracy versus Aryan supremacy; even President Franklin D. Roosevelt sent for Louis, felt his biceps and reminded: "Joe, we're depending on those muscles for America."[36] On June 22, 1938, seventy thousand partisan fans filled Yankee Stadium to see the fight, while many, many more listened to it on the radio. When Louis smashed Schmeling to the canvas four times amidst forty-one blows, delivering the KO at 2:04 of round one, celebration occurred everywhere.[37]

The victory greatly affected Louis, who became more sure of himself and at ease with others. He fully understood, possibly for the first time, his meaning for and commitment to black society. No longer isolated, he saw beyond family, friends, and personal pride a broader version of people and things black; "If I ever do anything to disgrace my race," he remarked later, "I hope to die."[38] Louis's triumph also appealed to white society's patriotism and need, outside of the South, to appear racially moral in the face of its Nazi-like values.[39] As an integrative force, he seemed capable of bringing the races together along commonly held ideals and against common enemies without challenging basic conditions of black life. In fact, 64 percent of all radio owners in the nation listened to the rematch—a figure exceeded in this internationally tense period only by two presidential broadcasts.[40]

Louis's mass appeal spread in 1939 and 1940, bringing him greater recognition. He drew honors from *Ring Magazine*—"Boxer of the Year" for the third time in six years—and from the Schomburg Collection of the New York Public Library and the Association for the Study of Negro Life and History for improving race relations.[41] Aware of his phenomenal popularity, particularly among blacks and white liberals, political brokers sought his support. In the hotly contested presidential campaign of 1940, Roosevelt's advisers shared NAACP spokesman Walter F. White's belief that northern black voters could decide the election.[42] Hence, they invited Louis to "thank the President for increasing Negro participation in defense" and "to offer his own services."[43] It was thought that such a gesture might parry criticism of Roosevelt's seeking a third term, appeals by challenger Wendell Willkie for black ballots, and pressure by black leaders for desegregation in the armed services and defense industries.

Nevertheless presidential aides sensed potential "dangers" and canceled the Roosevelt-Louis meeting.[44] Doubtless the dangers consisted of John Roxborough and his brother, Charles, a prominent Michigan figure in the Republican Party, who persuaded (more likely instructed) Louis to be "in Willkie's corner."[45] During the crucial, closing days of the campaign, Republicans used him as Democrats had hoped to. He stumped in Chicago, St. Louis, and New York, noting Roosevelt's failure to support an anti-lynch bill or get blacks off the WPA rolls; he predicted Willkie would "win by a knockout" and "help my people."[46] One concerned Democrat suggested a broadcast by vocalist Marian Anderson "to offset Joe Louis' influence."[47] Michigan state senator Diggs, however, assured Roosevelt that "the overwhelming majority" of black voters realized his record and Louis's political ignorance.[48] Diggs proved accurate, for blacks disregarded their hero's preference because it challenged their dreams for equal opportunity, which Roosevelt, however paternalistically, continued to act upon. Indeed, worried by Willkie's bid for black support, which included the strongest civil rights plank in political party history, Roosevelt followed the counsel of civil rights advocates and, among other concessions, promoted Colonel Benjamin O. Davis to be the first black brigadier general and appointed William H. Hastie civilian aide to the secretary of war.[49] Such was enough for blacks to place Louis in context and consider Roosevelt—in Willkie's phrase—"the Champ" of things political. Having to choose between heroes and a Republican Party that had not been responsive, they voted according to New Deal and wartime realities.

Louis retained his heroic stature, nonetheless. His endorsement of Willkie appeared orchestrated by someone selfishly willing to sell "this otherwise good boy down the river."[50] As significantly he remained humble in defeat: "I never alibi after a fight."[51] And he quickly returned to the ring, easily defending his title against Al McCoy in December. Sportswriter James P. Dawson hailed him as "the greatest 'fighting' champion" ever in the heavyweight class.[52] His elevation to truly national status was in the offing.

Such began to occur during 1941, a crucial year for Louis and society. As world war intensified abroad, so did black militancy and white soul-searching at home. Black leaders, faced with the dilemma of opposing the Axis while protesting homegrown racism, unveiled the Double V campaign for the purpose of channeling black frustrations into positive, patriotic actions.[53] By simultaneously seeking victory on two fronts—over foreign and domestic foes—they hoped to bolster black morale and promote racial equality; by linking the struggles and stimulating black defense of the country, they avoided charges of treason and claimed first-class citizenship. White leaders, meanwhile, understood the meaning of Nazism for white supremacy in the United States and the resistance by larger society to any suggestion of changes in the status quo.[54] Rather than chance alienating whites and hindering preparedness, they played up democratic rhetoric and, when forced by black pressure, compromised on symbolically important issues involving the armed forces and defense industries without fundamentally altering basic conditions.[55] In this context, Louis's forthcoming boxing feats served both personal and societal purposes. He mirrored the aggressiveness of the black masses and the patriotism of their leaders, bringing respect to the race; he embodied the fighting spirit and the interracial symbolism needed by white citizens and leaders during world crisis.[56]

Between January and June, he defended the championship monthly, keeping himself before the press and public. He fought Red Burman, Gus Dorazio, Abe Simon, Tony Musto, and Buddy Baer, in what some called the bum-a-month campaign, before meeting Billy Conn in a historic bout. No fight since the Schmeling rematch generated such excitement; Louis experienced difficulty defeating some of the "bums," and Conn, the 175-pound-light heavyweight champion, entered as the underdog. Indeed controversy swirled over whether Louis was slipping.[57]

On June 18, 54,487 people, including noted businessmen, politicians, "stars of stage and screen," and seven hundred sportswriters filled the Polo Grounds.[58] Most of them rooted for Conn, the cocky Irishman from Pittsburgh who spotted the Dark Destroyer twenty-five pounds and fought "a brand of battle" few expected. They supported Conn, local reporters opined, because of his dashing underdog appeal rather than his race; Louis believed otherwise, later referring to Conn as a "white hope."[59] No doubt both factors influenced the crowd, but after twelve spirited rounds by Conn, which left Louis "bewildered, dazed and on his way to a decisive defeat," the champion rallied.[60] In the thirteenth round Conn, whose speed had thus far carried the fight, ceased to box and threw a long left hook; Louis seized the opening, stunning his opponent with a devastating right cross followed by a fusillade of "crushing fire" with both hands "savagely, thudding home." Conn crumbled, ending one of the greatest heavyweight battles ever.

Louis reemerged even more heroic and popular among both races. Blacks in Harlem celebrated his victory according to formula: "shouting, dancing, pelting each other with torn paper."[61] Whites who saw, heard, or read about the match understood the epic dimension of Louis. His loss of speed, which probably reflected the smaller challenger's quickness more than the champion's aging, and come-from-behind win signaled human imperfection; but his courage throughout the bout and his awesome power and skill in the final round revealed godlike invincibility. His stepping back when Conn slipped in the tenth round (instead of attacking at a time when he was losing the championship), his praise for Conn as "an excellent ring general," and his admission of having declined as a fighter bespoke near-spiritual grace.[62] To the faithful, like Alabama-born actress Tallulah Bankhead, Louis loomed as one of the three greatest men in the nation.[63]

Even great men face difficulties, as Louis and his admirers discovered. In July, Marva filed for divorce. She charged "extreme and repeated cruelty" and estimated Louis's annual income from boxing at $250,000.[64] Over the next six weeks, reporters publicized their private relations and extravagant lifestyle. In mid-August they reconciled and, despite Marva's allegations that Joe acted ungodly by striking her, the champion remained as popular as ever. Maybe black fans believed the rumor that Marva had been "cutting some capers" with a prominent doctor while white supporters probably identified with the soft-spoken, magnanimous Louis they knew publicly.[65] Moreover, everyone could deduce from the reconciliation that charges of brutality were exaggerated. And all expected heroes who fight their way to the top to be wealthy.

Having weathered six title defenses, Conn's near-win, and marital problems, Louis now fought Lou Nova and reestablished his own indisputable supremacy. In predictable ritual, 56,549 persons jammed into the Polo Grounds on September 29 to see the champion drop Nova "like a deflated balloon" in the sixth round.[66] Celebrities abounded, including Louis's one-time paramour Sonja Henie and former challenger Billy Conn; even Roosevelt rearranged his travel schedule to hear the fight broadcast. In the aftermath, the *New York Times* editorialized anew about Louis's infallibility, and Detroit promoters planned a "white hope" tournament to find the next challenger.[67]

Increased renown continued to bring Louis into contact with black leaders and organizations, but his managers always stood between them. Detroit Urban Leaguer John C. Dancy, whose agency benefitted from Louis's generosity and who knew the champion well enough to pass along others' requests, observed that Roxborough handled all business matters.[68] The

NAACP also received donations via Black and Roxborough, who molded Louis's image while reducing his taxable income.[69] On occasion Walter F. White thanked Louis for helping the association financially, requested his autographed photo, and reprimanded journalists depicting him as "exceedingly stupid."[70] Black and Roxborough, nevertheless, protected Louis from controversial racial issues.

They permitted him more exposure in race relations as times changed but continued to shield him from militant protest. Aware of the strident Double V effort by White and others, Black and Roxborough aligned Louis with the more conservative, gradualistic National Urban League and Federal Council of the Churches of Christ. Hence he participated in the League's radio program on vocational education and, more significantly, solicited funds for the Council's Department of Race Relations.[71] "The hardest fight I ever had was against prejudice and discrimination," he informed Roosevelt in a request for money. Ironically, executive aides— doubtless smarting from the president recently having been forced by A. Philip Randolph and White to create the Fair Employment Practices Committee—suspected "the Italian hand" of White behind Louis's solicitation and advised against a contribution.[72] They misunderstood completely, because "in times like these" White believed in a "more dynamic and direct approach" to racial problems than efforts at Christian education.[73] Obviously displeased, he recognized the champion's right to place his assistance where he believed it would do "the most good."

As the national emergency bound Louis and society more closely together, White thought Louis could best serve black America in the armed forces. In the fall of 1941, he knew of the champion's 1-A classification and of increased violence between black servicemen and white citizens, police, and soldiers.[74] Behind the scenes he contacted Black and Roxborough, Eleanor Roosevelt, and military authorities, negotiating the possibility of commissioning Louis in the army's morale division.[75] Apparently all endorsed his proposal, particularly army commanders who had no other plans for controlling interracial conflict and imagined Louis capable of boosting black spirits.[76] White, of course, envisioned the champion as both a morale builder for blacks and an integrator for whites. One of the few blacks known and respected by both races, Louis could serve the Double V strategy by encouraging black participation and exemplifying black patriotism at a time when blacks appeared indifferent to the war and whites seemed vulnerable to civil rights propaganda. He fit the needs of black leaders, white liberals, and War Department officials.

For this reason, White became alarmed over Louis's image. His influential assistant, Roy Wilkins, warned that public reaction would be "very unfavorable" if Louis somehow avoided the draft.[77] People might resent his enormous income, widely publicized at two million dollars in seven years of professional fighting, and compare him with Jack Dempsey, who had evoked near-lasting criticism for refusing to serve during the previous war. Instead they would be "greatly impressed" if Louis entered the service as "a private just like Joe Doakes earning $18 a week"; by not accepting "some soft berth" made possible "though pull with Army higher-ups," he could follow the examples of Hank Greenberg, Winthrop Rockefeller, and other famous, wealthy individuals. White agreed with Wilkins and pressed the twenty-seven-year-old champion and his managers to squelch the story that talk of military service had been ballyhoo for the Nova bout.[78] And if Louis's age would prevent him from being called, White urged that he volunteer.

Black and Roxborough had other plans, however, indicating the limited influence of White and other leaders over themselves and their fighter. They opted for the draft and delayed Louis's November induction by signing a rematch with Buddy Baer. They arranged for Louis and promoter Jacobs to donate their purses for this twentieth title defense to the Navy Relief Society.[79] Such generosity and patriotism enhanced the champion's image and future, as well as their own and boxing's. It also brought raves from whites and sparked debate among Double V–minded blacks aware of the navy's discrimination.[80] Perhaps realizing the futility of stopping the bout, White complimented Louis for acting "far bigger than the Navy" and hoped his example might influence its policy of relegating blacks to messmen status.[81] He played on this theme in the wake of Japan's attack on Pearl Harbor; since "the unqualified support" of every citizen was needed in this national peril, he lectured leading editors, it was time to get rid of prejudice.[82] He later organized NAACP Youth Councils to distribute leaflets to boxing fans entering Madison Square Garden and asked Senator Arthur Clapper of Kansas to write the *New York Times* appealing for the removal of discrimination at "the psychological moment" of the bout.[83]

Louis held firm to his commitment despite some black criticism. Many things were wrong with America, he agreed, "but Hitler won't fix them."[84] When asked by reporters why risk his million-dollar championship for nothing, he corrected, "I ain't fighting for nothing, I am fighting for my country." On January 9, in "a flag-draped setting" hyped by the prefight rhetoric of Wendell Willkie, Louis destroyed Baer in round one, donated forty-seven thousand dollars to the Navy Relief Society, and received praise from some blacks for having drawn "loop rings" around "ding-donging and complaining" leaders.[85]

Three days after the Baer match Louis passed the army physical, ending his civilian period more popular than ever before. According to the nomination for the NAACP's highest award, the Spingarn Medal, it was his clean life, unprecedented title defenses, and Navy Relief Society bout that won the "respect of Americans and of people the world over."[86] By displaying traits—particularly love of country—admired by mainstream society, he conformed increasingly to its criteria for heroes; by enhancing his own and black esteem, while ignoring Double V protest, he avoided having to choose one race and set of ideas over another.[87] Honors came to him from all quarters, including the Edward J. Neil Trophy for outstanding contribution to boxing.[88] He also inspired suggestions that naval units bear his name and songs and posters that celebrated his patriotism.[89]

Although set in motion by the war crisis, his transition from sports hero to super patriot lay ahead. Some whites still perceived Louis as a great champion, nothing more; they denied him the Spingarn Medal for this reason. Anticipating strong backing for Louis and Randolph, White inquired about the possibility of naming two recipients for the award.[90] Such was impossible and Randolph emerged as the Spingarn Medal Committee's choice because he appealed to everyone, while the champion faced adamant opposition from white minister John Haynes Holmes of the Community Church in New York City.[91] Holmes admired Louis's ability, his "sense of propriety, personal honor and public spirit." Yet he considered boxing "bestial and degrading," appealing to base instincts; those concerned with "the serious business of life" should neither admire nor recognize it. Out of touch with black America and large segments of white society, the Park Avenue clergyman nevertheless represented those who, for similar or racial reasons, envisioned Louis as no more than an athlete.

Once Louis entered military service, this view of him eroded and, between 1942 and 1945, he became a national symbol. His physical on January 12 and assignment to Company C at Camp Upton, in Long Island, drew praise from reporters. Joining the service and being unable to fit into the uniform of "an ordinary man" enhanced his image and instilled national confidence.[92] U.S. senator Prentiss M. Brown of Michigan lauded his enlistment, which bandleader Lucky Millander memorialized in "Joe Louis Is a Mighty Man."[93] Few, if any, citizens realized how his managers stalled induction for months or how he awaited formal notice rather than volunteer. Instead they believed that he chose freely to forsake luxury, jeopardize life, and defend America; they knew of discriminatory military practices and of his segregated unit, making his action even more impressive. Indeed, the New York Times editor reminded readers resentful of war taxes of the champion's contribution.[94]

Even before completing basic training, Louis boosted the war effort by agreeing to speak for the Navy Relief Society. Before twenty thousand people on March 10, he stood erect in uniform and dismissed the idea that he was doing more than any other "redblooded American."[95] Everyone would do their part, he predicted, and "we'll win 'cause we are on God's side." His words stunned the Madison Square Garden crowd momentarily; then, jubilation—tears, laughter, applause, stamping, whistles. Louis's simple, touching greatness, explained columnist Bill Corum, could make him "a symbol" in troubled times. Indeed, he envisioned the global struggle a holy crusade, called it "God's War," and, in the process, fulfilled Roosevelt's request that newsmen find a name for the conflagration. Public relations consultant Carl Byoir celebrated the champion in "Joe Louis Named the War," a poem widely circulated, nationally broadcasted, and praised by the president.[96] He wrote that unlike others who fought and claimed "God is on our side," Louis spoke more modestly and reverently of being on God's side, drawing the war's name out of his humanity and "out of some instinct that reaches back":

> Back through all the struggle of mankind
> To establish the rights
> That we are fighting to keep now.[97]

Louis's influence continued well into the war as songwriters Sammy Cahn and Jule Styne highlighted his memorable words in "Keep Your Powder Dry."[98]

Fascination grew for Louis as he defined the crisis evangelically. Such beckoned black participation by challenging the argument that this was "a white man's war"; such soothed white consciences by engendering moral self-worth in a racist society fighting for democracy. Blacks understood what Louis meant by being on God's side, but did whites? Given "the downright oppression" in America, "the holier than thou attitude" expressed by some white writers about the champion's statement struck one black cleric as "sinful."[99] Whether or not whites took the opportunity offered by war "to get on God's side," Louis again bridged racial lines and continued to appear saintly.

He returned to Madison Square Garden on March 27 for another title defense. The event replicated that staged for the Navy Relief Society.[100] Flags, speeches, and government figures abounded, including Under Secretary of War Robert Patterson, who extolled Louis's patriotism over national and shortwave broadcasts. Civilians and combat soldiers listened as Louis dispatched Abe Simon in six rounds, donating his purse of $64,950 to the Army Emergency Relief Organization. Magnanimous as ever, he treated black GIs to almost three thousand dollars' worth of fight tickets.

Just as the military officials exploited Louis's commercial and patriotic value, so did black organizations. National Urban Leaguers hoped to capitalize on the Simon bout by raising funds for their program to place blacks in war jobs. They sought permission from Louis's managers for one hundred women of both races to solicit contributions from fans while distributing matchbooks bearing the message that defense and democracy necessitate the training and hiring of all Americans.[101] Despite cooperation from Louis's handlers, the request never received approval.[102] That project failing, NUL officials asked that Louis sign letters intended for potential contributors. This was the moment, Executive Secretary Lester B. Granger acknowledged, when "Joe's assistance could be of inestimable value."[103]

Military authorities also realized Louis's worth. Placing the champion in special services, they dampened charges of favoritism by treating him routinely. He completed boot camp, rose to corporal, and spoke uncomplainingly of needing to work harder for sergeant's chevrons.[104] A model soldier, he delighted army personnel, who assigned him several roles.

During and immediately after basic training, Louis stimulated the sale of defense bonds. Black disabled veterans in Milwaukee planned their drive around "Joe Louis Day," while he spoke before a predominantly black gathering of twenty thousand of his fellow Detroiters who bought bonds totaling $275,000.[105] Officials and private citizens requested his appearance at bond-selling rallies in New York and Memphis, claiming that such would increase sales and boost black morale.[106] All agreed with the Hutchinson, Kansas, correspondent that Louis stirred "the flame of patriotism" in the hearts of his people.[107] Much the same might have been said about his impact on whites, at least the sixty-five thousand patrons at the Tom O'Shanter golf tournament who purchased $933,000 worth of bonds at Louis's urgings.[108]

Representatives of labor, academy, and mass organizations also requested Louis's services. Members of Ford Local 600 desired his presence at their patriotic rally, and Malcom S. MacLean of Hampton Institute recommended he visit black colleges and uplift ROTC students with his simple talks that "weigh a ton."[109] More pointedly for race relations, White solicited Louis for NAACP-sponsored events; he believed the champion would help the association achieve an "affirmative note."[110] Only the United Automobile Workers' request appears to have been acted upon favorably by government officials, who preferred direct control of Louis's activities.

Military leaders, too, understood the value of Louis as morale builder and, especially during his first year of duty, image-maker. He promoted the service by appearing in the film *This Is the Army*, speaking on the broadcast "Army Hour," and participating in "I am an American Day."[111] In every instance he waxed patriotic: "This fight's the biggest ... I [have] ever been in, and ... I haven't any doubts about helping to win." Later, in the face of the Los Angeles and Detroit race riots, the War Department moved to bolster blacks and educate whites, using clips of Louis in the widely shown docudrama *The Negro Soldier*.[112]

Army officials also arranged for Louis to tour military camps in the United States beginning August 30, 1943. Over the next four months the champion boxed before thousands of soldiers. He visited the GIs in hospitals, lectured on good health, and sparred two or three rounds daily. Shortly thereafter he visited the British Isles, France, Italy, and North Africa, returning home in October of 1944. In all, he traveled fourteen months, covered thirty thousand miles, entertained two million troops, and fought nearly two hundred exhibition bouts overseas.[113] Servicemen flocked to watch him fight, "exchange quips, act in skits or just talk." Most appreciative were the wounded, one of whom begged to have his eyes unbandaged so he could see the champion and, having his wish fulfilled, exclaimed, "This is the happiest I've been."[114] Doubtless Louis provided "invaluable service" to the army.[115]

Most black spokesmen and white officials also recognized Louis's potential to incite, however unintended, yet check violence. Even as the champion's prestige grew among whites in the early 1940s, interracial conflict sprang from his victories over Conn and Baer in locales as far removed as Detroit and Gurdon, Arkansas.[116] Clearly Louis instilled pride, even assertiveness in some blacks, which many whites perceived as a threat to the racial status quo. "Since Joe Louis became so prominent every Negro goes around strutting his stuff," complained one Michigander.[117] Exactly because of the champion's influence among blacks, leaders of both races sought his assistance to curb discord. Following the spring riots of 1943 in Los Angeles, Detroit, and elsewhere, Roosevelt supposedly sent Louis as goodwill emissary to Pittsburgh, "the most sensitive spot for another outbreak."[118] Disorder came instead to New York, where Mayor Fiorello H. LaGuardia recruited celebrities to circulate through Harlem appealing for peace.[119] He called for Louis, who was out of town. Frightened by the specter of race war, scores of municipal officials created interracial committees, northern and southern liberals worked to "keep the lid on," and White sought Louis's participation in race relation programs.[120] Black editors retreating from direct action admonished rioters, particularly in Harlem, where blacks ignited the disorder, and invoked Louis's example and words: "You cannot expect to win a fight by hitting foul blows."[121]

Louis himself struck "fair" punches for black America. Besides promoting social control over black soldiers and civilians, he helped integrate society and change racial attitudes. Although organized protest lay behind Roosevelt's ordering the placement of black sailors in all naval branches, black newsmen and white officials agreed that Louis's benefit bout for the Navy Relief Society contributed to moving the race beyond messmen duty.[122] Neither black pressure nor Louis's magnanimity integrated the navy but, judged one editor, "he slapped Jim Crow in the face."[123] He weakened the segregated structure of civilian and military society elsewhere, expressing dissatisfaction with discrimination at bond rallies, integrating promotional golf tournaments, and boxing with soldiers of both races before integrated audiences only. Indeed, while the army used Louis to promote its image and the war effort, he turned the tables on more than one occasion; he informed twenty thousand Detroiters that if given defense jobs and "an even break in the Army," blacks, "would show the world how to win this war."[124]

When pressed by circumstances, he protested publicly. He ignored a "Whites Only" sign in the bus depot of Camp Sibert, Alabama (which resulted in his and Sugar Ray Robinson's arrest) and questioned Jim Crow theater seats in Salisbury, England.[125] More often he inquired privately as to why blacks of Jackie Robinson's athletic ability and education could neither play for post football teams nor attend Officer's Candidate School (OCS). Later Louis exaggerated his significance in correcting some of these wrongs. Rather than singlehandedly desegregating buses on Army posts, for example, his arrest merely reflected one of innumerable incidents of racial friction and low morale that dictated new policy; hence on July 8, 1944, the military command adopted the procedure of Brigadier General

George Horkan of Camp Lee, Virginia, who provided sufficient vehicles, on a first-come, first-served basis, for all soldiers traveling between post and town.[126] Nevertheless Louis assisted in bringing about minor, though far from insignificant, alterations. Robinson did play some football for Fort Riley, Kansas, and enter OCS, attributing the latter to Louis's efforts.[127] Certainly the champion's intervention on Robinson's behalf and his exhibitions with soldiers of both races "helped broaden the base of athletic competition of many posts."[128] He also might have been instrumental in Robinson going to OCS, but Robinson's ability and education must have been significant in themselves; in any case, military opposition to training more than token numbers of black officers continued throughout the war.[129] Not as assertively, consistently, dramatically, or effectively as many others, Louis interacted with racist institutions and turbulent times to advance the struggle for equality.

Such occurred for several reasons. In the service Louis found himself alone, making "all kinds of decisions."[130] While he completed basic training, Black faced charges and Roxborough served time for running numbers and, pushing Louis to his emotional depths, Blackburn died. Military duty kept him, his mother, and Marva apart, and ongoing marital problems ended in divorce two years later. Stripped of his guardians, Louis seemed more independent and concerned about racial justice, particularly for black soldiers and friends like Robinson. The war atmosphere affected him as well, for everyone from Roosevelt to Double V advocates espoused democratic principles. He became sensitized, fighting relief bouts, selling bonds, and bolstering morale while witnessing discrimination in the army; he believed that all servicemen should be treated identically "as American soldiers."[131] Perhaps worldwide fame also influenced him. French Tunisians asked every black soldier if he was the champion and a Soviet general looked for the man he had heard so much about: "No, not Eisenhower," he informed a CBS correspondent, "Joe Louis."[132] Despite being more independent, sensitive, and popular than ever before, he rebelled rarely.

During the last months of war, Louis continued to play the model soldier, contemplated civilian life, and basked in accolades. From his return to the United States in October 1944 until his discharge a year later, he visited defense plants to spur production or integrate labor forces.[133] He modestly parried efforts by admirers, like Congressman Adam Clayton Powell Jr., to promote him from technical sergeant (his rank for "excellent work overseas") to second lieutenant.[134] He joked about buying several civilian suits in "every color, except brown," but, not wanting special treatment, he preferred staying in uniform until victory.[135] He looked forward to boxing again, as did fans who believed him still capable of defending the title with "one hand."[136] Neither had long to wait, for he mustered out of the army on October 1 amidst great fanfare. Receiving the Legion of Merit "for exceptionally meritorious conduct in the performance of outstanding services" abroad, he expressed characteristic gratitude.[137] A medal and a military review, the presence of a brigadier general, and national broadcast coverage of the ceremony signified Louis's extraordinary prominence.

Quickly he returned to civilian life, as memories of his "meritorious conduct" lingered on and helped Americans adjust to peace. Many read Margery Miller's *Joe Louis: American* and news stories of "the nice things Joe has done."[138] They expressed pride in Louis for his character, his inspiration when "the Great War came" and his willingness to die so the nation might live.[139] Certainly citizens of both races associated themselves, their courage, and commitment in the face of disaster with the champion who represented "the best ideals of Americanism."[140] With victory in hand and reconstruction ahead, they again saw in him what they wanted to see in themselves: excellence.

Louis and society, then, interacted throughout the world crisis, helping to define one another. Initially, he made most blacks "unafraid of tomorrow" and some whites receptive to changing times.[141] Such was made possible by his awesome fistic skill and attractive human qualities; by his handlers, who understood—in the estimation of one white gradualist—"inter-racial relations and human psychology"; by black newsmen hungry for copy and their readers equally hungry for heroes; and by white promoters seeking profits and honest trainers wanting scandal-free bouts.[142] His politically symbolic victories over Carnera and Schmeling brought increasing respect from whites and near-universal decent treatment from daily presses.[143]

His Olympian demeanor and patriotic action thrust him into more historically significant and internationally prominent roles.

Preparedness and war engendered instability and heightened societal needs for someone of Louis's stature, a hero capable of pulling everyone into "a framework of comprehensibility and control."[144] In providing this function, he touched on "the range of values in society": patriotism and protest, continuity and change.[145] His enormous appeal and growth occurred because he identified himself with blacks personally and with all citizens representatively; he reflected both cultures and became their champion in and out of the ring.[146] Most importantly, he threatened neither race and unwittingly nurtured the status quo; one observer, expressing the feelings of many, extolled Louis for always having done "the right thing."[147] He pleased various segments of both communities who played on his prestige as a means to manipulate public behavior: black editors desiring democratic advances without rebellion, southern newsmen taking aim at Hitler without hitting Jim Crow targets, government officials seeking racial peace without social justice, white liberals wanting moral integrity without societal changes, and white citizens striving for respectability without recognizing black grievances.[148] Occasionally, he stepped out of character and challenged discrimination but only in military life and only very tentatively.

Genuinely the people's choice, Louis possessed that quality—"divine grace"—characteristic of heroic leadership.[149] He emerged more hero than leader, defining no ideology, presenting no strategy and organizing no constituency. Yet his historical significance lay in the symbolism he represented for black and white societies, their ideologies, their struggles, and their "assurances of success."[150] Traditionally, most prominent blacks "have been primarily spokesmen, symbolic leaders and propagandists, rather than individuals with a solid organizational base."[151] In his own way and for different racial constituencies, Louis functioned in all of these categories, played more than theatric parts in the life-and-death drama of war, and educated countrymen in decency and democracy. He also marked the transition from earlier, one-dimensional paragons to contemporary, many-faceted heroes who undertake several functions and reveal themselves "warts and all."[152] He laid, in a white admirer's words, "a red rose on Abe Lincoln's grave"; he became, from a black perspective, America's David.[153] When Billy Conn wished he could have the heavyweight crown, Louis joshed that he had it for twelve rounds of their fight but "didn't exactly know what to do with it!"[154] The same cannot be said of Joe Louis, multifarious hero of a society at war.

NOTES

(Information on the authors included in original footnote.)

1. See Harvard Sitkoff, "'No More Moanin': Black Rights History in the 1970s," *Prologue: The Journal of the National Archives* 11 (Summer 1979): 84–86, for the historiography of race relations. See also Richard Polenberg, *War and Society: The United States, 1941-1945* (Philadelphia, 1972), 99–130; and John Morton Blum, *V Was for Victory: Politics and American Culture during World War II* (New York, 1976), 182–220, for this interpretation.

2. See A. O. Edmonds, *Joe Louis* (Grand Rapids, 1973); Lawrence W. Levine, *Black Culture and Black Consciousness: Afro-American Folk Thought from Slavery to Freedom* (New York, 1977), 420–40; and Jeffrey T. Sammons, "Boxing as a Reflection of Society: The Southern Reaction to Joe Louis," *Journal of Popular Culture* 16 (Spring 1983): 23–33, respectively, for notable exceptions that provide a broad overview, the meaning of Louis for blacks during the Depression, and for white southerners from 1934 to 1941. See Al-Tony Gilmore, "The Black Southerner's Response to the Southern System of Race Relations: 1900 to Post-World War II" in *The Age of Segregation: Race Relations in the South, 1890-1945*, edited by Robert Haws (Jackson MS, 1978), 73, for the quotation.

3. Quoted in Gilmore, "Black Southerner's Response," 74.

4. Joe Louis with Edna Rust and Art Rust Jr., *Joe Louis: My Life* (New York, 1978) (hereafter cited as Louis, *My Life*), 3–33, 93. See also Joe Louis, *My Life Story* (New York, 1947) (hereafter cited as Louis, *Story*), for his initial, very guarded, and somewhat misleading autobiography. A comparison of these biographies reveals much about the champion's self-image and development at different stages of life.

5. Quoted in Margery Miller, *Joe Louis: American* (New York, 1945), 12; Louis, *My Life*, 5, 19.

6. See Al-Tony Gilmore, *Bad Nigger! The National Impact of Jack Johnson* (Port Washington NY, 1975), for the Johnson story. See Louis, *My Life*, 38–39, for

Roxborough's and Black's instructions and p. 36 for Blackburn's quotation. See Caswell Adams, "Introducing the New Joe Louis," *Saturday Evening Post*, May 10, 1941, 107; John C. Dancy to Ross Pascoe, January 16, 1946, reel 11, Detroit Urban League Papers, microfilm edition (hereafter cited as DULP); and Louis, *My Life*, 176, 185, for the significance of his handlers.

7. See Christopher F. Monte, *Beneath the Mask: An Introduction to Theories of Personality* (2nd ed.; New York, 1980), 224–62, for a summary of Erik H. Erickson's psychoanalytic ego psychology. See Erik H. Erikson, "Reflections on Dr. Borg's Life Cycle," in *Adulthood* (New York, 1978), 5, for the quotation that is applicable to Louis.

8. See Nancy J. Weiss, *The National Urban League* (New York, 1974), 266, for "political calculus," and see Robert L. Zangrando, *The NAACP Crusade against Lynching, 1909–1950* (Philadelphia, 1980), 98–165, for an example of it. See John B. Kirby, *Black Americans in the Roosevelt Era: Liberalism and Race* (Knoxville, 1980), 218–35; and Morton Sosna, *In Search of the Silent South: Southern Liberals and the Race Issue* (New York, 1977), 60–63, for white liberals. See Jeremiah Wilson Moses, *Black Messiahs and Uncle Toms* (University Park PA, 1982) for Louis as messiah. See Harvard Sitkoff, *A New Deal for Blacks: The Emergence of Civil Rights as a National Issue* (New York, 1978), 261–62, for black leaders. See August Meier and Elliot Rudwick, *Black Detroit and the Rise of the UAW* (New York, 1979), 35–107, for black awareness. See Martha Wilkerson and Richard A. Dodder, "Toward a Model of Collective Conscience and Sport in Modern Societies," *International Journal of Sport Psychology* 13 (1982): 272, for the quotation.

9. Roi Ottley, *"New World A-Coming": Inside Black America* (New York, 1943), 188.

10. See Louis, *My Life*, 270–77, for these and all other statistics regarding Louis's boxing record.

11. See Orrin E. Kapp, "Heroes, Villains, and Fools as Agents of Social Control," *American Sociological Review* 19 (February 1954): 61, for the interpretation that is applicable to Louis. See Lena Horne and Richard Schickel, *Lena* (Garden City NY, 1965), 75, for the quotation.

12. Ottley, *"New World A-Coming,"* 189. See Dixon Weeter, *The Hero in America: A Chronicle of Hero-Worship* (Ann Arbor MI, 1941), 7, 11, for the interpretation that is applicable to Louis.

13. Thomas Cripps, *Slow Fade to Black: The Negro in American Film, 1900–1942* (New York, 1977), 339.

14. Maya Angelou, *I Know Why the Caged Bird Sings* (New York, 1969), 129.

15. See Alexander J. Young. Jr., "Joe Louis, Symbol: 1933–1949" (PhD diss., University of Maryland, 1968), 83, for evidence of black elite reservation about Louis.

16. Angelou, *I Know Why the Caged Bird Sings*, 129; Mark D. Coburn, "America's Great Black Hope," *American Heritage* 29 (October 1978): 91.

17. See Young, "Joe Louis, Symbol," 82–83, for the letters and Levine, *Black Culture and Black Consciousness*, 437, for the lyrics.

18. Louis, *My Life*, 114, 119; Miller, *Louis*, 109; Levine, *Black Culture and Black Consciousness*, 436.

19. Horne and Schickel, *Lena*, 75; S. Res. 39, *Journal of the Senate of the State of Michigan: 1937 Regular Session*, 1641, Michigan State Library, Lansing.

20. Louis, *My Life*, 52, 67, 74, 80. See p. 121 for the "relatives." See Young, "Joe Louis, Symbol," 103, for the diet.

21. Langston Hughes, "Joe Louis" in *Black American Literature*, edited by Ruth Miller (New York, 1971), 550.

22. Alan Clive, *State of War: Michigan in World War II* (Ann Arbor MI, 1979), 11.

23. See Coburn, "America's Great Black Hope," 88, for the *New York Times* reference and the *Literary Digest* quotations.

24. Walter White to Earl Brown, June 19, 1940, box 365, National Association for the Advancement of Colored People Papers (General Office Files, 1940–1955), Manuscript Collection, Library of Congress, Washington DC (hereafter cited as NAACP).

25. Young, "Joe Louis, Symbol," 104, 116, 113.

26. See Sitkoff, *A New Deal for Blacks*, 190–215, for intellectuals. See Kirby, *Black Americans in the Roosevelt Era*, 218–35; and Sosna, *In Search of the Silent South*, 63, for the liberals. See Cripps, *Slow Fade to Black*, 257, for the quotation.

27. See Randy Roberts, "Jack Dempsey: An American Hero in the 1920s," *Journal of Popular Culture* 8 (Fall 1974): 420; and Roberts, *Jack Dempsey: The Manassa Mauler* (Baton Rouge LA, 1979) for Dempsey's life.

28. See Young, "Joe Louis, Symbol," 120; George Hutchinson, "The Black Athletes' Contribution towards Social Change in the United States" (PhD diss., United States International University, 1977), 86.

29. Miller, *Louis*, 35; Young, "Joe Louis, Symbol," 42; Edmonds, *Joe Louis*; 40; Sammons, "Boxing as a Reflection of Society," 26.

30. Louis, *My Life*, 58, 63, 90–91, 118–19.

31. Louis, *My Life*, 39, 65, 66–67, 81–83, 182–83.

32. Roxborough appeared Robin Hood–like to unemployed blacks; see Louis, *My Life*, 29–30. That Black, Blackburn, and he had police records partly explains

their attractiveness to the masses and entrepreneurs, who recognized shady dealings as an avenue for upward mobility in a society of limited opportunities; see David M. Katzman, *Before the Ghetto: Black Detroit in the Nineteenth Century* (Chicago, 1973), 171-74; and Allan Spear, *Black Chicago: The Making of a Negro Ghetto, 1890-1920* (Chicago, 1967), 71, 76-78. Their criminal activities aside, some professionals admired the all-black composition of "Joe Louis and Co."; see *Detroit Tribune*, June 22, 1940, 12.

33. See Earl Brown, "Joe Louis the Champion, Idol of His Race, Sets a Good Example of Conduct," *Life*, June 17, 1940, 52; and Marshall W. Fishwick, *American Heroes: Myth and Reality* (Westport CT, 1954), 228-29, for the contention that "skillful and faithful manipulators" lay behind all heroes creating "a mythical image and a second life for them." Parts of Louis's image and life—his humanitarianism, for example—were genuine, however.

34. Richard M. Dalfiume, "The 'Forgotten Years' of the Negro Revolution," *The Journal of American History* 55 (June 1968): 90-106.

35. Peter J. Kellogg, "Civil Rights Consciousness in the 1940s," *The Historian* 42 (November 1979): 31.

36. Jack Orr, "The Black Boxer: Exclusion and Ascendance" in *Sport and Society*, edited by John T. Talamini and Charles H. Page (Boston, 1973), 241. Quotation is from Louis, *My Life*, 137; the statistic is from p. 141.

37. Young, "Joe Louis, Symbol," 130.

38. See Erik H. Erikson, *Childhood and Society* (2nd ed.; New York, 1963), 263–66, for the concepts of isolation and intimacy. See Edwin R. Embree, *Thirteen against the Odds* (New York, 1944), 237, for the quotation.

39. Kellogg, "Civil Rights Consciousness in the 1940s," 33; Sammons, "Boxing as a Reflection of Society," 30.

40. *Time*, September 29, 1949, 60.

41. *New York Amsterdam News*, January 6, 1940, 15; *New York Times*, February 14, 1940, 13.

42. Walter White, *A Man Called White: The Autobiography of Walter White* (New York, 1948), 187–88.

43. Memo to Roberta Barrows (from H. K.), September 23, 1940, and Edwin M. Watson to Julian Rainey, September 25, 1940, both in box 13 of 300, Franklin D. Roosevelt Papers, Roosevelt Library, Hyde Park, New York (hereafter cited as FDRP).

44. Oscar R. Ewing to Edwin M. Watson, September 28, 1940, FDRP.

45. Quotation appears in *New York Times*, October 27, 1940, 37. See Louis, *My Life*, 158–59, for his version of the endorsement.

46. For the quotations see *New York Times*, October 31, 1940, 18; October 27, 1940, 37; and November 5, 1940, 21.

47. Anonymous telegram to Roosevelt, November 2, 1940, OF 4884, FDRP.

48. Diggs telegram to Roosevelt, November 1, 1940, OF 93, FDRP.

49. See Sitkoff, *A New Deal for Blacks*, 303-9; and Herbert Parmet, *Never Again: A President Runs for a Third Term* (New York, 1968), for the election results.

50. Diggs telegram to Roosevelt, November 1, 1940, OF 93, FDRP.

51. Quoted in Miller, *Louis*, 133.

52. *New York Times*, January 31, 1941, 22.

53. Lee Finkle, "The Conservative Aims of Militant Rhetoric: Black Protest during World War II," *The Journal of American History* 60 (December 1973): 702-4; *Forum for Protest: The Black Press during World War II* (Rutherford NJ, 1975), 88-128.

54. Neil A. Wynn, *The Afro-American and the Second World War* (New York, 1976), 99, 108-9.

55. See William H. Harris, *The Harder We Run: Black Workers since the Civil War* (New York, 1982), 117; and James A. Nuechterlein, "The Politics of Civil Rights: The FEPC, 1941-1946," *Prologue: The Journal of the National Archives* 10 (Fall 1978): 171-91, regarding Randolph, Roosevelt, and the Fair Employment Practices Committee.

56. Clarence Williams to the NAACP, January 3, 1942, box 549, NAACP; Walter H. Jacobs to Roosevelt, November 14, 1941, box 100, PPF 9-J, FDRP.

57. Bill White to the editor, *New York Times*, May 31, 1941, 18; John Kieran, "Sports of the Times," *New York Times*, June 18, 1941, 26.

58. See *New York Times*, June 18, 1941, 27, and June 19, 1941, 1, for the following quotation, and p. 27.

59. *New York Times*, June 20, 1941, 25; Louis, *My Life*, 167.

60. See *New York Times*, June 20, 1941, 25, for these quotations and June 19, 1941, 1, for the following quotations and description of the fight.

61. *New York Times*, June 19, 1941, 27.

62. *New York Times*, June 19, 1941, 27, and June 20, 1941, 25.

63. See *Pittsburgh Courier*, February 28, 1942, 1. Roosevelt and Willkie were the other greatest men.

64. *New York Times*, August 19, 1941, 23, and August 20, 1941, 21. See *New York Times*, July 3, 1941, 21, and July 10, 1941, 21, for Marva's quotation.

65. John C. Dancy to Presley S. Winfield, August 12, 1941, box 1, John C. Dancy Papers, Michigan Historical Collections, Bentley Historical Library, Ann Arbor MI (hereafter cited as JCDP).

66. See *New York Times*, September 30, 1941, 1, for the statistic and the quotation and p. 29 for information in the following sentence. See Louis, *My Life*, 81, for the Louis-Henie affair.

67. *New York Times*, October 1, 1941, 20; *Detroit Tribune*, October 4, 1941, 7.

68. John C. Dancy, *Sand against the Wind: The Memoirs of John C. Dancy* (Detroit, 1966), 186–88; Dancy to Julia Black, October 3, 1941, box 1, JCDP.

69. White to Louis, Roxborough and Black, December 12, 1941, box 365, NAACP.

70. White to Louis, February 16, 1940, and February 24, 1940, box 365, NAACP; *Life*, June 1940, 50. See White to editor, *Life*, June 18, 1940, for the quotation. See White to Earl Brown, June 19, 1940, box 365, NAACP, regarding the latter's "Joe Louis the Champion, Idol of His Race, Sets a Good Example of Conduct."

71. Guichard Parris and Lester Brooks, *Blacks in the City: A History of the National Urban League* (Boston, 1971), 312; Louis to Roosevelt, September 27, 1941, OF 93, FDRP.

72. Memorandum for Watson (from S.T.E.), October 2, 1941, box 5, OF 93, FDRP. Black militancy aside, Roosevelt must have recalled Louis's opposition to his reelection before informing the champion that he donated to relief organizations of broader scope; see Edwin W. Watson to Louis, October 7, 1941, box 5, OF 93, FDRP.

73. White to Robert D. Kohn, October 7, 1941, box 365, NAACP.

74. *New York Times*, September 10, 1941, 31; Richard M. Dalfiume, *Desegregation of the U.S. Armed Forces: Fighting on Two Fronts, 1939–1953* (Columbia MO, 1969), 64–68.

75. White to Eleanor Roosevelt, September 22, 1941, and White to Louis, Roxborough and Black, October 3, 1941, both in box 365, NAACP.

76. Brigadier General F. H. Osborn to White, October 1, 1941, box 365, NAACP.

77. Memorandum to White (from Wilkins), October 3, 1941, box 365, NAACP.

78. White to Louis, Roxborough and Black, October 3, 1941, box, 365, NAACP.

79. *New York Times*, November 13, 1941, 39, and December 17, 1941, 41. Baer agreed to donate 2.5 percent of his share to the society.

80. *Pittsburgh Courier*, December 6, 1941, 17, and December 13, 1941, 17.

81. White telegram to *Pittsburgh Courier*, November 15, 1941, box 365, NAACP.

82. White to editor, *New York Times*, December 15, 1941, box 365, NAACP; he sent an identical letter to several New York dailies, which was published by at least one newspaper, the *Herald Tribune*.

83. See Madison S. Jones, Jr. to Edna Scott, n.d., Memorandum to Miss Crump (from Mr. Morrow), January 9, 1942, and Memorandum to Mrs. Bowman (from Distribution Committee), January 19, 1942, all in box 365, NAACP, regarding

the leaflets. See White to Clapper, January 2, 1942, box 365, NAACP, for the quotation.

84. Quoted in "Our Joe," an unidentified press clipping, n.d., box 549, NAACP.

85. *New York Times*, January 10, 1942, 19; *New York Amsterdam News*, January 17, 1942, 1; *Pittsburgh Courier*, February 28, 1942, 5.

86. Memorandum (from the Secretary of the Spingarn Medal), January 26, 1942, box 549, NAACP.

87. See Wecter, *The Hero in America*, 1–16, 476–91, for the majority's criteria for heroes. See Erik H. Erikson, *Young Man Luther: A Study in Psychoanalysis and History* (New York, 1958), 259, for the theory of meshing with different groups and ideas.

88. *Pittsburgh Courier*, January 3, 1942, 16, February 14, 1942, 3, and January 10, 1942, 17.

89. See Spencer Page to Roosevelt, January 15, 1942, OF 4884, FDRP, and *Pittsburgh Courier*, January 31, 1942, 20, and February 7, 1942, 11, for the song and poster. The Boxing Writers Association of New York presented the Neil trophy.

90. White to Arthur B. Spingarn, January 22, 1942, and Spingarn to White, January 23, 1942, both in box 549, NAACP.

91. Holmes to White, January 27, 1942, box 549, NAACP.

92. *New York Amsterdam News*, January 17, 1942, 1, 3.

93. *Detroit Tribune*, January 17, 1942, 1; *Pittsburgh Courier*, January 31, 1942, 20.

94. Miller, *Louis*, 163.

95. *Pittsburgh Courier*, March 21, 1942, 17, and May 16, 1942, 17. Some reporters, including the *Courier*'s, misquoted Louis in their original stories.

96. Roosevelt to Byoir, May 4, 1942, and Byoir, "Joe Louis Named the War," both in PPP 2176, FDRP; Edward Anthony to Arthur B. Spingarn, May 5, 1942, box 365, NAACP.

97. Byoir guessed that Louis found inspiration in his great-grandfather, no doubt a slave; but columnist W. K. Kelsey opined that "consciously or unconsciously" he paraphrased Lincoln, who reputedly said something similar to a Southern delegation during the Civil War. However, Louis credited bandleader friend Lucky Millander for helping formulate ideas for the benefit speech; see Byoir, "Joe Louis Named the War," *Detroit News*, March 22, 1941, 6; and Louis, *My Life*, 173–74.

98. *Michigan Chronicle*, November 11, 1944, 14.

99. *Michigan Chronicle*, June 20, 1942, 6.

100. *New York Times*, March 28, 1942, 12; *Pittsburgh Courier*, April 4, 1942, 17; Louis, *My Life*, 174.

101. Lester B. Granger to Dancy, March 6, 1942, and Dancy to John Roxborough, March 6, 1942, both in reel 10, DULP.

102. Dancy to Lester B. Granger, March 9, 1942, and Ann Tanneyhill to John Roxborough, March 21, 1942, both in reel 10, DULP.

103. Granger to John Roxborough, March 30, 1942, reel 10, DULP.

104. *Pittsburgh Courier*, March 21, 1942, 20; *Michigan Chronicle*, June 6, 1942, 13. Privately, the army favored Louis with passes for Blackburn's funeral, his daughter's birth, and his wife's debut as a singer; see Louis, *Story*, 159, 166, 168.

105. *Pittsburgh Courier*, March 28, 1942, 16; *Michigan Chronicle*, June 6, 142, 1.

106. Summer A. Sirtl to Roosevelt, June 2, 1942, OF 4884, FDRP; Benjamin F. Bell, Jr., telegram to Roosevelt, September 6, 1943, OF 4408, FDRP.

107. Quoted in Memo (from M. H. McIntyre), July 11, 1942, OF 4884, FDRP.

108. *Detroit News*, July 20, 1943, 19, and July 31, 1943, 14.

109. Victor G. Reuther to John Gallo, March 11, 1942, box 31, United Automobile War Policy Collection, Archives of Labor and Urban Affairs, Detroit; Maclean to Marvin H. McIntyre, November 20, 1942, box 7, OF 93, FDRP.

110. White to Charles Poletti, April 30, 1943, box 248, NAACP.

111. "'Headliners,'" *New York Times Magazine*, May 24, 1942, 19. See *Pittsburgh Courier*, April 11, 1942, 20; *Detroit News*, June 11, 1943, 29; and *Michigan Chronicle*, May 16, 1942, 12, for the broadcast and following quotations.

112. Wynn, *The Afro-American and the Second World War*, 30, 83.

113. See *New York Times*, October 11, 1944, 25, for statistics and the following quotation, and September 24, 1945, 32.

114. Quoted in Miller, *Louis*, 179.

115. See *Michigan Chronicle*, October 28, 1944, 15, for the quotation from Col. Joe Triner, former chairman of the Illinois Boxing Commission.

116. *Detroit Tribune*, June 28, 1941, 3; *Pittsburgh Courier*, February 21, 1942, 11.

117. B. M. Merril to Edward J. Jeffries, Jr., March 2, 1942, box 9, Mayor's Papers, Burton Historical Collection, Detroit Public Library, Detroit.

118. Military Intelligence Division, War Department, "Race Riots," August 5, 1943, box 18, record group 319, Washington National Records Center, Suitland MD (hereafter cited as WNRC). It is unclear whether Louis visited Pittsburgh.

119. See Dominic J. Capeci Jr., *The Harlem Riot of 1943* (Philadelphia, 1977), 104, for LaGuardia following White's advice.

120. White to John Roxborough, August 18, 1943, box 365, NAACP. See Sitkoff, "Racial Militancy and Interracial Violence in the Second World War," 678–79; and Donald R. McCoy and Richard T. Ruetten, "Towards Equality: Blacks in the United States during the Second World War," in *Minorities in History*,

edited by A. C. Hepburn (New York, 1979), 148, for conflicting views of the significance of these committees. See Sosna, *In Search of the Silent South*, 108, for Jonathan Daniels's quotation.

121. Finkle, "Conservative Aims," 711. See *Michigan Chronicle*, August 7, 1943, 1, for Louis Martin's quotation.

122. Dalfiume, *Desegregation of the U.S. Armed Forces*, 54-55, 101; *Detroit Tribune*, April 11, 1942, 1; *Pittsburgh Courier*, April 18, 1942, 16; Special Services Division, Office of War Information, "Negro Organizations and the War Effort," April 28, 1942, box 1843, record group 44, WNRC.

123. *Michigan Chronicle*, May 23, 1942, 4.

124. *Michigan Chronicle*, June 6, 1942, 2.

125. See Louis, *My Life*, 185-86, for his view of the depot and theater incidents and pp. 177-79 for his recollection of the Jackie Robinson episode below. See Sugar Ray Robinson with Dave Anderson, *Sugar Ray* (New York, 1970), 122-24; and W. C. Heinz, *Once They Heard Cheers* (New York, 1979), 305-6, for their being provoked by a white military policeman at Camp Sibert.

126. Ulysses G. Lee. Jr. *The United States Army in World War II. Special Studies: The Employment of Negro Troops* (Washington DC, 1994), 323-24.

127. Jackie Robinson, *I Never Had It Made* (New York, 1972), 25, 28-29.

128. Lee, *Employment of Negro Troops*, 307.

129. See Lee, *Employment of Negro Troops*, 203-4, 211, 270-74; and Dalfiume, *Desegregation of the U.S. Armed Forces*, 63-74, for military policy.

130. Louis, *My Life*, 180-81.

131. Louis, *Story*, 169.

132. *Baltimore AfroAmerican*, May 22, 1943, 24. See *Michigan Chronicle*, May 29, 1944, 7, for the quotation.

133. *New York Times*, October 24, 1944, 14; Ottley, *"New World A-Coming,"* 299.

134. *New York Times*, March 8, 1945, 16, and April 10, 1945, 23.

135. *Michigan Chronicle*, April 7, 1945, 7; *New York Times*, July 16, 1945, 6.

136. *New York Times*, August 15, 1945, 22. See *Michigan Chronicle*, March 3, 1945, 4 for the quotation of Ford employee Arthur Mitchell of Detroit.

137. *New York Times*, September 24, 1945, 32.

138. Bernard B. Perry to White, September 18, 1945, box 365, NAACP; J. H. Eliashon to Dancy, January 22, 1946, reel 11, DULP.

139. See Elijah P. Marrs to White, April 29, 1946, box 91, NAACP, for an example.

140. Adam Clayton Powell, Jr. to Roosevelt, March 6, 1945, OF 4884, FDRP.

141. William Harrison to White, October 19, 1941, box 549, NAACP. See Ottley, *"New World A-Coming,"* 190, for the quotation.

142. Guy Wells to James E. Shepard, April 22, 1942, box 24, Howard W. Odum Papers, Southern Historical Collection, Wilson Library, Chapel Hill NC; Young, "Joe Louis, Symbol," 104. See St. Clair Drake and Horace R. Cayton, *Black Metropolis: A Study of Negro Life in a Northern City* (rev. ed., New York, 1962), II, 403, for an example—*Chicago Defender*, 1933–38—of the overwhelming coverage of Louis by black newspapers.

143. White to editor, *Life*, June 18, 1940, box 365, NAACP.

144. Sidney Hook, *The Hero in History: A Study in Limitation and Possibility* (New York, 1943), 12. See Kapp, "Heroes, Villains, and Fools as Agents of Social Control," 57, for the quotation.

145. Eldon E. Snyder and Elmer Spreitzer, *Social Aspects of Sports* (Englewood Cliffs NJ, 1978), 31.

146. See Erik H. Erikson, *Gandhi's Truth: On the Origins of Militant Nonviolence* (New York, 1969), 266; and *Identity: Youth and Crisis* (New York, 1968), 31–32, respectively, for the theories of individual-group identity and cultural consolidation.

147. Carl Rowan, "Nonsense about Joe" *Springfield (MO) Leader and Press*, April 2, 1981, A-5; John Kieran, "A Champion All the Way," *Opportunity: Journal of Negro Life* 20 (February 1942): 48.

148. See William J. Goode, *The Celebration of Heroes: Prestige as a Control System* (Berkeley CA, 1978), 1–2, 10, for this theory. One federal official even suggested that Louis ask black civilians to rid themselves of venereal disease as "a patriotic measure"; see J. M. Ragland to White, May 12, 1942, box 365, NAACP.

149. James MacGregor Burns, *Leadership* (New York, 1978), 243.

150. See Edmonds, *Joe Louis*, 86, for Louis as symbol. See Lewis M. Killian and Ralph H. Turner, *Collective Behavior* (Englewood Cliffs NJ, 1957), 465, for the quotation. See John William Ward, "The Meaning of Lindbergh's Flight," *American Quarterly* 10 (Spring 1958): 3–16, for the best example of the significance of heroism that does not imply leadership.

151. August Meier and Elliot Rudwick, *Along the Color Line: Explorations in the Black Experience* (Urbana, 1976), 2.

152. See Marshall Fishwick, "Prologue," in *Heroes of Popular Culture*, edited by Ray B. Brown, Marshall Fishwick, and Michael T. Marsden (Bowling Green OH: Bowling Green University Popular Press, 1972), 7, for characteristics of old and modern heroes; Louis presented an exemplary image but played numerous roles, thereby bridging the qualities of past and future heroes.

153. See *New York Times*, October 12, 1942, 12, for the quotation from James J. Walker, and May 13, 1979, V-3 for Reverend Jesse Jackson's view of Louis as David-like.

154. Quoted in Young, "Joe Louis, Symbol," 110.

4

Outside the Pale
The Exclusion of Blacks from the National
Football League, 1934–1946

THOMAS G. SMITH

With the exception of coaching and front office personnel, discrimination in professional football has virtually disappeared. Today 55 percent of National Football League rosters and 62 percent of all starters are African Americans. Blacks also constitute 81 percent of starting skill position athletes (quarterback, wide receiver, running back, cornerback, and safety). Only a few decades ago, however, professional football was a "popcorn" sport—played only by whites. Talented minority athletes performed for predominantly white colleges, but they were excluded from the professional game. Owners denied the existence of a color ban, but no blacks played in the NFL from 1933 to 1946. With the end of World War II and the emergence of a new league to compete with the NFL, the racial barrier was toppled. Many African Americans considered 1946 to have been a "banner year" because two professional sports—Minor League baseball and Major League football—were desegregated. This essay focuses on the efforts of blacks to expose and eradicate the policy of exclusion in professional football.[1]

During the 1920s and early 1930s, the formative years of the National Football League, a few blacks graced the gridiron. Robert "Rube" Marshall, the first black to appear in an NFL game, played for the Rock Island team. Fred "Duke" Slater, a premier tackle, starred for the Chicago Cardinals from 1926 to 1931. Paul Robeson, Fritz Pollard, and Jay "Inky" Williams were also standout professionals. After Ray Kemp and Joe Lillard were released in 1933, however, another black did not play organized professional football until 1946.[2]

A graduate of Duquesne University, where he played three years of varsity football, Ray Kemp signed with Art Rooney's newly created Pittsburgh Pirates in 1933. After playing two games at tackle, he was released by Pirates coach Jap Douds. Recalled to the team in December, Kemp played the final game against the New York Giants. When he attempted to join his teammates at the hotel in New York following the game, he was informed that no rooms were available. He reluctantly agreed to stay at a YMCA in Harlem. Released in 1933 after one season, he began a long career as a college football coach. In an interview, Kemp cited racism as the reason for his release. "It was my understanding," he noted, "that there was a gentleman's agreement in the league that there would be no more blacks."[3]

Joe Lillard's career, though more spectacular, was also cut short. A gifted athlete who excelled at baseball, basketball, and football, Lillard played for the Chicago Cardinals in 1932 and 1933. A star running back at the University of Oregon, his college career ended when a rival coach discovered that he had played baseball and basketball for semiprofessional black teams.

Signed by the Cardinals, Lillard was the only black man in the NFL in 1932. In a mid-October scoreless contest against the crosstown Bears, he gave a strong performance as a punt returner, kicker, and running back. The following week, he helped the Cardinals defeat the Boston Braves. An ebullient Boston columnist wrote, "Lillard is not only the ace of the Cardinal backfield but he is one of the greatest all-around players that has ever displayed his wares on any gridiron in this section of the country." Approximately one month later, Lillard was suspended by the Cardinals and out of football.[4]

Apparently, Lillard lost favor with teammates and management due to a lackluster effort and prideful attitude. Coach Jack Chevigny explained that Lillard disrupted practice by being tardy or absent, missed blocking assignments in games, and disobeyed team rules. The team's public relations officer, Rocky Wolfe, claimed that teammates resented his selfishness and swaggering style. They wanted Lillard to be more team-oriented, humble, and accommodating. "Football players, like anyone else, will always be jealous," remarked Wolfe. "But a fellow can always clear up such a situation by living, walking and breathing in a manner that does not bespeak supremacy—a thing Lillard hasn't learned." Worried that his cocky demeanor might deny opportunities to other minority athletes, black sports scribe Al Monroe urged Lillard to "learn to play upon the vanity" of whites. "He is the lone link in a place we are holding on to by a very weak string."[5]

The following year, Paul Schlissler, the new coach of the Cardinals, gave Lillard another opportunity. On October 7, Lillard threw three passes for 75 yards but missed a point after a touchdown in a 7–6 loss to Portsmouth, Ohio. The next week he drop-kicked a field goal to defeat Cincinnati 3–0. And the following week in a 12–9 loss to the Bears he kicked a field goal and returned a punt 53 yards for a touchdown. A black weekly, the *Chicago Defender*, described him as "easily the best halfback in football" during the 1933 season. Injuries limited his play, however, and his contract was not renewed the following year.[6]

The black press claimed that Lillard had been "Too Good For His Own Good" and that the "color of his skin had driven him out of the National Football League." In 1935 Coach Schlissler conceded that an unwritten rule barred blacks from the game for their own protection. Lillard, he said, had been a victim of racism. "He was a fine fellow, not as rugged as most in the pro game, but very clever," he explained. "But he was a marked man, and I don't mean that just the southern boys took it out on him either; after a while whole teams, Northern and Southern alike, would give Joe the works, and I'd have to take him out." Lillard's presence, the coach continued, made the Cardinals a "marked team" and the "rest of the league took it out on us! We had to let him go, for our own sake and for his too!"[7]

Professional football owners, like their baseball counterparts, denied the existence of a racial ban. "For myself and for most of the owners," Art

Rooney of the Pittsburgh Steelers explained decades later, "I can say there never was any racial bias." George Halas of the Chicago Bears declared in 1970 that there had "in no way, shape, or form" been an unwritten exclusionary agreement. Tex Schramm of the Los Angeles Rams did not recall a gentleman's agreement: "You just didn't do it [sign blacks]—it wasn't the thing that was done." Wellington and Tim Mara of the New York Giants also denied that minorities had been blackballed. Despite the disclaimers, however, blacks had disappeared from the game.[8]

The racial climate of the 1930s no doubt contributed to the policy of discrimination. True, blacks made important strides toward racial justice during the Roosevelt years. Above all, Roosevelt's New Deal offered hope. Encouraged by the New Deal promise of "no forgotten men and no forgotten races," blacks deserted their traditional allegiance to the Republican party. In 1936, FDR attracted about 75 percent of the black vote. New Deal relief programs, especially the Works Progress Administration headed by Harry Hopkins, helped blacks cope with hard times. In all, about 40 percent of the black population received some federal assistance during the Great Depression. Roosevelt appointed William H. Hastie, Mary McLeod Bethune, and other influential blacks to important government positions. And throughout the 1930s Eleanor Roosevelt denounced bigotry and worked for social justice.[9]

Despite modest gains and heightened expectations, African Americans continued to experience injustice. In agriculture, tenant farmers and sharecroppers suffered from plunging prices. In industry, the jobless rate soared as blacks were the "last hired and first fired." Some New Deal assistance programs discriminated against minorities. More than 60 percent of black workers were not eligible for Social Security benefits because the plan did not cover farm workers and domestics.[10]

In the South, where more than two-thirds of the black population resided, a vicious system of segregation existed. Blacks were terrorized and lynched. They were denied access to hospitals, colleges, hotels, restaurants, churches, polling places, playgrounds, and parks. Transportation facilities, public schools, and cemeteries were segregated. At the premiere of *Gone with the Wind* in Atlanta, Georgia, blacks were banned from the theaters.[11]

Discrimination extended beyond regional boundaries. "The Negro is a sort of national skeleton-in-the-closet," lamented one black editor. In the North, employers and unions, as well as schools and colleges, denied opportunities to African Americans. Motion pictures and radio shows portrayed blacks in stereotypical roles of Uncle Tom, Sambo, or Aunt Jemima. It is little wonder that some minorities found the celebration of the 150th anniversary of the United States Constitution hypocritical. Some drew parallels with the discriminatory treatment of Jews in Nazi Germany. Until Jim Crow ends, commented the *Pittsburgh Courier*, "only hypocrites will condemn the German Nazis for doing all of a sudden what America has been doing for generations." And when war erupted in Europe in 1939 the *Courier* cautioned that "before any of our people get unduly excited about SAVING DEMOCRACY in Europe, it should be called to their attention that we have NOT YET ACHIEVED DEMOCRACY HERE."[12]

Not surprisingly, discrimination and segregation extended to the sports field. While some blacks were distinguishing themselves in professional boxing and track and field, others were being denied opportunities in other sports. Most "major" colleges either excluded blacks or denied them a chance to participate on varsity teams. Professional sports such as basketball, baseball, and football also banned African Americans. In response, blacks organized their own professional teams and leagues. In football the most successful team was the New York Brown Bombers. Coached by Fritz Pollard, the Bombers attracted Otis Troupe, Joe Lillard, and other black stars. Black teams existed in many cities, but talented players were overlooked or shunned by NFL owners.[13]

Many reasons other than race prejudice were used to explain the absence of blacks from the professional game. Some blacks charged that NFL owners used Joe Lillard's volatile personality as an excuse to ban other minority athletes. Proud and hot-tempered, Lillard rarely overlooked a racial slur or dirty play. When wronged he retaliated and earned a reputation for being a "bad actor." In a game against the Pittsburgh Pirates in 1933 he was ejected for fighting. Lillard "was an angry young man," Ray Kemp has recalled, "and the players on the other teams knew what would set him off."[14]

During the 1920s, Fritz Pollard has observed, fledgling NFL teams may have signed black All-Americans to gain recognition and fan support. Having gained popularity and stability during the 1930s, the league no longer was willing to sign "name" black players. And during the Depression decade it was bad public relations to hire blacks when so many whites were without jobs.[15]

Other observers have blamed Redskins owner George Marshall for the color ban. The West Virginia–born owner, one of the most influential in the league, helped bring organization and structure to the NFL. During the 1920s there were numerous teams (as many as twenty-two in 1926), and franchises often went out of business or relocated. In 1933, at Marshall's request, the league was reorganized into two five-team divisions with a season-ending championship game. Four years later, Marshall established a franchise in the South by transferring his Boston team to Washington DC, a segregated city. To avoid offending Marshall and southern white players and fans, NFL owners may have tacitly agreed to shun black athletes. Marshall himself once publicly avowed that he would never employ minority athletes. Indeed, the Redskins were the last NFL team to desegregate, holding out until 1962.[16]

Some owners, like George Halas, unconvincingly attributed the absence of blacks in the NFL to the lack of quality college players. Others, like Art Rooney, claimed that financial constraints prohibited NFL teams from developing adequate scouting systems. Financial realities no doubt did discourage owners from scouting black colleges, but there were several standout minority athletes on major college teams in the 1930s. Since white players were scouted and signed, it seems reasonable to expect black athletes who played in the same conferences to have been discovered. But none were.[17]

Blacks had to have extraordinary ability and a serene temperament to play for desegregated college teams. At tryouts, they were quickly tested to see if they had the courage and perseverance to "take it." Harry Kipke, coach at the University of Michigan, ordered his veterans to pound a black candidate "without mercy" during practice. "If, at the end of the week," said Kipke, "he doesn't turn in his uniform, then I know I've got a great player." Coach Ossie Solem of Iowa confided, "There's no use kidding anyone—a colored player, even when opponents play cleanly, always gets plenty of bumps and particularly when he is the star."[18]

Black players also created logistical problems. Coaches had to deal with discrimination in travel, lodging, and restaurants. Should they insist upon equal treatment for all team members or ask minority players to endure humiliating Jim Crow laws? The black player, explained one coach, "through no fault of his own, but because of uninformed and prejudiced individuals, creates a problem for us, which we, in combating, frequently find so disagreeable that we wonder whether it is worth the battle we put up."[19]

Then, too, there were scheduling problems. Southern colleges usually refused to play against desegregated teams. Consequently, blacks were benched or games were canceled. Fitzhugh Lyons and Jesse Babb had to sit out when Indiana played Mississippi State in Bloomington. Windy Wallace and Borce Dickerson were benched when Iowa met George Washington University. The Iowa coach explained that he had "asked the boys to stay out of the contest for the good of the sport." The United States Naval Academy refused to play against Bill Bell of Ohio State but had no objections to NYU's Manuel Riviero because he was a "white Cuban." And despite heated protests from University of Michigan students, Willis Ward was not in uniform against Georgia Tech. "MICHIGAN U. BOWS TO DEMANDS OF SOUTH; WARD IS BARRED FROM GEORGIA TECH GAME," ran a front-page headline in a black newspaper.[20]

Finally, racial prejudice prevented minorities from winning the recognition they deserved. Those who excelled often did not win team captaincies, conference honors, or All-American recognition. They were rarely chosen to play in an annual game between the college All-Stars and the NFL championship team.[21]

Despite the obstacles, some blacks did play big-time college football, especially in the Big Ten Conference. Horace Bell and Dwight Reed of Minnesota, Clarence Hinton and Bernie Jefferson of Northwestern, and

Willis Ward of Michigan were all talented athletes who performed during the 1930s. None received NFL offers, although Jefferson, a gifted running back, was eventually signed by the Chicago Rockets in 1947, long after his prime.[22]

Oze Simmons, a 185-pound running back at the University of Iowa, was perhaps the most talented and celebrated player in the Big Ten in the 1930s. A four-sport high school star from Fort Worth, Texas, Simmons played on the team with his brother Don and two other blacks, Windy Wallace and Homer Harris. In his first varsity game, against Northwestern in 1934, he ran back a kickoff for a touchdown, returned 7 punts for 124 yards, and rushed for 166 yards on 24 carries. An elusive, speedy running back, he was nicknamed the "Wizard of Oze." The Northwestern coach, Dick Hanley, who had seen Fritz Pollard and Red Grange, called Simmons "absolutely the best I've ever seen."[23]

The following year the junior continued to impress, scoring 5 touchdowns on runs of over 50 yards. "Simmons is All-America, sure fire," wrote white scribe Harold Parrott of the *Brooklyn Eagle*. Simmons made the Associated Press second team and not the first team.[24]

Acrimony, more than accolades, surrounded Simmons during his varsity year. Rumors, which had begun in 1934, persisted that his teammates resented the attention he was getting and refused to block for him. He was the logical choice for team captain in 1936, but his teammates voted to do away with that honorary position for that year. At the end of the season, they selected Homer Harris, a black end, as the team's Most Valuable Player and captain for 1937. Harris became the first black player to captain a Big Ten football team.[25]

Simmons also had a falling-out with his coach, Ossie Solem. In mid-November, in the wake of a 52–0 loss to Minnesota, Simmons left the team after being berated by Coach Solem for a lack of effort. Reinstated for the final game against Temple, Simmons romped for a 72-yard touchdown. On the whole, however, it was a disappointing season. Despite considerable talent, he was bypassed for both the team's Most Valuable Player Award and for All-America honors. Shunned by the NFL, he signed with a black semiprofessional team, the Patterson Panthers, in 1937.[26]

Skilled black athletes also appeared on eastern college gridirons. Two of the best players, were Wilmeth Sidat-Singh of Syracuse University and Jerome "Brud" Holland of Cornell.[27]

The adopted son of a Hindu physician, Sidat-Singh attended Dewitt Clinton High School in New York. A basketball standout, he made the Syracuse varsity team as a sophomore but bypassed the football tryouts. A coach who noticed him playing intramural football urged him to go out for the varsity squad. In 1937 he made the starting backfield as a junior. He was coached by Ossie Solem, who had moved over from Iowa, and Charles "Bud" Wilkinson.

Sidat-Singh developed into one of the finest passers in the nation. Sportswriters compared his skills to those of Sammy Baugh, Sid Luckman, and Benny Friedman. "Singh's Slings Sink Cornell," ran one alliterative headline. "It Don't Mean a Thing If It Ain't Got That Singh," ran another. In 1937 Singh helped Syracuse beat Penn State and Cornell, two tough rivals. Against the University of Maryland, another strong opponent, Sidat-Singh was benched when the southern college objected to playing against an African American. Syracuse lost 14–0. The following year at Syracuse Sidat-Singh played against Maryland and led the Orangemen to "Sweet Revenge," a 51–0 victory.[28]

Sidat-Singh's most celebrated performance came against Cornell in October 1938. Heavily favored, Cornell led 10–0 with nine minutes to go in the fourth quarter. Sidat-Singh threw three passes covering 50 yards to narrow the score to 10–6. Cornell then ran back the kickoff for a touchdown to take a commanding 17–6 lead. Obtaining the ball on the 31-yard line, Sidat-Singh tossed two passes covering 69 yards for a quick touchdown that cut the score to 17–12. When Syracuse recovered a fumble on the 30-yard line of Cornell, Sidat-Singh promptly completed a touchdown pass to win the game, 19–17. In the final nine minutes of play he had thrown 6 passes for 150 yards that scored 3 touchdowns. Famed sportswriter Grantland Rice called the performance "one of the most amazing exhibitions of machine gun fire I've ever seen, where the odds were all the other way." And Sam Balter, a respected NBC radio broadcaster, proclaimed it "the outstanding one-man show of the gridiron season of 1938."[29]

Cornell, the team that had been victimized by Sidat-Singh, itself boasted one of the premier football players in the nation. Jerome "Brud" Holland from Auburn, New York, played end on the varsity squad from 1936 to 1938. Strong and agile, he was famous for the end-around play and excelled on both offense and defense. In his first season, he was voted to the All-Eastern college football team.[30]

In 1937 Holland led Cornell to a record of 5 wins, 2 losses, and 1 tie. In the team's biggest game of the year, against favored Colgate, he scored three touchdowns in a 40–7 victory. During the season his superb offensive and defensive play won plaudits from both black and white sportswriters. The Yale coach, Clint Frank, called him the best end in the nation. The black press touted Holland for All-America honors. The odds seemed "virtually insurmountable" because he was black and only a junior; nevertheless, he was named to five different All-American teams. He was the first minority athlete to win the honor since Paul Robeson in 1918. When he was again honored in 1938, he became the first African American since Robeson to be recognized in consecutive years.[31]

Despite the acclaim, Holland failed to receive an offer from an NFL team. Sidat-Singh also was snubbed. Both athletes were chosen by writers to play for the college All-Stars in a game against the New York Giants, the first time blacks had been invited. "Neither Holland nor Sidat-Singh will play in the National Professional Football League this season," lamented one black weekly, "but it's not because they haven't got what it takes."[32]

Like those in the East and the Midwest, western colleges had long produced talented gridiron athletes. In the late 1930s UCLA had three minority athletes with NFL potential: Jackie Robinson, Woodrow Wilson Strode, and Kenny Washington.[33]

A transfer student from Pasadena City College, Jackie Robinson was a year behind Strode and Washington, class of 1940. NFL owners had a chance to sign the "cyclone-gaited hellion" long before he broke Major League Baseball's color barrier in 1947. At UCLA he was the only athlete ever to letter in four sports: baseball, football, basketball, and track. He was the national champion in the long jump and the leading basketball scorer in the Pacific Coast Conference, and he still retains the school football record for highest average per carry in a season (12.2 yards in 1939). The assistant coach at Stanford University referred to him as "just about the best sprinter on the coast and he's a great ball carrier. He's rugged and can play just as hard and long as anyone. We are scared to death of him." Robinson appeared in the college All-Star game in Chicago in 1941 but was bypassed by the NFL. "In those days no major football or basketball clubs hired black players. The only job offered me was with the Honolulu Bears," Robinson recalled. The football Bears, his first professional team, "were not Major League but they were integrated." Robinson's football career ended in December 1941 with the bombing of Pearl Harbor.[34]

Woody Strode and Kenny Washington played together for the UCLA Bruins for three seasons (1937–1939). Strode was a 220-pound end with speed and sure hands. He also excelled defensively. He was not considered as talented as Brud Holland but did win selection to the Pacific Coast All-Star team in 1939. Overlooked by the NFL, he played with Minor League West Coast professional teams until 1946.

Washington, a 195-pound halfback, was one of the best players in college football in the late 1930s. Jackie Robinson described him as "the greatest football player I have ever seen. He had everything needed for greatness—size, speed, and tremendous strength. Kenny was probably the greatest long passer ever." In a game against USC in 1937 he won national attention by throwing a touchdown pass 62 yards in the air. He was also impressive in a game played in Los Angeles against SMU. Madison Bell, the coach at SMU, regarded him as "one of the best players I have ever seen." Washington and Strode even drew praise from the white Texas press. Horace McCoy of the *Dallas Daily Times Herald* wrote that the "two black boys were everywhere; they were the entire team; they were playing with inspiration and courage, and they cracked and banged the Mustangs all over the field." At the conclusion of the game, won by SMU 26–13, the Mustang supporters joined UCLA fans in giving Washington an ovation. "In that moment you forgot he was black; he was no color at all; he was simply a great athlete," McCoy wrote. The following year, his running and passing prowess earned him a spot on the Pacific Coast All-American team.[35]

In 1939 UCLA enjoyed an unbeaten season and Washington performed spectacularly. "King Kenny" led all college players in total yardage with 1,370. The University of Montana coach, Doug Fessenden, said he was "greater than Red Grange." West Coast sportswriter, Dick Hyland, described him as the "best all-around football player seen here this year." A victory over USC in the final game of the year would have sent UCLA to the Rose Bowl. Unfortunately for the Bruins, the game ended in a scoreless tie and USC received the invitation. Washington won praise for his spirited play. Syndicated columnist Ed Sullivan reported that when Washington left the field he was given a standing ovation from 103,000 spectators. "I have never been so moved emotionally, and rarely so proud of my country," he remarked.[36]

Sportswriters, both black and white, boosted Washington for All-America honors. Wendell Smith wrote that his ability surpassed that of Nile Kinnick of Iowa, Tom Harmon of Michigan, and Paul Christman of Missouri. "You can look this country over from coast to coast and back again, but you'll find nary a pigskin toter the likes of Kenny Washington!" Another writer declared that if Washington "is kept off this year's All-America then the West Coast has a right to secede from the football union." But Washington earned only second-team All-America recognition. Relegating the UCLA back to second honors infuriated the black press. Randy Dixon of the *Courier* called the slight "unadulterated hokum" and the "biggest joke of the year."[37]

Washington was ignored in the NFL draft despite setting UCLA records in career rushing and passing. NBC broadcaster Sam Balter blasted the NFL's black ban. In an "open letter" over the airwaves he asked NFL owners why "nobody chose the leading collegiate ground gainer of the 1939 season." Those who had seen him play agreed that he was "not only the best football player on the Pacific Coast this season, but the best of the last ten years and perhaps the best in all that slope's glorious football history—a player who has reduced to absurdity all the All-American teams selected this year because they did not include him—and all know why." NFL scouts, he continued, all ranked Washington the best player in the nation but "none of you chose him." Balter expressed bitter disappointment "on behalf of the millions of American sport fans who believe in fair play and equal opportunity." He concluded by offering airtime to owners to explain why neither Washington nor Brud Holland was "good enough to play ball on your teams." The offer was not accepted.[38]

Jimmy Powers, a columnist for the *New York Daily News*, also scolded NFL owners. After watching Washington play for the college All-Stars against the Green Bay Packers in 1940, he urged Tim Mara and Dan Topping, owners of the New York teams, to sign the UCLA star. "He played on the same field with boys who are going to be scattered through the league. And he played against the champion Packers. There wasn't a bit of trouble anywhere." The black ban, however, was not lifted.[39]

One owner, George Halas of the Chicago Bears, did agree to play a black All-Star team in a charity game at Soldier Field in 1938. Many African Americans saw this charity game as an opportunity to show that minority athletes could compete in the NFL. In fact, some black sportswriters predicted that the "sons of Ham" would "lambast the Bears."[40]

Coached by Duke Slater and Ray Kemp, and selected by popular vote, the All-Stars were made up of players who had already graduated. Many represented black colleges. The backfield consisted of Big Bertha Edwards of Kentucky State, Tank Conrad of Morgan State, Oze Simmons, and Joe Lillard. Unlike the backfield, the line was light, inexperienced, and no match for the Bears. Coach Ray Kemp, who had not played the game since 1933, toiled at tackle for nearly the entire game. Moreover, the team had less than two weeks of practice.[41]

The game was a rout, with the powerful Bears winning 51–0. The All-Stars made only four first downs and lost 51 yards rushing. The Bears, forced to punt only once, amassed 605 total yards. "We've just finished witnessing the most disappointing sports spectacle of the decade[,] . . . a 'promotion' which will set Negro college football back years," lamented William G. Nunn of the *Pittsburgh Courier*. Actually, most black fans took the game in stride. "Grin and Bear it," joked one sportswriter. Coach Ray Kemp pointed out that the Bears were a great football team. (Indeed, in 1940 they would defeat the Redskins in a championship game 73–0.) Still, he regretted the fact "that we didn't have a longer period to train." The game was a disappointing loss, but it seemed to make blacks more eager than ever to achieve desegregation in both professional and college football.[42]

Blacks and whites persistently denounced segregation on southern college gridirons. To be sure, some Dixie schools did play desegregated teams. For three consecutive years the University of North Carolina played against Ed Williams of NYU "and the sky didn't fall." In the Southwest, Southern Methodist University in 1937 "pushed aside petty prejudice" to play against Strode and Washington of UCLA. Madison "Matty" Bell, the long-time SMU coach, had played in the NFL with Pollard, Slater, and Robeson and opposed "drawing the color-line in sports ... , because when you do it takes something out of it. I think every boy should have his chance to participate regardless of color." An anomaly in the South, Coach Bell looked forward to the day when all gridirons would be integrated.[43]

Northerners, too, made headway against football segregation. Universities such as Notre Dame and Pittsburgh were ridiculed for their lily-whiteism. Northern college football teams that agreed to bench black players against Dixie schools were denounced. Boston College, coached by Frank Leahy, caused a furor when it benched Lou Montgomery against the University of Florida and Auburn. Despite the protest BC again submitted to southern custom when it agreed that Montgomery would not participate in the Cotton Bowl game against Clemson. BC administrators asked Montgomery to accompany the team to Dallas but to sit out the game. He would be able to sit with teammates on the bench but would not be allowed participate in pre- or postgame ceremonies, stay in the same hotel, or eat in the same restaurants. Montgomery refused to make the trip if he could not play. "To go down there under restrictions and possibly run into some embarrassing situations, that would be plain silly. Surely no one with self respect would place himself and his teammates in that position knowingly."[44]

The black and white press denounced the "cruel snub." The *Pittsburgh Courier* criticized Boston College for abandoning its democratic and Christian ideals. Jack Miley of the *New York Daily News* scored BC for one of the most "spineless, mealy-mouthed, weak-kneed, craven bits of business in the whole history of college football." College authorities should have rejected the Cotton Bowl bid, he said, rather than submit to race prejudice. "Even Hitler, to give the bum his due, didn't treat Jesse Owens the way the Cotton Bowl folk are treating Lou Montgomery—with the consent of the young Negro's alma mater. . . . For Adolf, at least, let Owens run, and . . . he had the good grace not to try to bar Jesse before the games got under way." Miley's sentiments were shared by many eastern sports fans. A white letter writer lamented to the *New York Times* the fact that Jim Crow "practices have become living denials of our democracy—the discrimination, with official tolerance, against Negro football stars, in particular."[45]

The Montgomery incident prompted the black press to intensify its attack on the NFL color ban. William Brower, writing in *Opportunity*, the magazine of the Urban League, denounced NFL owners for "cheating Negro players out of the opportunity to participate in their league." Football "bigwigs," the author feared, were trying to emulate the exclusionary policy of Major League Baseball. Yet there were "no arresting or rational excuses for professional football to follow the dubious precedent set by professional baseball." The explanation that desegregated squads would create discord and offend southern sensibilities was nonsense. Oze Simmons, who played for two years with the Paterson Panthers in the American Association, claimed that "not only did the southern boys block for me; they even fought for me." Then, too, with the exception of Washington DC, NFL franchises were located in northern cities, "where athletic miscegenation is not prohibited." Brower could not find "any authenticated commitment" to a racial ban by the NFL owners. Yet "one look at the workings of their draft system" was sufficient evidence to indicate that a gentleman's agreement existed. Halas, Marshall, and Rooney had made considerable contributions to the professional game, and it was hard to believe that they would continue "to flout fair-minded fans" or "injudiciously disregard the professional and commercial value of such Negro players of excellence as Kenny Washington, Brud Holland and Oze Simmons."[46]

World War II proved a major boon to sports integration. Not only did the war promote the ideals of democracy and fair play, it also gave blacks a chance to showcase their talents on college, semiprofessional, and service teams. In football, three of the most talented minority athletes during the war years were Bill Willis, Marion Motley, and Claude "Buddy" Young.

Football, like other aspects of American life, had to endure wartime hardships. Manpower difficulties forced NFL teams to reduce their rosters from 33 to 25. Some colleges ended football programs for the duration. And most college players had their education and playing days interrupted by wartime commitments.

Bill Willis, a native of Columbus, Ohio, was an exception. He entered Ohio State University in 1941 and graduated four years later. A 212-pound tackle nicknamed "The Cat" for his quickness, he played three varsity seasons. At OSU, Willis has related, he never experienced a racial slight from a teammate. "One reason was because I always attempted to show respect and conducted myself in such a way as to demand respect from my fellow players." Ohio State won conference titles in 1942 and 1944. As a senior Willis was regarded "one of the greatest tackles in football history" and was named to several All-American and All-Star teams. Although the NFL was desperate for competent players, it bypassed Willis. Upon graduation, he took a football coaching position at Kentucky State.[47]

Claude "Buddy" Young was perhaps the most sensational college gridiron star during the war years. A freshman running back at the University of Illinois in 1944, he captured national attention. "Not since the days when Red Grange was ripping up the sod . . . for Bob Zuppke and the Illini has there been so much pigskin excitement on the University of Illinois campus," wrote one sports columnist.[48]

A native of Chicago, the 5'5" "Bronze Bullet" had exceptional quickness and acceleration. A track star, he won the national collegiate championships in the 100- and 220-yard dashes, tied the world record for the 45- and 60-yard dashes, and was the Amateur Athletic Union's 100-meter champion.[49]

Young was equally impressive on the gridiron. In his first game against Iowa, he scampered 64 yards for a touchdown on the first play from scrimmage. On his second carry, he ran for a 30-yard touchdown. In all, he gained 139 yards on 7 carries, an average of 19.7 yards. Before the season concluded, he had touchdown runs of 93, 92, 74, 64, and 63 yards. He averaged 8.9 yards per carry and scored 13 touchdowns, equaling the Big

Ten Conference record established by Red Grange in 1924. Sportscaster Bill Stern called him "the fastest thing in cleats and the runner of the year." Ray Eliot, Young's coach, referred to him as "the best running back I have ever seen." Only a freshman, Young was named to several All-America teams.[50]

In late January 1945, Young was drafted by the navy. Initially he reported to the Great Lakes Naval Training Station but was eventually transferred to the naval base at Fleet City, California. Like many star athletes, Young played football for the service team. Coast service teams, one writer claimed, "unquestionably played the toughest football extant during the war. The personnel of the league was 30 percent All-America, 30 percent professional and 40 percent better than the average college squad."[51]

Coached by Bill Reinhart, the Fleet City Bluejackets were, in 1945, the best football team on the coast. Besides Young, the squad consisted of such NFL stars as Charlie O'Rourke (Bears), Aldo Forte (Bears), and Frank "Bruiser" Kinard (Redskins). College stars included Bill Daddio (Pittsburgh), Edgar "Special Delivery" Jones (Pittsburgh), Harry Hopp (Nebraska), and Steve Juzwick (Notre Dame). Games were scheduled against other service teams and one semiprofessional team, the Hollywood Rangers.[52]

The Bluejackets' toughest competitor was the El Toro, California, Marines. Like the Bluejackets, the El Toro team was brimming with talent: Paul Governali of Columbia, Elroy "Crazy Legs" Hirsch of Wisconsin, Bob Dove of Notre Dame, and Wee Willie Wilkin of the Washington Redskins. In mid-December, the two teams met for the championship. In an earlier contest the Bluejackets had prevailed 7–0. The championship game was played in Los Angeles at Memorial Stadium before sixty-five thousand fans. It was one of Buddy Young's greatest games. After a scoreless first quarter, Young returned a kickoff for a 94-yard touchdown. He ran back another kickoff for an 88-yard touchdown and took a hand-off from O'Rourke and scampered 30 yards for another. The Bluejackets won the game 45–28 to complete an unbeaten season. They challenged the unbeaten West Point team, but the cadets refused the invitation.[53]

Young's performance won accolades from players, coaches, writers, and fans. Charlie O'Rourke still talks excitedly about the game and Young's ability. Ernie Nevers had "never seen his equal," and Aldo Forte remarked, "I've seen the greatest in pro football. None can compare with Young." El Toro coach Dick Hanley, who had coached Northwestern, called Young "the greatest college back I've ever seen." Bluejackets coach Bill Reinhart declared that he had "never seen anything like Buddy Young . . . and I've seen Cliff Battles, Tuffy Lemmans, George McAfee, "Doc" Blanchard, Glenn Davis, and Bill Dudley, among others." Sports columnist Slip Madigan also considered Young superior to Blanchard and Davis. And comedian Bob Hope observed, "I'd heard of black magic. Now I've seen it."[54]

Rumors circulated that once Young fulfilled his service obligation he would be drafted by the NFL or lured to UCLA to play for the Bruins. Neither proved true. Young returned to the University of Illinois and helped the Illini win the 1947 Rose Bowl.[55]

Marion Motley was another superb service team player. A strong and swift 220-pound fullback from Canton, Ohio, he played briefly at the University of Nevada. During the war he joined the navy and was assigned to the Great Lakes Naval Training Station. There he played on the football team coached by Paul Brown, who was familiar with Motley's achievements as an Ohio high school player. Harry "Bud" Grant, an aspiring fullback, recalled that during tryouts Brown asked players to organize themselves by position. Motley walked to "where the rest of the fullbacks were, and at that moment I became an end because there was no way I was going to beat Marion Motley. I didn't know him and hadn't heard of him, but I knew he was awfully tough." Playing against college teams such as Illinois and Notre Dame, Motley was virtually unstoppable. And when Paul Brown became coach of the Cleveland Browns, he sought out the powerful, durable Great Lakes fullback.[56]

Minority athletes who had fulfilled or escaped their military commitment had an opportunity to play Minor League professional football on the West Coast. In 1944 both the American Professional League and the Pacific Coast Professional League fielded desegregated teams. Kenny Washington played for the San Francisco Clippers and Ezzrett Anderson for the Los Angeles Mustangs. The Los Angeles Wildcats and San Diego Gunners also had black players. In the Pacific Coast League, Jackie Robinson represented the Los Angeles Bulldogs and Mel Reid was one of twelve blacks on the Oakland Giants. The following year the two leagues merged into the Pacific Coast League. The Hollywood Bears, with Kenny Washington, Woody Strode, and Ezzrett Anderson, dominated play and won the title.[57]

The war years, as historian William Chafe has noted, "served as a crucial catalyst aiding black Americans in their long struggle for freedom." In 1941 black labor leader A. Philip Randolph proposed a march on Washington to protest the government's discriminatory hiring practices. That proposed action prompted FDR to issue an executive order creating the President's Committee on Fair Employment Practices. The FEPC and the wartime emergency sharply increased black employment. Lured by opportunity, millions of blacks migrated to northern and western cities. In some cities, such as Detroit, race prejudice provoked riots.[58]

Increasingly, blacks assailed the Roosevelt administration for failing to endorse a federal anti-lynching measure and refusing to support the elimination of the poll tax. Jim Crow policies in schools and the armed forces frustrated African Americans, as did Roosevelt's close association with "conspicuous Negrophobes" such as Senators Theodore Bilbo of Mississippi and Walter George of Georgia. Black columnist Ralph Mathews wrote that "after our armies have marched on Berlin and Tokyo, if the GI Joes, both colored and white, don't turn around and march on Washington and drive out the Fascist coalition of Southern Democrats and Republicans who are trying to Nazify America, they will not have learned what they were fighting for."[59]

Blacks, too, denounced the lack of opportunity in professional sports. For blacks the desegregation of Major League Baseball was of ultimate importance during the 1930s and 1940s. The national pastime was extremely popular among minority athletes, and dozens of qualified blacks played in the Negro leagues. Unlike football, however, blacks had never participated in Major League Baseball in the twentieth century. Indeed, during the early 1930s, when professional football was desegregated, minority writers condemned baseball for being the "only national sport that bars Race players." Even after the color barrier was established in professional football, blacks were slow to attack it because they were reluctant to admit that it existed.[60]

The black press, led by Wendell Smith of the *Pittsburgh Courier*, worked diligently for the desegregation of Major League Baseball. Some writers urged blacks to boycott games until the ban was lifted. Others wondered why owners would forego able-bodied, honorably discharged minority athletes to sign disabled veterans such as Chet Morrisey from Binghamton, New York. Finally, in November 1945 Branch Rickey, the owner of the Brooklyn Dodgers, broke the color ban by signing Jackie Robinson to a Minor League contract.[61]

Blacks also expected the fulfillment of the American ideal in professional football. In 1944 two leagues were created to compete with the NFL: the United States Football League and the All-America Football Conference. Red Grange, the president of the USFL, announced that "our new league has set up no barriers. Any athlete, regardless of color, will be invited to try out for our teams, and if he has the ability, he will be welcomed. The Negro boys are fighting for our country; they certainly are entitled to play in our professional leagues." Unfortunately, the USFL never became a reality.[62]

The AAFC, organized by Arch Ward, sports editor of the *Chicago Tribune*, was more successful than the USFL. Run by "men of millionaire incomes," franchises were created in New York, Chicago, Cleveland, Los Angeles, San Francisco, Buffalo, Brooklyn, and Miami. The fledgling league, which existed only on paper until 1946, drafted Steve Juzwick, Harry Hopp, Frankie Albert, Crazylegs Hirsch, and several other college stars who had played on service teams. Blacks, however, were initially ignored. Buddy Young was bypassed, perhaps because he still had college eligibility. But to the dismay of blacks, the AAFC overlooked Kenny Washington and Woody Strode.[63]

Desegregation hopes flagged when the Miami Seahawks entered the league in January 1946. Miami, wrote Wendell Smith, was the most "nazified of all the cities in the world on matters of racial equality." AAFC officials, like their NFL rivals, denied the existence of a color barrier. "But you can bet that Sunday topper," Smith continued, that blacks will be excluded. African Americans had hopes that the AAFC would be "operated by more liberal men—men who wouldn't draw the color line as the NFL has been doing for years. But it's the same old story. Negroes won't be permitted to play."[64]

Expectations ebbed, but blacks pushed for desegregation. In Los Angeles, two teams, the Rams of the NFL, recently transferred from Cleveland, and the Dons of the AAFC, hoped to use spacious Municipal Stadium. At a Coliseum Commission meeting, several black writers, including Halley Harding of the *Los Angeles Tribune* and Herman Hill, the West Coast correspondent of the *Pittsburgh Courier*, objected to the use of the coliseum by any organization that practiced racial discrimination. Since both leagues banned blacks, the journalists insisted, they should be denied the use of the facility. Representatives from the Rams and Dons promptly announced their intent to sign black athletes, and the Coliseum Commission allowed both teams to use the stadium.[65]

The breakthrough game came in late March 1946 when the Rams signed Kenny Washington. Rams backfield coach Bob Snyder later conceded that the team signed the twenty-seven-year-old black star as a precondition to obtaining a coliseum lease. He also believed that Washington would attract black fans and boost gate receipts. "I doubt we would have been interested in Washington if we had stayed in Cleveland," he stated.[66]

Not surprisingly, the black press hailed the signing of Washington. "Kenny finally gets a break," wrote Wendell Smith. Parallels were drawn with Jackie Robinson. "Both athletes had performed brilliantly at UCLA. Both became pioneers for their race in professional sports." In mid-May, the Rams purchased the contract of Woody Strode from the Hollywood Bears. But Strode was thirty-one years old and beyond his peak. And Washington was hampered by an injured knee. Both athletes spent several seasons with the Rams, but neither excelled.[67]

The AAFC delayed signing blacks. To obtain its lease from the Coliseum Commission, the Los Angeles Dons had agreed to provide blacks an opportunity to play. The Dons, however, violated that pledge. Sharply criticized by the black press, the Dons eventually relented, but not until the following year. Meanwhile, AAFC commissioner James Crowley reminded fans that the league had "no rule that bars a Negro athlete from playing." The AAFC, he informed a black newspaper, "is just what the name implies; it is All America in every respect." Only the Cleveland Browns, however, proved that point in 1946.[68]

In mid-August, Paul Brown, coach and part-owner of the Cleveland franchise, invited Bill Willis and Marion Motley to tryout camp at Bowling Green University. From the moment he was appointed coach in 1945, Brown has written, he was determined to sign the best athletes available regardless of color. He was aware of the unwritten black ban but had no intention of adhering to it. Both athletes impressed the coaches and were signed to contracts. Only a few owners, Brown recalls, took exception to his actions.[69]

The invitation to training camp caught Willis by surprise. Due to the black ban it was "inconceivable to me that I would play pro ball." In camp, he encountered few difficulties. He demanded respect and Brown insisted that all players be treated fairly. Invited to camp a few days after Willis, Motley ran the fastest times in the sprints and left little doubt that he had the ability to play professional football.[70]

Motley and Willis were well-liked and got along with teammates. Both men, however, often encountered race prejudice from opposing teams. Neither athlete was allowed to play in the game against Miami because state law forbade integration. Rival players sometimes taunted them with racial slurs and provoked them by stepping on their hands with cleats. Usually teammates "took care" of offending parties because Coach Brown warned them to be thick-skinned and composed. "If Willis and I had been anywhere near being hotheads," Motley recalled, "it would have been another ten years till black men got accepted in pro ball."[71]

Motley and Willis excelled throughout the season and helped lead the Browns to a conference title and the first of four consecutive league championships. Both athletes were named first-team All-Pros, an honor that became perennial.[72]

The black press considered the desegregation of professional football one of the top stories of 1946. Only the debut of Jackie Robinson with the

Montreal Royals was regarded as more important in the sports field than the signing of Strode, Washington, Willis, and Motley. According to Wendell Smith, Paul Brown "automatically becomes one of the 'men of the year' in sports because he voluntarily signed Motley and Willis." The Rams, on the other hand, "are not to be congratulated with the same enthusiasm as Brown" because they hired minority athletes under pressure.[73]

Many black Americans believed that desegregation in the sports field would promote the spirit of equality in other aspects of American life. "It has been proven time and again," wrote Bill Nunn, "that the athletic field has been the front line in this continued battle for racial tolerance." And Wendell Smith believed that athletic success was an "effective slap" at "racial mobsters" because "they know they can't explain these accomplishments and achievements, and at the same time convince you that some people are better than others by virtue of their racial heritage."[74]

The success of the Cleveland Browns, on the field and at the gate, led to the desegregation of other teams. In addition, the replacement of the Miami franchise with Baltimore also facilitated desegregation in the AAFC. Baltimore resisted signing blacks until it joined the NFL in 1953, but it had no objection to playing against minority athletes. In 1947 AAFC teams added more blacks to their rosters. The Browns signed Horace Gillom of the University of Nevada, the Buffalo Bisons selected Dolly King, and the Chicago Rockets took Bill Bass and Bernard Jefferson.

The Los Angeles Dons, who shunned blacks in 1946 in part because they wanted to avoid racial problems with the Miami team, offered contracts to Ezzert Anderson, John Brown, and Bert Piggott. Not to be outdone by the baseball team with the same name, the Brooklyn Dodgers signed Elmore Harris. And with considerable fanfare, the New York Yankees football team offered a multi-year contract to Buddy Young. A Rose Bowl hero and the Most Valuable Player in the college All-Star game against the Bears, Young had a successful rookie year. He finished fifth in the league in rushing and helped lead the Yankees to a division title. In 1948, the San Francisco 49ers, the only lily-white AAFC team besides Baltimore, signed Joe Perry. In its four years of existence, the AAFC helped prepare the way for desegregation by signing more than a dozen minority athletes. Not only did AAFC coaches seek talent in "white" schools, but they pursued athletes from black colleges as well.[75]

With the exception of the Detroit Lions, who signed two blacks in 1948, NFL owners did not actively pursue black players until the early 1950s. With the collapse of the AAFC in 1950, the NFL added new teams, including the Browns. Cleveland was nearly as successful in the NFL as it had been in the AAFC. Following Paul Brown's example, NFL owners gradually added black players.[76]

The democratic idealism sparked by World War II, the protests of writers and fans, the emergence of the AAFC, and the success of several minority athletes in college football all account for the collapse of professional football's racial barrier. In the eyes of most fans, owners who claimed that blacks were not qualified to play in the NFL had been discredited. NFL team rosters revealed that complete integration had not been achieved in the late 1940s. Yet blacks were no longer outside the pale. "The limitations have been lifted and, now, the sky's the limit," wrote an enthusiastic black sportswriter in 1947. "Come to think of it, that's all a plain Negro citizen needs in this country—a chance to get to the top."[77]

NOTES

1. Will McDonough in the Boston *Sunday Globe*, February 22, 1988. For "popcorn," I am indebted to Richard Pennington, *Breaking the Ice: The Racial Integration of Southwest Conference Football* (Jefferson NC, 1987), v.

2. For blacks in the early years of professional football, see Joe Horrigan, "Early Black Professionals" (unpublished paper, courtesy of Pro Football Hall of Fame, Canton OH); Bob Curran, *Pro Football's Rag Days* (New York, 1969), 50; "Top Negro Stars in Pro Football," *Sepia* 12 (November 1963): 76. For professional football in the 1920s and 1930s, see Ernest L. Cuneo, "Present at the Creation: Professional Football in the Twenties," *American Scholar* 56 (Autumn 1987): 487–501; George Halas, "My Forty Years in Pro Football," *Saturday Evening Post* 230, no. 21 (November 23, 1957): 34ff, and no. 22 (November 30, 1957): 34ff; "Increasing Popularity of Pro Football," *Literary Digest* 116 (December 9, 1933): 24ff; Benny Friedman, "The Professional Touch," *Collier's* 90 (October 15, 1932): 16–17, 46–47.

3. Bob Barnett, "Ray Kemp Blazed Important Trail," *Coffin Corner* 5 (December 1983): 3, 8; Mike Rathet and Don R. Smith, *Their Deeds and Dogged Faith* (New York, 1984), 220.

4. Al Monroe in *Chicago Defender*, October 15, 1932; and *Boston Evening American*, reprinted in *Defender*, October 22, 1932.

5. Al Monroe in *Chicago Defender*, December 3, 1932. See also Al Monroe in *Chicago Defender*, November 12, December 10, 1932.

6. *Chicago Defender*, October 7, 14, and 21, November 4, 1933, and January 6, 1934. In the off-season, Lillard played semiprofessional basketball for the Chicago Savoy Five. See *Chicago Defender*, December 10, 1932, December 16 and 30, 1933.

7. Al Monroe in *Chicago Defender*, September 29, 1934; Harold Parrott in *Brooklyn Eagle*, reprinted in *Defender*, November 23, 1935.

8. Art Rooney, letter to author, January 15, 1988; Halas quoted in Myron Cope, *The Game That Was: The Early Days of Pro Football* (New York, 1970), 7; Schramm quoted in Rathet and Smith, *Their Deeds*, 220: Tim Mara interview with Wendell Smith in *Pittsburgh Courier*, June 1, 1946.

9. FDR speech at Howard University in *Baltimore Afro-American*, October 31, 1936; Robert Divine et al., *America: Past and Present*, vol. 2, 2nd ed. (Glenview IL, 1987), 766–67; Harvard Sitkoff, *A New Deal for Blacks: The Emergence of Civil Rights as a National Issue* (New York, 1978), 326–35; Sitkoff, "The New Deal and Race Relations," in *Fifty Years Later: The New Deal Evaluated*, edited by Harvard Sitkoff (New York, 1985), 93–111.

10. Divine, *America*, 766; Mary Beth Norton et al., *A People and a Nation: A History of the United States*, vol. 2, 2nd ed. (Boston, 1986), 752.

11. Norton, *People and a Nation*, 721; *Pittsburgh Courier*, July 29, December 23, 1939.

12. *Pittsburgh Courier*, September 11 and 25, 1937, August 10, September 10, October 8, 1938, January 7, July 29, September 23, November 4, December 23, 1939; Stanley High, "Black Omens," *Saturday Evening Post* 210, no. 47 (May 21, 1938): 5–7, and no. 49 (June 4, 1938): 14–15ff; *Baltimore Afro-American*, December 5, 1936. On blacks and Jews, see *Chicago Defender*, October 5, 1935; Lewis K. McMillan, "An American Negro Looks at the German Jew," *Christian Century* 55 (August 31, 1938): 1034–36.

13. For the Bombers, see *Chicago Defender*, November 2, 1935; *Baltimore Afro-American*, November 9 and 16, 1935, September 26, October 24 and 31, November 21, December 5, 1936. For black achievements in boxing and track and field, see Edwin Bancroft Henderson, *The Negro in Sports*, rev. ed. (Washington

DC, 1949), 54–63; "Negro Stars on the Playing Fields of America," *Literary Digest* 119 (March 2, 1935): 32.

14. "Top Negro Stars in Pro Football," *Sepia* 12 (November 1963): 76; Barnett, "Ray Kemp," 3, 8.

15. Al Harvin, "Pollard, at 84, Reflects on His Days of Glory," *New York Times*, February 7, 1978, 7.

16. On Marshall, see Thomas G. Smith, "Civil Rights on the Gridiron: The Kennedy Administration and the Desegregation of the Washington Redskins," *Journal of Sport History* 14 (Summer 1987): 189–208.

17. Art Rooney, letter to author, January 15, 1988; Cope, *The Game That Was*, 7.

18. Kipke in *Baltimore Afro-American*, November 16, 1935; Solem in *Baltimore Afro-American*, November 17, 1934; Ira Lewis in *Pittsburgh Courier*, October 16, 1932.

19. Bill Gibson in *Baltimore Afro-American*, November 16, 1935.

20. *Chicago Defender*, October 15, November 5 and 19, 1932, October 14 and 28, 1933, September 22, October 20 and 27, 1934; *University of Michigan Daily*; November 3, 1934; *Baltimore Afro-American*, December 3, 1932.

21. Al Monroe in *Chicago Defender*, November 4, 1933, September 22, 1934. Jesse Owens won four gold medals in the 1936 Olympics but failed to receive the Sullivan Trophy. That honor, given to an American amateur athlete for contributions to sportsmanship, went to Glenn Morris, a Caucasian who won the decathlon at the Olympic Games; see *Baltimore Afro-American*, ed., January 9, 1937; Ollie Stewart in *Baltimore Afro-American*, January 16, 1937.

22. Henderson, *The Negro in Sports*, 114–18; Roy Wilkins, "Negro Stars on Big Grid Teams," *The Crisis* 43 (December 1936): 362–63 ff.

23. Al Monroe in *Chicago Defender*, October 13, 1934; Hanley quoted in *Chicago Defender*, October 20, 1934.

24. Parrott quoted in *Chicago Defender*, November 23, 1935. See also *Chicago Defender*, November 4 and 11, 1934, October 19, November 2, December 14, 1935; Bill Gibson in *Baltimore Afro-American*, November 17, 1934.

25. *Baltimore Afro-American*, October 24, December 5 and 12, 1936; *Chicago Defender*, October 27, 1934, November 23 and 30, 1935.

26. *Baltimore Afro-American*, November 14, 1936; F. M. Davis in *Baltimore Afro-American*, November 21, 1936; Frank Young of the *St. Louis Call* in *Baltimore Afro-American*, November 28, 1936; editorial in *Baltimore Afro-American*, December 5, 1936; *Pittsburgh Courier*, September 25, 1937.

27. Henderson, *Negro in Sports*, 108–10.

28. *Pittsburgh Courier*, November 6 and 13, 1937, October 22 and 29, 1938; *New York Times*, October 17, 1937, V-1.

29. Grantland Rice quoted in Henderson, *Negro in Sports*, 126; Balter quoted in Arthur L. Evans, *Fifty Years of Football at Syracuse University, 1889-1939* (Syracuse, 1939), 127-28, 130-31, 183-84; Rod Macdonald, *Syracuse Basketball: 1900-1975* (Syracuse, 1975), 36.

30. *Baltimore Afro-American*, November 7 and 14, 1936, December 5 and 26, 1936; *Cornellian* (Cornell University Yearbook) (Ithaca NY) for 1937, 364-71.

31. *Cornellian*, 1938, 390-99; Alison Danzig in *New York Times*, October 3, 1937, V-1; John Kiernan in *New York Times*, October 4, 1937, 27; Robert F. Kelley in *New York Times*, October 10, 1937, V-1; *Pittsburgh Courier*, October 9, 16, and 23, November 20 and 27, December 11, 1937; Heywood Broun column reprinted in *New York Times*, December 25, 1937; *New York Times*, September 24, October 8, November 19 and 26, December 3, 1938; *Cornellian*, 1939, 132-38.

32. Randy Dixon in *Pittsburgh Courier*, December 3, 1938; Chester Washington in *Pittsburgh Courier*, September 9, 1939; Ted Posten in *Pittsburgh Courier*, September 16, 1939. Rejecting offers to play semiprofessional football for a black team, Holland joined the faculty at Lincoln University as an instructor in sociology. He obtained his master's degree from Cornell in 1941 and his PhD from the University of Pennsylvania in 1950. From 1953 to 1963 he served as president of Delaware State College and headed Hampton Institute during the late 1960s. In 1970 he was named ambassador to Sweden by President Nixon. Educator, diplomat, and civil rights leader, Holland died in 1985.

Overlooked by the NFL, Sidat-Singh played semiprofessional basketball for the Syracuse Reds and the Harlem Renaissance. During World War II he joined the Army Air Corps and was killed in a training exercise over Lake Huron in June 1943.

33. Henderson, *Negro in Sports*, 119-21, 130-33.

34. *Pittsburgh Courier*, July 29, September 9, November 4, 1939; Hendrick Van Leuven, "Touchdown UCLA: The Complete Account of Bruin Football" (unpublished manuscript, Powell Library, UCLA); Jackie Robinson as told to Alfred Duckett, *I Never Had It Made: An Autobiography* (New York, 1972), 22-24.

35. Wendell Smith interview with Madison Bell in *Pittsburgh Courier*, October 29, 1938; Horace McCoy quoted by Ira Lewis in *Pittsburgh Courier*, December 4, 1937; Jackie Robinson quoted in Rathet and Smith, *Their Deeds*, 210; *Pittsburgh Courier*, December 11, 1937, October 15, November 26, 1938; *New York Times*, December 8, 1939.

36. Rathet and Smith, *Their Deeds*, 210; Fessenden quoted in *Pittsburgh Courier*, November 11, 1939; Hyland quoted by Wendell Smith in *Pittsburgh Courier*, December 23, 1939. See also *Pittsburgh Courier*, September 23, October 28, December 9 and 16, 1939; and *New York Times*, December 10, 1939, v-1.

37. Wendell Smith in *Pittsburgh Courier*, November 18, December 16, 1939; Randy Dixon in *Pittsburgh Courier*, November 4 and 11, December 16, 1939; Chester Washington in *Pittsburgh Courier*, November 18, 1939; Harry Culvert in *Pittsburgh Courier*, December 2, 1939; *New York Times*, December 9, 1939, 21.

38. For the NFL draft, see *New York Times*, December 10, 1939, v-1; Sam Balter broadcast reprinted in *Pittsburgh Courier*, January 13, 1940; Chester Washington in *Pittsburgh Courier*, December 23, 1939.

39. Powers quoted by William A. Brower, "Has Professional Football Closed the Door?" *Opportunity* 18 (December 1940): 376.

40. *Pittsburgh Courier*, August 6 and 27, September 3, 1938; *Chicago Defender*, August 6 and 20, September 10, 1938; Randy Dixon in *Pittsburgh Courier*, September 3, 1938.

41. *Pittsburgh Courier*, September 10 and 17, 1938.

42. William G. Ninn in *Pittsburgh Courier*, October 1, 1938; *Chicago Defender*, September 17 and 24, 1938; Fay Young in *Pittsburgh Courier*, September 3, October 1, 1938; John Lake in *Pittsburgh Courier*, October 1, 1938; Fay Young in *Pittsburgh Courier*, October 1, 1938. The game was ignored by the white press. See, for example, *Chicago Tribune*, September 1–5, 1938.

43. *Pittsburgh Courier*, ed., October 29, 1938; Madison Bell interview with Wendell Smith in *Pittsburgh Courier*, October 29, 1938.

44. *Pittsburgh Courier*, September 11, 1937, November 4, 1939; *Boston Traveller* in *Pittsburgh Courier*, October 26, 1939; Montgomery in *Pittsburgh Courier*, December 30, 1939.

45. Miley quoted in *Pittsburgh Courier*, December 30, 1939; letter to editor, *Pittsburgh Courier*, December 23, 1939.

46. Brower, "Has Professional Football Closed the Door?" 375–77; Ed Nace, "Negro Grid Stars, Past and Present," *Opportunity* 17 (September 1939): 272–74; Brower, "Negro Players on White Gridirons," *Opportunity* 19 (October 1941): 304–6.

47. Cope, *The Game That Was*, 250; Wendell Smith in *Pittsburgh Courier*, December 2, 1944; *New York Times*, November 1, 26, and 30, 1944, December 9 and 17, 1944, 19; *Baltimore Afro-American*, April 21, 1945.

48. Wendell Smith in the *Pittsburgh Courier*, October 7, 1944. Illinois had two other black players in 1944: Don Johnson and Paul Patterson. Other black

collegiate stars in 1944 and 1945 were Paul Robeson Jr. (Cornell), George Taliaferro (Indiana), Joe Perry (Compton Junior College), and Gene Derricotte (Michigan). See *Pittsburgh Courier*, September 30, October 7, 1944, September 29, December 8, 1945.

49. *Baltimore Afro-American*, December 16, 1944; Stanley Frank, "Buddy Totes the Ball," *Collier's* 118 (November 23, 1946): 21.

50. *Pittsburgh Courier*, October 14, 21, and 28, November 4, December 2, 1944; *Baltimore Afro-American*, November 4, December 2 and 23, 1944; Eliot quoted in Frank, "Buddy Totes," 109; Stern quoted in Wendell Smith, *Pittsburgh Courier*, October 21, 1944.

51. *Pittsburgh Courier*, January 27, 1945; *Baltimore Afro-American*, January 27, April 14, August 11, 1945; Frank, "Buddy Totes," 107.

52. *Pittsburgh Courier*, October 6 and 27, November 10 and 17, December 22, 1945; *Baltimore Afro-American*, December 8, 1945.

53. *Pittsburgh Courier*, December 15, 1945; *Baltimore Afro-American*, December 22, 1945; *New York Times*, November 27, 1945, November 19 and 28, 1945; "Buddy Young," *Sport* 3 (December 1947): 44; Hal Rosenthal, *Fifty Faces of Football* (New York, 1981), 76-77.

54. Charles O'Rourke, interview with author, February 3, 1988; *Pittsburgh Courier*, January 19, February 23, 1946; *Baltimore Afro-American*, December 22, 1945, January 12, February 16 and 23, 1946.

55. *Pittsburgh Courier*, December 29, 1945, January 26, 1946; Sam Lacy in the *Baltimore Afro-American*, January 12, 1946, January 11, 1947; Frank, "Buddy Totes," 108; *New York Times*, January 2, 1947, 17.

56. Cope, *The Game That Was*, 241; Paul Brown with Jack Clary, PB: *The Paul Brown Story* (New York, 1979), 114-15; Paul Brown, interview with author, February 8, 1988 (hereafter cited as Brown interview); *Baltimore Afro-American*, September 8, November 10, December 8, 1945.

57. On the Pacific Coast League, see *Pittsburgh Courier*, September 30, October 14, November 4, 11, and 18, December 2 and 16, 1944, January 13, August 4, September 22, October 13 and 20, November 3, 10, and 24, December 8 and 29, 1945, January 5 and 12, 1946.

58. William H. Chafe, *The Unfinished Journey: America since World War II* (New York, 1986), 18-21.

59. *Pittsburgh Courier*, September 30, October 14, 21, and 28, 1944; *Baltimore Afro-American*, ed., February 3, 1945.

60. *Chicago Defender*, October 28, 1933; Jules Tygiel, *Baseball's Great Experiment: Jackie Robinson and His Legacy* (New York, 1983), 30-46.

61. David K. Wiggins, "Wendell Smith, the *Pittsburgh Courier-Journal* and the Campaign to Include Blacks in Organized Baseball, 1933-1945," *Journal of Sport History* 10 (Summer 1983): 207-19; Sam Lacy in *Baltimore Afro-American*, January 20, February 3, March 31, April 7 and 14, 1945. On the signing of Jackie Robinson, see *Pittsburgh Courier*, April 21, November 3, 1945.

62. Grange quoted in *Pittsburgh Courier*, February 17, 1945, and *Baltimore Afro-American*, March 3, 1945; *New York Times*, November 20, 1944, November 18 and 28, 1944, June 2, 1945, 19.

63. *New York Times*, September 3, 1944, 1; *Baltimore Afro-American*, December 29, 1945; Fay Young in *Chicago Defender*, January 3, 1946.

64. Wendell Smith in *Pittsburgh Courier*, January 12, 1946.

65. *Pittsburgh Courier*, January 26, February 2 and 9, 1946; *Baltimore Afro-American*, February 23, 1946.

66. For Snyder's view, see Rathet and Smith, *Their Deeds*, 210-11. Snyder contends that the signing of Washington prompted Branch Rickey to obtain Jackie Robinson. That view, of course, is nonsense because Robinson's signing predated Washington's by nearly four months.

67. *Pittsburgh Courier*, March 30, July 6, 13, and 27, August 3, 10, and 24, 1946; *Baltimore Afro-American*, March 30, April 27, May 18, July 27, August 10 and 31, 1946; Wendell Smith in *Pittsburgh Courier*, August 3, 1946.

68. *Pittsburgh Courier*, August 24, October 19, 1946.

69. Brown interview; Brown, PB, 129; Al Dunmore in *Pittsburgh Courier*, August 17, 1946.

70. Brown interview; Brown, PB, 130.

71. Otto Graham, interview with author, February 11, 1988; Cope, *The Game That Was*, 241-45, 249-50.

72. *Chicago Defender*, September 7 and 21, October 26, 1946, January 4, 1947; *Baltimore Afro-American*, October 26, November 23, December 14, 1946, January 11, 1947; *Pittsburgh Courier*, September 1, October 19 and 26, December 7 and 14, 1946, January 11, 1947. Both Motley and Willis are members of the Pro Football Hall of Fame.

73. Wendell Smith in *Pittsburgh Courier*, January 4, 1947; *Baltimore Afro-American*, January 4 and 11, 1947; Fay Young in *Chicago Defender*, January 4, 1947.

74. Bill Nunn in *Pittsburgh Courier*, December 21, 1946; Wendell Smith in *Pittsburgh Courier*, December 14, 1946; Joseph D. Bibb in *Pittsburgh Courier*, December 7, 1946.

75. Al White, "Can Negroes Save Pro Football?" *Our World* 5 (December 1950): 60-65; *Chicago Defender*, April 12 and 26, August 23, 1947; *Pittsburgh Courier*,

January 11, March 29, 1947; *Baltimore Afro-American*, January 11, April 12 and 26, June 14, 1947. For Buddy Young, see *Chicago Defender*, January 25, February 1, May 10 and 24, August 30, 1947.

76. "New Faces in Pro Football," *Our World* 7 (December 1952): 62–64.

77. Lem Graves in *Pittsburgh Courier*, May 3, 1947. See, too, Ric Roberts in *Pittsburgh Courier*, March 1, 1947; Herman Hill in *Pittsburgh Courier*, April 19, 1947.

5

Democracy on the Field
The Black Press Takes On White Baseball

CHRIS LAMB AND GLEN L. BLESKE

More than a half-century has passed since Jackie Robinson went to spring training in 1946 to try out for the Montreal Royals, the top Minor League team in the Brooklyn Dodgers' organization. Baseball was integrated that spring in Daytona Beach, Florida, when Robinson became the first black in the twentieth century to share the field with whites in organized professional baseball.[1] This all happened deep in the Jim Crow South, where, as sociologist Gunnar Myrdal observed, whites rarely saw blacks except as servants or in other substandard conditions.[2] Segregation laws prohibited whites and blacks from sharing restaurants, hotels, theaters, water fountains, schools, and baseball fields.

Baseball was one of the first institutions in American society to become desegregated.[3] The integration of the sport has been called the "most widely commented on episode in American race relations of its time."[4] Robinson's name initiated discussions about national character, equality, democracy, and racism.[5] Many white Americans, including journalists of that era, opposed or feared integration of any kind. A *Richmond Times-Dispatch* editorial warned that any attempt to challenge segregation laws would result in violence that would leave "hundreds, if not thousands, dead."[6]

This essay explores press treatment of baseball's first integrated spring training from two perspectives—the advocacy role of the black press and the status quo role of the white, mainstream press. Robinson's first spring train-ing, more than a year before he played his first Major League regular-season game, represents a critical juncture in the story of the integration of baseball. It provides an opportunity to examine whether the press recognized what was happening and, if so, what journalists had to say about it. Did they capture its meaning, significance, and poignancy? More specifically, was it a different story for black journalists than it was for white journalists? Both black and white newspapers reflected and affected the beliefs and perspec-tives of their readers; therefore, a comparison of coverage between the black and white presses should demonstrate differences not only in press perspec-tives but also in the personal beliefs of journalists on the issue of integration.

Other studies of press coverage of the integration of baseball have shown that black sportswriters were more active in reporting the story than white sportswriters.[7] Historian Bill Weaver observed that no group had a greater responsibility as an organ of racial unity in the years after World War II than the black press, and "the extent to which it understood and met its responsibility can be observed in its handling of the assault on professional baseball's 'color line.'"[8] Another writer concluded that black sportswriters were instrumental in spreading the integration issue into mainstream society by campaigning for it in their columns and by appealing to sympathetic white sportswriters.[9]

For the black press, the news coverage of the Robinson story reflected a society in transition as equality on the baseball field became a metaphor for equality in civil rights. Black sportswriters used the success of blacks in sports to push for integration in all parts of society.[10] They reported the story with emotion, emphasizing its historical significance. They cast the story in terms of freedom, an important moment in a long struggle, while the white mainstream press generally viewed it as a curiosity or a publicity stunt.[11] White sportswriters, unsure or afraid of how their readers would react to the story, remained relatively silent on the issue.[12] To most of mainstream America at that time, the issue of civil rights was little more than a human interest story.[13]

For the black press, the Robinson story transcended sports and touched on racial issues neglected by both the mainstream press and the society at large. The mainstream press, on the other hand, rarely gave the story the social or cultural context it deserved. For example, an analysis of the signing of Robinson in 1945 concluded that black newspapers reported the news as historically significant while mainstream newspapers treated it as relatively unimportant.[14] This pattern of coverage is also confirmed in a study of newspaper coverage of the events that preceded integration in baseball and in a separate study of Robinson's two-day trip from his home in California to his first spring training in late February 1946.[15]

This analysis of press coverage of baseball's first integrated spring training focuses on a six-week period between March 1, 1946, when Robinson was scheduled to arrive in Daytona Beach for his tryout, until April 14, when the Montreal team left Florida to begin its regular season schedule. Twenty-eight newspapers were selected for the sample. It included the largest black weeklies in the country; New York City metropolitan dailies, which sent sportswriters to Daytona Beach to cover the Brooklyn Dodgers' spring training; Florida dailies to see how the story was reported throughout the state; two English-language dailies in Montreal, where Robinson would play that summer; the *Sporting News*, the prominent sports weekly at the time; and a few other dailies to get a sense of wire service coverage of the story.[16]

The integration of baseball meant more to black sportswriters in personal, societal, and journalistic terms than it did to white sportswriters. After a Major League team declined to sign him to a contract because of his race, Wendell Smith became a crusader for integration as sportswriter and editor on the *Pittsburgh Courier*, the most widely circulated black newspaper of its time. Smith has been described as the writer "who most doggedly fought for the inclusion of blacks in organized baseball."[17] Other black sportswriters, such as "Fay" Young of the *Chicago Defender*, Joe Bostic of the *People's Voice*, and Sam Lacy of the *Afro-American* chain, also campaigned for integration.

To black sportswriters and their readers, the country's mainstream press had different news values and different views on race relations. Unlike the white press, the black press made no attempt to be objective in its reporting; it was "a fighting press," largely circulated outside white America. Most white people in America were unaware of the black press's relentless criticisms of them and white society.[18] Black journalists such as Smith wrote about the need for black pride, self-confidence, self-reliance, and self-esteem.[19] They were not only more aware of progress in civil rights than white journalists were, but they also helped make progress possible.[20] By the spring of 1946, as hopes for racial equality increased, the circulation of black weeklies rose accordingly; several newspapers recorded their highest readership during this period.[21]

By contrast, the reporting in the white mainstream press was limited, both in content and context, by a mindset that kept white sportswriters, their newspapers, and their readers from appreciating the meaning of the story of the integration of baseball and its impact on the embryonic civil rights movement. Most white sportswriters, like the public they wrote for, either criticized integration, ignored the issue completely, or, as the *Sporting News*—the so-called bible of baseball—did in 1942, said that no good would come from raising the race issue.[22] The editor of *Sporting News* was J. G. Taylor Spink, who, according to one writer, reflected the voice of conservative reactionaries who wanted to keep the sport segregated.[23] Former *Washington Post* columnist Shirley Povich, one of the few white sportswriters who called for the integration of baseball in the 1930s and early 1940s, has said, "I'm afraid sportswriters thought like the club owners—that separate was better."[24]

Pittsburgh Courier columnist Wendell Smith distrusted the personal attitudes of white baseball writers who would report the Robinson story for New York dailies. In a column shortly before the beginning of spring training in 1946, he told his readers about a recent skit at the annual banquet of the New York chapter of the baseball writers organization, where a character identified as baseball commissioner Albert "Happy" Chandler summoned a black butler, who appeared in a Montreal uniform and said, "Yassah, Massa. Here ah is!" The Chandler character then responded, "Ah! There you are, Jackie. Jackie, you ole wooly-headed rascal, how long you been on the family?" And the butler answered, "Long time, Kun'l. . . . Evver since Mastah Rickey done bo't me."[25]

Smith, who was offended by the skit, recognized something the New York baseball writers did not: it reflected a personal disingenuousness, an insensitivity to racial stereotyping, and a lack of awareness to the larger issue of racism in general. He criticized the sportswriters for trying to hide their views on integration behind the guise of burlesque. If their columns had contained racist remarks, they would have been harshly criticized and their newspaper's circulation would drop, Smith wrote. But the white sportswriters had acted out their true feelings behind the closed doors of an annual dinner. "The next time you read a story in the *New York Times, News, Mirror, Journal, Herald-Tribune*, or any other 'highly regarded' New York publication, dealing with racial equality in baseball, just remember that it will probably come from the pen of a writer who was a part of that 'act' they pulled on Robinson and Rickey," he wrote.[26]

On October 23, 1945, a few months before the New York baseball writers' dinner, Brooklyn's top Minor League team, the Montreal Royals, announced it had signed Robinson, ending six decades of segregation in baseball. Black sportswriters emphasized the importance of the story, providing social and historical context. White sportswriters did not. One analysis of press reaction to the signing suggested that white sportswriters and white America in general were unaware of the severity and extent of prejudice and racism in the nation's social fabric.[27]

White sportswriters provided little enterprise reporting, and their editors gave the signing little recognition. New York metropolitan dailies reported it as if it were just another sports story.[28] Even journalists who supported the announcement, such as Red Smith of the *Herald-Tribune*, did so with little more than platitudes.[29] Others, such as Jimmy Powers of the *New York Daily News*, one of the highest-circulation dailies in the country, called the signing opportunistic and doubted whether Robinson would ever play in the Major Leagues.[30]

The *Sporting News* included several articles and columns on the signing of Robinson in its next issue, including reactions from the nation's sportswriters, but failed to capture the story's sense of history. In an editorial, it downplayed the story's importance and doubted whether Robinson was good enough to play in the Major Leagues. If he were white and six years younger, he might be good enough for Brooklyn's AA team, it said.[31] *New York World-Telegram* columnist Joe Williams wrote that Robinson must ignore "pressure groups, social frauds, and demagogues" who would try to exploit him to advance political and racial causes.[32]

By comparison, the news of Robinson's signing hit black newspapers "like a bombshell."[33] Black newspapers put the story on page one. Black sportswriters emotionalized the story and put it in historical context for their readers.[34] Ludlow Werner of *New York Age* said Robinson would be haunted by the expectations of his race. To millions of blacks, "he would symbolize not only their prowess in baseball, but their ability to rise to an opportunity."[35] Richard Hunt of the *People's Weekly* in New York City wrote, "While we are pleased, we want the world to know that we don't consider our fight won with the admission of just one player."[36] And Wendell Smith called the signing of Robinson "the most American and democratic step baseball has made in 25 years."[37]

The announcement had strong personal meaning to Smith, who had campaigned for integration for a decade and had recommended Robinson to Brooklyn president Branch Rickey. Smith was willing to put his personal beliefs ahead of his journalistic instincts. He knew that Rickey had quietly signed Robinson two months earlier but obeyed the baseball executive's wishes to suppress the news until the timing was right for the announcement. The journalist later said he would do whatever Rickey asked if it led to the integration of the game—and that included suppressing the biggest story of his career.[38]

The white publisher of the daily newspapers in Daytona Beach, Florida, the *Morning Journal* and the *Evening News*, also knew about the signing before the rest of the country and suppressed the news.[39] Herbert Davidson joined city officials in their talks with Rickey to prepare for the team's spring training, but nothing appeared in his newspapers. During the spring training of 1946, the newspapers published little about Robinson; when they did, it was often a wire service account. Davidson believed that the Robinson story should not incite troublemakers. He controlled news content to keep the city calm.[40] Other white sportswriters reported little about the developments of the story, probably because it made them uncomfortable—or because they did not want to risk upsetting their editors, advertisers, or readers.

A day after the Montreal press conference in October 1945, *Brooklyn Eagle* columnist Tommy Holmes wrote that Robinson's first big challenge would come during spring training in Daytona Beach. "Anyone who has ever traveled that far South can't help but wonder just how things can be arranged. Fundamental things such as where he will sleep and where he will eat. Not to mention what traveling accommodations they'll let him have in deepest Dixie," he wrote.[41] Rickey was aware of these issues. He signed black pitcher Johnny Wright to be Robinson's teammate. He also hired Smith and fellow *Courier* journalist Billy Rowe for the jobs of chauffeur, confidant, and father confessor for the ballplayers.[42] Smith was paid fifty dollars a week, or the same as his salary with the newspaper.[43]

The black journalists did not see this arrangement as a conflict of interest. The story was a personal one to them, one they reported subjectively, not objectively. They saw themselves as a counter to the coverage in the mainstream press. They thought white sportswriters wanted Robinson to fail.[44] If Smith, Rowe, and other black sportswriters were too close to the story that spring, the opposite appeared so for white sportswriters, who kept the story at arm's length. They rarely interviewed Robinson, receiving most of their information from Rickey, other team officials, and black sportswriters.

Black journalists such as Smith and Rowe even took an active role in shaping the story they covered. Robinson's first big challenge came not during spring training but on his trip to Florida from February 28 to March 2. Robinson and his wife, Rachel, faced repeated discrimination as they traveled from Los Angeles to Daytona Beach. Because of their skin color, they were prohibited from eating in restaurants and staying in hotels. They were twice bumped from planes and had to make the final sixteen hours of their trip riding in the back of a bus.[45] By the time they arrived in Daytona Beach, Jackie, humiliated by the ordeal, wanted to quit and return to California. Smith and Rowe talked him out of it.[46]

Black journalists understood that history was being made and reported it as it unfolded, including the discrimination. Mainstream journalists, on the other hand, published few details about the Robinsons' trip, relying principally on Rickey for their information. The Associated Press and New

York City dailies quoted Rickey as saying that Robinson had been delayed because of bad weather and bumped because of military priority.[47] Jack Smith, a Rickey critic, questioned the official explanation. "There was considerable mystery about his traveling difficulties," the columnist wrote in the *Daily News*. He also doubted the explanation that said Robinson had been bumped for military purposes.[48]

In contrast to most mainstream dailies, black newspapers wanted readers to understand the cruelties and ironies of segregation. The *Chicago Defender* said that Robinson had been bumped from an airplane in Pensacola with two other passengers "because the plane could not refuel with the weight of the three people aboard. That was the Dodgers' explanation."[49] Smith wrote that the Robinsons had been bumped on their way to Florida. When they could not find a train to Daytona Beach, "they reluctantly made the rest of the journey riding 'comfortably' on the back seat in accordance with the jim-crow laws in Dear Ole Dixie," he sarcastically reported.[50] Black newspaper readers, themselves victims of racism, understood that there was more to Robinson's late arrival than just bad weather.

When spring training began, black and white sportswriters continued to define news differently. Black newspapers treated the Robinson story as a top story; white newspapers did not. Shortly before the start of spring training, Rickey moved the Montreal team forty miles west to Sanford.[51] The New York City dailies left their top sportswriters in Daytona Beach to cover the opening of the Brooklyn Dodgers' spring training and relied on secondary writers, stringers, or wire service accounts to cover what Sam Lacy of the *Afro-American* newspapers would call "the Jackie Robinson beat."[52] Florida newspapers used wire service accounts of two or three paragraphs or said nothing. Editors could publish an Associated Press story without having to accept responsibility for it.

After Robinson and Wright arrived for spring training, the developments of the first day meant something different for black sportswriters than they did for white sportswriters. Black sportswriters reported the first day of spring training with more details. The *Washington Afro-American* included such mundane details as Wright jogging twice around the field alone because the other players had already done their calisthenics. When the pitcher finished, he joined a pepper game, fielding bunts with four other pitchers.[53] After practice, the white ballplayers went to a lakefront hotel while the black ballplayers stayed in private residences in the segregated part of town. The *Afro-American* described the private homes as "large, elaborately furnished and extremely clean."[54] Rickey visited the homes and found them impressive, the *Courier* told its readers.[55]

In addition, sportswriters had different interpretations of what happened when Robinson took his first swing against a batting machine. Lacy, an African American, wrote that Robinson lined the first pitch into left field, that his second swing produced a weak roller, and that in his third at bat, he hit an impressive fly to center field.[56] According to Tommy Holmes of the white-owned *Brooklyn Eagle*, Robinson bunted twice and swung at three or four others in his first appearance, making little or no contact with the ball.[57] The *Sporting News* said that the ballplayer "took several turns against the mechanical pitcher, smacking a number of pitches squarely."[58] Robinson, in one of his autobiographies, remembered hitting a couple long ones that impressed the white ballplayers standing nearby.[59]

Smith, Lacy, Fay Young, and other black sportswriters became emotionally involved in the story. They could not help it. They had campaigned for integration for years and reminded their readers of its ramifications. Smith praised the ballplayers for "their determined bid for sports immortality."[60] According to Lacy, Robinson was not just playing for himself; he was playing for something bigger. "It is easy to see why I felt a lump in my throat each time a ball was hit in his direction those first few days; why I experienced a sort of emptiness whenever he took a swing in batting practice."[61] In what read more like an appeal than an editorial or news story, Young cautioned his readers not to expect too much too quickly from the ballplayers. "Those wanting to see both men make good will do a heap of praying and hoping," he wrote in the *Chicago Defender*.[62]

Smith took such a personal interest in the story that he suppressed news again. He optimistically underestimated the racist attitudes of Sanford, at least in print, when he wrote that the city "was one of the most hospitable cities in the South and from all indications, Robinson will be free of the customary regulations which prohibit Negroes from mingling and associating with white people equally."[63] After the second day of practice, however, a delegation of Sanford citizens told Montreal team officials that they would not permit blacks and whites to play on the same field.[64] The team then returned to Daytona Beach. The Sanford incident went unreported. Several weeks later, Smith wrote about the incident and admitted he had withheld certain incidents for fear of jeopardizing the integration of baseball.[65] The white press never reported the story.

Stories in both the black and the white press gave the impression that all was well between the black and white ballplayers. An Associated Press story said that the team was treating Robinson and Wright no differently than anyone else.[66] The *Sporting News* wrote that no friction existed between Robinson and Wright and their white teammates during the early days of the spring season.[67] Black newspapers perpetuated the fiction. The *Pittsburgh Courier* published a series of photographs of Robinson interacting with white players.[68] In reality, Montreal's black players had little contact with their white teammates before, during, or after practices.[69] Smith and black sportswriters probably knew the truth and did not want to report it for fear of reflecting badly on integration. Black newspapers had long used the strategy of citing white support for integration as a way of legitimizing the fight for equality.[70] White sportswriters probably knew the truth and did not report it because of the sensitivity of the issue.

Coverage of Robinson's first game of the spring on March 17 reflected differences in the editorial philosophies of black and white newspapers and also editorial differences between dailies and weeklies. The press, including journalists from at least three wire services, the Associated Press, United Press, and American Negro Press, New York City dailies, the Daytona Beach newspapers, the *Sporting News*, and black weeklies watched as Robinson went hitless and played error-free ball during five innings at second base.

The mainstream daily press emphasized the historical significance of the game, the size of the crowd, the ballplayer's grace under pressure, and his inability to hit a curve ball. The *New York Daily Mirror* said it was the first time in fifty years that an African American played in a game that involved two teams in Organized Baseball.[71] The *New York Times* said the historic game was "seemingly taken in stride by a majority of the 4,000 spectators." It added that the Jim Crow section was inadequate and many blacks had to stand behind the right-field foul line.[72] The Associated Press said that Robinson was applauded by blacks during his first plate appearance, then applauded by both races during his next two at bats.[73] The *New York Daily Mirror* and the *Brooklyn Eagle* each mentioned that the nervous ballplayer struggled against the curve ball.[74] The *Sporting News* buried a three-paragraph account in the back of its following issue.[75] Not all newspapers thought the story was newsworthy. Nothing about the game appeared in newspapers in nearby Orlando and Jacksonville, and the *Los Angeles Times*, Robinson's hometown newspaper, published nothing about the game even though he had been a high school and college athletic star in Southern California.[76]

In contrast, black weeklies, even though the game was at least a couple of days old before they could publish anything, gave the story more space proportionately, published photographs, and included quotes. They emphasized the game's historical significance and the crowd's reaction, including that Robinson was cheered by all spectators, not just blacks. The *People's Voice* called Robinson the first black in a regularly scheduled spring training game.[77] The *Norfolk Journal and Guide* said it had predicted that Robinson would be booed by white southerners but that did not happen.[78] The *New York Age* said the game was like any other except that "one man on the field had a complexion a shade darker than every other player present."[79]

To Smith, the eternal optimist, the world seemed to begin the moment that his friend took the field. "Six thousand eyes were glued on the mercury-footed infielder each time he came to bat. His performance with the willow failed to provide any thrills, but, his vicious swings and air of confidence as he faced real major league pitching for the first time, won the admiration of a crowd that seemed to sense the historical significance of the occasion."[80] Rarely in baseball history has someone who went hitless in a game received such praise. Smith also quoted the opposing manager as saying that Robinson faced tremendous pressure and "came through it like a real champion."[81]

During the spring, the Jackie Robinson story remained little more than a minor human interest story to the mainstream press—with two exceptions: his first day of practice on March 4 and his first game on March 17. White sportswriters were more interested in reporting the developments of Major League teams such as the Brooklyn Dodgers, not Minor Leaguers such as the Montreal Royals. They were interested in the hundreds of servicemen returning from the war hoping to play professional baseball. And finally, there was the developing story of the Mexican Leagues trying to recruit Major Leaguers. To these journalists, this challenge to the national pastime represented a bigger story than what was happening in the Montreal camp. By comparison, the Robinson story was clearly the number-one story that spring in the black press. History has proven the black press was right.

While white sportswriters were clearly tentative writing about Robinson, they had no such qualms about Rickey, the architect of the integration effort. The Brooklyn president was part of baseball's white establishment and therefore represented acceptable and less risky subject matter for mainstream journalists and readers. The March 19 issue of *Look* magazine included a profile of Rickey, who was depicted as the Abraham Lincoln of baseball for integrating it.[82] New York sports columnists Jimmy Powers and Dan Parker used the article to attack Rickey. They called the signing of Robinson a publicity stunt. Powers again expressed his doubts that Robinson would ever play in the Major Leagues.[83] In addition, Parker said any resemblance between Rickey and Lincoln was strictly coincidental. He wrote that although there had been no unpleasantness on the surface, Robinson and Wright were clearly uncomfortable with the problems and pressures of southern segregation.[84]

To reporters of the black press, these comments typified the hostility of the white press. Smith responded viciously to Parker and Powers in two articles in the next issue of the *Courier*, calling them "smutty," "vicious," "putrid," "wacky," and "violently prejudiced."[85] For Smith, there could be no criticism of any aspect of the desegregation experiment. In addition, the *Washington Afro-American* published a report that quoted the Mayor's Committee on Baseball in New York, which had been created to study the integration of baseball, as calling Powers's column "untrue," "vicious," and "insidious." It said that his premise that "whites and colored players cannot compete against each other in sports without the danger of a race riot is against the evidence of well-proved facts."[86]

Robinson's second game on March 23 drew little of the attention of his first game. He was not mentioned in a *New York Times* story and only in passing in other newspapers, including the *Daytona Beach Sunday News-Journal*.[87] The *Brooklyn Eagle* said that the game was important if only because Daytona Beach permitted it.[88] The *Montreal Gazette*, however, summarized Robinson's five plate appearances and included a large photograph of Robinson and Wright with several of their teammates in the dugout before the game.[89] American dailies, by contrast, kept photographs of the ballplayers out of their respective newspapers.

Black weeklies and Montreal dailies felt the story was incomplete without photographs of the ballplayers. The *Pittsburgh Courier* ran a number of photographs of Robinson and Wright with its story on Robinson's second game. The *Norfolk Journal and Guide* ran a three-paragraph story and several photographs of the two ballplayers under a banner headline that said, "Democracy given tryout in Florida as baseball stars make bid for major league positions."[90] While neither Robinson nor Wright technically was trying out for the Major Leagues, the headline reflects the attitude of the newspaper that this was indeed an important story with significant ramifications.

Neither democracy nor integration would see much of a tryout over the next few weeks as one southern city after another would prohibit Montreal's black ballplayers from taking the field. The cancelations of several games generally received a mild response in the white, mainstream press, though the black press expressed a greater sense of outrage as the number of cancelations increased. The mainstream press, adhering to the journalistic practice of objectivity and the societal practice of racial indifference, reported the developments with little emotion. Black sportswriters suppressed their frustration until their patience toward segregationists became exhausted. Once Montreal began refusing to play if Robinson and Wright were prohibited, black journalists became more strident in their criticism.

Jacksonville became the first southern city to officially ban the black ballplayers when it canceled a game scheduled for March 24, the *New York Times* reported.[91] The *New York Daily News* and other newspapers reported that the game had been canceled because local laws prohibited games between blacks and whites.[92] The Associated Press circulated a detailed account of the ban, which included comments from Jacksonville city officials and Rickey.[93] Black weeklies downplayed the cancelation. The *Chicago Defender* published the Associated Press report. The *Norfolk Journal and Guide* published an equally mild piece by the American Negro Press Association.[94] But Joe Johnson of the *People's Voice* criticized the officials with the Dodgers and Giants for not supporting the ballplayers more than they had.[95]

Montreal's next road game was scheduled for March 25 in Deland, about thirty minutes west of Daytona Beach. It, too, was canceled. The city of DeLand said it had a night game scheduled the following night and needed to test the lights, which required digging up the cables under the field.[96] The United Press noted the irony of a day game being canceled because the lights were not working. The headline in the *New York Daily News* included the pun: "Good Night! Watt Happens Next!"[97] Young of the *Chicago Defender* was not amused. He said that at least Jacksonville had been honest enough to "come right out with the reason" for banning the player, while DeLand had used the lights as an excuse.[98]

Jacksonville canceled a second game on March 28. The *Times-Union* of Jacksonville blamed Montreal for the cancelation because it had insisted on challenging the city's segregation laws.[99] But at least one northern daily criticized Jacksonville. Under the headline "Rhubarbs abound in the South," Tommy Holmes of the *Brooklyn Eagle* told readers how Montreal had gone to Jacksonville for the game only to find the ballpark padlocked. The story included an interview with Rickey, who said that he was more encouraged than discouraged by the events of the spring. Holmes wrote that Rickey sounded like someone determined to fight all summer for his cause. "And," he added, "from what I have observed and from what I listened to in other baseball camps, he'll probably have to."[100]

This cancelation marked a change in strategy for Rickey, who decided to openly challenge Jacksonville's segregation laws, and also by the black press, which became more vocal in its criticism of segregationists. For instance, the *Chicago Defender* praised Montreal for its support of Robinson and Wright. "If Montreal had capitulated and left the Negro players behind, the setback would have encouraged the obstructionists to close the gates right against any additional dark aspirants."[101] Meanwhile, Wendell Smith called Jacksonville a city "festering from political graft and vice," while Daytona Beach, by contrast, was "Florida's most liberal and American city."[102]

On April 6, Montreal announced that the team had canceled its final away games of the spring season because city officials in Jacksonville, Savannah, and Richmond told them that Robinson and Wright would not be permitted to appear on the same field with whites. Black newspapers condemned the cancelations and supported Montreal for refusing to play the games with Robinson and Wright. In a passionate article condemning southern racism, Smith wrote that the games would have been played as scheduled if Robinson and Wright had been left behind but that Rickey had refused to compromise.[103] The *Norfolk Journal and Guide* said Richmond was apparently still "the capital of the Confederacy." It also printed a letter to the owner of the Richmond team that called the decision to cancel the game insulting and foolish.[104]

A brief account of the canceled games was distributed by the country's wire services. The white mainstream press clearly considered it a minor story or no story at all. This reflects the mainstream press's view of racial issues in postwar America, in general. While integration represented an open challenge to southern lifestyles and mores, the issue also made northerners uncomfortable. Journalists, including sportswriters like Red Smith, felt that integration was not something that should be challenged in the newspapers. There clearly existed a tacit conspiracy on the part of the white press to avoid reporting the substance of the integration story.

In the mid-1940s, the New York press had such widely read and influential sportswriters as Red Smith, Grantland Rice, Stanley Woodward, Arthur Daley, Frank Graham, Dick Young, and Joe Williams—some of the greatest names in the history of the profession. Yet they missed the story of the most important spring training in the history of the sport.[105] To these journalists, Robinson was strictly a Minor League story with few ramifications, or at least few worth writing about. Or perhaps they believed, as many players and managers, that the game should stay white. Most of these men were "closet racists," one writer has charged.[106] They were much slower than black journalists to understand what was happening. They avoided the story, at least in the beginning, and when they wrote about it, they identified Robinson as a "Negro" ballplayer. Other players were not identified by their ethnic background.[107]

According to Red Smith's biographer, the sportswriter was sympathetic to the race problem but did not think the issue should be challenged in print. When Smith was asked later how he felt about the story of Robinson trying to integrate the national pastime, he answered, "I don't remember feeling any way except having a very lively interest in a good story."[108] If he indeed had such an interest in the story, why did he not write anything about it?

The drama of baseball's first integrated spring training represents how the issues of integration and segregation were covered, or not, by the nation's black press and white mainstream press. It was clearly a different story for black sportswriters than it was for white sportswriters. In 1946, the objective, establishment press focused on hard news values: a history-making game, a game canceled. The reporting was limited, both in content and context, by a mindset that kept white reporters, their newspapers, and their readers from appreciating the historical significance and meaning of the story. To black sportswriters and their readers, the story symbolized the hopes and dreams of integration, not merely on a ballfield but in society. Black sportswriters and their newspapers recognized this critical juncture in the story of baseball and the fight for civil rights and shared the story with their readers.

NOTES

1. The term "organized professional baseball" was used to describe the Major Leagues and white-dominated professional baseball. Dozens of blacks played in organized professional baseball in the 1870s and 1880s. The ban on black ballplayers came as an unwritten agreement by the league's white owners and managers. Prohibited by Organized Baseball, blacks played in the Negro leagues.

2. Gunnar Myrdal, *An American Dilemma* (New York: Harper and Brother, 1944), 41.

3. Jules Tygiel, *Baseball's Great Experiment* (New York: Oxford University Press, 1984), 9.

4. William Simons, "Jackie Robinson and the American Mind: Journalistic Perceptions of the Reintegration of Baseball," *Journal of Sport History* 12 (Spring 1985): 40.

5. Simons, "Jackie Robinson," 40.

6. Tygiel, *Baseball's Great Experiment*, 8.

7. Bill Weaver, "The Black Press and the Assault on Professional Baseball's 'Color,' October 1945–April 1947," *Phylon* 40 (Winter 1979): 303. Other studies of the press coverage of the integration of baseball include William Kelley, "Jackie Robinson and the Press," *Journalism Quarterly* 53 (Spring 1976): 137–39; Patrick Washburn, "New York Newspapers and Robinson's First Season," *Journalism Quarterly* 58 (Winter 1981): 640–44; Patrick Washburn, "New York Newspaper Coverage of Jackie Robinson in His First Major League Season," *Western Journal of Black Studies* (Fall 1980): 183–92; David K. Wiggins, "Wendell Smith, The *Pittsburgh Courier-Journal* and the Campaign to Include Blacks in Organized Baseball," *Journal of Sport History* 10 (Summer 1983): 5–29; Glen Bleske, "Agenda for Equality: Heavy Hitting Sportswriter Wendell Smith," *Media History Digest* 13 (Fall-Winter 1993): 38–42; Chris Lamb and Glen Bleske, "The Road to October 23, 1945: The Press and the Integration of Baseball," *Nine: A Journal of Baseball History and Social Policy* 6 (Fall 1997): 48–68; Chris Lamb, "'I Never Want Another Trip Like this One': Jackie Robinson's Trip to Integrate Baseball," *Journal of Sport History* 24 (Summer 1997): 177–91; Chris Lamb and Glen Bleske, "A Different Story: How the Press Covered Baseball's First Integrated Spring Training" (paper presented to the Association for Education in Journalism and Mass Communication, Anaheim CA, August 1996).

8. Weaver, "The Black Press," 303.

9. Donald Deardorff, "The Newspaper Press and Black Athletes: Jack Johnson, Joe Louis, and Jackie Robinson" (master's thesis, University of Maryland, 1990), 108.

10. Bleske, "Agenda for Equality," 39.

11. Glen Bleske, "No Runs, No Hits, No Blacks: Wendell Smith, the Black Press, and a Strategy for Racial Equality in the Spring of 1946" (paper presented at the Association for Education in Journalism and Mass Communication Southeast Colloquium, Stone Mountain GA, March 1992).

12. Donald L. Deardorff, "The Black Press Played a Key Role in Integrating Baseball," *St. Louis Journalism Review*, July-August 1994, 12.

13. Taylor Branch, *Parting the Waters: America in the King Years 1954-1963* (New York: Simon and Schuster, 1988), 13.

14. Kelley, "Jackie Robinson and the Press," 137-39; Weaver, "The Black Press," 303-17.

15. See Lamb, "I Never Want Another Trip Like This One," 177-91.

16. The following newspapers were used in this study: *Pittsburgh Courier, Chicago Defender, Baltimore Afro-American, Washington Afro-American, Atlanta Daily World, Norfolk Journal and Guide, Amsterdam News, People's Voice, California Eagle, New York Times, Brooklyn Eagle, New York Daily News, New York Daily Mirror, New York Journal American, Daytona Beach Morning Journal, Daytona Beach Evening News, Tampa Tribune, Orlando Star, DeLand Sun-News, Florida Times-Union, Montreal Daily Star, Montreal Gazette, Sporting News, Los Angeles Times, Richmond Times-Dispatch, Philadelphia Record, Cleveland Plain Dealer,* and *Toledo Blade.*

17. Wiggins, "Wendell Smith," 6; Jim Reiser, *Black Writers/Black Baseball* (Jefferson NC: McFarland, 1994), 33-35. When Branch Rickey was working toward integrating professional baseball, he asked Smith to recommend an African American who had the necessary athletic skills and temperament to break the color barrier. Smith suggested Jackie Robinson.

18. Arnold Rose, *The Negro in America* (New York: Harper and Row, 1948), 289.

19. Wiggins, "Wendell Smith," 10.

20. One notable example of this is the Double V campaign, which was initiated by the *Pittsburgh Courier*. The newspaper achieved prominence through a series of editorials and articles aimed at gaining civil rights for blacks during World War II. The first V was for victory over Germany and Japan, the second V was for victory over racial prejudices in the United States. See Patrick Washburn, "The Pittsburgh Courier's Double V Campaign in 1942," *American Journalism* 3 (1986): 73-86.

21. Roland Wolseley, *The Black Press, U.S.A.* (Ames: Iowa State University Press, 1971), 56. World War II had stressed racial inequalities. Blacks fought valiantly during the war and considered social justice a reward for their sacrifice. The fact that the country was fighting totalitarianism abroad while denying racial equality at home was more than merely ironic to blacks and some sympathetic whites. See Oscar T. Barck Jr. and Nelson M. Bale, *Since 1900* (New York: Macmillan, 1976), 749.

22. *Sporting News*, August 6, 1942, 4.

23. Mark Ribowski, *A Complete History of the Negro Leagues* (New York: Birch Lane, 1995), 253.

24. Shirley Povich, telephone interview by author, July 8, 1996. Other white sportswriters who openly questioned the merits of segregation during the 1930s and 1940s included Jimmy Powers of the *New York Daily News*, Dan Parker of the *New York Daily Mirror*, Hugh Bradley of the *New York Post*, and Dave Egan of the *Boston Daily Record*.

25. *Pittsburgh Courier*, February 23, 1946, 12.

26. *Pittsburgh Courier*, February 23, 1946, 12.

27. Simons, "Jackie Robinson and the American Mind," 62.

28. Kelley, "Jackie Robinson and the Press," 139.

29. *Sporting News*, November 1, 1945, 6.

30. *New York Daily News*, March 12, 1946, 41. Ironically, Powers had been an early advocate of the integration of baseball but also had feuded with Brooklyn president Branch Rickey, regularly criticizing the penurious executive as "El Cheapo."

31. *Sporting News*, November 1, 1945, 12.

32. Quoted in *Sporting News*, November 1, 1945, 12.

33. Weaver, "The Black Press," 305.

34. Kelly, "Jackie Robinson and the Press," 139.

35. Quoted in *Sporting News*, November 1, 1945, 6.

36. Quoted in *Sporting News*, November 1, 1945, 6.

37. *Pittsburgh Courier*, November 3, 1945, 6.

38. Jackie Robinson and Wendell Smith, *My Own Story* (New York: Greenburg, 1948), 27.

39. Lamb and Bleske, "The Road to October 23, 1945," 61.

40. Lamb and Bleske, "The Road to October 23, 1945," 61. Rickey selected Daytona Beach as the spring training site for the Brooklyn organization because of its comparatively progressive racial climate. Blacks in Daytona Beach had achieved a measure of power and advantages largely unknown in other parts of Florida. City Manager James Titus and Mayor William Perry, who understood a spring training site would be a boon for the local economy, privately guaranteed Rickey that Robinson would be allowed to play that spring as long as the ballplayer obeyed the city's other segregation laws. Both Smith and Davidson probably knew about this quid pro quo but kept it to themselves.

41. Quoted in Tygiel, *Baseball's Great Experiment*, 99.

42. Billy Rowe, interview by author, September 14, 1990, Daytona Beach FL (hereafter cited as Rowe interview 1990).

43. Jerome Holtzman, *No Cheering in the Press Box* (New York: Henry Holt, 1995), 321.

44. Rowe interview 1990.

45. Tygiel, *Baseball's Great Experiment*, 99–101; Carl Rowan and Jackie Robinson, *Wait Till Next Year* (New York: Random House, 1960), 132–36; Rachel Robinson, interview by author, September 14, 1990, Daytona Beach FL; Rowe interview 1990.

46. Billy Rowe, telephone interview by author, March 12, 1993.

47. *New York Times*, March 2, 1946, 7.

48. *New York Daily News*, March 3, 1946, 80.

49. *Chicago Defender*, March 9, 1946, 9.

50. *Pittsburgh Courier*, March 9, 1946, 15.

51. Daytona Beach could not accommodate the hundreds of prospective ballplayers returning from the military service to try out for a spot in the Brooklyn organization. Sanford was less crowded and more remote than Daytona Beach. Rickey probably thought the beginning of his racial experiment would fare better in the relative obscurity of Sanford.

52. Sam Lacy, telephone interview by author, February 17, 1995.

53. *Washington Afro-American*, March 9, 1946, 31.

54. *Washington Afro-American*, March 9, 1946, 31.

55. *Pittsburgh Courier*, March 9, 1946, 15.

56. *Washington Afro-American*, March 9, 1946, 31.

57. *Brooklyn Eagle*, March 5, 1946, 11.

58. *Sporting News*, March 7, 1946, 17.

59. Robinson and Smith, *My Own Story*, 70.

60. *Pittsburgh Courier*, March 16, 1946, 17.

61. *Washington Afro-American*, March 16, 1946, 29.

62. *Chicago Defender*, March 9, 1946, 9.

63. *Pittsburgh Courier*, March 2, 1946, 12.

64. Robinson and Smith, *My Own Story*, 70–74.

65. *Pittsburgh Courier*, April 13, 1946, 14.

66. *Daytona Beach Sunday News-Journal*, March 10, 1946, 10.

67. *Sporting News*, March 14, 1946, 15.

68. *Pittsburgh Courier*, March 16, 1946, 17.

69. Jackie Robinson and Alfred Duckett, *I Never Had It Made* (New York: G.P. Putnam and Sons, 1972), 56; Tygiel, *Baseball's Great Experiment*, 107.

70. Bleske, "Agenda for Equality," 39.

71. *New York Daily Mirror*, March 18, 1946, 30.

72. *New York Times*, March 18, 1946, 16.

73. See *Florida Times-Union*, March 18, 1946, 10; *Tampa Tribune*, March 18, 1946, 9; and *Montreal Gazette*, March 18, 1946.

74. *New York Daily Mirror*, March 18, 1946, 20; *Brooklyn Eagle*, March 18, 1946, 11.

75. *Sporting News*, March 21, 1946, 22.

76. A *Los Angeles Times* editor of the era, Kyle Palmer, later showed his antagonism to integration during lunch with Supreme Court justice Earl Warren after the 1954 *Brown vs. Board of Education* decision. Palmer is reported to have told Warren that the decision would destroy the country and that God had not intended the races to mix. See David Halberstam, *The Powers That Be* (New York: Dell, 1979), 174–75.

77. *People's Voice*, March 23, 1946, 19.

78. *Norfolk Journal and Guide*, March 23, 1946, 19.

79. Quoted in Tygiel, *Baseball's Great Experiment*, 108.

80. *Pittsburgh Courier*, March 23, 1946, 17.

81. *Pittsburgh Courier*, March 23, 1946, 17.

82. Tim Cohane, "A Branch Grows in Brooklyn," *Look*, March 19, 1946, 70–76.

83. *New York Daily News*, March 12, 1946, 41.

84. *New York Daily Mirror*, March 20, 1946, 30.

85. *Pittsburgh Courier*, March 30, 1946, 16.

86. *Washington Afro-American*, March 23, 1946.

87. *Daytona Beach Sunday News-Journal*, March 24, 1946, 10.

88. *Brooklyn Eagle*, March 24, 1946, 25. Jacksonville had announced the day before that it would not permit Montreal to play in its municipal stadium if Robinson took the field on March 24.

89. *Montreal Gazette*, March 25, 1946, 17.

90. *Norfolk Journal and Guide*, March 30, 1946, 12.

91. *New York Times*, March 22, 1946, 25.

92. *New York Daily News*, March 21, 1946, 55.

93. *New York Times*, March 23, 1946, 17.

94. *Chicago Defender*, March 30, 1946, 10; *Norfolk Journal and Guide*, March 30, 1946, 12.

95. *People's Voice*, March 30, 1946, 29.

96. *Daytona Beach Evening News*, March 25, 1946, 10.

97. *New York Daily News*, March 26, 1946, 13.

98. *Chicago Defender*, April 6, 1946, 13.

99. See *Washington Afro-American*, April 6, 1946.

100. *Brooklyn Eagle*, March 29, 1946, 17.

101. *Chicago Defender*, April 13, 1946, 2.

102. *Pittsburgh Courier*, April 6, 1946, 16.

103. *Pittsburgh Courier*, April 13, 1946, 14.

104. *Norfolk Journal and Guide*, April 13, 1946, 12.

105. Peter Williams, *The Joe Williams Baseball Reader* (Chapel Hill NC: Algonquin Books, 1989), 203.

106. Williams, *Joe Williams Baseball Reader*, 203.

107. Williams, *Joe Williams Baseball Reader*, 203.

108. Ira Berkow, *Red* (New York: New York Times, 1986), 108–9.

....

6

A Nod from Destiny
How Sportswriters for White and African American
Newspapers Covered Kenny Washington's
Entry into the National Football League

RONALD BISHOP

More than a year before Jackie Robinson broke Major League Baseball's color barrier, his former UCLA teammate, Kenny Washington, was doing the same thing in professional football but with far less fanfare. Washington's contract with the Los Angeles Rams, signed in March 1946, ended an unwritten thirteen-year ban on African American players enforced by NFL owners. The last African Americans to play in the NFL before the ban were Ray Kemp of the Pittsburgh Pirates (later the Steelers) and "Smokey Joe" Lillard of the Chicago Cardinals. Kemp and Lillard were released in 1933. Both players claimed they were victims of racism. For their part, the owners denied the existence of a ban, although longtime NFL executive Tex Schramm once said about signing African American players, "You just didn't do it—it wasn't the thing that was done."[1]

Events leading up to Robinson's signing and his first season with the Dodgers drew extensive coverage from both white and African American newspapers. At the same time, African American sportswriters, particularly those working for the *Pittsburgh Courier* and two Los Angeles newspapers, the *Sentinel* and the *Tribune*, were working hard to expedite Washington's signing by the Rams. In this essay, I explore coverage of Washington by journalists from both white and African American newspapers but pay special attention to the work of three African American sportswriters:

Herman Hill of the *Courier*, Edward "Abie" Robinson of the *Sentinel*, and Hallie Harding of the *Tribune*. My exploration reveals that the story of Washington's signing includes a few more twists than the well-known story of Robinson and Branch Rickey. Like Robinson, Washington was celebrated as a top-flight collegiate athlete; he, not Robinson, was the first choice of some sportswriters to break Major League Baseball's color barrier. Washington's signing was overshadowed in part by the fact that professional football, still relatively new, was not the secular religion it is today. The sport was still searching for an audience. Further, the Rams were newcomers to Los Angeles and were faced with the daunting task of building a fan base. The Brooklyn Dodgers, who a little more than a decade after Washington's signing would end up in Los Angeles, were an established team, loved by their fans, playing a sport revered by millions of people. The skill and durability of the players was another key factor; Robinson went on to a Hall of Fame career with the Dodgers, while Washington's NFL career ended after three solid but unspectacular seasons with the Rams, in large part because of injuries suffered during several stellar seasons for the Hollywood Bears of the Pacific Coast Football League (PCFL).

Nevertheless, events surrounding Washington's signing offer a compelling story of dedicated African American journalists trying to right a thirteen-year wrong perpetrated by NFL owners. They acted as advocates for Washington, going beyond the journalist's traditional role as objective observer. They promoted Washington as the right person to end the NFL's unwritten ban on African American players. But while the African American press worked steadily to promote Robinson, its advocacy for Washington was sporadic and even waned for a time because of the presence of other qualified players and Washington's age and already long playing career. Only Harding, Hill, and Robinson remained committed to Washington. I will assess the shape and depth of their advocacy and probe themes in print coverage of Washington's signing, when he broke the NFL's color barrier for the second time.

The Goal Dust Twins

Washington was born in 1918; he grew up in Lincoln Heights, a predominantly white section of Los Angeles. He attended Lincoln High School in

Los Angeles, where he starred in football and baseball. He led Lincoln to the city football title in 1935. Washington's coach was Jim Tunney, whose son, Jim Jr., would go on to become a respected NFL referee. It was Tunney who convinced Washington to attend UCLA. African Americans who had followed Washington's stellar high school play came in droves to UCLA to watch Washington in part because UCLA was one of the first colleges "to really give the minority athlete a chance to play," according to Washington's friend and teammate Woody Strode. Bob Oates, then a sportswriter for the *Los Angeles Examiner*, said that UCLA enjoyed stronger support from local newspapers than did its crosstown rival, USC.[2]

A strong, swift runner with great lateral movement and a "knock-kneed" running style, Washington also had an extremely strong arm.[3] Jackie Robinson later said that with his athletic ability, Washington's future in baseball "seemed much brighter after his brief exposure to the college game than did mine."[4] Washington entered UCLA in 1936; he played left halfback, the featured position in the team's vaunted single-wing offense. At UCLA, Strode and Washington picked up the nickname "The Goal Dust Twins." The name, coined by *Los Angeles Examiner* sportswriter Bob Hunter, was an adaptation of an advertising slogan for Fairbank's Gold Dust, a brand of soap powder. Hunter's colleague, Melvin Durslag, criticized the nickname, calling it "a mocking appellation that might have been given a pair of black tap dancers working a nightclub in Reno."[5] Washington, called the "sparkling Westwood backfield ace" in a document detailing his selection as one of "Los Angeles' Greatest Athletes," had a stellar career at UCLA. He gained more than 500 yards rushing in 1937 and 1938, his sophomore and junior seasons, and scored 10 touchdowns in 1938. Documents obtained from UCLA's athletic department touted Washington's 62-yard pass to Hal Hirshon during a 1937 game against rival USC as "the longest verified pass, measured from point of throw to point of reception, in the annals of intercollegiate football." Strode recalled that the ball actually traveled 72 yards; Washington "received the snap 10 yards behind the line, and he backpedaled and sidestepped until he was boxed into a corner on [his own] 15."[6] Paul Zimmerman of the *Los Angeles Times*, using what today would be considered racist language, wrote,

Then in the winking of an eye black lightning struck the desolate scene. Black lightning in the mighty right arm of Kenny Washington, spectacular Bruins pass thrower.[7]

Strode would miss a fourth-down pass from Washington with 13 seconds left in the game that would have given UCLA a victory. Frank Finch of the *Los Angeles Times* wrote that Strode and Washington, "naked as a couple of chocolate cherubs as they sat dejectedly in their dressing room ... consoled each other over the failure to complete that fourth-down pass."[8]

Washington gained 812 yards during his senior season (1939)—at the time, a UCLA record—and led the Bruins to their first undefeated season (6-0-4). Robinson joined the "Goal Dust" backfield in 1939. Washington led the nation in total offense and was named second-team All-America by the nation's sportswriters. African American sportswriters were outraged that Washington was not named to the first team. In the estimation of *Courier* sportswriter Randy Dixon, the vote ignored the fact that Washington had "received the nod from destiny."[9] In each of his seasons at UCLA, Washington's name appeared "among the favored chattels for 'all' laurels." In each of those seasons, however, "the hazards of fame and the obstacles that must be hurdled on the rocky road to football's highest and most cherished niche, caught Kenny in its whirlpool."[10]

After graduating from UCLA, Washington bought a house in Los Angeles, married June Bradley, and joined the Los Angeles Police Department. He signed a one-thousand-dollars-a-game contract with promoter Larry Sunbrock to play in the new Pacific Coast Football League (PCFL). Thirteen African Americans would be playing in the league by 1945.[11] A knee injury suffered during the 1941 season kept Washington out of World War II.[12] Washington worked with the USO, traveling to segregated black military units to, as Strode claimed, "keep the black soldiers quiet by promising things would get better after the war."[13]

When the NFL's Cleveland Rams moved to Los Angeles for the 1946 season, African Americans and white liberals immediately began pressuring the Rams to add a black player to their roster.[14] African American sportswriters had for more than a decade been unsuccessfully pressuring the NFL to allow African American players to try out for NFL teams. The Rams won the NFL Championship in 1945, but poor attendance at Cleveland Stadium (only thirty thousand fans saw the Rams beat the Washington Redskins, 15–14, for the league title) convinced team owner Dan Reeves to move the Rams. Reeves, a grocery store magnate, knew that in order to fill the Los Angeles Coliseum, which seats more than ninety thousand fans, he would have to assemble a team of top players, regardless of color. "His goal," said Bob Oates, a veteran sportswriter for the *Los Angeles Times*, "was to get the best possible players he could."[15]

Despite the fact that Washington had played ten seasons of college and Minor League football, his supporters were confident that he still had the skills to play in the NFL. There was one minor catch: Washington was still under contract to the Hollywood Bears of the PCFL. Charles "Chile" Walsh, the Rams general manager, bought out Washington's pact with the Bears and signed Washington to a contract on March 21, 1946.[16] At Washington's request, the team later signed Woody Strode to room with Washington on the road. Jackie Robinson, playing with the Dodgers' farm team in Montreal, lauded Washington's signing, saying his former teammate was "a great football player" and that the Rams "will make a lot of money with him in the lineup."[17] Ironically according to Jules Tygiel, some felt that Washington would have been the better choice to break baseball's color barrier. Californians thought Washington was "a nice guy" where Robinson was a "troublemaker."[18]

The NFL welcomed the Rams' move to Los Angeles, since it helped the league head off competition from the newly created All-American Football Conference (AAFC). League officials also wanted to correct the misperception, nurtured by New York sportswriters, that the NFL "was not a Major League."[19] It wasn't until the late 1950s that these writers recognized the NFL as an established enterprise. While the Rams were selling out the Coliseum in the 1950s, the New York Giants had difficulty doing the same at the Polo Grounds. The city of Los Angeles, on the other hand, embraced professional football. According to Oates, "it was the first town to really understand that the NFL was the major leagues."[20]

But the Rams first had to secure the approval of the Los Angeles Coliseum Commission before they could occupy their new home. Commissioners were concerned that a new professional team would harm the gate for local college teams. Three locally based African American sportswriters—Herman Hill, West Coast editor of the *Pittsburgh Courier*; Halley Harding, sports editor for the *Los Angeles Tribune*; and Edward "Abie" Robinson, sports editor for the *Los Angeles Sentinel*—had on several occasions confronted Chile Walsh, demanding to know why the Rams had no African Americans on their roster and why the team, like the other teams in the NFL, had not allowed African American players to try out. The Rams' pragmatism would not endear the team to some African American sportswriters. Rams assistant coach Bob Snyder would later say that the team signed Washington only to finalize the lease for the Coliseum.[21] The team did not deserve praise, celebrated columnist Wendell Smith would later write, because they caved in to pressure from the African American community in signing Washington and Strode rather than acting on their own. Peterson claims that Washington and Strode "were forced" on the Rams.[22] Whatever the Rams' motives, Washington eventually got a tryout and later signed the contract that made him the first African American athlete to play a Major League professional sport. Oates, writing at the time for the *Los Angeles Examiner*, said that Washington and Robinson became "the first two members of their race to lead the way into modern day, big-time athletics."[23]

A Sure Thing?

Sports historians Chris Lamb and Glen Bleske have written extensively about Wendell Smith's efforts to integrate Major League Baseball through his well-known *Pittsburgh Courier* column, "Sports Beat."[24] Smith called on African Americans to work to eliminate the color line from baseball "until we drop from exhaustion." African American journalists "had different news values and different views on race relations."[25] These reporters "made no attempt to be objective" in their work. The passion and commitment they felt for the cause led them to unapologetically put aside journalistic conventions of objectivity and balance. Lamb and Bleske claim that reporters like Smith "wrote about the need for black pride, self-confidence, self-reliance, and self-esteem."[26] Remnants of their zeal appear today in the rise of "public" or "civic" journalism, through which journalists play an active role in creating solutions for problems facing the communities they cover. Harding, Hill, and "Abie" Robinson unabashedly acted as advocates for Washington, motivated by a desire to at least start a dialogue on the absence of African American players in professional football. Along the way, they hoped to galvanize their readers, who made up an important part of the Rams' new audience. African American newspapers, Robinson argued, "have no business being in business unless they're crusading for black people," a sentiment that would probably not sit well with those who believe that journalists should act as impartial observers.[27] "We were the crusaders," Robinson said of his work for Washington. "We were obligated to do it." The writers took a lesson from the movie industry, where blacks typically played small roles steeped in stereotype. "We were not going to let that happen in sports," Robinson said. Thus, the line between advocate and observer had been purposely blurred.[28]

Smith and other African American sportswriters thought it was inevitable that an NFL team would sign Washington, so they directed most of their energy toward Robinson's eventual signing, especially when Robinson struggled during spring training with the Montreal Royals in 1946.[29] The Courier ran regular updates on Robinson's progress and urged African American citizens to learn as much as they could about baseball and conduct themselves properly at the ballpark so that they would not humiliate Robinson or scuttle opportunities for other African American players.[30] For their part, white sportswriters covered the event, not the man. They tended to focus on Rickey, "the architect of the integration effort." Rickey "was part of baseball's white establishment and therefore represented acceptable and less risky subject matter" for white reporters, Lamb and Bleske argue.[31]

Despite the focus on Robinson, there was a great deal of outcry from sportswriters about the need for the Rams to sign an African American player. But because Washington had played so long, and because younger players, like University of Illinois standout Claude "Buddy" Young were available, Washington was not the top choice of many white and African

American sportswriters. The signing of an African American player might have been inevitable, but Washington's role in this drama was much less than a "sure thing." African American and white sportswriters in Los Angeles wanted the Rams to sign someone; it was only later, after Young decided not to transfer to UCLA—despite Washington's best efforts to help his alma mater by acting as tour guide for Young's family—that they jumped back on the Washington bandwagon constructed when Washington was passed over for the All-America team. Harding, Hill, and Robinson, however, never stopped supporting Washington.

"That Was Our Cue"

In an interview, Robinson claimed that from the beginning, Washington was the focus of their work. "We felt Kenny and Strode could distinguish themselves" in the NFL, Robinson said.[32] Coverage in the *Courier* for a time painted a different picture. *Courier* writers paid a great deal of attention to Buddy Young's performance. White sportswriters would later criticize Young for deciding not to transfer to UCLA, a move that they claim would have set the stage for Young's entry into the NFL.

Hill, editor for the *Courier's* West Coast bureau, was the first African American athlete recruited by the University of Southern California to play men's basketball.[33] Like Abie Robinson, Hill embraced his role as a civil rights activist and had no qualms about using his role as a reporter to help the cause. "You're out there and you see discrimination and injustice, and you have no choice but to use your talent and your influence to correct those wrongs," he said.[34] "As African American journalists, we often make news—good news—happen for our people." Hill went on to run his own his own public relations firm; his client list included Walt Disney Studios, 20th Century Fox, singer Nat King Cole, and the Rev. Martin Luther King Jr.

On January 15, 1946, Harding, Hill, and Robinson, along with several other journalists, attended a meeting with the Los Angeles Coliseum Commission. Robinson recalled that commission chair Leonard Roach tipped them off about the time and location of the meeting.[35] African American sportswriters were frustrated with their inability to convince NFL teams to give tryouts to African American players. "It wasn't practical to throw a picket line around the stadium," Robinson said. "The only weapon we had was to boycott the games."[36] Ironically, African American residents could not afford the price of a ticket to see the Rams play. The Rams' move to Los Angeles gave the writers a fresh opportunity to make their point, a point that enjoyed the unqualified support, Robinson claims, of local black churches and organizations. Robinson was also quick to recognize support from other African American sportswriters, even though some of them promoted Young. "Don't get the impression that we were doing this alone," he said. "We had the support of every black sportswriter in the country." But the writers also wanted to persuade white residents to recognize and even embrace their cause. "We were on the line," Robinson recalled. "We learned how to become visible in the eyes of whites." The writers wanted to do "the greatest good for the greatest number of black people. If you do that, you help whites as well," Robinson said.[37]

It helped the writers that the Rams, settling into their new home and trying to attract fans, were now an easier target. NFL and team officials "hid from writers back east" on the issue of racism. Now, with a team trying to build an audience in a new city, league officials were "more visible," according to Robinson. African American sportswriters on the West Coast negotiated more effectively than their East Coast colleagues because they made contact with the team through political figures like Roach. When the writers contacted Roach, they were told that commission meetings were open to the public. Robinson claimed that he and his colleagues were unaware of this policy and that they did not know that the commission met at the Coliseum, located in the heart of a predominantly African American section of Los Angeles, a quarter-mile from the *Sentinel*'s offices.[38]

At the meeting, the commission announced that it was prepared to accept the contract allowing the Rams to play at the Coliseum. Roach and the commission passed a resolution that barred teams that practiced discrimination from using the facility. Roach then gave the journalists the chance to make their case. Hill recalled:

> That was our cue. As a matter of fact, we had contacted Roach earlier and told him what we planned to do—and he said, "This will be your cue."[39]

Harding, Hill, and Robinson argued that the Rams and the Los Angeles Dons of the AAFC should not be allowed to use the Coliseum because they would not allow blacks to play for them. Harding, who had played football for two African American All-Star teams, the Chicago Black Hawks and the Harlem Brown Bombers, acted as the spokesperson for the trio, a strategy agreed on by the trio before the meeting.[40] Robinson said that he and Hill were just as committed as Harding to Washington's cause but that Harding received the nod as spokesperson because he had been an athlete. "He knew the trials and tribulations [faced by] athletes," Robinson said.[41] Minutes from the meeting refer to Harding's plea as one of several "short talks" given about the issue, but Harding's enthusiasm clearly caught Rams officials off guard.[42] "He just about upset the hearing with his Jim Crow allegations," Hill said.[43] Robinson was more emphatic: "You could have heard a rat piss on cotton" when Harding protested the proposed contract with the Rams.[44] Harding's zeal clearly unsettled Rams general manager Chile Walsh. "Walsh was really shook up. He turned pale and started to stutter. He denied any racial prejudice with the Rams or the NFL. He even went to the league's rule book," Hill said.[45] Walsh "was red-faced," Robinson said. Harding and Hill pointed out that the rule was not written down anywhere. The writers were simply seeking an opportunity for Washington and Strode. At that point, Roger Jessup, a member of the commission and a Los Angeles County supervisor, "asked whether or not the Rams would dare bar Kenny Washington."[46] Walsh said no. Then came a warning from Jessup: "I just want you to know if *our* Kenny Washington can't play, there will be no pro football in the Los Angeles Coliseum."[47] Roach and Washington were good friends, claims former *Sentinel* sports editor Brad Pye. Roach reportedly told the Rams "that if my friend Kenny Washington is not on the team, the Rams can't play in the Coliseum," Pye said.[48]

Walsh and Rams attorney Lloyd Wright emphatically denied that there was a ban on African American players "and further promised to give all such qualified players a chance to prove their worth."[49] According to Hill, "we won our case then and there."[50]

When the meeting ended, Harding stayed behind to push the case further. The writers were confident that they had at least started a dialogue on the issue. "We knew there would be some kind of discussion about it," Robinson recalled.[51] That dialogue produced results faster than the writers had imagined. "We will take any player of ability we can get," Walsh told the *Los Angeles Times*.[52] He continued,

> If we can get Buddy Young after he completes four years of college we will not only accept him but pay someone a bonus for getting him signed. And Kenny Washington is welcome to try out for our team anytime he likes.[53]

When Robinson returned to his office, he received a telegram from Walsh asking for a meeting at a local restaurant. At the meeting, Robinson said, Walsh told the writers that he would offer contracts to Washington and Strode. The *Times*'s Braven Dyer applauded Walsh's performance at the meeting. Walsh, he said, "made a masterful presentation of his case" to gain the right to use the Coliseum. "Chili did more than that—he did a whale of a job selling professional football to those present."[54]

Hill emphatically praised his colleagues—and himself—for their efforts on Washington's behalf. "The unsung heroes of the press did it again" in working toward Washington's signing, Hill wrote in a March 30, 1946, *Courier* column. "The gesture was done with a grand flourish of newsmen, flash bulbs clicking, handshaking, and backslapping by those present," Hill wrote.[55] Hill then walked the reader through the Coliseum Commission meeting, but not before another self-congratulatory flourish:

> Back of it all, however, is a story of three wide-awake progressive scribes (take a bow) in Los Angeles who probably will be forgotten in the shuffle, to say nothing of receiving a word of "thanks pal" from the player in question or other such athletes who will benefit by the democratic move of the Rams and the National Football League.[56]

Hill praised Roach for giving him and his colleagues the chance to express their opinions. As Hill recalled, the writers "cornered" Roach as he entered the room. "We explained in as few words as possible our mission and he listened," Hill recalled in his column. Roach said that he was "against Jim Crow not only in pro football but in all other forms."[57] The writers sat down and listened as representatives of the Rams and the AAFC's Dons argued for access to the Coliseum. Ironically, Harding was seated next to Walsh, the Rams general manager. Hill recalled that when Roach asked for additional comments,

> Brother, that was it, and Harding sprang to his feet, morally supported by [sportswriter J. Cullen] Fentress and myself. The rest is history. In a brief, but convincing talk in which he literally asked all the questions and gave all the stock answers on the League's past record as regards its policy toward Negroes, our spokesman scored a bulls eye.[58]

Harding's push to challenge the Rams' access to the Coliseum was "dramatic and unsuspected," the *Courier* reported.[59] Harding eloquently described for the commission how African American players like Fritz Pollard, Paul Robeson, and Duke Slater played key roles in the success of pro football. He laid the blame for the creation of the league's "Jim Crow policy" at the feet of George Preston Marshall, owner of the Washington Redskins. As part of an NFL reorganization plan he created in 1933, Marshall reportedly made an unwritten recommendation that African Americans be excluded from the NFL. African American sportswriters would later claim that Marshall, Halas, and Art Rooney, owner of the Pittsburgh Pirates, came to a gentleman's agreement to bar African Americans from the NFL. League commissioner Joe Carr endorsed the agreement.[60] Hallie Harding quickly reminded the commission of Washington's success and said he found it "singularly strange," according to the *Courier*, that no team had signed him. Ironically, John Carroll notes, Halas wanted to sign Washington in 1939 but could not get the support of other owners. One member of the Coliseum Commission, Roger Jessup, asked Harding whether it was true that players would refuse to play with or against Washington. Commission member John Ford "publicly praised Harding for his stand."[61]

Harding's speech stunned the commission. "Talk about hearing a pin drop. . . . Well you should have been there and listed to the silence that penetrated the conference room that fine day," Hill wrote. Most of the commissioners agreed with Harding; Walsh, to his "everlasting credit," denied the existence of a policy banning African Americans from playing in the NFL and offered to sign "any first-rate Negro player then and there," Hill recalled. In signing Washington, he made good on his promise and "rates aces in our book," wrote Hill. Efforts by the trio on Washington's behalf were "all in a day's work," Hill told his readers. "Such a conquest does make one's inner self feel mighty good." He, Robinson, and Harding "could just as well have stayed home, put our feet on the desk at the office and took it easy or stood on the corner and watched the fair ones breeze by," Hill wrote. Without their efforts, he said, it would have been "a lead-pipe cinch Kenny Washington or no other sun-tanned player would have seen the promised land." The *Courier* said Walsh's action "opened the way for race athletes to crash the hitherto locked gates of opportunity in big time profession [*sic*] pro football ranks."[62]

The commission granted the Rams a three-year lease to use the Coliseum, giving the team a priority on Sunday dates for the first two years of the pact. The *Courier* reported Walsh's guarantee that "any qualified Negro football player" had a standing invitation to try out for the Rams. *Examiner* sportswriter Bob Oates contends that Rams owner Dan Reeves, not Walsh, was the catalyst in signing an African American player.[63] Signing the best available players would help Reeves's team make a positive impression in its new home.

Not the Clear Choice

But Washington soon was no longer the choice of sportswriters to break the NFL's color barrier. Following the lead of white sportswriters in Los Angeles, the *Courier* shifted its focus from Washington to Buddy Young. As early as December 1945, the paper was telling its readers about the "battle for Young." According to the *Courier*, "the big question in the football world today is 'Where will Buddy Young attend college when he is released from the Navy?'" Young, who played for a military team, "has been feted by the most influential people on the 'Gold Coast' and they are leaving no stone unturned in an effort to lure the speed demon of the gridways to UCLA."[64] On January 26, 1946, the *Courier* reported that Walsh wanted to sign Young once he graduated from the University of Illinois.[65] Walsh would also consider signing Archie Harris, a star track athlete at Indiana University.

Vincent Flaherty of the *Los Angeles Examiner* urged Young to leave college early and sign with the Rams. Young "is the best potential buy for professional football's booming market right now," Flaherty wrote. If he returned to Illinois for his senior season, "Everybody will be shooting for him. . . . Coaches will be rigging up special defensive measures against the redoubtable Mr. Young."[66] Flaherty explained that there was no rule in the NFL against signing African American players but added that "there simply haven't been many truly great Negro stars in recent years."[67] He dismissed Washington and Strode, saying that they would not have been able to perform well in the NFL. In Young, however, the league had the chance "to snatch off the greatest individual attraction football has had since Red Grange stepped out of the same University of Illinois and created professional box office records which still stand." Of all the African American players, Flaherty wrote, Young "has the best chance of stepping straight into pro football because the rival All-America and National League will simply have to make a grab for his services in self-defense."[68] Fentress of the *Courier* called the January 1946 game between a service All-Star team (featuring Young) and the Hollywood Bears "the classic of the coast football season."[69] Cal Whorton, covering the game for the *Times*, referred to Young as the "19-year old sprint sensation."[70] The Bears, "showing entirely too much teamwork for the poorly coordinated service eleven," defeated the All-Stars, 14–0. Young played only sporadically, possibly because of a rib injury suffered early in the game. He carried the ball just five times. "However," Whorton wrote, "it must be surmised that the opposition respected greatly his known abilities because never once did the Bears kick anywhere near his position."[71] *Times* writer Paul Zimmerman blamed Young's teammates. "You can't bundle together a bunch of stars and expect them to provide the deception and interference necessary to make a specialist like Buddy click."[72] Two days later, Young visited the UCLA campus. The *Times* opened its story about the visit this way:

Buddy Young, together with his mother and stepfather, Mr. and Mrs. Robert Waterford, and a friend of the family named Kenny Washington, went sightseeing yesterday, and where do you suppose they wound up? Yep, UCLA![73]

Washington served as tour guide for Young and the Waterfords. The *Times* stressed that Young's presence would have been a boon for the university: "P.S.: UCLA 1946 football stock zoomed clear off the big board yesterday."[74] The paper actively promoted a February 1946 rematch of sorts between the service All-Star team and Kenny Washington's All-Stars. The *Times* called Young "the fastest human in football togs."[75] Playing in front of fifteen thousand fans at the Coliseum, the All-Stars exacted a measure of revenge, beating Washington's All-Stars 14–13. "The much heralded Buddy Young played more than he has in any game to date this season," the *Times*'s Dick Hyland wrote. The "little rambler" caught a 43-yard touchdown pass.[76]

A week after the January commission meeting, Walsh met again with African American sportswriters, this time at the Last Word Club in Los Angeles. He again expressed interest in signing Washington and two African American teammates from the Bears, Charles Anderson and Woody Strode. Walsh reminded the reporters that he could not sign Washington, Strode, or any other African American player if they were under contract to another team. Bears general manager Bill Schroeder said he would not stand in the way of his players if they decided to sign with the Rams, provided he received some consideration. Schroeder noted that Washington was "the highest paid football player in this part of the world."[77] In an article published the same day, February 2, 1946, the *Courier* reported that Buddy Young was set to transfer to UCLA. The *Courier*'s West Coast bureau was one of Young's stops on his impromptu tour. Washington and Young, along with Robinson, boxing great Joe Louis, and a number of other African American athletes and celebrities, were honored February 12, 1946, at the *Courier*'s first annual sports banquet, an event designed to raise money for African American students and athletes who wanted to attend college, which brought together "probably the greatest collection of sports figures in the history of Negro newspaper promotions."[78] The *Courier* said it was pleased that Young would attend.[79] At the event, the *Courier* received an award for its "farsightedness in staging the banquet" for needy African American students and athletes.[80] But the newspaper's efforts fell short: Young decided to return to the University of Illinois. He later signed a contract with the AAFC's New York Yankees. The Rams soon announced their decision to sign Washington.

Paid Off in Full

The *Tribune*, and in all likelihood Harding himself, trumpeted the sports editor's role in convincing the Rams to sign Washington in the lead to the paper's March 23, 1946, story about Washington's new contract:

> Yesterday, TRIBUNE sports editor Halley Harding's one-man crusade against the National Football League's patent, if unwritten, law against Negro players paid off in full.[81]

The *Tribune* reported Walsh's comment that "however bad it looked, there never was a rule against Negroes in the league and that actually no precedent was being set with the signing of Washington." Not only was Washington a gifted athlete, Walsh said, he was "a gentleman highly esteemed by all who have ever played against him."[82] A week earlier, Harding, in his column, "So What?" attacked *Examiner* columnist Vincent Flaherty for claiming that the league did not discriminate against African American players. "His thesis is about as sensible as saying there were no laws against the Jews in Germany during Hitler's reign," Harding wrote of Flaherty, whom he called "the most misinformed columnist this side of the Alleghenies." Harding also took Flaherty to task for suggesting that were no current African American players who could play well in the NFL. African American players were among "the founding fathers of the pro league," Harding argued.[83] Any number of players, including Washington, would acquit themselves well.

The *Courier*'s March 30, 1946, story announcing Washington's signing appeared adjacent to a lengthy Smith column on allegedly racist misstatements about Jackie Robinson made by New York newspaper columnists

Dan Parker and Jimmy Powers. The *Courier*'s J. Cullen Fentress began the article,

> To be the first Negro to play in the National Football League in more than twelve years, Kenny Washington, one of the greatest running and passing halfbacks in gridiron history, last week was signed by the Los Angeles Rams, world's professional champions.[84]

Fentress then reminded readers about the Coliseum Commission meeting at which Harding and Hill protested allowing the Rams to use the Coliseum if they refused to sign an African American player. Fentress quoted Walsh as saying he had heard "many fine things about Washington, both as a player and a man." Walsh was sure, Fentress wrote, that Washington "will be a credit to our ball club and to his race." Walsh said he hoped other teams would "accept him in good grace just as he has always been given fair treatment and won the respect of all who have played with and against him."[85]

In the *Los Angeles Examiner*'s story on the signing, reporter Bob Oates noted that Washington was the "first Negro brought into either major league football or baseball in more than a dozen years." Not since Joe Lillard played in Chicago, Oates wrote, "has a Negro athlete been observed in major-league football. None has yet appeared in major league baseball."[86] The *Los Angeles Times* reiterated the league's claim that there was no ban on black players. The NFL, wrote *Times* reporter Dick Hyland, "has never had a rule against the use of Negro players." By signing Washington, Hyland wrote, the Rams were not setting a precedent, "despite the fact that no member of his race has played in the league since 1933."[87] The Rams did not reveal the terms of Washington's contract, but Oates reported that the team was paying Washington handsomely to draw fans to the Coliseum; he quoted an unnamed Rams official as saying "Kenny asked for plenty and he got it."[88] Hyland reported that Washington's salary was in "keeping with the ex-Uclan's gridiron reputation."[89] Washington, then twenty-seven, was "generally regarded as the greatest halfback every produced in the far west," Oates said. The Rams could take comfort in the fact that he was also "the mightiest drawing card in Coast football."[90] Rams coach Adam

Walsh boasted to the *Los Angeles Times* that the 1946 version of the Rams would be better than the team that won the NFL title in 1945.[91]

Neither Hyland nor Flaherty, Oates's colleague at the *Examiner*, was convinced that Washington would succeed. In a column that ran the day after Oates's story, Flaherty said that while he was uncertain about how well Washington would perform in the NFL, he said he was "certain about one thing—and that is that he won't tear the league apart. Washington will put fans in the seats, and will help the Rams draw on the road," Flaherty acknowledged. "But Kenny is stepping into the toughest football he has ever faced."[92] Time was his biggest enemy, Flaherty wrote:

> Kenny is 27 years old. He has taken his quota of thumpings. He has a bad knee. As football players go, he is past his prime. It is unfair to judge Washington's performance now as against what he might have been a few years ago.[93]

According to Flaherty, it was the threat of competition to the NFL by the AAFC that indirectly motivated the Rams to sign Washington. The AAFC was "forcing the old league to do things that it wouldn't have condescended to do a couple of years ago"—chief among them, sign African American players. Thus, Washington could thank the fledgling league, rather than his skills or reputation, for his good fortune. In fact, many African American players were "grossly overrated," Flaherty wrote. They benefited from a friendly media: "The press bends over backward to give the Negro player a square deal."[94] For Flaherty, Washington's greatest accomplishment would have been convincing Buddy Young to attend UCLA. "Washington palled around with Young during his visits to Los Angeles," Flaherty wrote in early April 1946. "Washington is pretty much Young's idol."[95]

Dick Hyland of the *Los Angeles Times* was only a little kinder to Washington. The former UCLA star's break "is coming five or six years too late," he wrote in a March 22, 1946, column.[96] Had the Rams signed him in 1940, after he graduated from UCLA, "he would have undoubtedly been, with one year's experience, one of the greatest of professional backs and a drawing card from one end of the league to the other." But by 1946, after his stint with the Hollywood Bears, Washington "had become a beaten-up ballplayer who is neither so strong nor so quick in his reactions as he was before the war." Washington, he wrote, "has a trick leg which kept him out of games on many occasions last season." To make matters worse, "he has lost just enough of his speed to enable tacklers who would have missed him or run into his murderous straight arm when he was at his best, to nail him with punishing tackles."[97] Hyland applauded Washington's courage but predicted that Walsh would end up using Washington only as a part-time player, "entering games to heave long passes when [Walsh] thinks they might succeed," a tactic whose effectiveness Hyland doubted strenuously.

"It is my humble opinion that any time an 80-yard pass is completed the safety man should have his head examined," Hyland wrote. The fact that this play worked in the PCFL didn't mean it would work in the NFL. Still, Hyland lauded Washington's persistence and work ethic. Washington, he wrote, "will work his head off to prove this prediction wrong, and I hope he does."[98]

Wendell Smith congratulated Harding, Hill, and Abie Robinson in a January 4, 1947, *Courier* column that reviewed the progress made in 1946 by African American players in the world of professional sports. Smith wrote about the signing of Washington and Strode, as well as the signing of Marion Motley and Bill Willis by the Cleveland Browns. In Smith's estimation, Washington and Strode had subpar first seasons. Conversely, Motley and Willis played key roles in the Browns winning the AAFC title. Browns coach Paul Brown received Smith's vote for "Man of the Year" in sports because he voluntarily signed two African American players, while Walsh, on the other hand, had to be pressured into doing so. "This means, of course, that the Los Angeles officials are not to be congratulated with the same enthusiasm as Brown, the ex–Ohio State mentor and now the outstanding coach in professional football," Smith wrote.[99] Herman Hill's assessment of Walsh was far more favorable than Smith's; he called the Rams general manager "the Branch Rickey of pro football."[100] But according to Smith, it was Harding, Hill, and Robinson who deserved the credit for bringing about the signings: "It was through their untiring efforts that Los Angeles finally dropped the color-line and accepted the two Negro players."[101]

"A New Day Is Dawned"

But as Jackie Robinson's first game as a Dodger drew nearer in April 1947, the *Courier's* coverage of Washington waned. The *Tribune* and *Sentinel*, however, followed Washington's progress through the summer, even though Washington would enjoy only limited success in his first season with the Rams. "A new day is dawned," the *Tribune* reported in April 1946.[102] Washington "adds not only ploughing power but a passing arm that has completed six aerials of 60 yards or over."[103] Harding acknowledged, however, that Washington's performance in 1946 would depend on "whether his leg will stand up."[104] Washington had entered a Los Angeles hospital for minor surgery on his knees. The *Tribune* was optimistic about his recovery:

> Long suffering from double trouble of the knees, Washington will suffer no more if the minor operations performed on both his knees by Dr. D.H. Levinthal, crack orthopedician at Cedars of Lebanon Hospital last Thursday morning pan out.[105]

The *Tribune* took a swipe at other journalists for what it called "a sizable amount of propaganda to the effect that Washington is a has-been."[106] The April 27 issue of the *Tribune* featured a picture of Washington resting in his hospital bed, studying diagrams of the T-formation, a strategy endorsed by Rams coach Adam Walsh. "Busy recovering, Kenny is busier still learning football all over again from another angle," the photo caption read.[107] By July, Washington had almost completely recovered from his surgery. The *Sentinel* soon ran a two-column photo of Washington; its caption touted an upcoming game between the Rams and a team of college All-Stars. The paper also reminded readers that it was "the local sportswriters" who convinced Roach to insert the "no-discrimination clause" into the team's agreement to use the Coliseum.[108] Abie Robinson criticized Buddy Young for deciding to return to the University of Illinois, an institution "reeking with racial prejudice."[109] Robinson said the paper was "sorry to see him pass up UCLA, but we know he can do lots in breaking down the barriers at the college. . . . Good luck, kid."[110] In his July 13 column, the *Courier's* Smith also scolded Young. He pointed out that African American athletes were allowed to take part in only two sports at Illinois: track and football.[111]

Both the *Courier* and the *Tribune* ran stories about a preseason party thrown for Washington by Charles Hill, a prominent Los Angeles doctor. Washington "was given the psychological and heartwarming impetus of a pre-season social kickoff," the *Courier* reported.[112] Many of Washington's fans attended the party "to let him know that they will be in the Coliseum this fall in a solid group of rooters" as he and Strode "get their big chance to make good in the nation's oldest football league."[113] All three newspapers soon reported that Adam Walsh was set to give Washington a shot as the team's starting quarterback in the team's first 1946 intrasquad game. The *Tribune* and *Sentinel* ran the same story on the game, which would pit star quarterback Bob Waterfield and former top collegian Tom Harmon "against the wizardry of Kenny Washington" and former USC star Jim Hardy, "signed by the Rams in July 1946 to back up Waterfield."[114] Walsh later decided that Washington would not play in the game so that he could rest his knee. With such an array of offensive weapons, including Washington and Strode—"the most successful man-to-man passing team in Pacific Coast history"—the *Sentinel* reported that the Rams could be "the throwingest team in football—and the catchingest."[115] Meanwhile, the *Courier* questioned the wisdom of playing Washington in the T-formation. At UCLA, Washington had played tailback in the single wing formation, "where he could make equal use of his running and passing powers." In the "unfamiliar" T-formation, Washington would handle the ball on "virtually every play from center" and would "do nearly all of the passing, but very little running."[116] Walsh had designed plays that would make use of all of Washington's abilities while at the same time protect Washington's troublesome knees. Wendell Smith soon weighed in with a column on the importance of Washington's entry into the NFL. "Some great athletes," he wrote, "disappear as soon as they leave college. Washington and Robinson, however, are still going on. One is carrying the banner of his race in baseball and the other in football. They're still making history in the dizzy, stirring world of sports."[117]

In August, the Rams traveled to Chicago, where they were defeated, 16–0, by a team of college All-Stars before more than ninety-seven thousand fans. Smith wrote proudly about how "football history was made" when Washington and Strode came into the game with five minutes to play in the fourth quarter.[118] "For the brief time he was put in the collegiate fracas Washington shined," Harding wrote in the *Tribune*. "Even with his gimpy leg he went through the line for 12 yards, dragging half the opposition along."[119] Throughout the game, fans called for Walsh to put Washington in, but Walsh continued his plan to protect Washington's ailing knees. Washington "was still gimpy on the port side" despite the surgery, the *Tribune* reported.[120] Washington admitted that his knees were giving him trouble, Smith wrote, but he assured Smith that he would be all right when the Rams' regular season began.

The *Sentinel* assured its readers that Washington would get more playing time in the Rams' season opener against the Redskins. Washington and Waterfield both played quarterback in practice as Walsh juggled his lineup. "He lacks strength in one knee and does not have the drive of his collegiate days. But he can still wing those long passes," the paper reported.[121] The *Tribune* predicted Washington would start at quarterback for the Rams when they "play their inaugural league game with Los Angeles at homegrounds next Friday night."[122] The Rams beat the Redskins, 16–14, but Washington did not play. He played sporadically at running back in the team's next game, against the Philadelphia Eagles.

Washington ended up seeing only limited action for the Rams in 1946. He played in six games, and gained 114 rushing yards on 23 attempts. He completed one of eight passes for 19 yards, and caught six passes for 83 yards.[123] He scored one touchdown. The NFL was more successful; average attendance rose to its highest level (31,493 per game). On November 10, 1946, NFL games for the first time drew more than 200,000 fans on a single Sunday. The year's largest crowd—68,381—came to see the Rams play the Chicago Bears at the Coliseum. Meanwhile, the Cleveland Browns of the AAFC logged the two most well-attended games of the league's first year. Bill Willis and Marion Motley soon became mainstays in the Browns lineup. In 1946, they were both named All-Pro and led the Browns to the

AAFC championship.[124] Washington played 11 games in 1947, rushing for 444 yards on 60 carries (good for fourth in the NFL) and logging a 92-yard touchdown run, the longest of the season.[125] He scored five touchdowns and even completed two of five forward passes for 14 yards.[126] Washington played sparingly in 1948, catching just six passes for 104 yards and failing to complete the only pass he attempted.[127] Washington retired from professional football on December 12, 1948. The Helms Athletic Foundation named him and USC star Morley Drury the greatest football players in Los Angeles history.[128] The city of Los Angeles declared December 12 "Kenny Washington Day."[129] Washington later worked in the public relations department of Cutty Sark, a liquor company. He died in June 1971 at age fifty-two of a heart ailment. Shav Glick of the *Los Angeles Times* led Washington's obituary this way: "Kenny Washington, the legendary Kingfish, No. 13 for UCLA and the Rams, died Thursday night at UCLA Medical Center."[130] Rams great Bob Waterfield said that if Washington had come directly into the NFL from college, "he would have been, in my opinion, the best the NFL had ever seen."[131]

Conclusion

It is said that in life, timing is everything. Kenny Washington enjoyed a stellar playing career at UCLA only to be snubbed by the NFL in 1939. African American journalists failed in their efforts to convince their colleagues to name Washington first-team All-America and to pressure NFL team officials into drafting him. By the time Dan Reeves was ready to move the Rams from Cleveland to Los Angeles, Washington's opportunity to integrate football had passed. Most journalists—white and African American— had turned their attention to Jackie Robinson and the quest to integrate baseball. Robinson went on to have a Hall of Fame career. Only Harding, Hill, and "Abie" Robinson returned to act on Washington's behalf when the Rams completed their move to the West Coast. Convincing the Rams to sign Washington was part of a well-orchestrated campaign by these journalists to reintegrate professional football. They were just as zealous in their efforts to push Washington's signing as they and their colleagues were in pushing Branch Rickey to sign Jackie Robinson.

Washington received less national publicity than Robinson, but his story was quite well known on the West Coast. Harding, Hill, and "Abie" Robinson willingly stepped outside the conventional role of journalist as observer to act as advocates for Washington, motivated by an unstinting desire for fairness and equality. Unlike "public journalism," which is as much a product of marketing as it is of mission, these writers embraced the crusader's role out of a strong sense of obligation, setting aside journalistic conventions of objectivity and fairness. Washington was just as deeply committed to the cause, according to Robinson.[132] To be sure, Harding, Hill, and Robinson were helped by a touch of pragmatism; their purpose was renewed in large part by the Rams' decision to move to Los Angeles. One wonders how long the NFL would have remained segregated had the Rams not moved west. Team officials recognized that they would have to appeal to African American residents of Los Angeles if the Rams were to succeed. Thus, the writers capitalized on the NFL's desire for the Rams to make a strong showing in their new city—the "visibility" discussed by Abie Robinson. Washington, one of the city's most revered athletes, would help the Rams build an audience, they claimed.

Like Wendell Smith, who knew that Jackie Robinson would eventually integrate baseball, Harding, Hill, and Robinson focused on Washington long after they argued their case before the Coliseum Commission in 1946. However, some of their colleagues, and many sportswriters for Los Angeles's white newspapers, started looking elsewhere for a standard-bearer—not because Washington was undeserving; he was, to some, too old. This certainly makes Washington's story compelling, and somewhat sad. Had the push to integrate football been successful five years earlier, it is reasonable to argue that Washington, fresh from an outstanding career at UCLA, would have carved out a stellar professional career. But he would have to wait. By March 1946, his body battered by his seasons of semi-pro play, Washington was reduced to an option, one of many suggested by African American sportswriters who watched as Harding, Hill, and Robinson seized the opportunity to force the NFL to revisit integration. Only when Buddy Young decided not to attend UCLA did the door completely reopen for Washington. By that point, he was past his prime.[133]

Only Harding, Hill, and Robinson championed Washington from UCLA until he signed with the Rams and beyond. Thus, while it could be argued that they were living in the past by acting as advocates for Washington, it was a glorious past. Injuries and bad timing deprived Washington of a longer career but should not deprive him of recognition for his role in reintegrating football.

NOTES

1. Thomas Smith, "Outside the Pale: The Exclusion of Blacks from the National Football League, 1934–1946," *Journal of Sport History* 15 (1988): 258.
2. Bob Oates, interview with author, February 7, 2000.
3. Woody Strode, *Goal Dust: The Warm and Candid Memoirs of a Pioneer Black Athlete and Author* (Lanham MD: Madison Books, 1990), 58.
4. Quoted in Strode, *Goal Dust*, 56.
5. Quoted in Strode, *Goal Dust*, 63.
6. Strode, *Goal Dust*, 69.
7. Strode, *Goal Dust*, 69.
8. Strode, *Goal Dust*, 70.
9. Randy Dixon, "Kenny Washington Boards All-America Train," *Pittsburgh Courier*, November 4, 1939, 17.
10. Dixon, "Kenny Washington Boards All-America Train," 17.
11. Arthur Ashe, *A Hard Road to Glory* (New York: Warner, 1988).
12. Strode, *Goal Dust*, 134.
13. Strode, *Goal Dust*, 134.
14. A. S. Young, *Negro Firsts in Sports*, (Chicago: Johnson, 1963), 144.
15. Oates interview.
16. Young, *1963*, 144.
17. Arnold Rampersad, *Jackie Robinson: A Biography* (New York: Knopf, 1997), 148.
18. Jules Tygiel, *Baseball's Great Experiment: Jackie Robinson and His Legacy* (New York: Oxford University Press, 1983), 76.
19. Oates interview.
20. Oates interview.
21. Smith, "Outside the Pale," 287.
22. Robert Peterson, *Pigskin: The Early Years of Pro Football* (New York: Oxford University Press, 1997), 181.
23. Quoted in Strode, *Goal Dust*, 142.

24. Chris Lamb and Glen Bleske, "Democracy on the Field: The Black Press Takes on White Baseball," *Journalism History* 24 (1998): 51-59.

25. Lamb and Bleske, "Democracy on the Field," 52.

26. Lamb and Bleske, "Democracy on the Field," 52.

27. Edward "Abie" Robinson, interview with author, June 16, 2000.

28. Robinson interview.

29. Chris Lamb, interview with author, August 27, 1999.

30. Lamb and Bleske, "Democracy on the Field," 56.

31. Lamb and Bleske, "Democracy on the Field," 56.

32. Robinson interview.

33. Walter Renwick, "USC Alumnus, Black Journalist, Dies at Age 87," *USC Daily Trojan*, October 3, 1991, 1.

34. "Herman Hill; USC's First Black Basketball Player Was Activist," *Los Angeles Times*, October 1, 1991, A20.

35. Robinson interview.

36. Robinson interview.

37. Robinson interview.

38. Robinson interview.

39. Quoted in Young, *Negro Firsts*, 58.

40. John M. Carroll, *Fritz Pollard: Pioneer in Racial Advancement* (Urbana: University of Illinois Press, 1999), 201.

41. Robinson interview.

42. Minutes of the Los Angeles County Coliseum Commission, January 15, 1946.

43. Quoted in Young, *Negro Firsts*, 58.

44. Robinson interview.

45. Quoted in Young, *Negro Firsts*, 58.

46. Quoted in Young, *Negro Firsts*, 58.

47. Quoted in Young, *Negro Firsts*, 58.

48. Brad Pye, interview with author, June 13, 2000.

49. "Pro Grid Champs Say They Want Buddy Young," *Pittsburgh Courier*, January 26, 1946, 16.

50. Quoted in Young, *Negro Firsts*, 58.

51. Robinson interview.

52. Paul Zimmerman, "Rams Ask Five Dates in Coliseum," *Los Angeles Times*, January 16, 1946, 2:8.

53. Zimmerman, "Rams Ask Five Dates," 8.

54. Braven Dyer, "The Sports Parade," *Los Angeles Times*, January 17, 1946, 1:10.

55. Herman Hill, "Hill's Side," *Pittsburgh Courier*, March 30, 1946, 16.
56. Hill, "Hill's Side," March 30, 1946, 16.
57. Hill, "Hill's Side," March 30, 1946, 16.
58. Hill, "Hill's Side," March 30, 1946, 16.
59. Hill, "Hill's Side," March 30, 1946, 16.
60. Carroll, *Fritz Pollard*, 197.
61. Hill, "Hill's Side," March 30, 1946, 16.
62. Hill, "Hill's Side," March 30, 1946, 16.
63. Oates interview.
64. "UCLA Followers Try to Lure Young from Illinois," *Pittsburgh Courier*, December 29, 1945, 17.
65. "Pro Grid Champs," 16.
66. Vincent Flaherty, "Pro Football Should Hasten Star's Signing," *Los Angeles Examiner*, January 21, 1946, 2:5.
67. Flaherty, "Pro Football," 5.
68. Flaherty, "Pro Football," 5.
69. J. Cullen Fentress, "Buddy Young to Lead Stars against Hollywood Bears," *Pittsburgh Courier*, January 19, 1946, 17.
70. Cal Whorton, "Bears Defeat Service All-Stars, 14–0," *Los Angeles Times*, January 21, 1946, 7.
71. Whorton, "Bears Defeat Service All-Stars, 14–0," 7.
72. Paul Zimmerman, "Sportscripts," *Los Angeles Times*, January 22, 1946, 2:6.
73. "Buddy Young Visits UCLA," *Los Angeles Times*, January 22, 1946, 2:6.
74. "Buddy Young Visits," 6.
75. "Buddy Young in Action," *Los Angeles Times*, February 5, 1946, 2:11.
76. Dick Hyland, "Service Grids Nip Washington Stars," *Los Angeles Times*, February 11, 1946, 10.
77. J. Cullen Fentress, "Los Angeles Interested in Young and Kenny," *Pittsburgh Courier*, February 2, 1946, 12.
78. "Ranking Athletes Honored at Courier Spots Banquet," *Pittsburgh Courier*, February 23, 1946, 13.
79. "Lena Horne, King Cole, and Eddie Green Set For Sports Banquet," *Pittsburgh Courier*, February 2, 1946, 13.
80. "Ranking Athletes," 13.
81. "Kenny Washington Signs with the L.A. Rams," *Los Angeles Tribune*, March 23, 1946, 14.
82. "Kenny Washington Signs," 14.
83. "Kenny Washington Signs," 14.

84. J. Cullen Fentress, "Rams Sign Kenny Washington," *Pittsburgh Courier*, March 30, 1946, 16.

85. Fentress, "Rams Sign Kenny Washington," 16.

86. Bob Oates, "Rams Sign Washington," *Los Angeles Examiner*, March 22, 1946, 2:5.

87. Dick Hyland, "Washington Signed by Los Angeles Rams," *Los Angeles Times*, March 22, 1946, 1:6.

88. Hyland, "Washington Signed," 6.

89. Hyland, "Washington Signed," 6.

90. Oates, "Rams Sign Washington," 5.

91. "Walsh Predicts," *Los Angeles Times*, March 15, 1946, 1:6.

92. Vincent Flaherty, "Washington Won't Tear Pro Grid League Apart," *Los Angeles Examiner*, March 23, 1946, 2:3.

93. Flaherty, "Washington Won't Tear," 3.

94. Flaherty, "Washington Won't Tear," 3.

95. Vincent Flaherty, "Young, at Washington's Lead, to Join Bruins," *Los Angeles Examiner*, April 2, 1946, 2:5.

96. Dick Hyland, "The Hyland Fling," *Los Angeles Times*, March 22, 1946, 1:7.

97. Hyland, "The Hyland Fling," 7.

98. Hyland, "The Hyland Fling," 7.

99. Wendell Smith, "'46 Greatest Year for Negro Athletes," *Pittsburgh Courier*, January 4, 1947, 16.

100. Smith, "'46 Greatest Year," 16.

101. Smith, "'46 Greatest Year," 16.

102. "Rams Will Cash In on Kenny and the Coliseum," *Los Angeles Tribune*, April 4, 1946, 14.

103. "Rams Will Cash In," 14.

104. Halley Harding, "So What?" *Los Angeles Tribune*, April 6, 1946, 15.

105. "Kenny in Hospital; Gets Knee Fixed," *Los Angeles Tribune*, April 13, 1946, 14.

106. "Kenny in Hospital," 14.

107. "Kenny Mends; Bones Up on T-Formation," *Los Angeles Tribune*, April 27, 1946, 15.

108. "Kenny 'Kingfish' Washington," *Los Angeles Sentinel*, July 11, 1946, 22, photo caption.

109. Edward Robinson, "Abie's Corner," *Los Angeles Sentinel*, July 25, 1946, 22.

110. Robinson, "Abie's Corner," July 25, 1946, 22.

111. Wendell Smith, "Why Is Buddy Returning to Illinois?" *Pittsburgh Courier*, July 13, 1946, 16.

112. "Fans Give Kenny Good Luck Party," *Pittsburgh Courier*, July 27, 1946, 17.

113. "Fans Give Kenny Pro League Sendoff," *Los Angeles Tribune*, July 20, 1946, 15.

114. "Walsh to Try Kenny at Quarterback in Aug. 14 Game," *Los Angeles Tribune*, July 27, 1946, 14.

115. "L.A. Rams May Ring Up New Passing Mark," *Los Angeles Sentinel*, August 15, 1946, 22.

116. "L.A. Rams to Try Kenny as Quarterback," *Pittsburgh Courier*, August 3, 1946, 14.

117. Wendell Smith, "Kenny Finally Gets a Break," *Pittsburgh Courier*, August 3, 1946, 16.

118. Wendell Smith, "97,380 Fans See Negro Stars Play in 'Dream' Game," *Pittsburgh Courier*, August 31, 1946, 18.

119. Halley Harding, "So What?" *Los Angeles Tribune*, August 31, 1946, 16.

120. "Washington Not a Likely Starter in All-Star Game," *Los Angeles Tribune*, August 24, 1946, 15.

121. "Washington, Strode to See Plenty of Action Friday Night," *Los Angeles Sentinel*, September 1946, 22.

122. "Kenny Is Likely Starter against Redskins Friday," *Los Angeles Tribune*, August 31, 1946, 14.

123. Bob Carroll, Michael Gershman, David Neft, and John Thorn, eds., *Total Football: The Official Encyclopedia of the National Football League.* (New York: Harper Collins, 1997), 1273.

124. Smith, "Outside the Pale," 278–79.

125. Nick Peters, "Kenny Washington," *Touchdown Illustrated*, Fall 1989.

126. Carroll et al., *Total Football*, 1273.

127. Carroll et al., *Total Football*, 1273.

128. Peters, "Kenny Washington."

129. Shav Glick, "Kenny Washington, Former Bruin Star, Dies," *Los Angeles Times*, June 25, 1971, 3.

130. Glick, "Kenny Washington," 3.

131. Glick, "Kenny Washington," 3.

132. Peters, "Kenny Washington," 133.

133. Robinson interview.

....

7

Jackie Robinson and the American Mind
Journalistic Perceptions of the
Reintegration of Baseball

WILLIAM SIMONS

Jackie Robinson. For many the mere mention of that name conjures up a series of indelible tableaux. Yet the reintegration of Organized Baseball continues to attract an apparently inexhaustible supply of popular writers and scholars. A plethora of books and articles, even a Broadway musical, have examined the assault on baseball's color line from a variety of perspectives. *The Boys of Summer*, perhaps the most widely read account of the reintegration of baseball, is, by turns, memoir of Roger Kahn's youth, chronicle of Brooklyn baseball during the Robinson era, and a series of character studies focusing on the lives of former Dodgers. Kahn's poignant account of fathers and sons, men and time, and discrimination and justice always leads the reader back to Robinson and the lingering resonances he left for those who knew him. Jackie Robinson, embattled, courageous, and proud, appears a tragic hero. A very different albeit equally brilliant book is *Baseball's Great Experiment: Jackie Robinson and His Legacy* by Jules Tygiel. While Kahn's vantage point is the individual and personal sensibilities, public events and their societal consequences form Tygiel's frame of reference. *Baseball's Great Experiment*, a well-researched monograph, analyzes racial practices in baseball prior to 1945, factors that led to the signing of Robinson, stratagems employed by those who wanted baseball integration to succeed and those who wanted it to fail, the subsequent entry of other blacks into Organized Baseball, and the impact of Robinson's career on the latter history of sports and the larger American society.[1] Thanks to Kahn, Tygiel, and others we know much about baseball integration in terms of individual participants and social context.

Yet important phenomena defy definitive treatment. New questions and alternate approaches inevitably emerge. What, for example, did the controversy surrounding Robinson reveal about the ideology, assumptions, values, and perceptions of that era? By their content analysis of the media, Al-Tony Gilmore and Richard Crepeau, authors respectively of studies examining press images of black boxer Jack Johnson and of baseball during the Great Depression, demonstrate that sports can facilitate a more complete understanding of the American mind. A number of books dealing with the reintegration of baseball give attention to the reaction of the media; compilation of opinion, however, does not constitute systematic content analysis. Nevertheless, a few articles concerned with baseball integration make the media their major focus. The best of these, David Wiggins's study of the 1933–1945 campaign of a single black newspaper, the *Pittsburgh Courier*, to integrate Organized Baseball emphasizes strategy and tactics more than values and ideology. William Kelley's brief and disappointing survey of press reaction to the signing of Robinson concerns the number of stories and photographs publications devoted to the story while offering only the most minimal content analysis. Bill Weaver's examination of the black press coverage of baseball integration probes values and perceptions with intelligence. Weaver discusses four topics—the significance of the breakthrough, tributes to Dodgers president Branch Rickey, obstacles facing Robinson, and aspirations attached to Robinson by fellow blacks.[2] Still, Weaver has not exhausted the field. Additional concepts merit scrutiny, and the metropolitan and sporting press remain beyond Weaver's scope.

The integration of baseball was the most widely commented-on episode in American race relations of its time. At an October 23, 1945, press conference it was announced that Robinson had signed a contract to play baseball with the Montreal Royals, a Minor League affiliate of the Brooklyn Dodgers. Coming at the end of a war that had encouraged Americans to define themselves by a liberalism not found in Nazi Germany, the announcement that Robinson would become the first black to participate in Organized Baseball since the late nineteenth century generated extensive public discussion about consensus, conflict, equality, liberty, opportunity, prejudice, democracy, and national character. As an episode that encouraged articulation of important values, analysis of this phenomenon has the potential to deepen our understanding of American thought. Social scientists differ about the distinguishing characteristics of the American mind. Vernon Louis Parrington and Howard Zinn depict an enduring dualism in American thought between the forces of liberalism and conservatism. Conformity and an absence of ideology are described by Daniel Boorstin. An ability to harbor contradictory perceptions simultaneously, argues Michael Kammen, makes Americans a people of paradox. In *An American Dilemma: The Negro Problem and Modern Democracy*, published almost contemporaneously with the signing of Robinson, Gunnar Myrdal argues that most Americans believe in a shared creed. This "American Creed," contends Myrdal, endorses the "ideals of the essential dignity of the individual human being, of the fundamental equality of all men, and of certain inalienable rights to freedom, justice, and a fair opportunity."[3]

Employing the case study approach, this essay will focus on media reaction to the signing of Jackie Robinson. Media attention to the actual signing appeared during a chronologically circumscribed interval; during that interval, however, an abundance of commentary appeared. Utilizing the contemporary print media—metropolitan newspapers, black newspapers, sporting publications, and magazines—this essay will examine public reaction to the Robinson signing as a means of illuminating American thought at the opening of the postwar era.[4] Given that the announcement of the Robinson signing occurred in Montreal with notation that he would begin his Organized Baseball career in that city, the Montreal press also receives some attention.

This essay will seek to demonstrate that the tenets of Myrdal's American Creed significantly shaped contemporary press coverage of the reintegration of baseball. Newspaper accounts typically described an American public imbued with the belief that Robinson ought to succeed or fail on the basis of his abilities, not his color. According to the *Baltimore Afro-American,* "The signing of Jackie Robinson . . . has met with nationwide approval by fans all over the country."[5] And an International News Service article reported, "General approval was voiced today by baseball men to the signing of Jack Roosevelt Robinson."[6] Although the media certainly acknowledged criticisms of the signing, especially those that emanated from the South, few articles denied that a liberal consensus supported Robinson's entry into Organized Baseball.[7]

The conventional wisdom holds that baseball mirrors American values, and scholarship suggests that in some eras it has.[8] At the time of Robinson's signing, however, the media often asserted that baseball's conservative racial practices lagged behind practices already prevailing in America. Black journalists frequently termed baseball inferior to certain sports in living up to America's egalitarian beliefs. Although pugilism involved "brutal body contact," the *St. Louis Argus* argued that integrated boxing matches outside the South proceed "in grand style."[9] The *Pittsburgh Courier* also noted prior "achievements of colored men and women in various branches of sports."[10] A third black newspaper, the *Amsterdam News,* quoted Douglas Hertz, a promoter of interracial games: "It is extremely gratifying to see at this late date organized baseball has finally seen the light." And the black press reported a comment by a member of New York City's Mayor Fiorello LaGuardia's Committee on Unity, which suggested that baseball was tardy in conforming to practices long accepted by other sports: "There is every reason to hope that this will lead to a constructive solution by which organized baseball will be brought in line with those other sports in which Negroes have for a long time been participants."[11]

Not only did it appear negligent in comparison with other sports, baseball, asserted pundits, failed to keep pace with racial practices prevalent on a macrocosmic level. As "the nation moves toward a postwar lessening of discrimination," chided the *Brooklyn Eagle,* "the national game of Americans . . . cannot forever lag behind."[12] A letter to the editor of the *Detroit News* argued, "Colored artists and performers in all other fields have proved that the absence of a colored player in the major leagues of baseball is nothing more than the absence of the true American spirit in the greatest of American sports."[13] Aside from athletics, American blacks had already made notable contributions "in drama, opera, music, the stage," and other endeavors.[14] Beyond harboring reactionary attitudes, baseball, implied the press, practiced hypocrisy and irrationality in the enforcement of the color barrier. Writers frequently noted the participation of numbers of blacks in Organized Baseball before the establishment of the unofficial color line in the late nineteenth century.[15] Contemporary journalists also commented extensively on integrated play during postseason barnstorming, often featuring exhibition games that matched the ageless Satchell Paige against white stars.[16] When "baseball club owners are perfectly willing to take the money of Negro fans at the gate," editorialized the *St. Louis Post-Dispatch*, "while excluding them from the playing field, the failure of 'the Great American Game' to live up to its name became most evident."[17] Moreover, pundits acknowledged that a few twentieth-century blacks had entered Organized Baseball under the guise of an Indian or Cuban identity.[18] Negro newspapers and, indeed, most of the general-circulation press assumed blacks had earned the right to compete in the national pastime without concealing their identities. "We want Jackie to meet the test as a Negro," asserted a black journalist, "not as a sun-tanned white man or Eskimo."[19]

World War II, claimed the press, rendered arguments based on racial inequality un-American. Columnist Dink Carroll believed the war demonstrated that baseball segregation derived from southern exceptionalism, a violation of American democracy:

> Many Americans have criticized baseball for drawing the color line, and have argued that it couldn't truly be called America's national game because of this discrimination hostility to colored players didn't originate with the club owners or with the leagues, but with the players themselves. A good many of the players are Southerners. Part of the Japanese propaganda in the Pacific was to point out that colored people were discriminated against in the United States. Many Americans had to ask themselves should they not courageously back up their fighting men—of all races, creeds and color—by eradicating the color line at home?[20]

Indeed, asked the *Boston Daily Globe*, did "the masters of baseball" forget that America's mortal enemy, Nazi Germany, had been the "boastful headquarters of the 'master race' theory?"[21] Journalists frequently quoted the tribute by Hector Racine, president of the Montreal Royals, to black efforts during World War II: "Negroes fought alongside whites and shared the foxhole dangers, and they should get a fair trial in baseball."[22] A *Pittsburgh Courier* respondent employed similar rhetoric: "Those who were good enough to fight by the side of the whites are plenty good enough to play by the side of whites!"[23] Ironically baseball, which during World War II was frequently employed as a patriotic icon, at conflict's end came to appear as a transgressor of American values.

So pervasive was the liberal consensus that even opponents of baseball integration generally exhibited careful avoidance of public statements that violated egalitarian principles. Rather than attacking integration directly, opponents typically utilized more circuitous strategems. Critics sought to avoid the stigma of illiberalism. One tactic of obstructionists was to raise doubts about Robinson's baseball abilities. Ignoring Robinson's fine record in the Negro American League and employing sophistry to explain the failure of his own team to sign "Jackie" after having granted him a tryout, Eddie Collins, general manager of the Boston Red Sox, told the press, "Very few players can step off a sandlot or college diamond into a major league berth."[24] A United Press release implied that Robinson's baseball skills might not measure up to his proficiency in other sports by juxtaposing football, basketball, and track achievements with a former coach's observation that "Jackie didn't try too hard at baseball."[25] Terming Robinson's background in other sports a liability, Bob Feller, star pitcher for the Cleveland Indians, authored perhaps the most widely quoted expression of doubt about Robinson's baseball potential:

> He's a typical football player—they're all alike. . . . He is fast as blazes and a great athlete, but that doesn't make him a ball player. . . . Honestly, I can't see any chance at all for Robinson. And I'll say this—if he were a white man I doubt if they'd even consider him as big league material.[26]

Like others who questioned Robinson's future in baseball, Feller eschewed overt racism despite his belief that no contemporary black player possessed Major League skills: "When you say things like that, somebody usually accuses you of racial discrimination[,] . . . but I'm not prejudiced in the least."[27] And an editorial in "the baseball bible," the *Sporting News*, pontificated, "Robinson, at 26, is reported to possess baseball abilities which, were he white, would make him eligible for a trial with, let us say, the Brooklyn Dodgers' Class B farm at Newport News, if he were six years younger. . . . The waters of the International League will flood far over his head."[28]

Silence, however, constituted the most common public image of nonsupport. Journalists frequently perceived those who refused to comment as "cool" toward integration.[29] The *St. Louis Post-Dispatch*, believed, for example, that those who spoke "with extreme caution" left "the impression that they were pulling their punches."[30] Since reform could succeed only by eliciting a positive response from the public, reticence implicitly provided support for the existing arrangements that excluded blacks from Organized Baseball. With sophistry Bill Klem, chief of staff for the National League's umpires, reported the United Press, justified his "no comment" by arguing, "That's the proper stand for an umpire."[31] Connie Mack, dean of Major League managers, told the *Philadelphia Inquirer*, "I am not familiar with the move. I don't know Robinson and wouldn't care to comment."[32] A *Sporting News* editorial regarded those who "refused to comment" as more being diplomatic and effective than those openly "blasting the hiring of a Negro."[33] One could thus impede integration without appearing to challenge the liberal consensus.

Critics of the Robinson signing often tried desperately to portray themselves as opponents of discrimination and thus the true proponents of American values. A number of newspaper articles reflected the viewpoint of individuals concerned that Robinson's entry into Organized Baseball would undermine the Negro leagues; this line of argument purported that the Negro leagues provided important opportunities for black entrepreneurs and athletes. Tom Baird, white co-owner of the Kansas City Monarchs, the Negro baseball team for which Robinson played during 1945, protested the "steal" of Robinson by Rickey.[34] Angry that Rickey had not reimbursed the Monarchs for Robinson, the Kansas City co-owner feared that "if the wholesale robbery of Negro players from our league continues we may as well quit baseball."[35] A *Washington Post* editorial agreed: "A general competition among major and minor league owners for the best Negro players would certainly wreck the Negro leagues and with them the not inconsiderable capital investment of Negro entrepreneurs."[36]

Some prominent figures from Organized Baseball also expressed concern that the signing of Robinson would prove detrimental to Negro baseball. According to the *Brooklyn Eagle*, Larry MacPhail, president of the New York Yankees,

> took the view that signing Negroes at the present time would do the cause of Negro baseball more harm than good. He pointed out that Negro baseball is now a $2,000,000 business and Negro clubs pay salaries ranging up to $16,000 a year. He pointed out that comparatively few good young Negro players were being developed. He feared that if Organized Baseball raided the Negro League and took their good young players, the Negro Leagues would fold, the investments of the club owners would be lost and a lot of professional Negro ball players would lose their jobs.[37]

Journalists frequently quoted the caveats of Clark Griffith, seventy-five-year-old owner of the Washington Senators.[38] Condemning Rickey's signing of Robinson, Griffith denounced those who "steal" from the Negro leagues and "act like outlaws": "In no walk of life can one person take another's property unless he pays for it."[39] Griffith exhorted, "We have no right to destroy" the Negro leagues.[40] Griffith's dissatisfaction with the Robinson signing culminated in a long letter of counsel and praise for Negro baseball that the *New York Age*, a black newspaper, printed in its entirety. Part of the letter read,

> Your two (Negro) leagues have established a splendid reputation and now have the support and respect of the colored people all over the country as well as the decent white people. They have not pirated

against organized baseball nor have they stolen anything from them and organized baseball has no moral right to take anything from them without their consent....

Anything that is worthwhile is worth fighting for so you folks should leave not a stone unturned to protect the existence of your two established Negro leagues. Don't let anybody tear it down.[41]

Nevertheless, the press generally represented the attempt to link concern with the survival of Negro baseball with misgivings about the Robinson signing as a cynical distortion of American values. Negro newspapers in particular reflected a disdain for obstructionists who clothed themselves in the rhetoric of racial justice. Both the metropolitan and African American press noted that some blacks connected with Negro baseball, such as Effa Manley, co-owner of the Newark Eagles, felt Rickey was wrong to sign Robinson without compensating his former team. The media agreed, however, with near unanimity that black America viewed integration as a more important goal than the economic prosperity of Negro baseball. Earl Brown, a columnist for the *Amsterdam News*, pointed out the illogic of owners of Negro baseball teams posing as apostles of opportunity for black athletes: "Most Negro ball clubs are owned by enterprising white men who pay a few star exhibitionists, such as Satchel Paige and Josh Gibson, good salaries, but who pay the average player starvation wages."[42] The *St. Louis Star Times* pointedly noted "that Baird is white, not a Negro." And the *Chicago Daily News* said of Baird's original statement, "The attitude of the Kansas City Monarchs in the Negro National League ... for whom Robinson played last year ... is not commendable. They should be enough interested in what Robinson may accomplish in the majors ... both for himself and his race ... to let him go without any monetary furor about it."[43]

The Negro press argued that obstructionists were disingenuous about their motives. Attributing Griffith's support for Negro baseball to his rapacity, the National Negro Press Association stressed that rentals of Griffith Stadium to the Homestead Grays, a black team, constituted a significant source of revenue.

The Old Fox, as Griff is known in organized baseball, is a shrewd business man. It's his business acumen that causes him to compliment the National Negro League by saying it is well established and organized baseball shouldn't raid it by taking their players.... But Griff is no liberal by any means. Not until colored baseball made the turnstiles click in figures comparable to those of the Nationals did he allow colored clubs to play white clubs in Griffith Stadium.[44]

The *Amsterdam News* denounced the "unholy, reactionary, anti-Negro setup led by Clark Griffith" for attempting "to beat Rickey's attempts to Americanize baseball and allow all qualified to do so to participants [*sic*]."[45] In addition many general-circulation newspapers, such as the *St. Louis Globe-Democrat*, found Griffith's piety hypocritical given his disregard for the stability of Latin American baseball: "Certainly Clark Griffith of the Senator's [*sic*] should have little to say about that. He's been raiding Cuban, Mexican and even South American leagues for playing talent for years and up to now we've heard little about his buying the players' contracts."[46] Likewise, several newspapers, including the *Washington Post*, published Larry MacPhail's admission that self-interest influenced his position on the Robinson signing: "President Larry MacPhail of the Yankees admits that park rentals to colored teams at Yankee Stadium, Newark and Kansas City produce $100,000 in revenue for the Yankee chain annually."[47]

Negative images of the black leagues abounded in the black and general-circulation press, but they possessed an almost visceral intensity in African American newspapers. These criticisms extended beyond disappointment over black baseball's reaction to the Robinson signing. Noting the diffuse organizational structure of the Negro leagues, including an absence of binding player contracts and the dominance of white promoters and entrepreneurs, numerous articles quoted Branch Rickey: "There is no Negro league as such as far as I am concerned. Negro baseball is in the zone of a racket."[48] One of the most scathing indictments of Negro baseball appeared in the *Amsterdam News*:

Mr. Rickey said one thing about Negro baseball with which I emphatically and enthusiastically concur: it is a racket. At least it was when I used to play on Negro teams and recent checks with sports writers (Negro) and players (also Negro) corroborated Mr. Rickey's and my statements There is little or no discipline among the players. . . . The league had no constitution, by-laws or word of mouth customs by which to go . . . and the league is still about as stable as the smoke ascending from the mogul's stogie.[49]

But misgivings about Negro baseball extended beyond the issues of mismanagement and corruption.

Discrimination, contemporary black liberals assumed, came not from the American values but rather from their violation. The black press of the mid-1940s regarded integration as a fulfillment of national ideology. The distinctions that radicals of a latter generation would draw between separation and segregation were perceived as canards by contemporary black newspapers. Since the African American press termed segregation cruel, undemocratic, and anti-American, images of Negro league baseball connoted an accommodation to an unjust situation. Thus, a *Pittsburgh Courier* editorial condemned the "foolish protest" of those who felt protecting the sanctity of contractual agreements in the Negro leagues more important than advancing the cause of integration:

> For many years colored organizations and institutions have fought against jim crowism in major league baseball, and now that a small victory has been won with the selection of one colored player, it is annoying to have a wrench thrown into the machinery.
>
> Let us not at this juncture play the part of a crab in a barrel of crabs.
>
> Instead of trying to hamper those who have made a step forward, let us help them as much as we can.[50]

The assault against segregation, voluntary or involuntary, by several African American publications, included proposals to admit white players into black baseball and for the Negro leagues to become part of Organized Baseball.[51] A letter to the editor of the *Chicago Defender* reflects the disdain the black press typically directed at those who attempted to elevate "voluntary segregation" into a positive good:

There are occasions when segregation is practical, due to the existing laws and traditions that are next to impossible to contest openly. A Negro youth in a southern community wishing to attend a college and his funds are limited, naturally should take advantage of the nearest institution until time warrants his condition as to improve upon this condition.

But this is not enough. It is up to every Negro to aid himself and his entire group. If it's freedom from discrimination that we desire, then we should cast away all types of discrimination from our programs.

The protest of the Negro baseballers is as selfish as any plantation owner of slavery-bound men in the days prior to the Civil War. Their own interest is above that of their nation. This is an appeal to all Negroes to avoid this, for their freedom means freedom to all men, and courage to men of other lands. Segregate yourselves and others will do no better.[52]

The general-circulation press also overwhelmingly rejected, albeit with less vigor, attempts to portray black separation as compatible with American values. The *Boston Herald*, for example, related integration to "equal opportunity."[53]

Racism remained a national phenomenon during the mid-1940s. Race riots in New York City and Detroit reflected the intensity of group conflict. A shared consensus supporting the American Creed, brought to its zenith by World War II, made it difficult for Americans to acknowledge that their values deviated significantly from their behavior. A means was needed to recognize conflict without challenging the belief in consensus. An emphasis on southern exceptionalism became the means by which many Americans of the mid-1940s reconciled consensus and conflict. Racism and discrimination obviously existed, but they were typically termed southern, rather than American, phenomena. Newspapers did acknowledge obstacles, actual and potential, that were not exclusively southern—"icy stares and a boatload of caustic remarks," restrictive hotels in the North, "snobs and discrimination in cities where the Dodgers play other National League teams," "no little prejudice from a few members of his team," "insults," "racial strife in the grand stand," and a "terrible riding from the bench jockeys."[54] But references to racism outside the South were muted. Obviously the black press demonstrated a greater awareness of northern racism. Yet even commentary in the black press on northern racism lacked a certain precision. American racism during the Robinson controversy thus appeared an attribute primarily distinctive to the South; its people and its institutions, tarnished by segregation law and practice, deviated from the national consensus. Journalistic concern with southern exceptionalism took on great importance due to the perception that the region significantly shaped baseball's ambiance, thus threatening the game's position as the national pastime.

Despite the occasional use of code language, context left little doubt that phrases like "some parts of the United States where racial prejudice is rampant" meant the South.[55] "Although fans in Northern cities will be extremely friendly," the *Boston Herald* believed that "the Southern player and the Southern fan are in the wrong," ready to create "a most harrowing situation."[56] Journalists examining racism wrote of "the Southern attitude," "the Southern interests," "those in the South," and "the baseball constituency which hails from the South."[57] While not objecting to Robinson playing on integrated teams in the North, the sports editor of the *Spartanburg (SC) Herald Journal* warned, "Segregation in the South will continue to be an unalterable rule." The northern pattern of "Negroes and whites mix(ing) in practically every undertaking" was rejected by the *Jackson (TN) Sun*: "Here in the South we believe in the segregation of Negro and whites. This rule applies to baseball teams as well as to every other sport activity."[58] The press reported that both Branch Rickey Jr., head of the Dodgers farm system, and his father felt that most criticism of their actions would come from the South.[59]

As portrayed by the media, the South appeared a region apart. Judge William G. Bramham of Durham, the president of the National Association of Minor Leagues, received greater press visibility than any other advocate of separation to comment on the Robinson signing. Bramham, however, attempted to synthesize southern exceptionalism and American values. Bramham presented himself as committed to justice for all people, both black and white. After Bramham noted with undisguised disappointment that the rules of the National Association provided him with no basis for disqualifying Robinson's contract, he claimed that segregation provided the most beneficent context for the advancement of blacks:

> It is my opinion that if the Negro is left alone and aided by his unselfish friends of the white race, he will work out his own salvation in all lines of endeavor.
>
> The Negro is making rapid strides in baseball, as well as other lines of endeavor. They have their own form of player contracts and, as I understand it, their organizations are well officered and are financially successful. Why should we raid their ranks, grab a player and put him, his baseball association and his race in a position that will inevitably prove harmful?[60]

Utilizing Reconstruction imagery to demonstrate that southern paternalists understood blacks better than northern liberals, Bramham told the press, "It is those of the carpet-bagger stripe of the white race under the guise of helping, but in truth using the Negro for their own selfish interests, who retard the race."[61] Writing for the *Sporting News*, Jack Horner of the *Durham Morning Herald* praised Bramham:

> Bramham has been an outstanding fighter for the Negro cause during his 40-odd years of residence in Durham. Bramham helped the Negroes form their own separate fire department. He has been influential in assisting the Negro to better his conditions in many other ways.[62]

Outside of the South, however, the press generally viewed Bramham as spokesman for a regional code that defied the national consensus.

The press made clear that not all southerners camouflaged their racism in the paternalism and self-righteousness employed by Bramham. Unlike Bramham some southern whites quoted by the press did not leaven their advocacy of racial separation with the assumption that such an arrangement would produce equality.[63] Fred (Dixie) Walker, a popular Brooklyn Dodgers outfielder, for example, proclaimed that he most definitely did not want Robinson for a teammate: "As long as he isn't with the Dodgers, I'm not worried."[64] Likewise, Spud Davis, catcher-coach for the Pittsburgh

Pirates, responded, "So long as the Pittsburgh Club hasn't signed a Negro there's no need for me to worry now."[65] George Digby was more emphatic: "I think it's the worst thing that can happen to organized baseball. I think a lot of Southern boys will refuse to compete with Negroes in baseball."[66]

Many newspapers published a prediction by Branch Rickey Jr., which some mistakenly attributed to his father, that white southerners might refuse to play for the Dodgers: "If they come from certain sections in the South, they may steer away from a team with colored players."[67] The younger Rickey then added, "But, they'll be back in baseball after a year or two in the cotton mill."[68] Significantly those journalistic acknowledgements of southern resentment over the younger Rickey's remarks derived from his implication of a lack of resolve, not to his assumptions about regional racism. The *St. Louis Globe-Democrat*, for example, described the reaction of southern athletes to young Rickey's statement from an interesting vantage point: "If the subject had been left untouched especially the sneering part about the cotton mills, the boys probably would have taken it even if they didn't like it."[69] Likewise, a *Sporting News* article argued "ball players resented the comment, since the majority of Southern boys in baseball came off the farms."[70]

Due to "strict race segregation laws" in Daytona Beach, Florida, site of the Dodgers organization's preseason training camp, "the possibility was considered," reported the United Press, "that the team may have its new recruit train somewhere north of the Mason-Dixon line."[71] Journalists left little doubt that the South would enforce its "segregation rules" and that a black athlete would receive no exemption.[72] In Daytona Beach, commented *Montreal La Presse*, "Robinson will not be permitted to live in the hotel as the other players of the Montreal club because of a special law. The city has also special lines of buses for men of color and for the white race."[73] A myriad of articles quoted the Daytona Beach city manager's concept of "a very good situation between the races here: We never have had mixed teams."[74] With consistency media images cast the people, customs, and laws of the South as a threat to baseball integration.

Baseball, implied the media, had long violated the nation's egalitarian values due to the influence of the South. Often described as the national game, baseball, at this particular juncture, appeared in danger of becoming the southern game. Just as the press exaggerated the South's role in promoting racism in the nation at large so it also facilely attributed baseball's conservatism to the southern influence. Given that none of the sixteen Major League franchises were located further south than St. Louis, the press emphasis on southern exceptionalism takes on an insistent tone. But farm team nurseries for the big leagues, asserted the *St. Louis Post-Dispatch*, frequently "operate below the Mason and Dixon line."[75] And with the war over and travel restrictions lifted the South would once again provide spring training sites for Major League teams. Moreover, despite the Northeast and Midwest domiciles of Major League franchises, "many big leaguers," emphasized numerous articles, "are from Southern areas."[76] Various estimates of the number of Major League "players born below the Maxon-Dixon line" appeared in the press, ranging from "approximately 27 percent," a fairly accurate count, to "a guess . . . (of) 50 percent," a highly exaggerated figure.[77] The press could thus attribute baseball's conservatism to a regional aberration without questioning the national commitment to liberal values. Scribes found college football, track, boxing, and army athletics less restrictive than baseball. A *Detroit News* editorial stated, "More than most sports, organized baseball clings to . . . color line."[78] And a *Boston Daily Globe* editorial employed sarcasm: "In other fields of sport, news percolated around long ago that Grant had taken Richmond. Baseball has hitherto displayed hesitation about crediting that somewhat ancient news."[79]

Despite a predilection for identifying racism with southern exceptionalism, Americans tended to believe that in time the South would conform to national standards. Certain media images offered hope that, despite deep southern prejudice, the Robinson episode would eventually help move the South into the mainstream of American life. Some northern journalists suggested that segments of the southern press questioned the South's racial protocols. The *New York Age* generalized, "Sports writers by and large, North and South, gave Robinson good press."[80] The United Press also indicated, "With few exceptions . . . sports writers both north and south of the Mason Dixon line agreed that it was eminently fair that a Negro should have a chance to play in organized baseball."[81] A few African American and sporting publications even featured compilations of southern press opinion. Representatives of the southern press opinion most favorable to Robinson were assessments similar to the following: "If Jackie Robinson hits homers and plays a whale of a game . . . the fans will lose sight of his color"; "If he is qualified, then give him an opportunity"; "A star is a star no matter what his race"; and "It all makes far keener competition and most definitely will raise the standard of major league baseball."[82] Acknowledging that some southern journalists adopted a progressive stance on the race issue, however, did not fundamentally alter the media's perception of the region's dissent from national values. Nevertheless, paralleling the younger Rickey's "they'll be back" prognosis, several pundits hoped that a transformation of southern values would follow the initial period of turbulence. For instance, an editorial in the black *Michigan Chronicle* declared, "It is our guess, like that of the Dodger management, that the southern white boys who may be shocked will recover in due time. A good stiff democratic shock in the right place might do them a lot of good."[83]

Several black and general-circulation newspapers contended that Robinson had, and thus could again, help southerners to recognize the incompatibility of their regional code with national values. Jackie Reemes, *Amsterdam News* reporter, wrote, "I can recall Robinson's basketball days at UCLA. There were several southern white boys on the team with Robinson who handled any opposing players who unduly roughed up colored members of UCLA. If those lads, three of them from the heart of Texas, learned to overcome their prejudices others can and will learn the same lesson."[84] Southern exceptionalism thus obstructed the liberal consensus, but time and effort, suggested the press, would render justice triumphant over regional conservatism.

Not surprisingly, given the association drawn between baseball and southern exceptionalism, the press frequently depicted the redemption of the national pastime emanating from forces external to the game. Many images of Rickey as an emancipator appeared, and more than one pundit discovered Lincolnesque qualities in Rickey. Some journalists called the Dodgers president a "hero," a "savior," "courageous," "meritorious," "liberal," "sincere," "just," "democratic," "idealistic," "righteous," and "strong hearted."[85] Other images, however, leavened praise for Rickey's altruism and morality. Both the black and general-circulation press frequently suggested that Rickey was not the prime mover behind the game's belated experiment in integration. Many articles contained Rickey's denials that he had yielded to outside forces. "No pressure groups had anything to do with it," Rickey told the Associated Press.[86] Yet a wire service article reported his admission that macrocosmic considerations made integration an inevitability: "Racial equality in all sports must be an eventual fact."[87] Employing contradictory logic, Rickey steadfastly portrayed himself immune to influence emanating from outside Organized Baseball while acknowledging that "some of these owners who declared that they're not going to hire Negro players are going to run into difficulty. . . . This is a movement that cannot be stopped by anyone."[88] Referring to anti-discrimination legislation, the Dodgers owner confessed to the *Sporting News* that "the time is nearing fast when every professional baseball club operating in the state of New York will have to hire Negro players."[89] Thus, Rickey portrayed himself as a free agent while depicting societal pressures foreclosing traditional options to his fellow owners. Rickey's claims of exemption from external considerations, however, did not emerge as the dominant media perception of events. A plethora of articles served to undermine the inclination to view Rickey as a disinterested moralist. According to the Associated Press, for example, Rickey himself admitted, "I have never meant to be a crusader, and I hope I won't be regarded as one."[90] Typically journalists implied that forces outside of baseball were prodding the game to reflect the national consensus.

Although the normative media approach to this episode recognized the salutary influence of pressures external to baseball on the game, a minority response articulated misgivings about the impact of such outside forces. Ed Danforth, sports editor of the *Atlanta Journal*, warned, "The only menace to peace between the races is the carpet-bagger white press and agitators in the Negro press who capitalize on racial issues to exploit themselves."[91] Writing for the *Sporting News*, Joe Williams recalled instances of having witnessed "the Negro . . . cruelly victimized by pressure groups, social frauds and political demogogues."[92] Likewise, a *Cleveland Press* sportswriter denigrated "high-geared groups (who) tried to force their way into the major leagues."[93] Much more common in both the black and general-circulation press, however, was the belief that outside influences had a positive impact on the national pastime.

Journalists claimed "the long-sought opening wedge into the big leagues" "represents the first success scored by all the organizations and individuals who have been clamoring for big league baseball to end its ... discrimination against colored ball players."[94] Dave Egan, sportswriter for the *Boston Daily Record*, believed "major league moguls" would not truly accept integration "until public opinion forces them to accept the basic principles of such an old and conservative document as the Constitution of the United States of America."[95] Some general-circulation newspapers, including the *Philadelphia Record*, congratulated themselves for prompting Rickey's decision. More frequently, however, the white press attributed the integration of baseball to "all the recent laws and rulings aimed at an end of racial discrimination." The *Baltimore Morning Sun*, for example, noted "that the legislatures of many states had passed bills in recent years aimed at eliminating racial prejudice."[96] The *New York Post* acknowledged that the "anti-discrimination Ives-Quinn law, written into the New York State statutes this summer, increased the demands of those organizations, who now had the law on their side."[97] And some articles in general-circulation journals commented on black-led efforts to create opportunities for blacks in Organized Baseball.

For their part, black newspapers thanked white allies for their assistance. The *Amsterdam News*, for example, "spotlighted the liberal viewpoint of Gov. Thomas E. Dewey of New York, whose insistence that a State Fair Employment Practice Commission be established, formed the opening wedge by which Negroes are being integrated into all avenues of employment, including professional sports."[98] Similarly, the *Boston Guardian* praised the "Boston *Daily Record* ace sports columnist, Dave (The Colonel) Egan ... (who) led the fight in the daily newspapers."[99] To a much greater extent than the general-circulation press, however, the black press emphasized that the efforts of black themselves played a pivotal role in forcing baseball to acknowledge its delinquency. African American newspapers pointed to black civil rights organizations, black public opinion, and black standard bearers who contributed to the "long contending of Negroes for the white major leagues to take in qualified Negro players."[100]

The Negro press tended to view itself as the prime force behind the signing of Robinson. Sam Lacy, sports editor of the *Baltimore Afro-American*, remarked, "I have had a longtime connection with the campaign to break down the major leagues' color bar."[101] Similarly, a *Boston Chronicle* writer claimed, "This column has been hammering away for many seasons at the illogical viewpoint shown by those opposed to the integration of Organized Baseball."[102] The *Boston Guardian* also saluted the "efforts . . . of colored writers."[103] Readers of the *Amsterdam News* were reminded that "Dr. C. B. Powell, editor of the *Amsterdam News*[,] . . . was a member of the . . . commission against discrimination which drafted the Ives-Quinn Bill."[104] Don Le Leighbur wrote in the *Philadelphia Tribune*, "I have been in the forefront of the fight for years against these reactionaries in organized baseball to relax color bans."[105] The *Pittsburgh Courier* reminded readers of "its intensive campaign to smash the color barriers in organized major league baseball."[106] Although Negro pundits differed about the importance of their own individual contributions to the campaign against discrimination, they agreed that the collective efforts of the black press had a decisive influence on the signing of Robinson. A number of articles employed Robinson's tribute to the black press for confirmation: "I cannot thank the Negro press too much . . . for the wonderful things they have said and done in my behalf and in behalf of the hundreds of other Negro ball players down through the years."[107] Indeed, a *Baltimore Afro-American* headline exclaimed, "It's a press victory." Recent scholarship suggests that the black press did indeed make vital contributions to the long campaign to eradicate segregation from Organized Baseball.[108] The historian David Wiggins, for example, has documented the nearly twelve-year publicity campaign waged by the *Pittsburgh Courier* against Jim Crow practices in the national pastime.[109] As believers in the liberal consensus, black journalists congratulated themselves for forcing Organized Baseball to yield to national values.

American values synthesized self-interest and morality. Baseball integration, implied the press, would promote utilitarian benefits for both blacks and whites. By signing Robinson, suggested scribes, Rickey had chosen to transform blacks into an opportunity for the Dodgers specifically and for Organized Baseball in general. Both the black and general-circulation press gave much attention to the benefits they believed Rickey would soon derive. The *New York Times* depicted Rickey primarily motivated by a desire "to win baseball games."[110] Black players constituted a potentially rich reservoir of untapped talent for a man anxious to "win the pennant for Brooklyn."[111] In the *New York Age*, "Buster" Miller wrote, "He (Rickey) was in the market for a shortstop and went and bought what he thought was the best he could get for his money. Don't we all, whether its shortstops, shoes or sealing wax, cabbages or kings?"[112] Other newspapers, including the *Philadelphia Record*, reinforced the perception that integration would prove "profitable" to Organized Baseball.[113] Alluding to the growing presence of blacks in the urban North, several articles viewed the Robinson signing as a ploy to attract black fans: "If Negro players were included in the lineups of the major league teams, many new fans undoubtedly would be recruited from the large colored populations of cities like New York and Chicago."[114]

Perhaps the most representative media image germane to the Robinson signing derived from a widely quoted remark by Frank Shaughnessy, president of the International League. Shaughnessy endorsed racial integration "as long as any fellow's the right type and can make good and can get along with other players."[115] A *Sporting News* article, considering the various opinions expressed, declared, "Shaughnessy . . . seemed to strike the most intelligent note."[116] Numerous articles echoed Shaughnessy's assumption that Organized Baseball would give the "right type" of black a fair trial. With few exceptions the media employed phraseology, such as "right type of fellow," "right man," "right boy," "a credit to the race," "no better candidate," "ideal candidate," and "ideal Negro," that portrayed Robinson as a good choice to reintegrate baseball.[117] The Robinson portrayed by the media was "the right type" because rather than challenge the liberal consensus he appeared to apotheosize it.

Athletic skills alone were not sufficient to win Robinson "the right type" designation. Nevertheless, both the general-circulation and black press gave extensive and glowing attention to Robinson's accomplishments as a collegiate football, track, basketball, and baseball star and to his stellar performance for the Kansas City Monarchs, a Negro American League team.[118] Yet Rickey and much of the press knew that there were better and more experienced baseball players in Negro baseball than Robinson.[119] The Robinson described by the press in the aftermath of his signing was not the man the press would depict in later years. Recognizing that "the right type" of black would encounter fewer difficulties, the Dodgers president and the black athlete became collaborators.[120] Robinson's intelligence, poise, courage, and athletic ability were assets, but his independence and his anger, actually more radical in their intensity than their content, might have made him appear a critic of American values if not muted. As part of Rickey's stratagem for ameliorating opposition to the integration of Organized Baseball, Robinson, for a time, agreed to assume the personae of "the right type" of Negro.[121]

At times misinformation or omissions served to reinforce positive images of "Jackie's" personal history. Many articles referred to the migration of Robinson's family "when he was a year old" from Cairo, Georgia, to Pasadena, California.[122] Yet articles that appeared in print during 1945 failed to acknowledge one of the major reasons for the migration: Robinson's father had deserted the family.[123] The *Philadelphia Record*, for example, printed Robinson's fallacious account of the past: "I've never known my father. He died when I was a baby."[124] Miscegenation, like familial instability, might pose image difficulties for an individual seeking identification with the values integral to the national consensus. But the press clearly implied that nocturnal adventures, interracial or otherwise, obviously held little appeal for a man who planned to soon marry a woman he had known since his college days.[125] The *Philadelphia Evening Bulletin* went as far as to explicitly identify Robinson's fiancée as "a Negro."[126]

The building of a usable history extended to Robinson's education. Copious references to Robinson's association with the University of California at Los Angeles appeared in the press.[127] Repeated use of phrases such as "college bred," "an educated man," and "was educated" juxtaposed with references to "UCLA" implied Robinson graduated college.[128] Very few articles admitted that Robinson did not receive a degree, and even these extremely atypical accounts generally invented compelling excuses for Robinson's withdrawal from UCLA. The *Sporting News*, for example, gave the false impression that "he was a senior at University of California in Los Angeles" when he patriotically "enlisted" in the army.[129] Long after Robinson signed his first Organized Baseball career he candidly described his decision to quit college: "After two years at UCLA I decided to leave. I was convinced that no amount of education would help a black man get a job."[130] In 1945, such an admission by a black might have appeared as disillusionment with American values.

Likewise, journalistic ellipses and inaccuracies distorted Robinson's military record. Numerous articles noted that Robinson was a "former army lieutenant."[131] Yet sportswriters omitted the most significant aspect of Robinson's army career: he faced court-martial, "charged with willful disobedience and disrespect."[132] The episode evolved from Robinson's refusal to submit to racial discrimination on a bus at Camp Hood, and he was ultimately acquitted.[133] Acknowledging that baseball violated the liberal consensus was legitimate; the "right type" of black did not, however, suggest that national values were unjust. A number of journalists also attributed "31 months overseas service to Robinson although he remained stateside during the war."[134] The media Robinson was defender, not critic, of the American Creed.

"The right type" imagery enveloped every aspect of Robinson's personality and character. Almost uniformly the media portrayed Robinson's devotion to values sanctioned by the national consensus—patriotism, patience, self-denial, and hard work. Black newspapers often appeared even more eager than the general-circulation press to identify Robinson with these values. According to the *Pittsburgh Courier*, Robinson coupled gratitude toward Rickey with appreciation of country: "When I think of this opportunity, I'm very glad that I'm an American, because with all its so-called faults, it's the only place in the world where a young man can get such a chance—a chance to make a success out of life on his ability."[135]

Images of Robinson's "confidence," "self-assurance," "intelligent" manner, and determination to strive for his "best" appeared within a journalistic context that frequently alluded to the athlete's "level-headed," "shy," "well-behaved," "quiet," "modest," "responsible," and "sincere" demeanor.[136] Devoid of bravado, Robinson, as portrayed by the media, was "a high type of fellow" and "a high-class citizen."[137] His "good habits" and a "good character" encompassed abstinence from "drink or smoke."[138] Restraint and caution figured prominently among the traits newspapers attributed to this "fine type of young man."[139] The image of Robinson as deferential and soft-spoken that the press projected in 1945 differed markedly from the athlete's true self. Rickey and Robinson were thus successful in encouraging the press to view the athlete as "the right type" of black, one who sought to affirm, not challenge, American values. For the liberal consensus would reciprocate by demanding equality of opportunity for Robinson. In contrast the "bad nigger" imagery—carnality, miscegenation, bravado, iconoclasm, flamboyance, hostility toward whites, assertiveness, and irresponsibility—once embodied by boxer Jack Johnson, evoked fear from white Americans. Joe Louis, the current heavyweight champion, had already demonstrated the press's willingness to identity "the right type" of black with the liberal consensus.[140]

The American press displayed little sense of irony that a foreign country would host the integration of the national pastime. Some elements of the Canadian press did engage in self-congratulatory comparisons between the two nations, and the *Pittsburgh Courier* was also impressed by the benevolence of "French Canadian fans."[141] Nevertheless, typically American newspapers, including the black press, implicitly portrayed Montreal's ambiance as an extension of the racial practices normative north of the Mason-Dixon line. Newspapers perceived Rickey's assignment of Robinson to the Montreal Royals as an attempt to minimize southern interference with the integration of baseball. Both African American and general-circulation journals noted that, aside from the Daytona Beach training camp and a franchise in the border city of Baltimore, the Montreal Royals would avoid areas influenced by southern mores.[142] In addition to Montreal and Baltimore, the International League included Jersey City,

Newark, Toronto, Rochester, and Syracuse. Due to the nature of "International League membership," host cities other than Baltimore, reported the United Press, "were expected to show no unusual interest" in a black athlete.[143] Outside the South "the right type" of black, indicated journalists, could expect the fair trial dictated by national ideology.

While journalistic opinion overwhelmingly favored granting "the right type" of black "the chance . . . to make the big league grade," neither the general-circulation nor African American press suggested that a black athlete should receive special consideration.[144] The *St. Louis Argus* counseled blacks to remember that they shared in Robinson's testing and warned "Tan" fans of "Jackie's" against "loud provocative remarks" that would "stir race hatred."[145] The liberal consensus often encouraged those who espoused equal opportunity for Robinson to neglect the obvious: historical deprivation and endemic racism necessitated positive intervention on Robinson's behalf to create conditions amenable to equal opportunity. Endorsements for such positive intervention extended no further than supporting Rickey's pledge to take "adequate steps" against players in the Dodgers organization who "openly worked against Robinson."[146] Without hesitation, however, Rickey indicated that Robinson would not remain in Montreal "if he doesn't make good."[147] The press did not seek absolute assurances that Major League rosters would include black players. Media images reflected no significant pleas for guarantees in regard to outcome. Essentially the burden rested with Robinson to "go as far as he can."[148] A headline in the *Syracuse Herald-Journal*, for example, proclaimed, "Player Must Prove Worth on Diamond."[149] Although Arthur Siegel, *Boston Traveler* sportswriter, called the signing of Robinson "very nice," Siegel asked, "Is he (Robinson) of fast enough calibre to make the International League team?"[150] "Whether Jackie Robinson is or is not a good ballplayer," stated the *Saturday Review of Literature*, "is the only question at issue."[151] Robinson himself, suggested scribes, felt his fate should hinge only on his abilities.[152]

Nor did the black press ask any more for Robinson than a trial decided "solely on his baseball merits."[153] "Can Jackie Make the Grade?" questioned a *Detroit Tribune* article: "Branch Rickey may have opened the gates . . . but it is up to Jackie himself to prove whether he can stay inside the field."[154] The "End Jim Crow in Baseball Committee," stated the *Amsterdam News*, felt only a "competent Negro player who is qualified" should "play in the major leagues."[155] Likewise, the *Pittsburgh Courier* shared Rickey's aspiration that the Robinson's episode could become "just a matter of giving another young man a chance."[156] Unlike racial spokesmen of a latter generation the contemporary black press's interpretation of opportunity did not include quotas or affirmative action. All Negros wanted, indicated the *Michigan Chronicle*, was acceptance "on the basis of merit."[157]

The prevailing consensus largely checked the impulse to portray baseball segregation as a microcosm of American society. Instead the press generally depicted the Robinson signing as a stratagem for redeeming the national pastime. Relatively few media images suggested that the signing of Robinson was a disproportionately modest response to combat a problem so central to the social structure as racism. Even that media commentary most derisive of baseball's conservatism generally avoided placing such phenomena within a context that implied that the game merely reflected national life. Dave Egan, for example, of the *Boston Daily Record*, charged, "Generations of Jackie Robinsons now dead and gone must have smiled indulgently, when Christy Mathewson was called the greatest pitcher of all time, when they felt, all along the black Mathewson, Joe Mendez, was entitled to the place reserved for whites alone in the Hall of Fame."[158] Likewise, the *Cleveland Plain Dealer* believed, incorrectly as it turned out, that time had run out for the great Satchel Paige.[159] As the *Washington Post* noted, if Rickey truly regarded talent as the only germane criteria for evaluating an athlete, baseball integration might have occurred years ago.[160] These general-circulation newspapers, however, reminded readers that baseball had arrived too late for many great Negro athletes without characterizing national life off the diamond as suffused with racism.

Criticism of baseball's recalcitrance was more apparent in the black press than in the general-circulation press. Although accolades for Rickey appeared in the *Pittsburgh Courier*, this same newspaper carried lawyer Louis Nizer's statement "that what the Montreal Royals did in signing Jackie Robinson should have been done many years ago."[161] Earl Brown, a black columnist, expressed bitterness that "the fact that Jackie Robinson, a young Negro who is intellectually, culturally and physically superior to most white baseball players, has signed a contract to play in a minor league has caused a national sensation."[162] Similarly, the *Amsterdam News* printed the caveat of a civil rights group that "this is only the beginning."[163] Writing for the *Michigan Chronicle*, Horace White strongly argued that tokenism of the sort employed by Rickey exploited blacks:

> The minority groups usually succumb to these controls of the major-ity group. One way of succumbing to the controls of the majority is to bite for every sap that the majority group hands out. The assigning of a Negro to a berth in organized baseball is an example of what is meant here. The Negro population has been led to believe that Negroes have gained something by the very fact that the young man has been assigned to play with the Brooklyn Dodgers. Still, nothing has been gained.[164]

Even within the black press, however, White's tone was unusual. White clearly believed that the mere signing of a single black to Organized Baseball contract failed to address a problem with dimensions as broad as that of American racism. The extent of his resentment was atypical. In the black press strong disapproval of baseball's illiberalism almost always avoided suggesting a general disillusionment with American values.

The liberal consensus evident in press commentary on the signing of Robinson closely resembles the mid-1940s American Creed described by Gunnar Myrdal. Despite regional, class, and racial distinctions, Myrdal reported "that most Americans have most valuations in common." Myrdal argued that the prevalence of group and individual strife did not vitiate the consensus supporting the American Creed. Indeed, he perceived the need to reconcile belief with practice the nation's central dilemma. And no issue, Myrdal asserted, more vividly illuminated those contradictions than the status of the American Negro. World War II made domestic dis-sent from the tenets of the American Creed most difficult. "In fighting fascism and nazism," wrote Myrdal, "America had to stand before the whole world in favor of racial tolerance and cooperation and of racial equality" Even racists found it difficult to publicly disavow the creed.

Despite discrimination, blacks, argued Myrdal, endorsed the values of the American Creed: "Negroes show, by taking that position, that they have not lost their belief that ultimately the American Creed will come out on top." Northerners, contended Myrdal, exaggerated the South's contributions to contemporary racism. Perhaps even more significant, Americans, he reported, seriously minimized the extent of racial conflict in the North.[165]

Examination of press reaction to the Robinson signing suggests that Americans had little awareness of the extent and severity of racism in the nation's social fabric. The media fallaciously depicted prejudice as largely a regional problem. Race riots, housing discrimination, limited employment opportunities, and economic disparities make clear that the liberal consensus described a belief system rather than empirical phenomena.[166] Most Americans, however, mistook their values for both a system of belief and a method of operation while, in fact, it constituted only the former. By emphasizing unity, consensus, commonality and agreement, the liberal consensus obscured conflict. Analysis of the mid-1940s media attests to the pervasiveness of shared values. A people highly cognizant of their similarities found it difficult to acknowledge their differences. It was possible to acknowledge isolated defiance of the consensus, as with southern exceptionalism, but to acknowledge a sociological divergence from that belief system endemic to national life would throw into question the essence of the consensus, the belief that it could compel compliance from Americans. Furthermore, World War II encouraged Americans to view the United States in terms of characteristics antithetical to the racism and illiberalism of Nazi Germany. The crusade against Hitler nurtured a sense of national exaltation that acted as a deterrent against acknowledging the severity of America's domestic problems. Thus, in the mid-1940s a consensus about values flourished despite the existence of significant social conflict. Racism, a major contradiction to the consensus, could thus appear a manifestation of an atavistic region's refusal to conform to the consensus rather than as a criticism of the American way of life itself. Americans could then keep "to liberalism as a national creed, even if not as its actual way of life."[167]

In retrospect it is apparent that the signing of Robinson was primarily a symbolic breakthrough. Over the next decade integration in America proceeded slowly even within the context of baseball. Five years after the signing of Robinson, only a dozen blacks had played in the big leagues, and until late July 1959, fourteen years after the announced reintegration of baseball, the Boston Red Sox excluded blacks from their lineup. No blacks managed in the Major Leagues until 1975. Indeed, in the 1980s blacks remain grossly underrepresented at the coaching, managerial, executive, and entrepreneurial levels of baseball. And "stacking," the practice of concentrating black athletes at certain positions, still continues.[168] More significantly, the emphasis on symbolism obscured the irony that as the Dodgers accepted racial integration, de facto segregation increased in Brooklyn and in many other northern cities in the years following the signing of Robinson. The emphasis on symbolism detracted from attention to racism outside the South, contributing to the "invisible man" phenomena of the 1950s.

Extensive analysis of the contemporary print media reveals a nearly universal belief in the American Creed on both sides of the color line. As Myrdal recognized, blacks, as well as whites, tended to believe in the promise of the creed: "The American Negroes know that they are a subordinated group experiencing more than anybody else in the nation the consequence of the fact that the Creed is not lived up to in America. Yet their faith in the Creed is not simply a means of pleading their unfulfilled rights. They, like the whites, are under the spell of the great national suggestion. With one part of themselves they actually believe, as do the whites, that the Creed is ruling America."[169] Black and white journalists generally shared similar assumptions about the benevolence of the American Creed. Excerpts from two letters, one written to a black newspaper and the other to a general-circulation journal, reflect this common perspective. The *Chicago Defender* correspondent wrote, "The placement of a Negro in major league baseball is very encouraging. At last America's favorite pastime has accepted the democratic principle that accompanies the American ideal."[170] An epistle to the *Baltimore Morning Sun* articulated the same sentiment, "The recent signing of a Negro player by a major league baseball club was a definite step toward the attainment of that American way of life chartered by our forebears."[171] Unlike militants of the late 1960s, social critics of the mid-1940s reflected an ideological consensus; injustice, they believed, deviated from, rather than expressed, American values. Thus, "the right type" of black could redeem Organized Baseball from southern practices and allow the game to once again truly embody American values. Sportswriters were wrong, however. To deal with racism effectively, Americans had to acknowledge it as more than a regional malady. "The Negro problem," wrote Myrdal, "is an integral part of . . . the larger American civilization. It cannot be treated in isolation."[172]

The ideological consensus suggested by media reaction to the Robinson signing obviously did not signify social consensus. With the social science's "move away from a holistic view," "nowadays . . . the generalizations of consensus scholarship are out of fashion."[173] A generation of scholarship has ably documented the persistence of social conflict in the American past. Juxtaposing the near unanimity of the liberal response to the Robinson signing with the response to the race riots, housing and employment discrimination, the confinement of Japanese Americans to concentration camps, and other contemporary phenomena indicates consensus about values amid social conflict.[174] Unlike David Riesman, Daniel Bell, Sloan Wilson, William H. Whyte, and critics of the 1950s who found conformity a source of sterility, mediocrity, and stagnation, media reactions to the signing of Robinson criticized the particular, the South and Organized Baseball, while exalting the universal, the American Creed.[175] External conflict, according to Lewis Coser, stimulated internal cohesion, and World War II created a need to define America in terms diametrically opposed to those embodied by Nazi Germany.[176] My research for an earlier article, "The Athlete as Jewish Standard Bearer: Media Images of Hank Greenberg," identified a different relationship between the particular and the universal. During the divisive years of the Great Depression the particular, baseball, appeared an idealized League of Nations, able to diffuse social tensions while the universal, the larger American society, seemed to abound with unresolved strife.[177] Perhaps additional case studies will further clarify the symbiotic relationship between the American mind and perceptions of the national pastime.

NOTES

1. *New York Times*, November 18, 1981, 24; Roger Kahn, *The Boys of Summer* (New York: Harper & Row, 1971); Jules Tygiel, *Baseball's Great Experiment: Jackie Robinson and His Legacy* (New York: Oxford University Press, 1983).

2. Al-Tony Gilmore, *Bad Nigger: The National Impact of Jack Johnson* (New York: Kennikat, 1975); Richard Crepeau, *Baseball: America's Diamond Mind* (Orlando: University Presses of Florida, 1980); David K. Wiggins, "Wendell Smith, the *Pittsburgh Courier-Journal* and the Campaign to Include Blacks in Organized Baseball, 1933–1945," *Journal of Sport History* 10 (Summer 1983): 5–29; William Kelley, "Jackie Robinson and the Press," *Journalism Quarterly* 53 (Spring 1976): 137–39; Bill L. Weaver, "The Black Press and the Assault on Professional Baseball's 'Color Line,' October 1945–April 1947," *Phylon* 40 (Winter 1979): 303–17.

3. Harvey Frommer, *Rickey and Robinson: The Men Who Broke Baseball's Color Barrier* (New York: Macmillan, 1982), iii; John Higham and Paul Conkin, eds., *New Directions in American Intellectual History* (Baltimore: The Johns Hopkins University Press, 1979); Gunnar Myrdal with Richard Sterner and Arnold Rose, *An American Dilemma: The Negro Problem and Modern Democracy* (New York: Harper & Brothers, 1944), 4.

4. The author incurred debts to numerous libraries that made available bound, or, more commonly, microfilmed copies of old newspapers and magazines. Newspapers in cities with Major League teams generally exhibited the strongest interest in the signing of Robinson. Thus, this essay places primary emphasis on the black and general-circulation press of those cities.

5. *Baltimore Afro-American*, November 3, 1945, 23.

6. *Chicago Herald American*, October 24, 1945, 26.

7. *Boston Herald*, October 24, 1945, 24; *Detroit Tribune*, November 3, 1945, 11; *New York World Telegram*, October 25, 1945, 30.

8. Steven Riess, *Touching Base: Professional Baseball and American Culture in the Progressive Era* (Westport CT: Greenwood Press, 1980), 7; Richard Goldstein, *Spartan Seasons: How Baseball Survived the Second World War* (New York: 1980), 33.

9. *St. Louis Argus*, November 2, 1945, 17.

10. *Pittsburgh Courier*, November 3, 1945, 13.

11. *New York Amsterdam News*, November 3, 1945, 14.

12. Editorial, *Brooklyn Eagle*, October 25, 1945, 12.

13. Letter to the editor, *Detroit News*, October 30, 1945, 14.

14. *Pittsburgh Courier*, November 3, 1945, 13.

15. *Sporting News*, November 1, 1945, 6; *Philadelphia Record*, October 25, 1945, 18.

16. *New York World Telegram*, October 25, 1945, 30; *Washington Daily News*, October 25, 1945, 38.

17. Editorial, *St. Louis Post-Dispatch*, October 25, 1945, 26.

18. *New York World Telegram*, October 25, 1945, 30; *Washington Daily News*, October 25, 1945, 38; *Washington Evening Star*, October 25, 1945, 16.

19. *New York Daily Mirror*, October 25, 1945, 26.

20. *Montreal Gazette*, October 24, 1945, 14.

21. *Boston Daily Globe*, October 25, 1945, 14.

22. *Cleveland Press*, October 24, 1945, 16; *Montreal La Presse*, October 27, 1945, 36; *Washington Daily News*, October 24, 1945, 40.

23. *Pittsburgh Courier*, November 3, 1945, 12.

24. *Boston Daily Globe*, October 24, 1945, 17.

25. *Philadelphia Inquirer*, October 25, 1945, 24.

26. *Baltimore Afro-American*, November 10, 1945, 18; *Chicago Daily News*, October 31, 1945, 29; *Washington Post*, October 25, 1945, 22.

27. *Syracuse Herald Journal*, October 27, 1945, 6.

28. *Sporting News*, November 1, 1945, 12.

29. *Baltimore Afro-American*, November 3, 1945, 23; *Pittsburgh Courier*, December 1, 1945, 12.

30. *St. Louis Post-Dispatch*, October 28, 1945, B1.

31. *Detroit News*, October 25, 1945, 46.

32. *Philadelphia Inquirer*, October 24, 1945, 28.

33. *Sporting News*, November 1, 1945, 12.

34. *Cleveland Press*, October 24, 1945, 16.

35. *Washington Daily News*, October 24, 1945, 40.

36. *Washington Post*, October 27, 1945, 10.

37. *Brooklyn Eagle*, October 24, 1945, 17.

38. *Detroit News*, October 25, 1945, 46; *New York Herald Tribune*, October 25, 1945, 26; *New York Times*, October 24, 1945, 17.

39. *Boston Daily Globe*, October 25, 1945, 8; *Montreal Gazette*, October 25, 1945, 16; *Philadelphia Inquirer*, October 25, 1945, 24.

40. *Chicago Daily Tribune*, October 25, 1945, 29; *Cleveland Plain Dealer*, October 25, 1945, 16.

41. *New York Age*, November 17, 1945, 25.

42. *New York Amsterdam News*, November 3, 1945, 12.

43. *Chicago Daily News*, October 25, 1945, 33.

44. *New York Amsterdam News*, November 10, 1945, 10.

45. *New York Amsterdam News*, November 17, 1945, 24.

46. *St. Louis Globe Democrat*, October 25, 1945, 36.

47. *Washington Post*, October 27, 1945, 18; *New York World Telegram*, October 25, 1945, 30; *New York Sun*, October 25, 1945, 29.

48. *Chicago Defender*, November 3, 1945, 9; *Philadelphia Record*, October 25, 1945, 18; *Syracuse Post-Standard*, October 24, 1945, 10.

49. *New York Amsterdam News*, November 3, 1945, 12.

50. *Pittsburgh Courier*, November 24, 1945, 6.

51. *Philadelphia Tribune*, December 29, 1945, 9; *St. Louis Argus*, November 2, 1945, 17; *New York Amsterdam News*, November 3, 1945, 14.

52. Letter to editor, *Chicago Defender*, November 10, 1945, 14.

53. *Boston Herald*, October 26, 1945, 24.

54. *Baltimore Afro-American*, November 10, 1945, 18; *Boston Daily Globe*, October 24, 1945, 22; *Boston Guardian*, November 3, 1945, 4; Editorial, *Detroit Tribune*, November 3, 1945, 6; *New York Amsterdam News*, November 10, 1945, 13; *Brooklyn Eagle*, October 31, 1945, 17.

55. *Chicago Herald American*, October 26, 1945, 29; *New York Times*, October 25, 1945, 16.

56. *Boston Herald*, October 24, 1945, 24.

57. *Pittsburgh Courier*, November 3, 1945, 1; *Sporting News*, November 1, 1945, 12; *Chicago Daily News*, October 24, 1945, 26.

58. *Chicago Defender*, November 3, 1945, 7.

59. *Baltimore Morning Sun*, October 24, 1945, 1; *Chicago Daily News*, October 26, 1945, 33.

60. *Sporting News*, November 1, 1945, 4.

61. *Baltimore Morning Sun*, October 26, 1945, 20; *Chicago Herald American*, October 25, 1945, 22; *Cincinnati Enquirer*, October 26, 1945, 12.

62. *Sporting News*, November 1, 1945, 4.

63. *Baltimore Afro-American*, November 10, 1945, 18; Editorial, *Chicago Defender*, November 10, 1945, 14; *Detroit Tribune*, November 3, 1945, 6.

64. *Boston Chronicle*, November 3, 1945, 7; *New York Herald-Tribune*, October 25, 1945, 26; *Philadelphia Record*, October 25, 1946, 18.

65. *Boston Traveler*, October 24, 1945, 21; *Pittsburgh Post-Gazette*, October 25, 1945, 14; *Washington Daily News*, October 25, 1945, 38; *Washington Times Herald*, October 25, 1945, 38.

66. *New York Daily Mirror*, October 25, 1945, 34; *New York World Telegram*, October 24, 1945, 40.

67. *Chicago Daily News*, October 25, 1945, 33; *Cleveland Press*, October 24, 1945, 16; Editorial, *Washington Post*, October 27, 1945, 10; *Boston Chronicle*, November 3, 1945, 7.

68. *New York Age*, November 3, 1945, 6; *Philadelphia Tribune*, October 27, 1945, 1; *Brooklyn Eagle*, October 25, 1945, 17.

69. *St. Louis Globe Democrat*, October 25, 1945, C3.

70. *Sporting News*, November 1, 1945, 4.

71. *Boston Traveler*, October 24, 1945, 21.

72. *Detroit News*, October 25, 1945, 45; *Pittsburgh Post-Gazette*, October 25, 1945, 14; *St. Louis Star Times*, October 24, 1945, 21.

73. *Montreal La Presse*, October 25, 1945, 21.

74. *New York Daily Mirror*, October 25, 1945, 34; *Chicago Defender*, November 3, 1945, 9; *New York World Telegram*, October 24, 1945, 40.

75. *St. Louis Post-Dispatch*, October 25, 1945, C6.

76. *St. Louis Post-Dispatch*, October 28, 1945, B1; *Boston Daily Globe*, October 24, 1945, 22.

77. *Sporting News*, November 1, 1945, 6; *Sporting News*, November 29, 1945, 6; *New York World Telegram*, October 25, 1945, 30.

78. Editorial, *Detroit News*, October 26, 1945, 22.

79. *Boston Daily Globe*, October 25, 1945, 14.

80. *New York Age*, November 3, 1945, 6.

81. *Cleveland Press*, October 25, 1945, 26; *Detroit News*, October 25, 1945, 45; *Syracuse Herald Journal*, October 25, 1945, 38.

82. *Sporting News*, November 1, 1945, 5; *Chicago Defender*, November 3, 1945, 1.

83. *Michigan Chronicle*, November 3, 1945, 6.

84. *New York Amsterdam News*, November 3, 1945, 20.

85. *Boston Chronicle*, October 27, 1945, 1: *Boston Chronicle*, November 3, 1945, 7; *Boston Chronicle*, November 10, 1945, 7; *Boston Herald*, October 26, 1945, 26; *Chicago Defender*, November 3, 1945, 7; *Detroit Tribune*, November 24, 1945, 11; *New York Amsterdam News*, October 27, 1945, 1; *New York Amsterdam News*, November 3, 1945, 1, 17, 25; *New York Amsterdam News*, November 17, 1945, 24; *New York Herald Tribune*, October 26, 1945, 26; *New York Times*, October 25, 1945, 16; *Philadelphia Evening Bulletin*, October 26, 1945, 30; *Pittsburgh Courier*, November 3, 1945, 1, 4; *St. Louis Argus*, November 2, 1945, 17.

86. *Baltimore Morning Sun*, October 25, 1945, 20; *Philadelphia Inquirer*, October 25, 1945, 24; *Philadelphia Evening Bulletin*, October 25, 1945, 30.

87. *Philadelphia Inquirer*, October 24, 1945, 29.

88. *Pittsburgh Courier*, November 3, 1945, 1.

89. *Sporting News*, November 1, 1945, 4.

90. *Baltimore Morning Sun*, October 24, 1945, 15.

91. *Chicago Defender*, November 3, 1945, 1.

92. *Sporting News*, November 1, 1945, 12.

93. *Cleveland Press*, October 25, 1945, 26.

94. *Detroit News*, October 24, 1945, 21; *New York Post*, October 24, 1945, 68.

95. *Boston Daily Record*, October 25, 1945, 36.

96. *Baltimore Morning Sun*, October 24, 1945, 1.

97. *New York Post*, October 24, 1945, 68.

98. *New York Amsterdam News*, October 27, 1945, 1.

99. *Boston Guardian*, October 27, 1945, 1.

100. *New York Age*, November 10, 1945, 11.

101. *Baltimore Afro-American*, November 10, 1945, 18.

102. *Boston Chronicle*, November 3, 1945, 7.

103. *Boston Guardian*, October 27, 1945, 1.

104. *New York Amsterdam News*, October 27, 1945, 1.

105. *Pittsburgh Tribune*, December 29, 1945, 9.

106. *Pittsburgh Courier*, November 3, 1945, 12.

107. *Baltimore Afro-American*, November 3, 1945, 23; *Pittsburgh Courier*, November 10, 1945, 1; *Pittsburgh Courier*, November 3, 1945, 12.

108. *Baltimore Afro-American*, November 3, 1945, 1.

109. Wiggins, "Wendell Smith," 5–29.

110. *New York Times*, October 25, 1945, 17.

111. *New York Post*, October 25, 1945, 53.

112. *New York Age*, November 10, 1945, 11.

113. *Philadelphia Record*, October 24, 1945, 22.

114. *Pittsburgh Courier*, November 3, 1945, 12.

115. *Boston Christian Science Monitor*, October 27, 1945, 14; *Detroit News*, October 24, 1945, 21; *New York Sun*, October 24, 1945, 36.

116. *Sporting News*, November 1, 1945, 12.

117. *Syracuse Herald Journal*, October 27, 1945, 6; *Boston Daily Record*, October 24, 1945, 29; *New York Herald Tribune*, October 25, 1945, 26; *Brooklyn Eagle*, October 26, 1945, 15; Editorial, *Detroit News*, October 26, 1945, 22.

118. *New York Times*, October 24, 1945, 17; *Chicago Daily News*, October 25, 1945, 33; *Pittsburgh Sun Telegraph*, October 24, 1945, 20; *St. Louis Argus*, October 26, 1945, 1.

119. Tygiel, *Baseball's Great Experiment*, 58.

120. Tygiel, *Baseball's Great Experiment*, 67.

121. Robert Peterson, *Only the Ball Was White* (Englewood Cliffs, NJ: Prentice-Hall, 1970), 189–90: Arthur Mann, *Branch Rickey: American in Action* (Boston: Houghton Mifflin, 1957), 218.

122. *Michigan Chronicle* (Detroit), October 27, 1945, 1: *New York Daily Mirror*, October 24, 1945, 14; *Philadelphia Evening Bulletin*, October 24, 1945, 20.

123. *Sporting News*, March 20, 1971, 30.

124. *Philadelphia Record*, October 28, 1945, 23.

125. *Baltimore Afro-American*, November 3, 1945, 1; *Detroit Tribune*, November 17, 1945, 11; *Michigan Chronicle*, November 10, 1945, 6.

126. *Philadelphia Evening Bulletin*, October 26, 1945, 36.

127. *Washington Times Herald*, October 24, 1945, 22; *Washington Daily News*, October 25, 1945, 30; *New York Sun*, October 26, 1945, 34; *Detroit Times*, October 25, 1945, C18.

128. *Detroit Free Press*, October 27, 1945, 6; *Baltimore Afro-American*, November 10, 1945, 18; *New York Times*, October 25, 1945, 16.

129. *Sporting News*, November 1, 1945, 5.

130. Jackie Robinson and Alfred Ducket, *I Never Had It Made* (New York: G. P. Putnam's Sons, 1972), 23.

131. "A Negro on the Farm," *Newsweek* 26 (November 5, 1945): 95; "Jackie Robinson," *Life* 19 (November 26, 1945): 133; *Washington Daily News*, October 24, 1945, 40.

132. Jackie Robinson and Charles Dexter, *Baseball Has Done It* (Philadelphia: J. B. Lippincott, 1964), 37.

133. Jules Tygiel, "The Court-Martial of Jackie Robinson," *American Heritage* 35 (August-September 1984): 34–39.

134. *Philadelphia Evening Bulletin*, October 24, 1945, 20; *Philadelphia Tribune*, December 1, 1945, 13.

135. *Pittsburgh Courier*, November 3, 1945, 12.

136. *Baltimore Afro-American*, November 3, 1945, 1; *Chicago Herald American*, October 24, 1945, 26; *St. Louis Post-Dispatch*, October 24, 1945, C6; *Montreal La Presse*, October 30, 1945, 16; *New York Age*, November 3, 1945, 6; *New York Amsterdam News*, October 27, 1945, 5; *Brooklyn Eagle*, November 3, 1945, 6; *Philadelphia Evening Bulletin*, October 24, 1945, 20; *Pittsburgh Courier*, November 3, 1945, 12; *Sporting News*, November 1, 1945, 5.

137. *Pittsburgh Courier*, November 3, 1945, 1; *Brooklyn Eagle*, October 26, 1945, 15.

138. *Brooklyn Eagle*, October 25, 1945, 17; *New York Post*, October 25, 1945, 53; *Detroit Tribune*, November 17, 1945, 11; *Sporting News*, November 11, 1945, 6.

139. *Montreal Gazette*, October 24, 1945, 14; *Pittsburgh Courier*, November 3, 1945, 1.

140. Gilmore, *Bad Nigger*; Dominic Capeci and Martha Wilkerson, "Multifarious Hero: Joe Louis, American Society and Race Relations during World Crisis, 1935–1945," *Journal of Sport History* 10 (Winter 1983): 5.

141. *Montreal La Presse*, October 25, 1945, 20; *Montreal Gazette*, October 25, 1945, 16; *Sporting News*, November 1, 1945, 6; *Pittsburgh Courier*, November 10, 1945, 11.

142. *Montreal La Presse*, October 24, 1945, 18.

143. *Detroit News*, October 25, 1945, 45; *Syracuse Herald Journal*, October 25, 1945, 38.

144. *Pittsburgh Post-Gazette*, October 25, 1945, 6.

145. *St. Louis Argus*, November 2, 1945, 17.

146. *Detroit News*, October 25, 1945, 45; *New York Herald Tribune*, October 25, 1945, 26; *Brooklyn Eagle*, October 24, 1945, 17.

147. *Brooklyn Eagle*, October 25, 1945, 17; *New York Herald Tribune*, October 25, 1945, 26; *Boston Daily Globe*, October 24, 1945, 22.

148. *Washington Evening Star*, October 20, 1945, 12.

149. *Syracuse Herald Journal*, October 25, 1945, 38.

150. *Boston Traveler*, October 24, 1945, 20.

151. J. T. Winterich, "Playing Ball," *Saturday Review of Literature* 28 (November 24, 1945): 12.

152. *Chicago Herald American*, October 26, 1945, 12.

153. *Detroit Tribune*, November 3, 1945, 11.

154. *Detroit Tribune*, November 17, 1945, 11.

155. *New York Amsterdam News*, November 3, 1945, 14.

156. *Pittsburgh Courier*, November 3, 1945, 1.

157. *Michigan Chronicle*, November 3, 1945, 1.

158. *Boston Daily Record*, October 25, 1945, 36.

159. *Cleveland Plain Dealer*, October 26, 1945, 19.

160. *Washington Post*, October 27, 1945, 18.

161. *Pittsburgh Courier*, November 10, 1945, 11.

162. *New York Amsterdam News*, November 3, 1945, 12.

163. *New York Amsterdam News*, November 3, 1945, 14.

164. *Michigan Chronicle*, November 3, 1945, 6.

165. Myrdal, *An American Dilemma*, xlviii, 1004, 799, 600.

166. John Hope Franklin, *From Slavery to Freedom: A History of Negro Americans*, 5th ed. (New York: Alfred A. Knopf, 1980), 442–44.

167. Myrdal, *American Dilemma*, 12.

168. Merl Kleinknecht, "Integration of Baseball after World War II," *Baseball Research Journal* 12 (1983): 104–5; John Lucas and Ronald Smith, *Saga of American Sport* (Philadelphia: Lea & Febiger, 1978), 395.

169. Myrdal, *American Dilemma*, 4.

170. Letter to the editor, *Chicago Defender*, November 10, 1945, 14.

171. Letter to the editor, *Baltimore Morning Sun*, October 28, 1945, 12.

172. Myrdal, *American Dilemma*, liii.

173. John Ibsen, "Virgin Land or Virgin Mary? Studying the Ethnicity of White Americans," *American Quarterly* 33 (Bibliography 1981): 286.

174. David A. Noble, David A. Horowitz, and Peter N. Carroll, *Twentieth Century Limited: A History of Recent America* (Boston: Houghton-Mifflin, 1980), 298–303.

175. Alonzo Hamby, *The Imperial Years: The United States since 1939* (New York: Weybright and Tally, 1976), 225–35.

176. Lewis Coser, *The Functions of Social Conflict* (New York: Free Press, 1956).

177. William Simons, "The Athlete as Jewish Standard Bearer: Media Images of Hank Greenberg," *Jewish Social Studies* 44 (Spring 1982): 95–112.

8

"This Is It!"
The Public Relations Campaign Waged by Wendell
Smith and Jackie Robinson to Cast Robinson's
First Season as an Unqualified Success

BRIAN CARROLL

Few figures loom as large in American culture as Jackie Robinson, the
subject of poetry and a library shelf of books, Hollywood films and Broadway musicals, sermons and short stories, term papers and dramatic plays,
comic books and children's books. His journey to and with the Brooklyn
Dodgers is among America's most often told tales of heroism and courage,
and he has become shorthand for unflappable calm in the face of incredible adversity, including racism, irrational hatred, and even death threats.

This essay reveals and examines Jackie Robinson's little-known role
as columnist for the *Pittsburgh Courier* during his groundbreaking first
season with the Brooklyn Dodgers in 1947, the first for a black in Major
League Baseball since Moses Fleetwood Walker caught for the Toledo
Blue Stockings in 1884.[1] The twenty-five weekly columns are placed into
historical context by comparing their characterizations of the events of
that season against later, fuller, and in some ways more accurate accounts
from Robinson and others. Realizing that language is not neutral but active
and functional in shaping social realities and identities, this essay seeks to
hold up the picture or gallery of pictures Robinson wanted his readers to
see, pictures that framed the events of that first season. Framing theorists
have noted the power of media frames to "construct reality" for their
audiences through selection and emphasis of certain facts.[2] Identifying

what Robinson and longtime *Courier* sports editor Wendell Smith selected and emphasized, and what they cropped out of these pictures, will point to alternate texts and alternate meanings. Importantly, the absences and omissions could say as much as what Robinson did signify in presenting that first season in an unrelentingly positive light.

The columns are identified here as one prong of a three-pronged public relations campaign by Smith designed to ensure Robinson's success with the Dodgers and to leave no doubt in anyone's mind that the twentieth century's first black Major League Baseball player belonged in Brooklyn. The other prongs of Smith's campaign, in addition to ghostwriting the "Jackie Robinson Says" column examined here, were championing the player's every move in his own "Sports Beat" column in the *Courier*, which often ran on the same page as Robinson's, and ghostwriting Robinson's first autobiography, *Jackie Robinson: My Own Story*, written in 1947 and published the next year. This essay also compares that first autobiography with later, seemingly more candid, and clearly more comprehensive depictions of that first season in an effort to analyze how Robinson and Smith constructed a very particular social reality for *Courier* readers in 1947.[3]

In many ways, Jackie Robinson was the ideal candidate to break through baseball's color barrier. As UCLA's first four-sport letterman, Robinson was a national household name. Though he achieved most of his notoriety as an All-American running back for the Bruins football team, in a backfield he shared with another All-American, Kenny Washington, Robinson also was the Western Athletic Conference's most valuable player in basketball, and in track he set a conference record in the long jump. Importantly, with UCLA Robinson had already played on interracial teams. Though baseball seemingly was the sport with which he had the most difficulty in college, Robinson excelled in his one season of Negro league baseball, for the Kansas City Monarchs in 1945, and immediately in Major League Baseball's Minor Leagues. He led the Montreal Royals to the International League title in 1946, earning MVP honors along the way. During his ten-year career with the Dodgers, Robinson compiled a .311 batting average, became the National League's MVP in 1949, and played in six World Series and six All-Star games. Robinson was elected to baseball's Hall of Fame in 1962, the minimum five years after his retirement from the sport.

In characterizing Smith's and Robinson's efforts as a public relations campaign, this essay considers or regards Smith as a sort of press agent for Robinson, a role explained in the "Press Agentry/Publicity" model of public relations, one of the four classically understood approaches to or models of public relations.[4] In this approach, complete truth is not essential but is seen as subordinate to "spreading the faith" in the person or organization, an imperative compatible with and in some ways explained by the well-documented history of social and political activism in the black press.[5] Smith likely would not characterize his efforts as anything other than journalism, albeit a form or brand of activist journalism for which black papers were well known.

Literature Review

With ample help from black sportswriters, Jackie Robinson wrote extensively about himself, producing no fewer than four autobiographies. They were published in 1948, 1960, 1964, and 1972.[6] These accounts provided him the opportunity to revise depictions of his life and exploits, including those of his momentous first season in the Major Leagues. The Cairo, Georgia, native also has been researched and written about as extensively as any figure in American sports history, and across many academic disciplines. Robinson's column for the *Pittsburgh Courier* that first season in Brooklyn, however, has been only rarely mentioned and never systematically examined or analyzed. If journalism is in fact a first draft of history, as many have called it, Robinson's *Courier* columns represent the first rough draft of his own momentous history.[7]

The *Courier*, which in 1947 was a two-million-dollar business and the largest black newspaper in the country, gave Robinson the opportunity to reach more than 350,000 subscribers throughout the country, readers who counted on the black weekly to champion their causes.[8] Journalism historians David Wiggins, Chris Lamb, and Glen Bleske are among those who have examined this activism in the context of professional baseball.[9] These scholars deserve a great deal of credit for restoring Smith's and the

Courier's prominent place in the oft-told narrative of Robinson's relatively quick flight into the Major Leagues.[10] In examining *Courier* coverage of baseball between 1933 and 1945, Wiggins charted *how* the newspaper and Smith waged the campaign, finding the *Courier*'s approach to have been tactical, arranging player tryouts and meetings with baseball's officials, for example, as well as ideological and rhetorical.[11] In its examination of Smith's and Robinson's collaboration, this study supports Wiggins's findings.

Bleske's research complements Wiggins's by isolating and examining Smith's tactics to force baseball's desegregation. Bleske found that Smith used traditional news reporting to keep readers updated on progress. He noted Smith's tone and style as optimistic, observing that Smith routinely omitted racial prejudices from his coverage, a pattern this essay finds in Robinson's columns, as well. Bleske also described as tactical Smith's moralizing in instructing black fans as to how to behave at the ballpark.[12] Bleske and Lamb analyzed variances between the mainstream press and black newspapers in coverage of Robinson's debut in the Major Leagues. They found wide gulfs, determining the black press to have been much more cognizant of the historical context of Robinson's membership in a previously all-white league, a finding that helps explain Smith's role in ghostwriting Robinson's columns and his first autobiography.[13] Black sportswriters and editors "wrote with more emotion, emphasized the historical significance of the story, and included more personal insights on how the prospects . . . were coping," according to the authors, a finding supported by the research of Pat Washburn and, separately, of Bill Simons.[14] Lamb and Bleske found that the black weeklies "gave Robinson's first game more attention, stressed its historical importance, and mentioned that the ballplayer was cheered by all spectators, black and white."[15]

Bill Weaver in 1979 became one the first historians to examine the response of the black press to Rickey's and the Dodgers' decision to sign Robinson. Weaver described the responses as falling into one of four categories: comments on the breakthrough's significance, expressions of appreciation for Rickey's actions, expressions of racial hopes pinned on Robinson, and analyses of the intense pressure placed on Robinson to succeed.[16] Weaver also contributed one of the first examinations of the black press's columns and stories, finding that the weeklies urged fans to "keep [their] mouths closed and give Jackie the chance to PROVE he's major league caliber!" as Weaver quoted from the *Courier*.[17] The paternalistic attitudes of the press toward readers are an important thread here, too, particularly those communicated to readers of the *Courier*. Historian Jules Tygiel, who was among the nation's foremost Robinson scholars when he died in 2009, gave due credit in several of his books to Wendell Smith, *Afro-American* sportswriter Sam Lacy, Harlem *People's Voice* sportswriter Joe Bostic, and white sportswriters brave enough to join the crusade. For more than twenty years Tygiel was alone in recognizing the black sportswriters as having been victimized themselves by baseball's segregationist practices.[18]

All twenty-five of Robinson's eight- to ten-column-inch columns written for the *Courier* that inaugural season were examined, the first appearing on March 29, two weeks prior to the start of the 1947 season, and the last appearing at the end of the regular season on September 27.[19] Robinson did not continue the column into the postseason, during which the Dodgers lost the World Series to the New York Yankees four games to three, though he did write an advance story on the series, calling it "my greatest thrill."[20] Because the columns were written for a weekly newspaper and ghostwritten by *Courier* sports editor Wendell Smith, they likely are carefully considered texts, planned and shaped by Robinson and Smith.

Historical Background

In the fight for equal rights, Jack Roosevelt Robinson, a groundbreaking athlete and, after his playing career, an influential spokesman in the civil rights movement, proved a natural partner with the *Courier*, the nation's leading black weekly in 1947. By the time "Jackie Robinson Says" appeared in the paper's sports section, the *Courier* had firmly established its credentials as a fighting press. The weekly's "Double V" campaign during World War II, joined by black newspapers throughout the country, demanded that black soldiers risking their lives for democracy and victory abroad receive full citizenship rights, or victory, at home, as well.[21] Long before World

War II, in 1932, the *Courier* urged readers to switch from the Republican Party to the ticket of Franklin Roosevelt, and just a year earlier the paper had attacked the wildly popular *Amos 'n' Andy* radio show for the program's stereotypical and derogatory depictions of blacks.[22]

Robinson's and Smith's columns should be read within this context of social and political activism; they were written at a time of widespread race inequalities following a war fought to secure democracy on foreign soil. One scholar called this postwar period "an era of denial of diversity that lasted until the 1970s," a time of race-based discrimination and segregation in education, business, and social life.[23] The very existence of a vibrant black press points to a complex meshwork of discriminatory practices and of ideologies "directly enacted by text and talk" against minority groups by derogation, intimidation, inferiorization, and exclusion in everyday conversations and institutional dialogues.[24] The black press's vibrancy resulted in part from this exclusion as it served as a voice for the nation's black communities. In 1947, black newspapers were "understandably optimistic about the future," according to journalism historian Patrick Washburn, especially in fiscal terms.[25]

Because a discriminating, excluding dominant group does not normally admit the wrong in its practices, accounts of everyday discrimination from minorities themselves are important. Robinson's column represents this vantage point through most of the 1947 baseball season as he entered a sphere of racial and social consensus subscribed to by various elites, including politicians and the white-owned media, and baseball's Major League owners, officials, and white players. Though a wealth of scholarship addresses how the media systematically exclude minorities, racialize economic and social problems, and portray race and ethnic conflict, this research relies largely on the press. Individual writers and the texts and talk they produce have not been extensively studied. This project is part of an effort to correct this imbalance.

Serving as a sort of model for examining the discourse of a representative individual is the voluminous research on Martin Luther King Jr.'s "Letter from a Birmingham Jail," a letter of protest and statement of hope written in April 1963 that has fostered rich scholarship in rhetorical theory and criticism, social theory, and discourse. King had help editing the letter from local civil rights leaders, just as Robinson had Wendell Smith, himself a former black baseball player from Detroit, to edit and ghostwrite "Jackie Robinson Says."[26] A graduate of historically black West Virginia State College, Smith roared onto the baseball scene and into the sports pages of the *Pittsburgh Courier* in October 1937, writing with a force and flair that immediately distinguished him from his colleagues. Unlike Ches Washington, whom Smith would replace as the *Courier*'s sports editor in 1938, less than a year after arriving at the paper, the young writer did not reflexively accept segregation and with it the implicit subordination of blacks. Smith and his counterpart and contemporary at the Baltimore *Afro-American*, Sam Lacy, not only covered Negro league baseball's efforts to force integration, they became directly involved themselves. Smith's role as a sort of press agent to or for Robinson is evidence of this activism and intervention. In 1948, based on his work on the "Jackie Robinson beat," Smith became the *Chicago American*'s first black sportswriter and one of the first at a mainstream daily anywhere.[27]

In addition to his duties as sports editor for the *Courier*, "Smitty" worked for Branch Rickey and the Brooklyn Dodgers. Rickey added Smith to the Dodgers payroll after signing Robinson in October 1945, matching the *Courier*'s salary of fifty dollars per week. In their arrangement, Smith served as a companion to Robinson, securing accommodations and finding eateries on the road when whites-only hotels and restaurants barred the player, as was routine that first Major League season.[28] Smith, who later described himself as "Robinson's Boswell," also reported back to Rickey as a sort of talent scout for the Dodgers covering the Negro leagues, a role in which the writer took particular pride.[29] Unmentioned but implicit were Smith's services as a public relations practitioner on behalf of Rickey, Robinson, and the Dodgers, turning his and Robinson's weekly columns into regular, frequent forums for promoting the integration of baseball and, more particularly, Rickey's program for achieving it. This program included—in fact, centered on—Robinson's contrived gentle demeanor and ability to repeatedly turn the other cheek. In Smith's and Robinson's columns, the famously proud player comes off as unfazed by his victimization, the insults and isolation bouncing off like bullets shot at Superman. Robinson's "aw, shucks, everything is swell" serenity proved merely an illusion, however, or a carefully crafted façade to reduce potential causes—real or perceived—of failure, foment, or bad publicity.

Smith's approach to Robinson's first season mirrored his strategy to force baseball to integrate employed during a more than ten-year campaign that culminated with Rickey's signing of Robinson in October 1945. In his recollections years later, to Chicago sportswriter Jerome Holtzman, Smith said, "I always tried to keep [the crusade to integrate baseball] from becoming a flamboyant or highly militant thing. There were people who wanted to become a part of it, to push it faster. Fortunately, I managed to keep them away. If more people had been involved, it would have done more harm than good. That's one of the reasons we succeeded. We always tried to play it low-key."[30]

In Wendell Smith's April 12 column, the first published after the promotion of Robinson to the Dodgers had been announced in a press box in Daytona Beach, Florida, the long-time crusader for integration made it clear how high the stakes were, and not just for Jack Robinson: "If Robinson fails to make the grade, it will be many years before a Negro makes the grade. This is IT!"[31] Robinson recognized this responsibility, as well, and immediately. In his own *Courier* column the week prior, the then-Montreal Royal wrote, "I want to prove to those who resent me or other members of my race that we are not bad people at all. I want to prove that God alone has the right to judge a person."[32]

Smith had worked for more than a decade, both in print and behind the scenes, to make Robinson's entry into Major League Baseball possible. These efforts included arranging a tryout for Robinson and two other Negro league players with the Boston Red Sox in February 1945. For Smith, 1947 indeed was "IT!" which explains the boosterism in his own column, the ghostwriting he did for Robinson's first autobiography, *My Own Story*, and the ghostwriting he is believed to have done in and for Robinson's *Courier* column. There is no way to determine how much of Robinson's columns the player actually wrote himself. Neither Smith nor Robinson ever described how they worked together on the *Courier* coverage. Robinson's columns do have telltale signs of Smith's intimate and regular involvement, however. For example, Smith frequently picked up on coverage of black baseball in the white-owned press, excerpting and celebrating it in his own columns. This is a hallmark of Robinson's first autobiography, which Smith ghostwrote, and of several of his columns that first year with the Dodgers. The reflexive celebration of notice in the mainstream press is not found, however, in subsequent Robinson autobiographies, books Smith had no involvement in writing. Jonathan Eig flatly states in his biography of the player that "Robinson's [column] was ghostwritten by Wendell Smith," though the author provides no concrete evidence.[33]

For athletes writing newspaper columns at that time, it was typical for the ghostwriters they hired to do most of the writing.[34] In his third autobiography, *I Never Had It Made*, Robinson says he was "not ashamed of the fact that I am not a professional writer. I told [Harlem bookstore owner Lewis Micheaux] that I never hid the fact that Al Duckett ghosted my [*New York Amsterdam News*] column, but added that it was a joint effort, that the column never reflected anything that wasn't sincerely my conviction."[35] Robinson's columns likely were conceived as one piece of Smith's public relations campaign on behalf of the player, the newspaper, Rickey, and the Dodgers. The persuasive goals of the column perhaps explain why Robinson's accounts lack any real indication of the horrors of that first season, or of the very real possibility that he could fail. Robinson's Dodger story simply had to have a happy ending, and in the Robinson version, the story certainly had a Hollywood beginning.

"Next time I go to a movie and see a picture of a little ordinary girl become a great star, I'll believe it," he wrote in the April 19 *Courier*. "And whenever I hear my wife read fairy tales to my little boy, I'll listen. I know now that dreams do come true. I know because I am now playing with the Brooklyn Dodgers of the big leagues!"[36] The column's wide-eyed enthusiasm celebrated Robbie's introduction to the Dodger clubhouse at Ebbets Field and, inside that clubhouse, the "fellows on the club willing to help me. Eddie Stanky, a great ball player, helped me on the first day. Others have advised me and coached me since."[37]

If only this sense of fraternity had been real. As early as spring training in balmy Cuba and Panama, Robinson had noted the frigid reactions to his presence and to the possibility he might join the Dodgers, antagonism he omitted from his reports filed for the *Courier* from spring training.[38] He could not have been surprised, however. Shortstop Pee Wee Reese, the team leader, hailed from Kentucky. Outfielder Dixie Walker, the team's best hitter and highest-paid player, owned a hardware store back home in Alabama, where he grew up and where Stanky, the second baseman, spent his off-seasons.[39] Bobby Bragan, a utility infielder and catcher, also grew up in Alabama, where he was encouraged to believe in white supremacy.[40] Atlanta-born Hugh Casey, the team's top relief pitcher, owned a popular southern-style restaurant in Brooklyn, where the team would often gather after games, and he once told Robinson while playing cards on the train that when he ran into some bad luck back home in Georgia, "I used to go and find me the biggest, blackest nigger woman I could find and rub her teats to change my luck."[41] Pitching ace Kirby Higbe once told a radio interviewer that part of his pitching prowess could be traced back to his days growing up in South Carolina "throwing rocks at Negroes."[42]

Smith acknowledged the potential problems among Robinson's teammates but did not connect them to regional differences in ideology or upbringing. Eddie Stevens, the player Robinson would have to replace at first base to break into the starting lineup, was "definitely against Jackie" for that reason, Smith wrote. Stanky appeared to Smith to be prejudiced "but will play with him." Walker clearly was "against Robinson . . . but will tolerate him," while Reese's attitude had not yet been "revealed in any way."[43] Smith omitted, as did Robinson, a player protest against Robinson's promotion that was organized by Walker, who asked to be traded rather than play with Robinson. The protest, which Walker later called "the stupidest thing [I'd] ever done," was joined by most of the team's large southern bloc, as well as by Pennsylvania-born Carl Furillo, the Dodgers right fielder.[44] *Daily Worker* sports editor Lester Rodney in New York reported hearing Furillo say, "I ain't going to play with no niggers."[45]

In Robinson's contemporary version, however, the Dodgers, including those from the South, had shown themselves to be a "swell bunch. . . . We work together swell, all of them—Reese, Higbe, Stanky—they're wonderful guys to play ball with," he told the New York labor newspaper the *Union Voice*.[46] The "alleged [player] strikes" and some "threatening letters" had not distracted or deterred him, he wrote in his own column, so busy as he was playing baseball. "Everyone I have come in contact with since I joined the Dodgers has been all right," he fibbed in May.[47] The "alleged strikes" reference is Robinson's only acknowledgement of the petition drive, an incident he referred to equally opaquely in his first autobiography, or to the Phillies players' intent to boycott a series in Philadelphia against the Dodgers because of Robinson's presence. The Dodgers players opposed to his promotion, players he did not name, "suggested an organized move to keep me off the club," a move that was "quickly squelched."[48] Oddly, to support his claim of acceptance by teammates, Robinson cited in his own autobiography an Associated Press report of clubhouse harmony rather than testifying to it himself, a discursive move likely attributable to Smith, who closely monitored Robinson coverage in the mainstream press. The April 26 AP wire story declared that Robinson's teammates "have accepted him quite as readily as the Minor Leaguers did at Montreal last year.... There has been no unpleasantness about Robinson's advent."[49]

Perhaps no incident better demonstrates the rhetorical aims of Smith and Robinson that first season, or the illusion of reports like the wire story in April, than does the first visit to Brooklyn by the Philadelphia Phillies in late April. And perhaps no incident did more to give Robinson and his southern teammates a common enemy, an opposing "other" to galvanize the club. Led by their infamously racist manager, Birmingham, Alabama, native Ben Chapman, the visiting Phillies began riding Robinson long before the game even began, during batting practice. Chapman shouted, "Nigger, go back to the cotton fields where you belong." During the game, spewing from the Phillies dugout were catcalls and epithets:

"They're waiting for you in the jungles, black boy!"

"Hey, coon, did you always smell so bad?"

"Go back to the bushes!"

"Hey, snowflake, which one of you white boys' wives are you dating tonight."[50]

Over the course of the three games, during which Phillies players brought watermelon, fried chicken, and pork chops into the dugout, Chapman barked about Robinson's thick lips, a supposedly extra-thick Negro skull, and sores and diseases he said Robinson's teammates would be infected with, and he accused Robinson with breaking up his own Dodgers.[51] For his part, Robinson remained silent, even in print, in keeping with Rickey's "turn-the-other-cheek" strategy that first season. In his May 3 column, Robinson wrote that the bench jockeying "really didn't bother me.... The things the Phillies shouted at me from their bench have been shouted at me from other benches." In fact, the taunts "sound just the same in the big leagues as they did in the minor league," he wrote.[52] Smith, too, was uncharacteristically silent, using his May 3 column to instead reminisce about Robinson's Red Sox tryout two years prior.[53] In this same column, Smith went through Robinson's mail, indicating the intimacy of and partnership between the two men. In celebrating the "500 congratulatory messages" and excerpting some of the more memorable lines, Smith wrote nothing of the hate mail and death threats Robinson was receiving, threats that police had just begun investigating at Rickey's request.[54]

In his first autobiography, Robinson admitted to nearly losing his head against the Phillies and "taking a sock at one of them."[55] But he described Chapman as "a very able manager" and the Phillies as "great bench-riders." In a later autobiography twenty-five years after the fact, Robinson provided a more candid description of what he thought at the time. Recalling periods of "deep depression," Robinson remembered thinking to himself,

To hell with Mr. Rickey's "noble experiment." . . . It's clear it won't succeed. . . . My best is not good enough for them. . . . To hell with the image of the patient black freak I was supposed to create. I could throw down my bat, stride over to that Phillies dugout, grab one of those white sons of bitches, and smash his teeth in with my despised black fist.[56]

In his 1972 autobiography, which came out shortly before his and Smith's deaths that same year, Robinson said that "of all the unpleasant days in my life, [that first game against the Phillies] brought me nearer to cracking up than I ever had been."[57]

Though the abuse must have been terrible, and surely it contributed to a 0-for-20 hitless streak in April, a month during which he hit just .225, the persecution united the Dodgers around Robinson, if not with him. Of all people, Dixie Walker, a fellow Alabaman and close friend of the Philadelphia manager, criticized Chapman's and his team's behavior.[58] Eddie Stanky is believed to have yelled into the Philly dugout, "Listen, you yellow-bellied cowards. Why don't you yell at someone who can answer back?" (Other accounts of that first season, including one of Robinson's own, have Stanky saying something like this later in the season.)[59]

If Smith and Robinson were engaged in a public relations campaign to cast or frame that first season as a success, when the Dodgers traveled to Philadelphia on May 10, the team's first trip out of New York that season, the barrier breakers were walking onto hostile territory and into someone else's publicity stunt. The Phillies organization threatened not to take the field if Brooklyn brought its "nigger with the rest of the team," a sentiment attributed alternately by Harold Parrott, Brooklyn's traveling secretary, to Phillies general manager Herb Pennock and by Robinson to Phillies owner Bob Carpenter.[60] The Phillies players, including seven from the South, also threatened to boycott the series. Chapman clearly did not want to play against Robinson in Philadelphia either.[61] With Rickey threatening to claim any defaulted games as wins by forfeit, however, the games would go on.[62]

Robinson reported to Shibe Park that day from the Attucks hotel, one of the first establishments in Philadelphia to desegregate. The Benjamin Franklin Hotel had denied a room to Robinson even though the Dodgers had reserved rooms weeks in advance and despite the fact that Robinson's presence in baseball could hardly have been unknown to management. "Don't bring your team back here while you have any Nigras with you," the hotel's manager screeched, according to Parrott.[63] Robinson arrived at the ballpark and, in a publicity stunt brokered by Pennock and Rickey, was told to pose with Chapman—not because Chapman wished to apologize or had had any change of heart but simply to calm the controversy Chapman himself had caused with his bench jockeying.

Though they were asked to shake hands for the photo, Chapman refused. As a compromise the two held the same bat on the dugout steps. More than a dozen years later, Robinson recalled the humiliation of the photo shoot as the one occasion during which "I had more difficulty swallowing my pride" than any other, an occasion on which he was asked to pose for a photograph "with a man for whom I had the lowest regard."[64] In their weekly columns, both Robinson and Smith withheld complaint. Smith didn't comment on the Phillies series at all, while Robinson was ebullient in his weekly space: "I was glad to cooperate and when we got over to the Phillies' dugout, Chapman came out and shook my hand," Robinson lied in his *Courier* space. "Chapman impressed me as a nice fellow and I don't really think he meant the things he was shouting at me the first time we played in Philadelphia."[65]

A nice fellow? Philly pitcher Freddie Schmidt said he heard Chapman mutter during the photo shoot, "Jackie, you know, you're a good ballplayer, but you're still a nigger to me."[66] And when the game began, Chapman and his charges resumed their racist player riding, something he had no regrets about as long as twenty-five years after the fact.[67] In his 1948 autobiography, Robinson credited the Phillies for keeping "their verbal blows above the belt" during the series in Philadelphia, and the photo shoot for quieting the controversy. He also reprinted the Phillies' press statement from Chapman, knowing it to be a charade: "Jackie has been accepted in baseball and we of the Philadelphia organization have no objection to his playing and wish him all the luck we can."[68]

At the same time that the Dodgers wrangled with the Phillies, police began investigating hate mail sent to Jackie and Rachel Robinson at their McDonough Street address in Brooklyn, letters that included venomous race-based hate, a threat to kidnap the couple's son, Jackie Jr., and two in particular that threatened Jackie Sr.'s life. Smith omitted these from his April 26 column cataloging the player's fan mail, and Robinson in his first autobiography made only a passing reference to some "ugly letters" he turned over to Rickey at Rickey's request.[69] In his column, Robinson fielded the incident like a routine ground ball, saying that the hate mail likely was sent by "scatter-brained people who just want something to yelp about."[70] Only much later, in a 1964 autobiography, did Robinson reveal that one of the letters included a threat to shoot Robinson "if I dared play in a doubleheader against the Reds in Crosley Field."[71]

After uneventful trips to Pittsburgh and Cincinnati, cities in which everyone, according to Robinson in his column, "was very nice," the team returned to Brooklyn to play the St. Louis Cardinals just as stories broke about another Robinson-inspired boycott, this time by the Cardinals.[72] No Cardinal ever admitted to proposing the boycott or to seriously considering participating in one, but the rumors were thick enough to elicit from National League president Ford Frick a swift and definitive response, as well as a promise to suspend anyone who boycotted or struck:

> You will find that the friends you think you have in the press box will not support you, that you will be outcasts. I do not care if half the league strikes. Those who do it will encounter quick retribution. . . . This is the United States of America, and one citizen has as much a right to play as another. The National League will go down the line with Robinson no matter what the consequence.[73]

Again, Robinson and Smith, individually and collectively, simply brushed it off. In his first autobiography, Robinson credited the "short-lived" challenge with further solidifying his status on the team because of the solidarity it encouraged among his Dodger teammates. In his column, Robinson wrote that the Cardinals "were nice to me. . . . They seem to be a regular bunch of fellows and I still refuse to believe that they didn't want to play against me. . . . The issue wasn't really anything at all."[74] For Smith, the rumors were an opportunity to breathlessly praise Frick's statement, just as he had trumpeted Commissioner Happy Chandler's rebuke of the Phillies, which had been issued a week earlier, as "one of the most emphatic, clear-cut, and uncompromising mandates ever issued in the history of baseball."[75] Of Chandler's declaration, Smith wrote that it marked the "first time in the history of organized baseball that the commissioner has taken action in matters of a racial nature" and described it as "one of the most momentous steps he has taken."[76]

Both Robinson and Smith eagerly praised the Cardinals later, in June, when it was Brooklyn's turn to visit St. Louis. Robinson saluted the Cardinals, including catcher Joe Garagiola, who had not passed up an opportunity to ride, chide, or insult Robinson from his perch behind the plate. "They are a swell bunch of fellows," Robinson told Smith. "They treated me so nice I was actually surprised."[77] In his own column that same week, Robinson described the Cardinals as "classy club," but otherwise wrote only about the game action.[78] Robinson's columns for the rest of the season followed suit, focusing on the action on the field rather than relations with teammates or experiences in ballparks on the road. He also used his column to champion the signings by Major League teams of other black players, usually for their farm systems, including Roy Campanella, Sammy Gee, and Dan Bankhead (Dodgers); Willard Brown and Hank Thompson (St. Louis Browns); and, most spectacularly, Larry Doby (Cleveland Indians), who became the American League's first black player in July.

It was left to Smith, then, to demonstrate Robinson's seamless inclusion into the Dodgers' inner circle, his becoming "just one of the boys," as Smith liked to put it. Critical for the success of the great experiment, or perception of success, was proving that integration could occur without convulsion, without wrecking or dividing the team. Many naysayers had predicted just such an implosion, including Chapman, Yankees president Lee MacPhail, and even an attorney from Louisiana, who took the time to write to Rickey:

> Your decision to break big league tradition by playing a negro on the Brooklyn team is indeed deplorable. In fact, it is inconceivable that any white man would force a Negro on other white men as you have done. . . . I tell you Rickey anything the Negro touches he ruins and your club will be no exception.[79]

Reporting from St. Louis, Smith declared Robinson "definitely now one of the Dodgers. He is 'one of the boys' and treated that way by his teammates. No one on the team seems to resent his presence anymore, and Jackie seems to have won them over simply by being himself."[80] Of course, in swallowing his pride, in smiling at Chapman and Garagiola, in lying about the effects of the insults and humiliation, about the sense of threat in some of the mail he received, in eating and sleeping in separate quarters, Robinson was anything but himself. It was essential, however, at least to Smith, that Robinson be seen as a full-fledged Dodger, as being treated no differently than any other player. In his June 28 column, for example, Smith declared the Robinson "circus" over and that the player's trial with the Dodgers could no longer be considered "a side show," Robinson no longer a carnival "freak" or "two-headed man."[81] Finally, in June, a month during which Robinson hit a sparkling .381, Robinson belonged.

The centerpiece in Smith's case that Robinson had achieved a sort of normalcy as a big league ballplayer puts the sportswriter's persuasive goals on bald display. With some time to kill before an exhibition game against a Dodgers farm team in Danville, Illinois, Smith and Robinson decided to play some golf; both were good, avid golfers. As luck would have it, the two ended up teeing off behind Dodgers Pee Wee Reese, pitcher Rex Barney, and Harold Parrott, as well as *New York Times* reporter Roscoe McGowen. Though golfing's etiquette required the four to allow the two to play through, Reese invited the two to join his foursome, "against the rules," as Smith put it. In his sunny account, the gesture of friendship and inclusion proved without a doubt that Robinson had been accepted, ignoring the fact that far better proof would have been inviting Robinson and perhaps Smith along in the first place. None of the players, after all, had at any point during the season invited Jackie and Rachel to have dinner or go to the movies, and Rachel was without exception excluded from the circle of friends that united Dodgers players' wives. Throughout the round of golf, Robbie's Dodger teammates "joked and kidded with Jackie and he did the same with them. They were three baseball players and without actually saying it to each other, they admitted that each had something in common."[82] Robinson did not mention the golf outing in his own column.

The fiscal impact of Robinson on the Dodgers and on Major League Baseball in general provided Smith with an important piece of his program of persuasion, as economics did in each and every crusade and campaign

Smith waged.[83] As Robinson wrote in one of his autobiographies, blacks recognized that "money is America's God."[84] The *Courier* sports editor often led Dodger coverage with attendance figures, and the passage perhaps most often quoted from his weekly *Courier* articles, a snatch of verse from his May 31 column, highlights Robbie's box office draw:

Jackie's nimble,
Jackie's quick,
Jackie's making
The turnstiles click![85]

For the first three games of the year, exhibitions against the Yankees, Smith pointed out that nearly eighty thousand had filed into the intimate confines of Ebbets Field, making Robinson the "Peepul's Choice." A five-column banner headline on page one of the April 19 *Courier* trumpeted "Jackie Robinson Packing 'Em In," and Smith's story flatly stated, "Robinson is the attraction." The writer correctly predicted that Robinson would be "the best drawing card in baseball during the 1947 season."[86] The *Courier* headline for the Robinson's first game in Chicago was "46,572 Pack Wrigley Field."[87] Smith was merely highlighting the economic facts, leveraging them for future gains. On opening day April 15 against the Boston Braves in Brooklyn, nearly three-fifths of the attendees were black, meaning that only approximately twelve thousand white fans were on hand to twenty-seven thousand black patrons.[88] The Dodgers surpassed one million paid fans in July, faster than any other club, while Ebbets Field finished the season with 1.8 million tickets sold, more than any other National League ballpark ever. On the road, Robinson helped the Dodgers pull in 1.9 million, also a league record.

Toward the end of the regular season, when it became clear the Dodgers would take the National League pennant for a chance to face the Yankees in the World Series, Smith began lobbying for Robinson as Rookie of the Year, a campaign he kicked off in the August 9 issue of the *Courier*, knowing that the more accolades Robinson could earn, the stronger the case for baseball's further integration would become.[89] Robinson did his part, hitting .299 for the season, clubbing a dozen homers, and ably fielding his position at first, where he boasted a .989 fielding percentage. Smith and Robinson got help from a number of national publications, including *Time* magazine and *Ebony*, each of which trumpeted the player and his picture-perfect family in fluffy September cover stories.

Ebony led with a photograph of Robinson holding his baby boy next to Rachel and Jackie Jr.'s crib, all three beaming with ear-to-ear smiles. In the article's lead paragraph, the unbylined writer described Robinson as an "ex-Sunday School teacher," "a devoted malted milk devotee who insists he is just a 'home boy' with simple ambitions," and "a loyal family man warmly devoted to his pretty, trim, ex-nurse Rachel Annetta Isum."[90] On the Negro league circuit, Robinson was known as "quiet, modest, yet assured," someone "winning many friends and proving himself to be the exact opposite of all the stereotypes about ball players and about Negroes," according to the article.[91] (The article did not enumerate or elaborate on these stereotypes.) In a sidebar story appearing in the same issue, *Ebony* pointed out that neither of the Robinsons drank or smoked, that both "dislike nightclubs," and that in their "unpretentious life" together they often ate hamburgers and went to the movies.[92]

Even for an era when players' foibles were regularly overlooked by sportswriters, the *Ebony* coverage was unusually glossy, though not unique. Regular *New York Times* and *Sporting News* writer Roscoe McGowen wrote a laudatory spread on Robinson's successful, even heroic first season for *Sport* magazine.[93] Arthur Mann, who would write a Robinson biography of his own and cowrite a biopic movie screenplay in 1950, penned a similarly shiny spread for *Collier's* magazine in March 1946, just as Robinson was preparing to go north to Montreal to play for the Royals.[94] Accompanied by a photo of Robinson "going over his press clippings with [three] neighborhood boys," wearing his U.S. Army uniform, the article recounted the player's long journey into the Dodgers organization.[95] Highlighting primarily his athletic achievements, the article begins by comparing Robinson to football legend Jim Thorpe.

Reporting the player's Rookie of the Year award, *Time* magazine made Robinson its cover story in a September 22 issue. Like the coverage in *Ebony*, the *Time* article gushed about "the progress of Jackie Roosevelt

Robinson in the toughest first season any ballplayer has ever faced." And like *Ebony*, *Time* noted that Robinson neither smoked nor drank alcohol, reporting that the player preferred "a quart of milk a day" and going to bed early. "He had made good as a major leaguer, and proved himself as a man," read the unbylined article.[96]

The relentlessly positive coverage ensured Robinson's reception by all but the most prejudiced of observers. The *Sporting News*, which had for years resisted baseball's integration, named Robinson its Rookie of the Year. Ebbets Field held a "Jackie Robinson Day," during which the Dodgers' celebrated first baseman received a Cadillac, television, transistor radio, gold pen and pencil, gold watch, electric broiler, cutlery, and a check for $168 (to pay the inevitable taxes on all of the gifts). Plans were announced for a movie on his life, a vaudeville show, and a tour with the Harlem Globetrotters for more money than he made playing for Brooklyn.[97]

"Jackie Robinson Says" became the first of many journalistic endeavors for Robinson. He also provided bylined, firsthand accounts of the Dodgers-Yankees World Series that year for the *Courier*, and he continued writing "Jackie Robinson Says" throughout the 1948 season. He also briefly wrote a sports column for the *Saturday Evening Post* in 1964, in which he vigorously supported presidential candidate Barry Goldwater.[98] In 1953, while still playing for the Dodgers, Robinson became the founding editor of *Our Sports* magazine, a monthly that survived only a few issues. After retiring from baseball in 1957 after being traded to the crosstown rival New York Giants, Robinson's widest reach came with a nationally syndicated column for the *New York Post* in 1959 and 1960, and he used that reach to frequently write about civil rights and issues important to the black community.[99] When, unhappy with a piece Robinson did on anti-Semitism in Harlem, the *New York Post* discontinued his "Jackie Robinson" column in late 1960, he began writing a column for the black weekly *New York Citizen-Call*.[100] In 1962, Robinson and longtime ghostwriter Alfred Duckett teamed up for "Home Plate," a weekly column in the *New York Amsterdam News*, for which Duckett covered sports.[101]

In radio's first big serial hit, *Amos 'n' Andy*, listeners heard of and imagined an all-black world devoid of prejudice and discrimination, one in which blacks never encountered "the white world of strict segregation," as Michele Hilmes put it in her study of the program, though the show's characters, language, and descriptions were the basis of many of the most enduring and negative racial stereotypes.[102] Similarly, Robinson's *Courier* columns created for his national black audience an account of his first season in professional baseball as largely devoid of racial strife, one characterized by harmony among his teammates, fanatical support from the team's fans, and interactions with opponents Robinson almost uniformly described as "nice" or "swell." Smith followed suit, and in so doing he fulfilled a promise made to Robinson back in February as the two planned their collaboration beginning at spring training in Cuba. In a private letter, Smith encouraged the player: "All you have to do is take care of Jackie Robinson on the playing field and we will do the rest," referring to Rickey and himself.[103] The pair's depictions in columns, newspaper coverage, and autobiographies collectively served, as Gaye Tuchman termed it, as a type of shortcut to help readers interpret events beyond or outside their everyday experiences, the events of the Major League's first black baseball that century.[104]

Their constructed social reality was one in which Robinson inevitably, inexorably succeeded on baseball's biggest stage, proving that black ballplayers belonged and that integration could be won without disharmony or violence. In their process of selection, emphasis, and presentation, they revealed "tacit little theories about what exists, what happens, and what matters," as Todd Gitlin described in his study of the antiwar movement of the '60s.[105] The creators of *Amos 'n' Andy* left out of their frame any hint of racism or segregation in order to entertain and amuse, and perhaps to avoid the politics and problems of race. Smith and Robinson, however, cropped out racism in order to present the experiment as a success and in so doing to contribute and even achieve that success. As William Gamson found in elaborating what he called "collective action frames," Smith's and Robinson's frame identified racism as the problem, and it identified a solution—the addition of capable, law-abiding, family-loving black ballplayers who would help their teams win and put money in everyone's pockets.[106] In so doing, Smith and Robinson made it clear that it is possible to alter conditions and policies and that black Americans could become agents in their own history.

It is difficult to say whether manufacturing a veneer of harmony and acceptance and, therefore, essentially deceiving *Courier* readers was right or wrong. In conspiring to create the perception of success for the sake of social progress, the two sacrificed truth and accuracy, which were and remain hallmarks or at least goals of American journalism.[107] But the argument can be made that Smith and Robinson and, by extension, the black press as an institution was justified using any means necessary to fight the racism and separatism that had walled blacks off from professional baseball since 1889. Black newspapers took an advocacy approach since their inception, or since Samuel E. Cornish and John B. Russworm first published *Freedom's Journal* in 1827.[108] Given the fact that one of the primary arguments against baseball's integration had been that the presence of blacks would instigate race-based conflict on and between teams, it could also be argued that Smith and Robinson had little choice. They perhaps *had* to portray that first year in the majors as essentially trouble-free, portraying the "noble experiment," as it was called, as an unqualified success and not some sort of Frankenstein's monster.

NOTES

1. Sol White, *Sol White's History of Colored Baseball* (Lincoln NE: Bison Books, 1995), xxi. A barehanded black catcher from Mt. Pleasant, Ohio, Moses Fleetwood Walker represents both the beginning and end of the first era of integration at the Major League level. Before enrolling in the University of Michigan's law school, Walker was the first black to play at baseball's highest level, suiting up in 1884 for the Toledo Blue Stockings of the American Association. It is possible, however, that another player, William Edward White, preceded Walker as the first black player in the Major Leagues. White apparently played one game for the Providence Greys of the National League on June 21, 1879, five years before Walker played for the Blue Stockings, while enrolled as a student at Brown University. It has not yet been confirmed, however, that White, ironically, was indeed black (see Stefan Fatsis, "If Sleuths Are Right, Jackie Robinson Has New Company," *Wall Street Journal*, January 30, 2004,

A1). A native of Milner, Georgia, White got a hit in his one Greys game, scored a run, and fielded a dozen balls without error.

2. Peter L. Berger and Thomas Luckmann, *The Social Construction of Reality* (Garden City NY: Anchor Books, 1996); Gaye Tuchman, *Making News: A Study in the Social Construction of Reality* (New York: Free Press, 1978); R. Entman, "Framing: Toward Clarification of a Fractured Paradigm," *Journal of Communication* 43, no. 4 (Autumn 1993): 51–59; H. Johnston and John Noakes, *Frames of Protest: Social Movements and the Framing Perspective* (Lanham MD: Rowman & Littlefield, 2005); Stephen Reese, Oscar Gandy Jr., and August Grant, *Framing Public Life: Perspectives on Media and Our Understanding of the Social World* (Mahwah NJ: Lawrence Erlbaum, 2003).

3. It is acknowledged that all of Robinson's autobiographies were or are attempts at framing in particular ways his life and experiences, at least to some degree. It is clear, however, that Robinson's own descriptions of many of the negative experiences during his rookie season are described and reflected upon with increasingly more detail and depth in each successive autobiography.

4. See James E. Grunig and Todd Hunt, *Managing Public Relations* (New York: Holt, Rinehart & Winston, 1984), 22–43; in particular, for the Press Agentry/Publicity model, see pp. 22–24. The other models are "Public Information," "Two-way Asymmetric," and "Two-way Symmetric."

5. Quote from Grunig and Hunt, *Managing Public Relations*, 21. For one such documentation, see Patrick Washburn, *The African American Newspaper* (Evanston IL: Northwestern University Press, 2006).

6. Jackie Robinson, as told to Wendell Smith, *Jackie Robinson: My Own Story* (New York: Greenburg Publishers, 1948); Carl Rowan and Jackie Robinson, *Wait Till Next Year* (New York: Random House, 1960); Jackie Robinson, *Baseball Has Done It*, edited by Charles Dexter (Philadelphia: J. B. Lippincott, 1964); and Jackie Robinson and Alfred Duckett, *I Never Had It Made* (New York: G.P. Putnam's & Sons, 1972).

7. This "first draft" description of journalism has become cliché. See, for example, Bret Stephens, "A First Draft of History?" *Wall Street Journal*, March 8, 2005, accessed January 5, 2010, http://www.opinionjournal.com/editorial/feature .html?id=110006393.

8. For the circulation figure see Andrew Buni, *Robert L. Vann of the Pittsburgh Courier: Politics and Black Journalism* (London: University of Pittsburgh Press, 1974), 325.

9. Glen Bleske, "Heavy Hitting Sportswriter Wendell Smith," *Media History Digest* 13, no. 2 (Fall-Winter 1993), 38–42; Chris Lamb and Glen Bleske,

"Democracy on the Field," *Journalism History* 24, no. 2 (Summer 1998), 51–59; Lamb and Bleske, "The Road to October 23, 1945: The Press and the Integration of Baseball," *Nine: A Journal of Baseball and Social Policy* 6 (Fall 1997), 48–68; Lamb and Bleske, "Covering the Integration of Baseball—A Look Back," *Editor & Publisher* 27 (January 1996), 48–50; David Wiggins, "Wendell Smith, the *Pittsburgh Courier-Journal* and the Campaign to Include Blacks in Organized Baseball, 1933–1945," *Journal of Sport History* 10, no. 2 (Summer 1989), 5–29.

10. Robinson played less than one season in the Negro leagues, as a shortstop with the Kansas City Monarchs. By contrast, the move of black ballplayers into big league baseball was anything but quick, requiring more than a quarter-century after Negro league baseball organized in 1920.

11. Wiggins, "Wendell Smith," 28. Wiggins also wrote a series of eleven essays on the historical position of the black athlete in white society, *Glory Bound: Black Athletes in a White America*, (Syracuse NY: Syracuse University Press, 1997). The profile of Wendell Smith is pp. 80–103.

12. Bleske, "No Hits, No Runs, No Blacks: Wendell Smith, the Black Press, and a Strategy for Racial Equality in 1946," paper presented to the Southeast Colloquium of the Association for Education in Journalism and Mass Communication, Stone Mountain GA, March 26, 1992.

13. Lamb and Bleske, "Covering the Integration of Baseball."

14. Lamb and Bleske, "Covering the Integration of Baseball," 48. See William Simons, "Jackie Robinson and the American Mind: Journalistic Perceptions of the Reintegration of Baseball," *Journal of Sport History* 12, no. 1 (Spring 1985), 39–64; and Patrick S. Washburn, "New York Newspapers and Robinson's First Season," *Journalism Quarterly* 58, no. 4 (Winter 1981), 640–44.

15. Lamb and Bleske, "Democracy on the Field," 56.

16. Weaver, "The Black Press and the Assault on Professional Baseball's 'Color Line,' October 1945–April 1947," *Phylon* 40, no. 4 (Winter 1979), 303–17.

17. Weaver, "Black Press," 315.

18. See Jules Tygiel, *The Jackie Robinson Reader* (Oxford, England: Oxford University Press, 1983); *Baseball's Great Experiment: Jackie Robinson and His Legacy* (New York: Vintage, 1997); *Pastime: Baseball as History* (New York: Oxford University Press, 2000); and *Extra Innings: Reflections on Jackie Robinson, Race, and Baseball History* (Lincoln: University of Nebraska Press, 2002).

19. No column appeared on April 26, perhaps because the issue was published after Robinson's first week in Brooklyn; he was a busy man. In place of the column, the *Courier* ran a feature story on Robinson as a father to his five-month-old

son (Evelyn Sherrer, "Rachel's Dad Didn't Approve of Jackie At First . . . But Now!" *Pittsburgh Courier*, April 26, 1947, 13).

20. Jackie Robinson, "'Great to Be in World Series'—Jackie," *Pittsburgh Courier*, October 4, 1947, 1.

21. "Double V" signified Victory Abroad and Victory at Home. See Patrick S. Washburn, "The Pittsburgh Courier's Double V Campaign in 1942," *American Journalism* 3, no. 2 (Spring 1986), 73–86.

22. For more on the controversies surrounding the debut of Amos 'n' Andy, see Melvyn Patrick Ely, *The Adventures of Amos 'n' Andy: A Social History of an American Phenomenon* (New York: University of Virginia Press, 1991).

23. Quote from Michele Hilmes "Invisible Men: Amos 'n' Andy and the Roots of Broadcast Discourse," in *Critical Studies in Mass Communication* 10, no. 4 (December 1993), 315. See also T. Ella Strother, "The Race-Advocacy Function of the Black Press," *Black American Literature Forum* 12, no. 3 (Autumn 1978), 92–99; Charlotte G. O'Kelly, "Black Newspapers and the Black Protest Movement, 1946–1972," *Phylon* 41, no. 4 (fourth quarter 1980), 313–24; and Charlotte G. O'Kelly, "Black Newspapers and the Black Protest Movement: Their Historical Relationship, 1827–1945," *Phylon* 43, no. 1 (first quarter 1982), 1–14.

24. Quote from T. A. van Dijk, "Analyzing Racism through Discourse Analysis: Some Methodological Reflections," in *Race and Ethnicity in Research Methods*, edited by J. H. Stanfield II and R. M. Dennis (Newbury Park CA: Sage, 1993), 97.

25. Patrick S. Washburn, *African American Newspaper*, 179.

26. S. J. Bass, *Blessed Are the Peacemakers: Martin Luther King, Jr., Eight White Religious Leaders, and the "Letter from Birmingham Jail"* (Baton Rouge: Louisiana State University Press, 2001).

27. Interestingly, only after joining the *Chicago American*, which was a daily, did Smith become eligible to join the Baseball Writers Association and, therefore, gain access to Major League Baseball press boxes, more than a year *after* Jackie Robinson joined the Dodgers.

28. Letter from Rickey to Smith, January 8, 1946, Wendell Smith Papers, National Baseball Hall of Fame, Cooperstown NY, MS-1. Smith worked for the Dodgers in 1946 and 1947, including both spring training seasons.

29. "Boswell," Wendell Smith Papers, National Baseball Hall of Fame, Cooperstown NY, MS-1. For evidence of this pride, see correspondence to Rickey from Smith, dated June 3, 1948, and July 5, 1949, letters that also show Smith's grave concerns about the future of Negro league baseball.

30. "Boswell," Wendell Smith papers, MS-1.

31. "The Sports Beat," *Pittsburgh Courier*, April 12, 1947, 14.

32. "Jackie Robinson Says," *Pittsburgh Courier*, April 5, 1947, 14.

33. "Jackie Robinson Says," *Pittsburgh Courier*, April 5, 1947, 76.

34. Jonathan Eig, *Opening Day: The Story of Jackie Robinson's First Season* (New York: Simon & Schuster, 2007), 103.

35. Robinson, *I Never Had It Made*, 162. The *Amsterdam News* column was called "Home Plate" and ran throughout 1962.

36. "Jackie Robinson Says," *Pittsburgh Courier*, April 19, 1947, 18. Robinson's biographer, Arnold Rampersad, presents this and other excerpts from the player's *Courier* column but does not mention Smith's likely role helping Robinson write them (*Jackie Robinson: A Biography* [New York: Alfred A. Knopf, 1997], 167).

37. "Jackie Robinson Says," *Pittsburgh Courier*, April 19, 1947, 18.

38. For the acknowledgement, see Rampersad, *Jackie Robinson*, 163. For the omissions, see Jackie Robinson, "Batting It Out," *Pittsburgh Courier*, March 22, 1947, 15, which was filed from Havana, Cuba, and "Jackie Robinson Says," *Pittsburgh Courier*, March 29, 1947, 15, which was filed from Panama City, Panama.

39. Fred "Dixie" Walker's nickname certainly ensured attention to the player's views on Robinson and interracial baseball. It was a nickname he shared with his father, Ewart "Dixie" Walker, who pitched for the Washington Senators from 1909 to 1912.

40. Bragan died in January 2010 at the age of ninety-two. See Richard Goldstein, "Bobby Bragan, 92; Managed Three Teams," *New York Times*, January 30, 2010, A18.

41. Robinson, *I Never Had It Made*, 78.

42. Eig, *Opening Day*, 35.

43. "The Sports Beat," *Pittsburgh Courier*, April 12, 1947, 14.

44. Though Walker publicly denied organizing or even participating in the protest, which Rickey immediately quelled by promising to trade anyone who wanted out, he later asked baseball writer Roger Kahn to "please write that he [Walker] was sorry." See Harvey Araton, "The Dixie Walker She Knew: Re-examining a Legacy Tarnished by Opposition to Robinson," *New York Times*, April 11, 2010, Sports Sunday 2. Smith, who chaperoned Robinson for the Dodgers in Cuba, certainly believed Walker to have been the catalyst behind the petition. See "Dodgers Have Drawn 95,000 Fans in Four Exhibition Contests," *Pittsburgh Courier*, April 19, 1947, 1; "The Sports Beat," *Pittsburgh Courier*, May 17, 1947, 14.

45. Rampersad, *Jackie Robinson*, 171.

46. Marty Solow, "Meet Jackie Robinson," *Union Voice*, April 27, 1947, 3.

47. "Jackie Robinson Says," *Pittsburgh Courier*, May 17, 1947, 14.

48. Robinson, *My Own Story*, 120.

49. Robinson, *My Own Story*, 127–28.

50. *I Never Had It Made*, 71; William Ecenbarger, "First among Equals," *Philadelphia Inquirer Magazine*, February 19, 1995, 14.

51. These details were remembered by Harold Parrott, Brooklyn's traveling secretary, in his memoir, *The Lords of Baseball* (New York: Praeger, 1976), 194; and in his article for *Sporting News*, "Inside Jackie Robinson," February 3, 1973, 31–33. Some reports had the Phillies releasing a black cat onto the field, but it is not clear whether this actually happened. (See Mike Bruton, "Philadelphia Was the Worst of the NL for Robinson in '47," *Philadelphia Inquirer*, February 28, 1997, no page number available.) Though watermelon, fried chicken, and pork chops are often associated with the South, they are, as a racist stereotype, associated especially with southern blacks (see Alex Koppelman, "GOP Group Depicts Obama with Watermelon, Fried Chicken," Salon, October 18, 2008, accessed July 14, 2010, http://www.salon.com/news/politics/war_room/2008/10/16/newsletter).

52. "Jackie Robinson Says," *Pittsburgh Courier*, May 3, 1947, 15.

53. Wendell Smith, "The Sports Beat," *Pittsburgh Courier*, May 3, 1947, 14.

54. "Robinson Reveals Written Threats: Dodgers' Negro Star Told in Anonymous Letters to 'Get Out of Baseball,'" *New York Times*, May 10, 1947, 16.

55. Robinson, *My Own Story*, 128.

56. Robinson, *I Never Had It Made*, 72; "deep depression" from 87.

57. Robinson, *I Never Had It Made*, 71.

58. William Kashatus, *September Swoon* (University Park: Pennsylvania State University Press, 2006), 27.

59. Robinson, *I Never Had It Made*, 73. In Dodger manager Leo Durocher's autobiography, Stanky told Robinson at the start of the season, "Before I play with you, I want you to know how I feel about you. I want you to know I don't like it. I want you to know I don't like you" (*Nice Guys Finish Last* [New York: Simon & Schuster, 1975], 206). Robinson also wrote of Stanky saying something like this later in the season, during a game with the Cubs in response to riding from the bench from Cubs shortstop Len Merullo: "Listen, Merullo, why don't you jump on somebody who can fight you back?" Robinson recalls in *My Own Story* (p. 159), published twenty-six years before *I Never Had It Made*.

60. Harold Parrott, *Lords of Baseball*, 192; Jackie Robinson, *I Never Had It Made*, 74.

61. William Kashatus, *September Swoon*, 28.

62. For more on the threatened boycott and the Mexican standoff with Rickey over whether the games would be played, see Mike Bruton, "Philadelphia Was the Worst of the NL for Robinson in '47," *Philadelphia Inquirer*, February 28, 1997, no page number available; and Tim Cohane, "Jackie Robinson's First Year With the Dodgers," *Look Magazine* (Fall 1947): 48–51.

63. Harold Parrott, *Lords of Baseball*, 243.

64. Robinson, *Wait Till Next Year*, 184. This autobiography was published in 1960.

65. "Jackie Robinson Says," *Pittsburgh Courier*, May 17, 1947, 14.

66. In Jonathan Eig, *Opening Day*, 102; the author interviewed Schmidt.

67. Wayne Martin, "'Sure, We Rode Jackie,' Says Chapman," *Sporting News*, March 24, 1973, 36. Chapman attributes the photo shoot idea in this article to Pennock.

68. Robinson, *My Own Story*, 128.

69. Robinson, *My Own Story*, 145.

70. "Jackie Robinson Says," *Pittsburgh Courier*, May 17, 1947, 14.

71. Robinson, *Baseball Has Done It*, 67.

72. "Jackie Robinson Says," *Pittsburgh Courier*, May 24, 1947, 14. Pittsburgh players Hank Greenberg and Frank Gustine were "especially nice." In Cincinnati, Robinson had "a nice experience," including a friendly exchange with Happy Chandler, the commissioner of baseball.

73. Stanley Woodward, "Frick, Breadon Together Quash Anti-Negro Action," *New York Herald Tribune*, May 9, 1947, no page number available. Woodward's scoop established the *Herald Tribune* sports editor as one of the business's best. He certainly had Robinson's high regard (Robinson, *I Never Had It Made*, 75).

74. Robinson, *My Own Story*, 151; "Jackie Robinson Says," *Pittsburgh Courier*, May 31, 1947, 15.

75. Wendell Smith, "The Sports Beat," May 17, 1947, 14.

76. Wendell Smith, "Phillies Warned By Baseball Czar over Robinson Incident," *Pittsburgh Courier*, May 10, 1947, 1.

77. Wendell Smith, "The Sports Beat," *Pittsburgh Courier*, June 21, 1947, 14.

78. "Jackie Robinson Says," *Pittsburgh Courier*, June 21, 1947, 14.

79. Letter to Rickey, in Eig, *Opening Day*, 108.

80. Wendell Smith, "Chapman Says Jackie Keeping Brooklyn in Race by Brilliant Playing," *Pittsburgh Courier*, June 28, 1947, 14. Smith reported Chapman's effusive praise for Robinson and "the colored race," the latter for "their particularly fine actions at baseball games." Interestingly, Robinson's first autobiography uses remarkably similar language to Smith's, reporting that "no one on the club seemed to resent my presence any more. All of us were getting the pennant

fever, and the team became closer and more unified than it had ever been" (*My Own Story*, 149).

81. Wendell Smith, "The Sports Beat," *Pittsburgh Courier*, June 28, 1947, 14.

82. Wendell Smith, "The Sports Beat," *Pittsburgh Courier*, June 28, 1947, 14.

83. Attendance at Negro league games played in Major League ballparks became a central part of the economic case for integration made to Major League Baseball in the '30s and '40s. Attendance numbers often took precedence in headlines in the black press, even over the games' final scores. For examples, see Morgan S. Jensen, "Record Crowd at Yankee Stadium for 4-Team Card," *Pittsburgh Courier*, July 26, 1941, 16; and "10,000 See Satchel Paige Beat Chicago 2 to 1," *Chicago Defender*, May 24, 1941, 24. For much more on Smith's economic arguments articulated in his various crusades, see Brian Carroll, *When to Stop the Cheering? The Black Press, the Black Community, and the Integration of Professional Baseball* (New York: Routledge, 2007).

84. Robinson, *I Never Had It Made*, 10.

85. Wendell Smith, "Jackie Helps Dodgers Near Record Gate," *Pittsburgh Courier*, May 31, 1947, 15.

86. Wendell Smith, "Jackie Robinson Packing 'Em In," *Pittsburgh Courier*, April 19, 1947, 1, 4.

87. Wendell Smith, "46,572 Pack Wrigley Field," *Pittsburgh Courier*, May 24, 1947, 15.

88. Attendance figures from Eig, *Opening Day*, 195, 231.

89. Wendell Smith, "The Sports Beat," *Pittsburgh Courier*, June 28, 1947, 14.

90. Jackie Robinson, "Family Man Jackie Robinson: First Negro in Big Leagues Also Tops as a Father," *Ebony* 11, no. 11 (September 1947), 15–16.

91. Robinson, "Family Man Jackie Robinson," 15.

92. "Robinsons Plan for Day When They Have Own Home," *Ebony*, September 1947, 16.

93. Roscoe McGowen, "If You Were Jackie Robinson," *Sport*, September 1947, 41, 78–79.

94. Arthur Mann, *The Jackie Robinson Story* (New York: Grosset and Dunlop, 1950). This biography served as the basis for the movie version by the same name, a low-production film that starred Robinson as himself and came out also in 1950.

95. Arthur Mann, "Say Jack Robinson," *Collier's*, March 2, 1946, 67–68.

96. "Sport: Rookie of the Year," *Time*, September 22, 1947, http://www.time.com/time/magazine/article/0,9171,798173,00.html.

97. Wendell Smith, "Robinson May Earn $35,000," *Pittsburgh Courier*, September 24, 1947, 1. Robinson made five thousand dollars with the Dodgers and was promised six thousand dollars by Abe Saperstein's Globetrotters. The balance of the thirty-five thousand dollars was expected to come from "movies, stage and exhibition games."

98. For the magazine, Robinson wrote a "Speaking Out" column on politics, including the presidential race between Goldwater and Lyndon Johnson (*I Never Had It Made*, 180).

99. Jackie Robinson, "My Greatest Thrill, Jackie Tells the Courier," *Pittsburgh Courier*, October 4, 1947, 1.

100. The *Post*, one of the country's oldest newspapers at the time, apparently was not comfortable with Robinson's criticism of Harlem's black "nationalists" for anti-Semitism and, ironically, "bigotry" in criticizing and picketing white ownership of the Apollo Theater, among other ventures in Harlem (see Rampersad, *Jackie Robinson*, 353; and Robinson, *I Never Had It Made*, 159–61).

101. Duckett also ghosted Robinson's third autobiography, *I Never Had It Made*.

102. Hilmes, "Invisible Men," 309. Ironically, the radio show was the fantasy creation of two white men, Charles Gosden and Freeman Correll, who wrote all of the scripts and supplied all of the character voices.

103. Private letter dated February 4, 1947, Wendell Smith Papers.

104. Tuchman, *Making News*, 5.

105. Todd Gitlin, *The Whole World Is Watching: Mass Media and the Making and Unmaking of the New Left* (Berkeley: University of California Press, 1996), 6.

106. William H. Gamson, *Talking Politics* (New York: Cambridge University Press, 1992), 7.

107. See the Society of Professional Journalism's Code of Ethics, accessed on January 13, 2011, http://www.spj.org/ethicscode.asp, which begins, "Seek truth and report it."

108. See Jacqueline Bacon, *The First African American Newspaper: Freedom's Journal* (Lanham MD: Rowman & Littlefield, 2007).

9

....

Integrating New Year's Day
The Racial Politics of College Bowl
Games in the American South

CHARLES H. MARTIN

Early in the evening of November 23, 1948, a rapidly growing crowd of
agitated students gathered around a huge bonfire on the central quadrangle
of Lafayette College in Easton, Pennsylvania. Virtually the entire student
body soon assembled there, leaving nearby dormitories almost totally
deserted. The emotional issue that mobilized so many undergraduates
on that cool November evening was a controversial faculty decision made
earlier that day concerning the school's football program. In an unexpected
move that shocked the campus, the college faculty had voted to reject an
invitation for Lafayette's highly successful football team to participate in
the Sun Bowl football classic on New Year's Day. Since the Leopards had
not played in a bowl game for twenty-six years, students at the all-male
school had responded enthusiastically to news of the anticipated trip to El
Paso, Texas, and were bitterly disappointed by the sudden change in plans.
After much debate, nearly fifteen hundred concerned young men marched
to the nearby home of the school's president, Dr. Ralph C. Hutchison, to
demand an explanation. His dinner interrupted, Dr. Hutchison hastily
defended the unpopular faculty action by attempting to shift the blame
to narrow-minded Sun Bowl officials. The main reason that the faculty
rejected the bowl invitation, the beleaguered president explained, was
because southern racial customs would have barred senior halfback Dave

Showell, an African American, from the contest. "It is fundamentally wrong," Hutchison declared, "for any team to go and play a game and leave any player behind because of his race, color, or religion."[1]

Caught off guard by this revelation, the students urged Hutchison to inform Sun Bowl officials that the college still wished to participate in the January 1 game, provided that Showell could play. Impressed with the students' passion, and perhaps intimidated by their numbers, Hutchison agreed to reverse the faculty decision. The president then quickly placed a telephone call to the chairman of the selection committee, who curtly replied that Showell could not participate and that a replacement team had already been contacted. Disappointed by this negative response, the students subsequently marched to downtown Easton, where they held an orderly protest rally and sent off a telegram to President Harry S. Truman denouncing the Sun Bowl's action. The following day, nearly one thousand Lafayette students staged "a civil rights demonstration" in the school's auditorium, at which they adopted resolutions condemning intolerance in American society and endorsing the principle that "all Americans have equal rights under the law."[2]

The national publicity surrounding the Sun Bowl controversy of November 1948 deeply embarrassed Lafayette College administrators, bowl officials, and El Paso residents. More importantly, however, the incident is historically significant because it widely exposed the exclusion of African American football players from most college bowl games and dramatically highlighted the Deep South's fanatical insistence on maintaining segregation in all local sporting events. The controversy also demonstrated that northern students were increasingly willing to challenge the continuing presence of a color line in big-time college sports. By the fall of 1948, New Year's Day had become the single most important date in the college football season, with most of the top-ranked squads battling each other in a half-dozen or more bowl games. Since four of the five best-known postseason contests were held in the Deep South, southern racial policies controlled these events. This strategic grip on January 1 thus enabled whites in Dixie to impose their racial values on nonsouthern teams, in effect "southernizing" the national sport.

An examination of the rise and fall of racial exclusion in college bowl games held in the American South between 1935 and 1965 reveals much about the shifting trends in national race relations. During the 1930s and early 1940s, conservative white southerners demanded total conformity to Jim Crow and used the leverage of bowl games' profits and prestige to force opportunistic northern universities to abandon their black players. After World War II, northern colleges increasingly defended democracy on the gridiron, forcing southern bowl committees to modify segregation in order to recruit the top national teams. After 1954, however, militant segregationists, worried about the mounting threat to the foundations of the Jim Crow system, attacked this racial moderation in sports and attempted to reestablish a rigid color line. The eventual defeat of their conservative crusade finally permitted southern bowl games to implement a permanent policy of racial egalitarianism. This study will trace these events by focusing on the racial histories of the Cotton, Sugar, and Orange Bowls, the most prestigious southern classics of that era, and the Sun Bowl, the oldest and best-known of the so-called "second tier" bowl games.

During the 1920s college football captured the fancy of the American sporting public and became the nation's second most popular team sport, surpassed only by Major League Baseball, According to historian Benjamin G. Rader, "Between 1921 and 1930, attendance at all college games doubled and gate receipts tripled." This rapid surge in new spectators enticed many universities to launch a wave of stadium construction and expansion. The growing frequency of intersectional matches featuring North-South or East-West battles contributed substantially to this exploding fan enthusiasm. Despite several efforts to establish special postseason games, however, the famous Rose Bowl match remained the only continuous New Year's Day classic in operation. In the 1930s and 1940s, however, civic groups and individual promoters experimented with several new postseason contests. Festivals like the Dixie Bowl, Salad Bowl, Pineapple Bowl, Harbor Bowl, and Oil Bowl failed to attract enough fans to sustain themselves, as did the short-lived Bacardi Bowl in Havana, Cuba, and the Spaghetti Bowl in Florence, Italy.[3]

From this wreckage of failed dreams, four new postseason classics emerged as survivors—the Sugar Bowl in New Orleans, the Orange Bowl in Miami, the Sun Bowl in El Paso, and the Cotton Bowl in Dallas. Because all four host cities were located in the ex-Confederate South, they naturally adhered to the region's prevailing ideology of white supremacy, which prohibited all "mixed" athletic competition between blacks and whites. This custom dictated that if any northern team invited to a southern bowl game included African Americans on its roster, it would agree in advance to withhold them from the contest. Moreover, southern white college teams during the 1920s and 1930s went even further and demanded that nonsouthern teams bench black players for those intersectional games played north of the Mason-Dixon line. Until the late 1940s, most northern universities acquiesced to such demands, demonstrating that southern schools had succeeded in imposing their racial code on intersectional competition. This capitulation by northern coaches and administrators also reflected their tolerance for racial discrimination, the small number of black players on their squads, the marginal status of African American students on campus, and the growing lure of generous payouts and national prestige that bowl games provided.[4]

The Rose Bowl served as the model for these new regional ventures. However, on racial policy, the California classic took a more egalitarian position than did its southern imitators. Inspired by a one-time football match held in Pasadena in 1902, the modern Rose Bowl contest began in 1916 and was staged by the Tournament of Roses Committee, which already sponsored a wide variety of festivities in order to call attention to Southern California's mild winter weather. After a few lean years, the renewed game became a smashing success, attracting huge crowds and providing generous payments to participating teams. Although race relations in Southern California were far from ideal, the Rose Bowl accepted African American players from the start. In 1916 festival organizers invited Brown University to represent the East against host Washington State College, fully aware that Brown's star player was black halfback Fritz Pollard, a future All-American. Although Pollard encountered some discrimination in public accommodations while visiting California, the game's sponsors apparently made no efforts to prevent his appearance. This precedent of including black players was reinforced in 1922, when single-wing quarterback Charles West of Washington and Jefferson College played the entire game for the Presidents against the University of California.[5]

During the mid-1930s, promoters successfully launched four new bowl games in Deep South cities. These New Year's Day events were organized by businessmen and civic boosters who, seeking the Holy Grail of national press coverage, hoped to exploit the publicity generated by matches between top football powers to expand tourism and foster local economic growth. In Miami, civic leaders staged the Palm Festival in 1933 and 1934, with the local University of Miami squad hosting a visiting team from the North both years. In the latter half of 1934, these boosters and additional football fans formed the Orange Bowl Committee, which held its first contest on January 1, 1935. In New Orleans, a lengthy campaign by several journalists finally resulted in the creation of the Mid-Winter Sports Association, which organized its first Sugar Bowl game, also on January 1, 1935. The Sun Bowl in El Paso began operations on that same date, although its first contest matched two high school teams. In 1936 the West Texas festival hosted its first game between college teams. On New Year's Day in 1937, Texas oilman J. Curtis Sanford, inspired by Southern Methodist University's participation in the 1936 Rose Bowl, organized the first Cotton Bowl match in Dallas. Because of local skepticism about the venture's viability, Sanford personally financed the first few games before eventually turning the event's management over to the Cotton Bowl Association.[6]

All four of these new bowl games suffered problems with attendance and profits during their first few years. After Sanford reportedly lost $6,000 on the 1937 Cotton Bowl and $20,000 on the 1940 contest, critics jokingly referred to the event as "Sanford's folly." In Miami, the first Orange Bowl match drew a sparse crowd of only 5,135 fans, some of whom were curious neighborhood pedestrians admitted for free. Nonetheless, the creation of four new bowl games greatly expanded postseason opportunities for college football teams. At the same time, however, the fact that all four of the new events were located in the Lower South created possible conflicts for those northern schools whose rosters included one or more black athletes.'[7]

The 1940 Cotton Bowl and the 1941 Sugar Bowl revealed the fierce determination of white southerners to maintain the color line in college football and the willingness of ambitious northern universities to abandon their black players in pursuit of athletic success and financial rewards. Unlike intersectional games during the regular season, when northern teams possessed some leverage, bowl games in Dixie were controlled by white southerners who defined the "rules of engagement" to exclude blacks. Since the Cotton Bowl did not yet have an automatic contract with the Southwest Conference champion in 1940, the classic that year featured Clemson against Boston College. An emerging powerhouse in the Northeast, Boston College aggressively pursued its first-ever bowl bid, even though the team's starting lineup included black halfback Lou Montgomery. In preliminary discussions, Cotton Bowl officials made it clear that southern custom precluded Montgomery's participation. Although Coach Frank Leahy publicly grumbled about the exclusion, Boston College nonetheless quickly accepted the invitation. In reality, benching Montgomery presented no great moral dilemma for the Jesuit-run institution, since the school had already done so twice during the 1939 regular season for home games against Auburn and the University of Florida. The following year Boston College enjoyed even greater gridiron success, going undefeated and earning a bid to the 1941 Sugar Bowl. But once again, school administrators ignored criticism from a few sportswriters and students and cravenly agreed to withhold Montgomery from postseason play. As a small concession, New Orleans officials did permit him to accompany the team and watch the game from the press box.[8]

Although Boston College displayed no inhibitions about abandoning Lou Montgomery in 1940 and 1941, a few radical and liberal northern students did challenge racial exclusion in college sports during the immediate prewar years. Their numbers and clout grew enormously after 1945. As a result of the wartime campaign against Nazi doctrines of Aryan supremacy, liberal attitudes favoring equal opportunity in sports became commonplace on northern campuses. Consequently, northern teams stopped the custom of benching African American players for intersectional games at home, and some of these colleges also began to challenge this policy of racial exclusion for games played in Dixie. This new toughness by Yankee schools forced the cancelation of several games and the termination of a few intersectional rivalries in the late 1940s. The trend also forced southern bowl committees to reevaluate their commitment to racial purity on the gridiron, since it now threatened to interfere with their desire to offer the public the most exciting possible matchup and to maximize their own revenues. The first important defection from the traditional southern policy of racial exclusion came with the January 1, 1948, Cotton Bowl clash between Southern Methodist University and Penn State University. The game's tremendous success established a precedent for other southern bowl games and gave the Cotton Bowl a temporary recruiting advantage over them. Taking place just two and one-half months after the University of Virginia had shattered southern tradition by hosting an integrated Harvard team in Charlottesville, the SMU–Penn State showdown was reportedly the second integrated major college football contest ever held in the ex-Confederate South, and the first in Texas. In mid-November 1947, when the Cotton Bowl selection committee compiled the names of possible visiting teams, it placed Penn State at the head of the list. Winners of the Lambert Trophy, symbolic of football supremacy in the East, the Nittany Lions finished the 1947 season undefeated and ranked fourth in the Associated Press poll. However, the presence of two African Americans on the team's roster, fullback Wallace Triplett and end Dennis Hoggard, complicated the selection process.[9]

The Penn State administration and athletic department strongly supported the policy of racial egalitarianism in college sports. Located in an isolated spot in central Pennsylvania, the university was not the type of school normally associated with intellectual or political liberalism. Hence, Penn State's firm stand demonstrated the growing insistence on democratic ideals in sports that spread across most northern campuses after the war. The university had first confronted southern racism in 1940, when the U.S. Naval Academy refused to let sprint champion Barney Ewell run in a track meet at Annapolis. Refusing to compete without its African American sprinter, Penn State forced the academy to move the meet to State College. In the fall of 1946, a similar confrontation developed between the college and the University of Miami, after officials at the Florida school discovered that the Nittany Lion squad included Triplett and Hoggard. Miami authorities insisted that the two black players could not participate in their scheduled November matchup in the Orange Bowl Stadium because such a contest might result in "unfortunate incidents."[10]

Reflecting the new liberal attitude on northern campuses, Penn State students strongly criticized the Miami demand. One senior summed up this philosophy when he told the student newspaper that Penn State should play sports "the democratic way" or not at all, since "the ideals of Democracy are more important than any football game." After several weeks of negotiations, the two colleges finally called off the game. Afterward Penn State issued a formal statement that declared, "It is the policy of the college to compete only under circumstances which will permit the playing of any or all members of its athletic teams." In July 1947 the school reaffirmed this policy when the Athletic Advisory Board declined an invitation to send the school's boxing team to the 1947 Sugar Bowl boxing tournament, from which African American boxers were excluded. The action was based entirely on principle, since there were no black boxers on the current team. Penn State's position was well known nationally and understood by most Cotton Bowl officials from the start.[11]

Cotton Bowl officials were delighted when local favorite SMU, led by All-American halfback Doak Walker, captured the Southwest Conference title with an 8-0-1 record. As a result, the bowl could now showcase the third- and fourth-ranked teams in the AP Poll, creating "the top attraction in the nation on New Year's Day" and the most exciting matchup in the classic's brief history. (Number one–ranked Notre Dame did not participate in postseason play at that time.) After SMU coach Matty Bell and the Mustang players enthusiastically endorsed playing the Nittany Lions, the Cotton Bowl extended a formal invitation to the university.[12]

Although they quickly accepted the bid, Penn State administrators remained concerned about the rigid pattern of segregation and discrimination that characterized most aspects of Dallas life. Bowl officials worked carefully behind the scenes to ease their fears and avoid any unexpected confrontations with Jim Crow, especially in off-field social activities. Penn State coach Bob Higgins insisted that all of his players, including Triplett and Hoggard, stay together, but the major downtown hotels were segregated. Cotton Bowl planners cleverly resolved this issue by arranging for the visiting squad to reside in the bachelor officer quarters of the Dallas Naval Air Station near suburban Grand Prairie, fourteen miles from downtown. Bowl officials also scaled down some of the traditional social activities for the two teams, but all of the players, including Triplett and Hoggard, attended the postgame awards banquet at a downtown hotel, violating local segregation customs.[13]

The major Dallas newspapers openly reported the racial complications surrounding the possible selection of Penn State for the 1948 game. Once the Nittany Lions accepted the Cotton Bowl invitation, however, the white press temporarily refrained from making any references to Triplett and Hoggard or the larger significance of the racial milestone that was approaching. Since these newspapers did not report any local criticism of the decision to drop the color line, it seems likely that influential local whites preferred to downplay the impending racial change as much as possible, in order to avoid stirring up extreme segregationists. The *Dallas Morning News* did note one Pennsylvania sportswriter's description of the Nittany Lions as "a melting pot football team" composed of players from Polish, Irish, Italian, Ukrainian, and Negro lineage. Finally, on the day of the eagerly awaited showdown, the *Morning News* rediscovered Wallace Triplett, belatedly identifying him as Penn State's "star Negro fullback[,] . . . who is both a fast and elusive runner, and a superb defensive player." Unlike its mainstream counterparts, the black press paid close attention to the racial issue and interpreted the contest as an important step forward in race relations. The *Pittsburgh Courier* noted the game's larger significance and proudly reported that Triplett and Hoggard were always treated courteously by whites during their stay. The local black newspaper, the *Dallas Express*, praised SMU for its willingness to break with southern tradition and Coach Matty Bell for his "courage and character." Other newspapers around the nation, especially those with a liberal, assimilationist philosophy, also celebrated this racial breakthrough. Perhaps influenced by Jackie Robinson's integration of Major League Baseball earlier in the year, the *Christian Science Monitor* even argued that the integrated football game carried "more significance than does a Supreme Court decision against Jim Crowism or would a Federal Fair Employment Practices Act."[14]

The pairing of the eastern champion against local favorite SMU, as well as the substantial box office appeal of the Mustangs' All-American halfback Doak Walker, produced a record-setting demand for tickets. The Cotton Bowl ticket office received over 100,000 ticket applications in the first four days of mail sales, and one newspaper estimated that 150,000 tickets could have been sold if additional seats had been available. Penn State officials received 20,000 requests for its allotment of 3,000 tickets. An overflow crowd of nearly 47,000 packed the stadium on January 1 for what one sportswriter described as "a hell of a game." Paced by Doak Walker, SMU took an early lead, but Penn State rallied to tie the score at 13–13 on a third-quarter touchdown by Wallace Triplett. The game ended in a deadlock when a deflected last-second pass dramatically slipped off Dennis Hoggard's fingertips in the SMU end zone. The tremendous enthusiasm generated by the contest aided the Cotton Bowl in another area. Bowl officials had already planned to float a bond issue in order to expand the stadium's seating capacity, and the 1948 game's success made sale of the securities an easy task. By the time of the 1949 classic, the newly enlarged stadium now held just over 67,000 seats.[15]

Delighted with the game's tremendous success, the Cotton Bowl attempted to repeat this "milestone achievement" the following year when it invited another integrated team, the University of Oregon Ducks, to participate in the 1949 contest. The popular SMU Mustangs, ranked ninth in the nation, returned as the Southwest Conference champion, guaranteeing a large crowd. Moreover, the selection of SMU halfback Doak Walker for the Heisman Trophy, awarded annually to the top college player, fueled even greater interest in the match. The first team from the Pacific Coast Conference to visit the Cotton Bowl, Oregon had finished the season with a 9–1 record, a share of the league championship, and the number ten national ranking. However, the Ducks had been unexpectedly passed over in favor of the University of California for the conference's Rose Bowl slot. Paced by flashy quarterback Norm Van Brocklin, the Oregon squad contained three African American players, including starting halfback Woodley Lewis. Declining accommodations at the Naval Air Station, the visitors from the Pacific Northwest instead selected a downtown hotel. The three black players were housed separately at the private homes of prominent black Dallas residents but joined their teammates at the hotel for most of their meals. The bowl's reception committee included several African Americans, an interracial step bold for its day. The game itself provided exciting, hard-hitting play and was free of racial incidents. An overflow crowd of 70,000 applauded the action as the Mustangs posted a thrilling 21–13 victory. Clearly the Cotton Bowl and SMU had followed a policy of racial moderation, at a time and in a city where such flexibility was uncommon, and local politicians had not attempted to interfere. The gamble paid off handsomely, as the Cotton Bowl profited enormously from the two consecutive outstanding pairings. Although race relations in Dallas were conservative and paternalistic, bowl officials and city fathers understood the financial and public relations benefits that their city could gain from flexibility in athletic scheduling. The Cotton Bowl's willingness to breach the color line for one day each year also gave it a competitive advantage over the Sugar Bowl and Orange Bowl in recruiting top-ranked nonsouthern teams, since these two competitors retained their policies of racial exclusion.[16]

In El Paso, the Sun Bowl also directly confronted the problem of segregation in the late 1940s, but with less success than did the Cotton Bowl. The Southwestern Sun Carnival Association, which had been formed in 1934 by members of several local service clubs, sponsored the annual event. During the 1940s, the Sun Bowl pitted the champion of the Border Conference against a strong challenger, usually from a western conference. Although the Sun Bowl was located in far west Texas, it historically followed the prevailing southern and Texas custom of excluding black players. Since the game's venue was Kidd Field, on the campus of the Texas College of Mines and Metallurgy (later known as Texas Western College and now as the University of Texas at El Paso), which was a branch of the University of Texas at Austin, the bowl adhered to the University of Texas Board of Regents' standing policy against interracial athletic contests. This policy had come under fire in November 1947, when halfback Morrison "Dit" Warren of Arizona State College had been barred from a Border Conference match in El Paso. Arizona State officials and fans denounced the policy, as did many El Pasoans. Miner head coach Jack Curtice publicly noted that no one had "objected when we played against several Negroes in Tempe last year," and a campus poll at the College of Mines revealed that an overwhelming majority of students opposed the racial ban.[17]

The team-selection process for the January 1, 1949, Sun Bowl produced an embarrassing incident that briefly focused national attention on the continued exclusion of black football players from most southern bowl games. Since Border Conference champion Texas Tech declined its invitation to serve as home team, the selection committee eventually offered the host spot to the College of Mines, the conference runner-up. After talking with several teams from the East, the committee then extended a formal invitation on November 20 to Lafayette College, which had just completed a successful 7–2 season. Because the Pennsylvania university had not participated in a bowl game since 1923, its students responded enthusiastically to the news.[18]

An unexpected racial problem soon threatened to disrupt the Sun Bowl's plans. After receiving the official invitation, Lafayette president Ralph C. Hutchison informed College of Mines administrators about the presence of halfback Dave Showell, an African American, on the squad. Although apologetic about the exclusion rule, the El Pasoans nonetheless emphasized that Showell could not play and that there was nothing that local people could do about the regents' exclusion policy. When Lafayette officials told Showell about the ban, the popular World War II veteran graciously urged his teammates to carry on and make the trip without him. This burden lifted from their consciences, both the team and the athletic council voted to accept the Sun Bowl invitation. But the proposal still needed formal approval by the college faculty.[19]

On Tuesday afternoon, November 23, the Lafayette faculty met and debated the issue. Opponents of the El Paso trip stressed the school's tradition against postseason play, missed class time by athletes and students returning from the game, low grades by many football players, and the racial ban. After much discussion, the assembled professors voted overwhelmingly to reject the bid. President Hutchison promptly informed Sun Bowl officials of the negative faculty decision. He later claimed that he did not specifically cite the racial issue in his explanation to the El Pasoans, because he did not want to appear ungrateful for the invitation.[20]

Hutchison's announcement immediately sent the Sun Bowl selection committee into a frantic search for a replacement team and touched off the previously discussed series of demonstrations by Lafayette students. In interviews after the student protests, Hutchison carefully avoided mentioning any faculty concerns other than the racial issue. For their part, Sun Bowl officials desperately attempted to divert attention away from the regents' policy against interracial games and back to Lafayette's alleged indecisiveness.[21] The resulting national publicity about the incident created a public relations fiasco for the Sun Bowl. At the College of Mines, the student newspaper reported that most of the school's football players and students opposed the racial ban and were embarrassed by the affair. Many influential El Pasoans were also upset over the negative publicity that their city had received and resented the fact that the ultimate decision about who could play at Kidd Field remained in the hands of University of Texas regents, not local people. On November 24, West Virginia University agreed to play in the Sun Bowl as Lafayette's replacement, and eventually the controversy subsided.[22]

Two years later, however, another embarrassing incident over racial policies at Kidd Field further alarmed Sun Bowl officials and El Paso residents. After the 1950 fall season had begun, Loyola University of Los Angeles suddenly canceled its scheduled September 30 game against the Texas Western College Miners because local officials had barred African American halfback Bill English from the match. Although TWC administrators blamed Loyola for reneging on an alleged "gentlemen's agreement" not to bring English, most El Pasoans instead directed their criticism at the racial ban. The directors of the Sun Carnival Association, the city council, and several civic organizations adopted resolutions urging the board of regents to repeal the rule, warning that the current policy endangered the future of the Sun Bowl and Texas Western athletics. One month later, at their regular October meeting, the regents voted 6–3 to repeal the exclusion policy specifically for Kidd Field, but they retained the general rule for all other state university facilities. This modification greatly relieved the Sun Bowl's sponsors, since it now freed them to select teams from a much larger national pool. Just over a year later, the bowl invited its first integrated team, the College of the Pacific from Stockton, California. On January 1, 1952, Pacific halfback Eddie Macon became the first African American to play in the Sun Bowl when he took the field against host Texas Tech.[23]

The Orange Bowl classic in Miami experienced similar problems during the late 1940s and early 1950s. Since the Orange Bowl Stadium was owned by the city of Miami, the Orange Bowl Committee lacked the power to unilaterally set its own racial policies. Traditionally, all athletic competition in Florida had been segregated. Moreover, in the late 1940s, the State Board of Control adopted a formal policy specifically prohibiting all public colleges from hosting integrated home games. Despite a thriving tourist industry aimed at northern visitors, both Miami and sister city Miami Beach, located to the east across the bay, were very much southern cities with extensive segregation. The Orange Bowl Stadium, unlike most southern facilities, even lacked a segregated all-black spectator section until 1950, when it added one behind the east end zone. Florida's athletic color line first gained national exposure in the fall of 1946, when Penn State and the University of Miami canceled their scheduled intersectional football match at the Orange Bowl Stadium because of the racial ban. Embarrassed by the ensuing negative publicity, many Miami students criticized city officials and school administrators over the policy. Praising the student outcry, the sports editor of the college newspaper wrote that it had been most "heartening to note that a violation of one of the basic principles for which this last war was fought and for which over 250,000 Americans gave their lives, has caused a positive sentiment to sweep the campus." In January 1947 the local racial ban received additional national publicity when Duquesne University canceled an outdoor basketball game in the stadium against Miami. Duquesne decided not to make the trip south when it received confirmation that Charles Cooper, the college's black star, would not be allowed to play. Several other intersectional football and basketball games were canceled across the state in the late 1940s and early 1950s for similar reasons.[24] In a pivotal 1950 decision, however, the Miami *city* government reversed its position and permitted the private University of Miami to host the University of Iowa football team at the stadium. The Iowa traveling squad included five African American players, all of whom saw action in the Hawkeyes' loss to the Hurricanes.[25]

The Orange Bowl Committee successfully ducked the racial issue for several years by selecting all-white teams. Whether this invitational pattern represented a deliberate policy of avoiding integrated squads or merely reflected random chance (since several prominent northern teams lacked black players) is unclear. Nonetheless, ambitious bowl officials eventually adopted a colorblind policy when a major opportunity to enhance the bowl's national stature appeared. In November 1953 the festival pulled off a major coup when it signed an agreement with the Big Seven (later the Big Eight) Conference and the Atlantic Coast Conference to match their champions annually in Miami. Since all of the Big Seven schools except for Oklahoma and Missouri had recently begun to recruit African Americans for their football teams, the new contract guaranteed that most future Orange Bowl games would be integrated. This new lineup also brought the festival its first national television contract, another important milestone. Clearly then, the Orange Bowl Committee and the city government had jettisoned Jim Crow in order to elevate the bowl's national status and increase its financial strength. The city's expanding tourist industry and growing northern-born population may have aided this pragmatic decision. But Miami civic leaders acted without statewide support, as the rest of Florida firmly retained the traditional policy of exclusion.[26]

The Orange Bowl's first integrated game took place on January 1, 1955. In the second match of the new ACC–Big Seven series, the Nebraska Cornhuskers fielded two black players during their 34-7 loss to Duke. The local press did not take any special note of this racial milestone, perhaps to avoid stirring up segregationists around the state. Integrated games subsequently became the norm for the Orange Bowl in its city-owned stadium, while the University of Florida, Florida State University, other state colleges, and Florida high schools continued to prohibit mixed competition at their state-regulated facilities well into the 1960s. This loyalty to Jim Crow made scheduling additional intersectional games increasingly difficult. For example, in November 1958 the University of Buffalo rejected an invitation to play in the Tangerine Bowl in Orlando because of racial restrictions. Even though bowl officials were willing to host an integrated football match, the local school district, which owned the city's major stadium, refused to waive its ban against African American players.[27]

The Sugar Bowl in New Orleans experienced far more political interference from segregationist politicians than did all three of its major southern competitors combined. Local custom dictated that seating and other facilities at Tulane University Stadium, the game's annual site, be strictly segregated. By the late 1940s, Sugar Bowl tickets even stated, "This ticket is issued for a person of the Caucasian race" and warned that any other person using it could be ejected from the stadium. In the early 1950s, northern journalists began to criticize this seating policy. Even though not all northern colleges had African Americans on their team rosters, black students usually participated in marching bands and in fan delegations traveling to the games, thus creating a new source of potential conflict. In response to these complications, the Mid-Winter Sports Association quietly modified its guidelines for the January 1955 match, allowing unrestricted seating in the visitors' section while maintaining the traditional Jim Crow area for black fans in one end zone. This compromise allowed the U.S. Naval Academy, a recent convert to racial egalitarianism, and its integrated midshipman corps to participate in the 1955 New Year's Day classic against Ole Miss.[28]

The U.S. Supreme Court's *Brown v. Board of Education* decision declaring segregated public schools to be unconstitutional, announced in May 1954 and reaffirmed one year later, ignited an explosion of southern white resistance. This political crusade greatly complicated the Sugar Bowl's operations. For embattled segregationists, maintaining racial purity in athletics now became a crucial battle in the larger war to defend the entire

Jim Crow system. Alabama judge Hugh Locke, who in 1954 led a successful campaign to restore a Birmingham municipal ordinance barring interracial football and baseball games, voiced the extreme segregationist position when he warned ominously that "allowing a few Negroes to play baseball here will wind up with Negroes and whites marrying." Across the Deep South and also in Virginia, state legislators and political leaders eventually embarked on a sweeping campaign of "massive resistance" to federally mandated desegregation. According to one historian of the modern South, "Legislatures in the former Confederate states enacted some 450 segregationist laws and resolutions" during the ten years following the *Brown* ruling. This southern white backlash against racial change ran directly counter to the increasingly flexible athletic policies being implemented by southern bowl games and a few white southern universities.[29]

Sugar Bowl directors unintentionally crashed headlong into this tidal wave of massive resistance in late 1955 when they took the daring step of inviting an integrated University of Pittsburgh team to play Georgia Tech in the January 1, 1956, game. With the regular season champions of the ACC, the Big Seven, and the Southwest Conference all bound contractually to rival New Year's Day contests, the Sugar Bowl found it increasingly difficult to secure an attractive matchup for its game. Its task became even more difficult if it excluded integrated northern teams. Even though the Pitt squad included only one African American, fullback Bobby Grier, his solitary presence was sufficient to alarm rabid segregationists in both Georgia and Louisiana. Before Georgia Tech administrators accepted the bid, they prudently verified that key university boosters and Governor Marvin Griffin had no objections. But on Friday, December 2, 1955, after receiving complaints from influential segregationists, Governor Griffin unexpectedly reversed course and urged the board of regents of the university system to prohibit Tech's trip. In apocalyptic language, the governor warned,

The South stands at Armageddon. The battle is joined. We cannot make the slightest concession to the enemy in this dark and lamentable hour of struggle. There is no more difference in compromising the integrity of race on the playing field than in doing so in the classroom. One break in the dike and the relentless seas will rush in and destroy us.[30]

Griffin's dramatic shift outraged Georgia Tech students. That evening hundreds of young men gathered on the Tech campus, eventually burning Griffin in effigy. As more students and sympathetic residents joined their ranks, the crowd decided to march downtown to the state capitol. Eventually a mob of about two thousand people assembled at the capitol building, where they hanged another effigy of the governor and damaged a few doors and trash cans. Still not satisfied, part of the group then marched to the governor's mansion, where two dozen law enforcement vehicles and a phalanx of policemen greeted them. After voicing their complaints to reporters, the protesters peacefully dispersed and headed home in the early morning hours. The following Monday, the state board of regents met and debated Georgia Tech's Sugar Bowl invitation. Despite considerable pressure from the governor and militant segregationists, the regents approved the trip. However, the board did adopt formal guidelines requiring state colleges to honor Georgia's customs and traditions in all future home games.[31]

The so-called Tech riot and the larger political controversy over the Yellow Jackets' trip focused unusually heavy attention on the Sugar Bowl. In order to avoid patronizing segregated hotels in downtown New Orleans, Pitt established its team headquarters uptown at Tulane University, where it also held practices. Bowl officials again modified seating policies in the stadium for the visitors section, and increased attendance by black fans helped make the game a sellout. In a somewhat dull contest, Georgia Tech won a narrow 7–0 victory, with its lone touchdown being set up by a questionable pass interference call against Bobby Grier. That evening Grier broke another racial barrier by attending the awards banquet at a downtown hotel, mingling easily with several Georgia Tech players. However, he skipped the formal dance afterwards and instead attended a special party at historically black Dillard University.[32]

Militant segregationists in the Georgia state assembly and the Louisiana legislature refused to accept this abandonment of racial exclusion.

Members of both political bodies viewed integrated athletic competition as an opening wedge for further desegregation, and both were determined to do everything possible to protect the now-endangered Jim Crow system. The Georgia assembly responded with a flood of new laws reinforcing segregation, especially in the public schools. In early 1956 and again in early 1957, state legislators also debated, but narrowly failed to approve, a bill that would have outlawed all athletic competition between blacks and whites. Louisiana segregationists were more successful than their cracker cousins. In July 1956, as part of a wave of regressive legislation designed to forestall desegregation in the state, the legislature adopted bills that prohibited interracial sporting contests and required segregated seating at all public events. Despite pleas from Sugar Bowl officials that these measures would no doubt "seriously damage our sports program," Governor Earl Long reluctantly signed the bills into law. A few weeks later, though, a Long supporter privately offered financial assistance to the New Orleans NAACP if it would initiate a legal challenge to the sports ban, but the civil rights group responded that the governor should stand up for his convictions and file his own suit.[33]

The new Louisiana laws resegregated the Sugar Bowl and made it virtually impossible to attract nonsouthern teams to the New Year's Day game or any of the associated athletic events. Immediately after the legislature's action, three northern basketball squads pulled out of the December 1956 Sugar Bowl basketball tournament. Both the football game and the basketball tournament subsequently became regional events exclusively between all-white southern teams, thereby reducing their national visibility. Northern schools also canceled nearly a dozen scheduled football and basketball games with Louisiana colleges over the next two years. In 1958 a federal district court invalidated the sports segregation law, an action that the U.S. Supreme Court upheld in May 1959. This decision did not greatly aid the Sugar Bowl, however, since the segregated seating law remained intact and northern universities maintained their boycott. Finally, in January 1964, the Supreme Court struck down this law as well. With this racial burden now lifted from its back, the Sugar Bowl resumed a nondiscriminatory invitational policy and convinced Syracuse University, whose squad included eight African Americans, to play LSU in the 1965 match. The Syracuse invitation produced no public outcry, except for one complaint to Louisiana State University by the Southern Louisiana Citizens Council. After expressing its "sincere concern" over the school's decision to meet an integrated team, the Citizens Council warned that "LSU owes its greatness, academically and athletically, to its Anglo-Saxon heritage." The ensuing January 1, 1965, Sugar Bowl contest between Syracuse and LSU marked the end of "southern exceptionalism" concerning racial policy for bowl games and offered further proof that the high tide of racial resistance in the Deep South had now ebbed. Nonetheless, it still took the New Orleans classic several years to fully erase its previous stigma and reestablish strong television ratings.[34]

Racial controversy concerning the Sugar Bowl reappeared unexpectedly in the 1970s. These new incidents expanded the issue of racial exclusion far beyond the physical boundaries of the playing field. Just before the 1972 contest, African American players from the University of Oklahoma complained that only one black woman had been invited to any of the major social events held for the squad. In the fall of 1973, a New Orleans civil rights coalition threatened to picket the upcoming contest unless the Mid-Winter Sports Association appointed several African Americans as associate members of the group. In December, after extended negotiations, the organization named six prominent black civic leaders, including future mayor Ernest N. Morial, as its first nonwhite associate members, finally extending the principle of racial inclusion to its own ranks. Despite this concession, civil rights activists continued throughout the decade to press the sports association for greater black representation in its membership.[35]

During their early years, southern bowl games clearly reflected prevailing white racial values in the Deep South. To grant equality on the playing field, even if only for three hours, represented an unacceptable symbolic action because it suggested the possibility of equality in other areas of southern life. After 1945, however, as part of the crucial shift in racial values unleashed by World War II, northern universities gradually adopted an athletic policy of democratic egalitarianism. Confronted with a new firmness by these colleges, southern bowls began to waver in their loyalty to Jim Crow, fearing that they might lose the appeal and profits of attractive intersectional matchups if they did not modify their policies. Since the principal sponsors of these bowl games were urban business-men and civic leaders interested in attracting favorable national publicity and increased tourism to their communities, they tended to be pragmatic moderates on racial policy rather than rigid ideologues. Eventually they came to view the abandonment of traditional racial exclusion as a nec-essary concession to new national standards. The resulting integrated games began to acclimate some white southerners to black and white cooperation in one important aspect of social life. Thus, integrated bowl contests provided an important precedent for additional desegregation and reflected a modest liberalization in southern race relations.

The southern white response to the 1954 *Brown v. Board of Education* rul-ing brought this emerging trend to a sudden halt. During the ensuing period of "massive resistance," militant segregationists attacked all deviations from ideological purity in order to shore up the collapsing Jim Crow order. Postulating a racial "domino theory," they feared that integrated athletic events would serve as an opening wedge for more sweeping changes in southern race relations. This conservative counterattack interfered with intersectional competition at Deep South universities from Louisiana to South Carolina for up to a decade or longer. Yet because their host cities were located literally and culturally on the margins of the South, the Sun Bowl and the Orange Bowl remained unaffected by the segregationist counterattack. In Dallas, interracial athletic competition had become so deeply ingrained that the substantial local resistance to public school integration did not interfere with the Cotton Bowl's activities. But because it was located in Louisiana, one of the most recalcitrant Deep South states, the Sugar Bowl was seriously harmed by this white resistance well into the 1960s.

By 1964, however, even the Sugar Bowl had finally joined the other major southern bowls in adopting inclusive racial policies based on national, as opposed to regional, values. This successful transition from segregated to integrated competition represented a form of sectional reconciliation in athletics that indicated that the high tide of southern white resistance to racial change had ebbed. Yet it should be noted that, despite the widespread acceptance of integrated bowl games by the mid-1950s outside of Louisiana, most southern white universities did not rush to host integrated football matches on campus at that time or to recruit African American athletes for their own squads. In fact, many colleges still refused to accept black undergraduates, thereby revealing the limitations of this racial liberalization. Nonetheless, the triumph of pragmatism and self-interest that led to integrated bowl games reflected a strong desire by most white southerners to participate fully in the national sporting culture rather than maintain an extreme regional identity and risk further marginalization and isolation. Thus, each year on the sacred day of January 1, if not necessarily on the other 364 days, Dixie had become "Americanized."

NOTES

1. *New York Times*, November 24, 1948, 27. The team had earlier voted to accept the invitation, after Showell told them he would not object to sitting out the game.
2. *New York Times*, November 24, 1948, 27; *Lafayette* (Lafayette College), December 3, 1948; *El Paso Times*, November 23, 24, and 26, 1948; *El Paso Herald-Post*, November 23–24, 1948; *New York Times*, November 24, 1948, 27. The student telegram to the White House read, "Denied Sun Bowl game because we have a Negro on our team. Is this democracy?"
3. Historically black colleges also staged special postseason matches, the best known of which was the Orange Blossom Classic. Begun in 1933, the game was held at various Florida cities over the years and matched Florida A&M against a top-ranked black college team. See Benjamin G. Rader, *American Sports*, 2nd ed. (Englewood Cliffs NJ: Prentice Hall, 1990), 182–88; and Anthony C. DiMarco, *The Big Bowl Football Guide*, rev. ed. (New York: Putnam, 1976), 6–7.
4. For an overview of racial policies in southern college sports, see Charles H. Martin, "Racial Exclusion and Intersectional Rivalries: The Rise and Fall of the Gentlemen's Agreement in Big-Time College Football," paper delivered at the annual meeting of the Southern Historical Association, New Orleans LA, November 1995.
5. One California sportswriter joked about the relatively unknown Pennsylvania squad, "All I Know about Washington and Jefferson Is That They Are Both Dead." See DiMarco, *Big Bowl Football Guide*, 1–3; Joe Hendrickson, *Tournament*

of Roses: The First 100 Years (Los Angeles: Knapp Press, 1989), 1–42; and John
M. Carroll, *Fritz Pollard: Pioneer in Racial Advancement* (Urbana: University
of Illinois Press, 1992), 79–90.

6. DiMarco, *The Big Bowl Football Guide*, 3–4; Carlton Stowers, *Cotton Bowl Classic: The First Fifty Years* (Dallas: Host Communications, 1986), 7–16; Loran Smith, *Fifty Years on the Fifty: The Orange Bowl Story* (Charlotte NC: East Woods Press, 1983), 3–10.

7. Stowers, *Cotton Bowl Classic*, 10–11; Smith, *Fifty Years on the Fifty*, 5.

8. Despite Montgomery's absence, there still were sectional overtones to the 1940 match. At the pregame coin flip, one Boston College captain joked, "Let's not have any North–South bitterness. Remember, when your grandfathers were fighting Yankees, our grandfathers were in Poland and Czechoslovakia." See *Pittsburgh Courier*, December 23 and 30, 1939; Glen Stout, "Jim Crow, Halfback," *Boston Magazine*, December 1987, 124–31; Wright Bryan, *Clemson: An Informal History of the University 1889–1979* (Macon GA: Mercer University Press, 1988), 207.

9. *New York Times*, November 27, 1947, 51; *Daily Collegian* (Pennsylvania State University), November 25, 1947; *Pittsburgh Courier*, October 18, December 13, 1947; *Dallas Morning News*, November 24, 26–27, 1947.

10. *Centre (PA) Daily Times*, November 6, 1946; *New York Times*, November 6, 1946, 33.

11. The university did permit a popular distance runner on the track team to compete as an *individual* in the Sugar Bowl track meet, prompting complaints on campus that the school was being inconsistent on its racial policy. See *New York Times*, November 6, 1946, 33; *Daily Collegian* (Pennsylvania State University), November 1 and 6, 1946, July 29, September 26, November 25, December 10, 16, and 19, 1947, January 9, 1948; and *Pittsburgh Courier*, December 13, 1947.

12. *Dallas Times Herald*, November 25 and 27, December 9, 1947; *Dallas Morning News*, November 27, December 21, 1947.

13. Several of the Penn State players, mostly ex-servicemen, later complained about being housed on a military post, but their irritation was aimed more at the lack of evening entertainment, Coach Bob Higgins's rigorous training schedule, and military food than at their black teammates for causing the housing problem. See *New York Times*, November 27, 1947, 51; *Dallas Morning News*, December 21 and 24, 1947, January 6, 1948; Felix R. McKnight, telephone interview with author, April 23, 1996; *Daily Collegian* (Pennsylvania State University), January 6–7, 1948; Rich Donnell, *The Hig: Penn State's Gridiron Legacy* (Montgomery AL: Owl Bay Press, 1994), 186–87, 201–2.

14. *Dallas Morning News*, December 1–31, 1947, January 1, 1948; *Dallas Times Herald*, December 1–31, 1947; *Dallas Express*, January 10, 1948; *Pittsburgh Courier*, December 13, 1947, January 3 and 10, 1948; McKnight interview; *Christian Science Monitor*, quoted in *Centre (PA) Daily Times*, n.d., 1948.

15. The individual team payout was $66,453. See *Dallas Morning News*, January 2 and 6, 1948; *Dallas Express*, January 10, 1948; *Pittsburgh Courier*, January 3 and 10, 1948; Lee Cruse, *The Cotton Bowl* (Dallas: Debka, 1963), 36–39; Stowers, *Cotton Bowl Classic*, 77–78; McKnight interview; and Ridge Riley, *Road to Number One: A Personal Chronicle of Penn State Football* (New York: Doubleday, 1977), 305.

16. *Pittsburgh Courier*, December 4 and 11, 1948; *Dallas Express*, December 11 and 25, 1948, January 8, 1949; Cruse, *Cotton Bowl*, 39–41.

17. 1983 Sun Bowl Program, 44–47; *Prospector* (College of Mines), November 1 and 8, 1947; *El Paso Times*, November 4, 1947.

18. *Prospector* (College of Mines), November 20, 1948; *El Paso Times*, November 16 and 19, 1948.

19. The *Pittsburgh Courier* reported a rumor that state officials in Austin were worried that permitting an integrated football game in El Paso might undermine the university's defense against a pending lawsuit brought by the NAACP and plaintiff Heman Sweatt, which sought to integrate the University of Texas School of Law. See *El Paso Times*, November 22, 1948; *El Paso Herald-Post*, November 22 and 23, 1948; and *Pittsburgh Courier*, January 1, 1949.

20. Faculty Minutes, November 23, 1948, and Statement by the President, November 24, 1948, in College Archives, Skillman Library, Lafayette College, Easton PA; *El Paso Times*, November 24, 1948; *El Paso Herald-Post*, November 24, 1948.

21. *New York Times*, November 24, 1948, 27; *Lafayette* (Lafayette College), December 3, 1948; Albert W. Gendebien, *The Biography of a College* (Easton PA: Lafayette College, 1986), 234–35.

22. C. D. Belding, of the selection committee, accused Lafayette officials of attempting "to saddle me with the blame by trumping up this racial discrimination story" and claimed that Lafayette's original decision had been based primarily on nonracial factors. See *El Paso Herald-Post*, November 24, 1948; and *Prospector* (College of Mines), December 4, 1948.

23. Writer Larry Ring later recalled Texas Tech partisans yelling "kill that black ape" and other racial slurs at Macon early in the game but later applauding his excellent play. See *Prospector* (Texas Western College), September 30, October 28, 1950; *El Paso Herald-Post*, September 29, October 11, 12, and 28, 1950, December 26, 1951, January 2, 1952; *Oklahoma City Black Dispatch*, November

11, 1950; *El Paso Times*, September 30, October 28, 1950; and Larry L. Ring, *Confessions of a White Racist* (New York: Viking, 1971), 68.

24. Two University of Miami government professors, both World War II veterans, also publicly criticized the Penn State cancelation, asserting that the action was "contrary to the American tradition of democracy in education, and a perversion of the spirit of sport." See *Hurricane* (University of Miami), November 8, 15, and 22, 1946, January 9, 1947, December 8, 1950; *New York Times*, November 6, 1946, p. 33, January 10, 1947, p. 26, November 25, 1947, p. 41; Charlton W. Tebeau, *The University of Miami: A Golden Anniversary History, 1926-1976* (Coral Gables FL: University of Miami Press, 1976), 176-78, 236; Howard Kleinberg, telephone interviews with author, August 18 and 23, 1997; and Howard Kleinberg to author, August 29, 1997.

25. An editorial in the Miami student newspaper reported that the black players' participation took place "with a minimum of fanfare," adding that the contest "was a big, big step in the right direction." See *New York Times*, October 18, 1951, 39; *Pittsburgh Courier*, November 25, 1950, January 20, October 20, 1951; *Daily Iowan* (University of Iowa), November 25, 1950; and *Hurricane* (University of Miami), December 1, 1950. The five black Hawkeyes later reported that they did not experience any racial problems with Miami players or residents, but they were required to stay at a separate hotel.

26. Smith, *Fifty Years on the Fifty*, 83, 231; Bruce A. Corrie, *The Atlantic Coast Conference* (Durham NC: Carolina Academic Press, 1978), 49-50, Howard Kleinberg to author, August 27, 1997.

27. The Gator Bowl, founded in 1946 in Jacksonville, did not host an integrated game until 1961. FSU's first integrated home game finally took place in 1964 against New Mexico State. See A. S. "Doc" Young, *Negro Firsts in Sports* (Chicago: Johnson, 1963), 254; *El Paso Times*, January 2, 1955; *New York Times*, November 29, 1958, 22; Vaughn Mancha to author, January 31, 1995; and Smith, *Fifty Years on the Fifty*, 91, 178-79.

28. By the mid-1950s, the service academies had finally become sensitive to racial discrimination against any of their cadets, whether as competitors or spectators. See *New Orleans Times-Picayune*, January 1, 1984; *Atlanta Daily World*, January 8, 1955; *Pittsburgh Courier*, January 15, 1949; and *Miami Herald*, December 24, 1954.

29. William Warren Rogers, Robert David Ward, Leah Rawls Atkins, and Wayne Flynt, *Alabama: The History of a Deep South State* (Tuscaloosa: University of Alabama Press, 1994), 539; Numan V. Bartley, *The New South, 1945-1980* (Baton Rouge: Louisiana State University Press, 1995), 187-260.

30. *Atlanta Constitution*, December 1 and 3, 1955; "Tempest O'er the Sugar Bowl," *Tech Alumnus*, December 1955, 8; *Atlanta Daily World*, December 1, 1955.

31. *Atlanta Journal*, December 3, 5-6, 1955; *Atlanta Daily World*, December 7, 1955; *Atlanta Constitution*, December 3-6, 1955; Robert C. McMath Jr. et al., *Engineering the New South: Georgia Tech, 1885-1995* (Athens: University of Georgia Press, 1985), 283.

32. *Atlanta Constitution*, January 5, 1956; *Atlanta Daily World*, January 3, 1956; *Pittsburgh Courier*, December 10, 1955; *New York Times*, January 3, 1956, 33; Bobby Grier, telephone interview with author, June 23, 1994.

33. *Atlanta Constitution*, February 15-23, 1957; Charles H. Martin, "Racial Change and Big-Time College Football in Georgia: The Age of Segregation, 1892-1957," *Georgia Historical Quarterly* 80 (Fall 1996): 532-62; *New York Times*, July 17, 1956, p. 13, October 16, 1956, p. 14; *New Orleans Times-Picayune*, January 1, 1984; Adam Fairclough, *Race and Democracy: The Civil Rights Struggle in Louisiana, 1915-1972* (Athens: University of Georgia Press, 1995), 205-6, 232-33.

34. The *New York Times* strongly endorsed the 1959 Supreme Court ruling and suggested that expanded interracial contact through athletics would bring increased racial tolerance. The newspaper contended that "there has been no one channel of understanding that has been better than that of sport." See *New York Times*, October 16, 1956, p. 14, November 29, 1958, p. 22, May 26, 1959, p. 1, January 7, 1964, p. 20; DiMarco, *Big Bowl Football Guide*, 60-63; *New Orleans Times-Picayune*, January 1, 1984; *Red and Black* (University of Georgia), November 15, 1956; Fairclough, *Race and Democracy*, 219, 335-36; 1985 Sugar Bowl Media Guide; and Ken Rapport, *The Syracuse Football Stoly* (Huntsville AL: Strode, 1975), 254-56.

35. The Orange Bowl Committee eventually broadened its membership after receiving public complaints that it was not representative of the area's diverse population. See *New Orleans Times-Picayune*, January 1, 1984; Fairclough, *Race and Democracy*, 219, 335-36; *Los Angeles Times*, December 23, 1973, *New Orleans States-Item*, December 26 and 31, 1973, in Amistad Collection, Tulane University, New Orleans LA; and Howard Kleinberg to author, August 27, 1997.

10

....

Main Bout, Inc., Black Economic
Power, and Professional Boxing
The Canceled Muhammad Ali–Ernie Terrell Fight

MICHAEL EZRA

There was a major drift toward economic nationalism in many areas of
African American life during the 1960s. Though it was often viewed as
extreme at the time, scholars have come to place it within a constant
ideological struggle between black nationalism and integration going
back to the nineteenth century and later to the debates between Booker
T. Washington and W. E. B. Du Bois at the turn of the twentieth century
as well as the work of Marcus Garvey in the 1920s.[1] The issues involved
all areas of black life, and Muhammad Ali's embrace of black economic
nationalism in the 1960s demonstrates the saliency of nationalism as well
as Ali's role as a race leader.

At a press conference in January 1966, Muhammad Ali announced
that he had formed a new corporation, Main Bout, Inc., to manage the
multimillion-dollar promotional rights to his fights. "I am vitally interested
in the company," he said, "and in seeing that it will be one in which Negroes
are not used as fronts, but as stockholders, officers, and production and
promotion agents."[2] Although racially integrated, Main Bout was led by
the all-black Nation of Islam. Its rise to this position gave blacks control of
boxing's most valuable prize, the world heavyweight championship. This
essay examines how Main Bout embraced historical cooperative strategies
of black economic empowerment endorsed by Booker T. Washington,

Marcus Garvey, and Malcolm X. Muhammad Ali envisioned Main Bout as an economic network, a structure that would generate autonomy for black people.

From the beginning, Main Bout encountered resistance. Initially, it came from white sportswriters. But about a month after Main Bout's formation, Ali's draft status changed to 1-A, meaning he had become eligible for military service in the Vietnam War. He responded by publicly opposing the war. In response, politicians nationwide joined the press in attacking Main Bout. The political controversy surrounding Ali made it easier for Main Bout's economic competitors—rival promoters, closed-circuit television theater chains, organized crime—to run the organization out of business. Money and politics were important elements of white resistance to Main Bout, but we must also consider the organization's potency as a black power vehicle and its symbolic meaning to larger American publics.

Although Muhammad Ali's conviction for draft evasion in June 1967 would mean Main Bout's demise, the company's success in the face of corresponding political and economic attacks indicated the spirit of the civil rights movement and the tradition of cooperative black economic development. Why did Main Bout and Ali face massive resistance during this period? Certainly Ali's antiwar stance was vital to his potency as a symbol of the 1960s. This essay recognizes, however, that Ali's economic power as the world heavyweight champion was also essential to his significance as a race man. Ali demonstrated unprecedented professional, political, and personal autonomy for a black athlete by forming Main Bout and challenging the draft.

In their associations of Ali with the civil rights movement, scholars and journalists have emphasized Ali's draft resistance while overlooking the importance of Main Bout to Ali's vision as a race man. This focus on political protest over black economic nationalism parallels much of the scholarly literature and historical memory about the civil rights movement. Black leaders of the 1950s and 1960s often insisted that economic power was central to first-class citizenship, even as demonstrations and marches received the nation's attention.

This essay argues that Muhammad Ali's formation of Main Bout, Inc., embraced both the tradition of black economic development and its contemporary manifestations within the civil rights and black power movements. The formation of Main Bout, the resistance faced by the organization, and Ali's strategic counter-responses to his inquisitors during this period confirm Ali's importance to the African American freedom struggle. Within this context, Muhammad Ali must be treated as a race leader who was guided by a historical worldview that pursued black independence and freedom through economic empowerment.

In the United States, there has always been a strong element of economic nationalism in the programs of black leaders. At the turn of the twentieth century, Booker T. Washington modeled Tuskegee Institute as a center for black economic development and investment. Eschewing political protest in favor of business opportunities, Washington argued, "Brains, property, and character for the Negro will settle the question of civil rights."[3] At its peak in the early 1920s, Marcus Garvey's Universal Negro Improvement Association and its allied corporations operated three grocery stores, two restaurants, a printing plant, a steam laundry, and a clothing manufacturing department; owned buildings and trucks; published a newspaper; and employed one thousand black people in the United States.[4] In 1964, Malcolm X asserted, "The black man himself has to be made aware of the importance of going into business."[5] By this period, economic ventures had made the Nation of Islam the largest and wealthiest black nationalist organization in the country, with impressive real estate holdings, scores of commercial ventures, and its own bank.

Throughout the civil rights movement, organizations like Martin Luther King's Southern Christian Leadership Conference (SCLC) and the Student Nonviolent Coordinating Committee (SNCC) merged political action with economic goals. According to movement veteran Julian Bond, the campaign had an economic underpinning from the beginning. "When [SCLC] people were boycotting the Montgomery buses," Bond noted, "they didn't just want the front seats, they wanted bus driver jobs. When we [SNCC] were demonstrating at lunch counters in Atlanta, we didn't just want to sit at the lunch counters, we wanted jobs in the store."[6] In a

May 1965 newspaper editorial, SNCC chairman John Lewis wrote about the movement's increasing focus on black economic power: "In 1960 we were demanding the right to eat a hamburger at any lunch counter. It took us three years to discover that we could not afford the hamburger and that we needed money." According to Lewis, political and economic power were inseparable. "Money means economic power," he continued. "In order to get and to maintain economic power we have to bargain. Bargaining means political power. So it took us three years to understand that political power insures the stability of economic power."[7] Appearing on national television a year later, Lewis's successor Stokely Carmichael also underscored the relationships between politics and economics. "As I see the problem in this country it is an economic problem in terms of black people being forced, being exploited," he said. "We are property-less people in this country. We are property-less and we have to seek to redress that and the only means open to us now are political means. So we grasp that political power now and then we see . . . how we can work with that political power to then achieve economic power."[8] SNCC's 1965 campaign to form an independent black political party in Lowndes County, Alabama, coincided with its proposal for a Poor People's Land Cooperative in that area.[9] As part of its backing of the Mississippi Freedom Democratic Party's challenge of the white-supremacist Mississippi Democratic Party in 1964, SNCC proposed a Mississippi Farm League to "give Negroes economic, and therefore political power. A union of farmers will give Negroes economic autonomy. . . . As a strong organization it can give its members protection and effectively lobby for policies beneficial to them."[10]

Like SCLC and SNCC, Muhammad Ali also understood the importance of black economic control, and his formation of Main Bout had the potential to put increased economic power into the hands of blacks. At the press conference introducing Main Bout, Ali told reporters that the company would control the ancillary rights to his fights, starting with a multimillion-dollar March 29 match in Chicago against Ernie Terrell. Prior to 1966, Ali was managed by an all-white group of millionaires from his hometown called the Louisville Sponsoring Group. Most accounts indicate an amicable and profitable relationship between Ali and these backers.[11] But Ali's installation of Main Bout as his promotional team gave blacks unprecedented control of perhaps the most lucrative prize in sports: the ancillary rights to the heavyweight championship of the world. Main Bout's control of these ancillary rights gave them access to the vast majority of revenues from Ali's bouts. The ancillary promoter controlled the rights to live and delayed telecasts, radio broadcasts, fight films, and any further transmission or distribution of recordings of a bout—this as opposed to the local promoter, who produced the live event and controlled its on-site ticket sales. The major monies from big-time boxing matches during this period, including Ali's, came from closed-circuit television. Because seating at and revenue from the hundreds of closed-circuit theaters nationwide greatly outnumbered that which could be generated at the arena where a given fight took place, such fights usually had closed-circuit television takes much larger than the takes from other sources, such as radio broadcasts or live gates.

Ali's three previous bouts, the first of his championship career, were no exception. His last match before forming Main Bout, a November 1965 contest with former champion Floyd Patterson, grossed approximately $4 million. At least 210 closed-circuit television venues showed the match. Nearly 260 locations, with a seating capacity of 1.1 million, telecast Ali's May 1965 bout with Sonny Liston, and gross receipts for the fight were believed to approach $4.3 million. Ali's first title fight, against Liston in February 1964, was shown in about 250 theaters to nearly 550,000 spectators, and promoters estimated that the bout's gross receipts would be about $4 million. For all three of these fights, well over half of the total gross revenues came from closed-circuit television. By comparison, on-site ticket sales were only $300,000 for Ali's fight with Patterson, $200,000 for the Liston rematch, and $400,000 for the first Liston bout. Ali's purses also reflected the riches associated with this broadcast medium. He earned approximately $750,000 for the Patterson bout and $600,000 for each of the two Liston matches.[12]

Main Bout had five stockholders. Herbert Muhammad, son of Nation of Islam leader Elijah Muhammad, was its president. John Ali, the Nation of Islam's national secretary, was Main Bout's treasurer. Together, they controlled 50 percent of its stock and half of its board's six votes. The closed-circuit television operator Michael Malitz and his attorney Bob Arum were Main Bout's vice president and secretary, holding 20 percent of Main Bout's stock and one vote each. Jim Brown, the professional football player and Main Bout's vice president in charge of publicity, controlled one vote and 10 percent of the company. Malitz and Arum were Main Bout's sole white members. They came up with the idea for the enterprise while promoting a 1965 fight in which Jim Brown served as their broadcaster. Malitz and Arum asked Brown to carry to the champion a proposal for a company that would allow Ali to control the finances for his fights and potentially increase black participation in their production. Brown passed the idea to Ali. Ali and the Nation of Islam approved the measure and Main Bout was the result.[13]

Like Muhammad Ali, Jim Brown emphasized Main Bout's potential for increasing black economic power and control. He told a reporter, "Our goal is to use the money that we make—and hope to make in future ventures—to support the founding of business by Negroes. At first, we'll have to count basically on small businesses."[14] That summer, several months after Main Bout's formation, Brown retired from professional football and founded the National Negro Industrial and Economic Union. Although Main Bout was not formally connected to the National Negro Industrial and Economic Union, their goals were similar. Both wanted to increase black economic power in the United States. Muhammad Ali recognized this. In early 1967, he donated ten thousand dollars to Brown's group.[15]

White newspapermen constituted the first wave of opposition to Main Bout, as a number of reporters expressed fear over the Nation of Islam's ascent to power within professional boxing. Perhaps these reporters understood, like their contemporaries in the civil rights movement, that expanded economic power often brought with it influence in other areas of American life. Most were concerned with a black takeover of the sport, but others saw the Nation's rise within boxing as a portent of racial violence. Reminding readers that Elijah Muhammad's organization was "the group which advocates violence as the major weapon of racial war," syndicated *New York Daily News* columnist and virulent Ali critic Gene Ward argued that the development of Main Bout could destroy professional boxing. "Any way one sizes up this take-over of the heavyweight title by the Black Muslims," he claimed, "the fight game is going to be the worse for it. This could be the death blow." A longtime Ali nemesis, the eminent sportswriter Jimmy Cannon wrote in his syndicated column that Main Bout's rise not only had great symbolic value but also put power into the hands of evildoers. "The fight racket has been turned into a crusade by the Muslims. Their great trophy is Clay," shrieked Cannon. Assessing Main Bout's initial promotional venture, he insisted, "Herbert Muhammad, who is Elijah's kid, is the president of the firm that controls the Clay-Ernie Terrell promotion in Chicago. It is more than a fight. This is a fete to celebrate a religion that throws hate at people." Other reporters less specifically described their fears. Nevertheless, their columns revealed their nervousness over the new order in professional boxing. Doug Gilbert, the *Chicago American* boxing writer, believed "that if the Muslims own Clay, and also own the television rights to all of his fights, they have what amounts to a hammerlock on all that's lucrative in boxing." Syndicated *New York Herald-Tribune* writer Red Smith complained, "Except insofar as the Black Muslim leadership has a stake in the promotion, there is no good reason at present why the [Ali versus Terrell] match should not be accepted." Even the editorial boards of two Chicago newspapers, the *Daily News* and the *Tribune*, got into the act, urging Illinois governor Otto Kerner to ban the upcoming bout.[16]

Although Main Bout had critics within the black press, a number of writers welcomed its creation.[17] Cal Jacox, the *Norfolk Journal and Guide* sports editor and syndicated columnist, challenged the white press to cover Main Bout fairly. According to Jacox, "Boxing is in an uproar. It seems that pro football star Jim Brown has joined a group that will promote Cassius "Muhammad Ali" Clay's title bout with Ernie Terrell and includes members of the black Muslim sect among its officers; now, because of this alliance, the alarmist[s] are crying all over the place." Jacox assessed the fears of some white sportswriters: "They are saying that the Muslim philosophy will dominate Main Bout, Inc., and with this domination, they contend will come—via Cassius as the heavyweight champion—complete control of boxing." But to Jacox, this was not the issue. Main Bout's most important functions were outside professional boxing. "Jim Brown, in rebuttal, explained that the sole purpose of the new organization is to use its profits to generate capital for Negro businessmen," he continued, "and that explanation is good enough for this corner. And, from here, it should probably be sufficient for the critics, who are way off base in castigating the project before they've given it a chance to reveal its program to the public."[18] Two articles in the *Pittsburgh Courier* voiced similar support for Main Bout, adding that the organization was a necessary alternative to white rule of professional boxing, which had resulted in corruption and mob control of the sport.[19]

In February 1966, less than a month after Main Bout's formation, the United States Selective Service reclassified Muhammad Ali as draft-eligible for the Vietnam War. In 1960, at age eighteen, Ali had registered with Selective Service Local Board 47 in Louisville and in 1962 was classified as draft-eligible (1-A). In 1964, however, Ali failed the mental aptitude section of the induction exam. When asked to retest in front of army psychologists, Ali again flunked. He was then reclassified as unqualified to serve (1-Y). In need of more soldiers for the Vietnam War, however, the Army lowered its mental aptitude requirement in early 1966, and Ali's score became a passing one. With members of Congress calling for his reclassification, Ali's local draft board reviewed his case in February. After the fighter's request for an appeal hearing was denied, he was again declared draft-eligible.[20]

When reporters called Ali for comment, he signified his political and religious opposition to the Vietnam War. In a telephone interview with Tom Fitzpatrick of the *Chicago Daily News*, Ali claimed that he had seen "lots of whites burning their draft cards on television. If they are against the war, and even some congressmen are against the war," Ali asked, "why should we Muslims be for it?" According to Ali, the war violated the principles of the Nation of Islam. "Let me tell you, we Muslims are taught to defend ourselves when we are attacked," he added. "Those Vietcongs are not attacking me. All I know is that they are considered Asiatic black people and I don't have no fight with black people." Ali warned that his reclassification would incite the worldwide Muslim community: "I don't want to scare anybody about it, but there are millions of Muslims around the world watching what's happening to me."[21] Ali also asserted that he had been singled out for unfair treatment: "I can't understand why, out of all the baseball players, all of the football players, all of the basketball players—they seek out me, who's the world's only heavyweight champion?"[22] Ali's stand against the war produced a vicious backlash against him within the press and professional boxing.

White reporters nationwide dismissed Ali's stance as the result of fear and ignorance rather than principle. Elijah Muhammad, the Nation of Islam's leader, advised members of the organization to refuse military service in Vietnam. Not all Muslims refused military service, and some military people gravitated towards the Nation of Islam. But Ali's draft resistance conformed to the tradition established by Elijah Muhammad, who was imprisoned between 1942 and 1946 for his refusal to serve in World War II. Dick Young, the syndicated *New York Daily News* columnist and one of Ali's staunchest critics in the press, rejected this, asserting that there was "no evidence that [the Nation of Islam] is a pacifist organization, or that Cassius Clay is devoted to a policy of non-violence." *New York World-Telegram and Sun* scribe Jack Clary ("It's easy to see why Cassius [1-A] Clay flunked his Army mental.") and Red Smith ("It has been established to the satisfaction of most that Cassius Marcellus Clay is not a deep thinker.") claimed Ali was stupid. Gene Ward ("Cassius Clay is scared. There is a patina of panic glazing his eyes, as he talks compulsively in bursts of words.") and the important *New York Times* sportswriter Arthur Daley ("[Ali is] panic-stricken at the thought of military service.") felt that Ali was desperately afraid of combat duty.[23]

Another common supposition was that the Nation of Islam had manufactured Ali's draft resistance only to save the upcoming fight with Terrell. After that, claimed these reporters, Ali would drop his shenanigans and join the army.[24] To save their profits, Jimmy Cannon assured readers, "The Black Muslims will shut up Clay." Once again, the editorial boards of Chicago newspapers voiced their antipathy to Ali and the Nation of Islam. *Chicago American* claimed to be "sorry for Cassius Clay.... He is as innocent as a puppet compared to the gang of fanatics that now owns and operates him. In fact, he is a puppet." The *Chicago Tribune* asserted, "The Black Muslims have ordered [Ali] to appeal as a conscientious objector."[25] These writers disputed the sincerity of Ali's position and his understanding of the issues surrounding it.

In Chicago, Ali's draft resistance and an escalating distrust of Main Bout unleashed furious attacks by local newspapers and politicians who called for the banning of his upcoming match with Ernie Terrell. Editorials in two local dailies called for cancelation of the fight, citing Ali's anti-Vietnam stance and his new promotional scheme. *Chicago American* analyzed Ali's reasons for disputing the draft and concluded that "none of them [were] particularly convincing." The *Chicago Tribune* found it "deplorable that so many Chicagoans are unwittingly encouraging [Ali] by their interest in a fight whose profits will go largely to the Black Muslims." Twenty state newspaper executives released a joint announcement criticizing Governor Otto Kerner and the Illinois State Athletic Commission for allowing the bout to be sanctioned. For several days, the *Chicago Tribune* devoted its front page to opponents of the fight. It interviewed disgusted American GIs in Vietnam, highlighting their anti-Ali rants. An area Veterans of Foreign Wars district, representing 14,500 former soldiers, passed a resolution urging Mayor Richard Daley and Governor Kerner to "intercede" and cancel the fight. Politicians and government appointees also registered their displeasure. State Representatives Clyde Choate and Arthur Gottschalk threatened to investigate the Illinois State Athletic Commission for approving the contest. State Senator Arthur Swanson called for Kerner to remove the match from Chicago. Charles Siragusa, the Illinois Crime Investigating Commission's executive director, felt that "it is an insult to the people of this state to permit a man like Clay who swears allegiance to an admitted cult of violence to reap a harvest of cash from the very citizens he has insulted with his whining attempts to avoid the draft." Even State Auditor Michael J. Howlett hoped that the fight would be banned. Police Superintendent Orlando Wilson offered critical opposition, telling reporters, "My main concern is with the possibility of disorder arising from the bout, but I am also disturbed by the unpatriotic statements attributed to Clay." This intersection of professional duties and personal beliefs characterized official resistance to Ali. Daley leaned on the Illinois State Athletic Commission to "reconsider" the bout, claiming that Chicago "could well do without this fight." Kerner called Ali's comments "disgusting and unpatriotic." Aided by the local press, white city and state politicians formed a nearly united front against the match within a matter of days.[26]

Local boxing promoters Ben Bentley and Irving Schoenwald worked to save the bout, concocting a plan in which Ali would apologize for his antiwar statements in exchange for permission to fight in Chicago. Although the Illinois State Athletic Commission, the state agency in charge of regulating boxing, had the power to cancel the match, it agreed to this compromise. This made sense because the Illinois State Athletic Commission would not simply cancel a fight it had already sanctioned. Nothing new had happened regarding the fight's promotion that would give it legal reason to do so. Governor Kerner also had a lot to lose were he to intervene and bar the match. Such action could be seen as racial discrimination. Bentley circulated rumors of a telephone call between himself and Ali during which the fighter rescinded his antiwar statements. Bentley told reporters, "since he [Ali] doesn't understand politics he's not going to discuss them any further, and he promised he's going to stick to fighting." Bentley also claimed that Ali had admitted, "I went off half-cocked and didn't know what I was saying." Illinois State Athletic Commission chairman Joe Triner told the Associated Press, "Governor Kerner told me that he would be satisfied with an apology from Clay. So as of now, the fight hasn't been disapproved and it remains status quo." The United Press International quoted Ali: "If I knew everything I had said on politics would have been taken that seriously[,] . . . I never would have opened my mouth." Lester Bromberg of the *New York World-Telegram and Sun* detailed Ali's "newly-discovered humility" and reported the champion's assertion, "I ain't no authority on Vietnam. I ain't no leader and no preacher." With this narrative established, the Illinois State Athletic Commission announced that they would reconvene to hear Ali's apology for his "unpatriotic remarks."[27]

This scheme reflected the overriding feeling that Ali's draft resistance was insincere and offered him the chance to verify such speculation. If he were to go back on his beliefs, he could pursue his career without censure. White sportswriters, many of whom had already declared the folly of Ali's position, predicted that he would apologize to save the fight. They assumed that boxing, and the paydays that accompanied it, were more important to the champion than his antiwar stand. They wrote that he would withdraw from political matters in the future and that he had learned his lesson. These reporters also claimed that Ali would skip the Nation of Islam's Savior's Day Convention as a way of displaying this transformation.[28] Such predictions ignored *Miami Herald* reporter Pat Putnam's interview with the champion. Ali told Putnam that the reports were "not true. I'll be there. I've got to be there, I've got to. I'm going."[29] Unlike the white press, *Muhammad Speaks*, the Nation of Islam's official newspaper, reported that Ali had come to Chicago not only to attend the Illinois State Athletic Commission hearing but also to appear at the Savior's Day Convention, announcing that the champion "made preparations to fly into Chicago for a two-purpose visit, one of which included a meeting with the Illinois [State] Athletic Commission, the other with his leader and teacher, the Honorable Elijah Muhammad, during Savior's Day Convention."[30] His comments to Putnam notwithstanding, Ali agreed to the scheme, refusing further comment about the war until the hearing. He flew from his training camp in Miami to Chicago to testify. Promoter Bentley greeted the champion at the airport and plastered a piece of tape across his lips. Ali went along with the gag, responding to any questions by mumbling and pointing to his mouth.[31]

Before the Illinois State Athletic Commission, Ali refused to apologize. The hearing was a national event; fifty reporters, twenty-five lawyers, six state troopers, and several government officials packed the Illinois State Athletic Commission's Chicago office to hear Ali testify. The commission asked him if he were sorry for his antiwar comments. Ali answered, "I'm not apologizing for any remarks that were in the newspapers. I will take that up with government officials and officials of the draft board at the proper time." Ali expressed regrets, but not for his beliefs. He instead apologized "to the people who may be hurt financially. I am sorry I put the commission and Governor Kerner on the spot with my remarks. I did not mean to hurt the children and the sons of persons who are dying in Vietnam." Stunned, Triner asked Ali, "I want to know if you are apologizing to the people of the state of Illinois for the unpatriotic remarks you made." Ali insisted, "I'm not apologizing for anything like that because I don't have to."[32] To make himself clear, he added, "I'm not here to make a showdown plea. I'm not here to apologize in any way that the press has predicted I would apologize."[33] Flabbergasted by Ali's defiance, the Illinois State Athletic Commission adjourned the meeting and contemplated its next move.

About a half-hour after the hearing, Illinois attorney general William Clark declared the match illegal. Citing possible inconsistencies in the licensing procedures for Ali and Terrell and a widely ignored rule that any corporation promoting a boxing or wrestling event had to have at least fifty people in it, Clark advised the Illinois State Athletic Commission to "adjourn their meeting and to so advise the participants" that their promotion was finished in Chicago.[34] While Clark's legal claims were legitimate, such rules had always been loosely enforced, if not ignored. Almost certainly, Ali's draft resistance brought increased scrutiny over the licensing and promotion of his fight with Terrell. Mayor Daley backed the decision: "The attorney general has issued an opinion holding the fight illegal. All state officials are bound by the opinion of the attorney general. It seems to me the commission has no other choice but to follow the opinion."[35] The Illinois State Athletic Commission acquiesced and canceled the match. The *Chicago Tribune* praised Daley, Kerner, and Clark for intervening.[36]

Refusing to apologize reinforced Ali's defiance and engendered nationwide opposition to his upcoming title fight with Terrell. Unwelcome in Chicago, Main Bout shopped the contest around the United States with little success. In each city, local boxing people greeted Main Bout with interest, but state and local government officials rejected them. Main Bout's Bob Arum explained, "I got calls from promoters all over the country wanting to hold the fight, even from Huron, S.D." However, said Arum, "the day after a promoter would call me, the governor of his state or the mayor would announce there'd be no Clay fight in his town or state." Promoters in Louisville, for example, completed negotiations with Main Bout and the Kentucky State Athletic Commission agreed to sanction the bout. Influenced by local veterans groups, however, members of the Kentucky State Senate announced the next day that they would block the fight. The Kentucky State Senate also passed a resolution urging Ali to join the Army, and State Senator William L. Sullivan asked Ali to "abandon his reprehensible efforts to avoid duty in the country which afforded him the opportunity to achieve eminence." In Pittsburgh, promoters inquired about hosting the match. The next day, Pennsylvania legislators moved to bar it. After local promoters and the Maine State Athletic Commission announced their interest in sponsoring the contest, Governor John Reed rebuffed them. Promoters in South Dakota, Rhode Island, Oklahoma, and Missouri also asked about holding the bout in their states, but were blocked. The pattern was clear: as soon as the news broke that area boxing people were interested in the fight, local or state officials opposed them. With the contest less than a month away, Main Bout had yet to secure a site.[37]

At the Savior's Day Convention, which the champion attended, Elijah Muhammad blasted the government's war policy and the racist singling out of Ali; but some white sportswriters denied that prejudice had anything to do with the criticism of Ali. Before four thousand people, Muhammad asserted that whites only wanted Ali for service after "he entered the army of the Lord [the Nation of Islam]." He also claimed that white politicians had enforced an official policy that "the Negro should go to Vietnam and kill other Negroes while our sons stay home and go to colleges and universities." David Condon of the *Chicago Tribune* denied that racial or religious discrimination had anything to do with Ali's reclassification. Furthermore, he was appalled that "some of Champion Cassius Clay's admirers have bleated that the opposition to this fight is because it involves a great colored title holder. These admirers holler 'hate' and 'prejudice.'" To Condon, it was almost impossible for sportswriters to be racist. "A person would have to be naive, indeed, to believe that sports writers were becoming prejudiced at such a late date," he claimed. "No man of prejudice can be a sports writer today. The majority of the great athletes are colored men, and the sports writers associate with them daily."[38]

Meanwhile, Main Bout shopped the match around Canada. This was a risky move because it assumed that Ali's draft board would give him permission to leave the country. Fortunately, the Louisville Draft Board voted unanimously to let Ali perform in Canada because of its proximity to the United States and because the champion promised them that his stay there would be brief. The Louisville Draft Board ordered Ali to return to the United States by April 7 or face desertion charges.[39]

The same pattern developed in Canada as in the United States. Promoters in Montreal, Sorrels, Edmonton, and Verdun talked with Main Bout, but their city governments blocked the fight in opposition to Ali's antiwar stance.[40] Finally, the Ontario Minister of Labor agreed to host the contest. Even in Toronto, however, the fight stirred controversy. The management of Maple Leaf Gardens, where the bout would be held, became embroiled in a bitter struggle. Hockey legend Conn Smythe, the founder of the Toronto Maple Leafs franchise, resigned his position as the arena's director in protest.[41]

Almost immediately after Toronto approved the contest, Ernie Terrell withdrew, citing financial considerations, forcing Main Bout to find a substitute opponent, Canadian heavyweight George Chuvalo.[42] Sportswriters further hurt Main Bout's cause by labeling the fight a mismatch.[43] Chuvalo was not as attractive an opponent as Terrell from a boxing standpoint. He had lost his last bout to an unranked fighter. Therefore, it was unsurprising that sportswriters believed the contest to be uncompetitive. Despite this, it is unlikely that the substitution of Chuvalo per se would make the promotion unprofitable. First, the popular Chuvalo's fighting in his hometown for the championship would probably increase the live gate and Canadian closed-circuit television sales. Second, Chuvalo's whiteness was probably attractive to customers, black and white, who saw boxing as racial theater. Third, Chuvalo had previously fought in matches that had done well financially. His February 1965 bout with Floyd Patterson at Madison Square Garden drew 19,000 fans paying $165,000. Sixty-four closed-circuit television venues, with a seating capacity of 300,000, had screened the bout.[44]

Nevertheless, the promotion had gone bust. A month earlier, the Associated Press had predicted gross receipts of over $4 million and a minimum purse of $450,000 for Ali.[45] This was an excellent guarantee for a fight against Terrell, who was not as well known as Floyd Patterson or Sonny Liston. If the fight did better than expected, Ali's share would have been larger. The day after Main Bout announced that they had signed Chuvalo, however, the Associated Press reported that the fight's gross would be approximately $500,000.[46] Although there had been radio broadcasts of all of Ali's previous title matches, only a handful of the fight's forty-two sponsors agreed to support the bout. The radio broadcast had to be canceled.[47]

Critics of Main Bout, Ali, and the Nation of Islam proposed a boycott of the closed-circuit broadcast. In Miami, a 2,700-member American Legion post said that it would picket any theater that showed the fight. No Miami sites broadcast Ali versus Chuvalo. Other than a pair of demonstrators in Fort Worth and an unfounded bomb scare in Cleveland, however, the oft-threatened protests against operators showing the match did not materialize.[48] Some sportswriters asked readers to stay away from the bout. Eddie Muller, the *San Francisco Examiner*'s boxing writer, chastised any theater operators who "might take it upon themselves to accept the TV firm's promotion and make a quick dollar." Referring to a proposed local boycott of the fight, Muller commented, "If every state follows California's action perhaps it'll be a complete nationwide blackout, which is as it should be."[49]

The most crippling blow to the promotion, by far, was its abandonment by closed-circuit television theater chains. Main Bout had contracted 280 North American closed-circuit television venues to show the Terrell fight, but only thirty-two sites ended up showing the match against Chuvalo.[50] Several cities that normally hosted Ali title fights in at least one area venue, including Cincinnati, Milwaukee, Kansas City, and Minneapolis–St. Paul, did not screen the bout. California's two biggest boxing promoters, Don Chargin and Aileen Eaton, met on March 6 and agreed to block the broadcast in their state. They announced that they would meet with theater owners in an effort to make sure that no venues in California showed the March 29 contest, "in deference to the many families that have loved ones fighting and dying in Vietnam."[51] When Main Bout approached Ray Syufy, owner of twenty-one drive-in theaters in Northern California, to televise the match, it was turned down, although Syufy admitted that the company had made him a "lucrative offer." In total, the fight was shown in only two California venues, both of them independent theaters. By contrast, Ali's previous bout against Floyd Patterson was shown in thirteen Los Angeles–area theaters alone.[52] In New York, seven Loews' theaters withdrew thirteen thousand seats from the closed-circuit pool. Ernie Emerling, the firm's public relations vice president, claimed, "Too much silly-shallying over the site didn't leave us enough time to print tickets and advertise; we should have had six-to-eight weeks." Later, New York's RKO theater chain canceled their offer to show the fight in their ten area venues. While twenty-five New York City venues, with a seating capacity of eighty thousand, had shown Ali versus Patterson, only five New York City theaters, with a seating capacity of eleven thousand, hosted Ali versus Chuvalo. In Chicago, Ed Seguin, representing the Balaban and Katz chain of theaters, reported that his firm would not show the fight "because of all the uncertainty over where, and whether, it was coming off." Both the B&K and Warner theater chains canceled their arrangements with Main Bout nationwide.[53]

At this time, Main Bout needed cooperation from these chains because most of the theaters equipped to show fights belonged to motion picture concerns like Loews' and RKO. There were few independent operators capable of profiting from closed-circuit telecasts due to spatial and technical limitations. For example, when two locals produced a broadcast in Jacksonville of Ali's first fight with Sonny Liston, their fees and costs were difficult to overcome. The Jacksonville Coliseum had about nine thousand seats. The half-full arena produced about $17,300 in ticket sales. Federal and state taxes were about $1,000. Promoters had to pay the ancillary promoter, Theater Network Television, 55 percent of their gross receipts after taxes ($9,000). Although the Jacksonville Coliseum was equipped with a $675 RCA projector, Theater Network Television insisted that the promoters rent a state-of-the-art Eidophor projector to show the bout ($2,600). Theater Network Television owned the American rights to the Eidophor. Rental of the Jacksonville Coliseum cost $1,600. The promoters installed a phone loop that connected the fight's broadcast signal to the theater ($550). Insurance cost $300 and advertising was $750. The promoters also had to hire security, printers, ushers, a sound engineer, and ticket takers ($1,000). The Jacksonville promoters netted less than $500 for their enterprise. Theater Network Television probably made ten times this amount on the venture.[54] Main Bout hoped to do similarly well, but could only do so with the cooperation of properly equipped theater chains. Eventually, Main Bout hoped to encourage independent, black-owned theaters to get involved in Ali's fights, perhaps by lowering its percentage of the take.

The Ali-Chuvalo fight was financially disastrous, although fans saw an excellent boxing match that Ali won by fifteen-round unanimous decision.[55] The closed-circuit telecast sold about 46,000 tickets for $110,000. This gross take was twenty to forty times below closed-circuit revenues from each of Ali's three previous championship fights. The $150,000 on-site, live gate was also lower than for each of Ali's previous title bouts. Furthermore, Ali's $60,000 purse was approximately a tenth of those for each of his three previous bouts and at least three times less than for any fight of his championship career. The Associated Press summarized, "Theater-television of last night's Cassius Clay-George Chuvalo heavy-weight title fight proved a resounding dud, as expected." Eddie Muller crowed, "Forming the Main Bout, Inc., organization was a costly mistake. Whoever put money into the firm must wind up broke. There's no way, as far as we can see, of the organization recouping."[56] Michael Malitz of Main Bout disputed this claim, telling reporters that Main Bout "made enough to pay the bills" and break even. Nevertheless, even Malitz had to admit that his company was "grossly underpaid for the time and effort."[57] The fiasco illustrated Main Bout's lack of control over the terms of Ali's fights. The organization would have to weigh its next move carefully if it, and Ali's career, were to survive.

Several white sportswriters and at least one black reporter blamed Main Bout's incompetence for the promotion's collapse. Bob Stewart of the *New York World-Telegram and Sun* teased, "It all seemed so simple. You just formed a quickie corporation and put on a title fight." Eddie Muller called Main Bout a "fly-by-night enterprise which now louse[s] up the horizon." The syndicated *Los Angeles Times* reporter and Ali basher Jim Murray claimed, "Clay's corporation, which ironically, calls itself 'Main Bout, Inc.' and is run by a football player and a couple of guys whose sole qualification is they once subscribed to the Police Gazette." One of Ali's few consistent critics within the black press, A. S. "Doc" Young of the *New York Amsterdam News*, insisted, "It was the stupidest sort of publicity for the Black Muslims to publicize their association with Main Bout, Inc."[58] Other sportswriters compared Main Bout unfavorably to the Louisville Sponsoring Group.[59]

A number of black observers disagreed and identified racism and a possible criminal conspiracy as reasons for the financial failure of the Ali-Chuvalo fight. "There are some reports of possible court action or civil rights agencies may be looking into the cancelations of the closed circuit television showings to ascertain if there was any overt racial discrimination involved," according to Clarence Matthews of the *Louisville Defender*. "What columnists have tried to do is thwart the Black Muslims through castigation of Clay," Marion Jackson wrote in the *Atlanta Daily World*. "It seems as though the Black Muslims for the first time ha[ve] projected a Negro group—Main Bout, Inc., in control of a nationwide closed circuit telecast." *Muhammad Speaks* accused white reporters of hiding their racism through so-called patriotic attacks on Ali. "Outbursts over [Ali's] military draft status were [a] means of killing two birds with one red, white, and blue stone" and an "attempt to smear" Main Bout, according to the newspaper. The most strident response came from Moses Newson of the *Baltimore Afro-American*. Newson praised Main Bout for surviving "in face of the most vicious and concentrated 'kill them off' campaign ever joined in by the press, the Mafia, and politicians." He asserted that white "reporters, broadcasters, and others who tried to kill the fight scribbled and spouted bitter reams to a degree that they actually need to offer something more lest they themselves might be thought part of an unholy alliance that includes racists, hypocrites, and mobsters." On Capitol Hill, Main Bout's Jim Brown, in a press conference with Harlem Congressman Adam Clayton Powell, contended, "The ostensible reason" for the boycott "is because of Clay's so-called unpatriotic remarks about the draft, but that's just an excuse [to destroy Main Bout]." Powell vowed to have the U.S. Department of Justice and the Equal Employment Opportunity Commission investigate the situation, although it is unclear whether or not he did so.[60]

Although Main Bout had complained as early as January that the mob was sabotaging their promotion, white sportswriters denied such a conspiracy. Even Robert Lipsyte of the *New York Times*, one of Ali's strongest supporters in the white press, called such a possibility "imaginative" because it suggested "an improbable plot of enormous complexity." Jack Berry of the *Detroit Free Press* asserted that such a plot was "not evident here. There's only one difficulty in this whole affair and the name is Cassius Clay. He brought it all on himself." Jimmy Cannon denied that racism fueled anti-Main Bout sentiment but admitted that organized crime resented Main Bout's entry into boxing. "The fight mob detests Clay. Their revulsion isn't instigated by race," wrote Cannon in his syndicated column. "They want Chuvalo to beat him because Clay has made the greatest prize in sports worthless. This isn't temporary. He is in trouble for a long while."[61]

The Federal Bureau of Investigation (FBI) looked into the boycott. It suspected that Terrell withdrew not only because of financial concerns but also death threats to him and his manager Bernard Glickman by Chicago underworld figures that would no longer profit if the bout were moved to Canada.[62] The FBI inquiry, however, proved inconclusive and no further federal investigation of the fight took place.[63] The *Pittsburgh Courier* sighed, "As usual, the casting of light on supported underworld control of boxing still remains unfulfilled."[64]

In response to the FBI investigation, some members of the white press acknowledged the possibility of collusion to eliminate Main Bout and Ali from boxing. The difficulties surrounding Main Bout's initial closed-circuit venture were "apparently an outgrowth of boxing's current scramble for position in a future made uncertain by the troubles of Cassius Clay," wrote Robert Lipsyte. "To the underworld, the new organization meant only that 'a rival gang' had moved in and was in a position to 'ace them out' by not dealing with 'trusted' closed circuit television operators or exhibitors as well as the other businessmen who normally get pay days from a title fight." Similarly, United Press International reported, "New

York Mafia interests were enraged at the attempt of the Muslims to take over closed circuit television rights and other revenues from professional boxing through Main Bout, Inc."[65]

Realizing that he might not be able to fight under Main Bout at home, Ali considered matches outside the United States. At first, he was nervous about this possibility. "They want to stop me from fighting. They done run me out of the country. . . . This [the Chuvalo match] could be my last fight," the champion told Phil Pepe of the *New York World-Telegram and Sun*. He revealed to syndicated *New York Post* columnist Milton Gross, "I don't want to go [abroad]. I want to defend my title here somewhere or even in a phone booth or in a barge at sea."[66] By the end of March, however, Ali had reconciled his doubts. "I'm not fighting for money," he said, "but for the freedom of American black people to speak their minds."[67] To a Louisville reporter, he admitted that he would like to fight in the United States, "But they can put it in England, Nigeria, France, or Rome if they want to. I don't care about the money. It's a world title I got, not a U.S.A. title, and it can be defended anywhere in the world." During an interview with Larry Merchant of the *Philadelphia Daily News*, Ali fanned himself with a replica passport and insisted that he would fight wherever he would be allowed.[68] Ali's most eloquent expression of this outlook was recorded by Robert Lipsyte. "Boxing is nothing, just satisfying some bloodthirsty people. I'm no longer Cassius Clay, a Negro from Kentucky. I belong to the world, the black world. I'll always have a home in Pakistan, in Algeria, in Ethiopia. This is more than money," he said.[69] "I'm not disturbed and nervous. Why should I be? In a few hours I could fly to another country, in the East, in Africa, where people love me. Millions, all over the world want to see me. Why should I worry about losing a few dollars." The champion concluded, "I'm not going to sell my manhood for a few dollars, or a smile. I'd rather be poor and free than rich and a slave."[70] Ali's comments foreshadowed his and Main Bout's decision to take his next three matches to Europe, where there had not been a world heavyweight championship contest in more than thirty years. The three European fights earned Ali purses far more lucrative than he had received for the match in Canada with Chuvalo and reestablished him as the top drawing power in boxing.

Ali fought in May against Britain's Henry Cooper for a $350,000 purse, the first world heavyweight title fight in England since 1908. For the rights to the bout with Cooper, ABC paid Main Bout $75,000. Mexican and Canadian television stations that picked up the signal also had to pay Main Bout a fee. Although smaller than successful U.S. closed-circuit telecasts, this sum was comparable to the $110,000 grossed by the broadcast of Ali versus Chuvalo. Equally important, the deal gave Main Bout and Ali increased independence from oppositional forces in the United States. Primarily through a huge on-site crowd and a successful British closed-circuit telecast, the Cooper fight raked in money. About 46,000 fans packed Arsenal Stadium. The $560,000 live gate was almost four times greater than that of the Chuvalo fight and set a British boxing record. Sixteen English closed-circuit theaters generated approximately 40,000 ticket sales and $280,000 in revenues. In all, the fight grossed nearly $1.5 million.[71]

Ali fought again in England in August, garnering a $300,000 purse for his match against Brian London. Main Bout received fees in exchange for the European and foreign rights to the contest while Ali received a $270,000 minimum guarantee plus a share of the ancillary receipts. For the live North American television rights, ABC paid Main Bout $200,000. Ten thousand people paid to see the London fight, which took in $150,000 on-site. Closed-circuit returns neared $165,000.[72] Even Gene Ward had to admit, "In both of these European ventures, Clay will earn more than he ever could have in the United States, where his opposition to the draft has left him an unpopular figure."[73]

In September, he defended his title against Karl Mildenberger in Germany, where there had never been a world heavyweight championship fight, for a $300,000 purse. Once again, ABC agreed to pay Main Bout $200,000 for the live television rights to the match. Forty thousand fans paid $500,000 on-site to see it in person. Although there was no closed-circuit television broadcast, other ancillary revenues (not including Main Bout's $200,000 deal with ABC) brought $250,000.[74]

In these three cases, rather than trying to work with a corrupt and hostile closed-circuit television industry at home, Main Bout instead signed to air the bouts live on free television in the United States (made possible by the Early Bird Satellite's successful launch a year earlier), on closed-circuit television in Europe, and on the radio in Africa, the Middle East, and Asia. Main Bout and Ali's independence from the established network of promoters in the United States allowed their return to North America for three fights in late 1966 and early 1967 under favorable promotional terms. They earned millions of dollars without relinquishing any control of their prized championship commodity, and Ali became the most active heavyweight champion since Joe Louis. Even against overmatched and relatively unknown opposition, Ali was making good money.

Muhammad Ali's bout with Cleveland Williams in November 1966 did very well, thanks to a successful closed-circuit broadcast and Ali's popularity among blacks. Thirty-five thousand fans watched the contest at the Houston Astrodome, paying $460,000 and breaking the American indoor attendance record for boxing. One hundred twenty-five U.S. closed-circuit television venues, with a total seating capacity of 500,000, showed the match. In a number of cities, Main Bout worked with previously uncooperative theater chains. Twenty-four New York closed-circuit locations had a combined seating capacity of 68,000, with tickets priced between $5 and $10 each. Loews' and RKO, theater chains that had refused to show Ali-Chuvalo, hosted the fight. In New Jersey, three previously uncooperative Warner's theaters also telecast the match. Six Northern California venues showed the fight, and at least one did superb business. The Warfield Theater in San Francisco sold 2,000 of 2,600 available seats for the match. Jack Fiske of the *San Francisco Chronicle* observed, "The theater audience was at least one-fourth Negro, perhaps the largest turnout for any Clay fight I recall." At least fourteen Los Angeles area venues screened Ali-Williams; only two venues in California had shown Ali-Chuvalo. Chicago's B&K movie theater chain, which had declined to telecast Ali-Chuvalo, showed a feature movie before broadcasting to patrons the Ali-Williams fight. In total, seven Chicago-area venues hosted the match. Leo Brown, the manager of the State-Lake movie theater, told the *Chicago Tribune*, "It wasn't a full house, but a good house." The *Tribune* reporter noted, "an unusually large number of Negro fans paid $7.50 for reserved seats." Total closed-circuit receipts probably topped $1 million.

Main Bout also arranged for telecasts and films in forty-two countries. It sold live television rights to Mexican and Canadian stations and delayed privileges to ABC. There was also a live U.S. radio broadcast of the match, which brought in an additional $100,000. Main Bout pocketed 32.5 percent of the ancillary gross. Ali's purse probably exceeded $750,000.[75]

In February 1967, Ali's long-awaited match with Ernie Terrell also proved lucrative. Thirty-seven thousand fans at the Astrodome paid $400,000 on-site. One hundred seventy-eight North American closed-circuit venues took in approximately $1 million. Main Bout pocketed 30 percent of the ancillaries. Ali's purse approached $1 million. At Madison Square Garden, one of eleven New York City venues to show the bout, 5,500 (of a possible 10,000) fans paid between $7.50 and $10, despite inclement weather. Once again, Main Bout agreed to terms with previously uncooperative closed-circuit chains. In total, there were twenty-five New York Tri-State area venues, with a seating capacity of 95,000, not including a pay-per-view home TV arrangement in Hartford. Newark's Branford Theater, one of eight New Jersey venues, sold out. At least twelve Los Angeles area venues broadcast the bout. There was also a live U.S. radio broadcast.[76]

Ali's March 1967 contest with Zora Folley was not as big as the other two matches, but it yielded a solid $265,000 purse for Ali. The match was Madison Square Garden's first world heavyweight title bout in over fifteen years, but terrible weather in New York limited the crowd to 14,000. They paid $244,000, an arena record, to see it in person. RKO Pictures purchased the worldwide rights to the match from Main Bout for $175,000 and made Ali versus Folley the first ever heavyweight championship fight shown live on U.S. home television during prime time. Main Bout made no profit from the fight and did not promote it. The organization acted merely to broker the worldwide rights to RKO. Main Bout paid Ali $150,000 and Folley $25,000 of the fee it received. Ali also earned about 50 percent of the live gate.[77]

Following these successes, Main Bout arranged for a rematch between Ali and Floyd Patterson before the champion's May induction date. The Nevada State Athletic Commission agreed to sanction the April 25 bout in Las Vegas. Main Bout announced that it would be broadcast on closed-circuit television in the United States and beamed via satellite to Japan and Europe. Contracts called for Ali to receive $225,000. By April 11, according to Michael Malitz, Main Bout had contracted eighty-five venues in the United States and a "large number of foreign outlets" to show the bout. He estimated that Main Bout had already received $150,000 in fees.[78]

As in Chicago a year earlier, however, an anti-Ali backlash ensued and the fight never took place. The press and government officials called for the cancelation of the match. Jimmy Cannon labeled the bout a "sanctioned atrocity." Las Vegas sheriff Ralph Lamb warned local promoters that "they will not receive police protection from my department this time. Why should I risk some fine men getting hurt when the only ones who will profit from this fiasco will be the private promoters of the fight?" On April 11, Nevada governor Paul Laxalt requested that the Nevada State Athletic Commission cancel the fight, which it did. "It would give Nevada a black eye," claimed Laxalt. Main Bout then shifted its attention to Pittsburgh. The Pennsylvania State Athletic Commission agreed to sanction the match. Laxalt called Pennsylvania governor Raymond Shafer and asked him to block it, which Shafer did. New York was mentioned as a possible site. When asked about the fight, New York State Athletic Commissioner Edwin Dooley ended such speculation: "We have a reciprocity agreement with both the Nevada and Pennsylvania Commissions. They abide by our rulings and we abide by theirs." Although New Mexico governor David Cargo offered Albuquerque as a last-minute site, Main Bout had run out of time. They risked another Toronto-type flop with just two weeks remaining before Ali's induction ceremony. Main Bout threw in the towel. Malitz told a reporter, "Once Pittsburgh was a dead issue, I felt it was all over." With his career stalled, Ali turned his attention to his trial.[79]

Muhammad Ali's conviction on draft evasion charges in June 1967 ended Main Bout's run after only seventeen months and seven fights, and it is difficult to assess the company's impact on black economic power. Main Bout's economic goals seem to have been threefold: 1) negotiate good purses for Ali; 2) make money for its shareholders; 3) create wealth and employment for blacks. It would appear they accomplished the first two goals but not the third. Main Bout's early demise, however, makes it impossible to know whether it would have become a black economic institution capable of making money and creating jobs for substantial numbers of African Americans.

Ultimately, Main Bout's collapse stemmed from its lack of political power rather than from economic pressure. State athletic commissions nationwide unanimously refused to license Ali immediately following his indictment in May 1967. If any state athletic commission had sanctioned an Ali fight, he would have fought there. Following his conviction, Ali stayed out of prison on appeal, but his passport was invalidated, eliminating his chances of fighting abroad. Realizing Ali was finished, Arum, Malitz, and Brown left Main Bout to form their own company, Sports Action, Inc., which would promote the tournament designed to replace Ali as heavyweight champion.[80] The Nation of Islam and Ali were frozen out of professional boxing. For the next three and a half years, Ali did not fight professionally. Nevertheless, Main Bout's temporary success in the face of tremendous opposition was a symbolic victory for blacks. Like Ali and his contemporaries in the civil rights movement, the company faced challenges without compromising its principles. The story of Main Bout, Inc., reminds us how cultural sites, in this case professional boxing, can become key arenas for larger political and economic struggles.

NOTES

1. John Bracey, August Meier, and Elliot Rudwick, *Black Nationalism in America* (Indianapolis: Bobbs-Merrill, 1970); Wilson J. Moses, *The Golden Age of Black Nationalism* (New York: Oxford University Press, 1978); August Meier, *Negro Thought in America 1880–1915: Racial Ideologies in the Age of Booker T. Washington* (Ann Arbor: University of Michigan Press, [1963] 1966); August Meier and Elliot Rudwick, *Along the Color Line: Explorations in the Black Experience* (Urbana: University of Illinois, 1976); Sterling Stuckey, *Slave Culture: Nationalist Theory and the Foundations of Black America* (New York: Oxford University Press, 1987); Raymond W. Smock, ed., *Booker T. Washington in Perspective: Essays of Louis Harlan* (Jackson: University of Mississippi Press, 1988); David Levering Lewis, *W. E. B. Du Bois: Biography of a Race, 1868–1919* (New York: Henry Holt, 1993); Tony Martin, *Race First: The Ideological and Organizational Struggles of*

Marcus Garvey and the Universal Negro Improvement Association (Westport: Greenwood Press, 1976); Rodney Carlisle, *The Roots of Black Nationalism* (Port Washington: Kennikat Press, 1975).

2. Quoted in H. J. McFall, "Cassius Clay Tells Plans to Form a Negro Company," *Louisville Defender*, January 13, 1966, 1.

3. Quoted in Louis Harlan, *Booker T. Washington: The Making of a Black Leader, 1856–1901* (New York: Oxford University Press, 1972), 161.

4. Lawrence Levine, "Marcus Garvey and the Politics of Revitalization," in *Black Leaders of the Twentieth Century*, edited by John Hope Franklin and August Meier (Urbana: University of Illinois Press, 1982), 127.

5. Malcolm X, "The Bullet or the Ballot," reprinted in *The Norton Anthology of African American Literature*, edited by Henry Louis Gates Jr. and Nellie Y. McKay (New York: W.W. Norton, 1997), 92.

6. Julian Bond, interview by author, March 18, 2002.

7. John Lewis, "SNCC's Lewis: We March for Us . . . and for You," *New York Herald-Tribune*, May 23, 1965, subgroup A, series 1, reel 1, item 37, Student Nonviolent Coordinating Committee Papers (hereafter SNCC).

8. Transcript of Carmichael's June 19, 1966, appearance on CBS's *Face the Nation*, subgroup A, series 1, reel 2, item 58, SNCC.

9. Subgroup A, series 1, reel 2, item 52, SNCC.

10. Document dated August 7, 1964, appendix A, reel 70, item 534A, SNCC.

11. Thomas Hauser, who became an Ali spokesman during the 1990s and whose biography of the boxer helped spur that decade's Ali renaissance, called Ali's contract with the Louisville Sponsoring Group "fair and generous for its time." See Thomas Hauser, *Muhammad Ali: His Life and Times* (New York: Touchstone, 1991), 30. Claude Lewis's influential early biography commented, "There are eleven sponsors in the group, and at a time when the boxing world is beclouded by underworld dickerings, misappropriated funds, government investigation, and a general sorrowful malaise, they present an uplifting sight. . . . Not only does their private wealth insure Clay that he will never end up broke through any fault of theirs, but they surround him with a substantial moral and ethical environment, a rare commodity in boxing these days" (Claude Lewis, *Cassius Clay* [New York: MacFadden-Bartell Books, 1965], 39).

12. Discussion of the finances of Ali-Patterson can be found in Eddie Muller, "Fight Talk Today Is $," *San Francisco Examiner*, November 19, 1965, 58; Al Buck, "Cassius Clay: The 'Champion,'" *New York Post*, November 24, 1966, 48; "The Fight of TV," *Chicago Sun-Times*, November 24, 1965, 17; Associated Press, "Fight Facts and Figures," *Louisville Courier-Journal*, November 22, 1965,

B-7; and Paul Zimmerman, "Clay, Patterson to Offer Defense," *Los Angeles Times*, November 22, 1965, 3:1. Financial information on Ali's rematch with Liston can be found in Associated Press, "Facts on Title Fight," *New York Times*, May 26, 1965, 49, 54. For financial statistics on Ali's first bout with Liston, see Associated Press, "Fight Facts, Figures," *San Francisco Examiner*, February 25, 1964, 52; Robert Lipsyte, "Each Slice of Fight Pie Is Rich, But Promoter's Going Hungry," *New York Times*, February 24, 1964, 30; Leonard Koppett, "All the World's a Stage, via TV, for Title Fight," *New York Times*, February 23, 1964, 5:1.

13. Although Main Bout had only five members the organization was split into six voting shares in order to give the Nation of Islam 50 percent control. See Jimmy Cannon, "Theater TV, the Muslims . . . and Jim Brown," *Los Angeles Herald-Examiner*, January 10, 1966, C-2; Hauser, *Muhammad Ali*, 151–52; Robert Lipsyte, "Clay's Main Bout, Inc., Seen Final Step in a Project to Bolster Negro Business," *New York Times*, January 9, 1966, 5:4; and George Vass, "TV Firm Dictated Date of Title Bout," *Chicago Daily News*, January 28, 1966, 22.

14. Quoted in Vass, "TV Firm Dictated Date," 22.

15. Lipsyte, "Clay's Main Bout," 5:4; United Press International, "Cleveland Grid Star Brown Retires," *Montreal Star*, July 14, 1966, 21; Associated Press, "Brown to Help Negro Economy," *Baltimore Sun*, July 15, 1966, C-1; Earl Ruby, "Has Brown Left Door Ajar? No Ex-Athletes in His Plan," *Louisville Courier-Journal*, July 22, 1966, B-8; Milton Gross, "Curiouser and Curiouser," *New York Post*, February 3, 1967, 77.

16. Gene Ward, "Heavy Title TV and All, Taken Over By Muslims," *Chicago American*, February 13, 1966, 10; Jimmy Cannon, "Malice Disguised as Banter in Clay's Evil Strain of Wit," *Miami Herald*, February 19, 1966, C-2; Cannon, "Theater TV, the Muslims," C-2; Doug Gilbert, "Clay-Terrell Package Wrapped in Muslims?" *Chicago American*, February 5, 1966, 11; Red Smith, "N.Y. Merits Clay-Terrell, It's Claimed," *Chicago Sun-Times*, February 7, 1966, 72; editorial page, "Throw the Bums Out," *Chicago Daily News*, February 5, 1966, 14; editorial page, "Sucker Bait," *Chicago Tribune*, February 14, 1966, 1:20.

17. One critical article is "Clay Opens New 'Kettle of Fish,'" *New York Amsterdam News*, January 25, 1966, 25.

18. Cal Jacox, "From the Sidelines," *Cleveland Call and Post*, January 22, 1966, 22.

19. Ric Roberts, "Change of Pace," *Pittsburgh Courier*, February 19, 1966, 14; "'Mob' Ruled Boxers Retire Flat Broke," *Pittsburgh Courier*, February 12, 1966, 15.

20. Hauser, *Muhammad Ali*, 142; United Press International, "Clay, Namath Targets in Draft Legislation," *Louisville Courier-Journal*, February 10, 1966, B-5; Chip

Magnus, "Congressmen Seek Khaki for Clay, Namath," *Chicago Sun-Times*, February 10, 1966, 116; United Press International, "Draft Heat On, but Lip Still Zipped," *Los Angeles Times*, February 12, 1966, 2:7.

21. Quoted in Tom Fitzpatrick, "Cassius Appeals; 'Muslims Not at War,'" *Chicago Daily News*, February 18, 1966, 29.

22. Quoted in "Clay Sees Self as Boon to U.S. in Civilian Dress," *Chicago Tribune*, February 21, 1966, 1:3.

23. Dick Young, "Young Ideas," *New York Daily News*, December 31, 1966, 38; Jack Clary, "Frothy Facts," *New York World-Telegram and Sun*, February 21, 1966, 37; Red Smith, "Folk Hero," *New York Herald-Tribune*, February 21, 1966, 28; Gene Ward, "Ward to the Wise," *New York Daily News*, February 20, 1966, 153; Arthur Daley, "Instant Bile," *New York Times*, February 24, 1966, 42.

24. Examples of such articles include Melvin Durslag, "A Fight to Help the Worthy," *Los Angeles Herald-Examiner*, February 21, 1966, C-1; Milton Moss, "Emergency Operation on Clay," *Los Angeles Herald-Examiner*, February 22, 1966, C-2; Red Smith, "The Patrioteers," *New York Herald-Tribune*, February 23, 1966, 28.

25. Jimmy Cannon, "Too Much at Stake; Muslims Silence Clay," *Chicago Daily News*, February 22, 1966, 17; editorial page, "Clay's Tough Assignment," *Chicago American*, February 25, 1966, 10; editorial page, "He's All Yours, Louisville," *Chicago Tribune*, February 25, 1966, 18.

26. Editorial page, "Cassius vs. the Draft," *Chicago American*, February 19, 1966, 4; editorial page, "The Reluctant Hero," *Chicago Tribune*, February 19, 1966, 1:10; "News Chiefs Rap Kerner, Boxing Board," *Chicago Tribune*, February 21, 1966, 1:3; "VFW Urges Kerner to Block Clay Fight," *Chicago Tribune*, February 21, 1966, 1:2; "2 Legislators Rip Clay Bout License," *Chicago Tribune*, February 21, 1966, 1:1; "Senator Asks Kerner to Cancel Clay Bout," *Chicago Tribune*, February 22, 1966, 1:1; Charles Siragusa quoted in "Siragusa Raps Clay on Draft," *Chicago Tribune*, February 23, 1966, 1:1; Orlando Wilson quoted in "Wilson Fears Disorders at Clay Fight: Joins Opposition with Howlett," *Chicago Tribune*, February 24, 1966, 1:1; Richard Daley quoted in editorial page, "Mayor Daley's Good Advice," *Chicago Tribune*, February 23, 1966, 1:16; Otto Kerner quoted in "Clay Due Tomorrow as Fight Furor Grows," *Chicago American*, February 23, 1966, 37.

27. Ben Bentley quoted in Associated Press, "Cassius Is Still Single; Regrets Draft Popoff," *New York Daily News*, February 21, 1966, 117; Joe Triner quoted in Associated Press, "Clay Gives Apologies to Illinois," *Miami Herald*, February 22, 1966, B-1; Muhammad Ali quoted in United Press International, "Illinois Delays Fight Decision Pending Personal Clay Apology," *Miami Herald*, B-1;

Muhammad Ali quoted in Lester Bromberg, "Clay's New 'Quiet Man' Role May Save Fight," *New York World-Telegram and Sun*, February 22, 1966, 8.

28. Larry Merchant, "Clay Pigeon," *Philadelphia Daily News*, February 22, 1966, 58; United Press International, "Clay Apologizes for Draft Remarks," *Atlanta Daily World*, February 22, 1966, 1; Moss, "Emergency Operation," C-2; Cannon, "Too Much at Stake," 17; editorial page, "Whoever Wins, Illinois Loses," *Chicago Daily News*, February 23, 1966, 8; Ray Sons, "Shy Clay to 'Avoid' Muslim Meeting Here," *Chicago Daily News*, February 23, 1966, 49; Jack Mabley, "Plans Apology before Athletic Commission Here," *Chicago American*, February 24, 1966, 1; Associated Press, "Clay Not Expected to Attend Black Muslim Convention," *New York Times*, February 24, 1966, 44; Daley, "Instant Bile," 44; Sid Ziff, "One Fight He Wants," *Los Angeles Times*, February 25, 1966, 3:3.

29. Quoted in Pat Putnam, "Muslim Clay to Stay Away?" *Miami Herald*, February 24, 1966, D-5.

30. "News from the Camp of the Champ," *Muhammad Speaks*, March 4, 1966, 9.

31. "Champion Silent on Arrival for State Hearing," *Chicago American*, February 25, 1966, 1.

32. Ed Stone, "Suspicion Clouds Clay-Terrell Sanction Here," *Chicago American*, February 25, 1966, 25; "Champ Refuses to Apologize to Commission," *Chicago Daily News*, February 25, 1966, 3:25; Muhammad Ali and Joe Triner quoted in "Clay Fight Ruled Illegal," *Chicago American*, February 26, 1966, 1:1, 1:25; David Condon, "In the Wake of the News," *Chicago Tribune*, February 26, 1966, 2:1.

33. Quoted in Ed Sainsbury, "Illinois: Fight is Illegal . . . Clay No Apology," *New York World-Telegram and Sun*, February 25, 1966, 25.

34. Quoted in "Attorney General Clark's Statement," *Chicago American*, February 25, 1966, 25. Bentley and Schoenwald were the only members of the National Sports Promotion Corporation that promoted the live, on-site event. According to Clark, the licensing problems were the following: Ali didn't file a certificate of a resident physician with his license reapplication; Ali answered a 'moral character' question insufficiently; Ali failed to include his proper ring record in the license reapplication; and that he signed the application "Muhammad Ali" instead of "Cassius Clay." Clark also cited Terrell for failing to file a physician's certificate. See Jesse Abramson, "The Championship Fight Almost Nobody Wants," *New York Herald-Tribune*, March 2, 1966, 27.

35. Quoted in Doug Gilbert, "Clay Title Fight on Ropes Here, Pittsburgh Next?" *Chicago American*, February 26, 1966, 1:1.

36. Editorial page, "A Wise Decision at Last," *Chicago Tribune*, March 3, 1966, 20.

37. Bob Arum quoted in Jack Berry, "Clay: He Wouldn't Crawl," *Detroit Free Press*, March 10, 1966, D-2; Robert Lipsyte, "Clay-Terrell Fight for Title Is Shifted to Louisville for March 29," *New York Times*, March 1, 1966, 30; Robert Lipsyte, "Louisville Rejects Plans for a Clay-Terrell Go," *New York Times*, March 2, 1966, 36; William Sullivan quoted in United Press International, "Kentucky Senate Urges Clay to Enlist," *Philadelphia Daily News*, February 24, 1966, 58; Gilbert, "Clay Title Fight," 1; United Press International, "Clay-Terrell Bout Gets No Pennsylvania Welcome," *New York Times*, February 27, 1966, 5:2. Maine promoters' interest is detailed in Associated Press, "Boxing's Big Bout Bangor Bound?" *Los Angeles Herald-Examiner*, February 28, 1966, D-1. Maine State Athletic Commission support for the fight is in Associated Press, "No Decision on Clay Bout," *Baltimore Sun*, March 1, 1966, C-1. Governor Reed's opposition is detailed in Associated Press, "Heavy Fight Bounces Back," *Baltimore Sun*, March 2, 1966, C-1.

38. Elijah Muhammad quoted in "Muslim Leader Raps Viet Policy While Clay Listens," *Chicago Tribune*, February 27, 1966, 1:3; David Condon, "In the Wake of the News," *Chicago Tribune*, March 28, 1966, 3:1. Also see Paul Sisco, "Muslim Chief Backs Clay's Draft Stand," *Louisville Courier-Journal*, February 27, 1966, A-1.

39. United Press International, "Clay Is Granted Permission to Leave Country for Bout," *New York Times*, March 18, 1966, 47. Also see Milton Gross, "Cassius Clay at the Brink," *Chicago Daily News*, March 28, 1966, 29.

40. For explanations of the fight's rejection by various Canadian cities, some of which were political, some of which were logistical, see Jesse Abramson, "The License Hasn't Been Granted Yet," *New York Herald-Tribune*, March 3, 1966, 20; Combined Wire Services, "Funny Thing Happened To Clay Title Bout on Its Way to the Forum," *New York Herald-Tribune*, March 4, 1966, 21; Jesse Abramson, "Clay Fails to Pass at Verdun, Tries New Front," *New York Herald-Tribune*, March 5, 1966, 13; Associated Press, "5 Sites Considered for Clay Title Bout," *New York Herald-Tribune*, March 6, 1966, 4:6; United Press International, "Montreal May Take Clay Bout," *Los Angeles Herald-Examiner*, March 3, 1966, D-2; Norm Miller, "Ill. Wind Blows Clay-Terrell Go to Montreal," *New York Daily News*, March 3, 1966, 66; Associated Press, "Sorrels, Edmonton Display Interest," *New York Times*, March 5, 1966, 19.

41. Berry, "Clay: He Wouldn't Crawl," D-2; Lester Bromberg, "Toronto: We'll Accept Clay-Terrell Fight," *New York World-Telegram and Sun*, March 8, 1966, 18.

42. Lester Bromberg, "Clay-Terrell Fight for Title Appears Dead," *New York World-Telegram and Sun*, March 10, 1966, 12.

43. Jesse Abramson, "Clay Fights Chuvalo for Peanuts in Toronto," *New York Herald-Tribune*, March 29, 1966, 22; Arthur Daley, "Is This Trip Necessary?" *New York Times*, March 29, 1966, 47; Eddie Muller, "Clay-Chuvalo Talk Negative," *San Francisco Examiner*, March 25, 1966, 67; Lester Bromberg, "Price is 6–5 Chuvalo Will Go 15 Rounds," *New York World-Telegram and Sun*, March 28, 1966, 27; Prescott Sullivan, "Who'd Want to Miss It?" *San Francisco Examiner*, March 23, 1966, 61; Robert Lipsyte, "Bettor's Eye View of Chuvalo: A Big Bum with a Lot of Heart," *New York Times*, March 26, 1966, 19; Bob Stewart, "Just Maybe," *New York World-Telegram and Sun*, March 25, 1966, 27; John P. Carmichael, "The Barber Shop," *Chicago Daily News*, March 26, 1966, 3:29; Red Smith, "The Action," *New York Herald-Tribune*, March 29, 1966, 23.

44. Robert Lipsyte, "Patterson Gains Unanimous Decision Over Chuvalo in 12 Rounder," *New York Times*, February 2, 1965, 36; "64 Theater Sites to Show Patterson-Chuvalo Bout," *New York Times*, January 27, 1965, 39.

45. Associated Press, "Fight Facts and Figures," *Chicago Daily News*, February 9, 1966, 45.

46. Associated Press, "Fight Theater TV a Resounding Dud," *San Francisco Examiner*, March 30, 1966, 78.

47. "Advertisers Boycotting Clay Fight," *Chicago Tribune*, March 15, 1966, 3:3; Associated Press, "Ad Sponsors Cool to Bout," *Baltimore Sun*, March 16, 1966, C-3.

48. Associated Press, "Miami Legion Post to Picket Theaters," *New York Herald-Tribune*, March 6, 1966, 4:6; Berry, "Clay: He Wouldn't Crawl," D-2.

49. Eddie Muller, "Chargin, Ms. Eaton Swing Clay TV Ban," *San Francisco Examiner*, March 10, 1966, 56; Norman Ross, "How to Vote against Boxing: Don't Spend Money on It," *Chicago Daily News*, February 25, 1966, 12; Robert Lipsyte, "Coast Backs Boycott," *New York Times*, March 10, 1966, 37.

50. Abramson, "Clay Fights Chuvalo," 47; Associated Press, "Clay Beats Chuvalo in 15 Rounds," *Baltimore Sun*, March 30, 1966, C-1; Associated Press, "Theater-TV Lays an Egg at the Box Office," *New York World-Telegram and Sun*, March 30, 1966, 26; Associated Press, "Clucking Sound at Clay Box Office," *San Francisco Examiner*, March 12, 1966, 33.

51. Quoted in John Washington, "Olympic Bans Clay TV," *Los Angeles Herald-Examiner*, March 8, 1966, F-1; Eddie Muller, "Clay Fight Blackout," *San Francisco Examiner*, March 8, 1966, 51; Muller, "Chargin, Ms. Eaton," 56.

52. Quoted in Eddie Muller, "Syufy Spurns Clay Tee-Vee," *San Francisco Examiner*, March 19, 1966, 31; Sullivan, "Who'd Want to Miss It?" 61; Associated Press, "Experts Flock to Chuvalo Camp," *San Francisco Examiner*, March 22, 1966,

48; "Fight Tickets on Sale," *Los Angeles Herald-Examiner*, November 21, 1965, E-7.

53. Ernie Emerling and Ed Seguin quoted in Lester Bromberg, "Only 1 Local Theater Chain Has Clay TV," *New York World-Telegram and Sun*, March 9, 1966, 34; Paul Weisman, "Fight Facts . . . or Just Fiction?" *New York Herald-Tribune*, March 17, 1966, 24; Dick Young, "Young Ideas," *New York Daily News*, November 17, 1965, 113; Paul Weisman, ". . . Bout Also Flops on the Popcorn Circuit," *New York Herald-Tribune*, March 29, 1966, 23.

54. Figures from Red Smith, "The Zillion-Dollar Fight Gate, Jacksonville Style," *New York Herald-Tribune*, March 15, 1964, 4:2.

55. Associated Press, "Clay Beats Chuvalo," C-1; Melvin Durslag, "A Good Lively Match," *San Francisco Examiner*, March 30, 1966, 78; Robert Lipsyte, "Clay Outpoints Chuvalo in Bruising, No-Knockdown 15-Rounder at Toronto," *New York Times*, March 30, 1966, 49; "Clay Quiet, Chuvalo Proud," *New York World-Telegram and Sun*, March 30, 1966, 26.

56. Associated Press, "Fight Theater TV," 78; Abramson, "Clay Fights Chuvalo," 47; Associated Press, "Clay Beats Chuvalo," C-1; Associated Press, "Theater-TV Lays an Egg," 26; Associated Press, "Clucking Sound," 33; Muller, "Clay-Chuvalo Talk," 67.

57. Quoted in Dave Brady, "Home TV Carries Clay-Cooper Fight," *Washington Post*, April 27, 1966, C-3. If Malitz's claim was accurate, the profit margin for closed-circuit television was enormous.

58. Bob Stewart, "Flop in the Making," *New York World-Telegram and Sun*, March 9, 1966, 35; Eddie Muller, "Fight Empire Not That Bad," *San Francisco Examiner*, March 6, 1966, 3:8; Jim Murray, "'Enery Might Shut Him Up," *Des Moines Register*, April 26, 1966, S-2; A. S. Young, "Aw F'Heavens Sake," *New York Amsterdam News*, April 2, 1966, 31.

59. Larry Boeck, "Association With Muslims Has Cost Clay $2 Million over Last Two Years, Backer Says," *Louisville Courier-Journal*, November 20, 1965, B-9; "Clay, Muslim Pals Figure to Strike It Rich Here," *Chicago Tribune*, February 21, 1966, 3:1; "Clay Group to Stay with Him for Now; Reveal Appeal Plan," *Chicago Tribune*, February 22, 1966, 3:1; Gene Ward, "Ward to the Wise," *New York Daily News*, March 1, 1966, 51; Dick Young, "Young Ideas," *New York Daily News*, June 4, 1966, 35.

60. Clarence Matthews, "Muhammad Ali Wins," *Louisville Defender*, April 7, 1966, 30; Marion Jackson, "Views Sports of the World," *Atlanta Daily World*, March 13, 1966, 8; "Champ Ali on Threshold of New Achievements," *Muhammad Speaks*, April 5, 1966, 6; Moses J. Newson, "Cassius Clay, Main Bout, Inc.

and a Boxing World Miracle," *Baltimore Afro-American*, April 9, 1966, 10; Jim Brown quoted in "Jim Brown Charges Fight Foes Oppose Negro TV Promoters," *Chicago Daily News*, March 10, 1966, 27; "Jimmy Brown Defends Clay on Capitol Hill," *New York Herald-Tribune*, March 11, 1966, 20.

61. Robert Lipsyte, "Boxing's Bogeyman's Back," *New York Times*, January 30, 1966, s-3; Berry, "Clay: He Wouldn't Crawl," D-2; Jimmy Cannon, "This Mismatch Is for Title, Despite Toronto's Billing," *Chicago Daily News*, March 29, 1966, 40.

62. In a July 2002 interview with the author, Terrell denied being threatened by gangsters and claimed that Glickman had no mob ties. Terrell also denied talking to the FBI about his withdrawal from the Ali fight.

63. The FBI, with help from the U.S. Department of Justice (it is unclear whether they were responding to Powell's request) investigated the promotion and announced that it would hold grand jury hearings into death threats against Terrell. It also probed allegations that mobsters had threatened to kill Glickman for compromising the chances of a match between Ali and Terrell in New York, where the fight was originally scheduled to take place before being bumped to Chicago. The FBI also claimed that Chicago gangsters had threatened to murder Terrell if he faced Ali in Toronto. In all, eleven witnesses from the often-interrelated worlds of organized crime and professional boxing were on the docket. They were the following: Glickman; Irving Schoenwald; Bob Arum; Teddy Brenner and Harry Markson, who together ran Madison Square Garden's boxing division; Joseph Glaser, a New York theatrical agent and boxing manager; Julius Isaacson, Terrell's former manager and a New York underworld associate; Anthony Accardo, the Chicago crime syndicate's "Godfather"; Felix Alderisio, Accardo's second-in-command; Gus Alex, the boss of the Chicago crime syndicate's gambling operations; and Gus Zapas, a top Chicago aide to labor leader Jimmy Hoffa. The government wanted to know whether Accardo, Alderisio, Alex, Zapas, and perhaps some of their New York affiliates had violated federal gambling and racketeering laws in their attempt to hijack the March 29 promotion. U.S. Attorney Edward Hanrahan sought indictments against anyone who may have used "terror tactics" to tamper with "the arrangements to promote in New York City the ill-fated [Ali-Terrell] fight." The UPI claimed that a crime syndicate would have gotten half of Terrell's $300,000 purse had the fight been held in New York. The government's key witness was Glickman. If he would detail the processes by which mob involvement in boxing took place, it would have a chance at indicting the gangsters who may have interfered with the promotion. Witness Isaacson proved to be

no help, and Zapas and Alex exercised their Fifth Amendment rights rather than testify. The statements by Brenner, Markson, and Schoenwald were taken on March 30. Glickman told his story on March 31, discussing his entry into the fight game, his associations with boxers, and his relationships with fellow witnesses. After Glickman's testimony, Hanrahan announced that he would postpone further testimony to consider the evidence. He reserved the right to call the witnesses again and ordered federal protection for Glickman. On April 15, Glickman entered the hospital for exhaustion and released himself from the FBI's protective custody, which the government feared signaled a deal between the former manager and the gangsters he had offended. According to unnamed officials working the case, Glickman agreed not to implicate Accardo and Alderisio in exchange for his life. With its star witness suddenly uncooperative, the government wrapped up the investigation. It indicted Gus Alex on April 15. Members of the black press were disappointed by the government's failure to make more of an impact on mob control of professional boxing, while white reporters were silent on the investigation's conclusion. For descriptions of Terrell's and Glickman's problems in New York, see Ed Stone, "Glickman Denies Terrell Controlled by Underworld," *Chicago American*, November 19, 1965, 33; Associated Press, "Ernie Says Charge 'Lie,'" *Atlanta Journal*, November 19, 1965, 22; United Press International, "Deny Terrell License to Fight in New York," *New York World-Telegram and Sun*, January 28, 1966, 24; Jim McCulley, "N.Y. Denies Terrell's Bid For Title Bout with Clay," *New York Daily News*, January 29, 1966, 26; Robert Lipsyte, "State Commission Denies License to Terrell," *New York Times*, January 29, 1966, 17; Lipsyte, "Boxing's Bogeyman's Back," S-3; Dave Nightingale, "Ernie Denies Glickman Ties," *Chicago Daily News*, February 1, 1966, 31; Phil Pepe, "The Terrell Case," *New York World-Telegram and Sun*, February 17, 1966, 15; Jesse Abramson, "Terrell Lost Date By Coincidence," *New York Herald-Tribune*, February 17, 1966, 23. For discussions of the FBI grand jury hearings, see Cannon, "This Mismatch Is for the Title," 40; Associated Press and United Press International, "Probe on Terrell Death Threat," *San Francisco Examiner*, March 26, 1966, 31; Associated Press, "U.S. Probes Threat to Terrell's Life," *New York Herald-Tribune*, March 27, 1966, 4:1; United Press International, "Inquiry Ordered on Boxing Threat," *New York Times*, March 27, 1966, 5:1; "Who's Who in Federal Probe of Mob's Link to Boxing," *Chicago Daily News*, March 30, 1966, 5; Edmund J. Rooney, "Boxing Probe Opens Here after Last Minute Site Shift," *Chicago Daily News*, March 30, 1966, 1; "Glickman Tells Jury of Mob's Boxing Links," *Chicago Daily News*, March 31, 1966, 6; Norman Glubok, "I'll Talk, I'm Not

Afraid, Says Terrell," *Chicago Daily News*, March 28, 1966, 1; Robert Lipsyte, "Showdown in Boxing," *New York Times*, March 28, 1966, 45; United Press International, "Ring Pilot Gives Extortion Terms," *New York Times*, March 28, 1966, 45; United Press International, "In this Corner—the Mafia," *San Francisco Examiner*, March 28, 1966, 65; Edmund J. Rooney, "Glickman in City—Guarded by FBI," *Chicago Daily News*, March 29, 1966, 1; Combined News Services, "Glickman's Hobby Goes Sour, Business Fails," *St. Louis Post-Dispatch*, March 31, 1966, C-8; "Glickman Hospital Stay 'Indefinite,'" *Chicago Daily News*, May 4, 1966, 5; "Fear Mob Promised Glickman Protection to Stop Testimony," *Chicago American*, April 16, 1966, 3; "Boxing Jury Indictment," *Chicago Daily News*, April 15, 1966, 1. For reports of Glickman's hospitalization and his refusal to testify, see "Glickman Hospital Stay," 5; "Fear Mob Promised Glickman Protection," 3. For a note on the indictment of Gus Alex, see "Boxing Jury Indictment," 1.

64. "Terrell 'Intimidation' Exposes Ring Problem," *Pittsburgh Courier*, May 14, 1966, 14.

65. Lipsyte, "Showdown in Boxing," 45; United Press International, "Ring Pilot Gives," 45; United Press International, "In This Corner," 65.

66. Quoted in Phil Pepe, "Uneasy Lies the Head," *New York World-Telegram and Sun*, March 8, 1966, 16; quoted in Milton Gross, "Clay Distressed Now," *Chicago Daily News*, March 8, 1966, 35.

67. Quoted in Milton Gross, "Clay Heaviest of Career," *Chicago Daily News*, March 29, 1966, 39.

68. Quoted in Earl Ruby, "Ruby's Report," *Louisville Courier-Journal*, March 2, 1966, B-4; Larry Merchant, "A Day with Clay," *Philadelphia Daily News*, March 8, 1966, 64.

69. Quoted in Robert Lipsyte, "Youngsters Chatter Helps Clay Endure Camp Drudgery," *New York Times*, February 20, 1966, 4:3.

70. Quoted in Robert Lipsyte, "Clay Says He Is a Jet Airplane and All the Rest Are Prop Jets," *New York Times*, March 25, 1966, 49.

71. For reports on ABC's negotiations with Main Bout, see Brady, "Home TV Carries," C-3; Associated Press, "Clay, Cooper Home TV Is Discussed," *San Francisco Chronicle*, April 28, 1966, 56; United Press International, "Clay Bout on Satellite Relay to US," *San Francisco Chronicle*, April 29, 1966, 60; Milton Gross, "Rolling in the Isles," *New York Post*, May 24, 1966, 93. For financial particulars about the Ali versus Cooper fight, see Arthur Veysey, "See Sellout Crowd for Cooper and Clay Battle," *Chicago Tribune*, May 12, 1966, 3:1; Associated Press, "Cassius Wants Jones as Next Opponent," *Hartford Courant*, May 23, 1966, 22;

Gene Ward, "Clay in 6—Henry's a Bloody Mess," *New York Daily News*, May 22, 1966; "Cooper's Share May Remain a Secret," *Irish Times*, May 24, 1966, 3; "Big Fight Finance," *London Daily Express*, May 23, 1966, 4; Associated Press, "Clay 11–2 Choice to Retain World Heavyweight Crown over Cooper," *Wichita Eagle and Beacon*, May 15, 1966, D-5; John Rodda, "Why Clay Is Coming Here," *Manchester Guardian*, April 18, 1966, A-1; "Bookies Say It's Clay," *London Daily Mirror*, May 21, 1966, 2; "The Clay Fight May Go on TV," *London Daily Mirror*, May 9, 1966, 24; "British Broadcast Is Set Up for Clay-Cooper Title Bout," *New York Times*, May 9, 1966, 53; Ken Irwin, "Big Fight 'Live' on the Radio," *London Daily Mirror*, May 14, 1966, 11; Mike Grade, "Sportlight," *London Daily Mirror*, April 26, 1966, 20; Desmond Hackett, "'Enry's 'Arvest," *London Daily Express*, April 18, 1966, 18; Associated Press, "Clay, Beatles Rate Same Tax Category," *Wichita Eagle*, May 27, 1966, D-5; Eddie Muller, "Shadow Boxing: Clay's Purse Well-Bitten," *San Francisco Examiner*, June 7, 1966, 60; United Press International, "Title Bout May Pay $140,000 to Cooper," *Washington Post*, April 26, 1966, C-2.

72. "He's A Mere Mortal," *San Francisco Examiner*, August 5, 1966, 49; Arthur Daley, "A Visit with Brian London," *New York Times*, August 5, 1966, 22; Arthur Daley, "Britain Showing Little Interest," *New York Times*, August 6, 1966, 23; Sydney Hulls, "Frozen London," *London Daily Express*, August 8, 1966, 11; United Press International, "Clay-London Mismatch Was Financial Bomb, Too," *Washington Post*, August 10, 1966, D-3; Associated Press, "ABC to Televise Clay Title Bout," *Washington Post*, July 7, 1966, B-4; Associated Press, "Clay on TV," *Louisville Courier-Journal*, July 7, 1966, B-5; Associated Press, "Clay Title Bout on Live TV," *San Francisco Examiner*, July 20, 1966, 41; Milton Gross, "Cassius 203½, Karl 194¾," *New York Post*, September 10, 1966, 80; Sydney Hulls, "Angelo Predicts a K.O. Win," *London Daily Express*, August 4, 1966, 11; Red Fisher, "British Board Should Have Blocked Bout," *Montreal Star*, August 11, 1966, 26.

73. Gene Ward, "Terrell Outpoints Jones, Fans Boo 'Champ' for Fouls," *New York Daily News*, June 29, 1966, 107.

74. "Clay to Get 50 Percent for Bout with Mildenberger," *New York Times*, July 10, 1966, S-8; Fred Tupper, "Fight Expected to Draw 40,000," *New York Times*, September 10, 1966, 23; Gross, "Cassius 203½," 80; Hugh McIlvaney, "Clay Wins in 12th Round," *London Observer*, September 11, 1966, 20; Associated Press, "Mildenberger Accepts Sept. 10 as Date for Title Fight with Clay," *Washington Post*, June 25, 1966, E-1; Associated Press, "Clay Stops German in 12th Round," *Washington Post*, September 11, 1966, C-5.

75. Al Buck, "Cassius Puts Out the Cat; Terrell Next—in Garden?" *New York Post*, November 15, 1966, 96; "Title Crowd Shatters Indoor Fight Record," *New York Post*, November 15, 1966, 92; "Clay-Williams Bout Is Slated for 24 Metropolitan Theaters," *New York Times*, November 13, 1966, 5:2; Associated Press and United Press International, "Clay Rates Williams Fifth among Foes," *San Francisco Chronicle*, November 16, 1966, 50; Al Buck, "Cat Can't Win, Odds Insist," *New York Post*, November 14, 1966, 88; Associated Press, "Clay-Williams to Be on Radio Monday," *Newark Star-Ledger*, November 11, 1966, 36; United Press International, "Mutual Radio Carries Clay Bout," *Washington Post*, November 11, 1966, G-2; Gene Ward, "Clay 5-1 to Skin a Cat in Title Fight," *New York Daily News*, November 14, 1966, 72; Gene Ward, "Another Clay Pigeon: Cat KO'ed at 1:08 of the 3d," *New York Daily News*, November 15, 1966, 86; "Branford Set to Televise Clay-Williams," *Newark Star-Ledger*, November 13, 1966, 8:2; Jack Fiske, "A Shuffle, Some Fun, and a Fight," *San Francisco Chronicle*, November 15, 1966, 45; "Clay TV," *San Francisco Chronicle*, November 12, 1966, 39; Leo Brown quoted in Frank Mastro, "TV Viewers Cheer Clay's TKO Victory," *Chicago Tribune*, November 15, 1966, 3:2; "A Compound Problem Confronts Cassius!" *Los Angeles Herald-Examiner*, November 1, 1966, D-2.

76. "Facts on Houston Fight," *New York Times*, February 8, 1967, 23; "Fight Facts, Figures," *Houston Post*, February 8, 1967, 3:3; "Clay Now Eyes Old Man Folley," *Los Angeles Herald-Examiner*, February 7, 1967, B-3; Gerald Eskenazi, "Telecast Highlight: Close-Ups of Terrell's Face," *New York Times*, February 7, 1967, 46; Jesse Abramson, "Acoustical Dud in Garden," *New York World Journal Tribune*, February 7, 1967, 29; Jim McCulley, "Garden TV: A One-Rounder," *New York Daily News*, February 7, 1967, 52; George Bernet, "Ali's Crowd Cheers Hero in Theater," *Newark Star-Ledger*, February 7, 1967, 22; Steve Cady, "30,000 Expected at Houston Fight," *New York Times*, February 6, 1967, 36; "Garden among 25 Nearby Sites Presenting Title Fight on TV," *New York Times*, February 5, 1967, 5:3; Advertisement, *Los Angeles Herald-Examiner*, January 22, 1967, D-4.

77. Jim McCulley, "Clay Right to Jaw KO's Folley in 7," *New York Daily News*, March 23, 1967, 70; Kay Gardella, "Clay-Folley Bout to Revive Home TV," *New York Daily News*, February 22, 1967, 78; Jim McCulley, "Cassius Pockets $264,838," *New York Daily News*, March 24, 1967, 54.

78. "Champion Is Set for 10th Defense," *New York Times*, April 4, 1967, 51; "Clay and Floyd Do It Again on April 25 in Las Vegas," *New York World Journal Tribune*, April 4, 1967, 45; Robert Lipsyte, "After Patterson, the Field Lies Fallow," *New York Times*, April 3, 1967, 53; Joe O'Day, "Clay, Pat Sign for Encore; Ali's

Swan Song," *New York Daily News*, April 5, 1967, 99; Associated Press, "Clay and Patterson Sign for Rematch," *Chicago Tribune*, April 5, 1967, 3:1; Michael Malitz quoted in Deane McGowen, "Patterson Fight with Clay Is Off," *New York Times*, April 13, 1967, 56.

79. Jimmy Cannon, "Clay-Floyd Fight: A Sanctioned Atrocity," *New York World Journal Tribune*, April 5, 1967, 45; Ralph Lamb quoted in United Press International, "Won't Police Fight, Vegas Sheriff Says," *Philadelphia Daily News*, April 6, 1967, 53; Paul Laxalt quoted in United Press International, "Nevada Cancels Clay Title Bout," *New York Times*, April 12, 1967, 53; Edwin Dooley quoted in McGowen, "Patterson Fight," 56; United Press International, "Clay Title Fight Is Counted Out," *New York Times*, April 15, 1967, 23; Michael Malitz quoted in McGowen, "Patterson Fight," 56.

80. Gene Ward, "Ward to the Wise," *New York Daily News*, April 20, 1967, 95; Robert Lipsyte, "Boxing's New Era: The Gold Rush Is On," *New York Times*, April 30, 1967, 5:1; Robert Lipsyte, "Patterson Bout Slated July 15," *New York Times*, May 9, 1967, 58; Gene Ward, "Seven Stalking Clay's Title Willingly; Frazier Stalls," *New York Daily News*, May 10, 1967, 97; "'Not Guilty,' Says Clay in Draft Case," *Newark Star-Ledger*, May 9, 1967, 1, 14; United Press International, "Ring Tourney Moves Closer to Reality," *Louisville Courier-Journal and Times*, May 7, 1967, C-6; Nicholas Von Hoffman, "Clay Refuses Induction, Stripped of World Title," *Washington Post*, April 29, 1967, A-1, C-4; Dave Brady, "8 So-So Heavyweights Bounce into Title Picture," *Washington Post*, April 30, 1967, D-5.

....

11

A "Race" for Equality
Print Media Coverage of the 1968 Olympic
Protest by Tommie Smith and John Carlos

JASON PETERSON

On the night of October 16, 1968 at the Olympic Games in Mexico City, U.S. sprinter Tommie Smith set a world record for the 200-meter dash by finishing in 19.8 seconds.[1] The gold medal winner celebrated in a joyous embrace of fellow Olympian, college teammate, and good friend John Carlos, who won the bronze medal. However, Smith and Carlos had something other than athletic accolades or the spoils of victory on their minds. In the same year the Beatles topped the charts with the lyrics, "You say you want a revolution? Well, you know, we all want to change the world," Smith and Carlos sought to use their feats on the track oval to advance the mission of the Olympic Project for Human Rights, a group Smith helped start up. The principal driver behind the OPHR was sociologist and college professor Harry Edwards, who stated the group's mission as effecting the liberation of blacks in the United States and elsewhere by using the international platform provided by and in sports.[2]

Edwards, then a part-time sociology professor at San Jose State College, pursued an Olympic boycott even after an initial discussion of such a protest failed to generate much interest at the 1967 National Conference of Black Power held in Newark, New Jersey. Edwards, who once said that "sports were the only area of campus life where Blacks could exercise any political leverage," contacted sixty prominent college athletes and asked them to meet in Los Angeles at the 1967 Black Youth Conference.[3] Edwards led a workshop at the conference focused on whether or not black Americans should participate in the 1968 Olympic Games. He found that many of the athletes felt that despite their athletic accomplishments and the potential spoils their victories would bring to the United States, they were still treated as less than equals by white Americans. Edwards knighted the attending members as the Olympic Project for Human Rights and emerged from the meetings with a unified group of American athletes willing to go to extremes to point out the ills of American life for blacks.[4]

Edwards and OPHR members such as Smith, Carlos, and UCLA basketball star Lew Alcindor believed that human rights, not merely black civil rights, were being trampled on in the United States, in South Africa, and elsewhere.[5] From Paris to Prague, from New York to Los Angeles, and in Mexico City as well, the world's youth protested the Vietnam War, repression, and inequality that turbulent year of the Olympic Games. Martin Luther King Jr. had been assassinated in April. Robert F. Kennedy was gunned down in Los Angeles in June. Antiwar demonstrators disrupted the Democratic Convention in Chicago; students briefly took over Columbia University to oppose the construction of a gymnasium in Morningside Park, citing that the building's location and makeup was the administration's attempt to create a segregated environment, and CIA recruitment on campus; and protesters from the Women's Liberation movement threatened the Miss America pageant in Atlantic City—all in 1968. The Olympic Games themselves were threatened by a Mexican military assault on hundreds protesting government funds spent on the games.

Standout athletes such as Smith, fellow Olympic sprinter Lee Evans, and Alcindor joined Edwards's cause and supported his efforts, doing much to raise the organization's profile nationally. Edwards and the OPHR first used this newfound influence to boycott the New York Athletic Club's annual track meet in 1968.[6] Because of the group's prior threats of an Olympic boycott, its effort in New York was seen as a precursor of sorts to a withdrawal from the Mexico City games. Edwards also called for the resignation of then–International Olympic Committee president Avery Brundage. Edwards described Brundage as "a devout anti-Semitic and an anti-Negro personality."[7] Brundage openly supported South Africa's entry of an all-white team in the 1968 summer games and was once quoted as saying he would sell his home in a Santa Barbara Country Club before letting "niggers and kikes" become members.[8] The IOC ultimately revoked South Africa's invitation after other nations, including Ethiopia and Algeria, threatened to withdraw from the games in protest.[9] Edwards and members of the OPHR opposed the then eighty-year-old Brundage, in Smith words, as "our Hitler." Smith wrote, "as far as I was concerned, Avery Brundage was just another racist white man. Nothing I heard ever changed my mind about it. He thought white was it."[10] Smith's victory in the 200 meters, the first Olympic victory by a member of the Project, provided the group with the international platform it sought.

This essay examines newspaper coverage of Smith's and Carlos's Olympic solidarity demonstration in an attempt to determine how sportswriters and sports reporters handled the complexities of race and politics. Reporters for a number of major print publications in the United States expressed disdain and even anger toward Smith and Carlos. Sportswriters seemed to believe the U.S. sprinters had violated the sanctity of sports by inserting their own politics. These reactions point to an unwritten rule or norm in sports that its participants leave their politics and social activism at the arena or stadium gate. For example, Brent Musburger, then a reporter for the *Chicago American*, called the demonstration "an ignoble performance that completely overshadowed a magnificent athletic one." Smith and Carlos behaved like "a pair of dark-skinned storm troopers," in Musburger words.[11]

A sample of news accounts, columns, and opinions was drawn from fifteen U.S and world newspapers published between October 17, 1968, the first day the protest was reported, and October 29, 1968, when coverage of the last day of the Olympic Games ended. Because of the different political and racial contexts throughout the United States, a representative sample of newspapers in major markets throughout the country seemed appropriate. Newspapers examined included southern publications such as the *Atlanta Constitution*, the *Dallas Morning News*, and the *New Orleans Times-Picayune*; the *Boston Globe*, the *New York Times*, and the *Washington*

Post in the East; the *Milwaukee Journal Sentinel* and the *Chicago Tribune* in the Midwest; and the *San Jose Mercury News*, the *Oakland Tribune*, the *San Francisco Examiner*, and the *Los Angeles Times* in the West. These major market newspapers and those from the sprinters' home state of California were more likely to contain original reporting on the protest rather than merely wire reports from the Associated Press. English-language newspapers internationally were also included, newspapers such as the *London Times*, the *Sydney Mercury Herald*, and the *Montreal Gazette*. These newspapers provided important contrast to U.S. coverage, which helped to identify distinctly American themes in coverage.

On that warm October 16 evening, before Smith, Carlos, and Australian Peter Norman emerged for the medal awards ceremony, the two U.S. sprinters removed their shoes, rolled up their track pants, and exposed long black socks. The men then donned beads and scarves and fastened Olympic Project for Human Rights buttons on their U.S.A. warmup jackets (silver medalist Peter Norman, too, wore a button, in support of the Project). Finally, the two sprinters each slipped on one black glove.[12] Carlos told biographer C. D. Jackson that with their gestures and appearances he and Smith sought to defy the "hypocrisy" of the United States and "the way she treats people of color."[13]

The reaction in the Olympic stadium was one of shock, followed quickly by anger. At first, "the American people in the stands were shocked to silence," according to Carlos. "One could hear a frog piss on cotton it was so quiet in the stadium."[14] The silence was soon broken, however, by booing, while millions around the world watched on television in disbelief.

The press conference that followed quickly turned into a media frenzy. Carlos handled most of the questions, and he did so colorfully. "They [whites] look upon us as nothing but animals," he said at one point. "We are nothing but show horses for white people." Claiming he did not want the bronze medal, Carlos handed it to his wife, saying he would never attend another Olympics as a competitor.[15] For his part, Smith said very little at the press conference, only that he objected to being referred to as a "Negro" and would instead like to be referred to as "black." "If I do something bad, they won't say American, they say Negro," Smith explained.[16]

After the press conference, Smith elaborated for ABC sports reporter Howard Cosell:

> The right glove that I wore on my right hand signified power within black America. The left glove my teammate John Carlos wore on his left hand made an arc with my right hand and his left hand also to signify black unity. The scarf that was worn around my neck signified blackness. John Carlos and me wore socks, black socks, without shoes, to also signify our poverty.[17]

Members of both the United States Olympic Committee and the IOC were outraged; the two governing bodies acted quickly. Two days after their medal stand displays, Smith and Carlos were expelled from the Olympic Games and suspended from the U.S. Olympic team.

The Social Climate in 1968

Despite landmark legislation such as the Civil Rights Act of 1964 and the Voting Rights Act of 1965, by the late 1960s blacks in the United States had become disillusioned. For many, the civil rights movement had produced only the illusion of progress.[18] Some in the black community criticized the pervasive lack of enforcement of the civil rights–based legislation, allowing Jim Crow policies and norms to persist. Race riots in the Watts section of Los Angeles and in Newark, New Jersey, and the assassination of Martin Luther King Jr. on April 4, 1968, suggested that advances in civil rights were perhaps inciting more violence.[19] Evidence of the country's recalcitrance on civil rights abounded. In the South, colleges and universities continued to field white-only athletic teams. In addition, black athletes were denied product endorsements and coaching opportunities offered to their white counterparts.

Consistent with Edwards's belief and in the tradition of predecessors Jackie Robinson, Jesse Owens, and Joe Louis, many young black athletes began to see potential leverage in their roles as sports figures. "Blacks don't catch hell because we are basketball stars or because we don't have money," Alcindor said. "We catch hell because we are black. This is how I take my stand—using what I have," referring to his starring role on the

UCLA men's basketball team.[20] Alcindor eventually decided to not play for the United States in the Olympics, explaining that "until things are on an equitable basis, this is not my country. We have been a racist nation with first class citizens and my decision to not go to the Olympics is my way of getting my message across."[21]

Unlike Alcindor, Smith chose to participate in the summer games and fight for the cause of the OPHR. In his mind, something had to be done and done on a world stage.[22] Smith's justification for his affiliation with the OPHR's protest was the "contention that it [the protest] helped everybody, not just the black athletes."[23] Edwards's and the OPHR's objective in Mexico City could be summarized by a poster that hung in Edwards's San Jose office, a poster which read, "Rather than run and jump for medals, we are standing up for humanity."[24]

Literature Review

The work of sportswriters in the context of race has been studied before. Glen Bleske and Chris Lamb, for example, examined Jackie Robinson's 1947 debut in the Major Leagues from the perspectives of the white press and black press. Bleske and Lamb found that the black press was much more aware of the social significance of Robinson's appearance in Major League Baseball while white journalists failed to identify the historical context of the event.[25] Within the tumultuous and racially charged framework of 1968 and the Olympic protest, it is possible that a similar difference in coverage existed. While the black sports press may have identified with the overall political and social message being made by Smith and Carlos, the white press interpreted this historical moment as an act of disrespect, both to America and to the Olympics.

While the protest itself has been examined by sociologists and documented by historians, how the media covered the complex blend of politics, race, policy, and sports has not been studied. Sociologist Douglas Hartmann said that the protest was condemned because it forced the issue of racism into sports.[26] The negative response from mainstream America was "not surprising," Hartmann wrote, because "there was little sympathy or political support for those dramatizing the problems of race, much less for those who did so on the Olympic stage."[27] According to Hartmann, the American public misinterpreted the protest as an attack on sports rather than a social commentary on the racial strife that existed in America at the time. It is his belief that racial hegemony is manifest in and through popular culture, which is why the image of Smith and Carlos with fists raised has become so iconic.[28]

In her examination of race, national identity, and the 1968 Olympics, historian Amy Bass wrote that the emergent role of the black athlete as promoted by the OPHR sought "to make America fulfill its promises" of equality yet acknowledge that the mere presence of blacks in sports does not necessarily indicate a socially even playing field.[29] Bass suggested that the Black Power salute "challenged the flag, contesting and claiming a denied national identify and producing a dramatic reaction and consequences."[30]

Historian Mark Kurlansky included the protest in this book, *1968: The Year That Rocked the World*, writing that the protest "had the potential to politicize the [Olympic] games."[31] Kurlansky noted that OPHR member and 400-meter gold medal winner Lee Evans, along with 400-meter silver winner Larry James and 400-meter bronze winner Ron Freeman, were not punished for their mild protest because of their jubilant appearance. Evans, James, and Freeman wore black berets and posed in a similar manner as Smith and Carlos but removed the berets and bowed their heads as the United States National Anthem was played. "As it was in the days of slavery, the smiling Negro with a non-threatening posture was not to be punished," Kurlansky wrote.[32]

Sociologist Michael Lomax took a different view of the protest, examining Edwards's role in the OPHR. Lomax wrote that integration did not address the lack of equality that the black athlete faced and that the efforts of Edwards underlined "many aspects of the ongoing black freedom struggle."[33] Edwards, per Lomax, wanted to obtain basic human and civil rights through the OPHR. In fact, Lomax wrote that opposition to Edward's efforts came from other black athletes who feared that any radical action would only lead to racial prejudice in the one area that promised them a degree of social mobility.[34]

While Hartmann, Bass, and others have noted the very negative reactions in press reports and sports coverage to the U.S. sprinters' actions at the games, scholars have not studied how sportswriters handled the complexities of race, politics, nationalism, and activism. Examining news media coverage of Smith's and Carlos's gestures and statements can provide valuable insights, therefore, into how news media handled one of the first times that sportswriters, reporters, and columnists were forced in their daily journalism to make sense of overtly political statements made in the usually safe, apolitical haven of athletic competition. The 1968 games were only the beginning, as future Olympics would feature their fair share of political statements: the killing of Israeli athletes by Palestinian terrorists at the 1972 games in Munich, the U.S. Olympic boycott of the 1980 games in Montréal, and the Centennial Olympic Park Bombing in Atlanta at the 1996 games.

American Newspaper Coverage

Most news accounts of the protest portrayed Smith and Carlos in a negative light and offered little support for their efforts to advance equal rights for blacks.[35] Some print publications, regardless of geographic location, found the protest to be an embarrassment to the U.S. Olympic team and the United States in general, and sportswriters led the charge criticizing Smith and Carlos. Reporters took their focus off the Olympics as an athletic competition and emphasized instead their own positions on the appropriateness of Smith's and Carlos's actions.[36] Because of anger towards Smith and Carlos, news values such as balance and objectivity were often sacrificed. For example, in his article on Smith's victory, AP sportswriter Will Grimsley referred to Smith and Carlos as "militants" and described Carlos's comments during the press conference as a "bitter tirade against the white structure." Grimsley, who specialized in college football and the Olympic Games, spent over forty years with the Associated Press as a sportswriter and covered Freedom Summer in Mississippi and Muhammad Ali's refusal to join the military.[37] How Grimsley could discern bitterness in the medal stand actions of the two athletes is impossible to know, but because he wrote for the Associated Press, Grimsley's wire story was picked up by many newspapers throughout the United States. His characterization, then, was a potentially influential one in casting the events of the night of October 16. For this reason, then, it is also important that Smith's objection to being referred to as a "Negro," which can be found in other AP accounts of the press conference, was absent in Grimsley's, which described the one-fist gesture as a "Nazi-like" salute.[38]

Also writing for a national audience by virtue of syndication, *Washington Post* columnist Shirley Povich also condemned the actions of Smith and Carlos as particularly pernicious when juxtaposed with Australian Peter Norman standing in "respectful attention." The columnist did note, however, Smith's objection to being described as a "Negro."[39] Povich, who wrote columns for the *Post* for nearly seventy-five years, was one of the first white journalists to openly support the integration of baseball in the 1930s and 1940s and of the Washington Redskins in the early 1960s.[40] Povich would go on to cover the 1972 games in Munich and received the 1975 J. G. Taylor Spink Award from the National Baseball Hall of Fame.

In many instances, what a writer omitted is more significant than what she or he included. The *Chicago Tribune* diminished the importance of Smith's victory and the effects of Smith's and Carlos's actions by burying the news of the protest in its coverage. *Tribune* sports editor George Strickler did not mention Smith until the twelfth paragraph of his article, when he described the protest as a "discordant note" in the otherwise harmonious Olympics. Carlos "lost some cockiness" after Norman bested him for silver, Strickler wrote.[41] Bob Seagren's gold medal victory in the pole vault notwithstanding, there was no reason by the merits of athletic accomplishment not to lead with Smith's world record and gold medal victory. Stricker called Seagren's performance "the greatest in the history of the pole vault" but clarified that Seagren was awarded the gold medal because he had the fewest misses. In fact, Seagren's record of 17 feet, 8½ inches was shared with Claus Schiprowski of West Germany and Wolfgang Nordwig of East Germany. Based on Seagren's shared record, there is no journalistic justification for making his pole vault victory the focus of the article over Smith's win. Stricker would later become the Pro Football Writer's Association's first president and was awarded the Dick McCann Memorial Award in 1969 for excellence in reporting in professional football.[42]

Some newspapers included very little on Smith's and Carlos's display, seemingly as a means of protest. Sports columnist Sam Blair of the *Dallas Morning News* acknowledged on October 20 the lack of coverage in his newspaper, noting that a number of American journalists would likely withhold coverage.[43] Famed black U.S. Olympian Jesse Owens told the Associated Press that the news media should ignore the protest, thereby justifying *Dallas Morning News*'s blackout.[44] The *Dallas Morning News*, the *Atlanta Constitution*, and the *New Orleans Times-Picayune* published only wire accounts of the 200-meter race and subsequent protest in their October 17 editions.[45]

The *Boston Globe* also printed only AP copy in its October 17 edition; however, unlike the newspapers mentioned above, the *Globe* sent sportswriter John Ahern to Mexico City. Rather than cover the Smith and Carlos–spurred controversy himself, Ahern instead wrote only a sidebar on the protest from the perspective of Harvard University's crew team, members of the U.S. rowing team. The article did not mention Smith and Carlos by name, referring to them only as "two Negro trackmen" on first reference and as "two black athletes" afterward.[46] Ahern's choice of perspective—reporting only reactions from the Harvard crew team—could have been Ahern's or the *Globe*'s way of denying Smith and Carlos the forum they were seeking. (This approach also localized the story; Harvard University is in Cambridge, Massachusetts.)

Newspapers in and near Smith's and Carlos's home of San Jose, California, while not openly objecting to the protest, took a fairly neutral approach. The *San Jose Mercury Herald* had an obvious local angle; Smith and Carlos were both students at San Jose State College. Smith's victory was teased on the front page of the October 17 edition, and the sports section featured Povich's syndicated article with another article on the track races by sports editor Louis Duino under the headline "Tommie in Record 200 Win, then 'Salutes' Black Power." Duino's report made no mention of the protest, instead celebrating the victory by San Jose's own. The combination of Povich and Duino gave the sports page an interesting dichotomy, pairing Povich's bristling reactions with Duino's local pride.[47]

Published in Smith's and Carlos's backyard, the *Oakland Tribune* ran a story on Smith's victory and the subsequent podium protest on October 17 written by sportswriter Blaine Newnham, an article that covered the basic events of the evening. However, unlike many of the other writers, Newnham, who is white, never referred to Smith and Carlos as "Negroes" or as "militants."[48] According to Newnham, sportswriters knew usage of the term "Negro" had a negative connotation for many black athletes and black readers.[49] Newnham said in an interview that he chose not to use the term because of his knowledge of and sensitivity to his readers; Oakland was home to the Black Panther Party.[50]

Also published in the San Jose area, the *San Francisco Examiner* in its October 17 edition attempted to contextualize Smith's and Carlos's behavior, marking the newspaper's coverage as unique in the sample. *Examiner* sportswriter Bob Brachman, who began writing for the paper in 1937, pondered Smith's and Carlos's motivations, wondering what "deep emotional disturbances" they felt as they stood on the medal stand. Brachman also described Smith as being visibly upset after the protest.[51] Brachman, who according to Newnham was a close friend of Smith's, seemed to be explaining Smith's and Carlos's actions in support of the two sprinters by trying to identify with their feelings.[52]

Like his counterpart at the *Dallas Morning News*, *Los Angeles Times* sports editor Paul Zimmerman failed to mention Smith's gold medal victory or his world record run. Instead, Zimmerman led with Bob Seagren's record-setting victory in the pole vault. While writing only about the athletic aspects of the games, Zimmerman did mention in passing that Smith and Carlos had raised their fists during the national anthem, each with only one glove, explaining that "someone suggested that they buy one pair of gloves to save money."[53] Zimmerman, who died in 1996 at the age of ninety-two, covered eight Olympics, including the 1932 and 1984 games, both of which were held in Los Angeles.[54]

To now shift focus to the day after the medal stand controversy erupted on October 18, a number of newspapers ran an AP article on the United States Olympic Committee's apology to the IOC for Smith's and Carlos's actions and its warning to other U.S. athletes that similar displays would not be tolerated. The article, which ran in ran in the sports sections of the *Atlanta Constitution*, the *Chicago Tribune*, the *Los Angeles Times*, the *New York Times*, the *San Jose Mercury*, and the *Washington Post*, quotes Everett Barnes, then director of the USOC, as saying, "It [the protest] makes our country look like the devil." The unbylined story did not mention the names of Smith or Carlos until the fifth paragraph.[55]

While many major U.S. newspapers ran only wire copy on the Olympics on October 18, their first editorials and columns on the controversy began to appear on that date. One of the more outspoken sportswriters was *Los Angeles Times* columnist and 1990 Pulitzer Prize winner Jim Murray, who made light of the protest by writing that if his message wasn't clear, he should be excused for "wearing his black glove." Murray, who wrote for the *Times* from 1961 through 1998 and served as *Sports Illustrated*'s West Coast editor from 1959 through 1961, used sarcasm in addressing the protest, writing, "I don't care for the Star-Spangled Banner either. But I kept my shoes on."[56] Importantly, however, Murray acknowledged racial conflict in the United States: "Well, now our secret is out: we got race problems in our country This will come as a great astonishment to the reading public of the world, I am sure."[57]

Fellow *Times* veteran columnist John Hall echoed Murray's objections in writing that he was "sick of Smith and Carlos and their whining." Hall described Smith's and Carlos's outlook on the world as "shallow," and he said he "was sick of apologizing for the state of blacks in the United States."[58] While perhaps not as cutting as Murray, Hall clearly objected not only to the sprinters' protest but also to their views on race.

Perhaps because he was a veteran of politics in sports, having covered and even argued for blacks' entry into professional baseball in the 1930s and 1940s, Shirley Povich wrote one of the more balanced columns in the sample in the October 19 edition of the *Washington Post*. Povich questioned the USOC's decision to expel Smith and Carlos, but like Hall, Povich also second-guessed the sprinters' choice of time and place for their actions:

This, then was the chance for Smith and Carlos to tell the world of their militancy and protest with an impact never before offered by a Negro, athlete or otherwise. They took that chance, took the consequences, took their medals and were going home. It is not nice that they did not give their full attention to the American flag, but their sin otherwise was less than horrible.[59]

While sympathetic to Smith's and Carlos's grievances, the nationally syndicated columnist seemed more disappointed than anything else, believing that the Olympics were not the proper forum for an overtly political protest.

Murray followed up on October 20 with another column on the two sprinters' suspensions. Again using biting sarcasm, Murray wrote, "You remember when Tommie Smith and John Carlos were going to boycott the Olympics? Well, Friday the Olympics boycotted them."[60] Murray continued jabbing at the two runners, saying he didn't think a person could get into so much trouble over a pair of gloves. "The American blacks here have mistaken the International Olympic movement for the hierarchy of the state of Mississippi," he wrote.[61] Murray suggested that Carlos's negative views of white people could be perpetuated by the fact he lost the silver medal to one (Peter Norman), and he further insulted by questioning Carlos's and Smith's intelligence.[62]

Despite the lack of commentary on the controversy in his October 17 article, *San Jose Mercury* sports editor Louis Duino openly questioned the timing of Smith's and Carlos's protest in his October 18 column. Duino wrote that the protest had been conducted "in bad taste" and that it lacked "organization." While not objecting with the fervor of other sportswriters, Duino clearly believed that the protest was simply done in the wrong place at the wrong time.[63]

Almost every major newspaper ran an article on the suspensions of the two sprinters and their expulsion from the games. *New York Times* sportswriter Joseph Sheehan reported a mixture of reactions from Olympic Games participants: "Some hailed it as a gesture of independence and a move in support of a worthy cause. Many others said they were offended and embarrassed. A few were vehemently indignant."[64] On the same day, the *Los Angeles Times* sportswriter and columnist Charles Maher indicted Smith and Carlos for breaking an unwritten rule in sports by polluting the games with their political views. Maher also referred to a black reporter befriended by Smith and Carlos as a "Negro."[65] Maher gained a degree of notoriety earlier in the year for writing a five-part investigative series examining the possible athletic superiority of blacks over whites titled "The Negro Athlete in America."[66]

Some Olympic coverage, however, questioned the treatment of the two athletes, if not explicitly endorsing their behavior. The *Oakland Tribune*, for example, ran on October 18 an unbylined AP story critical of Smith's and Carlos's expulsion. There was no reason why Smith and Carlos could not have been allowed to stay in the Olympic Village as long as they were with their wives, according to the article, in clear violation of the journalistic standard of objectivity.[67]

The *Tribune*'s coverage was the exception, however. Overall, columns and editorials throughout the country put the blame on Smith and Carlos. An editorial in the *Chicago Tribune* on October 19 denounced the podium display as an "insult" to the United States and predicted that "when these renegades come home, they will probably be greeted as heroes by fellow extremists."[68] The *New York Times*'s 1956 Pulitzer Prize–winning columnist Arthur Daley wrote in his October 20 edition of "Sports of the Times" that Smith and Carlos brought their views where they didn't belong, describing the protest as "disgraceful, insulting, and embarrassing." He described Carlos as "ultra belligerent" and voiced pleasure over his expulsion from the games.[69]

In Dallas, Sam Blair wrote two columns on the podium protest, the first of which condemned it as "rude" and "deceptive." Blair, who spent forty-one years at the *Morning News*, wrote that Carlos "talks faster than he runs but not nearly as well," and he asked the sprinter to be sure to keep his promise to boycott the 1972 Olympics four years hence.[70] Blair's second column, which appeared on October 22, stated that despite the United States' many victories, the Olympics would best be remembered for "poor taste and bad manners." Smith's and Carlos's behavior was "sorry," and their actions were militant and ridiculous, according to Blair, who described Smith's and Carlos's positions on race as "insulting" and "distasteful."[71]

For the remainder of the Olympic Games, articles appeared on Smith and Carlos and their reception in the United States. Some of this coverage ran underneath critical headlines. An October 22 article on Smith's and Carlos's homecoming in the late edition of the *Dallas News* appeared with the headline "Smith, Carlos Silent."[72] For the early edition, the headline was more negative: "Irate Negro Sprinters Shut Mouths."[73] In an article on the sprinters' homecoming in the *Los Angeles Times*, Smith refused to discuss the protest or expulsion with reporters, then "led reporters on a broken field run." Smith was quoted by the *Times* as calling the news media "mean," which inspired the headline "Smith, Carlos in Flight from 'Mean' Reporters."[74] The *San Jose Mercury*, the hometown newspaper of Smith and Carlos, not surprisingly ran a much more thorough account of their return. The article noted Smith's silence, broken only to say he was tired. Smith then broke "into a fast walk," according to the account.[75] The United Press International's October 22 account of the homecoming in the *Washington Post* made no mention of the "mean" comment but did include gold medal pole vaulter Bob Seagren's description of the sprinters' actions as "cheap."[76]

In the most supportive editorial in this study, *Boston Globe* columnist Bud Collins's October 23 work sympathized with the San Jose contingent and blamed the format of the Olympic Games for the subsequent IOC outrage and eventual expulsion of the two sprinters.[77] The podium protest was "so mild that probably few would have noticed had the Olympic exactitudes not counter-punched in noble defense of their own standards—the standards of old, rich, unconcerned white men," he wrote, providing a refreshingly enlightened view compared to most of the reports in the sample. Collins also decried the suppression of individualism implicit in the condemnation of the two sprinters' actions, an individualism that Collins said resided at the very heart of the original Olympic spirit. "Olympic officials will tell you that they will allow no politics in their playpen, yet instead their very format encourages tasteless nationalism and stifling of individualism," he wrote. Collins, who after forty-six years still serves as a correspondent for the *Globe*, was often upset by the "strict code of denial that existed [in Boston] about confronting the racial problems" that were present in the city and the United States, and was often viewed by fellow journalists as "the moral voice" of Boston sports reporters because of his willingness to speak out on issues of race.[78]

To turn to Olympic wrap-up coverage, it is clear that many of the aforementioned journalists continued to paint the protest in a negative light. The *Los Angeles Times* indirectly included the sprinters only by briefly referencing the protest, calling it "a discouraging note" and saying that the controversy "threatened to rip the American teams apart."[79] The *San Jose Mercury News* published a different AP account from Los Angeles, calling the protest a "discordant note."[80] *Boston Globe* executive sports editor Jerry Nason wrote in his wrap of the games, "No one will forget that here the United States had to make a public apology for the boorish and misplaced 'black power' demonstrations."[81] The *Washington Post* also only briefly mentioned the 200-meter runners, focusing on their gestures rather than their athletic accomplishments: "The Games were marked by racial dispute, triggered when Tommie Smith and John Carlos gave a black power gesture during the gold-medal ceremony. Smith and Carlos were subsequently dropped from the U.S. team."[82] It is possible that in omitting Smith's and Carlos's athletic accomplishments, the newspapers were punishing the athletes for their activism, or perhaps attempting to distance the rest of America from the sprinters' embarrassing actions in Mexico City. Some newspapers, including the *Chicago Tribune* and the *New York Times*, simply omitted Smith and Carlos from any sort of summary Olympic accounts, leaving out of the summaries Smith's world record and gold medal victory.[83]

One of the few post-Olympic commentaries that discussed Smith and Carlos with any substance was in the October 29 edition of the *Milwaukee Journal Sentinel*. Oliver Kuechle's weekly sports column stated that there wasn't an unwanted event "except for the unfortunate insult before the world which sprinters Tommie Smith and John Carlos, accepting medals, gave this country."[84] Kuechle spent forty-seven years at the

Milwaukee-based paper and regularly covered the Milwaukee Braves and the Green Bay Packers.

The View Overseas

The foreign media examined were generally supportive of Smith and Carlos, even characterizing them as heroes to their cause. In its October 18 issue, for instance, the *London Times* covered the awards ceremony actions of the U.S. sprinters rather than running profiles of British Olympic athletes. *Times* sportswriter Neil Allen, who seemed to understand the significance of the protest in historical context in a way that most U.S. sportswriters seemingly could not, wrote that while individual Olympic events are generally forgotten over time, the 200-meter run in 1968 likely would be remembered forever.[85] Smith and Carlos made history by becoming the first Olympic champions to "make racial [and] political capital out of the most treasured moments of their sporting careers," he wrote, calling Smith "the most notable black champion of all."[86] Allen, who would become a veteran Olympic journalist, is a sportswriter at *The News* in Portsmouth, Great Britain.

The *Sydney Morning Herald*, too, endorsed the U.S. runners' actions, claiming that the IOC was "unwise" in suspending Smith and Carlos. The editorial writer or writers did recommend separating politics and sports but stated that only "racial bigots" should have been offended by the Smith's and Carlos's actions, calling the protest an "intensely human expression." The unbylined editorial also praised Australian native Peter Norman, the silver medalist, for his support of Smith and Carlos by wearing an OPHR button on his warm-up jacket.[87] Norman told reporters that he asked Smith for the button because he, too, "believed in human rights."[88]

Chris Allan, a columnist for the *Montreal Gazette* was not as understanding, writing that the U.S. track team members' "misguided" use of the Olympics for political theater amounted to a "cancer" on the games. Allan also reported comments from Canadian sprinter Jerome James, who compared the U.S. runners' one-fist gesture of "power" to a display of the swastika.[89]

Aftermath

Nearly four decades after the 1968 Olympics, former *Oakland Tribune* sportswriter Blaine Newnham was able to admit that he, too, had been angry with the U.S. sprinters and that his anger was shared by a number of fellow sportswriters who covered those same games. Newnham said in an interview in 2005 that many newspaper writers quickly tired of the controversy and, therefore, simply refused to cover Smith and Carlos after they had been suspended. Newnham said the one-fist black power protest was one of the first times that political action and sports intersected on such a grand stage, a complexity that left many writers angry and confused. "There was something special about the Olympics," he said. "You just don't violate that with politics."[90]

While Newnham's admission supports the notion that sportswriters viewed the protest as a blow to sports, Harry Edwards claimed in his 1970 book that a majority of white sports media in the United States were apathetic towards racial injustice, and that writers seemed to care more about pleasing editors and publishers than reporting the truth. Sacrificed, then, were the journalistic standards of objectivity and balance, in Edwards's view.[91]

Smith has stated on his website that people who viewed his actions on the podium as disrespectful misunderstood his purpose. He says that he was not behaving unpatriotically but rather demonstrating patriotism in his own way.[92] Smith said it was necessary to bring about their cause by making their protest when they had the largest audience. In 1998, Smith told the Associated Press that he and Carlos did what they did "to stand up for human rights and to stand up for black Americans."[93]

Following unsuccessful attempts at careers in the National Football League, both sprinters largely disappeared from the public eye, with the exception of the occasional update or "Where are they now?" article in newspapers and magazines. In some of these later accounts, Carlos acknowledged the negative reactions in the media but never blamed the media. While Newnham disagreed with the protest itself, looking back, he said he thought it had a positive effect. "The Olympics should rise above politics, but I think the two guys [Smith and Carlos] did a good thing," he said. "It was a world stage and they had something to say. The world had to listen and they forced us [Americans] to deal with it [the treatment of blacks]."[94]

Conclusion

During the two weeks that followed the protest, sportswriters, in general, objected to Smith and Carlos's demonstration and failed to contextualize the political statement behind their act. Rather than examining the protest for its meaning and considering the legitimacy of the OPHR's claims, sportswriters viewed the protest as a damning blow to the Olympic spirit. With few exceptions, sports reporters defended, perhaps unintentionally, the social climate of the United States by negating the racial content of protest with their steadfast objections. Emotionally biased journalism replaced the journalistic standards of fair and balanced reporting. Rather than pointing out the social legitimacy of the protest, sportswriters buried the messages and condemned Smith and Carlos. While the protest illustrated the potential power of the black athlete in sports, the message itself was lost. The strong political statement made by Smith and Carlos was simply damned by journalists as one of many negative occurrences in 1968. More comfortable covering clear winners and losers, these writers seemed unwilling or unable to understand the motivation for or goals of the two black athletes' actions.

Future research could examine the coverage in the black press and contrast it to how mainstream media covered the controversy. The black press likely was far more sympathetic to the sprinters' views and the OPHR's goals. An examination of black press coverage, then, could provide important insights into how or whether the protest resonated in black communities in the United States and into the ways black sportswriters viewed the athletes' actions. Another potential examination could include the 1972 Olympic Games in Munich, which was rife with political unrest and turmoil and included the aforementioned Munich massacre and the objections and potential protest of a Rhodesian contingent in Germany. Because of sportswriters' overall objections to the political context of 1968, it is possible that the further politicization of the sacred realm of athletics could have been met with similar disdain and contempt.

NOTES

1. "Smith and Seagren Win Gold Metals," *Atlanta Constitution*, October 17, 1968, 49; "Smith Wins 200 in 19.8," *Boston Globe*, October 17, 1968, 49–50; George Strickler, "Smith and Seagren Win Gold Medals," *Chicago Tribune*, October 17, 1968, 1, C3; "Two More Gold Medals," *Dallas Morning News*, October 17, 1968, B4; Paul Zimmerman, "Seagren Takes Pole Vault at 17-8½," *Los Angeles Times*, October 17, 1968, 3:1, 3:4; "Move to Avert Brundage Snub by Negroes," *London Times*, October 17, 1968, 17; Oliver Kuechle, "Gold Medals Won by 2 More Yanks," *Milwaukee Journal Sentinel*, October 17, 1968, 2:21; Joseph Sheehan, "Smith Takes Olympic 200 Meters and Seagren Captures Pole Vault," *New York Times*, October 17, 1968, 58; Louis Duino, "Tommie in Record 200 Win, then 'Salutes' Black Power," *San Jose Mercury News*, October 17, 1968, 73, 74; Blaine Newnham, "Incredible Smith in 19.8 Wins," *Oakland Tribune*, October 17, 1968, 37–38; Jim Webster, Ken Knox, and Australian Associated Press, "World Records at the Games," *Sydney Morning Herald*, October 19, 1968, 32; "Gold Total Rises Again," *New Orleans Times-Picayune*, October 17, 1968, 7:1. All accounts reported that Smith broke his own world record, which was 20.0 seconds. The previous Olympic record was 20.3, set by American Henry Carr in 1964.

2. Russell Wigginton, *The Strange Career of the Black Athlete: African Americans and Sports* (West Port CT: Praeger, 2006), 69–70; Harry Edwards, *The Revolt of the Black Athlete* (New York: Free Press, 1970), 128–29.

3. John Wilson, *Playing by the Rules: Sport, Society, and the State* (Detroit: Wayne State University Press, 1994), 56–57.

4. Michael Lomax, *Sports and the Racial Divide: African American and Latino Experience in an Era of Change* (Jackson: University Press of Mississippi, 2008), 55; Amy Bass, "Whose Broad Stripes and Bright Stars? Race, Nation, and Power at the 1968 Mexico City Olympics," in *Sports Matters: Race, Recreation, and Culture*, edited by John Bloom and Michael Nevin Willard (New York: New York University Press, 2002), 189; Kenny Moore, *Bowerman and the Men of Oregon: The Story of Oregon's Legendary Coach and Nike's Cofounder* (Emmaus PA: Rodale, 2007), 118–19.

5. Lomax, *Sports and the Racial Divide*, 55–56.

6. Bass, "Whose Broad Stripes and Bright Stars?" 185–86.

7. Bass, "Whose Broad Stripes and Bright Stars?" 185.

8. William L. Van Deburg, *New Day in Babylon: The Black Power Movement and American Culture, 1965–1975* (Chicago: University of Chicago Press, 1992), 88;

Mark Kurlansky, *1968: The Year That Rocked the World* (New York: Ballantine Books, 2004), 348; Blaine Newnham, interview by author, April 14, 2005. Newnham is an editor with the *Seattle Times* and former *Oakland Tribune* reporter who covered the Olympics in 1968.

9. Lomax, *Sports and the Racial Divide*, 79.

10. Tommie Smith and David Steele, *Silent Gesture: The Autobiography of Tommie Smith* (Philadelphia: Temple University Press, 2007), 165.

11. Smith and Steele, *Silent Gesture*, 165.

12. John Carlos and C. D. Jackson, *Why? The Autobiography of John Carlos* (Los Angeles: Milligan Books, 2000), 202.

13. Carlos and Jackson, *Why?* 202.

14. Carlos and Jackson, *Why?* 202.

15. Carlos and Jackson, *Why?* 208; Will Grimsley, "Olympic Village Stirred By Black Protest," *Baltimore Evening Sun*, October 17, 1968, D1, D11.

16. Carlos and Jackson, *Why?* 206.

17. Edwards, *Revolt of the Black Athlete*, 104.

18. Lomax, *Sports and the Racial Divide*, 60–61.

19. Lomax, *Sports and the Racial Divide*, 60–61.

20. Lomax, *Sports and the Racial Divide*, 71.

21. Amy Bass, *Not the Triumph but the Struggle: The 1968 Olympics and the Making of the Black Athlete* (Minneapolis: University of Minnesota Press, 2004), 187.

22. Smith and Steele, *Silent Gesture*, 22–23.

23. Smith and Steele, *Silent Gesture*, 33.

24. Smith and Steele, *Silent Gesture*, 33.

25. Chris Lamb and Glen Bleske, "Covering the Integration of Baseball—A Look Back," *Editor & Publisher* 130, no. 4 (January 27, 1996): 48–50; Chris Lamb, *Blackout: The Untold Story of Jackie Robinson's First Spring Training* (Omaha: Bison Books, 2006), 46–47.

26. Douglas Hartmann, "The Politics of Race and Sport: Resistance and Domination in the 1968 African American Olympic Protest Movement," *Ethnic and Racial Studies* 19, no. 3 (July 1995): 548.

27. Hartmann, "The Politics of Race and Sport," 556–57. Hartmann explained that, upon their return to the United States, both Smith and Carlos fell on hard times. Smith tried to register for U.S. Reserve Officers' Training classes in his final year at San Jose State. He was told to turn in his uniform and a verbal agreement to play football with the NFL's Los Angeles Rams was taken off the table because he was called "too eager," according to friend and future NFL Hall of Fame member Jim Brown. Carlos never finished college and had to

make ends meet by taking odd jobs. His wife committed suicide in 1977, an act he blames on the pressures he faced from his role in the protest.

28. Hartmann, "Politics of Race and Sport," 558.
29. Bass, "Whose Broad Stripes and Bright Stars?" 200.
30. Bass, "Whose Broad Stripes and Bright Stars?" 199.
31. Kurlansky, *1968*, 327.
32. Kurlansky, *1968*, 349.
33. Lomax, *Sports and the Racial Divide*, 85.
34. Lomax, *Sports and the Racial Divide*, 56–57.
35. Hartmann, "Politics of Race and Sport," 555.
36. Bass, "Whose Broad Stripes and Bright Stars?" 192.
37. Associated Press, *Breaking News: How the Associated Press Has Covered War, Peace, and Everything Else* (New York: Princeton Architectural Press, 2007), 147–48.
38. Will Grimsley, "Olympic Village Stirred By Black Protest," *Baltimore Evening Sun*, October 17, 1968, D1, D11; "Olympians Vary in Reaction to Protest," *Oakland Tribune*, October 17, 1968, E37, E38; "Black Fist Display Gets Varied Reaction in Olympic Village," *Los Angeles Times*, October 17, 1968, 3:1.
39. Shirley Povich, "Smith, Carlos Hold Black-Gloved Fists High during Star Spangled Banner," *Washington Post*, C1; Shirley Povich, "Black Power on Victory Stand," *Los Angeles Times*, October 17, 1968, 3:1, 3:4; Shirley Povich, "A Gesture of Protest," *San Jose Mercury News*, October 17, 1968, 73.
40. Shirley Povich, *All Those Mornings . . . at the Post: The 20th Century in Sports from Famed Washington Post Columnist Shirley Povich* (New York: PublicAffairs Publishing, 2006), 72, 203, 247.
41. George Strickler, "Smith and Seagren Win Gold Medals," *Chicago Tribune*, October 17, 1968, C1, C3.
42. Pro Football Hall of Fame, http://www.profootballhof.com, January 13, 2009.
43. Sam Blair, "Sprinters Back on Wright Foot," *Dallas Morning News*, October 20, 1968, B2.
44. Bill Tanton, "Press Irks Owens," *Baltimore Evening Sun*, October 17, 1968, D1.
45. "Smith and Seagren Win Gold Medals," *Atlanta Constitution*, October 17, 1968, 49; "Two More Gold Medals," *Dallas Morning News*, October 17, 1968, B4; "Gold Total Rises Again," *New Orleans Times-Picayune*, October 17, 1968, 7:1.
46. John Ahern, "Protest? Harvard Oarsman Too Busy," *Boston Globe*, October 17, 1968, 49, 50.
47. Duino, "Tommie in Record 200 Win," 73, 74.

48. Blaine Newnham, "Tommie Raises His Fist," *Oakland Tribune*, October 17, 1968, E37.

49. Edwards, *Revolt of the Black Athlete*, 29. Edwards described the word "Negro" as one assigned to blacks by white men as a shorter version of the word "nigger." Edwards said blacks objected to use of the word "Negro."

50. Newnham telephone interview with author, April 15, 2005.

51. Bob Brachman, "U.S. Apologizes for Protest," *San Francisco Examiner*, October 17, 1968, 27, 32.

52. Blaine Newnham, telephone interview with author, April 15, 2005.

53. Paul Zimmerman, "Seagren Takes Pole Vault," 3:1, 3:4.

54. Bill Dwyre, "Former Times Sports Editor Paul Zimmerman Dead at 92," *Los Angeles Times*, January 30, 1996, C2.

55. "U.S. Olympians Make Apology," *Atlanta Constitution*, October 18, 1968, 66; "U.S. Apologizes for Protest by Blacks," *Chicago Tribune*, October 18, 1968, 3:1, 3:3; "U.S. Apologizes for Athletes 'Discourtesy,'" *Los Angeles Times*, October 18, 1968, 3:1; "U.S. Leaders Warn of Penalties for Further Black Power Acts," *New York Times*, October 18, 1968, 59; "Yanks Apologize for Race Protest," *San Jose Mercury News*, October 18, 1968, 57; "U.S. Apologizes for Black Protest," *Washington Post*, October 18, 1968, D1.

56. Elizabeth A. Brennan and Elizabeth C. Clarage, *Who's Who of Pulitzer Prize Winners* (Westport CT: Greenwood, 1999), 65.

57. Jim Murray, "Excuse My Glove," *Los Angeles Times*, October 18, 1968, 3:1.

58. John Hall, "It Takes All Kinds," *Los Angeles Times*, October 18, 1968, 3:2.

59. Shirley Povich, "This Morning," *Washington Post*, October 19, 1968, C1.

60. Jim Murray, "The Olympic Games—No Place for A Sportswriter," *Los Angeles Times*, October 20, 1968, D1, D3.

61. Murray, "The Olympic Games," D1, D3.

62. Murray, "The Olympic Games," D1, D3.

63. Louis Duino, "Americans Boo Smith, Carlos," *San Jose Mercury News*, October 18, 1968, 58.

64. Joseph Sheehan, "2 Black Power Advocates Ousted from Olympics," *New York Times*, October 19, 1968, 1.

65. Charles Maher, "U.S. Expels Smith, Carlos from Olympic Team," *Los Angeles Times*, October 19, 1968, 2:1, 2:3.

66. The five part series, titled "The Negro Athlete in America," was published in the *Los Angeles Times* from March 24, 1968, through March 29, 1968. See also S. W. Pope, *The New American Sport History* (Champaign: University of Illinois Press, 1996), 320; Paul R. Spickard and W. Jeffrey Burroughs, *We Are a People:*

Narrative and Multiplicity in Constructing Ethnic Identity (Philadelphia: Temple University Press, 2000), 131; Bass, "Whose Broad Stripes and Bright Stars?" 199.

67. "Olympic Walkout Unlikely," *Oakland Tribune*, October 18, 1968, E55, E56.

68. "The Natural Right of Being a Slob," *Chicago Tribune*, October 19, 1968, 1:10.

69. Arthur Daley, "Sports of the Times," *New York Times*, October 20, 1968, 5:2.

70. Sam Blair, "Sprinters Back on Wright Foot," *Dallas Morning News*, October 20, 1968, B2.

71. Sam Blair, "Loud Mouths Taint U.S. Accomplishments," *Dallas Morning News*, October 22, 1968, B2.

72. "Smith, Carlos Silent," *Dallas Morning News*, October 22, 1968, B1.

73. "Irate Negro Sprinters Shut Mouths," *Dallas Morning News*, October 22, 1968, B1.

74. "Smith, Carlos in Flight from 'Mean' Reporters," *Los Angeles Times*, October 22, 3:6.

75. Scott Moore and Wes Mathis, "Newsmen Outrun Smith and Carlos," *San Jose Mercury News*, October 22, 1968, 1, 2.

76. "Smith, Carlos Back, Have 'No Comment,'" *Washington Post*, October 22, 1968, D2.

77. Bud Collins, "The Olympics Protesters Have Been Too Few," *Boston Globe*, October 23, 1968, 27.

78. Howard Bryant, *Shut Out: A Story of Race and Baseball in Boston* (Boston: Beacon, 2003), 48, 97.

79. "80,000 Watch Olympics End on Happy Note," *Los Angeles Times*, October 29, 1968, 3:3.

80. "Pageantry Ends Games," *San Jose Mercury News*, October 28, 1968, 45–46.

81. Jerry Nason, "Cheering Mexico City Bids Olympics 'Adios,'" *Boston Globe*, October 28, 1968, 1, 23.

82. "80,000 Watch Olympics Close," *Washington Post*, October 29, 1968, 3:1, 3:2.

83. Wrap-up articles that failed to mention the protest included George Strickler, "Bring Down Curtain on 1968 Festival," *Chicago Tribune*, October 28, 1968, 3:1, 3:5; Steve Cady, "Amid Gun Salutes and Music, Mexico Bids a Colorful 'Adios' to Olympics," *New York Times*, October 28, 1968, 59; Bob Brachman, "It's Adios to 1968 Olympics," *San Francisco Examiner*, October 28, 1968, 53, 58; and "Yanks Run on Gold Ends," *Oakland Tribune*, October 28, 1968, 37–38.

84. Oliver Kuechle, "Time Out for Talk," *Milwaukee Journal Sentinel*, October 20, 1968, 3:3.

85. Neil Allen, "After the Race, a Racial Gesture," *London Times*, October 18, 1968, 12.

86. Allen, "After the Race, a Racial Gesture," 12.

87. "Politics at the Games?" *Sydney Mercury Herald*, October 21, 1968, 2.

88. Jim Webster and Ken Knox, "Black Power Rears Its Head at Games," *Sydney Morning Herald*, October 19, 1968, 1.

89. Chris Allan, "Jerome Raps Affair as Misguided Power Play," *Montreal Gazette*, October 19, 1968, 3:27.

90. Newnham interview.

91. Edwards, *Revolt of the Black Athlete*, 33.

92. Tommie Smith, www.TommieSmith.com, April 24, 2005.

93. Kurlansky, *1968*, 350. Smith and Carlos were inducted into the San Jose State University Sports Hall of Fame in 1999.

94. Newnham interview.

12

Sports Illustrated's African American Athlete Series as Socially Responsible Journalism

REED SMITH

The year 1968 was a seminal one in United States history. Martin Luther King Jr. and Robert Kennedy were assassinated. There were riots at the Democratic National Convention in Chicago, and the Tet Offensive changed America's mind about the war in Vietnam. It also was an extraordinary year for African American athletes. Bob Gibson won Major League Baseball's Most Valuable Player Award, Arthur Ashe Jr. became the first African American to capture the U.S. Open Tennis Tournament, O. J. Simpson ran a football to the Heisman Trophy, and Sports Illustrated (SI) named pro basketball's Bill Russell Sportsman of the Year. Despite these accomplishments, all was not well with African American athletes or the media that reported about them.

Numerous journalism scholars have written about the complex relationship between African American athletes and the press during the twentieth century. They have documented how journalists reported Jackie Robinson's breaking of the baseball color barrier, and how Muhammad Ali redefined the relationship between sports, celebrity and journalism. Others have researched the role of the black press in informing the public about African American athletes.[1] They have not, however, investigated the role that SI—the so-called "bible" of sports journalism—may have played in extending the influence of the civil rights movement into the athletic realm with a landmark series of articles. That is the subject of this essay.

In the summer of 1968, *SI* published a five-part series that investigated the discrimination that African American college and pro athletes alleged was taking place. The 1960s had brought greater opportunities for on-the-field recognition for African Americans, but off-the-field racism remained an issue, just as it was on the streets of Selma, Detroit, and other racially divided American cities. This study examines the *SI* articles to determine how they addressed the issue of civil rights within American athletics. It compares the series with the activities of other publications and broadcasts during the period and examines reader feedback. The research also evaluates the series within the context of "socially responsible journalism" to determine whether the undertaking may have advanced the genre of sports journalism beyond primarily reporting athletic accomplishments and statistics and into social awareness.[2]

Background

Journalists who practice social responsibility reflect "cultural pluralism" in their work. Embracing this principle should have guided sports journalists to report the discriminatory practices that plagued African American athletes, but that had not been taking place. Following Robinson's entry into baseball in 1946, there had been more than twenty years of silence among white executives who controlled athletics and white journalists who dominated sports reporting. Jointly, they had led readers to believe that athletics was a unique arena in which African Americans had achieved equality. But the perception was a fabrication. In February 1968, the National Advisory on Civil Disorder (the Kerner Commission) found that the majority of African Americans considered the media "instruments of the white power structure." The average African American, reported the commission, "couldn't give less of a damn about what the media say."[3] The findings were based on an evaluation of daily news media content, but they were applicable to sports reporting as well.

The falsehoods about athletic integration had been contrived to a greater degree since Robinson joined the Brooklyn Dodgers. Sports journalists thereafter pointed to achievements such as his as evidence that athletics had found a way to transcend the racial issues that otherwise divided America. On the tenth anniversary of Robinson's first at bat, the *Sporting News* heralded baseball's record of "gradual, voluntary, and peaceful advance" as a contrast to the painful integration being contested in other segments of American society.[4] But, in reality, not until 1959 did all Major League Baseball teams integrate their rosters.[5]

During these years, white reporters wrote stories that were racially celebratory but superficial. They readily noted when an African American first participated in, won, or officiated an athletic event (tellingly, there were no African American coaches or managers at this time). At the same time, "rarely did they [reporters] tackle critical issues that affected the sport industry generally or African American athletes specifically," according to Lomax.[6] Collegiate and professional spokespersons successfully built a public perception that sports constituted "an institution which fashioned itself as the great leveler in society," by exemplifying "sportsmanship and fair play," write Eisen and Wiggins.[7]

The Controversy Begins

Journalists reported a limited number of race-related athletic incidents during the 1950s and '60s. Readers were seldom given the impression that a widespread problem was going unaddressed. But after decades of silence about the ambiguity of their situation, 1968 became the year in which African American athletes publicly spoke out, en masse, about their struggles. There had been an unwritten rule that because of the opportunity sports played in elevating African Americans' social status, according to Harry Edwards, they were not to complain but should express gratefulness for their position. But as African Americans across the nation were protesting and even giving their lives in the fight for equality in daily life, the hypocrisy of African American athletes' position became untenable. Although highly visible in media coverage of their athletic exploits, African Americans in sports had previously distanced themselves from the civil rights movement. But in 1968, in Edwards's words, "African American athletes began to shed their traditional conservative approach to racial matters."[8]

A San Jose State University sociology professor, Edwards helped precipitate the increased visibility when he attempted to organize an African American boycott of the 1968 Mexico City Summer Olympics. The boycott failed because of lack of a consensus among African American athletes. Nonetheless, the unexpected images of African American sprinters John Carlos and Tommie Smith raising clenched, black-gloved fists during the nationally televised 200-meter awards ceremony were burned indelibly into the consciousness of American viewers. The incident was one of a number that began to bring public attention to African American athletes' dissatisfaction. They were faced with the question of whether they should, according to Eisen and Wiggins, "go about their business, and represent the race through their ability.... [Or use] the platform of sports ... to make more expansive statements about race relations and social justice in America."[9]

Nevertheless, the disjointed Olympic boycott was indicative of the stillborn nature of the African American athletes' attempt at changing their status. The "movement" was a disorganized initiative in which a number of small groups of African American athletes around the country protested in a wide variety of ways. Without a leader to create a coalition, and more importantly, lacking national media attention, their hopes of securing support to address their problems were restrained.

Employing the same strategy as other media in the 1950s, *SI* had published its share of African American "firsts," but it began addressing athletic racism beginning in 1960. A search of the *SI* index reveals that the first story in this category appeared on March 21, 1960. "Private World of the Negro Ballplayer" noted that Major League Baseball teams were continuing to segregate African Americans within their clubhouses.[10] A month later, *SI* again reported that, despite a seemingly successful rookie season in the National Basketball Association, Wilt Chamberlain was announcing his premature retirement. He was doing so because of racial abuse he claimed he had suffered both on and off the court.[11] Over the next four years, *SI* did more stories involving race and athletics but only four that focused on it as an issue.[12]

During the same time period *SI* was following the blow-by-blow rise to ring success and growth of popular culture iconography of a larger-than-life young African American boxer by the name of Cassius Clay (later Muhammad Ali). In 1967, Ali became involved in a legal fight to retain his heavyweight crown after refusing to serve in the army because of his Islamic beliefs. Many sportswriters joined in the widespread criticism of Ali, labeling his position, according to Grabsky, "un-American."[13] While publishing stories about the charismatic Ali, *SI* had unwittingly provided him with not only a Vietnam War but a racial protest platform. The longer the magazine reported on the conflict between federal officials and Ali, the more it "lauded [his] nobility and sincerity, [and] mocked his opponents as self-righteous hypocrites," according to Spivey.[14] In 1965, racism and boxing coverage of Ali converged in a story that George Plimpton wrote for *SI*. Plimpton had witnessed firsthand discrimination against Ali when the champion and his entourage had stopped at a Florida truck stop to eat. "World Champion Is Refused a Meal" confirmed how, despite his fame among whites and African Americans alike, because he was an African American Ali remained a second-class citizen.[15] The experience of covering Ali collectively added to *SI* reporters' sympathy for African Americans.

This attitude was not shared, however, by *SI*'s upper management. The magazine's executives historically had been careful to act conservatively in covering African Americans in the pages of *SI*. Between its introduction in 1954 and 1959, only six of ninety-six front covers featured an African American face.[16] Management's view was not so much a facet of racism as an economic concern. Parent company Time Inc.'s market studies showed that nearly 99 percent of *SI* readership was white. Mac-Cambridge says executives did not want to alienate them.[17] Thus, a line of demarcation existed within the *SI* offices as to how to report on African American athletes. Publishing an investigative series on discriminatory practices was an idea that increasingly appealed to *SI* reporters because they considered it relevant to the world of sports they were covering. But *SI*'s management did not share the view.

Civil rights was a cause taking place in the streets of America but, for the majority of Americans, not in their athletic arenas. In 1968, despite the appearance of discrimination stories nationwide in daily newspapers, on TV news shows, and in news magazines, neither Time executives nor *SI* managers thought that a sports magazine should address the issue. Management believed *SI* was in the business of entertainment, not a change agent, but that is exactly what the magazine ended up acting as when it published "The African American Athlete: A Shameful Story." Given management's reticence, how could this have happened? It would require an amount of intra-office deception to accomplish the goal.

Sports Illustrated's Development

The introduction of television to Middle America following World War II coincided with a growth in middle-class spending power and a greater emphasis on enjoying increased amounts of leisure time. These elements benefited sports and led motivated non–sports fan Henry Luce to introduce a magazine, writes Spivey, that would take advantage of these developments.[18] Time advisors and Madison Avenue advertising agencies attempted to talk Luce out of the introduction, believing sports coverage was only for a blue-collar audience and beneath the attention of serious journalism. But Luce correctly saw that the time was right to fulfill a need for a more intellectual approach to sports activities. He envisioned that unlike daily newspaper pages and limited magazine coverage, *SI* would be more than just a chronicler of game results. An introductory article in *Time* noted that it would provide a "reevaluation of sport."[19]

SI struggled financially throughout the 1950s and into the '60s because management had trouble pinpointing its identity. In its early years, stories featured upper-class sports such as yachting and polo, and advertisers stayed away, doubting that true sports fans would read the in-depth stories Luce encouraged. To survive *SI* introduced several innovations as it moved into the 1960s. It made increased use of color photographs, in-depth scouting reports that previewed major events such as the World Series, and superior reporting and writing. Writers Robert Creamer, Tex Maule, and Dan Jenkins (and later Jack Olsen, Plimpton, and Frank Deford) soon set *SI* apart as not just a sports magazine but a superior journalistic enterprise. *SI* became a model for popular American magazines of all types, asserts MacCambridge.[20]

Luce's appointment of *Time*'s European correspondent Andre Laguerre as managing editor in 1960 was a turning point in defining the magazine's character. Under Laguerre's direction, reporters developed their own writing style and dared "to tell people what was important, and legitimized sports—and being a sports fan."[21] Laguerre challenged *SI* reporters to set the sports agenda, and they achieved that goal during his fourteen years of leadership. It became the only large-circulation publication to win consecutive National Magazine Awards for general excellence. Tennis star Chris Evert summed up the opinion of many readers and athletes when she called it "the Rolex of magazines."[22] But the *SI* African American series would be a completely different, even daring, step in *SI*'s growth into a serious journalistic endeavor. Against this growing esteem and level of influence on both readers and the world of athletics arose the civil right movement.

During the mid-1960s it became increasingly evident that racism in athletics, much as in other segments of American society, was headed toward a boiling point. The 1965 African American players' boycott of the American Football League All-Star Game in New Orleans made it clear to *SI* reporters that athletic racism was more than a single-person or limited-event issue. The AFL players declined to participate when they were denied hotel rooms comparable to those afforded white teammates. The following February, African American track and field collegians refused to run in the prestigious New York Athletic Club's One Hundredth Anniversary meet at Madison Square Garden. They did so because the club excluded African Americans. Concurrently, racial tension on college campuses across the nation widened to include athletic departments. More than three dozen predominantly white institutions witnessed protests related to African American athletes' dissatisfaction with their treatment by white coaches and administrators, according to Wiggins.[23]

Laguerre's reporters, who were witnessing the malfeasance firsthand, had already decided the issue could no longer remain unexplored. While other publications sought to "paint it [African American athletes' uprising] as a wild, militant Power thing," in Edwards's words, Laguerre believed a thoroughly researched investigation of the charges was the only way to get at the truth.[24] He commented to assistant Pat Ryan, "When everybody is saying one thing, you should look at the reverse and see if it's actually more true."[25] The magazine that had come to consider itself the definitive United States sports magazine undertook an exploration of the issue. Laguerre knew *SI*'s management well enough to believe that publishing the investigative treatment that the topic required would encounter resistance. He devised a scheme, which put his and several others' jobs on the line, to overcome the hurdle.

In November 1967, Laguerre, a white Frenchman, had assigned Olsen, a white Philadelphian, to research the topic. Olsen had been a newspaper crime and political reporter during the first ten years of his career before landing a job as an editor with *Time*. In 1957, he had covered the Little Rock school integration battle. He possessed, in the words of MacCambridge, "a muckraker's tenacity" and was a "tireless reporter."[26] It was a perfect assignment for Olsen because it "showed his conscience." Friend and fellow author David Guterson said that as a reporter Olsen "just couldn't deal with injustice. It haunted him."[27] Before beginning to write, Olsen traversed the country interviewing African American athletes, active and retired, and white collegiate and professional sports managers.[28] John Harris, who did research for a number of Olsen's later books, said Olsen was effective in gathering information for the series because "he could really get people to open up and trust him."[29]

While Olsen prepared the content, Laguerre executed his strategy for surreptitious publication. Contrary to the standard *SI* policy of previewing in the preceding week's edition what was forthcoming in the following week's issue, Laguerre and his colleagues did not publish a preview. He believed editor in chief Hedley Donovan would veto the project if he got wind of it because it "veered so far from the conventional wisdom of the times, and of Time Inc."[30] Laguerre believed Donovan was part of the white establishment. Doing stories about cultural icon Ali was one thing; accusing the American college and professional athletic institutions of perpetuating a racial conspiracy was quite another.

The series could be problematic because it represented an affront to the very sources that the magazine depended upon. Donovan did not believe *SI* was so powerful that it could thumb its nose at team owners and athletic directors, who could retaliate by closing their locker rooms to *SI*'s reporters. Doing so could damage *SI*'s ability to cover major stories, which could lead to decreased circulation and loss of advertising revenue. In addition, the series could alienate the largely white middle- and upper-class readership that had limited sympathy for the problems of African American athletes.

Laguerre, Olsen, and Ray Cave, who edited the series, all abruptly left New York for vacations at undisclosed locations just before the first installment of the series was published. Donovan was furious when he saw the cover and realized the scam the men had pulled off. But there was little he could do because *SI* was already hitting newsstands as he learned of the ruse.[31] A conspiracy by socially conscious white men within *SI*'s headquarters had been necessary for the magazine to expose a national athletic scandal. Donovan located and hurriedly called Cave back to his office, calling for an explanation. He demanded: "Are you confident about the reporting?" Cave replied: "Yes. I am totally confident."[32] To his credit, after the series ran Donovan grasped the significance of the series. He sent Cave a scribbled note that read, "The African American Athlete series is one of the most distinguished pieces of journalism in Time Inc.'s history."[33]

Other Outlets Seek to Co-opt the Issue

SI was not, however, alone in its decision to report the topic. Before the public could read the *SI* series, *Life* and *Newsweek* had already published articles on African Americans' motivation for boycotting the Olympics, and other media outlets would follow the *SI* articles with their own coverage. Had other media already done the job that Laguerre believed rightfully belonged to *SI*? An examination of the competition's coverage further elucidates the notoriety of *SI*'s examination.

Both the *Life* and *Newsweek* articles focused on individual African American athletes and the racism they encountered. The *Newsweek* story included comments from well-known former African American athletes, many of whom disagreed with the idea of an Olympic boycott. Written by former *SI* reporter Pete Axthelm, it outlined the issues involved in the controversy. But the article did not argue that the African American perspective was valid or explain that the controversy was related to larger societal issues.[34] Likewise, *Life*'s story seemingly sought to provide "objective coverage" of the controversy by including white coaches and administrators' rebuttals to African American criticism. UCLA football coach Tommy Prothro, for example, said, "Anyone could find athletes—white or African American—who were unhappy. [Likewise], where a white might say it was a personal matter . . . a Negro would say it was racial."[35]

The "African American said versus white said" journalistic strategy characterized both stories. This attempt to "balance" coverage of controversial stories traditionally has had a record of "undermin[ing] rather than advanc[ing] pluralism," according to Tuchman. Including opinion leaders' quotes that "subtly or blatantly denigrate . . . minority group ideas" has the ability to effectively undercut the minority agenda.[36] It appears that neither magazine provided the issue the context or advocacy journalism that the SI series displayed. *Life* and *Newsweek* readers had the African American athlete controversy presented as a tidy story in which two sides of an issue simply disagreed on the truth. It was not presented as a symptom of a larger more troubling societal development. Both publications limited their coverage to single articles.

In September 1968, a month after publication of the SI series ended, CBS News aired a half-hour primetime documentary titled "Body and Soul: Body of Black America." In an abbreviated treatment of the issue, seemingly motivated by the SI series, the program exposed television viewers to the same issues SI had divulged in print. Host Harry Reasoner even referred to the SI series when he observed that the magazine "recently brought to public attention that whites are prouder of being an integrating force of sports than are some black people." The program showed still photographs from the SI articles and did not provide insights beyond what SI had presented.[37]

Beginning two months later, in November and running until June 1969, the African American–targeted magazine *Ebony* published a seven-part series that traced the history of African American athletics from 1945 to 1969. Only in the final article in the series, "Stereotypes, Prejudices, and Other Unfunny Hilarities," did the magazine broach the contemporary issues addressed by *SI*. African American journalist A. S. "Doc" Young referred to the *SI* series but did not elaborate on the issues it raised. Instead, he focused on acknowledging the progress sports had made toward eliminating discrimination in America. He concluded that "America still has much work to do—to catch up with sports, imperfect though they are; and to end the lingering prejudices in sports as well."[38] None of the other media attempts provided the depth of coverage or issue analysis of the Olsen-*SI* series.

Details of the *SI* Series

SI publisher Garry Volk, in his letter to readers that accompanied the first article, called it "the most socially significant series this magazine has ever published." He said it would bring readers "a new appreciation of the problems and attitudes of the African American athletes whose performances all of us as sports fans cheer so enthusiastically but about whom we know so little." Olsen's introduction to the first article declared, "Sports Illustrated explores the roots and validity of the African American athlete's unrest—and finds them well founded."[39]

Striking black and white art of an African American athlete on the front cover of the issue heralded what waited inside. Similar to the two subsequent articles in the series, it focused on collegiate athletics. Olsen began by describing what athletic administrators thought about integration: "Every morning the world of sports wakes up and congratulates itself on its contributions to race relations. The litany has been repeated so many times it is believed almost universally. It goes: 'Look what sports has done for the Negro.'" But, according to Olsen, athletes themselves told a strikingly different story: "African American collegiate athletes say they are dehumanized, exploited and discarded, and some even say they were happier back in the ghetto.... They are underpaid, shunted into stereotyped positions and treated like sub-humans by Paleolithic coaches who regard them as watermelon-eating idiots."[40] Additional drawings of African Americans in purposefully disjointed athletic poses adorned the pages.

The article included statements from Edwards and from African American as well as white athletes. Much of it focused on how white coaches seemingly "used" African Americans during their four years of collegiate eligibility. Unless they were talented enough to advance to professional sports, many African Americans returned to a life of unemployment and even crime when they exhausted their eligibility. Few were prepared for academic rigor because of the deficiencies of the marginal public schools they had attended. Several African Americans related how they had never read a book before entering college. After arriving on campus, they were forced to cram into four years what they had missed in the classroom in the previous twelve. Many were faced with trying to understand a form of the English language they had not previously encountered. Olsen charged that universities were hiding embarrassing realities about their treatment of African Americans: "Some of the truths are painful. . . . Some show too clearly the heavy hand of white America."[41]

The article also described how "out of place" African Americans often felt trying to live in an alien society. Edwards called the African American athlete "the institutionalized Tom, the white man's nigger" and a college scholarship "merely a new form of indentured servitude." A white football official observed, "There is nothing in the world so forlorn and useless as a Negro college athlete who has used up his eligibility."[42] Olsen wrote that an African American who relied on athletics to define his future became a "caricature of his race."[43] Several professional African American athletes harshly criticized prominent African American athletes they considered reticent toward helping rectify the wrongs perpetuated against their race. Among those they disapproved of were Willie Mays, Jessie Owens, and Joe Louis. On the other hand, they praised Jim Brown, Bill Russell, and Oscar Roberson for their outspokenness.[44]

This kind of exposition is representative of socially responsible journalism.[45] Carrying out their moral right to correct a false picture was what the principals at *SI* were attempting to do with this series. *SI* was giving public voice to the plight of African American athletes, which had previously been concealed from readers. "The fact that everybody talked about, but nobody had previously delved deeply into it made it [the series] all the more commanding," according to Frank Deford.[46]

Part two of the series was published July 8. A diagonal banner in the top right corner of the magazine cover alerted readers that another installment of the series was inside. Subsequent issues featured similar banners. On the first page of this article a photograph taken on a college campus from behind clearly showed the images of an African American male with his arm around the back of a white female. On the same page, Olsen argued that "since the Renaissance, institutions of higher learning have been the scenes of social experiment." Therefore, he observed, no place in American society seemed to offer a more open-minded setting to reform race relations than a college campus, but this was not occurring. Moving beyond the discussion of African Americans as athletes, this article examined campus relationships between white and African American students, concluding that they were abysmal.[47]

Olsen asserted that each team's head coach served as the defining figure in African Americans' lives. He typically either failed to understand or ignored African Americans' social needs. As a result, most African Americans were provided with only a glimpse of what integration could be like. Many of them attended campuses in small rural towns where the population was almost 100 percent white. Townspeople were either unprepared or unwilling to make exceptions to integrate African Americans into their culture, leaving them ostracized and with no one to trust.

African Americans said a common message coaches delivered was "stay away from white girls." The racial stereotype that African American men were a sexual threat to white women lived on from nineteenth-century America. White coaches and white athletes still believed the only reason an African American male would approach a white woman was to violate her. Several instances were cited where African Americans who dared date white coeds were punished by either being demoted or dropped from teams. Olsen wrote that "the American sports establishment continues to hold its place as one of the bastions of deep, unsettling, sex-oriented prejudice."[48] African Americans also claimed that white coaches used more demeaning terms to discipline them than they employed with whites. Reportedly, one football coach, when criticizing the performance of white players, used the terms "dope," or "idiot," but when yelling at African American players called them "animals" or "niggers."[49] African Americans told Olsen that white athletes "were incapable of taking us as human beings." Whites were willing to play with African Americans because they helped win games, but they ostracized them otherwise. Retired University of Kansas basketball coach Dick Harp called "the concept of sports as an integrating force a myth." Several African American athletes said they coveted a single honest relationship with a white person, but few could accomplish it.[50]

African Americans were unanimous in asserting that to play they had to be physically superior to white teammates. They said the white perception of them was that they were "superhuman because you're African American, and that you're dumb." This meant that African Americans were "impervious to injury, insult and injustice." African Americans considered the latter point especially demeaning. They said coaches applied a double standard. Perceiving them as "workhorses," coaches thought African Americans were naturally lazy and feigned injury. African Americans said they feared getting injured because, regardless, they would have to play. Trainers and coaches refused to believe their injuries were real. African Americans who claimed they could not play because they were hurt ended up riding the bench or off the team.[51]

While African Americans said they rarely received verbal abuse from fans while on the field, booster influence impacted how coaches utilized them. Many insisted that teams maintained a quota system. "Fans don't want to see too many African American faces on the field at a time," said one player. Regardless of ability, only so many African Americans could be in an offensive backfield or on defense at one time. They also argued that "stacking" was a common practice. In this scenario, African Americans were put in only a few positions and left to compete with each other for a single starting role.[52] Skill positions such as quarterback, center, and linebacker were off limits. White coaches did not believe African Americans possessed the intelligence for independent thinking; positions that required speed and reaction but discouraged judgment were earmarked for them.

By publishing the articles, *SI* raised public awareness for an otherwise disorganized social movement. In *Making News*, Tuchman addressed what special-interest groups must do to secure a hearing for their agenda. In her research, she concluded that "lower class groups [especially minorities] . . . are cut off from the media . . . unless they recruit middle class supporters who . . . attack those who attract media coverage."[53] African American athletes had, in an informal way, "recruited" *si* to "assail" the sports establishment. Because of sports' popularity, it attracts a great deal of media coverage. This reality makes it easier to draw attention to a movement such as this than it might otherwise. Olsen's words demonstrated his ability to represent the previously unheard voices of African American athletes. In the memory of *si* veteran Deford, "Most reporters were pretty sympathetic to black athletes during this time. No less than news reporters were sympathetic to the general cause of civil rights."[54] As Baran and Davis note, journalists who undertake to act with social responsibility run the risk of antagonizing elites and reducing profits. But the practice appeals "to the idealism of individual media practitioners."[55]

The remaining articles in the series interspersed drawings and photographs of African American athletes with the narrative. The third installment focused specifically on racial problems within the University of Texas at El Paso "UTEP" (formerly Texas Western) athletic program. In 1965, the university's all–African American basketball starting five (the first in collegiate history) had defeated the all-white University of Kentucky squad. UTEP administrators and coaches considered themselves progressive because they represented the first Texas university to integrate athletics, but African Americans painted a conflicting picture. Former UTEP football player Fred Carr, who by 1968 was playing for the Green Bay Packers, said, "College [was] the time of my greatest suffering. I came to college and discovered prejudice." Willie Worsley, a member of the championship basketball team, said the triumph made little difference: "When the game's over they want you to come back to the dormitory and stay out of sight."[56]

The article further outlined how, early in the 1967 football season, African American UTEP team members staged what was probably the first collegiate athletic boycott. The players complained that there were no African American girls for them to date, and those who were married said their wives were compensated less than white players' wives for comparable campus employment. UTEP administrators attempted to keep the incident quiet and promised the athletes they would correct the inequities but by the following spring had taken no action.[57] That was when African American track team members, including the world's premiere long jumper, Bob Beamon, refused to travel to a meet at Brigham Young University. The athletes were disturbed that "the Book of Mormon . . . teach[es] that Negroes are descended from the devil." As a result, Coach Wayne Vandenburg, depending on who was telling the story, either kicked the boycotters off the team or they quit. UTEP president Joseph Ray supported Vanderburg: "This is a high price that no college athletes . . . have ever paid for a point on this issue. They were laying down their collegiate athletic lives, and they surely knew it."[58]

Part four of the series began a focus on professional athletics. It featured interviews with African Americans, some then playing but others retired. Those still playing asked that their names not be used, out of fear for their livelihood. Retired players identified themselves because they were, in their words, "no longer going along with the gag."[59] Olsen found that a professional African American had it better than his collegiate counterpart because "he has a degree of financial security . . . [and] he does not have to contend with the scholastic regimen." Conversely, the professional African American was helpless to stop the bigotry of both his teammates and team executives, was unequally paid, and could not share in the managerial and commercial rewards that white teammates enjoyed once their playing days ended.[60]

The article included statistics to document the extent of professional sports discrimination: "Only 13 of 207 pitchers on major league rosters . . . [were] Negroes." There was not a single starting quarterback or coach in the National Football League, and baseball did not have an African American manager. Only the National Basketball Association seemed to acknowledge both the athletic and intellectual abilities of African Americans. Its rosters were 50 percent integrated, and the Boston Celtics had named All-Star Bill Russell as the NBA's first African American head coach. Olsen asserted that "nothing is more obvious in professional sport than the fact that there are quotas—and few things are as hotly denied."[61]

Several African Americans said there were different rules for whites and themselves. Former All-League Baltimore Colts tackle Jim Parker said an African American has to "have the right attitude or you can't play." He became accustomed, he said, "to seeing African American teammates with ability disappear . . . over something to do with his attitude, but 'you don't ask . . . because you have a family to feed.'" Despite management's boast that professional sports were "a bastion of racial equality," the interviews revealed something quite different. "The overwhelming evidence is that sport has not been able to lead the way to new attitudes [for society at large]" concerning race because of its bigoted practices, wrote Olsen.[62]

The final article in the series focused on the St. Louis Cardinals football team, which had become the subject of news coverage in 1967 because of racial infighting. The Cardinals served as a case study. Olsen wrote, "Racism, a destroyer of both spirit and performance, exists to varying degrees on almost all professional athletic teams in the U.S. The Cardinals . . . provide a disturbing and poignant example of the chaos that can result."[63] Between late 1967 when the turmoil began and when Olsen wrote about it, the Cardinals had made progress in mediating the problems. Olsen acknowledged this and observed that the Cardinals' situation was probably worse but not unlike that on many NFL teams: "Prejudice is too common a commodity[,] . . . routine, expected. Almost every team . . . has a cell of white racists."[64] That the Cardinals had addressed the problem allowed *SI* to end its series with the impression that despite the institutionalization of athletic racism, there was hope for change. The article concluded with an observation from Prentice Gautt, an African American and former Cardinal player who had become a college coach: "If they [racial problems] can't be solved in sports, where can they be solved? Sports has been following when it's supposed to lead."[65]

Reader Reaction

Veteran CBS journalist Ted White has observed that investigative journalists believe the best indicator of whether they have done their job well is indicated by how much they agitate individuals on both sides of the issue.[66] The *SI* series generated both positive and negative reader comments.

Following the fourth article, *si* began printing reader reactions. A Chicagoan wrote, "I'm white. The message in . . . Jack Olsen's series was a long time coming from any national medium, sports or otherwise. Better late than anticlimactic." A New Yorker added, "The sports world has shown that African American and white can achieve together; it can credit itself with no more."[67] A college basketball coach observed that the series appears "destined to be remembered as the most significant statement ever published by *Sports Illustrated*." An Arkansas writer commented, "[Your series] ranks as one of the best in-depth treatments of any subject that I have ever read."[68] A UTEP faculty member replied: "I hope that *si* will continue to point out the weaknesses of our system. . . . Thank you for helping us to see ourselves as we are."[69]

But not all letters were complimentary. A white athletic director disputed the series' conclusions, calling them "a combination of half truths carefully selected from a group of exceptions and woven into a tale that does nothing but misrepresent the actions of collegiate athletics." He believed the articles would do great harm "due to the wide circulation of your magazine."[70] An African American New Jersey high school football coach, who had helped fifteen African American athletes gain entrance into colleges, called the series "yellow generalization" and asserted that it had "castrated him."[71]

In all, *si* received more than a thousand letters following publication of the series, the most it has received in reaction to any article or series published during its history.[72] It continued publishing readers' letters each week for a month after the series concluded. Feedback was overwhelmingly positive, but *si* also received negative letters that revealed a racist perspective. Representative of these were "[African Americans] should be damn glad their ancestors were brought over as slaves. . . . Instead of suffering through football at Kansas . . . they could be enjoying life in . . . the Congo or some other equally progressive, dignified African location"[73] and "I can't decide whether this Mr. Olsen is a sports writer or a civil rights leader."[74] Several readers charged that, regardless of its veracity, the series should not have appeared in a sports magazine. Those comments aside, there was recognition of the series' potential influence and quality. The president of the United Negro College Fund observed that *SI* "deserves the highest commendation and a Pulitzer Prize for having the insight to research the problem, the wisdom to assign a talented reporter to the job and the courage to report the story as it is."[75]

In an *SI* editorial that appeared a week after the series concluded, Volk wrote that it was intended to be "a first step, a beginning" toward righting a wrong. He listed a number of initiatives that readers had already either suggested or begun to address the issue. These included investigations of college athletic departments, inner city support groups for young African American athletes, and increased soul searching and accountability by athletic administrators.[76] Volk called on the National Collegiate Athletic Association (NCAA) to reform its standards to guard against future abuses.[77]

Olsen's *SI* colleagues admired the series. During a 2004 ESPN interview John Underwood said, "They [Olsen et al.] took on a true moral crisis. The series . . . was so new and so daring. It was less about what it exposed than that it exposed anything at all."[78] Deford remembers that the series "was a very big deal at the time." He believes that the fact that the topic was considered in five consecutive weekly issues added to its impact. "I don't think he [Olsen] cheated on any angle of the subject," said Deford, adding, "He just did a helluva job."[79] Soon after the series ran, Time published Olsen's extended work on the topic as a full-length book.

Conclusion

Thirty years after publication of Olsen's series, Edwards called 1968 "a watershed year . . . in the history of modern sports."[80] He was referring to the changes he believed African American protests helped bring about in the American sports establishment. But it is unlikely such change would have been possible without the awareness that *SI*'s articles helped create with the white sports public. *SI*'s series became part of an overall news media campaign that brought a variety of aspects of the civil rights movement into American homes. Many broadcast and print outlets became forums for dissent. The resulting exposure of racial issues encouraged individuals to join in the struggle, according to Gitlin.[81]

As significantly, Olsen's work was seminal because it represented an awakening for sports journalism. *SI* was America's most visible and influential sports magazine. The series helped make *SI* "the bible of the industry," in James Michener's estimation, because it assumed the journalistic role of the sports world's conscience.[82] Once *SI* had helped shine an investigative light on sports' "dirty secret," African Americans could begin to attain a level playing field both in and outside of the athletic arena. At the same time, sports journalists gained license to more aggressively pursue other issues that held sociological implications. This was *SI*'s first in-depth investigative series, but it would not be its last.[83] The magazine had begun to deal "openly with . . . topics which men in saloons [had previously only] talk[ed] about in whispers," in Michener's words.[84] Time executives who had feared the financial damage that publishing such a series would do to *SI*'s bottom line discovered that little harm resulted. There were a few canceled subscriptions and hate mail received in New York. But, according to Deford, *SI* received less negative mail after the series than "when it slighted some coach or team or city" in a less controversial article.[85]

In terms of impacting the issue it considered, the series could not, of course, singlehandedly bring an end to athletic racism. For that matter, extensive civil rights media coverage did not end racism in other areas of American society, either. *SI* could only reveal the situation to the public, which then had to act on the information. After centuries of assimilating racism into American society, it remains a predicament that continues to be slowly but gradually resolved. The best that can be said is that the *SI* series contributed to the process of ending blatant racism in athletics and began a course of action that continues to secure change. While integration began quickly in some areas of sports following its publication and has continued on all fronts, it has only recently occurred in others.[86] For instance, not until 2003 did a Southeastern Conference team hire its first African American football coach.[87]

In the final analysis, the *SI* series helped make 1968 an important year in sports journalism as well. Additionally, its foray into practicing socially responsible journalism would embolden it and other sports journalists for additional efforts in subsequent years. Olsen's "A Shameful Story," observed

Fitzpatrick, had "trod boldly where few other sportswriters had dared."[88] While there is no indication that Olsen or his editors were motivated by the Kerner Commission to undertake the series, by exposing a serious national issue they had acted in a socially responsible manner. They had acted out of a sense of personal and professional morality. While it probably was not exactly what Luce had in mind when he launched *SI* in 1954, his creation had fulfilled his vision of conducting, at least in this instance, a needed "reevaluation of sport."

NOTES

1. Examples of such work include, but are not limited to, Ronald Bishop, "A Nod from Destiny: How Sportswriters for White and African-American Newspapers Covered Kenny Washington's Entry into the National Football League," *American Journalism* 19 (Winter 2002), 81-106; William G. Kelley, "Jackie Robinson and the Press," *Journalism Quarterly* 53 (1976), 137-49; Chris Lamb, *Blackout: The Story of Jackie Robinson's First Spring Training* (Lincoln: University of Nebraska Press, 2004); Robert Lipsyte, *Covering Ali, Discovering an Era* (New Brunswick NJ: Transaction, 1998); John D. Stevens, "The Black Press and the 1936 Olympics," *American Journalism* 14 (1997), 97-102; and Patrick Washburn, "New York Newspaper Coverage of Jackie Robinson in His First Major League Season," *Journalism Quarterly* 58, no. 4 (1981), 640-44.

2. Commission on Freedom of the Press, *A Free and Responsible Press* (Chicago: University of Chicago Press, 1947), 13.

3. Philip J. Meranto, ed., *The Kerner Report Revisited* (Urbana: University of Illinois Press, 1970), 2, 31.

4. "Baseball Ten Years after Jackie Robinson," *Sporting News*, September 16, 1956, 22. For additional examples, see Jules Tygiel, *Baseball's Great Experiment: Jackie Robinson and His Legacy* (New York: Random House, 1984).

5. Jon Entine, *Taboo: Why African American Athletes Dominate Sports and Why We Are Afraid to Talk About It* (New York: Persceus Book Group, 2000), 210.

6. Michael E. Lomax, "Revisiting the Revolt of the African American Athlete: Harry Edwards and the Making of the New African American Sport Studies," *Journal of Sports History* 29 (2002), 473.

7. George Eisen and David K. Wiggins, *Ethnicity and Sport in North American History and Culture* (Westport CT: Greenwood Press, 1994), 133-34.

8. Lomax, "Revisiting the Revolt" 46, 473. "African Americans had been brainwashed so long and so completely about sports' supposed uniquely beneficent role in their lives that the very idea of . . . using sport as a protest vehicle . . . seemed to most as quite mystifying, to some ludicrous, and to yet others . . . treasonous," said Edwards. See Harry Edwards, "The Olympic Project for Human Rights: An Assessment Ten Years Later," *The African American Scholar* 9 (1979), 2.

9. David K. Wiggins and Patrick B. Miller, *The Unlevel Playing Field: A Documentary History of the African American Experience in Sport* (Urbana: University of Illinois Press, 2003), 271.

10. Robert H. Boyle, "Private World of the Negro Ballplayer," *Sports Illustrated*, March 21, 1960, 16, 84.

11. Jeremiah Tax, "Chamberlain's Big Mistake," *Sports Illustrated*, April 4, 1960, 58–59.

12. See Robert H. Boyle, "All Alone By the Telephone," *Sports Illustrated*, October 16, 1961, 37–43; Boyle, "The Ways of Life at the Country Club," *Sports Illustrated*, March 5, 1962, 68–74; Edwin Shrake, "Tough Cookie Marches to His Own Drummer," *Sports Illustrated*, December 14, 1964, 70–80; and Ron Mix, "Was This Their Freedom Ride?" *Sports Illustrated*, January 18, 1965, 24–25.

13. During this period of coverage Ali "became the most hated and reviled sports figure in American history." See Phil Grabsky, *Muhammad Ali: Through the Eyes of the World* (Hollywood: Universal Studios, 2001), 94 min.

14. Donald Spivey, *Sport in America: New Historical Perspectives* (Westport CT: Greenwood Press, 1985), 175.

15. George Plimpton, "World Champion Is Refused a Meal," *Sports Illustrated*, May 17, 1965, 24–27.

16. Amy Bass, *Not the Triumph but the Struggle* (Minneapolis: University of Minnesota Press, 2002), 213.

17. Michael MacCambridge, *The Franchise: A History of Sports Illustrated Magazine* (New York: Hyperion, 1997), 159.

18. Spivey, *Sport in America*, 175.

19. "The New Magazine of Sport," *Time*, May 17, 1954, 95.

20. MacCambridge, *Franchise*, 6, 27, 42.

21. MacCambridge, *Franchise*, 51.

22. MacCambridge, *Franchise*, 6, 8.

23. For details, see David K. Wiggins, "'The Year of Awakening': Black Athletes, Racial Unrest and the Civil Rights Movement of 1968," *The International Journal of the History of Sport* 9 (1992), 188–208; David K. Wiggins, "'The Future

of College Athletics Is at Stake': Black Athletes and Racial Turmoil on Three Predominantly White University Campuses, 1968–1972," *Journal of Sport History* 15 (1988), 304–33; and "Irate Black Athletes Stir Campus Tension," *New York Times*, November 16, 1969, 1, 85.

24. David Leonard, "What Happened to the Revolt of the African American Athlete? A Look Back Thirty Years Later: An Interview with Harry Edwards," *ColorLines* 1 (1968), 4.

25. Ray Cave, interviewed by Bob Lee, in *"Sports Illustrated" at 50*, ESPN, October 25, 2004.

26. The Jack Olsen Home Page, http://www.jackolsen.com.

27. Guterson quoted in Olsen's obituary, Gordy Holt, *Seattle Post-Intelligencer*, July 19, 2002, 5.

28. MacCambridge, *Franchise*, 159. Olsen later became renowned as "the dean of true crime authors" and a respected expert on the psychology of criminals. He published thirty-three books, and the *Philadelphia Inquirer* described him as "an American treasure." His *Sports Illustrated* series on African American athletes was published as a book, *The African-American Athlete: A Shameful Story: The Myth of Integration in American Sport* (New York: Time-Life Books, 1968). He died in 2002. See the Jack Olsen Home Page at jackolsen.com.

29. Quoted in Holt, Olsen obituary.

30. MacCambridge, *Franchise*, 160.

31. MacCambridge, *Franchise*, 160.

32. Cave interview.

33. Cave interview.

34. Pete Axthelm, "The Angry African American Athlete," *Newsweek*, July 15, 1968, 56–60.

35. "The Olympic Jolt," *Life*, March 15, 1968, 20–29.

36. Gaye Tuchman, *A Study in the Construction of Reality* (New York: Free Press, 1978), 201–2.

37. *Body and Soul: Body of Black America*, produced and directed by Andy Rooney (CBS News, BFA Distributors, 1968), videocassette, 30 min.

38. A. S. "Doc" Young, "The Black Athlete in the Golden Age of Sports," *Ebony*, June 1969, 114–24.

39. "Letter from the Publisher," *Sports Illustrated*, July 1, 1968, 4.

40. Jack Olsen, "The Cruel Deception," *Sports Illustrated*, July 1, 1968, 12.

41. Olsen, "The Cruel Deception," 13.

42. Olsen, "The Cruel Deception," 16.

43. Olsen, "The Cruel Deception," 17.

44. Olsen, "The Cruel Deception," 18.

45. For further information regarding the relevant points of the Hutchins Commission's findings about the press and representing minority interests, see Jerilyn S. McIntyre, "Repositioning a Landmark: The Hutchins Commission and Freedom of the Press," *Critical Studies in Mass Communication* 4 (1987), 137; Fred S. Siebert, Theodore Peterson, and Wilbur Schramm, *Four Theories of the Press* (Urbana: University of Illinois Press, 1956), 101; and Stanley J. Baran and Dennis K. Davis, *Mass Communication Theory: Foundations, Ferment, and Future*, 3rd ed. (Belmont CA: Wadsworth, 2003), 109.

46. Frank Deford, email interview with author, October 1, 2005.

47. Olsen, "The African American Athlete: Pride and Prejudice," *Sports Illustrated*, July 8, 1968, 20.

48. Olsen, "The African American Athlete," 24.

49. Olsen, "The African American Athlete."

50. Olsen, "The African American Athlete," 25–26.

51. Olsen, "The African American Athlete," 28.

52. Olsen, "The African American Athlete," 30.

53. Tuchman, *Study in the Construction of Reality*, 133.

54. Deford interview.

55. Baran and Davis, *Mass Communication Theory*, 110.

56. Olsen, "In an Alien World," *Sports Illustrated*, July 15, 1968, 31–36.

57. Olsen, "In an Alien World," 36.

58. Olsen, "In an Alien World," 42. Years later, several of the African Americans that Olsen interviewed for the series said he misquoted them, and they retracted their accusations. Olsen, however, stood by his story. See Frank Fitzpatrick, *And the Wall Came Tumbling Down* (New York: Simon & Schuster, 1999), 31–32.

59. Olsen, "In the Back of the Bus," *Sports Illustrated*, July 22, 1968, 28.

60. Olsen, "In the Back of the Bus."

61. Olsen, "In the Back of the Bus," 29–34.

62. Olsen, "In the Back of the Bus," 40.

63. Olsen, "The Anguish of a Team Divided," *Sports Illustrated*, July 29, 1968, 21.

64. Olsen, "Anguish of a Team Divided," 22.

65. Olsen, "Anguish of a Team Divided," 35.

66. For further discussion of this point, see Ted White, *Broadcast News: Writing, Reporting, and Producing* (Boston: Focal Press, 2002), 163.

67. Charles Bronz, "19th Hole: The Readers Take Over," *Sports Illustrated*, July 15, 1968, 94.

68. James R. Bowman, "19th Hole: The Readers Take Over," *Sports Illustrated*, July 22, 1968, 71.

69. Jean H. Miculka, "19th Hole: The Readers Take Over," *Sports Illustrated*, July 22, 1968.

70. Neil I. Cohen, "19th Hole: The Readers Take Over," *Sports Illustrated*, July 22, 1968.

71. Al Rinaldi, "19th Hole: The Readers Take Over," *Sports Illustrated*, July 22, 1968, 72.

72. MacCambridge, "19th Hole: The Readers Take Over," *Sports Illustrated*, July 22, 1968, 163.

73. Fred R. Davis, "19th Hole: The Readers Take Over," *Sports Illustrated*, August 25, 1968, 68.

74. J. P. Bonet, "19th Hole: The Readers Take Over," *Sports Illustrated*, August 25, 1968.

75. Stephen J. Wright, "19th Hole: The Readers Take Over," *Sports Illustrated*, August 25, 1968, 75.

76. Two letters to the editor in response to the series noted that readers did react to the injustices outlined. Bill Fromm of Kansas City, Missouri, wrote to say he had become involved with a group that had established the African American Athletes' Fund to help African American high school athletes better prepare for the challenges of college. See "19th Hole: The Readers Take Over," *Sports Illustrated*, July 22, 1968, 71. The second letter was from Ray Past, chair of the new Athletic Reevaluation Committee at UTEP. This was a biracial group made up of students and faculty that the campus administration had established to assure that UTEP's minority athletic problems were corrected. See "The 19th Hole: The Readers Take Over," *Sports Illustrated*, August 19, 1968, 63.

77. Gary Volk, "The Black Athlete: An Editorial," *Sports Illustrated*, August 5, 1968, 9.

78. John Underwood, interviewed by Bob Lee, "*Sports Illustrated*" at 50, ESPN, October 25, 2004.

79. Deford interview.

80. Leonard, "What Happened to the Revolt," 8.

81. Todd Gitlin, *The Whole World Is Watching: Mass Media in the Making and Unmasking of the New Left* (Berkeley: University of California Press, 1980), 1–4.

82. James Michener, *Sports in America* (New York: Random House, 1976), 322.

83. In 1971, *Sports Illustrated* published a series by Martin Kane about whether African Americans' physiology provided them with an edge in athletic competition,

and in 1976 *Sports Illustrated* investigated discriminatory practices against female athletes.

84. Michener, *Sports in America*, 322.

85. Deford interview.

86. See Jay Coakley, ed., *Sport in Society: Issues and Controversies* (New York: McGraw Hill, 2001); and Kenneth L. Shropshire, *In Black and White: Race and Sports in America* (New York: New York University Press, 1996), for thorough discussions of the progress that has been made and not made in the intervening years.

87. This is when Mississippi State University named Sylvester Croom its head man. For further discussion of developments (or lack thereof) in this regard, see Kathleen O'Brien, "Diversity Not Always Equal Deal on Front Office, Managerial Level," *Fort Worth Star-Telegram*, September 13, 2005, D-1.

88. Fitzpatrick, *Wall Came Tumbling Down*, 30. See also John Hoberman, *Darwin's Athletes: How Sport Has Damaged Black America and Preserved the Myth of Race* (New York: Houghton Mifflin, 1997), 31, 48.

13

Rebellion in the Kingdom of Swat
Sportswriters, African American Athletes, and Coverage of Curt Flood's Lawsuit against Major League Baseball

WILLIAM GILLIS

On January 2, 1970, veteran sports columnist Red Smith wrote, "Curtis Charles Flood is a man of character and self-respect. Being black, he is more sensitive than most white players about the institution of slavery as it exists in professional baseball."[1]

One day after Smith's words appeared in newspapers across the country, Curt Flood, a well-compensated All-Star baseball player, appeared on national television and told sports broadcaster Howard Cosell that he considered himself "a well-paid slave, but nonetheless a slave."[2] Both Flood, a thirty-one-year-old black athlete, and Smith, a sixty-four-year-old white sportswriter, believed that baseball's system—specifically its reserve clause that bound players to a team in perpetuity—was unfair and tantamount to slavery.

Flood, an All-Star center fielder who had played for the St. Louis Cardinals since 1958, was traded to the Philadelphia Phillies at the end of the 1969 season. Flood was not interested in playing for Philadelphia, but the reserve clause required that he play for the Phillies or not play at all. Instead of retiring, he decided that he would sue Major League Baseball for the right to play for any team that wished to employ him. Flood sat out the 1970 season while the lawsuit made its way through the legal system. Though the Supreme Court eventually ruled against Flood in 1972, the lawsuit led directly to collective bargaining between the owners and the Major League Baseball Players Association (MLBPA) on the reserve clause rules.[3] In 1975, an independent arbitrator granted free agency to two players, and by the end of the decade hundreds of players enjoyed free-agent status.[4] Today, even mediocre players sign multimillion-dollar contracts on the free-agent market.

Flood is widely credited by today's commentators, players, and fans for his willingness to sacrifice his career for a principle that has enriched thousands of baseball players. Since 2006, no fewer than four books about Flood's life and fight for free agency have been published.[5] Flood is also featured prominently in many books focusing on baseball and the players' union; free agency in sports; and sports, society, and race.[6] Among those who have told Flood's story and assessed the press coverage he received, there is nearly unanimous agreement that the sporting press of the era was overwhelmingly unsupportive of Flood because it believed that his lawsuit would destroy the national pastime. For example, Andrew O'Toole, author of the 2003 book *The Best Man Plays: Major League Baseball and the Black Athlete*, wrote,

> As could be expected, the game's commentators lined up in opposition to Flood's legal stance. The vast majority of baseball scribes viewed the lawsuit as a traitorous undertaking. . . . Change, especially change instigated by a Black man, offended the senses of the men who chronicled the game.[7]

This essay argues that the belief that "the vast majority" of sports columnists considered Flood's lawsuit "a traitorous undertaking" is simply false. The author examined the publications *Sports Illustrated*, *Sport*, and the *Sporting News*; the mass-market magazines *Time* and *Newsweek*; major newspapers including the *New York Times*, *Chicago Tribune*, *Los Angeles Times*, and *Washington Post*; several African American newspapers; and, using the Access Newspaper Archive, hundreds of small- to medium-sized U.S. newspapers.[8] He concluded that a majority of sports scribes both criticized *and* praised Flood, as well as the baseball establishment. And while a number of sports columnists unambiguously castigated Flood and his actions, nearly as many enthusiastically backed his lawsuit and rhetoric.

By 1970, the nation's sports pages contained more than scores, statistics, and innocuous profiles of star athletes; rather, they were as reflective of the upheaval in American society—particularly in regard to race—as front pages. Black athletes, such as Muhammad Ali, Dick (Richie) Allen, Jim Brown, Arthur Ashe, Dock Ellis, Duane Thomas, Kareem Abdul-Jabbar, and the Olympic athletes Tommie Smith and John Carlos, all rebelled against the sports establishment in the late 1960s and early 1970s.[9] The sportswriting beat was dominated by white males, and these men were compelled to deal with a new generation of outspoken athletes, many of whom were African Americans. A number of "old school" sportswriters, like Dick Young, Jimmy Cannon, Arthur Daley, and Bob Broeg, were dismayed by the changes they saw in society and sports, and they attacked such changes in their columns. Most contemporary writers telling Flood's story believe that such journalists were representative of an overwhelmingly white, aging, and borderline racist sportswriters corps that saw Flood as an ungrateful black man threatening the great American pastime. Yet, as author and *New Yorker* magazine editor David Remnick has shown, a number of formerly "old school" sports columnists like Cannon and Red Smith began to reassess their racial views and even question U.S. involvement in the Vietnam War in the late 1960s. Meanwhile, a younger generation of sportswriters emerged in the 1960s that was unafraid to tackle racial issues in their columns and supported rebels like Flood and Ali.[10]

It was Ali, Remnick believes, who spurred sportswriters to question their racial and cultural assumptions.[11] For this study, the author assessed a variety of opinions and attitudes of sportswriters on Flood and his lawsuit, six years after Ali first created controversy by changing his name from Cassius Clay and announcing his association with the Nation of Islam, and three years after Ali refused induction into the U.S. Army. This essay argues that the sporting press of the early 1970s was more socially aware and sensitive to racial issues, and demonstrated more empathy for an outspoken black man like Flood, than is commonly believed. The author suggests that the opinions of the white sporting press on the divisive issues of the era were as varied and intricate as those of the wider white American public.

The White Sporting Press and the Black Athlete

In his 1971 autobiography, cowritten with Richard Carter, *The Way It Is*, Flood imagined a white racist reading the sports page, where he would learn that Flood was suing baseball. "If the newspaper was typical," Flood wrote, "it lied that a victory for Flood would mean the collapse of our national pastime. God profaned! Flag desecrated! Motherhood defiled! Apple pie blasphemed! The animal was furious. Them niggers is never satisfied."[12] Flood granted that some journalists, namely Red Smith, Jim Murray, Leonard Koppett, and Howard Cosell, supported his lawsuit, but he concluded, "I can say with conviction that the preponderance of material I read and heard was distressingly cynical and ill-informed."[13]

Flood's indictment of the coverage he received from sports columnists is shared by many contemporary writers. In his 2006 biography *A Well-Paid Slave: Curt Flood's Fight for Free Agency in Professional Sports*, Brad Snyder characterized the sporting press of the 1960s and early 1970s as "firmly on the side of management" and suggested that "the bulk of the white media blasted Flood's 'well-paid slave' comment and backed the owners' contention that baseball needed the reserve system to survive."[14] Strangely, Snyder listed no fewer than eight names of sports journalists who supported Flood but provided only four examples of "anti-Flood" writers. At least one reviewer, however, accepted Snyder's argument. In the *New York Times Book Review*, David Margolick wrote that Flood's description of his situation as slavery "won Flood almost universal condemnation in the press and even from other ballplayers, past and present, white and black."[15] In 2006, the African American journalist William C. Rhoden declared in *$40 Million Slaves: The Rise, Fall, and Redemption of the Black Athlete* that the sports media helped baseball owners "destroy" Flood.[16] Other writers and commentators who have studied the Flood case, including O'Toole, Alex Belth, Charles P. Korr, and Bob Costas, also argued that with few exceptions sportswriters supported the owners and not Flood.[17]

Why do contemporary writers assume that the white sporting press of 1970 was overwhelmingly hostile toward Flood? The answer may lie in the ample evidence that prominent African American athletes of the 20th century were treated with both racist venom and paternalism by white sportswriters. Gene Roberts and Hank Klibanoff, authors of the 2006 book *The Race Beat: The Press, the Civil Rights Struggle, and the Awakening of a Nation*, argue that African Americans as a whole were largely ignored by the white press until the civil rights era.[18]

However, the success of African Americans in the sporting realm—a phenomenon called "muscular assimilation" by some scholars[19]—was impossible for the sports pages to ignore. Such coverage was often hostile. The African American heavyweight champion Jack Johnson, champion of the world from 1908 to 1915, attracted attention not only for his boxing prowess but also for his rejection of the racial norms of the day. He unabashedly dated white women, flaunted his wealth, and taunted his white opponents. As a result, the white press "ridiculed and deplored" Johnson's "wealth, glamour, and pretension."[20] Though Joe Louis, heavyweight champion three decades later, was nowhere near as controversial as was Johnson, his victories were covered by a white sporting press with often racist language. For example, *New York Daily News* columnist Paul Gallico described Louis as an "animal" and a "wild thing."[21]

Perhaps the most celebrated African American athlete of the twentieth century is Jackie Robinson, who integrated Major League Baseball by taking the field for the Brooklyn Dodgers in 1947. Though some publications, notably the *Sporting News*, insisted that segregation was good for baseball, most scholars agree that the white press largely backed Robinson, though sportswriters often used paternalistic, racist language to describe him.[22] Robinson himself wrote in his autobiography *I Never Had It Made* that both the black and white press supported him after Philadelphia Phillies manager Ben Chapman and his players taunted Robinson with racist invective during a game early in the 1947 season.[23] Years later, however, Robinson suggested that the white press didn't give black baseball players a fair shake. In a 1970 letter to Pittsburgh Pirates pitcher Dock Ellis, an African American embroiled in controversy, Robinson wrote, "The news media while knowing full well you are right and honest will use every means to get back at you."[24]

By necessity, both Louis and Robinson kept to themselves and avoided controversy. By the 1960s, however, black athletes were no longer keeping quiet, particularly Muhammad Ali, who seemed to represent all that was changing in American sports and society.[25] His 1966 declaration that he had "no quarrel with them Vietcong" was met with condemnation from legendary sports scribes, including Jimmy Cannon, Red Smith, and Arthur Daley.[26] Cannon, who wrote for the *New York Post*, had passionately backed Louis and Robinson, but Ali's militancy and calls for black separatism alarmed him.[27] Cannon—as well as the *New York Times*—insisted on calling Ali by his former name for years after his name change.[28] In a famous column that appeared after Ali refused induction into the military in 1967, Cannon connected "Clay" with the changes that alarmed many older Americans in the 1960s:

> Clay is part of the Beatle movement. He fits in with the famous singers no one can hear and the punks riding motorcycles with iron crosses pinned to their leather jackets and Batman and the boys with their long dirty hair and the girls with the unwashed look and the college kids dancing naked at secret proms held in apartments and the revolt of students who get a check from dad every first of the month and the painters who copy the labels off soup cans and the surf bums who refuse to work and the whole pampered stylemaking cult of the bored young.[29]

Similarly, Red Smith wrote in 1966 that "Cassius makes himself as sorry a spectacle as those unwashed punks who picket and demonstrate against the war."[30]

Sports columnists also reacted passionately to the meshing of sports and protest at the 1968 Olympic games in Mexico City. There, two members of the U.S. track team, the black athletes Tommie Smith and John Carlos, famously raised their gloved fists into the air in a black power gesture during the medal ceremony. Afterward, white sportswriters, and at least one black newspaper, argued that the demonstration was inappropriate.[31] *Time*, for example, ran an illustration that replaced a slogan accompanying the Olympic logo from "Faster, Higher, Stronger" with "Angrier, Nastier, Uglier."[32] Yet Red Smith, who blasted Ali just two years earlier, supported Carlos and Smith—a sign that his views may already have been changing.[33]

The adventures of Dick "Richie" Allen, an outspoken African American baseball player who was sent to the Cardinals in the trade that assigned Flood to the Phillies in 1969, were covered closely and often with hostility by the Philadelphia press. Allen, who joined the Phillies in 1963, was reviled by fans and many sportswriters in Philadelphia, despite being the team's best player during the '60s. Allen believed he was treated unfairly by the press and fans because he was black, and he began to rebel. In 1968, Allen missed games, set up a private dressing area in the Phillies locker room, demanded a trade, and late in the season, began scratching out messages in the infield dirt that made clear his desire to leave Philadelphia.[34] Though he was not appreciated by Philadelphia's sportswriters, sports columnists in other cities liked Allen's individuality, including Jim Murray of the *Los Angeles Times*, Art Spandler of the *San Francisco Examiner* and the *Sporting News*, and Melvin Durslag of the *Los Angeles Herald-Examiner*.[35]

The changing attitudes of writers like Jimmy Cannon and Red Smith, and the embrace of rebels like Allen by Murray, Spandler, and Durslag, suggests that the sporting press was more than just a bunch of conservative reactionaries by the end of the 1960s. Perhaps covering Ali did help to change the views of some of the men who wrote the country's sports columns. To be sure, Ali, Allen, Tommie Smith, and John Carlos had done little to change the conservative opinions of Dick Young, Bob Broeg, and Arthur Daley, or those of Larry Merchant and Bill Conlin of the *Philadelphia Daily News*, who regularly attacked Allen in their columns.[36] Yet a careful analysis of the coverage Curt Flood received from 1970 to 1972 shows that such scribes did not dominate the sportswriting profession in the early 1970s.

Baseball's Best Center Fielder

Curt Flood grew up poor but not impoverished in the black ghetto of West Oakland, California. In his late teens, Flood began to attract attention from Major League scouts, and in 1955 the Cincinnati Reds signed him to a one-year contract worth four thousand dollars.[37] Flood traveled to Florida in February 1956 to attend the Reds' spring training camp. For the first time, the teenager experienced the Jim Crow racial segregation then the norm in most southern states, and he would spend another painful two years playing Minor League baseball in the Deep South. In 1956, he was the only black player on the Hi-Toms of High Point–Thomasville, North Carolina. He was regularly subjected to racial abuse from spectators, even from Hi-Toms fans.[38] Flood somehow managed to concentrate on playing ball, and he played it well, winning the Carolina League Player of the Year Award.[39] After another difficult year playing in Savannah, Georgia, Flood was traded by the Reds to the St. Louis Cardinals.

Beginning in 1963, Flood won seven consecutive Gold Glove awards for defensive excellence, led the National League in hits in 1964, and was an All-Star three times for the Cardinals. His team won National League pennants in 1964, 1967, and 1968 and won the World Series in 1964 and 1967.[40] In August 1968, *Sports Illustrated* anointed him "the best center-fielder in baseball" on its cover, which showed Flood making a spectacular catch in Chicago's Wrigley Field.[41] As Flood's star rose, so did his salary. In 1958, his first year with the Cardinals, he made $5,000 a season; in 1965, $35,000; in 1967, $50,000; and by 1969, he was making $90,000.[42]

Flood was active in the black civil rights struggle of the 1960s. He spoke at a NAACP rally in Mississippi with Jackie Robinson, complained to reporters about the segregated spring training facilities in Florida, and in 1964 moved into a home in a previously all-white neighborhood in California despite death threats.[43] Though Flood experienced a fair share of racial slights in St. Louis, a city in the "border" state of Missouri, he was a popular figure.[44] In 1968, laudatory features on Flood appeared in both *Sports Illustrated* and the *Sporting News*. The stories celebrated his play on the field, leadership in the clubhouse, and his successful photography and portrait business. The *Sporting News* article declared, "Curt Flood is an artist with brush and oils as well as the fielder's mitt."[45]

In 1968, the Cardinals lost the World Series to the Detroit Tigers. In the off-season, Flood won a $90,000 contract for 1969—the second-highest on the team—after bitter contract negotiations with team management.[46]

The following season, however, was an unhappy one for Flood. His batting average dropped 16 points and the team—though the highest-paid in baseball—finished a disappointing fourth. Flood was thirty-one in 1969, and though still an excellent player, he had reached the twilight of his career. On October 8, 1969, Flood was telephoned by a mid-level executive in the Cardinals' front office, who told him that he had been traded to the Philadelphia Phillies. Flood wanted to continue playing baseball, but not in Philadelphia, a city that Flood would call the "nation's northernmost southern city" in *The Way It Is*.[47] He went to the players' association for advice.

The MLBPA had been a largely ineffective organization before it hired Marvin Miller, a sixteen-year veteran of the powerful steelworkers' union, as its executive director in 1966. In 1968, Miller negotiated a labor agreement that was the first of its kind in professional sports.[48] Yet Miller had not been able to pry concessions from the owners on the reserve clause. The reserve clause allowed a team to automatically renew a player's contract for one year for at least 80 percent of his previous season's salary if the player and the team could not agree to a contract. Players were not free to negotiate with other teams; the only way a player could join another team was if he was traded or released.[49]

In November 1969, Flood informed Miller that he wanted to challenge the legality of the reserve clause for the good it would do for fellow and future players, even if it meant his career was finished.[50] On December 24, Flood sent a letter to Major League Baseball commissioner Bowie Kuhn. The letter read in part,

> After twelve years in the Major Leagues, I do not feel that I am a piece of property to be bought and sold irrespective of my wishes. I believe that any system which produces that result violates my basic rights as a citizen and is inconsistent with the laws of the United States and of the several states.[51]

The letter asked Kuhn to allow Flood to negotiate with any team. A few days later, Kuhn responded with a letter that reminded Flood that he was bound to play for the Phillies.[52] On January 3, 1970, Flood and Miller appeared on ABC's *Wide World of Sports* with commentator and emerging national celebrity Howard Cosell, who asked Flood whether a man who made $90,000 (at a time when the median U.S. family income was $9,400) could really consider himself a slave. Flood replied, "A well-paid slave is nonetheless a slave."[53]

"Baseball Doesn't Need Their Kind"

In his biography of Flood, Brad Snyder argued that it was Flood's "well-paid slave" terminology that incensed sportswriters.[54] It is true that a fair number of writers were flabbergasted that a handsomely compensated sports star could call himself a slave. United Press International columnist Milt Richman wrote shortly after the Cosell interview,

> I can't believe Curt Flood, in all conscience, can argue he was treated like cattle since he's been in baseball. . . . That's where I stop feeling for Curt Flood. I know we're in the middle of a paralyzing inflation, but $90,000 for one head of cattle still staggers the imagination.[55]

Richman, along with Dick Young, Bob Broeg, and Bill Conlin, were the four writers Snyder cited for their pro-management, anti-Flood views.[56]

Broeg, who wrote for the *St. Louis Post-Dispatch* and the *Sporting News* and was considered one of the game's most knowledgeable historians, had long been a critic of those ballplayers he viewed as overpaid and greedy.[57] In February 1969, he had written about the "mountainous money demands" by the Cardinals players, in an article that quoted the Cardinals' owner and general manager but not a single player.[58] In his first column about Flood's lawsuit, Broeg sarcastically mocked "the poor victims of 'peonage and servitude.'"[59] He also questioned Flood's actual motives for suing baseball:

> So it is difficult indeed to be sympathetic to the little man, particularly when it really is not a matter of principle, but of principal.
> If principle were really involved in his legal assault on baseball's reserve clause as violating the federal antitrust laws, Flood would have asked for $1 and the right to negotiate for himself.[60]

Broeg's column was accompanied by a somewhat vicious cartoon by *Post-Dispatch* cartoonist Amadee Wohlschlaeger that depicted a beret-wearing Flood working on a canvas on which he had painted an enormous dollar sign. Flood tells his subject, a disheveled, hapless white male, "It keeps coming out that way."[61]

Flood's slavery rhetoric was also a major point of contention for the outspoken Dick Young, who opined that Flood "isn't helping his case with that tired slavery line" in the January 18, 1970, *New York Daily News*.[62] Young began writing his syndicated column "Young Ideas" in 1963, and it appeared in the *Sporting News*, the *Daily News*, and other newspapers. Young regularly attacked handsomely paid sports stars with anti-establishment views, such as Ali, whom Young insisted on calling by his former name of Clay. "What Young wanted, like television's Archie Bunker," baseball historian Ron Briley wrote, "was a return to the good ole' days, with values such as patriotism, hard work, obedience to authority, and standards of excellence."[63] Though Young criticized Flood and regularly attacked the demands of well-paid athletes, he also criticized owners for their unwillingness to negotiate with the MLBPA.[64]

Scattered among the country's smaller daily newspapers were sportswriters who also had problems with Flood's actions and rhetoric. Particularly venomous was Dick Maxwell of the *Athens (Ohio) Messenger*, who wrote that baseball had been "knifed in the back" by Flood and Denny McClain, a star pitcher who had been suspended for gambling.[65] Similarly, in the *Bennington (Vermont) Banner*, Hal March lumped Flood in with those athletes "criticizing, maligning, denouncing, spitting, quitting and generally crapping on their sport."[66] Stan Eames of the *Kennebec (Augusta, Maine) Journal*, Hank Hollingworth of the *Long Beach (California) Independent*, Jack Murphy of the Copley News Service, and Steve Tadevich of the *Fremont/Newark (California) Argus* all wrote columns questioning Flood's "slavery" claim. Tadevich asked rhetorically in his column, "Really, is there such an animal as a $90,000 slave?"[67]

Some writers linked the rebellion of athletes like Flood with the larger problems plaguing the country. Andrew Tully wrote in the *Lawton (Oklahoma) Constitution* that because of examples like Flood it was "small wonder that so many college kids . . . [spend] their spare time (which seems to be considerable) trying to tear down our capitol."[68] Holmes Alexander wrote in the *Argus* that Flood's slavery argument was "preposterous" and argued that "racial hysteria" had seized baseball and the country. "Race consciousness," Alexander wrote, "has increased, rather than lessened, in baseball. . . . Black players, like the Black Caucus in Congress, are racist aggressors. The fabric of the game, the fabric of politics, is warped."[69]

"Baseball's Arguments Are Pathetic"

One of the very first sports columnists to react to the news that Flood was challenging the legality of the reserve clause was Red Smith, whose syndicated column appeared in hundreds of newspapers nationwide. In several columns, including one published before Flood made his "well-paid" slave comment, Smith used phrases such as "strike off the fetters of baseball's reserve clause," "intolerable bondage," and "the slave trade" without a hint of irony.[70] Even before Flood did so, Smith was using forms of the word "slavery" to describe the conditions under which baseball players toiled. He wrote admiringly in one column, "Flood can still earn $90,000 a year but he is sacrificing the remainder of his career for a principle."[71] Smith's embrace of Flood's cause represented a dramatic transformation from the conservative columnist of only four years before, when he lashed out at Ali.

Another prominent scribe in Flood's corner was *New York Times* and *Sporting News* writer Leonard Koppett, who covered the Flood case closely for both publications. In his *Sporting News* columns, Koppett regularly attacked the baseball establishment and frankly broached the issue of race. "It is my contention that racial discrimination [in baseball] takes subtle forms, but is nonetheless real a full generation after the advent of Jackie Robinson," Koppett wrote in a March 1970 column.[72] Once Flood's trial began in New York City in May, Koppett filed near-daily articles for the *Times* and weekly opinion pieces for the *Sporting News*. The sub-headlines in Koppett's *Sporting News* columns that spring included "Baseball's Arguments Are Pathetic," "Baseball's Bias Is Subtle, Disturbing," and "Baseball Is Trailing Society."[73] However, Koppett felt that

Flood's use of the word "slavery" was "an emotion word, an unnecessary exaggeration."[74]

One of Koppett's *New York Times* colleagues, Robert Lipsyte, put Flood's lawsuit in the context of other "dramatic attack[s] on the sports system" by black athletes like Ali and Ashe.[75] "Common to each is the mounting demand by athletes that the principles they are paid to symbolize be applicable to them, too," Lipsyte wrote.[76] Another sports columnist, Shirley Povich of the *Washington Post*, pretended to be outraged by the actions of Flood, whom he facetiously called an "agitator, boat rocker and some kind of nut" in a January 26, 1970, column.[77] He clearly admired Flood, calling him "a committed man who is battling for a principle and is willing to take all the abuse he knew would come his way."[78] Povich, like other writers, ridiculed the claims of the owners that the game "would come tumbling down if there were no reserve clause."[79]

Though Robert Markus of the *Chicago Tribune* initially expressed support for the reserve clause and attacked Flood's motives, he came to believe that the reserve clause was unconstitutional. "I don't see how [the Supreme Court] can deny that the reserve clause is a form of slavery," he wrote.[80] Hearst syndicated columnist Bob Considine criticized those who attacked Flood on the basis of his handsome salary and wrote that if an ordinary Florida plumber was prohibited from moving to Alaska and practicing his trade, there would be "yells of rage" and "flutter[s] of subpoenas."[81]

Ed Levitt of the *Oakland Tribune* wrote at least a half-dozen columns about Flood and the reserve clause issue. Levitt recognized that the "average fan" would not sympathize with Flood because he had turned his back on the game that paid him $90,000 a year. However, he felt that anyone who had pulled himself "up from the poor area of Oakland, the way Curt Flood did, [knows] the value of a buck" and wrote that Flood "must be some kind of man to do what he's doing."[82]

Strong support for Flood could also be found in the pages of black newspapers. In a February 17, 1970, column in the *Philadelphia Tribune*, civil rights activist Bayard Rustin compared Flood to other courageous black athletes of the day:

Flood stands in the tradition of such black athletes as Jackie Robinson and Muhammad Ali who, in addition to achieving great status within their profession, took courageous stands on issues of human rights. For these reasons, Curt Flood deserves our support and our respect.[83]

The *Pittsburgh Courier*'s Bill Nunn Jr. wrote that Flood could be added to "a growing list of black athletes who have placed principle above personal gain" that included Robinson, Ali, Ashe, and football star Jim Brown.[84] Two years later, another *Courier* sportswriter, Jess Peters Jr., titled a section of his column "FLOOD FIGHTING SLAVERY." Peters wrote, "It is inconceivable to this column that the court will allow the cancerous [reserve] clause to enjoy the protection of the law."[85]

Columnists in general-circulation, small-market newspapers also rallied behind Flood. In the *Tri-City (Pasco, Washington) Herald*, columnist Joe Much recognized the significance the legacy of slavery would have on a black player like Flood. He called Flood "an honest, informed rebel [who] is challenging the '[reserve] clause' as a crusade against the slavery it represented in years past to his kind."[86] The syndicated black columnist Ken Richardson wrote, "Flood is to be admired," and "even if a man makes a million dollars, he is not totally free if he can be bought and sold."[87] Finally, Paul Mosnicka of the *Lowell (Massachusetts) Sun* warned athletes that they would have to accept the consequences if professional athletes were treated like any other worker but called for changes to the sports system: "It is about time professional athletes revolted against many rules and laws of their individual sport that are in direct opposition to the rules and laws of our country."[88]

Both Sides Are Overswinging

In his book on the players' union, *The End of Baseball as We Knew It*, Charles P. Korr cited an August 13, 1970, *Washington Post* editorial that said Flood was "not compelled by law or statute to play baseball for Philadelphia" and that he could choose to retire if he wished.[89] Korr suggested that this editorial is "representative" of the negative coverage Flood was subjected to by the press.[90] Though the journalist who wrote the *Post* column, Bob

Addie, was indeed skeptical about Flood's lawsuit, Korr failed to quote some of Addie's other remarks in the very same column, written after Flood lost his case in federal court. Despite Flood's defeat, Addie wrote, he "has hardly lost stature. He stood alone in his challenge and he should be remembered for that."[91]

Though he did not support Flood's cause, Addie was neither hostile to Flood nor was he a tool of baseball management. Most columnists who wrote about Flood took a similarly balanced view; some critiqued both sides, while others simply analyzed the situation without much in the way of editorial comment. Like Addie, many columnists who criticized Flood took pains to show that they admired Flood even if they disagreed with his actions. One such example was Richard Dozer of the *Chicago Tribune*, who feared that the abolition of the reserve clause might destroy the game. But Dozer had kind words for Flood: "One thing about Flood. It's obvious that it's not the money in his case. It's the principle of the thing."[92]

Charles Maher of the *Los Angeles Times* criticized both sides in the dispute. "The two sides in the Curt Flood case have started overswinging," he wrote on January 21, 1970.[93] Maher believed that Flood was not a peon because he made $90,000 a year, but he also argued that no player should be forced to play and live in a city in which he is unhappy. Writers who demonstrated similar views included North American Newspaper Alliance writer Milton Gross and Newspaper Enterprise Association (NEA) columnist Ralph Novak.[94]

Los Angeles Times writer and future Pulitzer Prize–winner Jim Murray used sarcasm to needle both Flood and the team owners. Because the reserve clause was just a "fancy name" for slavery, Murray wrote on January 21, all a player could do was "pick up [his] glove and hum spirituals."[95] Murray was certainly having some fun, but he also declared that the reserve clause was wrong and proposed a rule that no player could be traded against his will. "If Curt Flood wants to remain in St. Louis," Murray wrote, "baseball (and society) should let him."[96]

A few columnists attempted to assess the cultural, political, and racial ramifications of the *Flood v. Kuhn* lawsuit. The syndicated labor columnist Victor Riesel wrote that Flood "is truly the symbol of a new era" in which professional athletes were organizing themselves and searching for protection under federal labor laws.[97] NEA sports columnist Ira Berkow wrote that Flood's dispute boiled down to the feeling of many black athletes that sports owners and management lacked "insight into the black psyche."[98]

In the sporting press, *Sports Illustrated* offered little in the way of opinion on the lawsuit, but in its February 9, 1970, issue, it laughed off the "hysterical cries that baseball will die" if the reserve clause was abolished.[99] The St. Louis–based *Sporting News* has been cited as an overwhelmingly pro-management paper, but its editorials repeatedly called for compromise between the baseball establishment and players.[100] A January 24, 1970, editorial declared, "We must agree . . . that the high-priced player is indeed sitting pretty. He has no reason to rock the boat so far as his own financial welfare is concerned."[101] However, the *Sporting News* repeatedly called for negotiations between owners and the MLBPA, and one editorial criticized the rhetoric of both camps—both baseball's cries of "chaos and anarchy" and Flood's talk of "slave labor."[102] Though the *Sporting News* favored the arguments of the baseball owners, nowhere in evidence are characterizations of Flood as a man who was threatening the fabric of the game.

"As Sad As a Suicide Note"

On August 12, 1970, federal judge Irving Ben Cooper issued a forty-seven page opinion that ruled against Flood. Cooper ruled that only the Supreme Court could overturn its own rulings upholding baseball's antitrust exemption. But Cooper did not stop there; he also opined that the game was on "higher ground" and that any changes to the reserve clause would endanger baseball, "a fine sport and profession, which brings surcease from daily travail and as escape from the ordinary to most inhabitants of the land."[103] Charles Maher of the *Los Angeles Times* and others were baffled by the legal logic of Cooper's decision, and Maher called for some alternative to the current reserve clause system that would be fairer to players.[104] A *New York Times* editorial also argued for a modification of the clause, quoting former star player Hank Greenberg, who had testified in the Flood trial that the reserve clause is "obsolete, antiquated and definitely needs change."[105]

Immediately, Flood's lawyers began preparing an appeal, while Flood decided to spend some time in Denmark. In the closing months of 1970 he was contacted by Bob Short, owner of the Washington Senators, who had acquired Flood's rights from the Phillies. Short offered Flood $110,000 to play for the Senators in 1971. After Flood received assurances from Commissioner Kuhn that resuming his playing career would not prejudice his ongoing lawsuit, he signed a contract.[106]

Several writers thought that Flood's return to baseball was hypocritical. Arthur Daley of the *New York Times* wondered why Flood had decided that "twice-a-month checks from solvent ball clubs" no longer had a "slavish appearance."[107] Daley did call for a modification of the reserve clause, if the "baseball overlords had any sense—which they don't."[108] In the *Washington Post*, George Minot Jr. highlighted Flood's dignity and soft-spoken demeanor when the player met the press for the first time after signing with the Senators. "Curt Flood does not look like an earth-mover, an establishment-rocker," Minot wrote, in an article headlined "Flood Meets Press with Quiet Dignity."[109]

While Flood worked to get back in baseball shape, his autobiography, cowritten by Richard Carter, appeared in February 1971. *The Way It Is* was a startlingly frank book about Flood's harrowing experience playing Minor League ball in the South, the economics of baseball, his personal and financial troubles, and the sexual escapades of Major League players. The book also made it clear that Flood believed that the news media had treated him unfairly and viciously.[110]

Unsurprisingly, Red Smith's review of *The Way It Is* was positive. "When the best portrait artist and most resolute activist in baseball sets out to tell it the way it is, he levels," Smith wrote.[111] In the *New York Times*, Jonathan B. Segal was also impressed. He called Flood a "sensitive, artistic black man with a growing sense of pride" who wrote "an insightful book to explain his position."[112] In the first of two columns devoted to *The Way It Is*, Jim Murray wrote that parts of the book were "as sad as a suicide note."[113] With no sarcasm this time, Murray referred to the reserve clause as something "which makes a ballplayer a piece of property like a mule or a cow" and again called for modifications to the clause.[114] Murray was somewhat more critical of Flood a month later. Invoking a populist sensibility, he wrote, "Every $100-a-week hard hat who hates his job sits out there [in the outfield bleachers] and he may not be ready to understand why a $5,000-a-week outfielder hates his job."[115]

The views of the "hard hat" are perhaps in evidence in letters about the Flood lawsuit to newspapers and magazines by readers. A writer to the *Chicago Tribune* warned of the consequences if Flood won his lawsuit: "If [Flood] doesn't like being a 'slave,' he should quit and try making it elsewhere because if he carries successfully thru [*sic*] on the suit, then elsewhere is the place he'll end up when baseball is disbanded."[116] A reader from Carlstadt, New Jersey, wrote *Sport*, "Maybe [Flood] thinks he's worth more than $90,000 and could get it without the reserve clause. I don't think he's worth 90,000 peanuts with his attitude."[117] Yet not all letters were negative. Another writer to *Sport* supported Flood and adopted his slavery rhetoric: "Flood is so right—those who have this power [to control the players]—the slavemasters if you will—must be fought."[118]

Flood's lawsuit continued to move through the legal system in late 1970 and early 1971. After Cooper's ruling, Flood's team of lawyers appealed the case to the Court of Appeals for the Second Circuit. On April 7, 1971, hours before the Senators' second game of the season, Flood learned that the Appeals courts had affirmed Cooper's decision.[119] On the field, the situation was just as grim for Flood. Now thirty-three, he was playing sporadically and drinking heavily. On April 27, Flood fled the Senators and the country, boarding a flight to Spain. Before departing, he sent Senators owner Bob Short the following telegram:

> I TRIED A YEAR AND A HALF IS TOO MUCH VERY SERIOUS PERSONAL
> PROBLEMS MOUNTING EVERYDAY THANKS FOR YOUR CONFIDENCE
> AND UNDERSTANDING FLOOD.[120]

Some members of the press corps, including Charles Maher of the *Los Angeles Times* and Robert Markus of the *Chicago Tribune*, were exasperated by Flood's sudden flight from baseball and the country. Markus called Flood "the biggest turncoat since Judas," though he also wrote that the reserve clause is "obviously a form of slavery, however voluntary."[121] Other columnists were less hostile. In the *Washington Post*, Shirley Povich wrote that the "simple confessions of [Flood's] telegram showed class."[122] Red Smith defended Flood, calling his troubles "so many and so varied that it is no wonder his baseball comeback was going badly."[123] Smith boldly accused Flood's critics of racism: "Just about everybody interested in his case is a baseball fan, and baseball fans do not make their judgments objectively. Some are convinced that he must be in the wrong because he sleeps with white girls."[124]

Flood eventually settled in Majorca, an island off the coast of Spain, and ran a bar frequented by American military personnel. While Flood settled into expatriate life, his case was heard by the Supreme Court. On June 19, 1972, the Court ruled 5–3 to affirm the decisions of the lower courts.[125] Part 1 of the majority opinion, penned by Justice Harry Blackmun, was titled "The Game" and featured a list of no fewer than eighty-eight baseball greats and included the baseball poem, "Casey at the Bat."[126] Blackmun conceded that baseball's exemption was an "aberration" and an "anomaly" but did not want to overturn previous decisions because baseball had enjoyed its exemption for so long without Congress ever acting to overturn it.[127]

Arthur Daley of the *New York Times* questioned the logic of the decision, as did Jim Murray, who wrote that the decision "was handed down in the form of bubble-gum cards," clearly poking fun at Blackmun.[128] Both Shirley Povich and Red Smith called the decision a "cop-out" and called for changes to the reserve clause. The decision "is a disappointment," Smith wrote, "because the highest Court in the land is still averting its gaze from a system in American business that gives the employer outright ownership of its employees."[129]

In their responses to the Supreme Court decision, Dick Young and Bob Broeg agreed that Flood had been a lousy choice for a test case of the reserve clause. Broeg thought that a less well-paid player might have elicited more sympathy from the justice system.[130] In the *Charleston (West Virginia) Daily Mail*, sports editor Bill Smith reported that not one player on the Pittsburgh Pirates had commented on the decision, and few were even aware the case had been decided. Smith asked, "If the slaves aren't worried, why all the fuss?"[131]

Flood was interviewed in Majorca by Howard Cosell for ABC's *Wide World of Sports* in 1973, but he then disappeared from public view. He would spend the next two years in Spain and Andorra, drinking heavily, and upon returning to the United States in 1975 was nearly penniless. For the remainder of the 1970s and for much of the 1980s he struggled to find meaningful work and was beset by alcoholism. By the 1990s, however, he had quit drinking and had remarried. In 1994, he met Bill and Hillary Clinton at a White House ceremony celebrating the documentary *Baseball*, in which Flood's fight for free agency played a key role. Flood died in 1997 at the age of fifty-nine from throat cancer.[132]

What's Happening to Our Great Country?

Curt Flood played a game cherished by Americans, one that represented a simpler, idyllic era in the country's history. For some fans, baseball was an oasis from the troubles that plagued the country and the world. In the ten years Flood had played for the Cardinals, Americans had experienced, in the words of historian David Chalmers, "a civil rights revolution, an assault on poverty, campus unrest, an antiwar movement that sometimes threatened to become an insurrection, and an apparent cultural disaffiliation of the young that seemed to challenge the moral values of American society."[133] The debate over American involvement in the Vietnam War had fragmented society, and the riots in black ghettos in cities across the country seemed to bode ill for the future. The assassination of Martin Luther King Jr. and Robert F. Kennedy in 1968 shocked and dismayed Americans.

The outspoken demands of young people, particularly young blacks, were also startling for some. In the athletic arena, stars such as Ali, Ashe, Flood, and the Olympic medal–winners Smith and Carlos demonstrated that black athletes, once silent and grateful, were now often brash and outspoken. Sociologist Douglas Hartmann wrote in *Race, Culture, and the Revolt of the Black Athlete* that Smith's and Carlos's 1968 Olympics protest "was for many simply one more instance of the incomprehensible spectacle of social chaos and upheaval, another example of a world gone—or going—mad."[134] Similarly, for some white Americans, Flood's refusal to play for the Phillies was one more instance of black athletes going too far and asking for too much.[135] The change was bewildering for some, including St. Louis Cardinals owner Gussie Busch. Upset by the contract demands of players and Flood's lawsuit, he connected baseball's troubles with the nation's. "I'm disillusioned," Busch said in March 1970. "I don't know what's happening among our young people—to our campuses and to our great country."[136] A year later, Arthur Daley of the *New York Times* wrote about a growing resentment among sports fans. He wrote that Americans over the age of thirty "just can't get used to the way authority is challenged and eroded in sports just as it is to a greater extent everywhere else" and called the Flood case "the prime example" of this trend.[137]

The fans who wrote angry letters objecting to Flood's lawsuit were lashing out at the changes taking place in society that alarmed and frightened them. Baseball—the cherished national pastime—was seen as a bastion of traditional American values. Yet athletes like Flood appeared to be challenging those values. Many fans, and writers like Daley, Dick Young, and Bob Broeg, believed Flood was threatening *the* American game. Yet just as many if not more sportswriters argued that Flood was not an ungrateful black man attempting to destroy the American game but rather a man simply seeking fairness in a sporting industry badly in need of reform.

The variety of views found in the coverage of Flood and his lawsuit are not a discrete anomaly. Rather, they are reflective of the opinions, fears, hopes, and confusion of the American public during this period. Views among white Americans on the changes of the 1960s were not monolithic, with conservative, "silent majority" Americans on one side and liberal, racially sensitive do-gooders on the other. Several recent historical works examining political, cultural, and social change in the 1960s and 1970s show that whites living in the American South have too often been characterized simplistically as either racist resisters or liberal accommodationists. Matthew Lassiter, author of 2006's *The Silent Majority: Suburban Politics in the Sunbelt South*, argued that the complex emotions and concerns of a majority of white southerners have been largely ignored.[138] Lassiter told the *New York Times* in 2007, "There were a few white Southerners who were liberals, a larger number throwing rocks with the rioters, and the vast group in the middle were left out of the story."[139]

Historians like Lassiter and Jason Sokol, author of the 2006 book *There Goes My Everything: White Southerners in the Age of Civil Rights*, show that Americans in the South reacted to the sweeping changes of the 1960s in complex, various ways.[140] To be sure, most sportswriters in 1970 were not southerners accustomed to Jim Crow segregation. But the variety of reactions and opinions among sportswriters to an African American sports rebel like Flood reveals parallels with the stories told by Lassiter and Sokol. Certainly, some Americans, and some sportswriters, were appalled by Flood and other athletes, just as many were horrified by youth rebellion, protest against the war, urban riots, and black militancy. Yet "the vast group in the middle" had mixed feelings about changes in American society as well as the words and actions of a black man challenging the baseball system. The author does not deny or discount the racist treatment that African American athletes like Flood received from sportswriters or argue that racism does not exist to this very day in the sports pages and columns of American newspapers. But reducing Flood's story to a battle against intransigent racist enemies including those in the media simplistically tells a story that is far more complex. As Sokol told the *New York Times* in 2007, "You want to pry below these great narratives of good and evil and black and white."[141]

Despite its failure, Flood's lawsuit against Major League Baseball changed the game and sports as a whole. Yet today, many black athletes feel as trapped by the structure of professional sports as Flood once did. And there are perhaps just as many fans who view certain black athletes as overpaid, ungrateful, and greedy as there were in 1970. In 1999, Larry Johnson, a star basketball player, referred to himself and his teammates as "rebellious slaves." In the days that followed, several sportswriters—the spiritual descendants of Dick Young and Bob Broeg—excoriated Johnson in their columns. The criticism of Johnson, William C. Rhoden wrote, "boiled down to a recurring theme: How could an athlete making millions of dollars per season consider himself a common 'slave'?"[142] A few seasons later, a taunting fan called Johnson a "$40 million slave." More than thirty years after Curt Flood told Howard Cosell that he was nothing but a well-paid slave, rhetoric connecting professional athletes and slavery continued to spark controversy and debate among sports commentators and fans.

NOTES

1. Red Smith, "Views of Sport: Reserve Clause Hit By Super Team," *Washington Post*, January 2, 1970. Flood's birth name was Charles Curtis Flood. The title of this essay is taken from the headline of a January 6, 1970, Red Smith column about Flood. See Red Smith, "Rebellion in the Kingdom of Swat," *Philadelphia Inquirer*, January 6, 1970.

2. Brad Snyder, *A Well-Paid Slave: Curt Flood's Fight for Free Agency in Professional Sports* (New York: Viking, 2006), 104.

3. Because the baseball owners had conceded in their defense of Flood's lawsuit that the reserve clause rules were in fact a matter for collective bargaining, in 1973 owners agreed to use arbitrators to resolve disputes over player compensation for players with more than two years of experience. See Albert Theodore Powers, *The Business of Baseball* (Jefferson NC: McFarland, 2002), 176.

4. Charles P. Korr, *The End of Baseball as We Knew It: The Players Union, 1960-81* (Urbana: University of Illinois Press, 2002), 147-84.

5. See Snyder, *Well-Paid Slave*; Alex Belth, *Stepping Up: The Story of Curt Flood and His Fight for Baseball Players' Rights* (New York: Persea Books, 2006); Stuart L. Weiss, *The Curt Flood Story: The Man behind the Myth* (Columbia: University of Missouri Press, 2007); and Robert M. Goldman, *One Man Out: Curt Flood versus Baseball* (Lawrence: University Press of Kansas, 2008).

6. See for example Korr, *End of Baseball*, 84-101; Powers, *Business of Baseball*, 157-68; Andrew O'Toole, *The Best Man Plays: Major League Baseball and the Black Athlete, 1901-2002* (Jefferson NC: McFarland, 2003), 74-99; Marvin Miller, *A Whole Different Ball Game: The Sport and Business of Baseball* (New York: Birch Lane, 1991), 170-202; William C. Rhoden, *$40 Million Slaves: The Rise, Fall, and Redemption of the Black Athlete* (New York: Crown, 2006), 231-37; and Michael E. Lomax, "Curt Flood Stood Up for Us," in *Ethnicity, Sport, Identity: Struggles for Status*, edited by J. A. Mangan and Andrew Ritchie (London: Routledge, 2004), 44-70.

7. O'Toole, *Best Man Plays*, 95-97.

8. For this study, the author examined every magazine and newspaper article he found that contained some form of analysis, editorial opinion, or both on Flood and his legal battle. The articles cited and described in this study reflect the range of opinions found in the author's research. In several footnotes, the author provides further examples of articles reflecting similar opinions to the articles described in the main text. He used the following research methods to find relevant articles:

Using the ProQuest Historical Newspaper online database, he searched for all articles meeting the search term "Curt Flood" for the years 1969 through 1973 in the *New York Times, Chicago Tribune, Los Angeles Times*, and *Washington Post*. The same search term was used to find relevant articles via the Access Newspaper Archive online database for the period October 1969 through December 1973. The vast majority of articles meeting the search criteria in both the ProQuest and Access Newspaper Archive data bases were written in objective news writing style (many were Associated Press wire stories) and contained no opinion on Flood or his case.

Using the *Readers' Guide to Periodical Literature*, the author found all cited articles under the heading "Flood, Curt," for the years 1969 through 1973. This method yielded relevant articles in the magazines *Sports Illustrated, Sport, Time*, and *Newsweek*. The author also examined microfilm of the *Sporting News* from October 1969 through July 1971 and June 1972 through December 1972. The January 1972 through May 1972 period was not examined because Flood was no longer playing baseball and there were no new developments in his court case during that time. Flood-related articles in the *St. Louis Post-Dispatch* from 1969 through 1973 and the *Philadelphia Inquirer* from 1969 and 1970 were also examined, based on citations to specific articles found in various secondary sources. Finally, the author examined relevant articles on Flood in the black press based on citations found in various secondary sources, including the magazines *Jet* and *Ebony* and the newspapers the *Pittsburgh Courier, Philadelphia Tribune*, and *Baltimore Afro-American*.

9. A number of white athletes also rebelled during this period. Baseball pitcher Jim Bouton and former football player Dave Meggyesy wrote books in 1970 and 1971, respectively, that provided often uncensored, irreverent, and uncomplimentary inside views of professional sports and the owners and managers who ran the teams. Both books were controversial and were met with criticism from players and sportswriters. See Snyder, *Well-Paid Slave*, 211; Jim Bouton, "Foreword," in *The Hard Way: Writing by the Rebels Who Changed Sports*, edited by Will Balliett and Thomas Dyja (New York: Thunder's Mouth, 1999), viii–xii;

Thomas Dyja, "Introduction," in *Hard Way*, edited by Balliet and Dyja, 1–4; Jim Bouton, *Ball Four: My Life and Hard Times Throwing the Knuckleball in the Big Leagues* (New York: World, 1970); and Dave Meggyesy, *Out of Their League* (Berkeley CA: Ramparts Press, 1971).

10. David Remnick, "How Muhammad Ali Changed the Press," *SportsJones*, October 29, 1999, accessed October 23, 2006, http://www.sportsjones. com/ali4 .htm. Also see Remnick, *King of the World: Muhammad Ali and the Rise of an American Hero* (New York: Random House, 1998).

11. Remnick, "How Muhammad Ali Changed the Press."

12. Curt Flood with Richard Carter, *The Way It Is* (New York: Trident Press, 1971), 18. Weiss, author of *The Curt Flood Story*, stressed that *The Way It Is* was far from a balanced account. He wrote that Richard Carter "made no effort to check out and, if necessary, modify his friend's [Flood's] characterizations. He presented Flood's story as dramatically and sympathetically as his considerable skills would allow. It is not surprising then, that the book emerged not as balanced or even critically sympathetic but as an apologia, the story of Flood as the justifiably angry victim of persecution." See Weiss, *Curt Flood Story*, 199.

13. Flood with Carter, *The Way It Is*, 198.

14. Snyder, *Well-Paid Slave*, 111, 114.

15. David Margolick, "Fielder's Choice," *New York Times Book Review*, October 8, 2006, 17.

16. Rhoden, *$40 Million Slaves*, 234.

17. See O'Toole, *Best Man Plays*, 95–97; Belth, *Stepping Up*, 102, 159–60; Korr, *End of Baseball*, 96, 278; and Bob Costas, "Foreword," in Korr, *End of Baseball*, xii. Costas wrote in the introduction to *The End of Baseball as We Knew It*, "Flood's quiet courage was remarkable, especially since his stance was scorned by the vast majority of commentators and fans" (xii).

18. Gene Roberts and Hank Klibanoff, *The Race Beat: The Press, the Civil Rights Struggle, and the Awakening of a Nation* (New York: Vintage, 2006), 5. The white press was also indicted in the 1968 Commission on Civil Disorders report, popularly known as the Kerner Commission Report, which analyzed the causes of urban riots. The report concluded that "the news media have failed to analyze and report adequately on racial problems in the United States, and as a related matter, to meet the Negro's legitimate expectations in journalism.... The media report and write from the standpoint of a white man's world." See Commission on Civil Disorders, "The Role of the Mass Media in Reporting of News about Minorities," in *Killing the Messenger: 100 Years of Media Criticism*, edited by Tom Goldstein (New York: Columbia University Press, 2007), 256.

19. Patrick B. Miller and David K. Wiggins, "Images of the Black Athlete and the Racial Politics of Sport," in *Sport and the Color Line: Black Athletes and Race Relations in Twentieth-Century America* (New York: Routledge, 2004), 174.

20. Dave Zirin, *What's My Name, Fool? Sports and Resistance in the United States* (Chicago: Haymarket Books, 2005), 21. Also see pp. 20–23.

21. Remnick, *King of the World*, 225.

22. See Pat Washburn, "New York Newspapers and Robinson's First Season," *Journalism Quarterly* 58, no. 4, (Winter 1981): 640–44; and Jules Tygiel, "Jackie Robinson: 'A Lone Negro' in Major League Baseball," in Miller and Wiggins, *Sport and the Color Line*, 174. Writers coined nicknames for Robinson including "Black Meteor," "Ebony Ty Cobb," and "Bojangles of the Basepaths." The *Sporting News* named Robinson its 1947 baseball Rookie of the Year. See Tygiel, "Jackie Robinson," 174, 184.

23. Jackie Robinson as told to Alfred Duckett, *I Never Had It Made* (New York: G.P. Putnam's Sons, 1972), 74.

24. Donald Hall with Dock Ellis, *Dock Ellis: In the Country of Baseball* (New York: Coward, McCann and Geoghegan, 1976), 145. Robinson said in 1972, "The owners have the writers in their pockets. . . . After all, a player might be a hamburger from a writer. . . . but the owners feed [writers] steak." Quoted in Korr, *End of Baseball*, 8. Robinson publicly criticized the *New York Times* in 1965 in a regular syndicated column that appeared in several black newspapers. The *Times* had run stories on the Deacons for Defense and Justice, an armed black self-defense organization in Louisiana, but Robinson felt the *Times* was late to the story. "The *New York Times* may print 'all the news that's fit to [to print],' but it sure is late with this one. This column has been warning for many months—and so have out civil rights leaders—that Negroes are fed up being persecuted, bombed, burned out, flogged, and murdered while their Federal Government insists it is powerless to help." Quoted in Christopher B. Strain, *Pure Fire: Self-Defense as Activism in the Civil Rights Era* (Athens: University of Georgia Press, 2005), 107. Also see 214n39.

25. Miller and Wiggins, "Images of the Black Athlete and the Racial Politics of Sport," 270. Mike Marqusee argues that even before Clay changed his name to Ali, he "was beginning to change the way sports stars presented themselves. Hitherto, they were expected to be seen and not heard; modesty and deference had been the norm, for whites and especially blacks." Thus, Ali's name change was a "sinister transgression" for a "stunned white press." See Mike Marqusee, *Redemption Song: Muhammad Ali and the Spirit of the Sixties* (New York: Verso, 1999), 49, 85.

26. Remnick, *King of the World*, 287, 288.

27. See Tygiel, "Jackie Robinson," 173; Robert Lipsyte, "Covering Ali, Discovering an Era," in *Defining Moments in Journalism*, edited by Nancy J. Woodhull and Robert W. Snyder (New Brunswick NJ: Transaction, 1998), 25; and Remnick, "How Muhammad Ali Changed the Press."

28. See Remnick, "How Muhammad Ali Changed the Press"; and Zirin, *What's My Name, Fool?* 63.

29. Quoted in Remnick, "How Muhammad Ali Changed the Press."

30. Quoted in Ira Berkow, *Red: A Biography of Red Smith* (New York: Times Books, 1986), ix–x.

31. Amy Bass, *Not the Triumph, but the Struggle: The 1968 Olympics and the Making of the Black Athlete* (Minneapolis: University of Minnesota Press, 2002), 252–53.

32. Zirin, *What's My Name, Fool?* 76–77.

33. Berkow, *Red*, 189.

34. William C. Kashatus, *September Swoon: Richie Allen, the '64 Phillies, and Racial Integration* (University Park PA: Keystone, 2004), 183–200. Also see Powers, *Business of Baseball*, 153.

35. Powers, *Business of Baseball*, 166–67. Powers believes Allen and Flood were similar figures. "Curt Flood and Dick Allen, two seemingly dissimilar characters, had a front row seat for the most turbulent times in America and in baseball. Both Dick Allen and Curt Flood were their own men who joined Jackie Robinson in helping to liberate future generations of Major League baseball players." See Powers, *Business of Baseball*, 168.

36. Kashatus, *September Swoon*, 83–84, 176, 185–86.

37. See Flood with Carter, *The Way It Is*, 32; and Snyder, *Well-Paid Slave*, 151.

38. Flood with Carter, *The Way It Is*, 37–39.

39. See Flood with Carter, *The Way It Is*, 39; and Belth, *Stepping Up*, 35.

40. "Curt Flood," baseball-reference.com, accessed July 8, 2008, http://www.baseball-reference.com/f/floodcu01.shtml.

41. Front cover, *Sports Illustrated*, August 19, 1968.

42. Snyder, *Well-Paid Slave*, 151.

43. Snyder, *Well-Paid Slave*, 3.

44. See Snyder, *Well-Paid Slave*, 52; and Belth, *Stepping Up*, 118.

45. Nell Gross, "Cards' Flood: A Rembrandt Off Diamond," *Sporting News*, April 20, 1968, 9. Also see William Leggett, "Not Just a Flood, but a Deluge," *Sports Illustrated*, August 19, 1968, 20. A portrait of Martin Luther King Jr. that Flood claimed he had painted was widely reproduced and sold. However, Flood biographer Snyder revealed in 2006 that Flood did not actually paint the portraits

to which he signed his name. Instead, a California artist painted them and sent them to Flood, who then signed them. Flood, who died in 1997, never publicly revealed this secret. See Snyder, *Well-Paid Slave*, 9–10. Coretta Scott King kept a reproduction of the portrait of her late husband supposedly painted by Flood on one of the walls in her Atlanta office; she said it was one of her favorite portraits of Dr. King. See "Carrying on His Work" (photograph and caption), *Newport (Rhode Island) Daily News*, April 5, 1972.

46. Belth, *Stepping Up*, 138.

47. The passage in *The Way It Is* reads, "Philadelphia. The nation's northernmost southern city. Scene of Richie Allen's ordeals. . . . I did not want to succeed Richie Allen in the affections of that organization, its press and its catcalling, missile-hurling audience" (Flood with Carter, *The Way It Is*, 188).

48. Snyder, *Well-Paid Slave*, 18–19.

49. Though the 1890 Sherman Antitrust Act had prohibited the restraint of interstate commerce, the United States Supreme Court had ruled in a series of cases that baseball was not considered interstate commerce and was therefore exempt from anti-monopoly legislation. Oddly, no other professional sport was exempted from antitrust legislation. Baseball's exemption is what made the reserve clause legal. For a full explanation of the reserve clause and the antitrust exemption, see Morgen A. Sullivan, "'A Derelict in the Stream of the Law': Overruling Baseball's Antitrust Exemption," *Duke Law Journal* 48, no. 6 (April 1999): 1265–1304.

50. Snyder, *Well-Paid Slave*, 24–25.

51. Quoted in Snyder, *Well-Paid Slave*, 94–95. The letter was drafted by the lawyer Marvin Miller, hired for Flood's case; the former Supreme Court justice and ambassador to the United Nations Arthur Goldberg; and two of Goldberg's associates.

52. Kuhn wrote, "I certainly agree with you that you, as a human being, are not a piece of property to be bought and sold. . . . However, I cannot see its applicability to the situation at hand" (quoted in Snyder, *Well-Paid Slave*, 101).

53. U.S. Bureau of the Census, *Statistical Abstract of the United States: 1971* (Washington DC: U.S. Government Printing Office, 1971), 316; Snyder, *Well-Paid Slave*, 104. Using the consumer price index (CPI), Flood's 1969 salary of $90,000 would be $535,585 in 2009 dollars. Calculated on the Federal Reserve Bank of Minneapolis website, accessed June 12, 2009, http://www.minneapolisfed.org.

54. Snyder, *Well-Paid Slave*, 105.

55. Milton Richman, "Poor Curt Flood Has to Suffer under Harsh Baseball Rules," *Elyria (Ohio) Chronicle-Telegram*, January 11, 1970. Richman echoed such views

in another January column. See Richman, "Marvin Miller Proves Capable," *Hayward (California) Daily Review*, January 19, 1970.

56. See Snyder, *Well-Paid Slave*, 111-12. Conlin wrote for the *Philadelphia Daily News* and was a frequent critic of Dick Allen when he played for the Phillies.

57. *Washington Post* syndicated columnist Shirley Povich called Broeg the "foremost baseball historian of these times." See Povich, "Busch Takes Firm Stand against Player Demands," *Greeley (Colorado) Tribune*, March 24, 1972. During this period Broeg regularly wrote lengthy profiles in the *Sporting News* of baseball greats such as Bob Feller, Cy Young, and Jackie Robinson.

58. Bob Broeg, "9 Birds Ask $700,000," *St. Louis Post-Dispatch*, February 27, 1969.

59. Bob Broeg, "Does 'Principle' or 'Principal' Motivate Flood?" *St. Louis Post-Dispatch*, January 25, 1970. This article was reprinted in the *Sporting News*. See Bob Broeg, "Just What Prompted Flood Lawsuit?" *Sporting News*, February 2, 1970, 45.

60. Bob Broeg, "Does 'Principle' or 'Principal' Motivate Flood?"

61. Amadee Wohlschlaeger, untitled cartoon, *St. Louis Post-Dispatch*, January 25, 1970. An edition of "Berry's World," a Newspaper Enterprise Association cartoon that appeared in newspapers in February 1970, also appeared to lampoon Flood's claim that he was enslaved. It depicts a team owner speaking to a baseball team gathered in a locker room. He tells the team, "Just remember, until Curt Flood wins his case on the baseball reserve clause—you guys have to keep calling me 'massah'!" See Jim Berry, "Berry's World," *Los Angeles Times*, February 3, 1970.

62. Quoted in Snyder, *Well-Paid Slave*, 111.

63. Ron Briley, "Dick Young: Not So 'Young Ideas' on the Barricades in 1968," *Nine: A Journal of Baseball History and Culture* 15, no. 1 (Fall 2006): 50. Also see pp. 47-48.

64. Dick Young, "Time for Club Officials to Sit at Bargaining Table: A Way to End Impasse," *Sporting News*, April 4, 1970, 5.

65. Dick Maxwell, "Sportin' Comment: Baseball Doesn't Need Flood, McClain," *Athens (Ohio) Messenger*, September 27, 1970.

66. Hal March, "Sports Today: Age of the Anti-Hero—And the Big Sneer!" *Bennington (Vermont) Banner*, June 29, 1971.

67. Steve Tadevich, "Right On: Why Did Flood Wait to Challenge Reserve Clause?" *Fremont/Newark (California) Argus*, August 14, 1970. Also see Stan Eames, "Cut Pay, Watch Sox Players Move," *Kennebec (Augusta, Maine) Journal*, May 29, 1970; Hank Hollingworth, "Flood Out of Line Challenging Reserve Clause," *Long Beach (California) Independent*, February 4, 1970; and Jack Murphy, "Ferrara

Has Opposite View: It's Peculiar Form of Slavery When Only Rich Ones Protest," *Connellsville (Pennsylvania) Daily Courier*, March 26, 1970.

68. Andrew Tully, "Washington Report: Coaches Set Poor Example," *Lawton (Oklahoma) Constitution*, May 13, 1971. Also see Ray Berkow, "Flood's Book Will Leave Mark," *Abilene (Texas) Reporter-News*, February 16, 1971.

69. Holmes Alexander, "Baseball in Trouble," *Fremont/Newark (California) Argus*, March 28, 1972. The Black Caucus was an organization of black members of the U.S. House of Representatives.

70. Red Smith, "Views of Sport: Flood's Target," *Washington Post*, January 4, 1970. This column, under a different headline, appeared in the *Philadelphia Inquirer* on January 2, the same day that Smith's first column on Flood appeared in the *Washington Post* ("Reserve Clause Hit by Super Team"). See Red Smith, "Flood's Case Strongest Yet?" *Philadelphia Inquirer*, January 2, 1970.

71. Smith, "Views of Sport: Flood's Target."

72. Leonard Koppett, "Baseball's Bias Is Subtle, Disturbing," *Sporting News*, March 21, 1970, 4.

73. See Leonard Koppett, "Baseball's Arguments Are Pathetic," *Sporting News*, June 20, 1970; Koppett, "Baseball's Bias Is Subtle, Disturbing"; and Leonard Koppett, "The Hottest Issue of All," *Sporting News*, March 7, 1970.

74. Leonard Koppett, "Baseball Will Survive Law Suit," *New York Times*, June 14, 1970.

75. Robert Lipsyte, "Revolt of the Gladiators," *New York Times*, January 5, 1970.

76. Lipsyte, "Revolt of the Gladiators." Remnick wrote that Lipsyte made a point to learn about race and bring the subject into his columns for the *Times*. Lipsyte collaborated with African American comedian Dick Gregory on Gregory's autobiography, *Nigger*. See Remnick, "How Muhammad Ali Changed the Press."

77. Shirley Povich, "This Morning . . . with Shirley Povich," *Washington Post*, January 26, 1970.

78. Povich, "This Morning," January 26, 1970.

79. Povich, "This Morning," January 26, 1970.

80. Robert Markus, "The Sports Trail," *Chicago Tribune*, January 26, 1970.

81. Bob Considine, "On the Line: Day of Reckoning," *Van Wert (Ohio) Times-Bulletin*, October 26, 1971.

82. See Ed Levitt, "Flood, Part 2," *Oakland Tribune*, February 19, 1970; and Levitt, "Who's the Bad Guy?" *Oakland Tribune*, May 7, 1972.

83. Bayard Rustin, "In Support of Curt Flood's Anti-Trust Suit against Baseball," *Philadelphia Tribune*, February 17, 1970.

84. Bill Nunn Jr., "Change of Pace," *Pittsburgh Courier*, March 21, 1970.

85. Jess Peters Jr., "Jess' Sports Chest," *Pittsburgh Courier*, April 22, 1972. For another example of a pro-Flood column in a black newspaper, see "End of Line for Ali?" *Englewood (Illinois) Bulletin*, March 11, 1971.

86. Joe Much, "Column One: Glickman Strikes Blow for Owners," *Tri-City (Pasco, Washington) Herald*, December 19, 1971.

87. Ken Richardson, "Like It Is: Drafts—Either Military or Athletic—Are Necessary," *Fremont/Newark (California) Argus*, July 26, 1970.

88. Paul Mosnicka, "Curt Flood Spells Trouble," *Lowell (Massachusetts) Sun*, January 21, 1970.

89. Bob Addie, "Surprise in Court," *Washington Post*, August 13, 1970.

90. Korr, *End of Baseball*, 280.

91. Addie, "Surprise in Court."

92. Richard Dozer, "Some Assuring Words from Attorney for Curt Flood," *Chicago Tribune*, February 21, 1970.

93. Charles Maher, "Baseball Doomed?" *Los Angeles Times*, January 21, 1970.

94. See Milton Gross, "Compromise with Curt Flood Near?" *Pasadena (California) Star-News*, July 28, 1970; and Ralph Novak, "One, Two, Three Trials," *Columbus (Nebraska) Telegram*, November 8, 1971.

95. Jim Murray, "The Curt Flood Case: Lift That Bat, Chop That Ball . . ." *Los Angeles Times*, January 21, 1970.

96. Murray, "The Curt Flood Case."

97. Victor Riesel, "A New Era in Athletics," *San Mateo (California) Times*, April 16, 1971.

98. Ira Berkow, "Reggie's Problem," *Eureka (California) Times Standard*, July 18, 1970.

99. "Scorecard: Empty Issue?" *Sports Illustrated*, February 9, 1970, 9.

100. Korr, *End of Baseball*, 268n1.

101. "Genuine Bargaining Only Solution," *Sporting News*, January 24, 1970, 14.

102. "The Time for Talk Is Now," *Sporting News*, February 21, 1970, 14.

103. Quoted in Roger I. Abrams, *Legal Bases: Baseball and the Law* (Philadelphia: Temple University Press, 1998), 65. Also see Leonard Koppett, "Flood Whiffs, Goes into Extra Innings," *Sporting News*, August 29, 1970, 5.

104. Charles Maher, "'Fair and Equitable," *Los Angeles Times*, August 15, 1970.

105. "Batter Up in Court," *New York Times*, May 28, 1970. Though a few former players, including Jackie Robinson, testified on Flood's behalf at the trial, not a single active player testified on Flood's behalf, nor did any active players attend the proceedings. See Snyder, *Well-Paid Slave*, 175–76. Several notable active players, including star white players Harmon Killebrew, Gaylord Perry,

and Carl Yastrzemski as well as the black superstars Ernie Banks and Henry (Hank) Aaron, publicly questioned the MLBPA's support of Flood's lawsuit. See Richard Dozer, "Players Want Change, Not Death of Reserve Clause," *Chicago Tribune*, January 22, 1970; Ed Levitt, "Perry's Pitch," *Oakland Tribune*, January 23, 1970; Ed Wilks, "Player Opinion Divided Over Flood's Crusade," *St. Louis Post-Dispatch*, January 27, 1970; "Killebrew Seeks Poll; Jim Price for Flood," *St. Louis Post-Dispatch*, January 28, 1970; Will McDonough, "Player Group Off Base in Backing Flood, Yaz Charges," *Sporting News*, January 31, 1970, 36; and Snyder, *Well-Paid Slave*, 116–18. However, a few active players, including Dick Allen, the man who was traded to St. Louis in exchange for Flood; Cardinals stars Lou Brock and Bob Gibson; retired pitching ace Sandy Koufax; and football star Joe Namath were all quoted in the press for supporting Flood and his cause. Yet even some of Flood's closest friends who played on the Cardinals did not attend the trial, though they were in town playing the New York Mets during the proceedings. See Snyder, *Well-Paid Slave*, 121–22.

106. Snyder, *Well-Paid Slave*, 200–201.
107. See Dick Young, "Young Ideas," November 21, 1970, 16; and Arthur Daley, "Without Prejudice?" *New York Times*, November 29, 1970.
108. Daley, "Without Prejudice?"
109. George Minot Jr., "Flood Meets Press with Quiet Dignity," *Washington Post*, November 25, 1970.
110. Flood with Carter, *The Way It Is*, 198. The book was excerpted as a feature-length article in *Sports Illustrated* in February 1971. See Curt Flood with Richard Carter, "My Rebellion," *Sports Illustrated*, February 1, 1971, 24–29. In March 1970, *Sport* allowed Flood to tell his story in an article titled "Why I Am Challenging Baseball." See Curt Flood as told to John Devaney, "Why I Am Challenging Baseball," *Sport*, March 1970, 10–12, 62.
111. Red Smith, "Views of Sport: Cards Were Prejudiced—In Favor of Women," *Washington Post*, February 7, 1971. In *A Well-Paid Slave*, Snyder characterized the press reception of *The Way It Is*: "Other than Jim Murray, Red Smith, and Robert Lipsyte of the *New York Times*, most of the sporting press teed off on *The Way It Is*." But the only negative reactions to Flood's book cited by Snyder were columns by Broeg and *St. Louis Globe-Democrat* columnist Bob Burnes, who compared the book to Bouton's *Ball Four* and Meggyesy's *Out of Their League*. See Snyder, *Well-Paid Slave*, 210–11.
112. Jonathan B. Segal, "A Salvation and a Battlefield: The Way It Is," *New York Times*, May 16, 1971. Also see Robert Lipsyte, "The Way It Is: Sex, $, Politics," *New York Times*, May 1, 1971.

113. Jim Murray, "A Flood Warning," *Los Angeles Times*, February 23, 1971.

114. Murray, "Flood Warning."

115. Jim Murray, "$110,000 'Slavery,'" *Los Angeles Times*, March 26, 1971.

116. "Sound Off, Sports Fans!" *Chicago Tribune*, January 23, 1970.

117. "Letters to Sport: Flood Tide," *Sport*, May 1970, 12-13.

118. "Letters to Sport: Flood Tide," 12. Flood also received personal letters from fans. In January 1970 he said that 90 percent of the letters were "favorable" but the other 10 percent were costing him sleep. One of the unfavorable letters read, "Once you were compared with Willie Mays. Now you will be compared to Benedict Arnold." Another letter called him a "jerk." See "Curt Flood Having Some Second Thoughts," *Salisbury (Maryland) Sunday Times*, January 25, 1970.

119. Snyder, *Well-Paid Slave*, 221-22.

120. Snyder, *Well-Paid Slave*, 231.

121. Markus, "Along the Sports Trail," *Chicago Tribune*, October 21, 1971. Also see Charles Maher, "Complaint Dept.," *Los Angeles Times*, May 5, 1971.

122. Shirley Povich, "This Morning . . . with Shirley Povich," *Washington Post*, April 29, 1971.

123. Red Smith, "Views of Sport: Flood's Deficiencies Overridden by Principle," *Washington Post*, May 5, 1971.

124. Smith, "Views of Sport: Flood's Deficiencies Overridden by Principle."

125. Justice Lewis Powell excused himself from the case because of a conflict of interest: he owned stock in Anheuser-Busch, which owned the St. Louis Cardinals. See Snyder, *Well-Paid Slave*, 285.

126. Flood v. Kuhn, 407 U.S. 258, 260-64.

127. "The Chance of a Called Strike," *New York Times*, June 25, 1972.

128. Arthur Daley, "The Sad Story of the Leaky Umbrella," *New York Times*, June 22, 1972; Jim Murray, "High and Flighty," *Los Angeles Times*, June 22, 1972.

129. Red Smith, "The Buck Passes," *New York Times*, June 21, 1972. Also see Shirley Povich, "Baseball Antitrust Decision: Supreme 'Copout'?" *Pasco (Washington) Tri-City Herald*, June 20, 1972.

130. See Bob Broeg, "Broeg on Baseball," *Sporting News*, July 8, 1972, 16; and Dick Young, "Young Ideas," *Sporting News*, July 1, 1972, 14.

131. Bill Smith, "All Bases," *Charleston (West Virginia) Daily Mail*, June 27, 1972.

132. Snyder, *Well-Paid Slave*, 313-47.

133. David Chalmers, *And the Crooked Places Made Straight: The Struggle for Social Change in the 1960s* (Baltimore: Johns Hopkins University Press, 1991), xvii.

134. Douglas Hartmann, *Race, Culture, and the Revolt of the Black Athlete* (Chicago: The University of Chicago Press, 2003), 176.

135. Flood made his way into novelist Philip Roth's 1971 best-selling parody of politics, *Our Gang*. Tricky Dixon, the nation's president, blames a protest demonstration in Washington DC by Boy Scouts on Flood, prompting Dixon to order one hundred thousand troops into Denmark, where in real life Flood maintained a residence. See Miles A. Smith, "Book Review," *Eureka (California) Times-Standard*, October 31, 1971.

136. Bob Broeg, "Redbird Owner Busch Admits 'I'm Disillusioned,'" *Sporting News*, March 28, 1970, 5. Also see Povich, "Busch Takes Firm Stand against Player Demands."

137. Arthur Daley, "Paging Sigmund Freud," *New York Times*, February 3, 1971.

138. Matthew Lassiter, *The Silent Majority: Suburban Politics in the Sunbelt South* (Princeton NJ: Princeton University Press, 2006).

139. Patricia Cohen, "Interpreting Some Overlooked Stories from the South," *New York Times*, May 1, 2007.

140. Jason Sokol, *There Goes My Everything: White Southerners in the Age of Civil Rights*, 1945–1975 (New York: Vintage, 2006), 195.

141. Cohen, "Interpreting Some Overlooked Stories from the South."

142. Rhoden, *$40 Million Slaves*, 240.

14

Chasing Babe Ruth
An Analysis of Newspaper Coverage of Hank Aaron's Pursuit of the Career Home Run Record

MAUREEN SMITH

Baseball has long been enamored with home runs and, subsequently, home run records. To begin with, the "Sultan of Swat," Babe Ruth, established the home run as his signature swing, with the 1920s marking his domination of the long ball, hitting 60 home runs in 1927 to set the standard for his peers and future ballplayers and finishing with 714 when he retired in 1935.[1] Jimmie Foxx and Hank Greenberg both threatened Ruth's single season record with 58 home runs each, in 1932 and 1938 respectively, but it didn't happen until 1961, when New York Yankees teammates Roger Maris and Mickey Mantle dueled, with Maris finally besting Ruth's record with 61 home runs. Mark McGwire and Sammy Sosa's 1998 pursuit of Roger Maris's single-season record of 61 home runs set in 1961 is credited with bringing baseball back to life, a sign of full recovery from the player strike in 1994–1995.[2] Only three years later, Barry Bonds broke McGwire's short-lived season record with 73 home runs and appeared to have a realistic shot at breaking the all-time record of 755 career home runs set by Hank Aaron in 1976. When Bonds broke Aaron's record in 2007, much of the debate and sentiment focused on his rightful ownership of the record, with some fans and sportswriters claiming Aaron's record should stand due to Bonds's alleged steroid use.[3] Much of this media coverage of McGwire, Sosa, and Bonds reveals the multiple ways race and ethnicity have been and continue to be discussed in the sporting press. For decades, race has played a factor in the coverage of sporting events in America and in the establishment of favored athletes and news coverage of their athletic accomplishments.

Media coverage of these recent turn-of-the-century home run chases offers sports historians an opportunity to revisit an old challenge to one of baseball's most hallowed records—Ruth's all-time home run record of 714 home runs, broken in 1974 by Hank Aaron. This essay examines American newspaper coverage of Aaron's pursuit of Ruth's record throughout the 1973 season and extending into the first week of the 1974 season. How was the challenge of a Ruth-owned record by Aaron, an African American athlete, covered in the newspapers? Specifically, how was Aaron's skin color a factor in the media coverage? During the 1970s, when Aaron was in pursuit of Ruth's record, there were a significant number of successful newspapers owned and operated by African Americans. What were the differences and similarities between the African American and mainstream newspapers in their coverage of Aaron's chase and the subsequent breaking of the record? Black newspapers and mainstream United States newspapers from six American cities were examined to explore the ways in which race was discussed in the coverage of Aaron's home run chase. The six cities and their respective newspapers were selected as representative of American urban centers: the *Chicago Defender* and *Chicago Tribune*, *Los Angeles Sentinel* and *Los Angeles Times*, the *Washington Afro-American* and the *Washington Post*, and *Amsterdam News* and *New York Times*. The *Milwaukee Courier*, *Milwaukee Journal*, *Milwaukee Sentinel*, and the *Atlanta Daily World*, *Atlanta Constitution*, and *Atlanta Journal* were also included as the newspapers that covered Aaron's career with the Milwaukee Braves and then the Atlanta Braves (the Milwaukee Braves relocated to Atlanta at the end of the 1965 season). The entire 1973 season beginning in March until two weeks after the record was broken in April 1974 was examined. Focus here is given to four themes that emerged in the newspapers: the role of Babe Ruth as Aaron approached the record, the hate mail Aaron received in 1973, the role of baseball commissioner Bowie Kuhn, and conversations around race and the home run chase.

Hank Aaron Chases Babe Ruth: Prequel

At the start of the 1973, Atlanta Braves outfielder Hank Aaron had tallied 673 home runs over his nineteen-year career, needing 41 home runs to tie Ruth's record and one more to own the record by himself. He had hit 31 home runs in 1972, but as he approached the ripe old age of 40, Ruth's record appeared both attainable and challenging. Aaron's Major League Baseball career had begun in 1954, a year he hit 13 home runs, with the Milwaukee Braves. He was an All-Star player from 1955 until his retirement in 1976. On May 17, 1970, Aaron hit his 3000th hit, joining baseball's elite, and would eventually finish his career with 3771 hits. His accumulation of home runs came as a result of steady performances year after year, reaching 500 home runs on July 14, 1968. He was only the eighth player to achieve this feat, and on July 31, 1969, he hit his 537th home run to move past Mickey Mantle into third place on the all-time list behind Willie Mays and Ruth. In 1971, Aaron hit a career high 47 home runs.[4]

Regarding his pursuit of the all-time home run record, Aaron revealed in a June 1973 interview that he was "spurred" by a lack of recognition, noting that his name always came up last in discussions of Mantle and Mays. He lamented, "I figured the only way to get the recognition others get was to accomplish something nobody else did," and admitted he thought he might have a chance at finishing second behind Ruth.[5] Of his prospects to get the job done during the 1973 season, Aaron claimed he wasn't a "cinch" and that if it didn't happen in 1973, it "will be a real chore . . . because I'm 39 now, and it's tougher when you're 40. Nobody respects a man 40 years old, you know."[6] Aaron was cognizant of the significance of his athletic achievements and how his successes were meaningful to the black community, acknowledging, "It will mean a hell of a lot not only to me but to black people all over the world. Not only because the record is held by a white man, but because we as blacks didn't get a chance to get into baseball until the late forties."[7] As to the comparisons being made between himself and Ruth, the all-time standard bearer, Aaron explained, "I always said I wasn't a home run hitter, and I still say it, in the sense that I consider myself more of an all-around player. I'm not a slugger like Babe

Ruth was, but I've got 3000 hits (3423 to be exact), and he didn't, so that's one thing I can brag about. I'm more proud of my overall accomplishments. . . . I know how tall he was, 6-2. I also know he was fat and puggy [sic], and that's about it. Shucks, I never heard of the man until six years ago."[8] At thirty-nine years old, Aaron finished the 1973 season with 40 home runs, leaving him just one home run shy of Ruth's record, delaying the inevitable over a long, long winter.[9] At the close of the 1973 season, an editorial in the *Chicago Defender* stated, "714 will have to wait," exclaiming, "He finished the season just short of the mark with 713 home runs to his credit. That is mighty close and so suspenseful that we don't know if we can hold our breath until the next episode of the drama takes place!"[10] When Aaron finally hit the record-breaking home run, Bruce Bakke of the *Milwaukee Journal* considered it "the greatest moment in Atlanta sport history. It was unquestionably one of the great moments in baseball history. Through it all, Hammerin' Hank Aaron remained poised, calm. For three minutes the fans screamed."[11]

General Patterns in Black and White

When examining the coverage of Aaron's pursuit of Ruth's record, it is important to note that each mainstream newspaper was published daily, while the African American newspapers were published less often, most often weekly.[12] Another notable difference during this time period was the news reported on the front pages of the newspapers, with mainstream newspapers providing extensive coverage of the Patty Hearst kidnapping and African American newspapers covering more regional news of the local black communities.[13]

The newspapers that had the most Hank Aaron coverage, in terms of pages and number of articles were, unsurprisingly, Aaron's "hometown" newspapers, the *Milwaukee Journal, Milwaukee Sentinel, Atlanta Constitution*, and *Atlanta Journal*.[14] All four mainstream dailies covered each of Aaron's homeruns during the 1973 season and his final swings in 1974 and, additionally, carried stories of interest related to Aaron and his home run record pursuit. The remaining mainstream newspapers, the *Chicago Tribune, Los Angeles Times, New York Times*, and *Washington Post*, provided regular coverage, reporting on each home run, with special features and editorials. Most mainstream newspapers published columns by at least two columnists, offering differing viewpoints. Of the six African American newspapers, Aaron's local *Atlanta Daily World* offered the greatest number of articles, with the *Chicago Defender* and *Los Angeles Sentinel* also writing a good deal on Aaron. None of the three rivaled their daily counterparts in the amount of coverage but did offer additional perspectives in the national and racial dialogues. The *Washington Afro-American* provided readers with a weekly update on Aaron's 1973 season, with regular columns by noted sportswriter Sam Lacy. A surprising finding was the lack of coverage in New York's *Amsterdam News* as well as in the *Milwaukee Courier*, which barely fielded a sports section and focused largely on community politics. The *Amsterdam News* was a rarity among the newspapers, failing to feature Aaron on the front page after his historic home run. From the newspaper that billed itself as "America's Largest Weekly Newspaper," only nine issues over the course of 54 weeks included any mention of Aaron, including only one column about him. While most other newspapers had detailed coverage of Aaron's 714th and 715th home runs, the *Amsterdam News* did not cover the record-tying home run.

Beyond the amount of coverage from each newspaper, there were differences and similarities between the newspapers in the ways Hank Aaron and his pursuit of the record were presented. While many of the newspapers reported on the same incident, there was sometimes a difference of perspective offered by the columnists, sometimes within the same newspaper. The attitudes and ideas expressed by the newspapers and columnists cannot be easily categorized by mainstream (read white) versus African American—instead the reader is presented with a diaspora of ideas between and within the fourteen newspapers and their respective writers.

The Shadow of Babe Ruth

Babe Ruth was a constant shadow in the newspaper coverage of Aaron's assault on the Babe's all-time home run record. Comparisons between Ruth and Aaron relied on statistics to establish that while Aaron would eventually end up with more home runs than Ruth, he would not really be the record-holder. These constant comparisons were attempts by sportswriters writing for the mainstream press to minimize Aaron's accomplishment. Red Smith of the *New York Times* claimed that while "Babe never bore the black man's burden," he was called "nigger" by opponents.[15] Less than a month later, Smith wrote a column listing his readers' arguments in support of Ruth and against Aaron, such as Aaron's low average, his selfishness for focusing on the record, and his obsession with home runs.[16] Smith stood up for his readers, explaining "defending Ruth's place in history is not racist. . . . There can never be another like the Babe." He noted that Ruth would have hit more home runs had he not wasted a few seasons as a pitcher and reminded readers Aaron played in more games than Ruth.[17] Dave Anderson, Smith's colleague at the *Times*, noted that "skeptics, some traditionalists, some racists, minimize his accomplishments as a hitter" and presented an alternative view of Aaron as durable, consistent, and dignified.[18] Another article noted that Aaron was low-keyed and lacked the flamboyance of Ruth, symbolic of a type of comparison of the two athletes' demeanor and presence.[19] Ruth was portrayed as a larger-than-life personality who played for the nation's best team, the New York Yankees, in the largest media market, a notable contrast with Aaron, who played his entire career for small-market teams, in Milwaukee and Atlanta, with few endorsements until the last few years of his career.

The *Los Angeles Times* offered another point of view of the two sluggers. Charles Maher wrote "apart from rednecks who want no black man messing with a white god's record, some fans probably regard Ruth's accomplishments as an exception to the rule that records are made to be broken. This is one they don't want broken."[20] He listed the arguments presented by Ruth's supporters: Aaron will have 3,000 more at bats; Ruth hit a home run every 12 times at bat while Aaron was every 16; Aaron was playing in the live ball era, and the fences have been brought in. Maher states the list isn't exactly true and points out Ruth was walked 2,000 times, concluding it is difficult to compare two generations of players but largely placing the arguments as the folly of fans and not his own. A *Los Angeles Times* editorial simply stated, "When Aaron hits No. 715, he will have the most home runs, lifetime. Period."[21] Columnist Jim Murray offered his sarcastic take on the reaction of fans to Aaron breaking Ruth's record, saying it was like finding out Santa Claus is not real. In support of Aaron, Murray noted that Babe never played against black players and that was a major difference that ought to be considered. He added that Babe was walked so many times and that a walk should not be counted as an at bat.[22] When all was said and done and the record was in the books, the *Los Angeles Times* wrote, "Aaron's 714th, 11,289 at bats vs. Ruth 8,399—the difference in times at bat did not lessen the magic of the moment."[23] One Aaron fan, writing in response to what he viewed as flawed cross-generational comparisons, asked, "How many 400–500 foot parks did the Babe hit in? Also, when did the Babe ever see the likes of a Tom Seaver, Bob Gibson or Sandy Koufax and their 100 plus mile an hour fireballs that they threw—and throw—at Hank?"[24] The *Atlanta Journal*'s Jesse Outlar rose above the debate, claiming, "Debating the merits of Henry Louis Aaron and George Herman Ruth is similar to arguing about Michelangelo and Da Vinci, Jones and Nicklaus, Hemingway and Faulkner, hamburgers and hot dogs, and Secretariat and Man O' War," framing the issue of greatest home run hitter more in terms of personal preference.[25]

Fred Down, writing for the *Milwaukee Journal*, thought that once Aaron set the record, he should be automatically inducted into baseball's Hall of Fame, to "seize the opportunity created by Aaron's assault on Ruth's record," eschewing any discussion that Aaron's accomplishment was somehow less worthy.[26] The *Atlanta Constitution* used the renewed attention on Ruth as an opportunity to offer their readers a six-part series on the superstar. In their ad promotions for the series, the newspaper contended, "While Braves' rightfielder Hank Aaron will probably break Ruth's home run record this year, no one has yet come close to the magnetism of the Babe."[27] George Cunningham, writing for the *Constitution*, admitted that Aaron may be the greatest player ever but that he was largely to blame for the poor performance of the Braves.[28] When Aaron hit his 700th home run, the "South's Best Sport Pages" placed an image of Aaron adjacent to Ruth's with the phrase "Countdown: 14" in between the images of the two players.[29] The day after Aaron tied Ruth's record, the *Atlanta Constitution* published an editorial cartoon that showed Aaron rounding third with a ghostlike Ruth, twice the size of Aaron, patting him on the back, with the caption, "... One More Time."[30] In the same issue, on the front page of the daily, with the headline "Aaron Hits 714," a photo of Aaron is on the left side of the page, with a smaller photo of Ruth on the right, with the caption, "Babe Ruth Held Record 39 Years," with another headline reading, "Mrs. Ruth: 'I Wish Him Luck.'"[31]

No columnists in any of the African American newspapers made such hierarchical comparisons between the two players, nor did they question or entertain the idea that Aaron's record would somehow be tarnished based on more at bats or games played. As a group, they were supportive of Aaron, responding to the comparisons, often expressing racial pride in Aaron. Norman Unger, writing for the *Chicago Defender*, wrote, "Hank Aaron turns the clock back as he nears the record of not just another baseball player, but that of Babe Ruth, the baseball idol of kids for more than 50 years. Shame on him to do such a thing. The bigots of Atlanta only needed an excuse and now they have one."[32] Milton Richman, a United Press International writer whose articles appeared in the mainstream press and black press, thought the only thing Aaron and Ruth had in common was their record-breaking home runs came as players with the Braves organization.[33] He also thought "Hank's glory outshines the 'at bat' controversy."[34] Carl Chamberlain, another writer for the *Defender*, chided, "These cynics are the same people who constantly compare him to Babe Ruth, who died before cars went 60 miles an hour and before the world heard of Count Basie. They drag out long lists of statistics to show that Ruth hit homers at a faster rate than Aaron but they fail to point out that he struck out at a faster rate too."[35] Richman, this time in the *Los Angeles Sentinel*, suggested "Ruth never really was one to throw a wet blanket over anything, but there was some human vanity in him, too, and were he alive today it might be only natural for him to hope deep down that nobody would ever break his all-time home run record." He reported that single-season home run record-holder, Roger Maris, who also endured constant comparisons with Ruth during his 1961 chase, suggested Aaron would "find out the only time he's going to get any relief is when he's out on the field. He'll never be able to enjoy himself either before or after the ball game. He'll never be allowed to relax."[36] Sam Lacy, a big supporter of Aaron during his home run chase, dismantled the arguments from mainstream columnists and concluded using the words of his colleague Arthur Lewis: "Heck, let 'em put an asterisk besides Hank's name if they wish. . . . Who cares? . . . They can't erase that 715."[37]

Hank Aaron's Mailbox

At the beginning of May 1973, Aaron began to speak out against fans who yelled racial slurs at him during Atlanta's home games.[38] Four days later, Wayne Minshew brought attention to the hate mail Aaron was receiving as he pursued the home run record. According to Minshew, Aaron speculated that half of his mail was of a racist nature, and the columnist saw this as proof that the chase was "not all fun."[39] Both the *Los Angeles Times* and *Defender* noted that Aaron received hate mail every day berating him for approaching a white man's record. Aaron was quoted as saying, "If I were a white man, all America would be proud of me. But I'm black. You have to be black in America to know how sick some people are. I've always thought racism a problem, even with as much progress as America has made."[40] Aaron reported that in one day he received 416 piece of mail, and over 600 the next, with 60 percent of the letters being of a racist nature. Unger, of the *Defender*, provided readers with Aaron's mailing address to encourage readers send letters of support to the ballplayer.[41] Three months later, the *New York Times* reported Aaron was receiving police protection because of the hate mail, while the *Los Angeles Sentinel* mentioned Atlanta fans who heckled Aaron in right field, calling him "nigger" and "s.o.b." and telling him he was nothing compared to Ruth, but making no mention of the hate mail.[42] The *Sentinel* also reported that Roger Maris was pulling for Aaron and that during his 1961 chase of Ruth's single-season record, he had also received hate mail.[43] The *Amsterdam News* mentioned the hate mail for the first time in October 1973, quoting Aaron as saying, "It would not have been a public matter had it not been that I was asked the casual question: how were the fans taking my chase at Ruth."[44]

In what can only be described as ironic, Aaron was honored with a "Postal Service plaque recognizing him as 'America's No. 1' in fan mail as well as home runs," owing to the 900,000 pieces of mail he received in 1973. After this honor was reported, Mary Keas, in a letter to the editor, complained about the government's keeping track of such data and noted, "Not all fan mail is complimentary—and I understand this was particularly the case concerning some of Mr. Aaron's mail."[45]

Commissioner Kuhn's Snubs

As commissioner, Bowie Kuhn played a central and always controversial role during Aaron's season-long pursuit. In June 1973, he threatened pitchers with suspensions if they helped Aaron hit home runs. In response to a story quoting several pitchers who stated they would help Aaron reach the record, the *Los Angeles Times* reported Kuhn would punish pitchers with long-term suspensions, reminding the players of Major League rule 21, for serving Aaron "fat" pitches.[46] Just two months prior, Aaron had been worried of the opposite, quoted in the *Amsterdam News* saying he was "worried about the pitchers trying to prevent" him from breaking Ruth's record.[47] One newspaper identified Kuhn's mood over the pitchers supposed aid as "boiling."[48] Norman Unger read Kuhn's warnings as not exactly saying "break a leg" but as "less than complimentary and totally unnecessary."[49] Three weeks after Kuhn issued his warning, Aaron hit home runs 695 and 696 against the New York Mets and said he "hoped the commissioner was watching. Neither one was down the middle."[50]

When Aaron became only the second player in Major League Baseball history to hit 700 home runs, several newspapers noted that Kuhn had failed to congratulate Aaron on his accomplishment and that the slight was a disappointment to Aaron.[51] The *Chicago Defender* noted Kuhn was the only "VIP" to overlook Aaron's 700th home run.[52] Of the snub, Aaron claimed, "I'm not agitating him and I'm perfectly serious. I mean this sincerely, regardless of how small he thinks it is, hitting that home run, it wasn't small to me. I feel he should have acknowledged it somehow."[53]

As the 1973 season closed and Aaron edged closer to the record, falling one shy of the record by season's end, the *Tribune* provided an interesting follow-up. Richard Dozer reported Kuhn was a captive audience in Atlanta waiting for the record, in large part because he had missed Aaron's 700th home run. Dozer commented that Kuhn would much rather be in Chicago or Pittsburgh, where the outcome of games would determine division winners.[54] During his time in Atlanta, Kuhn invited Aaron to throw out the first pitch at the World Series, and it appeared the men had smoothed over the commissioner's absence earlier in the season.[55]

Kuhn's wasted no time in stirring up controversy at the start of the new season. The Atlanta Braves opened the 1974 season in Cincinnati, and in an effort to allow Aaron to break the record in front of a home crowd, manager Eddie Mathews planned to sit Aaron for two of the three games in the opening series. The Los Angeles Sentinel issued an article titled "They're Still Picking on Hank Aaron." Aaron commented that neither Stan Musial nor Roberto Clemente was given a hard time when they decided to hit their 3000th hit at their home fields.[56] As the season began, other newspapers picked up the story. At the start of the opening series with the Reds, Kuhn ordered Mathews to play Aaron or face serious penalty. John Husar, of the Tribune, reported on Mathews's reaction to the order, "The commissioner has unlimited powers to impose very serious penalties. For the first time I realize that these penalties are not only fines, but also suspensions and other threats to the franchise itself. Because of this order and the threatened penalties, I intend to start Hank Aaron tomorrow."[57] The title of another Husar column the same day read, "Mathews Is Man Caught in the Middle."[58] David Condon, Husar's colleague at the Tribune, posited that Kuhn should have avoided the controversy and scheduled the Braves opening series for Atlanta.[59] In an Associated Press poll, fans were critical of both Aaron and Kuhn, stating that Kuhn should not order him to play but that Aaron should want to play.[60] Norman Unger, of the Chicago Defender, was by far the harshest critic of the commissioner when he wrote, "The game's highest ranking official, who has often likened himself to 'Hitler' with his idiotic statements, topped himself by ordering that Aaron be in the lineup in Cincinnati."[61] When Aaron tied the record in Cincinnati, with Kuhn in attendance, Red Smith saw the events as "Kuhn's finest hour."[62]

The final controversy occurred when Aaron broke the record in his first swing in Atlanta. Kuhn was noticeably absent. The *Chicago Tribune* and *Los Angeles Times* noted that the absent commissioner was thrilled and proud.[63] It was reported that Kuhn was invited to both Cleveland and Atlanta, opting for Cleveland because he had seen Aaron's record-tying home run in Cincinnati. Robert Markus, a columnist for the *Tribune*, believed Kuhn showed he had a backbone through the series of events, by ordering Aaron to play.[64] Dave Anderson, of the *New York Times*, reported that in the ceremonies following the home run, Aaron was presented with a wristwatch from the commissioner, who had Monte Irvin represent his office at the event. As Irvin gave the watch to Aaron and Kuhn's name was announced, a roar of boos filled the stands. Aaron said he was "smiling from the boos."[65] Brad Pye Jr., of the *Los Angeles Sentinel*, stated that the celebration was a "tribute to baseball, even though the commissioner to the game, Bowie Kuhn, was too busy elsewhere to be on hand for this historic moment." He noted two signs in the stands that read "Phooey to Bowie," and "Aaron 715, Kuhn 0."[66] Kuhn was a favorite target for editorial cartoonists. The *Amsterdam News* published an editorial on Kuhn's role in the home run chase adjacent to a cartoon that pictured Aaron's 715th home run ball firmly planted in Kuhn's mouth.[67] In another, on the front page of the *Milwaukee Journal*, with the caption, "A game of giants . . . and midgets," a drawing of Aaron swinging was imposed on a ghostlike image of Ruth swinging and a small man dressed like Napoleon in the corner with his thumb in his mouth and a hat that read "Bowie Kuhn."[68]

Conversations around Race and the Home Run Chase

Much of the dialogue, whether it was hate mail, the comparisons of Ruth and Aaron, or even the role of the baseball commissioner, was presented in a manner that focused on Aaron as an African American. Aaron's racial identity was critical in the analysis of his pursuit of the record, and in the interpretations of his efforts. Mainstream newspapers tacitly acknowledged the racism Aaron faced, while black newspapers were much more willing to identify and discuss not only the racism Aaron faced but also the significance of his accomplishment for the black community, within baseball history as well as American history.

As several newspapers made their comparisons between Aaron and Ruth, it was revealed that as a child Aaron had no real knowledge of Babe Ruth, and the ensuing discussion around Aaron's inspiration provided insight into the segregated years of Major League Baseball and the Negro leagues. In a feature on Aaron's career, a *Los Angeles Times* article also focused on Aaron's childhood lack of familiarity with Ruth. The ballplayer was quoted as saying, "I know I never remember hearing the name of Babe Ruth when I was younger. What he accomplished was virtually meaningless to black kids. We paid little attention to the records of white professional players."[69] Cleon Walfoort said that he thought it would be "nice to report that the mighty Babe Ruth" was Aaron's childhood hero but that it would be "completely untrue." Aaron told Walfoort, "We all knew that Ruth was a great home run hitter and the most famous player in baseball, but we didn't pay much attention to Major League records. It wasn't until Jackie Robinson became the first black player in the Major Leagues, in 1947, that I started thinking of playing in the big leagues myself."[70]

It was reported early in the 1973 season that Atlanta fans were yelling racial slurs at Aaron. Aaron was very forthcoming about the slurs and his honesty made it difficult for any newspaper to dispute the attacks were racist. When asked what the fans yelled, Aaron replied, "I'll tell you what they call me. They call me nigger. They say I'm not as good as Babe Ruth. I never said I was, did I? Then they say I'm paid too much money. They call me a S.O.B. . . . . I'm not going to take no more of that. Why should I? It doesn't happen in other cities." He believed that his race, and that of Ruth, were the motivation for the fans' abuse, explaining, "Look, I'm no damn fool. I'm getting too close to Ruth's record, infringing on an area where no black man has ever been before. If I were a white boy, it'd be fine. If this were someone like Killebrew or Mantle doing it, everything would be all right. But they can't accept the fact I'm black and I've got this chance to do it."[71] Norman Unger identified the abuse as "Jim Crow" at work.[72] A *Washington Afro-American* editorial argued that Hank Aaron's "crime . . . is not that he threatens to destroy a white legend. Rather, it is that he is black and threatens to destroy a white legend."[73]

Some fans refused to see racism in the treatment of Aaron. Brian Boettcher, in a letter to the editor, sarcastically claimed, "White people still drive Cadillacs and eat fried chicken. Some even eat watermelon and listen to Ray Charles or James Brown records." He angrily concluded his letter, "I'm getting pretty damn tired of getting the past 300 years thrown up in my face and I'm sick of black nationalism and soul food. My ancestors fought to free the slaves and abolish slavery."[74] Of this sort of racial resentment, A. S. Doc Young posited that "with Ruth's record almost certain to fall, there are people who feel compelled to dig up other old records which, they hope, will preserve in their minds the lilywhite era of the game."[75] Chalmers Roberts explained his and others' reluctance to embrace Aaron as being "captives to our memories," as less about race and more as a "matter of moorings." He plainly admits, "It isn't anything personal and it isn't racial; there just will be one thing less for me to cling to."[76] Jesse Outlar liked to believe the accomplishments of Aaron, and his demeanor, were what made him a credit to his race—"the human race."[77]

An example that exemplifies the racial dialogue around Aaron appears in the coverage of opening day in April 1974. On the opening day of the 1974 season, and the day that Aaron would tie Ruth's record, Aaron was honored by the Cincinnati Reds during a pregame ceremony. Aaron asked for a moment of silence to honor the anniversary of civil rights leader Martin Luther King Jr.'s assassination, which was refused. Several newspapers reported on this slight.[78] The *New York Times* reported on the record-tying home run but also noted that "Aaron's pleasure in tying Ruth's record also was dampened by the refusal of Reds management to comply with his request for a moment of silence during the pregame ceremonies on the 6th anniversary of Dr. Martin Luther King's assassination." On the slight, Aaron commented, "For some reason, they found that their schedule wouldn't permit it. . . . It would have been appropriate. We were all very disappointed about it. I'd spoken with Jesse Jackson about it before the game."[79] The *Los Angeles Times* reported the same comment from Aaron but included that other African American players had been involved in the request.[80] Husar, of the *Chicago Tribune*, claimed that some of the Braves were not even aware of the request but also included a statement from the Reds vice president, Dick Wagner, who said, "As a policy, we do not want to get into religious, political, or racial things. We don't do it for Kennedy, for Lincoln, or anyone else. It's not because of the men or what they stand for. We just don't think our fans want that at the ballpark. They come here to be entertained. This is really a personal thing of Mr. Aaron's. We believe Mr. Aaron has to decide his own way to pay tribute to Mr. King. But I don't believe it belongs in the ballpark or in the baseball business."[81]

Both the *Chicago Defender* and *Los Angeles Sentinel* framed the record within the context of race and what the accomplishment meant to the black community. Unger of the *Defender* saw Aaron as a "symbol of excellence to blacks in or out of the game."[82] He saw the event as the right time for "a black man to make the front page of every newspaper in the country."[83] Carl Chamberlain, Unger's colleague at the *Defender*, prior to Aaron breaking the record, urged Aaron to "do it for all the little black boys in ghettoes who don't have a dream. Hit it for Cool Papa Bell, Josh Gibson, Satchel Paige and Jackie Robinson, and when you round the bases think of them. Think of them and all the millions of black hearts that smile and feel proud."[84] Writing for the *Sentinel*, Vernon Jordan called Aaron an "Authentic American Hero" and described his accomplishment as "a visible reminder that black baseball players have reached a crucial importance to the game and ought to get the kind of treatment that stature deserves. . . . America has always accepted, if grudgingly, black superstars. It's just beginning to come around to accept average players and people. If Hank Aaron's breakthrough into immortality is to have deeper meaning for the game and for the country, the pace of that acceptance must be accelerated."[85] Brad Pye Jr., also writing for the *Sentinel*, offered his perspective of what Aaron's record meant to black Americans with a front page story, "Hank Aaron Joins MLK as a Legend."[86] Pye believed that, with the record-breaking him run, "Aaron became the second black man to become a living legend in his own time. . . . Aaron's blow reached into the graves and brought joy to men like the late civil rights battler, Walter White of the NAACP, Lester Granger of the Urban League, Medgar Evers, the slain Mississippi civil rights crusader, and even little Emmitt Till."[87] Pye reminded his readers of the significance of Atlanta in the sports drama, as the city had also just elected Maynard Jackson as the nation's first (and youngest) black mayor of a major southern city. Across town, writing for the *Los Angeles Times*, Roy Wilkins, in an editorial, hailed Aaron's accomplishment as a cause for celebration for all Americans: "America and America's world were in the slump of slumps: inflation, an oil boycott, the Watergate scandal, the slicksters and the schemers. . . . Aaron had been building up to this muddle and, like the incomparable Joe Louis, brought to white Americans a vindication of their better selves. To black Americans he brought hope that by keeping their specialties they could win."[88] Louis Martin, in the *Chicago Defender*, claimed "The ghosts of Jackie Robinson and the smiling face of Roy Campanella seemed to intrude on my TV screen as I saw Hank Aaron come to bat. They too cracked an enormous amount of ice. Perhaps no one is more sensitive to the contributions of these pioneers than the thoughtful, gentlemanly new home run king."[89]

Mainstream newspapers also saw the racial significance of Aaron's accomplishment, and in an editorial celebrating the record, the *Milwaukee Journal* lauded their city's former star in the language of the politics of respectability: "Ruth's record had become ancient history—so old that it came to look invincible. . . . Aaron has said that he was inspired more by Jackie Robinson, the first black to play in the major leagues, than by Ruth. And No. 44's achievement must be seen as a contribution to the struggle for black-identity. But Aaron is also the kind of self-effacing hero that all America wants. Nice guys should finish first. Henry Aaron has. Way to go, Hank."[90]

Conclusion

When Aaron finally hit home run number 715, owning the all-time title outright, Ross Newhan commented on the attendance, noting it was a "record baseball crowd in a city that had displayed a measure of apathy toward Aaron's pursuit last year."[91] The abundant attention Aaron received in the Atlanta newspapers as Aaron played for the Atlanta Braves provides a hometown lens from which to examine the home run chase. Other newspapers located around the country, including several of the nation's top black newspapers, provide additional perspectives on Aaron's chase as well as the significance of his accomplishments in baseball, a sport that once banned African American players. In considering more recent assaults on baseball records, most notably Aaron's own all-time home run record and the establishment of a new record set by Barry Bonds in 2007, we can gain some nuanced understandings, and perhaps greater appreciation, of how newspapers in the 1970s discussed race and racism in American sports.

NOTES

1. There are hundreds of books that focus on the home run. A sample includes Lew Freedman, *Going Yard: The Everything Home Run Book* (Triumph Books, 2011); Eldon L. Ham, *All the Babe's Men: Baseball's Greatest Home Run Seasons and How They Changed America* (Potomac Books Inc., 2013); Greg Jacobs, *The Everything KIDS' Baseball Book: From Baseball's History to Today's Favorite Players—with Lots of Home Run Fun in Between* (Adams Media, 2012); Bill Jenkinson, *The Year Babe Ruth Hit 104 Home Runs: Recrowning Baseball's Greatest Slugger* (De Capo Press, 2007); Bill Nowlin, *521: The Story of Ted Williams' Home Runs* (Rounder Books, 2013); Mitchell S. Soivenski, *New York Yankees Home Runs: A Comprehensive Factbook, 1903-2012* (McFarland, 2013); Tom Stanton, *Hank Aaron and the Home Run That Changed Everything* (It Books, 2005); and David Vincent, *Home Run: The Definitive History of Baseball's Ultimate Weapon* (Potomac Books Inc., 2007).
2. For more on the McGwire-Sosa home run chase, see Shelley Lucas, "Lost in Translation: Voice, Masculinity, Race, and the 1998 Home Run Chase," in *Fame to Infamy: Race, Sport, and the Fall From Grace*, edited by David C. Ogden and Joel Nathan Rosen (University Press of Mississippi, 2010), 61-75. Also see Lisa Doris Alexander, "Mark McGwire, Sammy Sosa and the Politics of Race and Nationality," in *When Baseball Isn't White, Straight and Male* (McFarland, 2013), 11-30.
3. For more on the media coverage of Bonds's pursuit of Aaron's record, see Matt Ventresca, "There's Something about Barry: Media Representations of a Home Run King," *NINE* 20, no. 1 (Fall 2011): 56-80.
4. For an excellent biography of Aaron, see Howard Bryant, *The Last Hero: A Life of Henry Aaron* (Pantheon Books, 2011). Bryant does a nice job of capturing the

stress Aaron experienced during the home run chase as well as his reflections on the breaking of his record by Bonds. Additionally, the reader will get a very good understanding of Aaron's early days in Negro league baseball as well as his overall career achievements.

5. Bob Wolf, "Lack of Recognition Spurred Aaron," *Milwaukee Journal*, June 3, 1973, 1.

6. Wolf, "Lack of Recognition Spurred Aaron," 1.

7. Wolf, "Lack of Recognition Spurred Aaron," 6.

8. Wolf, "Lack of Recognition Spurred Aaron," 6.

9. At least one television channel saw the winter wait as an opportunity to produce programming related to the home run chase. See "TV Documentary Looks at Aaron's 'Long Winter,'" *Washington Afro-American*, October 23, 1974, 10.

10. "714 Will Have to Wait," *Chicago Defender*, October 3, 1973, 15.

11. Bruce Bakke, "Aaron's Quest Ends in an Instant," *Milwaukee Journal*, April 9, 1974, 2:7, 2:10.

12. Black newspapers published at varying frequencies. For example, in 1973 and 1974, the *Atlanta Daily World* was published on Tuesdays, Thursdays, Fridays, and Sundays. The *Amsterdam* was published weekly. The *Chicago Defender* was published daily, though it is now published weekly.

13. According to Henry LaBrie, the black press in 1970 comprised 173 daily and weekly newspapers, with a readership of over 3.5 million. LaBrie, on the state of the black press, commented, "There are those who believe the Black press is on a downhill skid and as the Black American continues to become a greater part of the mainstream of our society, he will less and less need his own newspaper." See Henry LaBrie, "Black Press: Substitute or Supplement," *Milwaukee Courier*, March 16, 1974, 13. Also see Vernon Jordan, "Millions Depend on Black Press," *Milwaukee Courier*, March 16, 1974, 12; Carlton B. Goodlett, "The Black Press: Voice of 25 Million Who Earn over $50 Billion a Year," *Milwaukee Courier*, March 16, 1974, 2:10–11. For more on the black press, see Armistead S. Pride and Clint C. Wilson, *A History of the Black Press* (Howard University Press, 1997); Patrick S. Washburn, *The African American Newspaper: Voice of Freedom* (Northwestern University Press, 2006); and Todd Vogel, ed., *The Black Press: New Literary and Historical Essays* (Rutgers University Press, 2001).

14. The *Atlanta Journal* was published in the afternoon, with the *Atlanta Constitution* published in the morning. The two newspapers offered a combined weekend edition. The two newspapers merged in 2001 to offer a morning newspaper, *Atlanta Journal-Constitution*. The *Milwaukee Journal* was published

in the afternoons, while the *Milwaukee Sentinel* was published each morning. The two newspapers merged in 1995 to form the *Milwaukee Journal-Sentinel*.

15. Red Smith, "Henry, Babe and All Those Homers," *New York Times*, July 16, 1973, 37.

16. Red Smith, "Intruder on This Hallowed Ground," *New York Times*, August 8, 1973.

17. Smith, "Intruder."

18. Dave Anderson, "The Sound of 715," *New York Times*, April 9, 1974.

19. "Modest Man Alone at the Top," *New York Times*, April 9, 1974.

20. Charles Maher, "Aaron vs. Ruth: The Argument Rages," *Los Angeles Times*, June 18, 1973, 3:1.

21. "Viewpoint: Putting It Simply," *Los Angeles Times*, August 11, 1973, B3.

22. Jim Murray, "Bad Henry He Isn't," *Los Angeles Times*, August 19, 1973, C1.

23. Bob Oates, "Aaron Catches a Legend," *Los Angeles Times*, April 5, 1974, 10–11; also see "Vic Raschi Was First Victim: Aaron's Trail to Immortality Took 20 Years," *Los Angeles Times*, April 5, 1974, 1, 13.

24. "Coach Irks Hair Corps; Letters to the Sports Desk," *Milwaukee Journal*, June 1, 1973, 26; Letter from Dean Mayer.

25. Jesse Outlar, "From Ruth to Aaron," *Atlanta Journal*, June 19, 1973, D1.

26. Fred Down, "Why Not Hall of Fame If Aaron Sets Record?" *Milwaukee Journal*, April 22, 1973, 2:5.

27. Advertisement, "The Truth about Ruth," *Atlanta Constitution*, August 1, 1973, D6.

28. George Cunningham, "Too Much Talk Too Soon," *Atlanta Constitution*, July 7, 1973, D2.

29. See images above Wayne Minshew, "Aaron Slams No. 700, But Phillies Celebrate," *Atlanta Constitution*, July 22, 1973, D1. For a sample of other articles in the mainstream press that address the comparisons between Aaron and Ruth, see Robert Akerman, "History Will Love Henry, Too," *Atlanta Journal and Constitution*, April 14, 1974, A23; David Condon, "Hank: How about All in One Game?" *Chicago Tribune*, September 19, 1973, 3:15; Joseph Durso, "Aaron—Like Ruth—Had Modest Start to Top," *Chicago Tribune*, April 9, 1974, section 3; David Condon, "Babe and Hank: As Seen by Hitting Expert Fonseca," *Chicago Tribune*, April 10, 1974, 3:3; Leonard Koppett, "Who's Following Aaron's Footsteps—Nobody at Present," *Chicago Tribune*, April 14, 1974, 3:2; Bob Addie, "Old Records Never Fade," *Washington Post*, July 11, 1973, D1; Bob Addie, "Babe Ruth's Waning Days—Can Aaron Expect Likewise?" *Washington Post*, September 20, 1973, D12; Letter to editor, "E. Howard Hunt . . . Civil Rights . . . Living

Tradition . . ." *Washington Post*, October 4, 1973, A19; William Gildea, "Aaron Fated to Stay Second in Fan Hearts," *Washington Post*, September 14, 1973, D1, D3; William Barry Furlong, "Aaron Embodies Era Irrespective of Ruth," *Washington Post*, April 8, 1974, D1; Letter to editor, "Watergate and Chappaquiddick . . . Babe Ruth's Record," *Washington Post*, July 20, 1973, A20; "Ruth RBI Mark Also in Danger," *Washington Post*, September 8, 1973, D9; and Tony Petrella, "Henry Keeps on Hammering," *Atlanta Constitution*, May 14, 1973, D1, D5.

30. "One More Time," April 5, 1974, *Atlanta Constitution*, A4. The artist's last name is Baldy.

31. Jesse Outlar, "Aaron Hits 714," *Atlanta Constitution*, April 5, 1974, 1; "Mrs. Ruth: 'I Wish Him Luck,'" *Atlanta Constitution*, April 5, 1974, 1. Ruth's widow may have wished Aaron luck, but she did not attend the events; see "Ruth's Widow Didn't Watch," *Milwaukee Journal*, April 9, 1974, 2:10. By the time Aaron broke the record, most columnists were resigned to a new record-holder and paid appropriate respect. For example, see Dave Anderson, "Aaron Steps Forward as a Man of History," *Milwaukee Journal*, April 7, 1974, 2:2; Thomas Boswell, "The Amazing Aaron: Improving with Age," *Los Angeles Times*, September 19, 1973, 3:1–2; Joseph Durso, "Aaron Hits 715th, Passes Babe Ruth," *New York Times*, April 9, 1974, 1; David Moffit, "Aaron Will Not Rest on His Laurels," *Los Angeles Sentinel*, April 11, 1974, B1; Ross Newhan, "Aaron: A Quiet Man Pursues a Legend," *Los Angeles Times*, September 25, 1973, 3:2; and Red Smith, "Henry, Babe and All Those Homers," *New York Times*, July 16, 1973, 37.

32. Norman Unger, "Baseball: The Game's No Longer Kids' Stuff," *Chicago Defender*, May 12, 1973, 29.

33. Milton Richman, "Hank's Glory Outshines the 'At Bat' Controversy," *Chicago Defender*, April 13, 1974, 20.

34. Richman, "Hank's Glory," 20.

35. Carl Chamberlain, "Hank May Pass Babe's Mark This Season," *Chicago Defender*, September 8, 1973, 20.

36. Milton Richman, "Roger Maris Pulls for Hank Aaron," *Los Angeles Sentinel*, July 19, 1973, B1.

37. Sam Lacy, "Let Em Put Asterisk If They Wish," *Washington Afro-American*, April 16–20, 1974, 9. Also see Sam Lacy, "I Have Had Egg on My Face, but . . . ," *Washington Afro-American*, July 17–21, 1973, 7; Sam Lacy, "Found: A Guy Rapping Hank," *Washington Afro-American*, April 16–20, 1974, 9; Sam Lacy, "Homer Hitters of Both Races Rally to Aaron," *Washington Afro-American*, June 5–9, 1973, 7; Sam Lacy, "They Mean Well but They Can't Know," *Washington Afro-American*, May 26, 1973, 7.

38. Wayne Minshew, "Aaron Charges Racism," *Atlanta Constitution*, May 3, 1973, D1. Also see "Bigots, Racists Upset Hank Aaron," *Los Angeles Sentinel*, May 10, 1973, B1.

39. Wayne Minshew, "Hank's 714 Homer Chase Stamps Him with Trouble," *Atlanta Constitution*, May 7, 1973, D6. For more on Aaron's outfield hecklers, as well as the hate mail, see Wayne Minshew, "Aaron: 'I've Earned Respect,'" *Atlanta Constitution*, May 8, 1973, D1; Al Thomy, "Aaron Baiters," *Atlanta Constitution*, May 12, 1973, D1. One California legislator, Democratic Rep. Glenn Anderson, proposed a resolution to salute Aaron, largely in response to the hecklers. See Bob Fort, "Californian Wants Aaron Resolution," *Atlanta Journal and Constitution*, July 4, 1973, E2.

40. "Hate Mail Grows as Aaron Nears the Babe's Record," *Los Angeles Times*, May 17, 1973, 3:1.

41. *Los Angeles Times*, May 17, 1973; Unger, "Hank Aaron Needs Help from His Loyal Fans," *Chicago Defender*, May 19, 1973, 29. A similar call was made in Atlanta; see "Mail Call for Aaron: Swarmed with Encouragement," *Atlanta Constitution*, May 21, 1973, D5. Milwaukee also promoted a letter-writing campaign to support Aaron. See "'Cards for Hank' Idea Proposed; Letters to the Sports Desk," *Milwaukee Journal*, May 20, 1973, 3:3.

42. "People in Sports: Aussies Call on Laver," *New York Times* August 14, 1973; "Bigots, Racists Upset Hank Aaron," *Los Angeles Sentinel*, May 10, 1973, B1.

43. Milton Richman, "Roger Maris Pulls For Hank Aaron," *Los Angeles Sentinel*, July 19, 1973, B1.

44. Sam Lacy, "No Help for Aaron, Kuhn Says," *Amsterdam News, Dawn Magazine*, October 27, 1973, insert.

45. George Minot Jr., "House Salutes Aaron, Its Flag Day Speaker," *Washington Post*, June 14, 1974, D3; "Letter to editor (Mary Keas)," *Washington Post*, July 2, 1974, A21.

46. "Hurlers Who Give Aaron 'Fat' Pitch Will Be Suspended," June 19, 1973, *Los Angeles Times*, 3:2. Rule 21 reads, "Every player must give his best efforts toward the winning of any baseball game for which he is involved." This edict was published in several newspapers. For example, see Norman O. Unger, "Kuhn Warns Pitchers on Helping," *Chicago Defender*, June 19, 1973, 25. A. S. Doc Young identified some of the pitchers—Andy Messersmith, Tug McGraw, and Reggie Cleveland—as hoping Aaron would hit a home run off their pitchers as a means to increase their own value. See A. S. Doc Young, "More Home Run Talk," *Chicago Defender*, June 21, 1973, 36. For more on Kuhn's response, see "Hank's Help Draws Fire," *Atlanta Journal*, June 21, 1973, 2; "Helping Aaron

Called Joke," *Milwaukee Journal*, June 19, 1973, part 2; "Kuhn Warns Aaron 'Help,'" *Washington Post*, June 19, 1973, D2; Wayne Minshew, "'Grooving' Remarks Make Aaron Wince," *Atlanta Journal*, June 21, 1973, D1, D10; "No Help for Aaron," *Chicago Tribune*, June 19, 1973, 3:5; "Pitchers Say They'd Groove Aaron's 715," *Atlanta Constitution*, June 17, 1973, D1; A. S. Doc Young, "Bowie Goofs . . ." *Chicago Defender*, June 27, 1973, 28.

47. *Amsterdam News*, April 13, 1973.

48. "Bowie Boils: Threatens 'Helping' Hurlers," *Atlanta Constitution*, June 19, 1973, D1.

49. Unger, "Kuhn Warns Pitchers on Helping," 25.

50. Joseph Durso, "Aaron's 695th and 696th Subdue Mets," *New York Times*, July 9, 1973.

51. Richard Dozer, "Aaron, Mays Rap Kuhn and Baseball Bosses," *Chicago Tribune*, July 24, 1973, 3:2. Also see David Condon, "Baseball's Boss Excels at Doing the Wrong Thing," *Chicago Tribune*, July 18, 1973, 3:3; Dozer, "Aaron, Mays Rap Kuhn and Baseball Bosses," 3:2; and Bob Addie, "Aaron Irked by Kuhn's Silence," *Washington Post*, July 24, 1973, D2.

52. "Kuhn Only 'VIP' to Overlook Aaron's 700 Mark," *Chicago Defender*, July 24, 1973, 26.

53. "Kuhn Only 'VIP' to Overlook Aaron's 700 Mark," 26. Also see James D. Heath, "Hank Aaron Snubbed by Commissioner," *Atlanta Daily World*, July 26, 1973, 5.

54. Richard Dozer, "Bowie Kuhn Is Captive Audience," *Chicago Tribune*, September 29, 1973, 2:3.

55. "Kuhn Invites Aaron to Series," *Chicago Defender*, September 19, 1973, 28. Kuhn is quoted in this article as "jokingly" telling Aaron, "You're a showoff" after Aaron hit home run number 711. Also see "First World Series Ball to Be Thrown by Hank Aaron," *Atlanta Daily World*, September 20, 1973, 10.

56. Milton Richman, "They're Still Picking on Hank Aaron," *Los Angeles Sentinel*, March 22, 1974, B3. Weeks earlier, and with still a month before the season was set to start, the controversy was already being discussed in the *Washington Afro-American*; see "Commissioner Kuhn Irked by Braves' Holdout of Aaron," *Washington Afro-American*, February 26, 1974, 14.

57. John Husar, "Kuhn: Hank Must Play Today," *Chicago Tribune*, April 7, 1974, 3:1. Also see "Aaron to Play on Kuhn's Order," *Milwaukee Journal*, April 7, 1974, 2:1; "Aaron's Name in the Lineup," *Milwaukee Journal*, April 4, 1974, sports section, 1; Joseph Durso, "Braves Bench Aaron but Kuhn Orders They Play Him Today," *New York Times*, April 7, 1974, 5:1; "Mathews to Ignore Order,"

Milwaukee Journal, April 6, 1974, 12; and Chuck Johnson, "The Sports Journal: Mathews' Tortured Logic Defies Explanation," *Milwaukee Journal*, April 7, 1974, 2:2.

58. John Husar, "Mathews Is a Man Caught in the Middle," *Chicago Tribune*, April 7, 1974, 3:3.

59. David Condon, "Kuhn Should Have Had Braves Open in Atlanta," *Chicago Tribune*, April 4, 1974, 3:1, 3:8.

60. "Poll Shows Fans Critical of Both Aaron and Kuhn," *Chicago Tribune*, April 7, 1974, 3:3.

61. Norman O. Unger, "All Eyes on Hank Aaron, the Greatest," *Chicago Defender*, April 6, 1974, 19. Although Kuhn did not attend the opening series in Cincinnati, Vice President Gerald Ford attended the opening day game. See "Ford Ready, Aaron May Be," *Milwaukee Journal*, April 3, 1974, part 2.

62. Red Smith, "Hank's Day Kuhn's, Too," *Milwaukee Journal*, April 5, 1974, 17.

63. "Absent Kuhn is 'Thrilled, Proud,'" *Chicago Tribune*, April 9, 1974, 3:2; Ross Newhan, "No. 715 Belongs to Aaron and Nobody Else," *Los Angeles Times*, April 9, 1974, B1.

64. Robert Markus, "Bowie Kuhn Shows He Has a Backbone," *Chicago Tribune*, April 9, 1974, 3:3. Markus also stated that Kuhn had been the "constant target of snipers almost since he was elected." Also see George Minot Jr., "Cincinnati: Suspense," *Washington Post*, April 4, 1974, D1; William Barry Furlong, "Waiting for No. 715: Poor Bowie's Almanack," *Washington Post*, April 5, 1974, D1; George Minot Jr., "Kuhn Orders Aaron Play Today," *Washington Post*, April 7, 1974, D1; Sam Lacy, "Aaron Homers but Kuhn Fans," *Washington Afro-American*, April 9, 1974, 1; David Condon, "Kuhn Should Have Had Braves Open in Atlanta," *Chicago Tribune*, April 4, 1974, 3:1; John Husar, "Kuhn: Hank Must Play Today," *Chicago Tribune*, April 7, 1974, 3:1; "Kuhn Said He Had 'No Commitment' to Be in Atlanta," *Milwaukee Journal*, April 9, 1974, 2:7, 2:10.

65. Dave Anderson, "The Sound of 715," *New York Times*, April 9, 1974.

66. Brad Pye Jr., *Los Angeles Sentinel*, April 18, 1974, B1.

67. "A Well Directed Hit," *Amsterdam News*, April 13, 1974, A4. Artist is Melvin Tapley.

68. "A game of giants . . . and midgets," cartoon, *Milwaukee Journal*, April 10, 1974, 1. At least one other athlete has faced the hostility of the commissioner. When Roger Maris broke Ruth's single season record in 1961, he was framed by the news media as the villain, partly because he was breaking a hallowed record also held by Ruth but equally so because his main competition for the record was his more-popular teammate Mickey Mantle. Maris received hate mail

and death threats as he approached the record. Prior to Maris's even breaking the record, Ford Frick, the commissioner, ordered that the record would be accompanied by an asterisk, indicating that it took more games for the new home run record than it had taken for Ruth.

69. Bill Livingston, "Mom's Mop Handle Was First Bat for Young Hank Aaron," *Los Angeles Times*, April 9, 1974, B1.

70. Cleon Walfoort, "Aaron Hardly Knew Who Ruth Was," *Milwaukee Journal*, April 5, 1974, 17. Walfoort was among those columnists who provided his readers with a listed-out comparison of Aaron and Ruth by year, age, and number of home runs.

71. Milton Richman, "Aaron Tires of Insults," *Milwaukee Journal*, May 8, 1973, 16.

72. Norman O. Unger, "'Jim Crow' Starts Work on Aaron," *Chicago Defender*, May 9, 1973, 28.

73. "Editorial: Hank Aaron's Crime," *Washington Afro-American*, May 29, 1973, 4.

74. "What Our Readers Are Saying" (a letter from Brian Boettcher, "Racism Killing Sports?"), *Milwaukee Journal*, April 9, 1973, 1:14. Boettcher's letter was in response to an article previously published, Edward H. Blackwell, "Trends in Sports Are Color Coded."

75. A. S. Doc Young, "Appraising Records . . . ," *Chicago Defender*, August 28, 1973, 24.

76. Chalmers M. Roberts, "Worried Memories of a Baseball Nut," *Washington Post*, July 14, 1973, A18.

77. Jesse Outlar, "They're in Left Field," *Atlanta Journal*, May 9, 1973, C1. Outlar was paraphrasing a similar comment made by Jimmy Cannon about boxer Joe Louis.

78. The *Amsterdam News* did not, nor did the *Milwaukee Sentinel*. In the case of the *Sentinel* and other newspapers, they covered the game but focused on the hitting of 714 as opposed to the pregame festivities and MLK snub.

79. Dave Anderson, "Aaron Ties Babe Ruth with 714th Homer," *New York Times*, April 5, 1974, 43.

80. Bob Oates, "Aaron Catches a Legend," *Los Angeles Times*, April 5, 1974, 11.

81. John Husar, "Aaron Tried Hard to Hide Emotions," *Chicago Tribune*, April 6, 1974, 2:3.

82. Norman O. Unger, *Chicago Defender*, May 19, 1973, 29.

83. Unger, "All Eyes on Hank Aaron, the Greatest," 19.

84. Carl Chamberlain, "Open Letter to Hank Aaron," *Chicago Defender*, September 1, 1973, 7.

85. Vernon Jordan, "Hank Aaron: He's an Authentic National Hero," *Los Angeles Sentinel*, April 18, 1974, A2. Jordan's article was reprinted in the *Washington*

Afro-American; see Vernon Jordan Jr., "Hank Aaron Is Authentic National Hero," *Washington Afro-American*, April 16–20, 1974, 4.

86. Brad Pye Jr., "Hank Aaron Joins MLK as a Legend," April 11, 1974, *Los Angeles Sentinel*, A1, B1.

87. Brad Pye Jr., "Hank Aaron Joins MLK as a Legend," A1, B1.

88. Roy Wilkins, "A Good Thing for America," *Los Angeles Times*, May 16, 1974, B7.

89. Louis Martin, "Hank Aaron Also Cracked Some Ice," *Chicago Defender*, April 13, 1974, 3. "Cracking some ice" refers to a statement made by Shirley Chisolm, who explained she had run for president as a means to crack some ice—in essence, to open up more opportunities and possibilities for black Americans.

90. Editorial, "Hank Overtakes the Sultan," *Milwaukee Journal*, April 10, 1974, 26.

91. Ross Newhan, "No. 715 . . . It Belongs to Aaron and Nobody Else," *Los Angeles Times*, April 9, 1974, 3:1. Newhan noted the attendance was 53,775. In 1973, the Braves finished 11 of 12 National League teams in home attendance. This is in sharp contrast to Bonds's 2007 pursuit, for which the San Francisco Giants sold out game after game as fans packed the stands to be in attendance for any Bonds home run.

15

Arthur Ashe
An Analysis of Newspaper Journalists'
Coverage of *USA Today*'s Outing

PAMELA C. LAUCELLA

Arthur Robert Ashe Jr., the first black man to win a Grand Slam title in men's professional tennis, is known for his 33 singles titles, including the U.S. Open, Wimbledon, and Australian Open, his commitment to civil rights, and a sense of humanity that transcended sport. Ashe remained resolute in advocating equality and progress throughout his life and used his celebrity status for changing perceptions and policy (Leavy 1993). He raised global awareness on such issues as acquired immunodeficiency syndrome (AIDS), apartheid, the treatment of Haitian refugees, and college graduation rates among black athletes. Ashe's indefatigable strength of spirit endured despite the forced revelation of his AIDS diagnosis.

On April 7, 1992, Ashe saw childhood friend Doug Smith, a tennis writer at *USA Today*. Ashe thought he was being interviewed about *A Hard Road to Glory*, his three-volume set on African Americans in sport. Instead, Smith asked him to confirm or deny an anonymous tip that he was HIV-positive. After talking on the telephone to Smith's sports editor, Gene Policinski, Ashe knew he had no choice but to go public with his diagnosis. Policinski viewed Ashe as a public figure, saying, "Anytime a public figure is ill, it's news. . . . We have no special zone of treatment for AIDS. It's a disease, like heart disease. It is news." (Ashe and Rampersad 1993, 8). Policinski (1992) defended the decision in *USA Today*: "There was no question that this was a significant news story," he said. "A great U.S. athlete could be critically ill. If he had cancer or a heart attack—as he did in 1979—it was and is news. AIDS is a disease." (p. A2). Ashe previously confided in close friends and family. Others in the tennis, medical, and journalism communities knew or suspected; however, none betrayed his privacy.

Generally, an outing occurs when a "closeted" celebrity or public figure is exposed in the media as being gay. For Ashe, however, it was different. He described the outing in his memoir *Days of Grace*. While he believed in freedom of speech and freedom of the press, he thought that ethically no one had a right to know. The outcast label or stigma did not bother Ashe. He merely wanted to protect his family's privacy and his busy schedule as a commentator for HBO Sports and ABC Sports and as a writer for the *Washington Post* and *Tennis Magazine* (Price 1994). He chose HBO as his medium and scheduled the press conference at 3:30 on the next day, April 8, 1992. Ashe later compared the outing to a Catholic confession. While he felt relieved, he did not feel "cleansed." Ashe said he was made to feel guilty without even committing a sin. There was stigma about AIDS linked to drug abuse and to homosexual sex. Ashe also felt guilty for maintaining his privacy and initially not telling the public (Ashe and Rampersad 1993). Regardless, Ashe did not resent Smith and merely dismissed it as him doing his job. Smith (1992) wrote a retrospective piece in which he said, "Eight months later, I'm still troubled by the experience" (p. C3).

While scholars have referenced Ashe's outing in articles about ethics and privacy, no study has analyzed newspaper journalists' reactions to *USA Today* or media portrayals of Ashe during this time. Specifically, this research seeks to expand knowledge of the outing, newspapers' coverage of the event, and how journalists framed Ashe in news stories.

This research poses the following questions:

RQ1: How did newspaper journalists portray *USA Today's* outing of Arthur Ashe and AIDS?

RQ2: How did newspaper journalists frame Ashe in their news stories?

Research Methodology

For this study, a qualitative textual analysis was conducted, drawing from Altheide's (1996) work on framing and qualitative analysis. This qualitative method was selected for its depth and breadth of detail and absoluteness (Alasuutari 1995). The sample included articles from April 8, 1992, the day of Ashe's press conference, until April 15, 1992. I used both LexisNexis and ProQuest databases to verify the sample and only included articles with bylines. I analyzed newspapers from two major markets on the East Coast and one regional market in the South for variances in market size and location. The *Richmond Times-Dispatch* is Ashe's hometown newspaper, and the *New York Times* and the *Washington Post* are among the ten daily newspapers with the highest circulations. According to the Audit Bureau of Circulations, the *Times* is the third-largest newspaper, the *Post* is number seven, and the *Times-Dispatch* is number fifty-five (Audit Bureau of Circulations 2006).

Altheide stressed the importance of frames, themes, and discourse in the presenting of information, but the study of frames originated in the 1970s (p. 29). Goffman (1974) used frame analysis to describe individuals' ways of defining events in accordance with the organization of social events and their subjective involvement in those situations (pp. 10–11). Additionally, McCombs and Ghanem (2001) recognized its cognitive components and linked framing with agenda-setting, denoting "mental images of events" as their common ground (p. 67). Maxwell McCombs and Donald Shaw's (1978) pioneering agenda-setting study showed that the topics covered most frequently in news stories are those designated the most pressing among audience members. According to McCombs and Shaw, "Readers learn not only about a given issue, but also how much importance to attach to that issue from the amount of information in a news story and its position" (p. 176). Frames both create and restrict meaning (Tuchman 1978). They make the world seem natural and influence how we perceive events, individuals, and the society in which they coexist (Gitlin 1980). Gaye Tuchman (1978) believes "news is a window of the world" (p. 1) and that, like a picture or window frame, news frames offer a selective vista of a scene and a lens for the exploration and understanding of events (p. 29). Framing defines events and issues and lays out terms for deliberation (Tankard 2001). Todd Gitlin called the media "mobile spotlights" that actively mirror society and select what they perceive as important (1980, p. 49). The story is a choice since it adopts a frame and then highlights and enhances certain material and downplays other information deemed as less newsworthy. According to Birrell and McDonald (2000), "Stories are always presented within frames, and these frames guide and limit public understandings of events and personalities" (p. 6).

Communicators use framing judgments in word choice and selection decisions (Entman 1993). How the media cover an event and issue affects how the public perceives it (Hardin and Zuegner 2003). Facts take on meaning by being rooted in a frame or story that organizes them in a cohesive way (Gamson 1989). Journalists' use of language and choice of words create an image based upon the values of those in dominant positions in society, and according to sociologist Michael Messner (1988) they afford "frameworks of meaning which . . . selectively interpret not only the athletic events themselves but also the controversies and problems surrounding the events" (p. 205). The journalists and their ability to define the situation is a vital element in social power, and these definitions, the themes and discourse we use, and how we frame the experience are key in determining what an audience believes is true.

This research will offer an analysis of one event and will show similarities and variances between journalists at three publications. It will use Altheide's (1996) definition of frames as the "focus, a parameter or boundary, for discussing a particular event" (p. 31). The key stages are data collection and analysis. Next, I categorized elements and wrote summaries and comparisons. This stage involved reading, sorting, and studying documents to understand themes and to create frames. The final stage was the integration of findings with interpretation (Altheide 1996). This entire process of qualitative media analysis will elucidate journalists' perceptions of Ashe, the outing, and AIDS as well as the articles' potential significance in terms of information provided and perspectives conveyed.

The AIDS Crisis

HIV/AIDS became a worldwide public health challenge that has afflicted black Americans disproportionately more greatly than white Americans. In 2005, in the United States, 12,689 white Americans and 22,030 black Americans were diagnosed with AIDS (CDC 2005). The crisis was markedly worse on the continent of Africa. At one point, six Africans contracted HIV every minute. A Kaiser Family Foundation survey found that 72 percent of Americans obtain most of their information on HIV/AIDS from the media (Brodie, M., et al. 2004). Media attention in the United States has focused on public opinion and publicity surrounding key admissions from individuals like "Magic" Johnson and Arthur Ashe. Effects of announcements and ensuing media coverage of public figures could potentially prevent risky behaviors by the general public. Whether it is a change in attitude about AIDS (recognizing everyone is susceptible, understanding the disease) or a change in behavior (e.g., practicing safe sex, becoming monogamous, getting tested), announcements from public figures have been shown to help decrease the stigma and increase awareness (Hollander 1993; Tesoriero and Sorin 1992; Langer et al. 1992).

Johnson influenced public opinion after his announcement in 1991. Early media reports linked the disease to the gay community, especially after actor Rock Hudson's death to AIDS in 1985 (Albert 1989; Jelen and Wilcox 1992; Kinsella 1989; Le Poire et al. 1990; Pollock, Lillie, and Vittes 1993; Pryor et al. 1989; Shilts 1987; Stipp and Kerr 1989). Johnson was viewed as the epitome of heterosexuality as an athlete and sports celebrity, and the "heterosexual symbolism" of his message shifted values and opinions about the disease (Pollock 1994). On foxsports.com, Elliott Kalb (2006) called the announcement that Johnson had HIV "the day Magic Johnson changed the world" and praised the athlete's courage and commitment to raising money and awareness of HIV and AIDS. Coverage of Johnson's announcement composed 15 percent of stories about HIV/AIDS in 1992 (Brodie, M., et al. 2004). AIDS has become a "narrated disease," with language playing a key role in stories of healing and damage (Dawes 1995). It has been discussed in relation to race, media coverage, and privacy. This study examines how newspapers covered Ashe from two perspectives—as a media subject and as a human with AIDS.

Ashe as an Activist Athlete

Ashe was born in Richmond on July 10, 1943, and endured discrimination firsthand in a segregated South. Unable to play tennis on "whites only" tennis courts, Ashe used his life experiences for personal growth and change. *Time* magazine called Ashe a "paradigm of understated reason and elegance" (Witteman 1993, 70). He learned this from father Arthur Sr., who instilled in him the importance of reputation and compassion. Ashe's mother, Mattie, died before his seventh birthday. Ashe was close to his father, who was a policeman and ran a playground and park for African Americans. Dr. Robert Walker Johnson of Lynchburg, Virginia, was also one of Ashe's mentors, and through his guidance the tennis racquet became his "rod and staff" (Ashe and Rampersad 1993, 128). He sponsored Ashe and enabled him to play tennis in tournaments nationwide. Ashe was the first African American to win the NCAA singles crown as a junior at UCLA and graduated college in 1966. In 1968, he won the U.S. Open while still a lieutenant in the U.S. Army. Ashe also won the Australian Open in 1970 and Wimbledon in 1975. Ashe was the first black man to win a Grand Slam title. Althea Gibson held this honor for women with her victory in 1956 at the French championships.

Ashe spoke publicly for the first time about race and politics after the 1968 assassinations of Martin Luther King Jr. and Robert F. Kennedy. While Ashe praised Jackie Robinson and Bill Russell as pioneering black athletes in professional baseball and basketball respectively (Ashe and Rampersad 1993), he believed it was his duty to make a difference in his community, state, country, and world. According to Ashe, he was not for "black or white, nor even for the United States of America, but for the whole of humanity" (Ashe and Rampersad 1993, 153). While Ashe professed an all-inclusive philosophy, race became the center of his identity as a black man in a white man's sport (Djata 2006). He became first black man to win the U.S. Open and Wimbledon and the first to play for the U.S. Davis Cup team (Carter 2005). He was often identified in marked language like

"American Negro," "first black male," and "black athlete." Romanian player Ilie Nastase even called him "Negroni." Ashe dismissed his friend's demeanor as tactless (Ashe and Deford 1975, 99).

Ashe retired from tennis in 1979 after suffering his first heart attack. Subsequently, he had two heart bypass operations in 1979 and 1983, and when he was admitted to the hospital for brain surgery in 1988, it was discovered he had AIDS. A blood transfusion from the second bypass surgery was the suspected cause since HIV testing for donated blood did not begin until 1985 (La Prensa San Diego 2003; Ashe and Rampersad 1993; Schwartz n.d.). According to Ashe, "From what we get, we can make a living; what we give, however, makes a life" (Ashe and Rampersad 1993, 196). Ashe clearly saw the "bigger picture" (Heller 2006). He helped form the Ashe-Bollettieri Cities tennis program, the Safe Passage Foundation, the Athletes Career Connection, the Arthur Ashe Institute for Urban Health, and the Ashe Foundation for the Defeat of AIDS.

Ashe also took a strong stance against South African apartheid. He persevered in obtaining a South African visa and played in the 1973 South African Open (and was also there in 1974, 1975, 1977). He insisted that his matches be desegregated, so fans could see a free black man. While the black press and activists criticized his stance, Ashe did things his way (Garber 2003). Later, Ashe changed his position and joined the boycott against South African sports after being told to buy tickets from an "Africans only" counter (Lapchick n.d.). According to Richard Lapchick, who heads the Institute for Diversity and Ethics in Sport, "He taught me the power of being able to say that you have been wrong and changing direction. . . . He never stopped protesting injustice in America, South Africa, Haiti, or anywhere else people were oppressed" (Lapchick n.d.). Ashe befriended South African president Nelson Mandela and marched in protest against apartheid and the American treatment of Haitian refugees (and was arrested twice). He was one of the founders of Artists and Athletes against Apartheid with actor and activist Harry Belafonte. He also joined TransAfrica, which focused on the U.S. policies towards Africa and the Caribbean islands (Ashe and Rampersad 1993; Carter 2005; "Grand Slam" 1993; Moore 1992; Roach 2005).

Additionally, Ashe was committed to improving graduation rates among black athletes. He supported higher academic standards for athletes with Proposition 42, siding with Pennsylvania State football coach Joe Paterno over basketball coaches John Thompson and John Chaney of Georgetown and Temple, respectively. Ashe received an honorary degree from Princeton, turned down Yale to teach at Florida Memorial College, and also supported the United Negro College Fund. He created the African American Athletic Association (AAAA), which mentored student-athletes of color and helped them find jobs. In 1992 alone, he won the Helen Hayes Award, the AIDS Leadership Award of the Harvard AIDS Institute, the American Sportscasters Association Sports Legend Award, and *Sports Illustrated*'s "Sportsman of the Year" (Ashe and Rampersad 1993; Hawkins 1995). That same year, Ashe was forced to acknowledge that he had AIDS.

Discussion and Findings: Media Portrayal of the Outing

Overall, the media response to the USA *Today* story was overwhelmingly favorable to Ashe. USA *Today* received more than seven hundred letters with approximately 95 percent opposing Policinski's actions. Journalists Ellen Goodman of the *Boston Globe*, syndicated columnist DeWayne Wickham, Michael Olesker of the *Baltimore Sun*, Jonathan Yardley of the *Washington Post*, and Raymond R. Coffee of the *Chicago Sun-Times* all opposed USA *Today*'s decision (Ashe and Rampersad 1993). Lance Morrow of *Time* wrote, "Everyone is not fair game to be dragged onstage for involuntary exposure.... That Arthur Ashe is a 'public figure' whom people recognize as he walks down the street is precisely the best argument for any decent human being's not informing the whole world that the man has AIDS" (1992). Joan Ryan of *Sporting News* asked, "Was the public interest served in pursuing the story? In withholding it, would the editors have betrayed their readers' right to know? The answer, on both counts, is no" (1992, 213, 216). William C. Rhoden (1992b) of the *New York Times* believed the media war sparked competition that forces reporters to cover more intimate stories. Fred Bruning of *Maclean's* supported the decision based on journalists' role as "custodians of the facts." "We can lament the terrible turn of events that threaten the life of so fine a man as Arthur Ashe but we do not honor him—or the freedom he championed—by confusing sympathy with self-censorship," wrote Bruning (1992, 13).

The journalists from the *Richmond Times-Dispatch* and the *Washington Post* especially disparaged Policinski and the outing. This was not a sports story—it was a story about Ashe and a story about privacy and betrayal. A subplot was AIDS, however, it was not entirely a primary theme. Newspapers provided reactions from other journalists, pundits, and tennis players, which strongly backed Ashe. From Stan Smith and Cliff Drysdale to Billie Jean King, Chris Evert, and Tracy Austin, all revered and respected Ashe. Most journalists also admired Ashe and did not write detached, fact-based articles. While some used the outing as a means to discuss concerns about journalism, their roles as journalists, and ethics in the profession, more wrote about Ashe's contributions to tennis, the United States, and the world. While journalists noted the importance of First Amendment freedoms, most said they would not have "ratted" on Ashe nor forced him to divulge personal details about his illness. Journalists exhibited sympathy, especially the ones who knew him personally like Michael Wilbon of the *Washington Post*, Bill Rhoden of the *New York Times*, and Bob Lipper and Bill Millsaps of the *Richmond Times-Dispatch*. Conversely, Michael Freeman in the *Washington Post* and Bill Rhoden in the *New York Times* wrote fact-based, detached accounts of the press conference and key details about the outing.

Many journalists grappled with their varying roles as watchdog and public servant while striving to maintain morals and ethics. The ones who did not support the outing rationalized that Ashe was no longer a current athlete and that he sought to live a private life with Jeanne and daughter Camera, who was five. Writers like Ray McAllister of the *Times-Dispatch*, Michael Freeman of the *Post*, and William C. Rhoden and Anna Quindlen of the *Times* tried to present both sides for balance, but many journalists merely took a stance against the outing and explained why. Journalists like Richard Cohen of the *Post* and Bruce Potter and Douglas Durden of the *Times-Dispatch* referenced news stories about the extramarital affairs of politicians such as President Bill Clinton and U.S. senators Gary Hart and Chuck Robb. Most writers mentioned that the Los Angeles Lakers' "Magic" Johnson was the first prominent athlete to publicly announce he had AIDS, five months prior to Ashe. Some used Johnson and Ashe as a platform for promoting AIDS education and awareness. A few gave details about blood-screening tests and AIDS statistics and trends. Robin Herman of the *Post*, Anna Barron Billingsley, Olivia Winslow, and Beverly Orndorff of the *Times-Dispatch*, and Kathleen M. Berry of the *Times* all focused on health issues.

All journalists lauded Ashe as an athlete and individual and stressed that his achievements transcended tennis. They viewed him as an important, pioneering tennis player and a dedicated family man who spoke his mind freely and exhibited integrity, class, and grace. Race was not an issue in the stories, however, most noted the significance of Ashe as the first black man to win a Grand Slam event. This was the only marked language. While Ashe devoted an entire chapter to race in his memoir and freely discussed it throughout his life, journalists did not stereotype him or question details on how he contracted AIDS.

Berkow, Rhoden, Lorge, Lipper, McAllister, Wilbon, Freeman, Kornheiser, and Ashe himself mentioned wife Jeanne Moutoussamy-Ashe and daughter Camera. The *Times-Dispatch* included references or quotes from his stepmother, Lorraine Ashe; his aunt Dorothy Brown; his uncle Horace; and his tenth-grade geometry teacher, Ruth E. Richardson. In addition to intimate family coverage, other topics included competition for stories, forcing journalists to delve into more personal and provocative issues.

As far as the total number of stories, the *Richmond Times-Dispatch* had the most with thirteen, the *Washington Post* had nine, and the *New York Times* had seven. Of the twenty-nine stories, nine female journalists (including two on coauthored pieces) contributed to the sample. Most women, however, wrote on AIDS rather than the Ashe angle. The Richmond stories took on more personal frames and had a local angle despite Ashe's stature globally. The *Washington Post* stories, especially Wilbon's and Kornheiser's, praised Ashe and set his feats in historical context. The *New York Times* had the fewest stories, yet Berkow and Lipsyte's articles effectively captured Ashe's personality, perspectives, and plight.

There was ambivalence in journalists' coverage of the outing, since some believed *USA Today* should have pursued the story while others questioned the decision. Whether the press was viewed in an adversarial role or as a public servant, journalists exhibited mixed reactions. *Times-Dispatch* columnist Bob Lipper (1992) called Ashe's contraction of AIDS "terribly and capriciously unfair" yet mentioned in passing *USA Today's* tip (p. D1). At the other end of the spectrum, Jonathan Yardley (1992) of the *Washington Post* used a stern, caustic tone to reprimand journalists and specifically *USA Today*. He discussed double standards for public figures and journalists and cited editor Reid Beddow as an example. Beddow died from AIDS without being outed by fellow journalists. Yardley wrote, "He [Ashe] was bullied into his public statement" and said the newspaper "went after the story with all the fury of a cur attacking a T-bone because the story had sensational potential" (p. C2). He called Policinski self-righteous and his rationale for reporting an illness cold. Yardley concluded, "That he [Ashe] responded so civilly and forthrightly to the threat of exposure that *USA Today* held over him is still further evidence of his dignity and character. These qualities stand in stark and revealing contrast to the people who so cynically and cruelly used him" (p. C2). Richard Cohen of the *Post* wrote, "Nothing in *USA Today's* explanation of why it pursued the Ashe story is convincing," (p. A27). While Cohen believed decisions depend on circumstances, he wrote, "We balance the pain we inflict against the certainty that the public has a stake and has to be informed. When Arthur Ashe appeared before the cameras and announced he was HIV positive, anyone could see the pain. What was not so clear is why we had to know" (p. A27).

Kornheiser focused on Ashe rather than the outing yet mentioned Doug Smith in his conclusion. "I know how hard it was for Doug to tell Arthur that his paper was working on this story," said Kornheiser. "I know Doug took that unhappy responsibility, feeling that if questions had to be asked, if there was no way to stop them, they would be better coming from a friend" (p. F1). Rhoden's article in the *Times* began with Ashe's press conference. He did not address Smith nor Policinski until the middle of the article but failed to pass judgment. Rhoden mainly detailed the facts of

Ashe's telephone conversation with Policinski after meeting with Smith. Since Ashe offered no confirmation, Policinski said he would not "print unconfirmed stories from unattributed sources" yet would pursue the story (p. B9).

Lipsyte, on the other hand, showed deep sympathy. He wrote that Ashe would no longer be "free to act and react without being judged and assaulted by yet another broadside of other people's assumptions and demands" (p. B13). Lipsyte empathized since he had battled cancer and maintained his privacy. Nevertheless, Lipsyte did not even mention Policinski or USA Today. Lorge discussed Ashe's appreciation for journalists' earlier "conspiracy of compassion" to withhold his illness from the public. He discussed the journalist-source relationship and noted that tennis had an "insular" community in the 1960s and 1970s (1992, 358). The 1990s, however, were different. Quindlen (1992) noted the challenges of journalists' jobs, from deadline pressure to covering controversial topics and grappling with roles of person vs. reporter. "Naming rape victims. Outing gay people. The candidate's sex life. The candidate's drug use. Editors are making decisions they have never made before, on deadline, with only hours to spare, with competitors breathing down their necks," she wrote (p. 168). While Quindlen said she would have withheld the information, she covered the story from the journalists' perspective and posed numerous questions and ideas for contemplation. "We tell people what we think they need to know. We hurt people, sometimes without reason. Sometimes we are kind," she wrote. "Arthur Ashe has already begun to turn his exposure into education. I hope we manage to do the same" (p. 168).

Berkow started with imagery of the press conference, focusing on wife Jeanne as her husband of fifteen years addressed the public. With little emotion, Ashe said, "'I have known since the time of my brain surgery in September 1988 that I have AIDS" (p. B9). Lawrence Altman of the Times led with Ashe's loss of feeling in his right hand, which subsequently led him to a brain surgeon where he discovered he had AIDS. News of the outing appeared only in the sixth paragraph. Ross Mackenzie of the Times-Dispatch mentioned the outing and how Ashe's life changed in the first paragraph. He showed empathy in revealing his struggle with a life-threatening disease (no details). "I view Arthur Ashe's predicament with particular sympathy and particular dismay," he wrote (p. 10). As far as Ashe's comment about being exposed, he wrote, "His bitterness is perhaps properly directed at the individual. It is improperly directed at the press. The press was doing its job" (p. 10). Like other journalists siding with freedom of the press, he argued, "Arthur Ashe is news—whether the news about him has to do with his views on tennis and apartheid, or with his heart condition and (now) his invasion by the virus called AIDS" (p. 10). Mackenzie did not mention USA Today nor Smith by name.

Paul Woody in the Times-Dispatch, on the other hand, sided with Ashe as far as privacy. He wrote, "Yesterday, Ashe told the world of his illness. And he did it entirely against his will" (p. 25). Woody mentioned USA Today but not Policinski or Smith. He just focused on how Ashe overcame adversity throughout his life (p. 25). Ray McAllister was the only journalist to discuss the true definition of the term "outed." He began, "Arthur Ashe, to put a '90s spin on an '80s word, has been 'outed.' That's exactly it. 'Outed'" (p. B1). While he criticized USA Today, he wrote, "THE USA TODAY POSITION is not atypical in the news business: A public figure who falls ill is news" (p. B1). McAllister interviewed a sports editor, who would have had a difficult time with the decision, and Robert Haiman of the Poynter Institute for Media Studies, who called it a "tough call" (McAllister, p. B1). McAllister ended by saying the dilemma was not over Ashe's status as a public figure. "The difficulty is that Ashe is such a very good human being . . . and that is such a very bad thing to happen to him . . . and society still tends to make it even worse," he said. "Only one good thing can come of it. And that is, we begin dealing better with AIDS victims . . . and we start with Ashe and his family" (p. B1).

Bruce Potter, a political writer for the Times-Dispatch, believed the public's right to know only goes so far. "Arthur Ashe is a public figure. He was a star tennis player. He is a role model, an author and an advocate for a variety of worthy causes," he wrote. "But in none of these roles was it important or necessary for us to know he has the AIDS virus" (p. 15). He distinguished Ashe from President Clinton and other politicians since he had no desire to seek or hold public office. Politicians spend public money and the public entrusts politicians with their lives, so they should have stricter standards. He credited Smith towards the end of the story, however, since he asked Ashe before writing a story.

Durden noted that Ashe resented the press rather than feeling bitterness toward AIDS. While Durden named Policinski, he did not detail the outing. He interviewed Ted J. Smith, a mass communications professor at Virginia Commonwealth University, who contended that Ashe's privacy should have been observed on three grounds. Smith believes someone does not relinquish basic human rights as a public figure, and Ashe's desire for privacy therefore should have been respected. Smith also dismissed the justification of the public's right to know since Ashe's illness was not vital as public knowledge. Smith also noted the hypocrisy of such a story started by an unnamed source.

Howard Kurtz of the *Post* took a different stance and was sympathetic toward the other newspaper. "USA *Today* found itself in the uncomfortable position yesterday of being blamed by tennis star Arthur Ashe for forcing him to disclose that he has the AIDS virus," wrote Kurtz (p. C1). He noted that Smith and Ashe were childhood friends and that Policinski invited Ashe to write a column for the newspaper. Michael Freeman of the *Post* questioned Ashe's belief that the transfusion caused AIDS. While Freeman included Ashe's statement of cause, he included a statement of dispute from Dr. Hutchinson, who performed the 1983 surgery. Hutchinson would not confirm whether blood was used in the surgery. Officials at St. Luke's Hospital, where Ashe had the transfusion, also refused to comment (Altman 1992, B15). Altman's article also created doubt about Ashe's assertion of how he contracted AIDS.

As noted earlier, Ashe occasionally wrote columns for the *Post* and he discussed the outing on April 12, 1992. He began by discussing how he and *Newsweek* writer Frank Deford spent time together before the press conference. He told his good friend, "I'm pissed off that someone would rat on me, but I'm even more angered that I would have to lie to protect my privacy" (p. D1). While Ashe understood the watchdog role of the press, he did not want to be "sacrificed for the sake of the public's right to know" (p. D1). Ashe's statement from the *Post* article was dramatic: "Going public with a disease such as AIDS is akin to telling the world in 1900 that you have leprosy," he wrote (p. D1). He also called it "mysterious, so daunting and so potent. So final" (p. D1). While AIDS activists pressured Ashe to get involved, he sought to get involved only in "efforts to educate, clarify and dispel" (p. D1).

Michael Wilbon wrote about the impact of the respective diagnoses of "Magic" Johnson and Arthur Ashe. "It's gotten to the point where we're scared to pick up the phone or turn on the news. First Magic, now Arthur. Who's next? AIDS has become to the '90s what assassination was in the '60s," Wilbon wrote (p. D1). Bob Lipper called AIDS "insidious" and "a killer" (p. D1). He said that AIDS did not discriminate. He personalized AIDS by adding faces to the disease and the randomness and divergent circumstances. Paul Woody asked, "What do you do when you go from being Arthur Ashe, former tennis star, to Arthur Ashe, AIDS patient and AIDS victim?" (p. 25). With no detail of the disease, Woody simply labeled Ashe. It was apparent that in the early 1990s, there were still stigmas. McAllister called it "no ordinary disease" (p. B1), while Lipsyte compared it to cancer. Many writers listed the cause of AIDS in Ashe's case. Altman listed AIDS statistics in his article, writing that 214,000 Americans reported having AIDS as of March 1, 1992, and that only 2 percent of cases contracted AIDS from a blood transfusion (p. B15).

Orndorff quoted American Red Cross spokeswoman Liz Hall, who said, "More people are killed by lightning or die from a penicillin reaction than get the AIDS virus from a transfusion" (p. D6). Like Freeman's article, this calls into question how Ashe contracted AIDS. The article, however, included AIDS facts, how people contract HIV, and AIDS hotline numbers. Herman discussed the pre-1985 and post-1985 situations and the importance of HIV blood screening (p. A1). Winslow specifically discussed AIDS trends in Virginia and quoted the executive director of Central Virginia AIDS Services and Education and his concerns on how it impacts the black community. The article also noted that 22.2 percent of HIV cases are women and protection is vital. Winslow added that she hoped Ashe's admission created dialogue that would hopefully promote prevention and AIDS awareness and education (p. A1). According to Billingsley, there were "inadequate resources" to deal with AIDS. Whether it's increased testing or treatment facilities, she said, more services and resources were needed (p. 1). Surprisingly, no journalist mentioned that Jeanne and Camera had HIV tests and they came back negative.

A *People* magazine reporter asked Ashe whether AIDS was the heaviest burden for him. "You're not going to believe this," he responded, "but being black is the greatest burden I've had to bear. . . . Race has always been my biggest burden. Having to live as a minority in America. Even now it continues to feel like an extra weight tied around me" (Ashe and Rampersad 1993, 139). Ashe thought he was accepted due to racial tipping, where blacks are accepted if they constitute a small percentage or token of people in a group. And according to Djata (2006), "Playing tennis, being articulate (in a manner acceptable to whites), and being soft-spoken made Ashe a prime candidate to be viewed in a way that boxer Muhammad Ali or other outspoken black athletes or visible personalities could not be viewed, although they may have been just as articulate" (p. 55).

Ashe voiced concerns over political issues, racism, and social concerns throughout his life. Conversely, Althea Gibson remained silent and did not view herself as a racially conscious person. Michael Jordan also received criticism for not speaking out on political and social issues. Black athletes face added pressure to participate in discourse since American mainstream media has limited divergent voices. Many fear they will lose endorsements or public support if they are vocal. Black athletes also face pressure to give back to the black community. Ashe discovered French tennis star Yannick Noah in Cameroon and was also a role model for current American player James Blake. Said Blake, "I think being African American, I owe him a great debt of gratitude for being able to deal with the pressures and situations. . . . We are so fortunate today to have had him as that role model, as that person to do that, to really break the color barrier in tennis and be such a great champion" (United States Olympic Committee 2004).

According to Ashe, there was "absolutely no escape from race" in his life (Ashe and Rampersad 1993, 145). Even though AIDS should be a medical and scientific issue, race overshadowed it since the disease emerged as a disease of drug users, gays, and people of color (Haitians first and then sub-Saharan Africans). Due to its link to Africa, black Americans and Africans felt stigmatized by an image of Africa that was ignorant and misinformed. In fact, Austin (1989) found that racist messages appear in mainstream American media reports of AIDS in Africa. She found the characters to include the "philandering urban male," "the female prostitute," "the victimized wife," and the "male homosexual" (p. 129). The setting is usually the African city within black Africa and the urban center in the United States within white society.

After Ashe's death on February 6, 1993, flags flew at half-staff in Virginia. Ashe was the first athlete to lie in state at Virginia's executive mansion in Richmond, once the capital of the Confederacy. L. Douglas Wilder (former governor of Virginia and now mayor of Richmond), broadcaster Bryant Gumbel, former Atlanta mayor Andrew Young, journalist Frank Deford, and tennis players Yannick Noah, Donald Dell, Stan Smith, and Charlie Pasarell all celebrated Ashe's life with his wife, Jeannie, daughter, Camera, and many others. A monument to Ashe lies in Richmond on Monument Avenue with statues of Confederate war heroes Stonewall Jackson, Robert E. Lee, Jefferson Davis, and J. E. B. Stuart. In 1996, sculptor Paul DiPasquale erected a twelve-foot bronze statue of Ashe in tennis gear, holding books in one hand and a tennis racquet in the other. The structure symbolizes Ashe's commitment to making a difference not only as an athlete but as a compassionate individual and humanitarian (Price 1994; Ashe and Rampersad 1993; CNN 1996; Leavy 1993; Roach 2003; Williams 1993).

Conclusion and Opportunities for Research

According to James H. Frey and D. Stanley Eitzen (1991), sports are a microcosm of society and the media's attention to sports molds images and perceptions (pp. 503, 510). Ashe himself talked about the importance of studying sports and especially sports history. He stressed that historians should study sports despite "academic snobbery and timidity" (Ashe and Rampersad 1993, 195). By studying an event like the Ashe outing, we can learn more about the press and its role in relaying key information to the public and more about one of the key athletes in sports history. While this pilot study was not free from bias due to its interpretive nature and limited sample, it helped reveal the prominent frames emerging from primary newspaper documents during the week Ashe publicly revealed he had AIDS. Additionally, it offered insight into how journalists portrayed Ashe, the USA Today outing, and AIDS. By analyzing language, tone, inclusions, and exclusions, we can grasp the nuances of the journalists' works while seeking to understand the implications of their views for readers and their pictures of reality.

This research is intended to serve as a foundation for future studies, which could expand the sample with the *Los Angeles Times* for West Coast perspectives or the *Chicago Tribune* from the Midwest. The study could also increase its longitudinal reach by analyzing newspapers two weeks before the outing and two weeks after the outing. Additionally, it would be interesting to investigate coverage around Ashe's death to see how journalists framed him later. Triangulation of research also would add to its efficacy. Adding in-depth interviews of journalists who covered Ashe or personal stories from family, friends, and colleagues would supplement the texts. Another related study could analyze press treatment of Ashe's trips to South Africa in the 1970s.

This study revealed the emotion surrounding such issues as privacy and AIDS. It showed just one example of difficult decisions journalists make and the diverse roles they hold in informing the public. While there was no clear-cut answer on the outing, the study shows the complexities of media issues. For journalists, the outing shows the importance of ethical decision-making in selecting and pursuing stories. In pursuing stories involving privacy, journalists need to fully consider their sources and the nature of their preferences, the significance and context of the issue and the information, and whether disclosure will serve the public good. While the outing was a two-sided betrayal for Ashe since Smith was a friend and Ashe was a member of the media, he became openly involved in AIDS activism. His Arthur Ashe Foundation for the Defeat of AIDS Inc. raised $5 million, and a $1 million endowment was created at New York Hospital–Cornell Medical Center where he was treated (Ashe Foundation for Defeat of AIDS). Additionally, while his situation was different from Johnson's (Johnson contracted AIDS from sex and willingly disclosed it), cases of public figures can help increase AIDS education and public awareness. This was especially important during the 1990s, as the study showed a lack of knowledge about AIDS. A few writers discussed statistics and causes, yet there was a dearth of AIDS awareness and education. Writers did not discuss treatments, challenges, implications, or historical and long-standing significance. While drawing attention to AIDS is positive, the media's discussion of ordinary citizens battling the disease—men, women, and children from all ethnic and racial backgrounds—will further expand public knowledge.

This study found that, surprisingly, media coverage of Ashe's outing did not reinforce racial stereotypes. While writers mentioned that Ashe was the first black man to win a Grand Slam tournament, this was the only mention of race. There was no racially marked language otherwise. This could indicate progress, or it could indicate denial since Ashe was accepted by everyone due to his intellect, demeanor, diverse interests, and success on and off the tennis court. The research especially reinforced Ashe's character and impact. While journalists did not detail the outing or information on AIDS, they effectively captured Ashe's life perspectives and spirit. Journalists clearly indicated that Ashe was a free and independent thinker by incorporating themes of tolerance, altruism, activism, and strength. Ashe was a pioneer on the tennis court, yet he did not want to be known or remembered as a tennis player or athlete. He used sports as a platform for growth and progress and left a legacy for all to emulate.

REFERENCES

Alasuutari, P. 1995. *Researching Culture: Qualitative Methods and Cultural Studies.* London: Sage.

Albert, E. 1989. "AIDS and the Press: The Creation and Transformation of a Social Problem." In *Images of Issues*, edited by J. Best. New York: Aldine De Gruyter.

Allen, E. W. 1922. "The Social Value of a Code of Ethics for Journalists." *Annals of the American Academy of Political and Social Science* 101 (May): 170–79.

Altheide, D. L. 1996. *Qualitative Media Analysis*. Vol. 38, *Qualitative Research Methods*. Thousand Oaks CA: Sage.

Altman, L. K. 1992. "Ashe Received a Transfusion before Blood Supply Was Tested for H.I.V." *New York Times*, April 9, B15.

Arthur Ashe Website. n.d. "Biography (page 2)." Accessed March 19, 2006. http://web.archive.org/web/20070823181910/http://www.cmgworldwide.com/sports/ashe/about/bio2.htm.

Ashe, A. 1992. "Secondary Assault of AIDS Spells the Public End to a Private Agenda." *The Washington Post*, April 12, D1.

Ashe, A., and F. Deford. 1975. *Arthur Ashe: Portrait in Motion*. Boston: Houghton Mifflin.

Ashe, A., and A. Rampersad. 1993. *Days of Grace: A Memoir*. New York: Ballantine Books.

"Ashe Foundation for Defeat of AIDS Will Close." 1995. *Jet* 87, no. 13 (February 6).

Audit Bureau of Circulations. "Top 200 Newspapers by Largest Reported Circulation." Accessed January 31, 2007. http://web.archive.org/web/20070201233133/http://www.accessabc.com/reader/top150.htm.

Austin, S. B. 1989. "AIDS and Africa: United States Media and Racist Fantasy." *Cultural Critique* 14: 129–52.

Barney, R. K. 1985. "Beyond Physical Performance: Theoretical Criteria: Ideals in the Appraisal of Sport Heroes." In *Proceedings and Newsletter of the North American Society for Sport History*, 45–47.

Bates, Stephen. 1995. *Realigning Journalism with Democracy: The Hutchins Commission, Its Times, and Ours*. Washington DC: The Annenberg Washington Program in Communications Policy Studies of Northwestern University. Accessed March 19, 2006. http://www.annenberg.northwestern.edu/pubs/hutchins/hutch01.htm.

Bennett, L. W. 2005. *News: The Politics of Illusion*, 6th ed. New York: Pearson.

Berkow, I. 1992. "Sports of the Times. Ashe: A Pawn of History." *New York Times*, April 9, B9.

Berry, K. M. 1992. "The Business of Tracking Deadly Viruses." *New York Times*, April 12, 120.

Billingsley, A. B. 1992. "Ashe Reaction Highlights Scarce Resources." *Richmond Times Dispatch*, April 9, 1.

Birrell, S., and M. G. McDonald. 2000. "Reading Sport, Articulating Power Lines: An Introduction." In *Reading Sport: Critical Essays on Power and Representation*, edited by S. Birrell and M. G. McDonald. Boston: Northeastern University Press.

Brennan, C. 1992. "Ashe Told Friends in '88; Stan Smith Says Media Forced Public Disclosure." *Washington Post*, April 9, D1.

Brodie, M., E. Hamel, L. A. Brady, J. Kates, and D. E. Altman. 2004. "AIDS at 21: Media Coverage of the HIV Epidemic 1981–2002." *Columbia Journalism Review* 42, no. 6: A1–8.

Bruning, F. 1992. "How a Private Citizen Lost His Privacy Rights." *Maclean's* 105, no. 18 (May 4): 13.

Carter, B. n.d. *Sportscentury Biography: Ashe's Impact Reached Far beyond the Court.* ESPN Classic website. Accessed June 9, 2005. http://espn.go.com/classic /biography/s/Ashe_Arthur.html.

Centers for Disease Control and Protection. 2005. "Basic Statistics." Center for Disease Control and Protection Home Page. Accessed April 17, 2015. http:// web.archive.org/web/20060206163000/http://www.cdc.gov/hiv/topics /surveillance/basic.htm#aidsrace.

Coakley, J. 2004. *Sports in Society: Issues and Controversies.* 8th ed. Boston: McGraw Hill.

Cohen, R. 1992. "Did We Have to Know?" *Washington Post*, April 10, A27.

Coleman, R. 2003. "Race and Ethical Reasoning: The Importance of Race to Journalistic Decision Making." *Journalism & Mass Communication Quarterly* 80, no. 2: 295–310.

Dawes, J. 1995. "Narrating Disease: AIDS, Consent, and the Ethics of Representation." *Social Text* 43: 27–44.

Djata, S. 2006. *Blacks at the Net: Black Achievement in the History of Tennis*, Vol. 1. Syracuse NY: Syracuse University Press.

Domke, D. 2001. "The Press, Race Relations, and Social Change." *Journal of Communication* 51, no. 2: 317–44.

Douglass, F. 1857. "West India Emancipation." Speech presented in Canandaigua NY on August 3. Accessed March 27, 2007. http://www.blackpast.org /?q=1857-frederick-douglass-if-there-no-struggle-there-no-progress.

Du Bois, W. E. B. (1903) 1989. *The Souls of Black Folk*. New York: Bantam Books.

Durden, D. 1992. "VCU Professor Assails Press Intrusion on Ashe's Privacy." *Richmond Times-Dispatch*, April 10, D13.

Edwards, H. 1973. *Sociology of Sport*. Homewood IL: Dorsey.

Entine, J. 2000. *Taboo: Why Black Athletes Dominate Sports and Why We're Afraid to Talk about It*. New York: Public Affairs.

Entman, R. M. 1991. "Framing U.S. Coverage of International News: Contrasts in Narratives of the KAL and Iran Air Incidents." *Journal of Communication* 41, no. 4: 6–27.

———. 1993. "Framing: Toward Clarification of a Fractured Paradigm." *Journal of Communication* 43, no. 4: 51–58.

Entman, R. M., and A. Rojecki. 2000. *The Black Image in the White Mind: Media and Race in America*. Chicago: The University of Chicago Press.

Evans, A. 1985. "Joe Louis as a Key Functionary: White Reactions toward a Black Champion." *Journal of Black Studies* 16, no. 1: 95–111.

Evans, A. S., Jr. 1997. "Blacks as Key Functionaries: A Study of Racial Stratification in Professional Sport." *Journal of Black Studies* 28, no. 1: 43–59.

"Even after Death, Arthur Ashe Topples Another Barrier." 1996. CNN. July 11. Accessed March 23, 2007. http://web.archive.org/web/20070323181323/http://www.cnn.com/US/9607/11/ashe.

Farmer, R. 1992. "Revered, Respected, Honored." *Richmond Time-Dispatch*, April 9, D4.

Finnegan, R. J. 1942. "Social Responsibilities of the Newspaper." *Annals of the American Academy of Political and Social Science* 219: 166–68.

Freeman, M. 1992. "Arthur Ashe Announces He Has AIDS." *Washington Post*, April 9, A1.

Frey, J. H., and D. S. Eitzen. 1991. "Sport and Society." *Annual Review of Sociology* 17: 503–22.

Gamson, W. A. 1989. "News as Framing." *American Behavioral Scientist* 33, no. 2: 157–61.

Garber, G. 2003. "Ashe's Activism Helped Mold the Future." espn.com, February 6. Accessed March 30, 2007. http://web.archive.org/web/20070224234008/http://espn.go.com/tennis/s/2003/0205/1504540.html.

Gauthier, C. C. 2002. "Privacy Invasion by the News Media: Three Ethical Models." *Journal of Media Ethics* 17, no. 1: 20–34.

Gitlin, T. 1980. *The Whole World Is Watching: Mass Media in the Making and Unmaking of the New Left*. Berkeley: University of California Press.

Goffman, E. 1974. *Frame Analysis: An Essay on the Organization of Experience*. Boston: Northeastern University Press.

Goodale, J. C. n.d. "The First Amendment and Freedom of the Press." USIA *Electronic Journal* 2, no. 1. Accessed March 19, 2006. http://web.archive.org/web/20060322044301/http://usinfo.state.gov/journals/itdhr/0297/ijde/goodale.htm.

"Grand Slam." 1993. *U.S. News & World Report* 114, no. 7 (February 22): 20.

Gray, H. 1989. "Television, Black Americans and the American Dream." *Critical Studies in Mass Communication* 6: 376–86.

Gregor, Chris. 2003. "Q&A with Tennis' James Blake on Davis Cup and Arthur Ashe." U.S. Olympic Fan Club website. Accessed March 20, 2006. http://web .archive.org/web/20060909090957/http://www.usoc.org/27555_12353.htm.

Hall, R. E. 2001. "The Ball Curve: Calculated Racism and the Stereotype of African American Men." *Journal of Black Studies* 32, no. 1: 104–19.

Hall, S. 2003. "The Whites of Their Eyes: Racist Ideologies and the Media." In *Gender, Race, and Class in Media.* 2nd ed. Edited by G. Dines and J. M. Humez. Thousand Oaks CA: Sage.

Hardin, R., and C. Zuegner. 2003. "Life, Liberty, and the Pursuit of Golf Balls." *Journalism History* 29, no. 2: 82–90.

Hardy, M., and M. P. Williams. 1992 9. "Ashe Sure AIDS Came from Transfusion." *Richmond Times-Dispatch*, April, A1.

Hawkins, B. D. 1995. "Arthur Ashe Jr.: The Lessons He Taught and Learned." *Black Issues in Higher Education* 12, no. 3: 10.

Heller, D. 2006. "Ashe Was More Than an Athlete." *Washington Times*, February 9.

Herman, R. 1992. "In 1983, HIV Blood Screening Was Nonexistent." *Washington Post*, April 9, A1.

Hodges, L. 1994. "The Journalist and Privacy." *Journal of Mass Media Ethics* 9, no. 4: 197–212.

Hollander, D. 1993. "Publicity about Magic Johnson May Have Led Some to Reduce Their Risky Behavior, Request HIV Testing." *Family Planning Perspectives* 25, no. 4: 192–93.

James, M., T. Hoff, J. Davis, and R. Graham. 2005. "Leveraging the Power of the Media to Combat HIV/AIDS." *Health Affairs* 24, no. 3: 854–57.

Jelen, T. G., and C. Wilcox. 1992. "Symbolic and Instrumental Values as Predictors of AIDS Policy Attitudes." *Social Science Quarterly* 73: 737–49.

Jones, D. A. 2004. "Why Americans Don't Trust the Media." *Press/Politics* 9, no. 2: 60–75.

Kalb, E. 2006. "The Day Magic Johnson Changed the World." Foxsports.com. Accessed March 1, 2007. http://web.archive.org/web/20061107194750/http:// msn.foxsports.com/nba/story/6141830.

Kinsella, J. 1989. *Covering the Plague: AIDS and the American Media.* New Brunswick NJ: Rutgers University Press.

Kornheiser, T. 1992. A Tear for a Hero. *Washington Post*, April 12, F1.

Kurtz, H. 1992. "USA Today Lobs a Tough One." *Washington Post*, April 9, C1.

Langer, L. M., R. S. Zimmerman, E. F. Hendershot, M. Singh. 1992. "Effect of Magic Johnson's HIV Status on HIV-Related Attitudes and Behaviors of an STD Clinic Population." *AIDS Education and Prevention* 4, 295–307.

Lapchick, R. n.d. "Arthur Ashe: A Legacy of Hope and Change." *DeVos Sport Business Management.* Accessed March 15, 2007. http://web.archive.org/ web/20060830035623/http://www.bus.ucf.edu/sport/cgi-bin/site/sitew. cgi?page=/news/articles/article_32.htx.

La Prensa San Diego. 2003. "Arthur Ashe's Legacy Lives On." February 7. Accessed March 19, 2006. http://www.laprensa-sandiego.org/archieve/february07-03 /ashe.htm.

Leavy, W. 1993. "Arthur Ashe: The Gentle Warrior, 1943-1993." *Ebony* 48, no. 6 (April): 110-11.

Le Poire, B. A., C. K. Sigelman, L. Sigelman, and H. C. Kenski. 1990. "Who Wants to Quarantine Persons with AIDS? Patterns of Support for California's Proposition 64." *Social Science Quarterly* 71: 239-49.

Lipper, B. 1992. "Ashe Knew Life Wasn't Fair—And Now the Rest of Us Know." *Richmond Times-Dispatch*, April 9, D1.

Lipsyte, R. 1992. "None of Us Needs Other People's Fears." *New York Times*, April 10, B13.

Lorge, B. 1992. "Tennis's Conspiracy of Compassion for Arthur Ashe." *New York Times*, April 12, 358.

Mackenzie, R. 1992. "Arthur Ashe: Class Act." *Richmond Times-Dispatch*, April 9, 10.

McAllister, R. 1992. "AIDS 'Outing': When Is It News?" *Richmond Times-Dispatch*, April 10, B1.

McCombs, M., and S. I. Ghanem. 2001. "The Convergence of Agenda Setting and Framing." In *Framing Public Life: Perspectives on Media and Our Understanding of the Social World*, edited by S. D. Reese, O. H. Gandy Jr., and A. E. Grant. Mahwah NJ: Lawrence Erlbaum.

McCombs, M. E., and D. L. Shaw. 1972. "The Agenda-Setting Function of Mass Media." *Public Opinion Quarterly* 36, no. 2: 176-87.

Messner, M. A. 1988. "Sports and Male Domination: The Female Athlete as Contested Ideological Terrain." *Sociology of Sport Journal* 5, no. 3: 197-211.

Meyers, C. 1993. "Justifying Journalistic Harms: Right to Know vs. Interest in Knowing." *Journal of Mass Media Ethics* 8, no. 3: 133-46.

Moeller, S. 2000. "Coverage of AIDS in Africa: The Media Are Silent No Longer." *Nieman Reports* 54, no. 3: 89.

Moore, K. 1992. "Sportsman of the Year." *Sports Illustrated*, December 21. Accessed March 19, 2006. http://web.archive.org/web/20060518190140 /http://sportsillustrated.cnn.com/tennis/features/1997/arthurashe /sport1.html.

Morrow, L. 1992. "Fair Game?" *Time* 139, no. 16 (April 20): 74-75.

Murphy, S. T. 1998. "The Impact of Factual versus Fictional Media Portrayals on Cultural Stereotypes." *Annals of the American Academy of Political and Social Science* 560: 165–78.

Orndorff, B. 1992. "HIV Bombs Still Detonating from Pre-1985 Blood Transfusions." *Richmond Times-Dispatch*, April 9, D6.

Packett, J. 1992. "Family, Some Others Aware of Condition." *Richmond Times-Dispatch*, April 9, D4.

Pedersen, P., K. Miloch, and P. Laucella. 2007. *Strategic Sport Communication.* Champaign IL: Human Kinetics.

Pedrick, W. H. 1970. "Publicity and Privacy: Is It Any of Our Business?" *The University of Toronto Law Journal* 20, no. 4: 391–411.

Policinski, G. 1992. "Sports Editor: It's a News Story. Would Be News No Matter Disease." *USA Today*, April 9, A2.

Pollock, P. H., III. 1994. "Issues, Values, and Critical Moments: Did 'Magic' Johnson Transform Public Opinion on AIDS?" *American Journal of Political Science* 38, no. 2: 426–44.

Pollock, P. H., III, S. A. Lillie, M. E. Vittes. 1993. "On the Nature and Dynamics of Social Construction: The Case of AIDS." *Social Science Quarterly* 74: 123–35.

Potter, B. 1992. "Arthur Ashe Did Nothing That Gave the Public a Right to Know All." *Richmond Times-Dispatch*, April 10, 15.

Price, S. L. 1994. "Arthur Ashe." *Sports Illustrated* 81, no. 12 (September 19): 116–17.

Pryor, J. B., G. D. Reeder, R. Vinacco Jr., and T. L. Kott. 1989. "The Instrumental and Symbolic Functions of Attitudes towards Persons with AIDS." *Journal of Applied Social Psychology* 19: 377–404.

Quindlen, A. 1992. "Journalism 2001." *New York Times*, April 12, 168.

Randolph, L. B. 1993. "On Love, Loss and Life after Arthur." *Ebony* 48, no. 12: 27–31.

Rhoden, W. C. 1992a. "An Emotional Ashe Says That He Has AIDS." *New York Times*, April 9, B9.

———. 1992b. "Media Twitch Is Turning into a Dangerous Reflex." *Sporting News*, April 27, 213, 217.

———. 2006. *Forty Million Dollar Slaves: The Rise, Fall, and Redemption of the Black Athlete.* New York: Crown.

Roach, R. 2003. "Keeping the Ashe Legacy Relevant." *Black Issues in Higher Education* 20, no. 4: 18.

Ruby, M. 1992. "The Private Life of Arthur Ashe." *U.S. News & World Report* 112, no. 15: 84.

Ryan, J. 1992. "The Greatest Tragedy Is That Ashe Didn't Have a Choice." *Sporting News*, April 20, 213, 216.

Sabato, L. J. 1991. *Feeding Frenzy: How Attack Journalism Has Transformed American Politics*. New York: Free Press.

Schwartz, L. n.d. "Sportscentury Biography: Althea Gibson Broke Barriers." ESPN Classic website. Accessed March 27, 2006. http://espn.go.com/classic/biography/s/gibson_althea.html.

Shilts, R. 1987. *And the Band Played On*. New York: St. Martin's.

Smith, D. 1992. "Ashe's Elegance Helps Ease the Anguish." *USA Today*, December 10, C3.

Stipp, H., and D. Kerr. 1989. "Determinants of Public Opinion about AIDS." *Public Opinion Quarterly* 53: 98–106.

Tankard, J. W., Jr. 2001. "The Empirical Approach to the Study of Media Framing." In *Perspectives on Media and Our Understanding of the Social World*, edited by S. D. Reese, O. H. Gandy Jr., and A. E. Grant. Mahwah NJ: Lawrence Erlbaum.

Tesoriero, J. M., and M. D. Sorin. 1992. "The Effect of 'Magic' Johnson's HIV Disclosure on Anonymous Testing Services in New York State." *AIDS & Public Policy Journal* 7: 216–24.

Tuchman, G. 1978. *Making News: A Study in the Construction of Reality*. New York: Free Press.

White, D. M. 1950. "The 'Gate Keeper': A Case Study in the Selection of News." *Journalism Quarterly* 27: 383–90.

Wilbon, M. 1992. "Hero's Biggest Challenge." *Washington Post*, April 9, D1.

Wilkins, L. 1994. "Journalists and the Character of Public Officials/Figures." *Journal of Mass Media Ethics* 9, no. 3: 157–68.

Williams, J. 1993. "Friends and Fans Say Farewell to Arthur Ashe." *Jet* 83, no. 18: 10–20.

Winslow, O. 1992. "HIV Figures Don't Look Good for Minorities." *Richmond Times-Dispatch*, April 10, A1.

Witteman, Paul A. 1993. "A Man of Fire and Grace: Arthur Ashe, 1943–1993." *Time* 141, no. 7: 70.

Woody, P. 1992. "Dignity Is Ashe's Ally in Struggle with AIDS." *Richmond Times-Dispatch*, April 9, 25.

Woolley, W., and T. Lemons. 1992. "At Decision Time, Ashe Put Family First." *Richmond Times-Dispatch*, April 9, 13.

Yardley, J. 1992. "Arthur Ashe and the Cruel Volleys of the Media." *Washington Post*, April 13, C2.

Yarros, V. S. 1922. "Journalism, Ethics, and Common Sense." *International Journal of Ethics* 32, no. 4: 410–19.

16

Michael Jordan's Family Values
Marketing, Meaning, and Post-Reagan America

MARY G. MCDONALD

Michael Jordan's body is one of the most visible and celebrated bodies of recent times, thanks to the National Basketball Association's (NBA) clever promotion of appealing personalities, creative commercials produced by Nike and other commercial sponsors, and his own marketing savvy. Jordan's fame has translated into 1995 endorsement earnings estimated to be $40 million (Lane and McHugh 1995). As Michael Eric Dyson (1993) and David Andrews (1993, 1996) argue, Michael Jordan represents more than a successful marketing campaign that sells Nike sneakers, the NBA, Wheaties, Hanes underwear, Coca-Cola, Gatorade, Chevrolets, and McDonald's hamburgers: Jordan's body is a culturally significant site for the commodification and subsequent consumption of black masculinity.

The marketing appeal of Michael Jordan is worth exploring given the historically complex representations of black masculinity. Henry Louis Gates (1994) cites critic Barbara Johnson in suggesting that African American men embody an "already read text." That is, images of African American men carry historically forged racist and sexist meanings that associate African Americans with nature, animality, hypersensuality, and eroticism. Once used to legitimate slavery and white supremacy, these representations persist in the visual media and hold particular significance within the conservative-backlash climate of post-Reagan America: the bodies of African American men (and women) have been made to serve as "symbolic icons for the nation's ills" (Golden 1994, 22). For example, Wilt Chamberlain stands for "perverse promiscuity," Clarence Thomas for sexual harassment, Mike Tyson for date rape, and O. J. Simpson for spousal abuse (Golden 1994).

Given this historical legacy and current hysteria, how and why is it that Michael Jordan manages to be marketable and extremely successful as a cultural symbol? On one level, exploring the popularity of Michael Jordan is a seemingly simple task. Jordan offers a fresh, more tolerant, and thus more marketable vision of black masculinity because he has achieved an extraordinary level of success in a culture that celebrates masculine achievements like those romanticized in sports. Off the court and in commercial endorsements, Jordan appears as an engaging, thoughtful, private family man. This portrait of Jordan apparently counters and challenges the socially constructed representations of African American men as dangerous, incompetent, and overtly hypersexualized. Still, given the unstable, contextual state of cultural meanings, Jordan's public persona as an exceptional athlete and private family man cannot be blithely celebrated as a positive portrayal of African Americans nor for that matter simply dismissed as reactionary Reaganism. Rather, making sense of Michael Jordan's ubiquitous presence within popular media necessitates exploring the historically specific, often contradictory economic rationales, social relations, and ideologies in which Jordan and his image are embedded.

Informed by cultural studies sensibilities, in this essay I explore the public persona of Michael Jordan in selected sporting and advertising accounts to critically interrogate the image(s) we are being offered to consume. What makes representations of Michael Jordan so complex and intriguing for cultural analysis is that they offer a unique opportunity to illuminate the complicated political status of popular culture and identity. To interrogate the ideologies of race, class, masculinity, and sexuality inscribed on Michael Jordan's commodified body is to acknowledge that relations of power are always multiple and contradictory. We cannot fully understand Michael Jordan if we focus only on the socially constructed representations of his identity as an African American, or as a heterosexual, or as a man, or as a member of the capitalist class. While that sort of analytical compartmentalization may be appealing, its simplicity fails to provide an accurate reflection of the complex, inter-related, and fluid character of cultural meanings and power relations (Birrell and McDonald 1993).

This analysis of Michael Jordan benefits from the concept of articulation, which suggests that cultural meaning does not inhere in texts, identities, or practices and that, rather, it is produced through their interactions (Hall 1985; Hall 1986a; Hall 1986b; Hall 1991; Howell 1990; Grossberg 1992). An articulation is an association or a link between distinctive ideological elements that operate in a specific historical place and time with identifi-able consequences. Methodologically, this suggests that cultural analysis is an interpretive act requiring the exploration of both texts and contexts. The cultural process is further complicated by the incessant generation of new meanings and fresh associations.

In this essay I trace the contradictory ways in which representations of gender, race, class, and sexuality are articulated through the phenomenon of Michael Jordan within the context of post-Reagan America. Specifically, I explore the ways media accounts of Jordan's basketball talents reinforce lingering stereotypes that equate natural athleticism with men—particularly African American men—and suggest people of color have privileged access to bodily pleasures and expressions (see Harris 1991; Birrell 1989; Wiggins 1989; hooks 1992; West 1993). Likewise, the off-court persona of Jordan as a private family man participates in contemporary popular discourses on the family, engaging a variety of racial, class, gender, sexual, and national ideologies. The definition of what constitutes the family continues to be reformulated from a variety of positions, while dominant cultural portrayals of the nuclear family proclaim it is "in crisis," or "on the decline," or just plain "broken." The alleged decline of the traditional nuclear family—a heterosexual couple with children featuring a breadwinner father and housewife mother—has been successfully deployed by the conservative New Right as the commonsense explanation for social problems ranging from crime, poverty, and sexual "promiscuity" to drug abuse (Reeves and Campbell 1994).

Jordan and his promoters play up his seemingly natural athleticism while down playing any suggestion of excessive sensuality. An apparent devotion to "traditional family values" serves to further distance Jordan from the stereotypical portrayal of black masculinity as hypersexual, immoral, and irresponsible, the very demonic characteristics members of the New Right claim threaten the nuclear family and, by association, the very moral fiber of America itself. In post-Reagan America, where traditional family values and the public hysteria surrounding AIDS suggest sexuality is both immoral and life-threatening, Jordan's commodified body is culturally coded as natural in ways that are socially sanctioned and culturally envied.

Here Comes Mr. Jordan: The Marketing of Black Masculinity

Understanding Michael Jordan's status as a cultural and marketing icon in post-Reagan America means acknowledging the tremendous significance of both sports and advertising in the national consciousness. Mark Dyreson (1989) traces the symbiotic relationship between consumerism and sports to the 1920s, where Americans increasingly understood sports "as a vehicle of entertainment—one of the many items available for amusement in a culture which glorified consumption" (p. 261). The form and content of sports as a commodity have varied and shifted over the years, just as the crafting of Jordan as an appealing persona to be marketed and consumed has its own unique history. Exploring the convergence of the historical with the economic and biographical suggests that much of Jordan's appeal can be attributed to his athletic status: professional basketball offers a prominent site for African American men such as Jordan to be visible, culturally lauded, and clearly successful.

Michael Eric Dyson (1993) notes that Jordan represents the hope of freedom and ultimate escape from the pernicious beliefs and social structures that stand between African Americans and economic prosperity as well as physical and psychological security. Jordan's commodified body is, therefore, the "symbolic carrier of racial and cultural desires to fly beyond limits and obstacles ... and thus the player's achievements have furthered the cultural acceptance of at least the Black athletic body" (p. 71). While acknowledging Dyson's arguments about the resistant potential of the black athletic body, cultural critic bell hooks (1994) suggests the selling of Michael Jordan is best understood as the signpost and reinforcement of overtly depoliticized times. Beginning in the late 1970s, market forces coopted much of the subversive potential of black masculinity while male athletes increasingly espoused politically neutral positions in an effort to secure financially lucrative endorsement deals.

Significantly, the increasing numbers of black male athletes endorsing products parallels the ascent of the Reagan era, a unique historical epoch characterized by a shift in the national zeitgeist. First emerging under the leadership of President Ronald Reagan, this shift in the national consciousness suggests movement away from the overt political activism of the 1960s toward an era of backlash politics that also served to justify economic policies favoring the wealthy. By the 1980s, conservative voices had positioned a pro-business agenda as tantamount to the emotionally cherished ideals of family, respectability, and nation (Hall 1988; Reeves and Campbell 1994).The underlying rationale was that corporate expansion and freedom strengthened not only the economy but also the nuclear family and, by association, the very moral fiber of America. According to key members of the New Right, economic problems such as inflation or the budget deficit could be traced to the "permissive" and "hedonistic" politics of big government. Bleeding-heart liberalism, characterized by the expansion of the state's social entitlement programs like the New Deal, the Great Society, and the War on Poverty, merely undermine the values of hard work, family, and nation. Illegitimate birth rates, joblessness, and welfare dependency were all created and reinforced by "economic incentives to bear out-of-wedlock children and disincentives to work created by the Great Society" (Edsall and Edsall 1991, 15).

While always contested, challenged, and resisted, increasingly socially conservative worldviews gained popularity among a broad segment of the American population. According to Grossberg (1992), these positions include the growing acceptance of social and economic inequalities for various subordinated groups, the attempt to impose a narrowly defined notion of morality on all of society, the justification of inequality in the name of economic competition, and the demonization of activist groups who challenge the political and conservative status quo. Distancing himself from potentially controversial issues and espousing benign views (see Cole and Andrews 1996), Jordan fits neatly with the regressive political climate of post-Reagan America. Andrews (1996) argues that Jordan's successes on the basketball court and in the advertising world offer apparent "proof" of a racially tolerant and colorblind society. Read from this perspective. Jordan's popularity is both the product of, and reinforcement for, New Right strategies to maintain white interests by suggesting that racism has been eradicated (Andrews 1996).

The commodification of Michael Jordan also signals the loss of political agency and the once-radical political potential of black athletes. Michael Jordan as a spectacular athlete and willing corporate apologist stands in stark contrast to another powerful vision of yesteryear: that of African American athletes as political activists and outspoken critics of the establishment (hooks 1994). Perhaps no one individual athlete better embodied the civil rights era and mandate for social change of the 1960s and 1970s than boxer Muhammad Ali. Ali spoke out against the war in Vietnam and in support of Black Power, willingly sacrificing fame for his convictions. Ali's conversion to the Nation of Islam and refusal to serve in the Vietnam War cost him the heavyweight boxing title and a prison term (Harris 1995). While Ali no doubt embodied the sexism of professional boxing (see Sammons 1995) and earned a tremendous amount of money at the prime of his athletic career, he also offered a decidedly subversive persona as an outspoken critic of the racial status quo. Othello Harris (1995) suggests that Ali countered stereotypes of African Americans while moving beyond "white limits of acceptability in his beliefs and behavior" (p. 66).

While I don't wish to oversimplify complex cultural meanings, especially in light of feminist critiques of both sports and history, suffice it to say these contrasts between Ali and Jordan exemplify distinctions between the two divergent eras: where Ali embodied the pride of black resolve in the 1960s, the commodification of Michael Jordan in the 1980s and 1990s is a sign of increasingly reactionary times. While also commodified, Ali was among a group of African American athletes who helped publicize issues like economic stratification and racial segregation (hooks 1994). Contrast the image of "rebellious masculinity" (hooks 1994, 133) embodied by Ali to that of the genial association created by Nike in pairing Michael Jordan with Bugs Bunny in the "Hare Jordan" campaign. As hooks (1994) sees it, in those commercials where Jordan

> speaks to the cartoon figure of Bugs Bunny as though they are equals—peers—his elegance and grace of presence is ridiculed and mocked by a visual aesthetics which suggests that his body makes him larger than life, a fantasy character. This visual image, though presented as playful and comic, in fact dehumanizes. (p. 134)

Creating appealing fantasy characters also was a key strategy employed by the NBA in the 1980s in an effort to revive the once-floundering, financially strapped league of the 1970s. As Cheryl Cole and Harry Denny (1994) note, a key element of the league's resurgence lies in the ability of promoters to distance the NBA from previous racist associations conflating the predominantly black athletic labor force with an "undisciplined" style of play and the stigma of drug abuse. Cole and Denny suggest that during the 1980s marketers and an equally invested sports media promoted professional basketball as an appealing cultural event complete with stylized play and extraordinary, larger-than-life personalities like those of Earvin "Magic" Johnson of the Los Angeles Lakers and Larry Bird of the Boston Celtics. With an assist from Nike, fresh meanings were associated with black masculinity in an effort to court white middle-class audiences. New narratives suggested that NBA athletes possessed exceptional skill, hard work, dedication, and determination. The presentation of NBA players as idealized athletic heroes committed to competition and meritocracy also suggests the New Right's understanding of a racially harmonious country (Cole and Denny 1994).

By the time Jordan entered the league in 1984, the NBA was well on its way toward transforming games into spectacular entertainment events. Just as this time period saw the explosion of special effects in *Raiders of the Lost Ark* (1981), *ET* (1982), *Ghostbusters* (1984), *Back to the Future* (1985), *Batman* (1989), and other top-grossing blockbuster Hollywood films of the era, so too did the NBA exploit the spectacular, employing laser shows, dramatic player introductions, energizing music, half-time contests, and sideshows. The NBA changed basketball games into a unique type of athletic escapism. In doing so, NBA commissioner David Stern makes it clear that the NBA is targeting the entire family:

> They have themes parks, . . . and we have theme parks, only we call them arenas. They have characters: Mickey Mouse, Goofy. Our characters are named Magic and Michael [Jordan]. Disney sells apparel; we sell apparel. They make home videos; we make home videos. (quoted in Swift 1991, 84)

That Stern would choose to align the NBA with Disney, the corporate exemplar of wholesome entertainment, is particularly telling. Disney's wholesomeness, excitement, and eternal optimism are the antithesis of the racist characterizations of "undisciplined" blackness associated with the NBA of the 1970s. The reference to Disney also helps identify the NBA's idealized, target audience—Disney productions "relentlessly define the United States as white, middle-class, and heterosexual" (Giroux 1994, 31).

By the 1990s, the NBA had been successfully "Disneyfied." The complete reversal of financial fortunes included a complete line of commodities: NBA-licensed caps, jerseys, t-shirts, basketballs, videos, and so on. To this day, however, the most valuable commodities continue to be the players themselves; the now-global NBA has successfully created a sense of audience identification and name recognition. Thus, the NBA has followed the long-established capitalist logic of the film and television industries. As David Lusted (1991) argues in regards to television, "a stock of recognized names acts as an assurance that audiences will return again (and again) to their role as viewers. Perpetuating—via advertising or license revenue—the flow of cash to maintain the institution" (p. 251).

Still, this remaking of the NBA did not displace the themes most commonly connected to professional basketball, including those of masculine prowess and competitive capitalism. Henry Giroux's (1994) analysis of Disney's sanitized aura can be applied to the NBA's complicity in what Giroux terms the "politics of innocence." Behind Disney's guise of naiveté rests a multinational conglomerate that wields enormous cultural and political power:

> Disney's power and its reach into popular culture combine an insouciant playfulness and the fantastic possibility of making childhood dreams come true—yet only through the reproduction of strict gender roles, an unexamined nationalism, and a choice that is attached to the proliferation of commodities. (p. 31)

Similarly, NBA promotional strategies entice fans in ways that appear benevolent yet mask particular relations of power. Underlying the visible space of the game is a semipublic masculinized and heterosexualized culture displayed through "a 'politics of lifestyle' marked by the semipublic sexual exchange of a conspicuously displayed network of adoring, supportive female fans, girlfriends, and/or wives: it is a masculine lifestyle meant to be embraced, admired, envied, and consumed" (Cole and Denny 1994, 128). This masculinist preserve of the NBA is further complicated by the stereotypical association that equates people of color with sensuality and physicality. Thus, perceptions of hypersexuality and eroticism persist as powerful racist undercurrents within the consumer culture and the commodified space of the NBA (Cole and Denny 1994).

Cole and Denny's (1994) contention that these racist assumptions are constantly being managed through the marketing of particular player personalities is important for understanding the cultural appeal of Jordan. The very public depiction of Michael Jordan as a wholesome family figure helps stabilize the league's hoped-for clean-cut image just as it diffuses lingering impressions of black hypersexuality. Indeed, one of the first snapshots of Jordan in the NBA features the nuclear family: parents James and Deloris attended the 1984 press conference to witness the announcement of the $6 million contract awarded by the professional Chicago Bulls to Michael. Over the course of the next several years, even after the tragic murder of James Jordan in 1993, the pair provided affirmation of Jordan's All-American persona.

In *Michael Jordan: Come Fly with Me* (Sperling 1989), a video produced by NBA Entertainment, basketball game footage is juxtaposed against voiceover narratives outlining Jordan's personal virtues. Accompanied by piano music and film of his own aesthetically pleasing body running and leaping on the court. Jordan states assertively that his parents' influence continues: "I was always taught never to forget where you came from. My parents, if I change as a person, they would be the first to tell me that, and they have not told me that yet. So, I'm doing well" (Sperling 1989). This persona is an enticing portrait of black masculinity, highlighting "natural" athleticism and family sentiment in ways designed to provoke "desire without evoking dread" (Jackson 1994, 49).

Body Language: Cultivating Michael Jordan's "Natural" Physicality

One of the most enduring and seemingly endearing aspects of the Michael Jordan phenomenon are the words and phrases coined to describe his particular type of physically expressive basketball talent. The most popular and lasting nicknames connote flight for Jordan—"Air," "Air Jordan," "His Airness," a "Flyer" who operates in either "Air Time" or "Rare Air" or is perpetually "Talking to the Air." Of course, these phrases did not originate out of thin air. References to flight are testimony to the tremendous role of advertising discourses in generating Jordan's image. "Air Jordan" is part of Nike's clever plan to market an air-sole shoe to challenge Converse, long the leader in the gym shoe segment of the market (Raissman 1984). In 1984, Nike transferred a lion's share of their advertising budget into one preeminent multimillion-dollar five-year deal, an agreement sealed before Jordan's rookie year in the NBA. David Falk, Jordan's agent then with ProServ, explained the cultural logic of this marriage:

> Because of Michael's style of play—we like to call him a flier—he fits in well with the whole line of the shoe [Air Shoe] which is high tech. That's where the upper end of Nike's marketing strategy is going. (quoted in Raissman 1984, 1)

Two early Air Jordan TV commercials, first "aired" in the spring of 1985, helped construct Jordan's public persona. One commercial was created as a response to the NBA's "uniformity of uniform" clause when commissioner David Stern banned the original red-and-black Technicolor Nike Air Jordan shoes. The voiceover states, "On October 18, the NBA banned Michael Jordan from wearing these shoes. But the NBA can't stop you from buying these shoes. Air Jordan. Basketball by Nike" (Murphy 1985, 34). In this commercial, Jordan is presented as a menacing figure—even angry—with a scowl, presumably in response to the authoritarian stance taken by the league in banning the Nike shoes. This portrayal of Jordan plays on racist depictions of black men as threatening and intimidating. Significantly, it also is the last time Jordan is presented as an intimidating figure in an advertisement (Murphy 1985). In subsequent promotional campaigns, Jordan would be represented as approachable and likable, an everyday American with extraordinary athletic talents.

The archetype that Nike, the NBA, and subsequent advertisers seized upon appeared in another early Nike commercial from the spring of 1985 entitled "Jordan Flight." It features Jordan moving across a black-topped basketball court at twilight with the Chicago skyline in the background. The sound of jet engines revving to an increasingly higher pitch reaches its zenith when Jordan slam dunks the basketball. Jordan remains in the air with his legs apart for the final ten seconds of the commercial, an apparent testimonial to both his incredible athleticism and the power of the red-and-black Technicolor Nike athletic shoes he wears (Katz 1994). The voiceover booms, "Who said man was not meant to fly" (Murphy 1985, 34). This commercial presents an affable Jordan as the quintessential "natural athlete," for as the rather hyperbolic claim goes, he can literally fly through the air.

A quick read of this Nike commercial suggests Michael Jordan's celebrated and commodified physicality is dramatically embellished in basketball and advertising discourses through catchy narratives and phrases, slow-motion replay, and special effects. These commercials, along with video highlights and televised NBA games, use multiple camera angles, slow-motion replays, and personalized narratives to create the illusion of an intimate, revealing, and pleasurable encounter with Michael "Air" Jordan. The ways in which Jordan is represented also assist in the reconstruction, legitimation, and embellishment of larger cultural associations between natural athleticism and masculinity (especially black masculinity) that play a significant role in the area of contemporary gender relations. "Symbolic representations of the male body as a symbol of strength, virility, and power have become increasingly important in popular culture as actual inequalities between the sexes are contested in all areas of public life" (Messner 1988, 212).

Images of masculinity as powerful and "natural" on televised sporting spectacles offer men of all socioeconomic backgrounds one of the most powerful sites to collectively identify with masculinity and an ideology of male physical and cultural superiority (Messner 1988; Theberge 1991). Still these representations offer contradictory meanings when connected with commonsense perceptions of African American men. Traits such as aggression and brute strength have historically been associated with both African American men and athleticism (Sabo and Jansen 1992). Television sports commentary, for example, more often credits white basketball players with exhibiting "intelligence" while explaining the success of African Americans in terms of their "innate" physicality (Jackson 1989; Harris 1991). This seemed to be the implicit message of the 1989 NBC television special *Black Athletes: Fact and Fiction*, according to Laurel Davis (1990). Relying heavily on questionable bioscientific discourses, NBC focused an entire show exploring the presumed link between racial difference and athletic performance. This quest downplayed human agency and dismissed sociopolitical issues, including the very racist preoccupation with the alleged "naturalness" of African Americans (Davis 1990). As Andrews (1996) has recently demonstrated, the media reinforces this type of pseudoscientific, essentialist logic with repeated references to Jordan as someone who was seemingly "born to dunk."

Media images, such as Nike commercials, have a powerful effect, subtly influencing our perceptions of the body. Here technology merges with ideology to reify notions of African Americans as naturally athletic. For example, slow-motion replay offers a particularly compelling dramatic aesthetic. Margaret Morse (1983) argues that the conventions of slow-motion replay allow for an analysis of "body movements which are normally inaccessible to view; this capacity has justifiably lent slow motion an aura of scientificity" (p. 49). The video *Come Fly with Me* (Sperling 1989) offers many examples of how slow-motion replay creates the dramatic, aesthetic athleticism of Jordan's athletic body. A scene near the end of the video features four different examples of Jordan dunking the basketball in slow motion, each from a dramatically different camera angle.

Slow motion's aura of scientific legitimacy helps to strengthen the illusion that Jordan can defy the laws of gravity. This presentation has proven to be persuasive. On June 13, 1991, for example, the ABC television show *Primetime Live* aired a segment narrated by Diane Sawyer in which several people were asked, "Why does Michael Jordan seem to fly?" The broadcasted responses:

> First Fan: Michael Jordan hangs in the air for at least eight to ten seconds.
> Second fan: Six seconds.
> Third Fan: Ten seconds.
> Fourth Fan: 4.56 seconds.
> Fifth Fan: Oh, his hang time's got to be at least 8 seconds.
> Sawyer: Eight seconds? Is it possible Michael Jordan is airborne that long? Is he exempt from gravity? In other words, if Michael Jordan had fallen from that apple tree, would Sir Isaac Newton still be waiting for a bop on the head? (*Primetime Live* 1991)

The scene shifts to Peter Brancazio, a professor in the Department of Physics at Brooklyn College, who assures the audience that the "laws of physics apply to everyone, even Michael Jordan." Using basic physics, Brancazio concludes that a three-foot leap leaves Jordan in "flight" not for the three to ten seconds believed by the audience but for about nine-tenths of a second.

By the time of Jordan's October 6, 1993, initial retirement from professional basketball, this reputation for flight had long been well established: basketball and advertising discourses drawing on commonsense assumptions about athleticism repeatedly constructed Jordan as the ultimate natural athlete. Even the nickname "Air" suggests an aura of naturalness and reinforces the rather hyperbolic notion that Jordan could defy gravity via his uncanny "hang time," the seeming ability to remain suspended in space as if in flight.[1]

Still, these characterizations of flight are far from innocent, communicating much more than Michael Jordan's great athleticism and symbolic worth. Historically, African Americans have been linked with nature in racist ways that seemingly suggest extraordinary "sexuality, sensuality, and an alternately celebrated or denigrated propensity for physical ability" (Desmond 1994, 43).

These associations are rooted in the racist assumptions that black men are "closer to nature" than white men and in Victorian notions that Africans have a different genetic makeup than their more genteel and intellectual European counterparts. Rooted in allegedly natural differences, these ideologies have helped to restrict black men to certain occupational niches such as sports, music, and entertainment. Crucially, these ideologies operate by making the connection between sporting and sexual prowess (Jackson 1994, 54).

The black athletic body is often referenced in terms of an extraordinary physicality. According to critic Peter Jackson (1994), the dominant perspective of white heterosexual masculinity still expects superior sexual performance from people of color. The marketing strategy applied to Jordan suggests an apparent awareness of these larger issues. Under the direction of his original marketing agency, ProServ, and agent David Falk, and thanks partially to the promotional apparatuses of the NBA and sports media, Jordan has played up the "natural" black athletic body while simultaneously repudiating any suggestion of culturally inappropriate sexuality. This serves to undermine stereotypical associations of black sexuality with destructive and predatory behavior (Jackson 1994).

The cultural power of these depictions of black sexuality derives from America's simultaneous obsession with sex and fear of black sexuality (West 1993). The "exotic" images of African American sexuality thus also speak to the paradox of sexuality and race in America. According to Cornel West (1993), behind "closed doors the dirty, disgusting and funky sex associated with Black people is often perceived to be more intriguing and interesting while in public spaces talk about Black sexuality is virtually taboo" (p. 120). Sexual myths about African Americans, invented during Reconstruction to maintain white cultural and financial privilege, present them as either oversexed, threatening personas or as desexed individuals committed to serving white interests. Although the former might be the most pernicious, all of these types of representations distort and dehumanize African Americans.

These myths flourish in professional sports where African American male athletes make disproportionate contributions, most notably in baseball, football, and basketball. The masculinist culture of professional sports also encourages men of all backgrounds to treat women as sexual conquests (Curry 1991). Too often being a male athlete means that one has power over and entitlement to women's bodies. Still, the stereotypes of black sexuality ensure that African American men disproportionately bear the pejorative label of hypersexuality (Rowe 1994). In sport, there is a long history in which gender, race, and sexuality have been articulated to suggest depravity. For example, Jack Johnson became the heavyweight boxing champion of the world in 1908 when the pseudoscience of eugenics seemed to "prove" the mental and physical inferiority of African Americans. While Johnson gained a measure of material success from boxing and performing in Vaudeville, he was perhaps as much a draw (and certainly more infamous) for his sexual relations with white women (Roberts 1983).

Lest the Johnson story seem like old history, consider also that the Associated Press named boxer Mike Tyson's rape trial and conviction as its 1992 story of the year in sports, despite considerable debate over whether a rape trial even belonged on the sports pages. Tyson was convicted of raping Desiree Washington after the failure of a defense strategy that presented him as pathologically incapable of sexual control. While undoubtedly a white defendant would never have to bear the burden of overcoming stereotypes of hypersexuality, the strategy used by Tyson's lawyers actually played into racist and sexist worldviews. Tyson's trial provided a convenient link between criminality, race, sexuality, and sports (Birrell and McDonald 1993). Angela Davis (1984) maintains the myth of the black rapist has been historically conjured up to maintain white privilege and justify white violence and terror against the black community. Far more African American women were raped by white men than white women by black men, yet this idea still persists. Who better represents the stereotype of the black rapist than Mike Tyson (Birrell and McDonald 1993)? Alongside Willie Horton, the convicted rapist whose parole was used during the George H. W. Bush presidential campaign to portray opponent Michael Dukakis as soft on crime, the Mike Tyson case has become "evidence" to justify white America's commonsense perception of violence among blacks. This concept is especially powerful during a time when many civil rights advances have stagnated or been reversed by Reaganite economic and social policies (Birrell and McDonald 1993).

While the Tyson case represents the most glaring association of sexual deviance and sport, representations of sexual prowess echo throughout the culture. The linkage between African Americans' "innate" physicality and sexuality were perhaps most crudely articulated in 1988 in the words of sportscaster Jimmy "The Greek" Snyder:

> The Black is a better athlete to begin with because he's been bred to be that way because of his thigh size and big size. . . . [The advantage] goes all the way back to the Civil War, when during the slave period the slave owner would breed his big Black buck with his big woman so that they could have a big Black kid. That's where it all started. (quoted in Harris 1991, 25)

These words provoked national outrage, resulting in the sportscaster's dismissal from CBS television. Rather than reflecting the words of one misinformed individual, however, the sentiment expressed by Snyder crudely represents a lingering cultural commonsense belief that African Americans are more animalistic as the very terms "bred" and "buck" suggest. The underlying message is that African Americans have privileged access to bodily expressions and pleasure (hooks 1992).

Critic bell hooks (1992) explains the paradoxical implications of this image of black masculinity.

It is the young Black male body that is seen as epitomizing this promise of wildness, of unlimited physical prowess and unbridled eroticism. It was this Black body that was most "desired" for its labor in slavery, and it is this body that is most represented in contemporary popular culture as the body to be watched, imitated, desired, possessed. (p. 34)

Indeed, sensuality and sexuality offer one of the few resources African American men and women have been able to parlay into wider popularity in the entertainment industries (hooks 1992; Rowe 1994). African American actors, musicians, and athletes often are impelled to walk a narrow and ambiguous line between the suggestion of threat and the allure of desire, particularly in attempting to appeal to a wide range of audiences (Rowe 1994).

The salience of the black body has, if possible, magnified in an era where bodies have increasingly become available for inspection and comparison (see Foucault 1978; Watney 1989; Theberge 1991; King 1993). The fitness boom in the late 1970s and early 1980s, coupled with the AIDS crisis, have added to an overall obsession with the fit, healthy body and with reasserting the superiority of the heterosexual body. Male athletes, especially African American athletes, stand for the commodification of the hard body and an active heterosexuality.

Peter Jackson's (1994) analyses of British athletes Daley Thompson and John Barnes help elucidate the ways Jordan's athletic body negotiates notions of sensuality, sexuality, and athleticism. According to Jackson, both Thompson and Barnes are presented in advertising discourses as the "acceptable face" of black masculinity, their presumed sensual energy coupled with impeccable moral reputations and pleasing personalities. The well-known athletes' personas defuse any perceived sexual threat and defy the "conventional mapping of the mind-body dualism on to White and Black men respectively" (p. 56). Described in various media accounts as "supple and muscular" (Norment 1991), "sexy" (Naughton 1992), and offering basketball audiences "pleasure, sheer delight, and wonderment" (Vancil 1992), Jordan's body offers consumers a voyeuristic encounter (see hooks 1994). His carefully cultivated persona as a devoted son, husband, and father is a key component of this process serving to distance Jordan from any overt association of hypersexuality (see Jackson 1994; Cole and Denny 1994).

"Just Wait until We Get Our Hanes on You"

Two commercials for Hanes underwear illustrate the ways Jordan is marketed to exploit the black body as safely erotic. The Hanes campaign offers some of the most overtly risqué representations of Jordan. While other athletes have made a career out of revealing their bodies in underwear ads (witness the meteoric rise in popularity of baseball player Jim Palmer after he posed in scant briefs several years ago), Jordan is presented rather modestly in Hanes commercials. Maintaining Jordan's wholesome person in the Hanes campaign must have provided a bit of a challenge because sensuality and eroticism are closely aligned with advertising campaigns for underwear. Over the past fifteen years, Calvin Klein has parlayed America's uncomfortable titillation with youthful sexuality into a business empire (Ingrassia 1995). Calvin Klein launched a controversial campaign in the mid-1980s featuring young men in their "Calvins" as the object of an erotic gaze. More recently, white rap star Marky Mark was featured in Calvin Klein ads on billboards across the country. Dressed only in a pair of Lycra boxer shorts that hugged his muscular thighs and bulged provocatively at his crotch, Mark stood laughing with his baggy pants twisted around the ankles as if someone had just pulled his trousers down (Harris 1993). His muscular body and apparently delighted reaction suggest agency, power, and approval: Mark appears as a willing and wanton accomplice in the ad's scenario.

In sharp contrast to the provocative profiles of the white entertainers, Jim Palmer and Marky Mark, Jordan appears in Hanes television commercials fully clothed. Where Mark's image of phallic power is representative of the larger cultural trend to position men in (hetero) sexualized yet assertive ways to sell products, Jordan's modest attire is representative of the cultural anxiety around black masculinity and sexuality. Hanes advertisers have clearly decided to play it safe, locking into already well-established images of Jordan's athleticism and position in the nuclear family.

For example, a commercial produced in 1992, opens with a voiceover: "Michael Jordan in Hanes briefs." The camera focuses on a smiling Jordan clutching a basketball, dressed in suit coat, white (presumably Hanes) undershirt, and slacks. This casual suit reveals far less flesh than does the sleeveless jersey and long, modest baggy shorts of the Chicago Bulls uniform. Both a voiceover and graphic proclaim, "Michael Jordan in NEW IMPROVED Hanes briefs." Jordan then leaps into the air as special effects technologies produce the illusion of flight. With background noise of a jet engine, Jordan continues to "fly" through the rafters of a basketball gymnasium, which resembles an airplane hangar complete with an indoor runway. Jordan circles several times over the basket before slamming the ball through the hoop and returning to the ground. The good-natured parody of the ads implies that "New Improved" Hanes underwear can somehow improve performance.

Another Hanes commercial with Jordan alludes to the subject of sexual performance. The scene opens with the words: "Michael Jordan for Hanes fashion briefs." Wearing loafers, long casual shorts, a bright blue shirt, and a baseball cap, Jordan dribbles a basketball into a tastefully, expensively decorated room, apparently his own house. Jordan shoots the basketball into a laundry basket and sits down next to his father. James Jordan puts down his newspaper, reaches into the laundry basket, and picks up a pair of red bikini briefs from a pile of blander underwear. The elder Jordan asks, "Michael, are these your Hanes? Son, is there a reason why you wear them?" At this point Michael's wife, Juanita, enters the room, embraces her husband, and with a firm kiss on Michael's cheek says, "Definitely." Given this feminine approval, James Jordan asks his son, "Do you think Mom would like me in these?" Michael replies hesitantly, "Maybe," at which point the word "definitely" flashes across the screen. The commercial concludes with slow-motion footage of Jordan bashfully smiling as the familiar Hanes jingle rings the sexually suggestive words, "Just wait until we get our Hanes on you."

This father-and-son bonding episode, complete with Michael Jordan's shy, sheepish expressions and repeatedly raised eyebrows, distances Jordan from both the overtly sexist views of many professional athletes and the racist vision of hypersexuality. Rather, this commercial promotes the notion of sexual restraint and a stable family relationship with James Jordan as a strong, sensitive father figure. This sets Michael Jordan apart from the homogenized and simplistic media portrayal of African American families in post-Reagan America that suggests that strong men and father figures are nowhere to be found, having "vanished," abdicating their responsibility and abandoning their own families.

In contrast, James and Michael's conversation about Hanes is reminiscent of father-son talks about responsible sexuality. The generational signs are carefully crafted and are readily displayed in the divergent ways in which the two men are dressed. Michael Jordan's attire suggests boyhood and innocence, especially the casual shorts, loafers, and a baseball cap without any professional team affiliation. This ensemble sharply contrasts with James Jordan's clothing, which evokes the adult business world: a button-down, lightly colored Oxford shirt and nicely creased slacks. Their short dialogue suggests awkwardness and modesty. The younger Jordan appears uncomfortable with this parental query into his underwear choice and the resulting unspoken association of his own sexuality and his father's sexuality.

However modest, this short discussion represents a twist on intergenerational male bonding over female sexuality. Each man is looking for ways to dress in order to please a woman. Juanita is portrayed as the most actively sexual of the three, with the embrace and approval of a boyish and innocent, albeit sexy, Michael Jordan. Yet, even this portrayal is tempered by the white, long-sleeved, high-necked blouse and white slacks she wears. The white color suggests virginal restraint, or perhaps even a sanitized presence. The affectionate embrace and brief kiss on the cheek are devoid of any obvious reference to unbridled passion. Rather, intimacy is suggested as both Michael and Juanita knowingly raise their eyebrows, give each other sideways glances and, thus, allude to excitement and heterosexual intimacy (apparently thanks to the racy red bikini Hanes underwear). The unspoken suggestion is that sexual passion is a personal issue and, thus, any tantalizing detail beyond innuendo is not for public discussion; rather it is best expressed and experienced in private.

Placed within the nuclear family, Jordan offers quite a different aura than does Marky Mark and professional (male) sports. The presence of Michael Jordan's wife and father evoke the socially constructed sentimental images often associated with the family, including warmth, emotional support, respectability, love, and sexual restraint. This blissful restraint between Juanita and Michael Jordan promotes what has, in the age of AIDS, become the ideological bastion of safe sex: the presumably monogamous heterosexual marriage. Magic Johnson's revelation of his HIV status no doubt adds to the common sense of this connection (see Cole and Denny 1994). Johnson's public announcement occurred in November 1991, ironically the very month in which *Ebony* magazine featured a cover shot of Michael and Juanita Jordan embracing happily under the headline "Michael and Juanita Jordan on Marriage, Love, and Life after Basketball." In this piece, Juanita speaks at length about the loving support husband Michael gives to her and their children (Norment 1991).

Still, the contrast between the two basketball players may be diminishing. After revealing that he acquired HIV through unprotected sex in the effort to "accommodate" many women, Johnson is now increasingly referenced from a position within the nuclear family (see King 1993; Cole and Denny 1994; Rowe 1994). In an effort to deflect criticism away from queries about Johnson's sexual identity, his wife Cookie has become increasingly visible:

> Frequent images of Johnson and family in the media and statements like, "Cookie is a very strong woman. Marrying her is the smartest thing I've ever done," have cemented the public respectability, which was undermined by his HIV status. Anchoring Johnson inside the family immediately temporizes his promiscuity, with his "bachelor's life" safely consigned to the past. (Rowe 1994, 16)

Jordan has been repeatedly referenced within the nuclear family and pictured off-the-court with children throughout his basketball career. Early in his career Deloris and James Jordan praised Michael as a loving, moral son, as the elder Jordan's wholesome appeal seems to explain their son's success. The Jordans embody the seemingly lost ideal of family values. Consider, for example, the words of sportswriter Curry Kirkpatrick (1991):

Jordan takes his sense of humor from his dad, who used to work around the house with his tongue hanging out (sound familiar?), his sense of business from his mom, and his work ethic from both. "The Jordans are from the old school where education and teachers and administration meant something to parents," says Laney High principal Kenneth McLaurin. (p. 72)

It is not widely known that Jordan and his wife, Juanita Vanoy, transgressed one of American society's moral rules in 1989 by having their first child out of wedlock. Jordan suffered relatively little adverse media publicity in this matter; he was reportedly urged by several business associates to marry Vanoy in order to protect his carefully cultivated moral image (Naughton 1992). Even the source of this cynical assessment assures us that, once married, Jordan matured thanks to wife Juanita's influence (Naughton 1992). Once married, the Jordan familial bliss means partaking in the good life afforded by the consumer culture and in the promise of greater material rewards: In the *Ebony* piece there is discussion of a dream home to be constructed for Michael and Juanita Jordan and their children, with six bedrooms, a guest house, an indoor/outdoor swimming pool (with Jacuzzi and sauna), and ample parking space for the Jordans' dozen or so cars, including Porsches, Mercedes-Benzes, Testarossas, and a Jeep or two (Norment 1991).

The Black Family as Contested Terrain

Nowhere is an image of harmonious family life more obviously represented than in a recent advertisement for Ball Park Franks. In that ad, a casually dressed Michael and Juanita Jordan stand with a small child (presumably one of their young sons), all smiling gleefully at the camera while clutching hot dogs. Reminiscent of a family portrait, Jordan has one arm draped over Juanita's shoulder; she similarly places a tight touch on the shoulder of the child. The headline reads, "Michael's Family Values." The scripted text proclaims, "Enjoy Ball Park Franks, Fat Free Classics, and kid-size Fun Franks, all with the delicious Ball Park taste that your family values."

In this advertisement, the Jordans lend support to one of the most ubiquitous themes of post-Reagan America: a vocal rhetoric that calls for a return to "traditional" family values. While never explicitly defined, the word "values" suggests a link between morality and responsibility; the entire phrase advises Americans to hearken back to bygone eras when family life was presumably simpler, purer, and more enjoyable. This emphasis on "pro-family" issues and traditional values can be partially seen as conservative backlash aimed at advances of women and political minorities and the perceived challenge to the hegemony of heterosexual love and marriage. Returning to the past means returning to the rigid gender role conformity and racial segregation reasserted in the wake of World War II (Reeves and Campbell 1994). By aligning himself with the term "family values," Michael Jordan joins a whole host of individuals who have exploited a storybook fantasy of family, hearth, and home. Realizing the powerful emotions and sentiment that could be mobilized around appeals to a mythical nuclear family, Ronald Reagan coopted images of harmonious domesticity as the presumed ideal American way of life. Despite the recent numerical decline of the nuclear family and Reagan's tumultuous relationship with his own children, as well as his status as the only divorcee to serve as president, appeals to a nostalgic, conflict-free family life proliferated throughout the Reagan-Bush era (Jeffords 1994; Fiske 1994). The 1990s continued to be fraught with nostalgic depictions of the family as the ultimate refuge of the traditional American values of hard work, discipline, and self-denial.

The conservative political agenda of the New Right, developed under the tenure of Presidents Reagan and Bush and continuing through the 1990s under the direction of Newt Gingrich, politicized notions of family in particular ways. The presumed breakdown of the seemingly stable family unit with the never-divorced breadwinner/husband and housewife/ mother continues to be used by conservatives to explain many of the social ills exacerbated by a rapidly deindustrializing economy and conservative political policies that privilege a corporate worldview (Fiske 1994). Ironically, the profile of the ideal nuclear family celebrated by Reagan might best be described as representing "the way we never were," to borrow

Stephanie Coontz's (1992) phrase. Until the nineteenth century in Western industrialized countries, both women and men worked inside or around the home. Only during the Industrial Revolution did "men's work" move outside the home while middle-class white women remained confined and enshrined within the domestic sphere. By the early portion of the twentieth century, consumerism, a developing youth culture and women's suffrage all contributed to the contestation of the extended family as the dominant norm. According to Elaine Tyler May (1988), only in the wake of World War II did Cold War fears, increased prosperity, new technologies, and fears over women's emancipation help fuel conformity to the suburban family ideal. Thus, this much-debated nuclear unit has only recently come into existence and has almost never been experienced by the vast majority of poor and disenfranchised people at any time. Furthermore, the romanticized ideal of the nuclear family, with the breadwinner husband/father and the wife/mother who does not work outside the home, now accounts for only 7 percent of American families (Hoff and Farnham 1992).

Despite these numbers, the nuclear family continues to serve as the beacon of presumed morality in an era fraught with all sorts of changes and challenges. Under the guise of morality, fairness, and a commitment to family values, a whole host of regressive social policies have been enacted. For example, women's access to legal abortions has been greatly curbed, civil rights legislation has been rolled back, and anti-pornography campaigns have been waged against artists, while corporate freedom and capital expand (Clarke 1991; Reeves and Campbell 1994; Faludi 1991). The New Right's claim of declining family values can thus he seen as a way to legitimize a series of policy changes enacted to expand capital as well as a way to remain staunchly antiwelfare, antiabortion, anti–affirmative action, and antigay (Reeves and Campbell 1994). The classic example of this type of reductive reasoning is found in the statements made after the Los Angeles riots in 1992 by then–vice president Dan Quayle, who noted that "the anarchy and lack of structure in our inner cities are testament to how quickly civilization falls apart when the family foundation cracks" (quoted in Hoff and Farnham 1992). This isolated focus on the family renders invisible political, economic, and cultural issues, which all continue to have enormous impact on the poor, people of color, and women.

Images of Jordan within the nuclear family contrast strikingly with the suggestion of the black family's decline and destruction. The well-publicized "decline" of the African American family is a notion that itself is class-based, a strategy used by conservatives and liberals alike to marginalize the increasingly large number of people of color who find themselves in poverty. Rather than blaming poverty on larger economic changes—such as deindustrialization, a rapidly globalizing economy, or continuing political issues, including institutional racism and the gendered division of labor—the rhetoric returned to a classic blame-the-victim scenario. In post-Reagan America, renewed attacks were launched against the black family as pathologically weak, indicative of what then–vice president Dan Quayle would call "a poverty of values" (Fiske 1994).

These politicized notions of the family reinforced the conservative moralism of Reaganism, which operates on the assumption of a binary logic privileging those who espoused the "traditional" virtues of hard work, determination, and loyalty while demonizing those who need legal, social, or financial assistance. Susan Jeffords (1994) argues that this dialogical reasoning of Reaganism positions individual Americans in two fundamentally different camps, separating the privileged "hard bodies" from the errant bodies. These "soft" and undesirable bodies are those that are infected—containing sexually transmitted diseases, immorality, laziness, and illegal chemicals. In a culture marked by race and gender, the soft body usually belonged to a woman or person of color, whereas the prototype hard body was invariably male and white. According to Jeffords (1994), the classic example of the Reaganite hard body can be seen in some of the most popular Hollywood films of the era. The action film hero Rambo is the quintessential success story of the period: a muscular hard body—white, male, heterosexual—committed to military strength while fighting against the ineptitude of excessive governmental regulation and other bureaucracies (Jeffords 1994). Jordan's hard-body masculinity is much more consistent with the "kinder, gentler" version that Jeffords (1994) argues attracted popular appeal during the Bush presidency and continues into the 1990s. This prototype offers a twist on the classic masculine "hard body" of Rambo, a shift not toward softness but toward an increased commitment to self-reflection, the nuclear family, and intimacy. This "gentler" version of masculinity is less intimidating and, thus, partially explains how an African American man could gain mainstream support without much white uneasiness.

By contrast, the mythical profile of the welfare mother represents the iconic soft body of Reaganism, a site where pro-family discourses intersect with racism, sexism, and classism. This depiction rests on stereotypical racist and sexist images of the (assumed) black matriarch, domineering, castigating, and lazy, who robs a husband or lover of his "rightful" role as head of the family while depending on welfare for sustenance (Reeves and Campbell 1994). According to black feminist Patricia Hill Collins (1989), gender plays an important role in the commonsense depiction of poverty. Poor African American women, the quintessential soft bodies of post-Reagan America, are often portrayed as overly masculine, apparently "choosing" to head the household in domineering ways. This inappropriate gender socialization is then said to be passed on to their impressionable offspring, who repeat the cycle by marginalizing the importance of the traditional male provider. The result, according to both conservative and many liberal voices, is a life of welfare dependency (Collins 1989). Thus, by appealing to circular reasoning, this discourse offers the absence of patriarchal power relations in these families as the apparent "proof" of black cultural deficiency (Baca Zinn 1989; Collins 1989). Or in the words of then–vice president Dan Quayle, "for those concerned about the children growing up in poverty, marriage is probably the best antipoverty program of all" (quoted in Hoff and Farnham 1992, 8).

The Jordan family serves as the moral obverse of this stereotypical vision of the black family. This portrait is readily apparent in one *Newsweek* account, published in March of 1995 just as Jordan was contemplating a return to professional basketball after a brief sabbatical/retirement. A picture of Jordan holding his daughter Jasmine as he raises his retired jersey to the rafters is juxtaposed with a text that records reactions of young Jordan fans from "the beleaguered" Houston projects where teens stand around "drinking malt liquor from brown paper sacks" (Leland 1995, 54). In addressing the issue of what Jordan meant to them,

> a few of the players cited Jordan's game. But all talked about his life off the court: about his character, his family, and especially about his relationship with his father, James Jordan, who was murdered in 1993. "He's got a good attitude, he don't smoke, he don't drink," says Robert Taylor, 11, who considers Jordan his hero. "He's got two kids—*and* a wife." (p. 54)

As this passage suggests, the ideological salience of the Jordan familial bliss lies in the enticing depictions of harmony built on the traditional gender roles that middle-class men and women have been encouraged to follow when married. Juanita raises the children with love while Michael takes his role as the family's provider very seriously: "I've got to do more for her, because this is what she expects of her husband—to be taken out to dinner, to movies, on vacations. . . . From a husband's point of view, I've got to improve" (quoted in Norment 1991, 70).

While Jordan's position within the nuclear family represents an ideal that only a tiny minority of Americans can achieve, the image of Jordan as a private family man articulates a conservative moral agenda. The visibility of an African American family like the Jordans reinforces the desirability of consumer comfort, patriarchal privilege, and familial bliss, all hallmarks of America, especially post-Reagan America (McDonald 1995). The Jordans offer a particularly powerful image masking what Reeves and Campbell (1994) identify as the perils of "reverse Robin Hoodism." Despite significant challenges, post-Reagan America has seen budget cuts, program changes, and reorganizations in social programs, coupled with increased public opposition to welfare, affirmative action, and civil rights laws. These changes and challenges have disproportionately and adversely affected people of color (Shull 1993). As Andrews (1993, 1996) also has argued in an era increasingly committed to corporate freedom and individualism, the happiness of the Jordan family seemingly offers "proof" that the American Dream is available to those people of color who are apparently committed enough to pull themselves up by their bootstraps.

Concluding Remarks: Family Matters

In discussing representations of Michael Jordan, I have attempted to highlight some of the historically specific economic rationales and dominant cultural beliefs that constitute and are reciprocally reinforced through these depictions. Michael Jordan is popular precisely because his commodified persona negotiates historically specific and complex gendered, racialized, and sexualized meanings in ways that are socially accepted and culturally envied by mainstream audiences. The appealing persona of Jordan suggests that black masculinity, which historically has been viewed as inappropriate to white and middle-class America, is represented in an attractive albeit still highly ideologically charged way. Given the intense focus on Jordan's "natural body," representations of the nuclear family serve a key role in this process. Jordan's status as a family man assists in suppressing the socially constructed portrait of a threatening black sexuality. This idealized vision of Jordan within the nuclear family also reinforces the pro-family discourses of the New Right.

Cultural analysis suggests that particular popular figures are linked to a variety of discourses, suggesting multiple, often contradictory meanings and the need to explore representations within a variety of contexts. Given this insight, it is possible to acknowledge both politically progressive and regressive elements within the phenomenon of Michael Jordan. Indeed, representations of Jordan defy racist sexual stereotypes just as these depictions assist in furthering a reactionary agenda in regard to U.S. families. Still, because cultural processes are fluid, there is no guarantee a specific version and vision of Michael Jordan will remain etched in history forever. Meanings are never essential for all time; rather they have to be constantly renewed and remade. Fresh associations will be forged because the "text" of Jordan is a boundless one, subject to rearticulation in accordance with a variety of historically specific needs and individual circumstances, including Jordan's own human agency. To locate representations within the realm of the historical and political also is to locate the commonsense meanings circulating in the wider culture within the realm of construction, contestation, and change. From this critical perspective, to interrogate representations of Michael Jordan is to offer cultural criticism as a strategy of intervention in the politicized terrain of commodified popular culture. This conceptualization alerts us to the contested character of social relations, so that we can envision alternative forms of cultural practices as well as the insight necessary to engage critically in the practice of social change.

NOTES

1. It is interesting to note the ironic rearticulation of "hang time" to describe Michael Jordan's athletic talents. In this country's sordid history of race relations, to speak of hanging, especially in relationship to African American men, is to suggest lynching. That an African American man is marketed for his "hang time" complete with a protruding tongue is ironic given the historical lethal power of lynching to reinforce ideologies of white dominance.

REFERENCES

Andrews, D. 1993. "Deconstructing Michael Jordan: Popular Culture, Politics, and Postmodern America." Unpublished doctoral dissertation, University of Illinois, Urbana-Champaign.

——. 1996. "The Fact(s) of Michael Jordan's Blackness: Excavating a Floating Racial Signifier." *Sociology of Sport Journal* 13 (2): 125–58.

Baca Zinn, M. 1989. "Family, Race, and Poverty in the Eighties." *Signs: Journal of Women in Culture and Society* 14 (41): 856–74.

Birrell, S. 1989. "Racial Relations Theories and Sport: Suggestions for a More Critical Analysis." *Sociology of Sport Journal* 6 (3): 212–27.

Birrell, S., and M. McDonald. 1993. "Privileged Assault: The Representation of Violence and the Inadequacy of Segmented Category Analysis." Paper presented at the meeting of the National Girls and Women in Sport Symposium, February, Slippery Rock PA.

Calo, B., segment producer. 1991. "The Puzzle of Michael Jordan: Why Does He Seem to Fly?" Transcript #197. *Primetime Live.* June 13. Denver CO: Journal Graphics.

Clarke, J. 1991. *New Times and Old Enemies: Essays on Cultural Studies and America.* London: Harper Collins Academic.

Cole, C., and D. Andrews. 1996. "Look—It's *NBA ShowTime*! Visions of Race in the Popular Imaginary." *Cultural Studies: A Research Annual* 1 (1): 141–81.

Cole C., and D. Denny. 1994. "Visualizing Deviance in Post-Reagan America: Magic Johnson, AIDS, and the Promiscuous World of Professional Sport." *Critical Sociology* 20 (3): 123–47.

Collins, P. H. 1989. "A Comparison of Two Works on Black Family Life." *Signs: Journal of Women in Culture and Society* 14 (41): 875–79.

Coontz, S. 1992. *The Way We Never Were: American Families and the Nostalgia Trap.* New York: Basic.

Curry, T. J. 1991. "Fraternal Bonding in the Locker Room: A Profeminist Analysis of Talk about Competition and Women." *Sociology of Sport Journal* 8: 119–35.

Davis, A. 1984. "Rape, Racism, and the Myth of the Black Rapist." In *Feminist Frameworks: Alternative Accounts of the Relations between Women and Men.* 2nd ed., edited by A. Jaggar and P. Rothenberg, 428–31. New York: McGraw-Hill.

Davis, L. 1990. "The Articulation of Difference: White Preoccupation with the Question of Racially Linked Genetic Differences among Athletes." *Sociology of Sport Journal* 7 (2): 179–87.

Desmond, J. 1994. "Embodying Difference: Issues in Dance and Cultural Studies." *Cultural Critique* 26: 33–62.

Dyreson, M. 1989. "The Emergence of Consumer Culture and the Transformation of Physical Culture: American Sport in the 1920s." *Journal of Sport History* 16 (3): 261–81.

Dyson, M. 1993. "Be Like Mike? Michael Jordan and the Pedagogy of Desire." *Cultural Studies* 7 (1): 64–72.

Edsall, T., and M. Edsall. 1991. *Chain Reaction: The Impact of Race, Rights, and Taxes on the American Public.* New York: W.W. Norton.

Faludi, S. 1991. *Backlash: The Undeclared War against American Women.* New York: Anchor.

Fiske, J. 1994. *Media Matters: Everyday Culture and Political Change.* Minneapolis: University of Minnesota.

Foucault, M. 1978. *History of Sexuality: An Introduction.* New York: Vintage Books.

Gates, H. L. 1994. "Preface." In *Black Male: Representations of Masculinity in Contemporary Art*, edited by T. Golden, 11–14. New York: Whitney Museum of American Art.

Giroux, H. 1994. *Disturbing Pleasures.* New York: Routledge.

Golden, T. 1994. "My Brother." In *Black Male: Representations of Masculinity in Contemporary Art*, edited by T. Golden, 19–43. New York: Whitney Museum of American Art.

Grossberg, L. 1992. *We Got to Get Out of This Place: Popular Conservatism and Post-modern Culture*. New York: Routledge.

Hall, S. 1985. "Signification, Representation, and Ideology: Althusser and the Post-structuralist Debate." *Critical Studies in Mass Communication* 2: 91–114.

———. 1986a. "The Problem of Ideology: Marxism without Guarantees." *Journal of Communication Inquiry* 10 (2): 28–44.

———. 1986b. "On Postmodernism and Articulation: An Interview." *Journal of Communication Inquiry* 10 (2): 45–60.

———. 1988. *The Hard Road to Renewal: Thatcherism and the Crisis of the Left*. London: Verso.

———. 1991. "Signification, Representation and Ideology: Althusser and the Post-structuralist debates." In *Critical Perspectives on Media and Society*, edited by R. Avery and D. Eason, 88–113. New York: Guilford.

Harris, D. 1993. "The Current Crisis in Men's Lingerie: Notes on the Belated Com-mercialization of a Noncommercial Product." *Salmagundi* 100: 131–39.

Harris, O. 1991. "The Image of the African American in Psychological Journals, 1825–1923." *The Black Scholar* 21 (4): 25–29.

———. 1995. "Muhammad Ali and the Revolt of the Black Athlete." In *Muham-mad Ali: The People's Champ*, edited by E. Gorn, 54–69. Urbana: University of Illinois Press.

Hoff, J., and C. Farnham. 1992. "Sexist and Racist: The Post-Cold War World's Emphasis on Family Values." *Journal of Women's History* 4 (2): 6–9.

hooks, b. 1992. *Black Looks: Race and Representation*. Boston: South End.

———. 1994. "Feminism Inside: Toward a Black Body Politic." In *Black Male: Rep-resentations of Masculinity in Contemporary Art*, edited by T. Golden, 127–40. New York: Whitney Museum of American Art.

Howell, J. 1991. "A Revolution in Motion: Advertising and the Politics of Nostalgia." *Sociology of Sport Journal* 8 (3): 258–71.

Ingrassia, M. 1995. "Calvin's World." *Newsweek* 126 (11): 60–66.

Jackson, D. 1989. "Calling the Plays in Black and White." *Boston Globe*, January 22, A30–33.

Jackson, P. 1994. "Black Male: Advertising and the Cultural Politics of Masculin-ity." *Gender, Place, and Culture* 1 (1): 49–59.

Jeffords, S. 1994. *Hard Bodies: Hollywood Masculinity in the Reagan Era*. New Bruns-wick NJ: Rutgers University.

Katz, D. 1994. *Just Do It: The Nike Spirit in the Corporate World*. New York: Random House.

King, S. 1993. "The Politics of the Body and the Body Politic: Magic Johnson and the Ideology of AIDS." *Sociology of Sport Journal* 10: 270-85.

Kirkpatrick, C. 1991. "The Unlikeliest Homeboy." *Sports Illustrated* 75 (27): 70-75.

Lane, R., and J. McHugh. 1995. "A Very Green 1995." *Forbes* 156 (14): 212-32.

Leland, J. 1995. "Hoop Dreams: Will Michael Jordan Return to Basketball?" *Newsweek* 125 (12): 48-55.

Lusted, D. 1991. "The Glut of Personality." In *Stardom: The Industry of Desire*, edited by C. Gledhill, 251-58. London: Associated University.

May, E. T. 1988. *Homeward Bound: American Families in the Cold War Era*. New York: Basic Books.

McDonald, M. 1995. "Clean 'Air': Representing Michael Jordan in the Reagan-Bush Era." Unpublished doctoral dissertation, University of Iowa, Iowa City.

Messner, M. 1988. "Sport and Male Domination: The Female Athlete as Contested Terrain." *Sociology of Sport Journal* 5: 197-211.

Morse, M. 1983. "Sport on Television: Replay and Display." In *Regarding Television: Critical Approaches—An Anthology*, edited by A. Kaplan, 44-66. Los Angeles: American Film Institute.

Murphy, T. 1985. "On the Rebound." *Madison Avenue* 27 (June): 28-34.

Naughton, J. 1992. *Talking to the Air: The Rise of Michael Jordan*. New York: Warner.

Norment, L. 1991. "Michael and Juanita Jordan Talk about Love, Marriage, and Life after Basketball." *Ebony* 47 (November): 68-76.

Raissman, R. 1984. "Jordan Soars for Nike Deal: New Strategy Seen." *Advertising Age* 1 (October 18): 58.

Reeves, J., and R. Campbell. 1994. *Cracked Coverage: Television News, the Anti-cocaine Crusade, and the Reagan Legacy*. Durham NC: Duke University.

Roberts, R. 1983. *Papa Jack: Jack Johnson and the Era of White Hopes*. New York: Free Press.

Rowe, D. 1994. "Accommodating Bodies: Celebrity, Sexuality, and 'Tragic Magic.'" *Journal of Sport and Social Issues* 18 (2): 6-26.

Sabo, D., and S. Jansen. 1992. "Images of Men in the Sport Media: The Social Reproduction of the Gender Order." In *Men, Masculinity, and the Media: Research on Men and Masculinity*, edited by S. Craig, 169-84. Newbury Park CA: Sage.

Sammons, J. 1995. "Rebel with a Cause: Muhammad Ali as Sixties Protest Symbol." In *Muhammad Ali: The People's Champ*, edited by E. Gorn, 154-80. Champaign: University of Illinois Press.

Shull, S. 1993. *A Kinder, Gentler Racism? The Reagan-Bush Civil Rights Legacy*. Armonk NY: M.E. Sharpe.

Sperling, D., executive producer. 1989. *Michael Jordan: Come Fly with Me*. New York: CBS/Fox.

Swift, E. M. 1991. "From Corned Beef to Caviar." *Sports Illustrated*, 74 (27): 54–58.

Theberge, N. 1991. "Reflection on the Body in the Sociology of Sport." *Quest* 43: 123–34.

Vancil, M. 1992. "Playboy Interview: Michael Jordan." *Playboy* 39 (5): 51–64.

Watney, S. 1989. *Policing Desire: Pornography, AIDS, and the Media*. 2nd ed. Minneapolis: University of Minnesota.

West, C. 1993. *Race Matters*. Boston: Beacon.

Wiggins, D. 1989. "Great Speed but Little Stamina: The Historical Debate over Black Athletic Superiority." *Journal of Sport History* 16 (2): 158–85.

17

Rush Limbaugh, Donovan McNabb, and "A Little Social Concern"
Reflections on the Problems of Whiteness in Contemporary American Sport

DOUGLAS HARTMANN

On Sunday, September 28, 2003, just a few weeks into the conservative radio talk show host's new gig as a studio commentator on ESPN's *NFL Countdown*, Limbaugh offered this contribution to a panel discussion of the early season struggles of the Eagles and their quarterback:

> Sorry to say this, I don't think he's been that good from the get-go. . . . What we have here is a little social concern in the NFL. The media has been very desirous that a Black quarterback can do well—Black coaches and Black quarterbacks doing well. . . . There's a little hope invested in McNabb, and he got credit for the performance of his team that he didn't deserve. The defense [has] carried this team.[1]

No one in the studio pushed Limbaugh to elaborate or defend his claims. However, when told of Limbaugh's comments, McNabb himself had this to say, "It's somewhat shocking to hear that on national TV from him. It's not something I can sit here and say won't bother me." The racial aspects of the criticisms were what bothered McNabb. "It's sad that you've got to go to skin color. I thought we were through with that whole deal." Later in the week, McNabb worried that Limbaugh's comments might discourage young African Americans from wanting to play quarterback, on the grounds that they might "be looked down upon because of the color of [their] skin."[2]

McNabb's response touched off a national firestorm of controversy and critical commentary. Many were quick to recall Limbaugh's past record of inflammatory racial remarks and anti-black attitudes—"Who cares about [African Americans]," he once famously said in what was perhaps the most widely cited quote, "they're only 12 percent of the population." The National Association for the Advancement of Colored People (NAACP) characterized Limbaugh's comments as "both bigoted and ignorant" and called for Limbaugh to be fired or at least for the network to provide an opposing point of view. In the middle of the campaign for the Democratic presidential nomination, several candidates took up the mantle and vied for the most compelling sound bite: Wesley Clark characterized the remarks as "hateful and ignorant speech," Howard Dean called them "absurd and offensive," and the Reverend Al Sharpton announced that later in the week he would hold a news conference in front of ABC headquarters in New York where he would call for a national boycott of the network if Limbaugh wasn't released. (ABC and ESPN are corporate cousins, both owned by Walt Disney Company.) As these and other comments made their rounds, sports reporters, columnists, and other writers all across the country began to solicit comments and reactions from players and weigh in with their criticisms.[3]

Not even the NFL was happy about this publicity. Eagles owner Jeffrey Lurie characterized Limbaugh's remarks as "despicable" and spoke of the "institutional racism" of the network and its executives. And Joe Browne, the league's executive vice president of communications and public affairs, released an official statement that put the blame as much on the network as on Limbaugh himself: "Donovan's stature as a top quarterback reflects his performance on the field, not the desire of the media. . . . ESPN knew what they were getting when they hired Rush Limbaugh. ESPN selects its on-air talent, not the NFL."[4]

Having already been barraged with thousands of negative e-mail messages on the matter, ESPN had to do something.[5] They had *Countdown* anchor Chris Berman, whom the network described as a "self-described New England Democrat," hold a news conference. His main message was that he didn't think "Rush was malicious in intent or in tone." "As cut and dry as it seems in print," ESPN's star announcer explained, "I didn't think so when it went by my ears." Berman went on to say that the network was sorry to have upset McNabb "in the middle of his travails" and reiterated that he didn't think Limbaugh's comment "was meant the way it came out. I don't think that defines the way Rush feels about people." Limbaugh himself had a similar message on his nationally syndicated radio talk show on Wednesday. "My comments this past Sunday were directed at the media and were not racially motivated." "This is such a mountain out of a mole hill," he told his listeners. "There's no racism here. There's no racist intent whatsoever."[6]

But the damage was done. Behind-the-scenes talks between Limbaugh and ESPN about an exit strategy began on Wednesday morning, October 1. By the end of the day, Limbaugh had announced his resignation via his website. While still insisting that his comments were directed only at the media and not racially motivated, he acknowledged,

> I offered an opinion . . . [that] has caused discomfort to the crew, which I regret. I love NFL Sunday Countdown and do not want to be a distraction to the great work done by all who work on it. Therefore, I have decided to resign.

ESPN and ABC sports president George Brodenheimer had this to say: "We accept his resignation and regret the circumstances surrounding this. We believe that he took the appropriate action to resolve this matter expeditiously."[7] The following day (Thursday), in a previously scheduled appearance in front of the National Press Association, however, Limbaugh reiterated his previous claims and mused, "All of this has become the tempest that it is because I must have been right about something. If I wasn't right, there wouldn't be this cacophony of outrage that has sprung up in the sportswriter community." In fact, Limbaugh was quoted in *Newsweek* magazine as saying, "I know I'm right. . . . I'm not going to retract anything."[8]

The Working of Whiteness

On initial reflection, the lessons of this incident for our understanding of the relations between sports and race in American culture appear to be fairly clear and straightforward—and, perhaps more importantly, make the sports community look enlightened and progressive. When a popular African American athlete objects to the racially inflammatory comments of a controversial political pundit turned sports analyst, the sports media and opinion-makers rise to condemn the comments, the commentator, and his network as racist. In spite of the attempts of the offending parties to deny the racial intent of the remarks and downplay their anti-black thrust, the opposition holds firm; in fact, public opinion in and around the sporting community hardens in support. The network is forced to take action and works out a deal where the commentator—albeit without repudiating his comments—resigns his post. Thus, the drama was quickly and decisively resolved in favor of what would seem to be the forces of racial progress.

The only real question, it would seem, is how the commentator (and his erstwhile network supporters) believed he could get away with insisting—repeatedly and with a straight face—that his remarks were neither racially motivated nor at all racist. And here, I believe, is the first lesson in how the erstwhile normativity of whiteness typically operates to assert its authority and, by extension, to support and maintain white social supremacy.

Part of the explanation for Limbaugh's self-righteousness stems from the fact that his television commentary was not directed against McNabb personally. But Limbaugh also believed he was in the right. In the conservative pundit' s worldview—which we must take seriously if we are to understand the cultural power of whiteness and its relationship to structures of white supremacy—racial fairness is about treating individuals of all races exactly the same, judging each only on the basis of his or her merits and performances. Limbaugh believed his remarks about what he perceived to be the media's overly sympathetic assessment of McNabb were not only defensible but in fact virtuous—because they emanated from colorblind, individualistic values. Anything else, in this view, was actually its own version of racism, a classic case of reverse racism. Although Limbaugh did not use this phrase, there were those on his side who claimed that if racism was involved in this incident, it was in the denial of Limbaugh's right to criticize an African American if he believed the statistics and results warranted it.[9]

Here it is important to point out that Limbaugh was not lacking for evidence in support of his claim that McNabb—one of the most popular figures in the league as judged by jersey sales and the popularity of his Chunky Soup commercials—was overrated. McNabb's early season performance had not only failed to live up to his previous All-Pro standards, but the Eagles signal caller actually had the lowest statistical rating of any quarterback in the league over the first two weeks of the season. Limbaugh was hardly the first critic to point this out. McNabb had long been subject to criticism from his (notoriously fickle) hometown media, and that fall I heard an eminent sociologist present a statistical analysis of the performance of NFL quarterbacks over several seasons that was unable to definitely reject Limbaugh's claims (Walker 2003).[10] Moreover, a recent sociological study (Buffington 2005) found that the rise of black quarterbacks in the NFL tends to be celebrated in the media as a positive development, and some economists claimed that television audiences increased significantly if at least one team started a black quarterback (Vigdor 2003). Indeed, race-critical sports scholars have been talking for at least a decade about the inordinate popularity of superstar African American athletes such as Michael Jordan, what Michael Eric Dyson (1993) called the "pedagogy of desire" (for a fuller treatment, see Hartmann 2006).

For all of its supposed evidence and logic, however, the shortcomings of Limbaugh's colorblind appeal are both manifest and legion from a more critical, sociological perspective. Perhaps most obvious is the fundamental inability of an individualist, race-neutral perspective to grasp and grapple with persistent inequalities of race. A noble aspiration, colorblindness is far from an accurate description of the racial realities of the United States today—and this applies to sports as much as to society at large. Whether it involves stacking, differential treatment by coaches, management, league officials, or stereotypes in the media, sociological research has consistently demonstrated clear patterns of racial discrimination in sports (for a review, see Hartmann 2000); and this is to say nothing of the disadvantaged social backgrounds and institutional barriers that many African American athletes have to overcome. Even the celebration of black athletic success can take on troubling racial overtones and connotations. The same sports scholars who have detected a tendency to romanticize certain celebrity African American athletes have also documented that the media and American public turn on black athletes quickly when shortcomings on or off the fields of competition are exposed (e.g., Cole and Andrews 1996; Cole and Denny 1994; see also Andrews 1996).

In the absence of interviews or other behind-the-scenes data, it is impossible to say for sure just how conscious and strategic Limbaugh's deployment of colorblind discourse and ideals was. But their impact on audiences and the general American public is well known among race scholars. Not only does colorblindness blind regular folks to existing racial injustices and inequalities, it can make it seem as if the existing racial status quo and white supremacy itself is acceptable. This legitimation function has led sociologist Eduardo Bonilla-Silva (2001; see also Bonilla-Silva and Forman 2000) and others (Carr 1997; Crenshaw 1997) to argue that "colorblind racism" is the most pervasive and problematic racial discourse of the post–civil rights movement era.

And even if Limbaugh conceived of his initial remarks to be in defense of race-neutral values, this still raises the question of why he refused to explicitly defend his colorblind racial vision, instead hiding behind the claim that he was not talking about race at all. Even colorblindness, after all, is a vision of race and racial justice. The answer takes us deeper into the heart of Limbaugh's whiteness. Beyond its colorblind individualism, Limbaugh's ideology and discourse were based in the comfortable assumption that his worldview and way of talking were simply true, so commonsensical and taken for granted that they didn't need to be articulated or elaborated, much less defended. Such an assumption is made possible, as critical whiteness scholars have analyzed in some detail (see Goldberg 1993), both because whites occupy a dominant social position and because of the abstract, universalist conceptions of knowledge and subjectivity that are associated with their liberal individualism. Whiteness, in short, is a cultural vantage point so deeply privileged that it is able to disavow its own social location and cultural specificity. And it is precisely this normativity, this perceived universality and transcendence, that allowed Limbaugh, as Dave Roediger (2002) has commented on the pundit's ill-fated television show, to "walk the tightrope between the unspoken and the largely unspeakable" (p. 54).

Limbaugh's unacknowledged white normativity had additional social functions as well. At their most basic, they placed the seemingly objective, disinterested white commentator in the position of being the ultimate arbiter of black America. Limbaugh's comments not only put McNabb in his place (and conveniently forgot McNabb's previous seasons of earned merit on the gridiron), they resonated with the sense of victimization, outrage, resentment, and resurgent—if misplaced—pride of white racial projects. Whether intended or not, they reflected and reinforced a subtler, more entrenched resentment about the successes of African Americans both in sports and society in general. This is, of course, a difficult point to prove conclusively, but perhaps a counterexample will provide some empirical ballast. I am thinking here of Brett Favre, the much-celebrated quarterback of the Green Bay Packers. In recent years, Favre's performance decline has been both more obvious and precipitous than McNabb's was then or now. Yet Favre—who has refused to retire or have his playing time reduced (and this is not even to get into his onetime addiction to painkillers)—has not only escaped substantial or sustained criticism, he has actually been mythologized by the league and the media for his grit and determination. Furthermore, when the subject of retirement is brought up by disgruntled fans or commentators, Favre's desire to continue playing is defended on the grounds that he has "earned the right" to decide for himself by virtue of his previous accomplishments, which include leading the Packers to two Super Bowls in the 1990s. I do not know what Limbaugh thinks of Favre, but clearly he did not extend such an allowance for past performance to McNabb.[11] In any case, the more general point is that Limbaugh's whiteness not only denied its own cultural biases and social location, it also served to assert white privilege and dominance over African Americans—even in an arena where African Americans have made tremendous progress and enjoy a high degree of power and influence.

Some Questions about Whiteness and the World of Sport

Of course, the real question for this analysis is whether the leaders and opinion-makers of the sporting establishment realized and repudiated Limbaugh's whiteness and its associated supremacist functions, as might be inferred from the eventual and seemingly decisive resolution of the controversy he provoked. Several questions and factors complicate such a straightforward, heartwarming rendering of the sports community as a critic of whiteness and its privileges.

For one thing, Limbaugh's rebuke did not come immediately. Not only did Limbaugh's in-studio colleagues—African American analysts Michael Irvin and Tom Jackson among them—fail to register an on-air complaint, the national media didn't pick up the story until prompted by McNabb's observations and complaints. A LexisNexis search reveals that the articles and commentaries in the two days after Limbaugh's initial comments could be counted on one hand. The full barrage of public commentary and criticism didn't come until the end of the week (thirty-two articles on Thursday, forty-eight on Friday), after Limbaugh had already resigned his position. If the sports world—or at least the NFL and its reporters and commentators—was (or is) so racially attuned and committed, why the hesitation?

And then there is the question of why Limbaugh—with his history of inflammatory racial opinions and remarks—was hired by ESPN in the first place. The *New York Times* was obsessed with "unanswered questions" about how much network executives knew about Limbaugh's "record of racial commentary" when he was brought on. But the real mystery is how the network could have failed to consider the racial views of the most popular and controversial talk show host in the nation. The explicit justification provided by ESPN for the hiring was that Limbaugh was brought in to be "the voice of the fan," the regular guy, the six-pack Joe—much like what ABC had said of the hiring of Dennis Miller for *Monday Night Football* two years previously (a position for which Limbaugh himself had famously interviewed and campaigned).[12] This blatant disregard for the African American football fan may not constitute blatant, out-and-out racism (as

Kimberle Crenshaw [2003] charged); however, one must acknowledge that casting Limbaugh as the "everyman" of American sports fans clearly normalized and naturalized the whiteness of the league's fan base and its cultural commonsense.

A third point has to do with the blunt label and accusations of racism leveraged against Limbaugh—a framing, not incidentally, that seems to have become story line for the incident in the collective memory of the sporting establishment.[13] Let me preface this point by reiterating that there is no doubt in my mind that Limbaugh's comments—which emanate from a normative position designed to privilege whiteness, keep African Americans in their place, and maintain and legitimate the broader racial status quo—were racist in their social function if not their actual intent. In this respect, the sporting establishment got it right in castigating Limbaugh. However, in terms of their expressed rhetoric and underlying ideology, I think things are a bit more complicated. There are two reasons for this. One is that if Limbaugh's comments were indeed ideologically racist, it is a brand of racism that went well beyond the usual individualist, anti-black sentiments of traditional, referential definitions of racism. Connected with this, branding Limbaugh (or anyone else, for that matter) as racist made it far too easy for the sporting establishment to absolve itself of the troubles and complications of race—much as the disavowal of the Holocaust allowed Europe to wash its hands of the other stains of race throughout the second half of the twentieth century.

So the question now becomes twofold: (a) What, precisely, did the sporting establishment see as problematic about Limbaugh's comments? (b) What does this tell us about the relationships among race, racism, whiteness, and white supremacy in contemporary American sports? To address these questions, I conducted a close reading and basic content analysis of the forty-four commentaries preserved in the LexisNexis database on the episode written in the week immediately following Limbaugh's comments. I will turn to that analysis now. What is at stake here is less a matter of being politically correct (once again, in terms of a progressive racial politics, the sporting establishment was clearly on the right side in opposing Limbaugh) than it is of a proper understanding of the subtle and complicated ways in which race and whiteness are implicated in the culture and practices of the American sporting establishment if not American society more generally.

The Perceived Problems with Limbaugh and the Problems with Those Perceptions

The first and most obvious objection I anticipated, given the initial sound bites, was that of sportswriters and columnists who described Limbaugh and his comments as racist. And indeed there were some who took this line. One of them was Bob Raismann of the *New York Daily News*, who called Limbaugh, among other things, a "two-bit bigot." "Strip away all of Limbaugh's media mumbo-jumbo," Raismann insisted, "and what you have is someone who believes McNabb is an inadequate quarterback because he is black."[14] However, there were far fewer of this sort of accusation than might have been expected. Only six of the forty-four commentaries in the sample explicitly condemned Limbaugh for being racist, and three of these references came from columns penned by the *Daily News*'s Raismann.

The limited accusations of racism could have resulted from the fact that the sporting establishment did indeed possess a subtle, sophisticated understanding and critique of race and racism and Limbaugh's self-satisfied whiteness. One might infer this, for example, from Lurie's somewhat cryptic mention of institutional racism or from the tantalizing, much-quoted comment offered by Eagles defensive end N. D. Kalu: "He speaks well. He's well-read. But he's an idiot. That's dangerous."[15] Somewhat in this vein, Thomas George, writing in the *New York Times*, used the incident to highlight ongoing racism in the league. "Among the black quarterbacks and the three black head coaches on the 32 NFL teams," George reported, "there is a definitive feeling that they are on shorter leashes than their white counterparts. For every push from the news media, they say, there is a blistering pull."[16] But very few writers went this route. Rather than delving into the subtleties and complexities of Limbaugh's white normative appeal and its perpetuation of white privilege, in fact, most critics had very little at all to say about race.

The most basic, nonracialist criticism was that Limbaugh was a sports novice who had no place commenting on football in the first place. At least a half dozen columnists made this problem their central theme, and many others made mention of it, often quoting Washington linebacker LaVar Arrington: "Who is Rush Limbaugh to make a statement like that? He needs to stay in his area of expertise because he's out of it right now."[17]

One of the broader points for those who saw Limbaugh as somehow out of his element was that the sports world was simply not the proper place for Limbaugh's brand of commentary, that Limbaugh and his views were "too controversial" for the arena of sports. A half dozen writers made this their primary thesis. Here, the point had less to do with Limbaugh's sports expertise (or lack thereof) and more to do with the fact that he was raising so-called controversial issues in an arena that many considered somehow special or sacred, above politics, either because it was a sacred cultural space or because it was an arena for entertainment pure and simple. It was the latter point that was made by a sportswriter out of West Virginia named Jason Martin:

> That's why many skip to the sports page—to avoid the mindless jibber-jabber of political positioning and redundant self-promotion that plagues most of the rest of the [newspaper's] sections.[18]

Although there is nothing inherently objectionable about either of these responses, there is certainly nothing particularly progressive or inspiring about them in racial terms. Even worse, in advocating for an uncontroversial, apolitical sports world, these sports-as-somehow-special critics actually let Limbaugh and his racial opinions off the hook. Martin, it is worth noting, was as frustrated with the demands for Limbaugh's dismissal as he was with Limbaugh's initial comments because the whole controversy, for him, had nothing to do with sports. The ultimate function of positing the world of sports as off-limits to any non-sports issue that might be considered controversial is that sports is rendered an irrelevant, if not essentially conservative social institution—one that turns a blind eye to the social status quo, racial or otherwise. In terms of its social effects, the outcome is little different from Limbaugh's privileged, colorblind complacency. It is the kind of agnostic, apolitical vision that is most easily accepted by those who are privileged and empowered to begin with.

The fourth and most popular criticism of Limbaugh—expressed by slightly more than half of the commentaries in the sample (twenty-three of forty-four)—appears a good deal more engaged and progressive and is both revealing and dangerous precisely because of that. Somewhat like the previous set of responses, this group held that Limbaugh shouldn't have brought race explicitly into the sacrosanct world of sports. But these critics did not justify their claim on the grounds that sports was apolitical or somehow off-limits to non-sports controversy but rather on the grounds that there wasn't any racism in sports in the first place. More than this, they argued, sports was a paragon and model for appropriate race relations. Thomas Boswell, writing in the *Washington Post*, was one of these critics. Boswell began his condemnation of Limbaugh by saying that the race of quarterbacks was "a dead horse, a forgotten issue" in the NFL, but it was the higher ideals of the league and sports more generally that he felt Limbaugh had really violated:

> Despite its violence, the NFL does possess a purity. Merit is honored. Race, religion, and origin are, largely, ignored. Best of all, like sports in general, every premise is measured against reality, not molded to ideology. On days like this, as Limbaugh leaves us, that sounds mighty pure.[19]

Eagles defensive tackle Corey Simon supplied one of the favorite quotations to this effect:

> The athletic arena is the one thing that unites us. It takes away racial and religious affiliation. To bring this guy out of the political arena to the purity of football I think is uncalled for. . . . It kind of sickens you.[20]

It almost goes without saying that this idealization of sports as Mecca of racial purity and justice presents a serious impediment for grasping the persistent problems of race and racism in sports and in sports' relation to racial formations in society at large. But what is more troubling about this belief in the racial sanctity of sports, at least in the context of this case study, is that it is based on a colorblind, individualist set of ideals not so different from some of Limbaugh's own. For these critics, Limbaugh's central offense was not his racism. It was not his political posturing or his lack of football acumen or even his underlying white normative vision and privilege. Limbaugh's real offense was violating sports' colorblind, race-neutral language and discourse, exposing for all the world to see and in fact have to discuss the realities of race in operation in the NFL, especially at the skill position of the quarterback. He violated the colorblind code that says you can't call attention to race openly and explicitly, even when it is right there in front of you.

This colorblindness runs deep in American sports culture. Although a full treatment of the point is well beyond the confines of this analysis, it is instructive to note that such an individualist, meritocratic ethos was even apparent in McNabb's initial comments to the media ("I thought we were through with all of that") and at the core of his subsequent clarifications and discussions.

> I'm a football player and that was my dream. My dream was to play pro football in the NFL ... [and] to become a great human being, a person that people can rely on and trust and a good football player.

He also noted he wanted people to "see him as a quarterback not a black quarterback."[21] McNabb's reaction and attitude, according to *Monday Night Football*'s Al Michaels, "spoke volumes about the kind of guy he is" and was obviously a big part of the quarterback's popularity and appeal.[22] The only difference between Limbaugh and the sporting establishment on this front is that Limbaugh believed these ideals were being violated by the media, whereas his critics believed they were being upheld.

I have already suggested the sociological shortcomings of colorblind discourse and rhetoric in previous sections. Here, I want to make a couple of additional points. First is how this avowed race neutrality stands in contrast to the way in which the NFL and its media partners regularly celebrate African American stars such as McNabb and construct narratives of racial uplift and progress around them. Though often conveyed through cultural codes that have their own dangers and abuses (Wheelock and Hartmann 2007), there is nothing, in my view, necessarily wrong with this practice. In fact, I think even subtle narratives of progress can serve a useful, even progressive role in reminding white audiences of ongoing struggles for racial justice. However, it is clearly not consistent with a strict, literal interpretation of colorblind ideals. This brings me to what I believe is one of the real ironies or perhaps tragedies of the entire Limbaugh-McNabb affair: there should have been nothing for liberals in the sporting establishment who were active supporters of McNabb and other black quarterbacks to be ashamed about. In a society marked by historical and persistent inequalities, the defense of McNabb could well have been seen as a very good, very progressive thing. Indeed, meaningful racial resistance and change requires some degree of this kind of color consciousness and political commitment. Yet the liberal colorblind ideology made the leaders and opinion-makers of the sporting establishment—even by those who may have been championing the position for progressive reasons—embarrassed to the point of an inability to maintain and defend the courage of their political passion and personal commitment.

Making the absence of a meaningful politics of racial resistance in sports all the more problematic is how colorblind idealism can work in tandem with the views that sports should not deal with issues that are controversial or with issues not bearing directly on the world of sports. Together, as I put it in my study of the 1968 African American Olympic protest movement (Hartmann 2003, chap. 3), this combination of ideals about sports being both racially progressive and yet somehow above or beyond the complexities of everyday politics and social life allows sports elites and sports fans to have their cake and eat it too—to believe that sports can at once be a paragon of racial virtue and simultaneously never be required to take a stand on any potentially progressive issues or incidents. The net result is that the ideologies and discourses of the sports world cause its adherents to misunderstand the problems of race in the United States and, even worse, to accept and endorse the legitimacy of the racial status quo and its associated white dominance. And in all of this, the most disturbing discovery is how much the critics who rejected Limbaugh actually had in common with his ideology and discourse.

Discussion and Conclusion: Ideologies, Inequalities, and Institutional Practices

In a rightfully cautious commentary on the rise of whiteness studies among sports scholars, C. Richard King (2005) argues that the focus of analytic work should not be on the concept of whiteness per se but rather on white supremacy as a structural problem. The proper object of study for whiteness scholars, in other words, should be "the attitudes, ideologies and policies associated with the rise of blatant forms of white or European domination over non-white populations" (p. 401, quoted in Fredrickson 1981).

I agree with King's point—that the ultimate focus and payoff in studying whiteness should not be on the structure and meaning of white culture and identity but rather on how whiteness, a whole set of ideologies, discourses, and identities, serves to produce and perpetuate existing racial hierarchies and white domination more specifically. It is, in other words, the relationship between white cultural forms and the social structures of white privilege and power that is most important to analyze and dissect, the proper project of critical whiteness studies (for a recent review and commentary, see Roediger 2006). However, I have a bit of trouble with King's further suggestion that white supremacy is "self-conscious" as well as systemic (p. 402). In my view, the whole idea of whiteness as an analytical category is to focus attention on ideas, ideals, ideologies, and discourses that are not fully understood by their advocates and adherents and that, in their unthinking embrace, serve to mystify, misconstrue, and accept the realities of race in the United States. Whiteness, in this sense, is less an identity than the absence of identity (see Doane 1997; Lewis 2004) and more accurately conceived as an ideology and discourse—or set of ideologies and discourses—that limit and constrain consciousness, that get in the way of a fuller understanding and a more progressive vision of racial justice and change. The essence of critical whiteness studies is to grasp the power of these taken-for-granted, commonsensical ideologies and discourses, to understand how these ways of thinking and talking serve to perpetuate the unequal and unjust social hierarchies of race in the

United States through processes—of both mystification and legitimation—neither grasped nor intended by the actors themselves.[23]

The most basic purpose of focusing on media responses and public reactions to Rush Limbaugh's racially charged comments has been to illustrate this point—to show how deeply engrained and largely unrealized the discourses and ideologies that perpetuate white cultural power and social privilege are in the American sporting establishment and its attendant media. And my broader ambition has been to demonstrate and explore some of the specific ways in which the American sports world both complies with and advances the cultural formations of whiteness. Based on both critical theory and the empirical data of this case, I have argued that the unique power and analytical problematic of whiteness in the context of American athletics derive from two key features: its complicity with sports' colorblind ideals and discourse and the belief or claim that sports is somehow a sacred or special cultural space. Moreover, I have suggested that taken together these beliefs and ideologies constitute the crucial, consequential paradox of sports' social power as it pertains to race: it is a cultural arena that can be taken seriously and highly valued even as it is dismissed as trivial and unimportant.

But I have still only scratched the surface of the problem of whiteness and its relation to the world of American sports. Whiteness is far more fluid and multifaceted than this particular case reveals (see Kusz 2006). And, as George Lipsitz (1998) writes in his seminal *Possessive Investment in Whiteness*, "whiteness never works in isolation; it functions as part of a broader dynamic grid created through intersections of race, class, gender and sexuality" (p. 72). For reasons that should by now be obvious, sports scholars have focused on the ideological and identity aspects of the categories Lipsitz highlights (for a discussion and examples, see McDonald 2005). And where I believe there are real contributions left to be made is in the institutional realm—the social structures and organizational arrangements that white ideologies and identities take shape in and help to reproduce. And no institution is more important and pervasive in this respect than the market-based economy of the American sporting scene. I am thinking here of the institutional practices and cultural assumptions about a sporting world driven and sustained by a for-profit, capitalist ethos.

Explicating the connections among whiteness, white supremacy, and the market-obsessed sporting establishment obviously requires far more time and space than is possible in the conclusion of a case-based analysis like this one. But let me illustrate by recalling why ESPN hired Rush Limbaugh—whose only meaningful experience in the world of sports was a once-upon-a-time stint as the PR man for the Kansas City Royals—in the first place.[24] The racial and political dynamics may have been complicated, but the bottom line was not. The rationale was entirely economic. ESPN believed that Limbaugh would generate interest and intrigue and thus increase market share of their studio show. Many critics of Limbaugh's comments about McNabb immediately pointed this out. In the NAACP's initial statement on the matter, in fact, Kweisi Mfume speculated the whole thing was a publicity ploy. "It is appalling that ESPN has to go to this extent to try to increase viewership."[25] The *Daily News*'s Raismann predicted that ESPN would not only refuse to fire Limbaugh but would likely give him a raise because of how all of the controversy and attention was almost sure to promote the ratings boost the network was looking for in bringing in Limbaugh.[26] The sports economist Jacob Vigdor (2003) went so far as to suggest that if the NFL was promoting African American quarterbacks such as McNabb, it was not for high-minded, liberal principles but for base economic motives: teams with starting black quarterbacks, according to his analysis of television ratings, actually outperformed white quarterbacks in terms of audience viewership and fan interest.

What stands out about these and other references to Limbaugh's market appeal is how deeply taken for granted or matter-of-fact all interested parties were about the profit motive. The need to increase market share and make as much money as possible is simply not something that anyone felt could be challenged or changed. This is not to suggest that the profit motive is the only interest organizing the production and promotion of NFL football—if nothing else, the Limbaugh-McNabb incident illustrates that there are limits even to this. But economic gain is clearly pervasive and, more to the point of this essay, deeply bound up with both the demographic and cultural dominance of whites in sports as in the society more generally.

Whiteness functions in a wide variety of forms and contexts in the United States—in ideologies and discourses, in popular cultural practices, and in institutional arrangements and the cultural logics that animate them. The challenge for the critical race scholar is not so much to find whiteness but rather to figure out the insidious, nefarious, and not-so-obvious ways it works to perpetuate the normativity of white worldviews and maintain the privileged position of whites, even without many whites themselves realizing what is going on.

NOTES

1. The data and information on which this description and analysis are based come from a fairly extensive reading of the mainstream media coverage. Many of the basic details and most publicized quotations are archived on ESPN's website ("News Services," espn.com, retrieved November 2005). Sources for other factual information and quotations are cited as appropriate.
2. *Philadelphia Daily News*, September 30, 2003.
3. Associated Press, October 1, 2003.
4. *Washington Post*, October 2, 2003.
5. *New York Times*, October 3, 2003.
6. Associated Press, October 1, 2003.
7. *Washington Post*, October 2, 2003.
8. *Newsweek*, October 13, 2003, 25; *Washington Post*, October 2, 2003.
9. One such example came from a conservative public relations executive who believed Limbaugh should not have bowed to the pressures to resign:

    Can a prominent white person in America criticize a prominent black person in America without being told his speech is impermissible? He's got a right to be wrong but he shouldn't lose his job because some hypocritical, pinheaded Congressmen and presidential candidates become the speech police. (*New York Times*, October 3, 2003)

10. That such criticisms still circulate was exemplified most recently and dramatically by a column in the *Philadelphia Sunday Sun* (December 4, 2005), wherein Whyatt Mondesire, then head of the Philadelphia chapter of the National

Association for the Advancement of Colored People (NAACP), called McNabb a "mediocre talent" who was "hiding behind excuses dripping in make-believe racial stereotypes" by refusing to run the ball as often as he did earlier in his career. This commentary prompted an apology from Bruce Gordon, CEO of the NAACP: "The NAACP has many civil rights issues that require our attention. Criticizing Donovan McNabb is not one of them" (*Sports Illustrated*, January 6, 2006, 25).

11. My thanks to Kyle Kusz, who not only suggested this point but also provided the example and some of the language to illustrate and explain it.

12. *Sports Illustrated*, August 7, 2003.

13. A recent profile on McNabb made for the ESPN series *Beyond the Glory*, for example, showed clips of players, reporters, and commentators dismissing Limbaugh as "a racist" and an "idiot." "To McNabb," the narrator in this reconstruction intoned, "the words were the latest version of a familiar refrain . . . in a lifetime of overcoming barriers." Despite the allusion to McNabb's "lifetime" of struggle, the dominant rhetorical theme of dismissing Limbaugh as a racist is to render racism itself as essentially outdated, a thing of the past.

14. *New York Daily News*, October 2, 2003.

15. Associated Press, October 1, 2003.

16. *New York Times*, October 3, 2003.

17. *Washington Post*, October 2, 2003.

18. *Charleston Daily Mail*, October 2, 2003.

19. *Washington Post*, October 3, 2003.

20. *Washington Post*, October 3, 2003.

21. Agence France Presse (English edition), October 2, 2003. McNabb echoed similar themes in the interviews that were part of his subsequent *Beyond the Glory* profile on ESPN (2005). The complicity of colorblindness and whiteness were even clearer (if more uncomfortable) in this context, as illustrated in the star quarterback's conception of audience and use of pronouns in the following quote: "I'd like people to understand, you know, I'm just like you. Although we're of a different race, another ethnic background, I like to do some of the same things you like to do."

22. ESPN, "Donovan McNabb," *Beyond the Glory*, season 4, episode 1, aired March 14, 2004.

23. For a prescient commentary on how racial and other social ideas can be circulated and reproduced in public discourse without the discussants even realizing it, see Goldberg's (1998) discussion of sports talk radio.

24. *Sports Illustrated*, August 7, 2003. This story also laughably points out that Limbaugh was the place kicker for his high school football team and that he played touch football for the Royals staff in their annual contest against the personnel of Kansas City's professional football team, the Chiefs.

25. Associated Press, October 1, 2003.

26. *New York Daily News*, October 2, 2003.

REFERENCES

Andrews, V. 1996. "Black Bodies—White Control: The Contested Terrain of Sports-manlike Conduct." *Journal of African American Men* 2 (1): 33–59.

Bonilla-Silva, E. 2001. *White Supremacy and Racism in the Post–Civil Rights Era*. Boulder CO: Lynne Reinner.

Bonilla-Silva, E., and T. Forman. 2000. "'I'm Not a Racist but . . .': Mapping White College Students' Racial Ideology in the U.S.A." *Discourse and Society* 11 (1): 53–85.

Buffington, D. 2005. "Contesting Race on Sundays: Making Meaning out of the Rise in Black Quarterbacks." *Sociology of Sport Journal* 21: 19–37.

Carr, L. G. 1997. *Colorblind Racism*. Thousand Oaks CA: Sage.

Cole, C. L., and D. Andrews, D. 1996. "Look—It's *NBA Showtime*! Visions of Race in the Popular Imagery." *Cultural Studies Annual* 1: 141–81.

Cole, C. L., and H. Denny III. 1994. "Visualizing Deviance in Post-Reagan America: Magic Johnson, AIDS and the Promiscuous World of Professional Sport." *Critical Sociology* 20 (3): 123–47.

Crenshaw, K. W. 1997. "Color-Blind Dreams and Racial Nightmares: Reconfiguring Racism in the Post–Civil Rights Era." In *Birth of a Nation'Hood: Gaze, Script and Spectacle in the O.J. Simpson Case*, edited by T. Morrison, 97–168. New York: Random House.

———. 2003. "Bad Calls on the Racial Playing Field." Common Dreams, October 11. Accessed October 12, 2003. http://www.commondreams.org/scriptfiles /views03/1011-08.htm.

Doane, A. W., Jr. 1997. "Dominant Group Identity in the United States: The Role of 'Hidden' Ethnicity in Intergroup Relations." *Sociological Quarterly* 38: 375–97.

Dyson, E. M. 1993. "Be Like Mike? Michael Jordan and the Pedagogy of Desire." In *Reflecting Black: African-American Cultural Criticism*, 64–75. Minneapolis: University of Minnesota Press.

Fredrickson, G. M. 1981. *White Supremacy: A Comparative Study in American and South African History*. Oxford, UK: Oxford University Press.

Goldberg, D. T. 1993. *Racist Culture*. Oxford, UK: Blackwell.

———. 1998. "Call and Response: Sports, Talk Radio, and the Death of Democracy." *Journal of Sport and Social Issues* 22: 212–23.

Hartmann, D. 2000. "Rethinking the Relationships between Sport and Race in American Culture: Golden Ghettos and Contested Terrain." *Sociology of Sport Journal* 17: 229–53.

———. 2003. *Race, Culture and the Revolt of the Black Athlete: The 1968 Olympic Protests and Their Aftermath*. Chicago: University of Chicago Press.

———. 2006. "Bound by Blackness or Above it? Michael Jordan and the Paradoxes of Post-Civil Rights American Race Relations." In *Out of the Shadows: A Biographical History of African American Athletes*, edited by D. K. Wiggins, 301–23. Fayetteville: University of Arkansas Press.

King, C. R. 2005. "Cautionary Notes on Whiteness and Sport Studies." *Sociology of Sport Journal* 22: 397–408.

Kusz, K. W. 2006. "Dogtown and Z-Boys: White Particularity, and the New, *New* Cultural Racism." In *Visual Economies of/in Motion: Sport and Film*, edited by C. R. King and D. Leonard. New York: Peter Lang.

Lewis, A. E. 2004. "'What Group?' Studying Whites and Whiteness in the Era of 'Color-Blindness.'" *Sociological Theory* 22: 623–46.

Lipsitz, G. 1998. *Possessive Investment in Whiteness: How White People Profit from Identity Politics*. Philadelphia: Temple University Press.

McDonald, M. G. 2005. "Mapping Whiteness and Sport: An Introduction." *Sociology of Sport Journal* 22: 245–55.

Roediger, D. R. 2002. "White Looks and Limbaugh's Laugh." In *Colored White: Transcending the Racial Past*, 44–54. Berkeley: University of California Press.

———. 2006. "Whiteness and Its Complications." *Chronicle of Higher Education*, July 14, B1, B6–7.

Vigdor, J. L. 2003. "Quarterback Draw: Media Executives Want Black Quarterbacks to Succeed Because of Rating, Not 'Social Concern.'" *American Prospect*, October 7. Accessed October 12, 2003. http://www.prospect.org/article/quarterback-draw.

Walker, H. 2003. "Is Rush Right? Double Standards and Stable Expectations." Department workshop series, Department of Sociology, University of Minnesota, Minneapolis.

Wheelock, D., and D. Hartmann. 2007. "Midnight Basketball and the 1994 Crime Bill Debates: The Operation of a Racial Code." *Sociological Quarterly* 48 (2): 315–42.

18

I'm the King of the World
Barry Bonds and the Race for the Record

LISA DORIS ALEXANDER

It was inevitable—though not entirely welcomed. As long as Barry Bonds remained healthy and pitchers threw pitches in the general vicinity of the strike zone, Bonds would break Hank Aaron's Major League Baseball (MLB) all-time home run record. There were a few other predictable certainties to the 2007 season: despite the fact that Bonds has not failed a drug test, the issue of performance-enhancing drugs would dominate the discussion; the media response to Bonds breaking the record would range from benign indifference to outright hostility; and race would exist just below the surface of the discussion but rarely be talked about.

As media continues to encroach into citizens' everyday lives via television, radio, internet, and smartphones, how an event is covered by media representatives becomes just as important as, if not more important than, the event itself. This means, in a sports context, that sportswriters and commentators have tremendous power to influence the ways in which fans and the general public view persons and events. Anyone who has read a Spiderman comic book or seen the immensely popular films of the same name is familiar with the adage "with great power comes great responsibility." Unfortunately, sportswriters and commentators have not always framed sporting events and controversies in a "fair and balanced" manner, particularly when race and ethnicity intersect with sports (e.g., the Duke Lacrosse case, the NBA dress code issue). One possible explanation for the racial blind spot comes from critical race theorist Charles R. Lawrence III, who argues that

> Americans share a common historical and cultural heritage in which racism has played and still plays a dominant role. Because of this shared experience, we also inevitably share many ideas, attitudes, and beliefs that attach significance to an individual's race and induce negative feelings and opinions about nonwhites. To the extent that this cultural belief system has influenced all of us, we are all racists. At the same time, most of us are unaware of our racism. We do not recognize the ways in which our cultural experience has influenced our beliefs about race or the occasions on which those beliefs affect our actions. In other words, a large part of the behavior that produces racial discrimination is influenced by unconscious racial motivation.[1]

If Lawrence is correct, then race permeates all of our actions whether we want it to or not and whether we are conscious of it or not. It stands to reason that unconscious racial attitudes influence the ways in which sportswriters discuss sports issues involving race and ethnicity generally and more specifically the ways Bonds's home run chase has been framed. When MLB began the integration process and sportswriters began paying attention to athletes of color, racist attitudes were the norm and could be expressed freely. Since overt racism is no longer tolerated, the negative attitudes created by the shared racist history will find an outlet, and in this case, the ways in which Bonds's pursuit of Aaron's record has been framed provide such an outlet.

The year 2007 was a banner year for race in sports—in both good and bad ways. The year began on a hopeful note when the Chicago Bears' Lovie Smith and the Indianapolis Colts' Tony Dungy became the first African American head coaches in the National Football League to reach the Super Bowl.[2] Unfortunately it took only two months for the glow of Smith's and Dungy's accomplishment to fade. On April 3, 2007, while the Rutgers women's basketball team was playing its first championship title game, radio talk show host Don Imus and his producer Bernard McGuirk referred to the team as "nappy-headed hos."[3] Less than two weeks later, MLB celebrated the sixtieth anniversary of Jackie Robinson's first regular-season game with the Brooklyn Dodgers. Many players, coaches, and managers opted to wear the number 42, including the entire Houston Astros team, which did not have any U.S.-born black players on its roster.[4] MLB began the anniversary season by holding an inaugural Civil Rights Game between the St. Louis Cardinals and Cleveland Indians, the first American League team to sign a U.S.-born black player in the twentieth century. Despite the franchise's history, the inclusion of Cleveland, whose name and mascot is an affront to many people of color, was viewed by some as hypocritical and disingenuous in terms of honoring civil rights. The disturbing saga surrounding Atlanta Falcons quarterback Michael Vick's involvement in dogfighting has produced its own racial commentary. Lastly, Detroit Tigers DH Gary Sheffield created quite a stir when he not only claimed that the increasing number of Latin players has to do with their pliability but also charged Yankees manager Joe Torre with racial bias against black players. Though sports often frames itself as a bastion of fair play and equality, according to espn.com columnist Pat Forde, "you'd have to go straight ostrich to escape the current crossfire over race, race relations, racial dynamics and racial viewpoints in sports."[5] Race has always intersected with sports in one form or another, which leaves us with the question, how does race influence portrayals of Barry Bonds's chase for MLB's career home run record?

I'm the King of the World

When the 2007 season began, Barry Bonds was second on the MLB career home run list with 734 and was a mere stone's throw away from Hank Aaron's hallowed 755. The fact that Bonds pushed Babe Ruth to third on that list last season was disturbing to many sportswriters, and those sentiments not only produced their own racialized commentary but also fanned the steroid discussion flames. At this point, the BALCO trial had concluded without any concrete evidence that Bonds knowingly took steroids, and the fact that federal agents tried and failed to force former Diamondbacks pitcher Jason Grimsley to gather incriminating evidence on Bonds was common knowledge.[6] Though many bemoaned Bonds's passing of Ruth and denounced the slugger's "tainted" record, the fact that Ruth's record is tainted by the fact that he played during the Jim Crow era was rarely mentioned.

Prior to the 2007 season, Bonds certainly could not be described as the most well-liked person in baseball. To say that Bonds's relationship with sportswriters was acrimonious would be kind. ESPN *The Magazine*'s Robert Miles remarked, "Your image rivals Mel Gibson's, post-DUI rant. You're in a worse spot than a couch-jumping Tom Cruise or a crotch-flashing Britney Spears. Thing is, people don't think you're crazy, they think you're just mean."[7] Tony Kornheiser of the *Washington Post* and ESPN's *Pardon the Interruption* remarked that Bonds "has been a cold, angry, condescending person for most of his career. He's not lovable and he wants it that way and has wanted it that way," and *Sports Illustrated*'s Jeff Pearlman remarked that "Bonds had an unmatched record of standing up reporters, of blowing off autograph seekers, of dogging teammates, of taking every opportunity to remind everyone that there is only one Barry Bonds—and *you're not him*."[8] Even people outside of sportswriting circles have commented on Bonds's persona. In the *Chronicle of Higher Education*, Warren Goldstein commented that Bonds "appears to be a genuinely unpleasant human being, who reserves special hostility for the reporters charged with covering his exploits,"[9] and Todd Boyd, professor of critical studies at the University of Southern California, wrote on espn.com that

> there has long been a notion among certain members of the African-American community that once a successful black person manages to make it to the top of his respective field, there is a vested interest among other people outside of the community to see this person fall. Barry Bonds is only the most recent example of such a notion. The vehemence with which these outside forces seem aligned in their interest to go after Bonds has helped to fuel such thinking.[10]

Regardless of whether anyone actually wanted to see Bonds break the record and irrespective of whether people believed he deserved the record, on August 5, 2007, Bonds tied Aaron's mark. Commissioner Bud Selig was in Petco Park during the game and his reaction was puzzling: he looked confused, and only after being prodded by Rangers owner Tom Hicks he stood but kept his hands in his pockets. Though it was widely believed that most fans outside of San Francisco would boo Bonds when he tied the record, most fans in San Diego cheered while Selig looked on with disgust. When Bonds broke the record two days later, Selig was not in attendance but the antipathy was still evident.

Jim Reeves from the *Ft. Worth Star-Telegram* arguably had the most extreme reaction when he wrote, "It is now officially a national day of mourning. Black bunting should hang from every ballpark in America. A riderless black horse, its saddle empty, its stirrups filled by a pair of Hank Aaron's cleats turned backward, should be led around every warning track tonight. The greatest record in sports has fallen to a liar and a cheat."[11] On his ESPN television program, Jim Rome began his show by saying "congrats on the asterisk" and Gene Wojciechowski wrote on espn.com that "Bonds and his career numbers are a fraud," said the slugger was "as embraceable as a cactus," and called the entire evening "a make-believe piece of baseball drama."[12] Mike Lupica proclaimed on ESPN's *The Sports Reporters* that in light of Bonds's accomplishment, Joe DiMaggio's fifty-six-game hit streak was now the greatest record in sports.[13] Lupica failed to remember or neglected to mention that DiMaggio's streak is tainted by the fact that it too was accomplished during the Jim Crow era. Dave Zirin observed the visceral reaction to Bonds's achievement and wrote,

> Nothing is off-limits. I've seen it all: comparing [Bonds] to O.J. Simpson? Sure. Comparing him to a child molester? Sure. Call for a lynching? These are the words of John Seibel on ESPN radio: "If [Bonds used steroids], hang him. Now I'm not saying hang him. I'm saying hang him from a tree. I'm not saying strap him to a gurney and inject poison in his veins."[14]

The response to Bonds's accomplishment is not surprising despite the fact that Bonds has never tested positive for performance-enhancing drugs and has never admitted to knowingly taking steroids. Many sportswriters point to Lance Williams and Mark Fainaru-Wada's *Game of Shadows* as gospel for the steroid era though the authors included sealed grand jury testimony in their work. Despite discussions surrounding the morality of athletes taking performance-enhancing drugs, there was no discussion surrounding the ethics of using illegally obtained evidence. Because an overwhelming majority of sportswriters and sports reporters are white, 90 percent and 87.5 percent respectively, while players of color make up approximately 40.5 percent of MLB's rosters, the selected reporting illustrates George Lipsitz's concept of the possessive investment in whiteness.[15] Lipsitz argues that "racial injuries . . . originate from the indirect, inferential, institutional, and systemic skewing of opportunities and life chances along racial lines. Whiteness is the most subsidized identity in our society; the most powerful identity politics are those that protect the value of whiteness. White advantages come from favoritism, not fitness, fortitude, or family formations."[16] By focusing on Bonds, sportswriters diverted attention from any unethical/illegal practices their fellow journalists employed to get the story. This diversion perpetuates a racial system where mostly white sportswriters can frame issues about athletes, the majority of whom are men of color, without equitable accountability.

Lies, Damned Lies, and Statistics

Fan reaction to Bonds's feats was usually measured by the boos leveled at the slugger in every National League ballpark that wasn't in San Francisco; and in May 2007 sports fans chimed in on Bonds's quest. An ESPN/ABC poll found that 37 percent of fans wanted Bonds to break the record and 73 percent of fans believed that Bonds used steroids.[17] But those statistics tell only part of the story. The poll also found a drastic difference in the responses along racial lines: 74 percent of black fans wanted Bonds to break the record and only 37 percent believed that Bonds used steroids, and black fans were nearly twice as likely as white fans (46 percent vs. 25 percent) to believe that Bonds has been treated unfairly.[18] When asked for the reasons behind Bonds's treatment 41 percent of black fans blamed steroids and 25 percent blamed race while "virtually none" of the white fans attributed Bonds's treatment to race.[19]

Methodologically the poll is problematic because it perpetuates the myth that race in the United States is simply a black/white issue by not including Latina/o, Asian American, or Native American fans as part of the sample. However, in all honesty, no one should have been surprised that black fans were more likely than white fans to support Bonds. What was surprising was the fact that over one-third of the total respondents actually *wanted* Bonds to break the record and it raises the question of whether or not sportswriters and commentators did fans a disservice by framing Bonds in such a negative manner. Equally startling was the fact that *none* of the white respondents who stated that Bonds has been treated unfairly believed that race had nothing to do it. In response to the poll results, ESPN's Jayson Stark wrote, "For nearly all white fans who think Bonds has been treated unfairly to say race has nothing to do with it is stunning. We say to those fans: You're kidding yourselves if that's what you truly think."[20] As previously noted, the poll results were not that much of a surprise—it simply provided the most recent evidence that blacks and whites often view the world differently. At the same time, the inability/unwillingness of white fans to even entertain the possibility that race could have anything to do with the ways Bonds has been framed highlights Kimberlé Crenshaw's notion that there is a "deep dissonance between conventions built on the fantasy that racism is a thing of the past or the preserve of the crazies, and the reality that racist influences are as enduring as Old Glory."[21] People who believe that racism no longer exists in the United States or who define racism in terms of the most egregious acts (e.g., racial death threats against Hank Aaron) would have no reason to suspect that race impacts how Bonds is framed. On the other hand, the very notion of unconscious racism supposes that we will not recognize the role race plays in our everyday lives.

It is possible that fans are taking their cue from sportswriters themselves. Gene Wojciechowski wrote,

> While I hate to disappoint the racial-conspiracy theorists, this isn't about his being an African-American. If this were the very freckled and very white Mark McGwire in Bonds' cleats, I'd be saying the very

same thing: that you can't celebrate the accomplishments of someone who allegedly used illegal performance enhancers.[22]

But one only has to go back to the 1998 home run chase to see that McGwire's public acknowledgement that he used andro did little to damper sportswriters' enthusiasm. The *Sporting News*'s Steve Marantz and Michael Knisley were explicit about their support of McGwire when they wrote,

> Not that [McGwire's] perfect. His use of the over-the-counter supplement, androstenedione, makes us wonder about his judgment. A substance incompletely researched, banned from the NFL, NCAA and Olympics, barred from the shelves of major dietary supplement chains, is dubious. We question that blind spot, yet perversely, find him more appealing because of it, in the way Cindy Crawford's mole accents her beauty.[23]

Sportswriters cannot claim ignorance of McGwire's andro usage, but even with McGwire's legal yet potentially unethical use of performance-enhancing drugs, the slugger was revered by fans and journalists alike. Was McGwire's acceptance because andro was legal, because everyone within the baseball establishment wanted the sport to recover following the 1994 strike, because McGwire is white, or some combination of the three? To be fair, McGwire is certainly being punished now for using performance-enhancing drugs by being denied entry into the Hall of Fame during his first year of eligibility. Wojciechowski is correct to a certain extent: as with any other issue, the subject of what role race plays in the Bonds story does not have a simple answer. On the other hand, framing those who suggest that race could play a role in the Bonds as "racial conspiracy theorists" is telling and highlights the fact that many sportswriters, like fans, are reluctant to at least acknowledge the *possibility* that race plays a role in how Bonds is framed and perceived.

There's No Need to Fear: A-Rod is Here

One person who unexpectedly benefited from the ways in which Bonds's record-breaking has been framed is Yankees third baseman Alex Rodríguez.

On the August 5, 2007, edition of *The Sports Reporters*, John Saunders, Michael Kay, William C. Rhoden, and Mitch Albom contemplated the fact that Bonds tied Aaron's record. Mitch Albom argued that "the saddest part is on the same day that Bonds ties this record, A-Rod hits his 500th and half the country is going hit em faster A-Rod, hit em faster," and Rhoden replied, "And the strange thing is that Bonds has turned a guy like A-Rod into a hero."[24]

When Rodríguez signed the largest contract in sports history in 2000, he was lambasted from every direction. Despite being one of the best players in the game it was said that he was not "worth" $25 million per season—a framing which has racial connotations as well. When he was traded to New York, Yankees fans and the New York media were less than hospitable. Granted, Rodríguez's lackluster playoff performances did not help, and *SI*'s Tom Verducci points out that

> A-Rod routinely is treated like the guy in the dunk tank at the county fair, even, most incriminating of all, by his peers. In the past two years he's been called out by Boston pitcher Curt Schilling ("bush league"), Red Sox outfielder Trot Nixon ("He can't stand up to Jeter in my book, or Bernie Williams or Posada"), Chicago White Sox manager Ozzie Guillen ("hypocrite") and New York Mets catcher Paul Lo Duca (who accused him on the field of showing up the Mets by admiring a home run too long).[25]

When it seemed that the only thing that could redeem Rodríguez was carrying the Yankees to another World Series title, Barry Bonds breaking Aaron's mark came along. If Rodríguez continues his current pace and does not suffer any serious injuries, he is on pace to hit well over eight hundred home runs.

The embracing of A-Rod's quest for baseball immortality brings up an important point. As previously mentioned, there are those sportswriters who argue that Bonds's perceived link to performance-enhancing drugs is the only reason why his accomplishment was framed as tarnished. If that is the case then it stands to reason that A-Rod's record should be viewed as tainted as well. Atlanta third baseman Chipper Jones expressed a similar sentiment when he noted that "all of us who did something great in this era are in effect suspects."[26] If we define the steroid era from the 1980s through 2005 then any and all offensive and defensive numbers gained during that era are suspect, including Roger Clemens's and Greg Maddux's wins, Craig Biggio's hits, and home runs from a variety of players, including Sammy Sosa, Ken Griffey Jr., Frank Thomas, Jim Thome, and Alex Rodríguez. Sportswriters who frame Bonds's record as tainted are rather disingenuous in their pleas for A-Rod to break the record and hypocritical for not calling attention to other "tainted" records. In order for the home run record to be framed as "pure," it would take the heroics of someone who matriculated into the majors after steroid testing was implemented, like the Brewers' Prince Fielder or the Phillies' Ryan Howard—though the latter began his career in 2004.

Bonds is a complex human being and the issues that surround his all-time home run record are complicated. There are myriad different reasons why some sportswriters and fans have not embraced Bonds and the record. Perceptions about steroids, surliness, and race influence the way fans and sportswriters think, talk, and write about Bonds. No one is going to be able to point to one factor and say that is the single reason why sportswriters frame Bonds the ways they do. Sportswriters and fans are not willing to admit the possibility that race plays a part in how athletes are perceived. Race, however, permeates every aspect of U.S. history, institutions, politics, economy, and culture. Regardless of whether people choose to admit it, race influences our perceptions and seeps into sports culture as well. And as author Dave Zirin points out, "to argue that race has nothing to do with the saga of Barry Bonds is to embrace ignorance frightening in its Rocker-esque grandiosity."[27]

NOTES

1. Charles R. Lawrence III, "The Id, the Ego, and Equal Protection: Reckoning with Unconscious Racism," in *Critical Race Theory: The Key Writings That Formed the Movement*, edited by Kimberlé Crenshaw et. al. (New York: New Press, 1995), 246.

2. Cole Wiley, "Let Us Be Wary of Celebrating Too Much," espn.com, February 28, 2007, http://sports.espn.go.com/espn/blackhistory2007/columns/story?id=2782051.

3. Pat Forde, "Sports World Is Incubator for Larger Discussions to Come," espn.com, May 14, 2007, http://sports.espn.go.com/espn/columns/story?columnist=forde_pat&id=2881430&sportCat=mlb.

4. Barry M. Bloom, "Many to Take Part in Honoring Robinson," mlb.com, April 15, 2007, http://mlb.mlb.com/news/article.jsp?ymd=20070410&content_id=1890656&vkey=news_mlb&fext=.jsp&c_id=mlb; Ben Walker, "Astros Roster Has No Black Players," Associated Press, October 26, 2005.

5. Forde, "Sports World Is Incubator."

6. Joseph A. Reaves and Craig Harris, "Grimsley's Lawyer Says Feds Targeted Bonds," USA Today, June 9, 2006, http://www.usatoday.com/sports/baseball/2006-06-08-grimsley-bonds_x.htm.

7. Robert Miles, "Hollywood Ending," ESPN the Magazine, June 4, 2007, 48.

8. Tony Kornheiser and Michael Wilbon, "Does Barry Deserve More Love?" Pardon the Interruption, aired September 13, 2004; Jeff Pearlman, "Appreciating Bonds," Sports Illustrated, June 5, 2000, 51.

9. Warren Goldstein, "The Conundrum That Is Barry Bonds," Chronicle of Higher Education, June 8, 2007.

10. Todd Boyd, "You Can't Discuss Bonds without Race," espn.com, May 9, 2007, http://sports.espn.go.com/espn/page2/story?page=boyd/070508.

11. Jim Reeves, "Bonds Cheated and Disgraced the Game and Hank Aaron," Fort Worth Star-Telegram, August 8, 2007, http://www.star-telegram.com/sports/story/194941.html.

12. Jim Rome, Jim Rome is Burning, aired August 12, 2007; Gene Wojciechowski, "Bonds' Record Homer Doesn't Enhance Baseball," espn.com, August 8, 2007, http://sports.espn.go.com/espn/columns/story?columnist=wojciechowski_gene&id=2963913&sportCat=mlb.

13. John Saunders, Bob Ryan, Mike Lupica, and Dan LeBatard, The Sports Reporters, aired August 12, 2007.

14. Dave Zirin, Welcome to the Terrordome: The Pain, Politics, and Promise of Sports (Chicago: Haymarket Books, 2007), 160.

15. Richard Lapchick, "Who's Covering Whom? Sports Sections Lag in Diversity," espn.com, June 22, 2006, http://sports.espn.go.com/espn/news/story?id=2496651; Richard Lapchick, "The 2006 Racial and Gender Report Card: Major League Baseball" (Orlando: Institute for Diversity and Ethics in Sport, 2006), 1.

16. George Lipsitz, "The White 2K Problem," *Cultural Values* 4, no. 4 (2000): 521.

17. ESPN News Services, "Americans Conflicted about Bonds' Home Run Chase," espn.com, May 16, 2007, http://sports.espn.go.com/mlb/news/story?id=2861930.

18. ESPN New Services, "Americans Conflicted."

19. ESPN New Services, "Americans Conflicted."

20. Jayson Stark, "Racial Issues Hover over the Chase," espn.com, May 16, 2007, http://sports.espn.go.com/mlb/columns/story?columnist=stark_jayson&id=2861938.

21. Kimberlé Crenshaw, "Bad Calls on the Racial Playing Field," Common Dreams, October 22, 2003, http://www.commondreams.org/views03/1011-08.htm.

22. Wojciechowski, "Bonds' Record Homer."

23. Steve Marantz and Michael Knisley, "American Hero," *Sporting News*, September 21, 1998, 21.

24. John Saunders, Michael Kay, William C. Rhoden, and Mitch Albom, *The Sports Reporters*, aired August 5, 2007.

25. Tom Verducci, "A-Rod Agonistes," *Sports Illustrated*, September 25, 2006.

26. John Saunders, Michael Kay, William C. Rhoden, and Mitch Albom, *The Sports Reporters*, ESPN, aired August 5, 2007.

27. Zirin, *Welcome to the Terrordome*, 162.

19

Redemption on the Field
Framing, Narrative, and Race in Media
Coverage of Michael Vick

BRYAN CARR

Despite his numerous and significant athletic accomplishments on the football field, the name Michael Vick still carries with it a significant asterisk. In 2007, police and federal officials raided a Virginia property and found several neglected dogs and evidence that the animals had been used in illegal dogfighting activities. Further investigation showed that the property had been purchased five years earlier by Vick and his business partners for the purposes of beginning a dogfighting operation (Associated Press 2009). Prior to his appearance before the grand jury where he denied accusations of betting on the fights, Vick claimed that he knew nothing about the actions happening on his property and that he seldom visited it (Associated Press 2009; ESPN 2007). Vick was suspended from the NFL and indicted in August of 2007; his sentence was eventually set at twenty-three months in jail (Associated Press 2009; Mihoces 2007). He also pleaded guilty to charges brought against him by the state of Virginia a year later ("Vick to Enter Guilty Plea in Va. Court Tuesday" 2008). Vick, who had been a college standout at Virginia Tech and the overall first pick in the 2001 NFL draft, was now considered a criminal (Alden n.d.).

Following his sentencing, Vick served time in a minimum-security prison in Kansas and entered bankruptcy protection (Associated Press 2009). Many of Vick's assets were put up for sale, and three banks filed lawsuits, stating that he had defaulted on loans (Pasquarelli 2007). Vick also donated $1 million to help treat and rehabilitate the dogs owned by the operation and made an appearance in a federal bankruptcy court stating he would repay his debts and resume his NFL career (Associated Press 2009; Humane Society of the United States 2011). Later, after serving the house arrest portion of his sentence, Vick was released and reinstated into the NFL by Commissioner Roger Goodell on a provisional basis, signing a contract with the Philadelphia Eagles (Associated Press 2009; espn.com News Services 2009). Following a productive season in which he was named the starting quarterback for the team, the Eagles offered Vick a $100 million contract, putting Vick among the highest-paid quarterbacks in the league (Katzowitz 2011). Following his return, the public conversation over Vick ranged from his role on the team to the ethical dimensions of his reinstatement to, as Piquero et al. (2011) suggest, whether he should have been allowed to play again at all.

Among those taking a moral objection to Vick's reinstatement was the animal rights organization People for the Ethical Treatment of Animals (PETA), which accused Vick of being a "psychopath" and refused to allow Vick to work with them on a public service announcement (Goldstein and Burdick 2009). Following President Barack Obama's statement to Eagles owner Jeff Lurie that he was enjoying Vick as quarterback, PETA softened their position somewhat but stated that Obama's endorsement "cannot let us forget" (Weigel 2010). While PETA may have been the most vocal critic of Vick's reinstatement, similar sentiments were found across the media and in other organizations.

However, the notion of Vick as a redemptive figure was another popular narrative. A *Sporting News* article contended that Vick's story was an example of a "true redemption story," citing Vick's willingness to "become a contributing member of society" and his desire to "make amends" for his crimes (Whitley 2011, 63). Cultural critic and author Touré contributed to this narrative by saying that Vick has become a "heroic" figure (Touré 2011). Mike Freeman, a blogger for CBS Sports, called Vick's story "stunning" and "American," stating it was "an ugly fall from grace due to some ugly actions and a return" (Freeman 2011). Moreover, Vick's success was closely tied to the success of others, with no more authoritative source than the Philadelphia Eagles' own website stating in 2011 that Vick "must be a 'great quarterback' week in and week out for the Eagles to reach their full potential" (Spadaro 2011). The implication at the time was that Vick became something bigger than himself, a mythic figure on the cusp of remaking his life.

These narratives are intriguing in light of Vick's actions on and off the field. The media coverage of Vick's return to professional football took many different forms. But, other than a provocative ESPN piece that asked whether Vick would have been treated differently if he were white, the question of whether Vick's ethnicity informed the media coverage surrounding him went largely unasked. The article, which included an unfortunate and largely unrelated digitally photomanipulated image of Vick with white skin that sparked a minor media controversy, concluded that simply switching the ethnic experiences of Vick from an African American experience to a white experience was a largely ineffective intellectual exercise in no small part because "switching someone's race changes his entire existence" and "sets his life trajectory in an entirely different direction" (Touré 2011). The question, Touré suggests, is whether class and socioeconomic situation may have had a more significant impact than race; considering that Vick left college his sophomore year to help his family members living in poverty, it is impossible to discount his background and life experience in the narrative (Alden n.d.). This debate indicates that the Vick situation offers a unique opportunity to investigate the development of media narratives surrounding black athletes and the degree to which those narratives are influenced by player ethnicity.

Race and Sports

The relationship between race and sports has been a substantial one, as athletic competition and involvement has often been used as a means of acculturation for ethnic minorities (Adair and Rowe 2010; Stodolska and Alexandris 2004). The notion of stratification and separation between ethnic groups is a recurring theme throughout sociological literature. Alba and Nee (2003) suggest that even as systemic barriers between races break down society is still headed towards a segmentation based on economic factors that correlate with race. Even if racial discrimination is no longer codified, its influence on socialization and neighborhoods is still felt as African Americans in particular become significantly more segregated from their white neighbors, further limiting economic and educational opportunities (Alba et al. 1999; Charles 2003; Pager and Shepherd 2008; Pattillo-McCoy 2000). Such notions are furthered by the phenomenon Bonilla-Silva (2010) calls "colorblind racism," a psychological perspective that justifies discrimination or dominant race perceptions of minorities through characteristics other than skin color—work ethic, and so on—that ignores the notion of white privilege and suggests that the problems with minority groups are their own making. Doane (1997) makes a similar argument, suggesting that the dominant white ethnic group in a culture does not see itself or its successes through the lens of ethnicity because their ethnicity is not socially defined; therefore they are less likely to see differences in societal experience and assume that ethnicity is not an important social factor. Such perspectives help to explain why rare opportunities such as participating in professional athletics are seen as a means of equalizing and advancing minorities in contemporary society.

The notion of athletics as a panacea to solve issues of racial stratification and advancement is not a new one. Smedley and Smedley (2011) argue that the economic and educational limitations imposed on young black men in post–Civil War America created a cultural environment in which success could only be found through the avenues of athletics or entertainment. Eitle and Eitle (2002) hypothesized that differences in cultural capital made a more significant difference in whether black men participated in sports to compensate for a lack of "resources necessary to perform well academically" (p. 142). Harris (1994) found that coaches encouraged young black men to participate in sports in hopes of the possibility of professional opportunity. The perception of sports as a rare meritocracy in which black athletes were able to succeed on an equal playing field further promoted a sort of "psychic dependence" on athletic success among many African Americans (Brown 2005, 126). Certainly, it could be argued from the outside looking in that a young Michael Vick may have been influenced by this perspective, viewing an NFL career as a means of advancing himself and providing for his family (Alden n.d.). Still, from a young age even this "even" playing field brings with it stratification and the baggage of culture. Elling and Knoppers (2005) found that while sporting activities had the potential to promote integration and cooperation between youth of different ethnic groups, they also further delineated social classes, with participation falling along socially defined expectations.

To that end, sports are often viewed as a "contested terrain" in which racial issues are clearly present and "struggled on and over" (Hartmann 2000, 241). Even so, athletics are often portrayed as one of the few avenues in which blacks and minorities can succeed in a manner that is "nonthreatening" to the white establishment (Hardin, Dodd, Chance, and Walsdorf 2004, 223). Despite this notion of sports as an equalizer or opportunity for advancement, there still exists a significant gap in life experience between minority athletes and white athletes, particularly in compensation. Berri and Simmons (2009) found that while the overall salaries were comparable between white and black quarterbacks, the number of black athletes playing the lucrative positions was far smaller than the number of white athletes playing the positions. However, the distinction between race and racial experiences may be no starker than in the area of media representation.

Sports, Race, and the Media

Historically, sports media have influenced not just the business of sports but also society on a larger scale. During the 1920s, Negro league baseball was portrayed in black newspapers by team owners as a means through which community was fostered and social change could be advocated (Carroll 2006). Articles published by *Sports Illustrated* in 1968 investigating and condemning unfair treatment of African American players on the part of various league and team authorities, and articles exposing the racist treatment of then-heavyweight boxing champion Muhammad Ali, made positive contributions to the overall media coverage of the civil rights movement (Smith 2006). However, the sports media have not always played a positive role in race relations.

Much of the negative impact of sports media comes when the media reinforce racial constructs and categories from outside the sports world

(Sterkenburg, Knoppers, and De Leeuw 2010). Often, minority athletes are described in analogical and often animalistic terms—for example, the black athlete as "talented gazelle"—that place the roots of their success in biological differences rather than hard work, thereby normalizing the white majority's narratives about race (Bruce 2004, 872). This delineation was found again when Murrell and Curtis (1994) observed that the media credited successful performance of black NFL quarterbacks to innate and natural skills and characteristics, while performance among white quarterbacks was credited to effort and determination. Such narratives are prominent and recurring, with Mercurio and Filak (2010) observing that black quarterbacks were often championed in the media for their athletic prowess but rarely for their intellect. It is worth noting that there is some argument about this point—an analysis by Byrd and Utsler (2007) found little variance in the way the intellect of African American and white quarterbacks was discussed, for example—but it is difficult to deny that there is a historical precedent for athletes of different ethnicities being covered differently in the press. Such distinctions are not lost on the audience—Rainville, Roberts, and Sweet (1978) found that student participants were able to correctly determine the ethnicity of an athlete more than half of the time based on commentator statements alone.

The idea of black athletes having innate characteristics that make them different from whites is not limited to the sports arena; it has also been used by the media as a means of explaining the causes of criminal behavior among black athletes (Enck-Wanzer 2009). It is worth noting, however, that Seate, Harwood, and Blecha (2010) found that race did not necessarily influence audience perceptions of guilt in stories pertaining to athletes accused of crimes in all cases. However, when exposed to an accusatory message and a framing that emphasized the athlete's being black, participants were still more likely to have negative perceptions of black athletes (Seate et al. 2010). Such perspectives may be influenced by the racial makeup of the audience. In a study of media coverage in the Michael Vick case, Piquero et al. discovered that whites felt that Vick served too light of a sentence and should not have been allowed to play in the NFL again while nonwhites generally disagreed (Piquero et al. 2011).

The largely white sports media do their part to influence these perceptions as well; as Lapchick (2009) suggests, this dominant racial perspective may reflect and reinforce particular stereotypes or perceptions.

The difference in portrayal of white and minority athletes manifests in many ways throughout the sports media. In their analysis of the 2004 Summer Olympics, Billings and Angelini (2007) found that white athletes, and particularly American ones, were more prevalent in NBC's coverage. Ironically, even though African American players dominate many major sports, they were not covered in feature articles in sporting publications nearly as often as their white counterparts (Lumpkin 2009). Coverage of the 1998 home run battle between Mark McGwire and Sammy Sosa was also influenced by racial frames and white privilege—sportswriters cast McGwire as "the archetypal American hero[,] ... the fact of his whiteness taken for granted; and Sosa as the grateful, dark-skinned buddy just happy to be along for the ride" (Butterworth 2007, 238). Halone and Billings (2010) identified these and similar phenomena as rhetorical frames used in coverage of minority athletes, suggesting the importance of framing as a theoretical perspective.

The Significance of Framing

Framing theory suggests people use certain assumptions and expectations to simplify the world around them and make sense of events, selecting a "few elements of perceived reality" and developing a narrative that establishes and identifies connections between those elements "to promote a particular interpretation" (Baran and Davis 2006; Entman 2007, 164). Entman (1993) also suggests that framing involves the selection of elements that are then made more important and relevant in the text. It is worth noting, however, that individual writers and reporters may not be solely responsible for the implementation of frames. Rather, the systemic processes and interaction between "professional and organizational processes in the newsroom" may have a good deal of influence on the development of frames (Vliegenthart and van Zoonen 2011, 111). Regardless, journalists and other creators of media content are in the unique position of being able to "draw attention and confer legitimacy to one aspect of reality . . . while marginalizing other aspects" (Jackson 2011, 170). This power becomes especially noteworthy and a matter of concern when it is considered that frames effectively represent that which is perceived to real (Young 2010). Therefore, frames can be a powerful means of orientation within the media environment.

Frames effectively work on three levels: the cognitive (in which the frame tells the recipient of the message what to focus on as well as how to activate and tie together previously existing "thematic elements"), the rhetorical (focused on the content and quality of arguments as well as how they are structured), and the ideological level (in which frames explain how society should ideally function); regardless of the level frames operate on, they influence perception of an issue in terms of its importance and interpretation (Waller and Conaway 2011, 87). Entman (1993) identifies the four components that create a frame: the communicator (makes the decision of what to say and how to say it), the text (where the frames are located and what is communicated), the receiver (the audience for the message that uses their own individual frames to analyze a message), and the culture (the surrounding context of frames); these components explain both where the frame comes from and how it is delivered.

This essay will focus on the frames created by the media that tell audience members how to approach a given subject or issue. Frames by their nature select specific parts of an issue and make them more important than others or make them the focus of a given article or analysis, thereby encouraging the audience to analyze a situation in a manner concordant with the frame. This essay, as a largely textual and rhetorical exercise, considers frames to be the overall context and characteristics of a story and how the story is presented to the audience. More specifically, frames are the manner in which the issue is shown to be important and relevant to the audience.

Analyzing Media Coverage of Michael Vick

Close examination of the literature provides some recurring themes and avenues of inquiry for this project. The recurring theme of sports as an advancing and redeeming factor for black athletes is certainly one of them—after all, a significant portion of the literature focuses on the sociological factors and outcomes that perpetuate such a perception. As the literature suggests, the construction of race is a significant component of the African American experience to a degree that is not seen in other ethnicities; because whites do not generally see ethnicity as a major issue, the possibility exists that white sportswriters may bring their own perceptions to their writing (Doane 1997; Lapchick 2009). Therefore, even though it may not be easy or possible to compare Vick's situation directly to that of a non–African American player, there is significant evidence to suggest that racial frames may exist in the coverage nonetheless.

This qualitative analysis of the media narratives surrounding Michael Vick focused on the time period spanning his return to the NFL to the start of his first full season as the quarterback for the Philadelphia Eagles. First, the analysis will ask whether positive or negative frames are more prominent in media coverage of Michael Vick, determining authorial intent retroactively based on the language and content of the articles— and while this may be somewhat subjective, the language used in stories and the choice of which aspects of Vick's career and which activities they cover can generally tell us whether the article is pro-Vick or not. This analysis also seeks to uncover the most common narratives and frames in media coverage, identifying four main frames pulled from the literature and body of work on the subject. These frames include Vick's possibility for *redemption*, Vick's *athletic and professional skills*, the *morality and crime* frame that focuses primarily on his legal issues, and finally the *race* frame that focuses most significantly on Vick's ethnic identity. While a story may fall into more than one category, the focus of the story is what is most important for this analysis—that is, if a story is predominantly about race in its headline and lead paragraphs, that will be considered to be the frame even if it becomes a discussion of Vick's athletic capabilities later on.

However, the literature suggests that athletics are often seen as a source of advancement and legitimization for minority athletes, raising the question of whether Vick's redemption may also be tied to his athletic accomplishments and how likely such claims are to appear in the body of articles on Vick's return to the NFL. This question is necessary because redemption appears to be a primary narrative in the Vick story and deserves further inquiry. Again, the dominance of the frame is important here—if there are multiple lines in a redemption narrative regarding Vick's athletic talents and comparatively few regarding his other efforts, the narrative's view of redemption is tied to Vick's football accomplishments. This question could provide a significant contribution to the discussion of the perception of sports as a source of assimilation and acculturation.

This analysis also seeks to determine whether differences in the coverage and perception of Michael Vick exist between different kinds of media outlets, including predominantly mainstream news outlets, sports-focused outlets, and minority-controlled media. It is reasonable to infer that different organizations that have different goals and serve different audiences should have different means of covering the Vick story. Moreover, the impact of time on media coverage of Michael Vick cannot be discounted, and as such this analysis will look at three primary points in time: Vick's reinstatement to the NFL, his first season as the Eagles' quarterback, and the start of the 2011 season, where he earned a $100 million contract (Murphy 2011). These timeframes offer a rough estimate of Vick's career at a given point in time.

To find a body of articles to analyze, a LexisNexis database search was conducted. To ensure stories related directly to Vick's return to the NFL and his start as the official starting quarterback for the Philadelphia Eagles, the timeframe for stories was limited to stories between July 28, 2009, (the date of Vick's conditional reinstatement into the league) and September 11, 2011 (the first game of the first regular season in which Vick was the full-time starting quarterback). I searched through stories from major newspapers using the term "Michael Vick." From this sample, a quarter of the stories were selected. Duplicate stories and letters to the editor were discarded, as were stories that did not directly pertain to Vick's incarceration and return. This search returned both mainstream, general news and more sports-centric stories. In order to ensure representation for minority-controlled media, I performed separate LexisNexis inquiries into the archives of *Jet* and *Ebony*, due to their status as respected, long-running magazines aimed at an African American audience (Johnson 1992). When these sources did not return a substantial amount of stories, a search was conducted on the website for Black Entertainment Television, chosen for its status as a well-established, long-running television network (BET Networks n.d.). The combination of these sources resulted in a study sample of 139 stories, which were coded and analyzed for their textual content.

Frames and Contexts

In terms of positive and negative frames, the analysis showed that the plurality of stories was framed positively (46 percent), while stories that were unbiased or neutral composed 36 percent of the sample. Negative frames were the least likely to be present in this sample, with just 18 percent of stories fitting a negative frame. At the textual level, positive stories ranged from discussing Vick's attempts to redeem himself through community service to more general philosophical writings on forgiveness and redemption; negative articles tended to use more hostile language, with one article referring to animal lovers waiting to see Vick "squirm" during an interview with Oprah Winfrey (Murphy 2011). Overall, however, positive frames appeared to be the norm in coverage of Michael Vick's return.

Table 1: Positive, Negative, and Neutral Frames in Vick Coverage

Media type	Mainstream	Sports	Minority-controlled	Total
Positive frames	13	39	12	64
Negative frames	5	16	4	25
Neutral frames	8	31	11	50
Total	26	86	27	139

As was suggested in the literature, redemption was by far the most popular narrative in stories about Vick, with 52.5 percent of the stories focusing on Vick's attempts to rehabilitate his image. The second most common frame focused on Vick's athletic prowess or other professional concerns, with 35 of the 139 stories using some manner of this frame. Close behind was the morality and crime frame, in which Vick's story was discussed in terms of ethics or as a criminal action (20 percent). Surprisingly, race was rarely used as a framing device at all, with only 3 of the 139 stories using race as a primary focus of discussion. Of the 73 total redemptive narrative frames, the majority focused on Vick's redemption through athletics (55 percent) while comparatively fewer focused on redemption through off-field activities (45 percent). This analysis suggests that the media cast Vick's path to redemption largely as a function of his athletic achievement rather than any off-field activity.

Table 2: Narrative Frame Types in Media Coverage of Michael Vick

Media type	Mainstream	Sports	Minority-controlled	Total
Redemption	12	48	13	73
Athletic/professional	7	22	6	35
Morality/crime	7	16	5	28
Race	0	0	3	3
Total	26	86	27	139

Table 3: Sources of Redemption in Vick Coverage

Media type	Mainstream	Sports	Minority-controlled	Total
Athletic	5	31	4	40
Service/non-athletic	7	17	9	33
Total	12	48	13	73

In terms of positive and negative frames, more positive stories by number existed in sports-oriented media than in minority-controlled media, though the percentage was relatively similar between the two. Interestingly, positive stories were more likely to be present in the mainstream media, at least in terms of percentage. Again, however, because positive stories were generally the norm across the board, it may be difficult to make the argument that any of the forms of media were any more or less likely to report positive stories in general. If there is a difference between the positivity with which different kinds of outlets covered the Vick story, it was not obvious from this analysis.

In terms of narrative frame types, redemptive frames were by percentage most present in the sporting media (56 percent), followed by minority-controlled and then mainstream media. In terms of the source of Vick's redemption, it is perhaps unsurprising that frames discussing Vick's athletic and professional acumen were more likely to be present in sports media by percentage (26 percent), followed by mainstream and then minority-controlled media. The morality and crime frame was relatively uncommon across all forms of media, though slightly more likely by percentage (27 percent) to show up in the mainstream media. Conspicuous by its absence, however, is the lack of race as a framing narrative in both the mainstream and sports media. Neither of these forms of media used race as a narrative frame in the sampled articles, and even in minority-controlled media such frames were unlikely to be present. The analysis suggests the frames were distributed more or less as expected in accordance with the primary goals and audiences of the different types of media. However, the absence of race as a narrative frame suggests some support for the notions of "hidden ethnicity" and "colorblind racism" discussed in the literature review, an idea we will come back to in a moment.

Finally, time had some influence on the presence of frames. Positive frames increased by percentage steadily across the three time periods, ending with 60 percent of the stories about Vick in the 2011 time period fitting into the definition of a positive frame. This could suggest that the overall perception of Vick became more positive as time progressed. By percentage, negative frames about Vick stayed more or less consistent across the three time periods. Finally, the percentage of neutral stories decreased across the three time periods, hitting its lowest point in 2011 (23 percent). This could suggest that the general media perception of Vick had more or less crystallized.

Table 4: Positive and Negative Frames across Time

Time period	2009	2010	2011	Total
Positive	25	18	21	64
Negative	12	7	6	25
Neutral	29	13	8	50
Total	66	38	35	139

In terms of narrative type, redemptive frames made up the largest number of stories in all three time periods, in each case making up over half of the frames in each set of stories. Frames pertaining to Vick's athletic and professional skills were the second most prevalent type of frames in the 2009 and 2011 time periods, though in the 2010 time period there was one more example of a morality and crime frame. Race was essentially nonexistent across the board but most prevalent in 2011. Again, the numbers suggest media coverage of Vick over time became more positive and crystallized, and that redemptive frames were the most common type of narrative frame across the three time periods. However, there did not appear to be a linear progression in terms of the sources of redemption across the time periods.

Table 5: Narrative Frames across Time

Time period	2009	2010	2011	Total
Redemption	34	21	18	73
Athletic/professional	19	8	8	35
Morality/crime	12	9	7	28
Race	1	0	2	3
Total	66	38	35	139

Table 6: Sources of Redemption in Vick Coverage

Time period	2009	2010	2011	Total
Athletic	17	15	8	40
Service/non-athletic	17	6	10	33
Total	34	21	18	73

What the Coverage of Vick's Return Says about Race and Sports

The findings of this study reflect the socially constructed notion of athletics as a significant means of advancement and acculturation into society for African Americans and supports the concept in the literature of sports as a platform in which racial issues are brought to the forefront (Brown

2005; Eitle and Eitle 2002; Hardin et al. 2004; Harris 1994; Hartmann 2000; Lapchick 2009). The findings suggest that across the various forms of media, athletics was seen as a way in which Vick could shed the weight of his criminal convictions and build a positive future. Looking at the evidence, it appears that the media more or less agreed that success on the football field afforded Vick the potential for a second chance and absolution of his legal sins. That this narrative existed beyond sports media provides further support for this concept as one that permeates society and is socialized even to the level of educational practices (Harris 1994). Such a notion is problematic for two reasons.

The first is that it takes the focus away from educational and economic advancement, strengthening the existing socially constructed barriers that effectively segregate African Americans from other races (Alba et al. 1999; Charles 2003; Pager and Shepherd 2008; Pattillo-McCoy 2000). The media worldview that focuses less on Vick's intellect or service as a means of atoning for his past transgressions and more on whether he can throw a football does not challenge systemic stratification or segregation but instead reinforces it. The other problem is that the continuing presence of this narrative in the media further encourages worldviews based around Bonilla-Silva's (2010) concept of "colorblind racism" and Doane's (1997) notion of hidden ethnicity. If the media reinforce the idea that football is effectively a catch-all solution to problems faced by minorities, the worldview in which these problems are innate within minority groups rather than the outcome of an unequal socioeconomic system becomes further legitimized.

From a media criticism perspective, the ubiquity of redemption as a narrative frame could mean the media have both reinforced and legitimized the aforementioned views, thereby supporting the argument of Sterkenburg et al. (2010) that the media reinforce racial constructs and categories. Beyond this, however, it can be argued that the media have romanticized the Vick saga by turning it into a narrative of redemption and marginalizing the societal factors and impact. Textual analysis of the articles turned up little discussion of the socializing factors of Vick's background or critical analysis of the factors that allowed Vick to participate in dogfighting activity. Rather than examining what the Vick case illustrates or explains about society and differences in racial experience, the media instead chose to emphasize the mythic elements and dramatic aspects of his return. While such a tactic works for telling a compelling story, it marginalizes discussion of important issues. As time goes on, the crystallization of views toward Vick and the nature of the news cycle further divorce the story from its original social context.

Germane to both interests is the surprising lack of discussion of race in the sample. As explored in the literature review, there is a significant degree of overlap between racial issues and the field of athletics. What few discussions of race existed were found in the minority-controlled media and were focused on what the Vick story meant to the perception of African Americans and African American athletes. Such discussions are valuable but few and far between and likely nonexistent in the mainstream media. In this case, the silence of the media serves to further strengthen and legitimize racial separation and friction.

It is worthwhile to discuss the media coverage of Michael Vick from an ethical and moral standpoint, as it raises interesting questions about both. Vick's ability to use football and community service as a means of rehabilitation makes for a compelling media narrative, yet it is also a unique and privileged position. Lost in this narrative is discussion of the availability of redemptive and rehabilitative opportunities for nonathletes. In keeping with the literature, it could be argued that Vick was afforded unique opportunity and status based on his abilities and status as a skilled and well-known football player. Textual review of the stories in this sample showed little discussion of the differences in opportunities between Vick and other men convicted of such crimes. Again, the media have missed an opportunity to contribute to social understanding and illuminate significant social issues in the hopes of providing possible solutions.

This essay is far from the last word on the subject, as media coverage of the Michael Vick issue provides ample fodder for sociological inquiry and media criticism with implications beyond football. Since the timeframe covered by this study, Michael Vick's star has faded, the result of lackluster regular-season performances, injury, and increased competition for his position from younger players (Garafolo 2013). Yet, the coverage of Vick's return to football following his incarceration remains a perfect case study for the myths and narratives created by media coverage of embattled athletes and the evocation of athletic accomplishment as a socializing force for black men in American society. Vick's crime and punishment may be a closed issue, but the implications of his return are anything but.

REFERENCES

Adair, D., and D. Rowe. 2010. "Beyond Boundaries? 'Race,' Ethnicity, and Identity in Sport." *International Review for the Sociology of Sport* 45 (3): 251–57.

Alba, R. D., J. R. Logan, B. J. Stults, G. Marzan, and W. Zhang. 1999. "Immigrant Groups in the Suburbs: A Reexamination of Suburbanization and Spatial Assimilation." *American Sociological Review* 64 (3): 446–60.

Alba, R., and V. Nee. 2003. *Remaking the American Mainstream: Assimilation and Contemporary Immigration.* Cambridge MA: Harvard University Press.

Alden, J. n.d. "Michael Vick Photo Biography: Michael Vick Rookie Season." About. com Football website. http://football.about.com/od/nflplayerprofiles/ig /Michael-Vick-Photo-Gallery/Michael-Vick-Rookie-Season.htm.

Associated Press 2009. "Timeline of Michael Vick Dogfighting Case." piloton-line.com, July 27. http://hamptonroads.com/2009/07/timeline-michael -vick-dogfighting-case.

Baran, S. J., and D. K. Davis. 2006. *Mass Communication Theory: Foundations, Ferment, and Future.* 4th ed. Belmont CA: Thomson Wadsworth.

BET Networks. n.d. "Corporate Fact Sheet." BET Networks website. Accessed January 21, 2012. https://web.archive.org/web/20120121112951/http://bet.media room.com/index.php?s=45.

Bonilla-Silva, E. 2010. *Racism without Racists: Color-blind Racism and Racial Inequality in Contemporary America.* 3rd ed. Lanham MD: Rowman & Littlefield.

Brown, J. 2005. "Between the Lines: The Impact of Blacks in Sports." *Ebony* 61 (1): 126.

Bruce, T. 2004. "Marking the Boundaries of the 'Normal' in Televised Sports: The Play-by-Play of Race." *Media, Culture & Society* 26 (6): 861–79.

Butterworth, M. L. 2007. "Race in 'the Race': Mark McGwire, Sammy Sosa, and Heroic Constructions of Whiteness." *Critical Studies* 24 (3): 228–44.

Carroll, B. 2006. "From Fraternity to Fracture: Black Press Coverage of and Involvement in Negro League Baseball in the 1920s." *American Journalism* 23 (2): 69–95.

Charles, C. Z. 2003. "The Dynamics of Racial Residential Segregation." *Annual Review of Sociology* 29: 167–207.

Dickey, J. 2011. "Your Collection of 'What If White Michael Vick Were . . .' Photoshops." *Deadspin*, August 26. http://deadspin.com/5834782/your-collection-of-what-if-white-michael-vick-were-photoshops.

Doane, A. W. 1997. "Dominant Group Ethnic Identity in the United States: The Role of 'Hidden' Ethnicity in Intergroup Relations." *The Sociological Quarterly* 38 (3): 375–97.

Eitle, T. M., and D. J. Eitle. 2002. "Race, Cultural Capital, and the Educational Effects of Participation in Sports." *Sociology of Education* 75 (2): 123–46.

Elling, A., and A. Knoppers. 2005. "Sport, Gender, and Ethnicity: Practices of Symbolic Inclusion/Exclusion." *Journal of Youth and Adolescence* 34 (3): 257–68.

Enck-Wanzer, S. M. 2009. "All's Fair in Love and Sport: Black Masculinity and Domestic Violence in the News." *Communication and Critical/Cultural Studies* 6 (1): 1–18.

Entman, R. M. 1993. "Framing: Toward Clarification of a Fractured Paradigm." *Journal of Communication* 43 (4): 51–58.

———. 2007. "Framing Bias: Media in the Distribution of Power." *Journal of Communication* 57 (1): 164–73.

espn.com News Services. 2007. "Vick Faces Prison Time after Agreeing to Plead Guilty." espn.com, August 21. http://sports.espn.go.com/nfl/news/story?id=2983121.

———. 2009. "Vick, Eagles Agree to 2-Year Deal." espn.com, August 14. http://sports.espn.go.com/nfl/news/story?id=4397938.

Freeman, M. 2011. "Mike Vick: Redemption Almost Complete." cbssports.com. http://www.cbssports.com/mcc/blogs/entry/6264363/31613979.

Garafolo, M. 2013. "Eagles Restructure Michael Vick's Contract." *USA Today*, February 11. http://www.usatoday.com/story/sports/nfl/eagles/2013/02/11/michael-vick-one-year-contract/1909695/.

Goffman, E. 1974. *Frame Analysis: An Essay on the Organization of Experience*. New York: Harvard Press.

Goldstein, K., and D. Burdick. 2009. "PETA: Michael Vick Eagles Signing Has Disappointed 'Millions of Decent Football Fans.'" *Huffington Post*, August 14. http://www.huffingtonpost.com/2009/05/01/michael-vick-peta-spokesm_n_194700.html.

Halone, K. K., and A. C. Billings. 2010. "The Temporal Nature of Racialized Sport Consumption." *American Behavioral Scientist* 53 (11): 1645–68.

Hardin, M., J. E. Dodd, J. Chance, and K. Walsdorf. 2004. "Sporting Images in Black and White: Race in Newspaper Coverage of the 2000 Olympic Games." *Howard Journal of Communications* 15 (4): 211–27.

Harris, O. 1994. "Race, Sport, and Social Support." *Sociology of Sport Journal* 11 (1): 40–50.

Hartmann, D. 2000. "Rethinking the Relationship between Sport and Race in American Culture: Golden Ghettos and Contested Terrain." *Sociology of Sport Journal* 17 (3): 229–53.

Humane Society of the United States. 2011. "Michael Vick and the HSUS's Work to End Dogfighting." The Humane Society of the United States website. Accessed January 27. http://www.humanesociety.org/issues/dogfighting/qa/vick_faq .html.

Jackson, D. 2011. "Strategic News Frames and Public Policy Debates: Press and Television News Coverage of the Euro in the UK." *Communications: The European Journal of Communication Research* 36 (2): 169–93.

Johnson, J. H. 1992. "Founder's Statement." *Ebony* 48 (1): 29.

Katzowitz, J. 2011. "Report: Vick Signs 6-Year, $100 Million Deal." cbssports.com, August 29. http://www.cbssports.com/mcc/blogs/entry/22475988/31614019.

Lapchick, R. E. 2009. "Sport in America: The New Racial Stereotypes." In *Rethinking the Color Line.* 4th ed., edited by C. A. Gallagher, 327–34. New York: McGraw-Hill.

Lumpkin, A. 2007. "A Descriptive Analysis of Race/Ethnicity and Sex of Individuals Appearing on the Covers of *Sports Illustrated* in the 1990s." *Physical Educator* 64 (1): 29–37.

Mercurio, E., and V. Filak. 2010. "Roughing the Passer: The Framing of Black and White Quarterbacks prior to the NFL Draft." *The Howard Journal of Communications* 21 (1): 56–71.

Mihoces, G. 2007. "Vick's Status Uncertain as Jail Term Begins." *USA Today*, November 20. http://www.usatoday.com/sports/football/nfl/falcons/2007 -11-19-vick-surrender_N.htm.

Murphy, P. 2011. "Michael Vick Comeback Pays Off Handsomely." *Christian Science Monitor*, August 30.

———. 2011a. "Michael Vick Opts Out of 'Oprah' Appearance; Did Eagles, Dog Owners Force Him to Scramble?" *Christian Science Monitor*, February 17.

Murrell, A. J., and E. M. Curtis. 1994. "Causal Attributions of Performance for Black and White Quarterbacks in the NFL: A Look at the Sports Pages." *Journal of Sport and Social Issues* 18 (3): 224–33.

Pager, D., and H. Shepherd. 2008. "The Sociology of Discrimination: Racial Discrimination in Employment, Housing, Credit, and Consumer Markets." *Annual Review of Sociology* 34, 181–209.

Pasquarelli, L. 2007. "Vick Hoping to Get $4.5 Million for Sale of Lakefront Georgia Home." espn.com, October 20. http://sports.espn.go.com/nfl/news/story ?id=3071572.

Pattillo-McCoy, M. 2000. "The Limits of Out-migration for the Black Middle Class." *Journal of Urban Affairs* 22 (3): 225–41.

Piquero, A. R., N. L. Piquero, M. Gertz, T. Baker, J. Batton, and J. C. Barnes. 2011. "Race, Punishment, and the Michael Vick Experience." *Social Science Quarterly* 92 (2): 535–51.

Rainville, R. E., A. Roberts, and A. Sweet. 1978. "Recognition of Covert Racial Prejudice." *Journalism Quarterly* 55 (2): 256–59.

Seate, A. A., J. Harwood, and E. Blecha. 2010. "'He Was Framed!' Framing Criminal Behavior in Sports News." *Communication Research Reports* 27 (4): 343–54.

Smedley, A., and B. D. Smedley. 2011. *Race in North America: Origin and Evolution of a Worldview*. 4th ed. Boulder CO: Westview.

Smith, R. 2006. "*Sports Illustrated*'s African American Athlete Series as Socially Responsible Journalism." *American Journalism* 23 (2): 45–68.

Spadaro, D. 2011. "Vick Becoming a Complete QB." philadelphiaeagles.com, November 5. http://www.philadelphiaeagles.com/news/dave-spadaro/article -1/Vick-Becoming-A-Complete-qb/aec78fe8-0602-4fc8-ae2e-7299d 155559c.

Sterkenburg, J. V., A. Knoppers, and S. De Leeuw. 2010. "Race, Ethnicity, and Content Analysis of the Sports Media: A Critical Reflection." *Media, Culture & Society* 32 (5): 819–39.

Stodolska, M., and K. Alexandris. 2004. "The Role of Recreational Sport in the Adaptation of First Generation Immigrants in the United States." *Journal of Leisure Research* 36 (3): 379–413.

Touré. 2011. "What If Michael Vick Were White?" *ESPN Commentary*, August 25. http://espn.go.com/espn/commentary/story/_/id/6894586/imagining -michael-vick-white-quarterback-nfl-espn-magazine.

"Vick to Enter Guilty Plea in Va. Court Tuesday." 2008. *Atlanta Journal-Constitution*, November 24. http://www.ajc.com/sports/content/sports/falcons/stories /2008/11/24/vick_virginia_court.html.

Vliegenthart, R., and L. van Zoonen. 2011. "Power to the Frame: Bringing Sociology Back to Frame Analysis." *European Journal of Communication* 26 (2): 101–15.

Waller, R. L., and R. N. Conaway. 2011. "Framing and Counterframing the Issue of Corporate Social Responsibility." *Journal of Business Communication* 48 (1): 83–106.

Weigel, D. 2010. "PETA Forgives Michael Vick, So Why Can't You?" *Slate*, December 28. http://www.slate.com/blogs/weigel/2010/12/28/peta_forgives_michael _vick_so_why_can_t_you.html.

Whitley, D. 2011. "Michael Vick Is a Story of Redemption—Whether We Like It or Not." *Sporting News*, September 12.

Young, A. A. 2010. "New Life for an Old Concept: Frame Analysis and the Reinvigoration of Studies in Culture and Poverty." *Annals of the American Academy of Political and Social Science* 629: 53–74.

20

Weighing In on the Coaching Decision
====================================

Weighing In on the Coaching Decision
Discussing Sports and Race Online

JIMMY SANDERSON

Sports have long been considered to reflect the racial hierarchy of a society (Frey and Eitzen 1991; Lapchick 1986). The belief that issues of "race" are no longer present in sports (Leonard 2004; Springwood 2006) is consistent with contemporary U.S. beliefs that racism has vanished from the social scene (Bonilla-Silva 2001; Carr 1997; Crenshaw 1997). This perception has become so entrenched that questionable racial practices made by sports organizations often go unquestioned, whereas those who publicly contest these decisions endure harsh criticism for attacking "American values" (Butterworth and Moskal 2009; King 2006). Although scholars have explored how these beliefs have become (re)produced through the organizational policies of sports organizations (Hughes 2004; Ruggiero and Lattin 2008) and throughout the media (Halone 2008; Zagacki and Grano 2005), the Internet has become an overlooked space for examining issues of race in sports. This study examines how sports fans used computer-mediated communication (CMC) channels to discuss allegations of racism in the face of American Division I College Football hiring practices.

Race and Ethnicity in Sport(ing) Culture

Contrary to popular belief, issues of race are firmly embedded in the sports world (Springwood 2006). The domain of sports has become historically linked to an American identity that has promoted a dominant white ideology (Gemmell 2007; Staurowsky 2007). For example, King (2006) contended that sports teams that used American Indian names and mascots (e.g., Atlanta Braves, Washington Redskins) reinforced dynamics of whiteness by conjuring up frontier-conquering images and stereotypes of American Indians. King (2007) further noted that—although these names and mascots are offensive to many American Indian groups—when critiques of these "naming" practices are extended, those "sounding the alarm" are often condemned as attacking American identity and values, ideas that have become deeply intertwined with sports (Butterworth and Moskal 2009). Similarly, Newman (2007) profiled how flying the Confederate flag at University of Mississippi football games reconstituted the vestiges of both the Confederacy and a privileged white ideology. In two years of systematic observation of this practice, it was never challenged, implying a promotion and maintenance of a Dixie Civil War identity (Newman 2007).

These aforementioned dynamics have been further reinforced throughout sports media (Billings 2004; Buffington 2005; Halone 2008). Invoking stereotypes is one of the primary ways that televised sports both promulgates and reinforces troublesome representations for its viewing audience. Sports broadcasts, for example, have depicted black athletes as having physical superiority, whereas white athletes have been depicted as possessing intellectual superiority (Billings 2008; Hermes 2005; Li, Harrison, and Solman 2004). Although these trends are problematic, the belief that racism does not affect sports continues to exist (van Sterkenburg and Knoppers 2004). Indeed, people are socialized to these "colorblind" discourses at an early age (Glover 2007), leading to the prevailing ideology that "American sport is an arena, in the popular imagination, which simultaneously celebrates itself as a racial utopia while erasing race and racism" (Springwood 2006, 365).

Race and Ethnicity in Sports Organization

Sports organizations also have enacted policies that privilege unquestioned forms of whiteness (Hughes 2004). Newhall and Buzuvis (2008), for example, chronicled Penn State University's dismissal of women's head basketball coach, Rene Portland, who observed that Penn State University enforced standard policies about hair and beauty that silenced the identity expression of black athletes. Similarly, in 2005, the National Basketball Association (NBA) amended its dress code to require inactive players sitting on the bench to be dressed in business professional attire (Wise 2005). This change was largely attributed to the NBA's attempt to pacify concerns from corporate sponsors that many inactive players wore clothing that resembled that worn in "the ghetto" (McCarthy 2005).

Los Angeles Lakers coach Phil Jackson reinforced such perceptions when he stated, "The players have been dressing in prison garb the last five or six years. . . . All the stuff that goes on, it's like gangsta, thuggery stuff" (J. Wilson 2005, 21). Jackson's choice of words—associating players' attire with "prison," "gangsta," and hence criminal activity (rather than with what had become trendy or fashionable)—intimates the presence of racial overtones. Jackson certainly could have connected their attire with fashion trends or the desire to wear casual clothing when off the court; yet his comments demonstrate how prevailing notions of race and ethnicity at a societal level affect decision making at an organizational level. In this case, the NBA implicitly reinforced whiteness through the dress code, as players subsumed their cultural clothing to align with the interests of the league's white corporate sponsors.

The argument that racism also has trickled down to the hiring of head coaches has prompted some to contend that such practices have become normalized (Fort, Lee, and Berri 2008; Scully 1989). In light of this, some sports organizations are taking steps to promote more racial diversity within the coaching ranks. Consider the National Football League's (NFL) implementation of the "Rooney Rule," which requires teams to interview at least one minority candidate for a head coaching vacancy unless the team is promoting an assistant (Smith 2009). However, despite a recent surge of black head coaches hired in the NFL, questions still remain about the rule's effectiveness. For instance, some teams willingly circumvent the rule and accept fines issued by the league for bypassing this process, or by merely granting "token" interviews to minority candidates who are not seriously being considered for the coaching vacancy (Rhoden 2008).

Although some progress has been made in coaching opportunities for minorities in the NBA, the NFL, and Major League Baseball among others, American Division I College Football—commonly referred to as the Football Bowl Subdivision (FBS)—has not followed suit (Berkotwitz and Wieberg 2009). Indeed, at the present time, only 14 (or 12 percent) of the 120 available head coaching positions in the FBS are held by minorities (Wieberg and Brady 2010). However, this marks a significant increase in minority hiring at FBS programs over the past year, even though a clear discrepancy still exists (Wieberg and Brady 2010).[1] Despite a host of reasons why racial diversity within the FBS coaching ranks remains low, it is unclear how this disparity continues to remain unquestioned by the general public. Two candidate explanations surface for this disparity. First, as fans are conditioned to accept sports as a "racial utopia," they also may perceive that workplace opportunities in sports are no longer influenced by issues of race (Berry and Bonilla-Silva 2008; Bonilla-Silva 2002). Second, given the strong identification fans have with the sport they support, such questionable practices become passively accepted and, therefore, persist (Newman 2007).

In the past, fans were limited to calling in to talk-radio shows or writing letters to the editor of the newspaper to broadcast their opinions about sports organizations decisions. The Internet now enables them to voice commentary, almost instantaneously, on these decisions with other fans across the globe. Thus, when allegations of racial discrimination are made against a sports organization, fan commentary can provide a micro-level view of how fans respond to the organizational (meso-level) practices enacted by sports organizations.

Sports Fans and Computer-Mediated Communication

Within the past decade, sports media has experienced exponential growth to the point that an abundance of sports information is now available on demand from a variety of media outlets. Much of this expansion has resulted from traditional mass media organizations increasing their programming options (e.g., ESPN developing a host of channels, sports leagues establishing their own networks). Internet technology increasingly shares responsibility for being able to usher in the current era of instantaneous and continuous sports news availability (Butler and Sagas 2008; Dart 2009; Galily 2008). Whereas fans were once dependent on waiting for evening news telecasts or local newspapers to obtain their sports information, they can now access this data immediately via the Internet, cell phones, and other technological devices. This alteration has prompted some scholars to suggest that the proliferation of Internet sites devoted to sports is creating a vast digital environment for fans to consume, as well as interact with each other about, sports (Hutchins and Rowe 2009).

Not surprisingly, research is attending to these recent changes in the sports media landscape. Research has discovered, for example, that sports fans employ CMC to discuss their experiences at sporting events (Dart 2009), parasocially interact with athletes (Kassing and Sanderson 2009; Sanderson 2008), and contest hegemonic knowledge produced and distributed by sports organizations (Plymire 2008). Fans' increasing use of computer-mediated forums to consume sports (Clavio 2008; Dart 2009) is so widespread that traditional mass media outlets have developed web-based sports sites to remain competitive in this growing sports media market (Butler and Sagas 2008).

One of the more prominent outcomes of sports-related CMC is that it enables fans to connect with others to discuss sports. The ability for fans to interact with others about sports—across time and space—creates a community-building function wherein meaningful discussions on sports can take place. W. Wilson (2007), for example, analyzed an Internet discussion board devoted to the U.S. Major League Soccer (MLS) league. Here, it was found that virtual communities that formed around teams lacking strong social identities enabled fans to hold meaningful discussions about professional soccer's struggle to gain mainstream acceptance in the United States (W. Wilson 2007). Ferriter (2009) also examined fans' narratives posted on retired NFL players' Wikipedia pages and found that they used such digital spaces to (a) collectively celebrate and debate the athletes' achievements and (b) construct representations of these athletes that stimulated future online interaction.

The interactivity and access afforded by CMC enables a multitude of voices to emanate from these sites for researchers to investigate. This, combined with sports' links to fan identity and the fact that it is widely held to be a racial utopia, means that CMC sites can provide valuable insight into fan reactions when the racial sanctity of sports is publicly challenged. What remains unknown, however, is how CMC practices are used among sports fans when this challenge occurs. Such an incident occurred on December 15, 2008, when former NBA player Charles Barkley publicly criticized Auburn University, his alma mater, for hiring a white candidate (Gene Chizik) instead of a black candidate (Turner Gill) as their head football coach.

Auburn's Search for a Football Coach

On December 3, 2008, after a disappointing season with a record of five wins and seven losses, Auburn University head football coach Tommy Tuberville resigned (Thamel 2008). After Tuberville's resignation, Auburn began a national search to find a replacement. During the search, Turner Gill, who had rebuilt the University of Buffalo's football program, publicly emerged as a popular choice to become Auburn's next head football coach, where he was subsequently interviewed for the job (Hickey 2008). On December 13, 2008, however, Auburn announced that they had hired Iowa State University head football coach Gene Chizik as their new head coach. Chizik's hiring was promptly criticized, with some detractors pointing to Chizik's record at Iowa State (5–19 in two seasons) as evidence that he was unqualified (Glier 2008). Criticism was also directed toward Auburn for failing to hire a qualified black candidate, drawing further attention to the issue of black coaches in the FBS.

One of the more prominent critiques came on December 15, 2008, when former NBA star and Auburn alumnus Charles Barkley publicly chastised the school for hiring Chizik. In commenting on the story to ESPN, Barkley declared that "race was the No. 1 factor" in Chizik's hiring, that he was "disappointed" in the hire, and that he:

thought Turner Gill would be the perfect choice for two reasons: He's a terrific coach and we needed to make a splash. I thought we had to do something spectacular to bring attention to the program. Clearly, if we'd hired a black coach, it would have created a buzz. (Schlabach 2008, para. 7)

Barkley's comments were reported by major mass media outlets, which prompted a multitude of fans to go online and respond to his allegations. Considering the large participation that resulted from Barkley's criticisms (9,005 total postings on espn.com alone), this event appeared to prompt strong fan reactions about the role of race in sports (Douglas and Jamieson 2006; Springwood 2006). The corpus of fan commentary that resulted from this story offers a salient opportunity to examine how sports fans discuss issues of race in sports online.

Method

Data, obtained from the ESPN website, consisted of online postings that responded to ESPN college football reporter Mark Schlabach's (2008) article that reported Barkley's criticisms.[2] The ESPN network is considered "the single most successful sports enterprise in the world" (Perez-Pena 2007, 1) and has multiple distribution formats, such as ESPN television programming, ESPN *The Magazine*, and espn.com. As the dominant U.S. site for online sports consumption (Lemke 2008), espn.com was an appropriate choice for data collection. espn.com enables audience members to post comments to stories reported on their website, and, in order to do so, one must create a user account by providing personal information (e.g., date of birth, gender, e-mail address) while entering a username that is linked to the comments that one posts.

At the time of analysis, there were a total of 9,005 postings, which spanned 2 days, 11 hours, and 37 minutes.[3] Given the large number of available postings, data were randomly selected for analysis. A 20 percent stratified random sample was employed, with every fifth posting selected for inclusion ($n = 1,801$ postings). This procedure mirrors prior strategies to systematically examine large amounts of online fan communication (Kassing and Sanderson 2009; Sanderson 2008). Participation in the forum ranged from people making 1 comment ($n = 548$) to 37 comments ($n = 1$). Table 7 depicts the participation frequencies in the data.

An online post served as the unit of analysis. Each post was initially read to see how participants reacted to Barkley's allegations. Postings that did not contain messages meaningful to the study ($n = 547$; e.g., "Go Gators," commentary about other sports stories) were excluded from analysis. This left 1,254 online postings available for analysis. Although the postings appeared to be from fans, it remains a possibility that some of the postings were authored by espn.com personnel attempting to manage the discussion, a trend that has been observed in other sports media research (Mean, Kassing, and Sanderson 2010). However, the number of postings combined with the stratified sampling technique minimized the impact of this on the findings.

The remaining postings were subjected to a thematic analysis (Boyatzis 1998). First, two subsamples of 100 postings were initially selected to develop inductively derived themes. Next, candidate themes from within each subsample were compared across each subsample to ascertain potential similarity. After this, once candidate themes were determined ($n = 4$), each subsequent posting was carefully read and placed in a candidate theme. Finally, formal codes for each theme were developed (Boyatzis 1998).

Results

Four general themes emerged as follows: (a) transference ($n = 524$), (b) irrelevance ($n = 194$), (c) reverse racism ($n = 198$), and (d) recognition ($n = 338$). An illustration of each theme is located in table 8. Each of these themes is now discussed along with exemplars drawn from the postings. To indicate the number of the posting in the data, a number is attached following each exemplar, indicating where the posting fell in the data set. Postings are reported verbatim from the data; spelling and grammatical errors were left intact.

Table 7. Commentary Frequencies in Participants Responding to espn.com

Number of comments	Number of people
1	548
2	114
3	53
4	32
5	15
6	13
7	12
8	4
9	3
10	5
11	4
13	2
14	3
15	1
16	1
17	2
18	2
19	2
22	1
23	1
26	1
33	1
37	1

Transference

A predominant theme that surfaced was *transference*. This theme suggested that blacks were to blame for their lack of representation in FBS head coaching positions.[4] These postings contended that the lack of coaching diversity was because of the actions of blacks, rather than through any systematic or institutional racism, thus transferring accountability to those affected by racism instead of to those who actually benefit from such racism. This form of redirection became specifically manifest through: (a) criticism ($n = 396$), (b) minimization ($n = 98$), and (c) the "race card" ($n = 30$).

Criticism

Some individuals used Barkley's comments as evidence that allegations of racism were a tool that blacks used to avert accountability for social problems. For instance, "the bottom line is you don't want to get over it because you like having someone to blame for your problems" (600); "Black people have EVERYTHING handed to them and they still manage to lead the country in murders, teen pregnancy, high school drop outs, and unemployed. STOP POINTING THE FINGER AT OTHER PEOPLE...IT'S YOUR OWN FAULT" (674); and "Why do blacks always feel like they are getting screwed?" (915). Fueled by these claims, other individuals then claimed that past allegations of racism had resulted in the underrepresentation of blacks in FBS head coaching circles. For example, "Black people are not worth the risk because they can cause soooooo much trouble screaming racism. I'm sorry but they do it to themselves" (482) and "There arn't as many black coaches because there arn't as many good black coaches" (411).

People also criticized blacks by contending that they had more pressing social issues that needed to be solved before attention could be devoted to racial discrepancies in coaching: "We should first worry about the percentage of black prison guards compared to black prisoners. Lets take care of your societal problems before we move into college sports" (442) and "I've never heard Barkley talk about all the black on black crime. The hundreds of young men killed each day in the streets by other black men. At least he and all the other complainers have their priorities straight" (502). People then leveled specific criticisms at Barkley for having the audacity to question that racism may have played a role in Auburn's hiring process. For example, "Charles Barkley sit you big fat A** down and shut up! No one gives a rats A** what you think, you piece of dog shi*" (817); "Barkley can rot in hell" (239); and "anything an alcoholic, gambling maniac says can't be taken seriously either" (302).

Others declared that Barkley needed to "Shut up" (311, 417, 835) or "Shut his big mouth" (221), as "no one cares what an overweight has been has to say" (610). Additionally, other people concluded that Barkley's allegations were racist: "I am sorry, when you say that the only reason someone got hired is because of race makes you racist" (559); "Charles Barkley is the racist in this story" (643); and "Charles Barkley is the BIGGEST RACIST I have ever heard from. NO BLACK MAN IS MORE RACIST towards white people than him" (909).

These criticisms essentially shifted the issue back to blacks. Thus, rather than it being acknowledged that institutionalized practices may be racist, discriminatory actions were validated as the natural consequences of previous (unwarranted) claims of racism. In other words, this commentary framed the underrepresentation of black head coaches in the FBS as resulting from previous concerns and allegations raised about the lack of diversity in FBS coaching circles. This framing has been historically observed as a convenient way for whites to deflect blame for racism onto minority groups (Foster 2009; Renzetti 2007). Thus, although Auburn may have had the noblest of intentions in hiring Chizik instead of Gill, the current situation surrounding minority coaches in the FBS suggests that Barkley's critiques certainly had merit. Rather than opting to pause for reflection and actually consider what changes *could* be made to bring more racial equity to the FBS, online participants collectively (re)produced messages that minorities were to blame for their lack of representation in certain fields of employment.

The public rebuke of Barkley's criticism may prevent other individuals who share similar feelings from actually speaking out, particularly if such backlashes label them in a way that prevents them from being considered for future employment opportunities. For instance, individuals who perceive race and ethnicity as legitimate barriers that also contribute to differential treatment of coaches (Kamphoff and Gill 2008; Mixon and Trevino 2004) may refrain from speaking out about racism for fear of being negatively labeled. Such personal silence, in light of such lingering public messages, maintains the status quo by reifying the notion that what constitutes racism is the act of speaking out about it.

Table 8. Coding Elements for Participant Themes

Category label	Number of incidents	Definition	Indicators	Differentiation	Example
Transference	524	Postings that suggested that blacks were to blame for lack of diversity in fbs head coaches or for racism in society	Postings that criticized, trivialized, or attributed racism allegations to use of the "race card"	Postings that invoked reverse racism, irrelevance, or agreement with Barkley	"Racism does not exist."
Criticism	396	Postings criticizing blacks or Barkley for contending racism factored in Auburn's decision	Postings that criticized the allegation of racism	Postings that did not directly criticize blacks or Barkley	"Just another stupid comment by Sir Charles."
Minimization	98	Postings that minimized the experiences of blacks and other minorities	Postings that intimated that racism no longer occurred, was no longer relevant, or was not problematic	Postings that did not trivialize the experience of blacks and other minorities with respect to racism	"Are you kidding me? It's the 21st century no one cares about that stuff anymore."

Race card	30	Postings attributing racism or Barkley's comments to use of the "race card"	Postings that considered Barkley's remarks or charges of racism as evidence of use of the "race card"	Postings that did not mention the "race card"	"Barkley again shows his ignorance by again using the race card."
Irrelevance	194	Postings suggesting that racism had no bearing on Auburn's decision to hire Chizik	Postings that attributed Chizik's hiring to other factors, such as tenure	Postings that invoked racism as the reason for Chizik's hiring or did not address the hiring process	"Gill has no history with Auburn, Chizik does."
Reverse racism	198	Postings suggesting that whites were bearing the consequences of racism in sports, society, or both	Postings that detailed some type of discrimination that whites experienced	Postings that did not shift the blame for racism to blacks or that agreed with Barkley's criticisms	"I'm outraged because there aren't enough white running backs in the nfl."
Recognition	338	Postings that acknowledged that the lack of diversity within fbs coaching was problematic	Postings that agreed with Barkley or emphasized the diversity problem in the fbs	Postings that did not consider the lack of diversity to be problematic	"Explain to me how 60 percent of the players are black, yet only 3 percent of the coaches are black."

Note: FBS = Football Bowl Subdivision; NFL = National Football League.

Minimization

Some participants minimized the contention that racism still exists in American society. As such, for them, any allegations that racism factored in Auburn's hiring decision (or others) represented a crutch that blacks used to compensate for their shortcomings and lack of achievement. For example, "Racism is much much lower than you believe but it makes ALOT of people feel better when they have something or someone else to blame it on" (1,131) and "Let the race issue go away please. Everyone is tired of hearing it. No one hires because of race anymore" (856). Because issues of race allegedly had no bearing on individual opportunity, charges of racism were viewed as an excuse to mask one's personal deficiencies. For example, "Any person today has the opportunity to go as far as their desire will take them. It's all up to you and you have no one left to blame" (136) and "Americas' promise is true for everyone who chooses to stay the course" (824). Interestingly, some considered the election of Barack Obama to the United States presidency as evidence of racism's exit from American society. For example, "Hey Charles, did you see the election? White people like Black people now" (210) and

> I am quite frankly tired of him [Barkley] and other high-profile black people making comments claiming racism or prejudice keeps other blacks from getting jobs. Recently with the "hiring" of the first black President, that accusation has become void of any credibility. (902)

Scholars have suggested that minimization claims reduce perceptions that racism still functions, which frames instances of racism as rare, isolated incidents that are deemed fluke occurrences (Bonilla-Silva 2003; O'Brien and Korgen 2007). Although this became manifest in the data, it was also interesting that people pointed to Barack Obama's election to the United States presidency as evidence that racism had diminished. In offering these arguments, this commentary reflected an ideology that conflates American culture and white culture (Nakayama and Martin 2007). By presenting Barack Obama's election as evidence that *any* individual can aspire to anything they wish, the perceived relevance of racism was greatly reduced; in minimizing racism's relevance, these discussions perpetuated an ideology that anyone can overcome any barrier to achieve success (Gandy and Li 2005; Renzetti 2007).

Here, any racial discrepancy that allegedly existed throughout the FBS was merely a by-product of individuals not (a) working hard enough or (b) possessing the merit to be a head coach. By conflating the issue with American ideals (Butterworth and Moskal 2009), any potential dialogue for exploring legitimate reasons for existing racial inequities in the FBS was silenced, which, in turn, absolved institutional culpability for the current situation. Highlighting the successes of a few minority individuals was "evidence" enough that the system was working, which silenced the need to actually address these inequitable barriers.

The Race Card

Categorizing Barkley's critiques specifically, and racism allegations generally, as uses of the race card was another way that online discussion shifted responsibility for racism back onto blacks. Some contended that "using the race card" performed an excuse-making function: "When you say they should of hired a black coach instead of a better coach you have pulled the race card for no apparent reason" (271); "everytime a black man doesn't receive some ptye of recognition, or isnt hired as a coach, chosen for awards, or is being 'singled out' by the media, theres charles barkley crying race . . . stop playing the race card" (113); and "if you don't get what u want, just play the race card" (904). For others, talking about the race card was a way of expressing their general frustration with the topic of racial issues: "I am sick and tired of somebody always throwing up the race card" (1,052); "I'm so tired of the race card being played, not just in sports, but in society as a whole" (207); and "I am so damn sick of people playing the race card" (1,187).

Accusing others of playing the race card provided a strategic way to both dismiss and silence challenges surrounding the status quo around the hiring of FBS head coaches. Rather than engage in a meaningful online conversation about the racial discrepancies in the FBS head coaching ranks and exploring viable options to ameliorate this issue, legitimate questions to these longstanding issues seemed to be conveniently discarded and categorized as race card displays that people were "damn sick" of discussing. Here, online participants further voiced support for the notion that coaching opportunities in this realm are equally available to people of all racial and ethnic backgrounds, despite the fact that, as previously noted, only 12 percent of these jobs are held by minorities. These online postings corroborate research that suggests that accusing someone of playing the race card is employed in discussions in order to undermine criticism of current policies (Hurwitz and Peffiey 2005). The commentary in these posts claimed that there was no need for future legislation or policy revisions, such as the "Rooney Rule," because there was simply not a problem that warranted any action.

Irrelevance

Some participants quickly dismissed the relevance of racism in Auburn's hiring decision. Although some individuals acknowledged that Gill seemed to be a more qualified candidate than Chizik, they believed that factors other than racism accounted for Auburn's final selection. For example, "This is a case of stupidism not racism" (929) and "This is either blatant racism or complete stupidity. Stupidity is my vote" (263). Yet others contended that Chizik's hiring was merely an issue of the best candidate being selected: "It is sad that is still brought up whether the coach, player, scout, whatever is black or white. What happened to being the best candidate?" (154) and "I can see where Auburn is coming from by hiring Chizik, he was their DC [defensive coordinator] when they went 14-0" (531). Still others posited that Gill was not hired because he was simply not qualified to be the head coach at Auburn: "I think Auburn believing that going from the MAC to the SEC is too big a step was the reason Gill wasn't hired, not b/c of Gill's race" (940); "Turner Gill's 'record' was compiled in the pee wee leagues. Gene Chizik helped Auburn to an undefeated season in the 'big leagues'" (1,045); and "Gill is an alright coach but coaching at buffalo and then auburn is a lot different in the sense of competition played" (45).

Commentary that contended that racism did not enter into Auburn's hiring equation reflects how the prevalence of racism becomes underestimated in society (Steinhorn and Diggs-Brown 2000). Although disparate hiring practices toward minorities clearly still exist (Berry and Bonilla-Silva 2008; Jackson 2008), these participants argued that race could not have been a consideration because it paled in comparison with other factors (i.e., previous tenure, work experience). Although the hiring decision could have been possibly influenced by these components, suggesting that racism had *no* role in the hiring decision inhibited meaningful discussion from taking place, thus reinforcing an ideology that employment decisions are void of racial biases.

Reverse Racism

Online participants also contended that elements of reverse racism were present. These claims suggested that whites were the group who were encountering racism in sports. These messages shifted focus from the core issue (i.e., lack of minority head coaches) to the white sporting experience. For instance: "The number of white RB's [running backs] in the NFL is absolutely unacceptable" (24); "I think the only reason I did not get recruited to play running back at Auburn is because I am white. I want justice, I have been discriminated against" (835); and "I will think about hiring a black head football coach when half the players in an NBA game are white and not on the bench" (229). People also argued that this discrimination extended beyond sports and was a result of societal policies, most notably, affirmative action. For example: "if our ancestors would have known that this is what would have happened to our country, they never would have adopted slavery" (96); "the bottom line is that when things go bad for whites, they have to deal with it. When they go wrong for blacks, the entitlement mentality kicks in" (841); "what do all the white coaches that didn't get the job get to blame it on?" (110); and

> To all blacks, I, as a short white boy, with no ball skills, understand your plight, have been a victim of racism myself and therefore ask that you stand with me in protest and help me to start an affirmative action program to stamp out the obvious racism in pro basketball. (141)

These claims suggested that whites no longer had equal opportunities for athletic participation and, therefore, were confronted with an unequal playing field. This, ironically, appeared to have trumped the real issue at hand: the lack of minority coaches in the FBS. Although racial inequity within FBS head coaching circles may have been a salient issue, the more pressing matter for these online participants was the diminished participation opportunities for whites. Despite the fact that whites have enjoyed a monopoly on sports participation throughout sporting history, such contentions dismiss the years of discriminatory practices and struggles that minorities have encountered to gain an equal footing in sports (Simpson 2008). Messages such as these, in turn, further enable discussions of racism to emanate from a white point of view (Deleuze and Guattari 1987).

Recognition

Some individuals acknowledged that the lack of coaching diversity within the FBS was problematic and, thus, warranted corrective action. Some audience members conveyed that the small number of black head coaches in the FBS was a significant problem and stressed that this situation could no longer be ignored. Some individuals expressed that the low number of black head coaches was "indefensible" (1,035), "truly ridiculous" (40), and "a joke" (5). Others more emphatically noted, "Get your heads out of the sand minority candidates are being passed up. these schools aren't going after the best candidates they get and are not being inclusive. 4 out of 119 c'mon!!!" (994); "You hire a white coach with a losing record over a black coach with a winning record? There's something wrong here" (148); and

> Why are there so few Black head coaches??? Throw out the qualified argument because this story obviously defeats that defense, easily. Seriously, explain why isn't the ethnicity of the majority of football players represented in the coaching ranks? (1,569)

Another stated the following:

> Can somebody please explain to me how there are only 4 african-american coaches in a sport which has had a large percentage of

african-american participants for over 30 years? And if your answer is something along the lines of "the best candidate always gets the job" can you please explain to me how Charles Barkley is wrong for pointing out that in the last two coaching searches at Auburn, the worst candidate, who happens to be white, was offered the job over legitimate and established minority candidates? (43)

These messages used language that conveyed the need for increased racial diversity within the FBS. That is, by labeling the current situation as "ridiculous" and "a joke," these participants argued strongly that the racial disparity in the FBS head coaching ranks could no longer be tolerated. Moreover, there appeared to be a strong emphasis placed on pointing out facts about the state of FBS head coaching hiring. With the commenter's highlighting the numerical fact that only "4 out of 119" coaches were black, a vividness emerges that is absent from other generalized postings. Although many had suggested that racism was not a relevant sports topic and had largely disappeared from American society, these voices challenged such messages by acknowledging a need for dialogue. Despite prevalent postings suggesting that Barkley and others had greatly exaggerated the issue, these voices eloquently articulated why conversation about racism in sports is needed (Cole 2008).

Conclusion

This study examined how fans discussed allegations of racial impropriety in sports via computer-mediated discussion forums. Sports fans reacted to Charles Barkley's implication that racism was a factor in Auburn University's hiring of Gene Chizik by entering into computer-mediated forums to differentially voice dissent against or agreement with Barkley's claims. The large number of online responses to this one story clearly demonstrated both how relevant the issue of race in sport actually is and the utility that CMC forums potentially hold for facilitating such discussions. Although fans presumably did respond to this story using traditional media outlets (e.g., writing a letter to the newspaper editor, calling in to a sports radio talk show), these channels inherently limit the number of people who get published or who receive airtime. By going online, fans were able to participate in a public discussion that was not as limited by issues of access, time, or space.[5] They were personally able to comment on a story however they wished as well as collectively engage in a pertinent discussion about the relevance of race in sport while remaining comparatively anonymous.

Although meaningful sports discussions on this topic can certainly take place in other venues, the ability to enter online forums seemed to promote more openness in participants' commentary, possibly allowing for a more accurate societal barometer of fans' views on the relevance of race in sports. This is not to say that fans cannot be more open about their feelings in other venues, but the relative sensitivity of the topic may make the comparative anonymity and immediacy of CMC more likely to facilitate politically incorrect and less socially censored views. In other words, people who possess beliefs about racism that may be considered socially unacceptable (e.g., blacks are actually the ones to blame for racism) may be more likely to express these opinions in an environment where they are afforded anonymity (Peter and Valkenburg 2007; Scott 2004, 2009). Although this does not justify the perpetuation of such views, it does provide public access to those views that some individuals otherwise hold privately. This access provides valuable insight into how sports fans communicate about the role of race in sports while uncovering prevailing ideologies that collectively govern views of race in a given society.

This "openness" that is stimulated vis-a-vis online anonymity provides some valuable insights into the ways people discuss issues of race in sport and society. Scott (2004), for example, made distinctions between "visual" and "discursive" forms of anonymity, suggesting that visual anonymity lacks a visual representation of the person (e.g., appearance, ethnicity), whereas with discursive anonymity—although it reveals something about the message source—users often feel anonymous as their personal information is being withheld. In this study, it appeared that discursive anonymity certainly emboldened audience members to voice controversial and problematic beliefs and opinions about the role of racism in sports, and—though sometimes troubling—they nonetheless demonstrated that racism still surfaces throughout sports. Similarly, the participants in this study appeared to sanction and defend organizational decisions that may perpetuate such practices. For instance, much of the discussion in the forum collectively served to (a) produce and reproduce ideological positions that claim racism as nonexistent, (b) blame the victims of racism for their underrepresentation, and (c) suggest that any lingering racism is against whites (e.g., that whites are victims of reverse discrimination). The presence of such commentary essentially silences dialogue and ultimately diverts attention away from current sports practices that reinforce such racial imbalances.

Participants, moreover, sought out the Internet to defend and protect the identity of college football by contending that the domain of sport is a haven free of racial strife. Given that sports are strongly linked to identity (Gemmell 2007; Halone 2010; Staurowsky 2007), fans were quick to rebuff Barkley's criticisms by contending that the actual problem was with those accusing the systems of unfairness, not with the system itself. By rising up to quell racist allegations, participants (re)directed attention away from the issue at hand and positioned any racial problems as emanating from those who were questioning the system. In suggesting that racism does not enter into the sporting landscape and that its presence surfaces among those who cannot achieve on their own merits, a negative stigma was placed on those who actually raised the question. This may prompt people to perceive that overcoming racial inequities is a hopeless cause (Gazel 2007), which may perpetuate unquestioned instances of hiring discrimination and collective feelings of hopelessness toward racism. And yet, important questions must be asked in situations such as Auburn's hiring process. For instance, although Gill was positioned as merely one person amidst a larger pool of candidates who were passed over for the job, why was Gill the only black candidate considered for the job?

Scholars have contended that research needs to critically examine how media channels marginalize minorities (Bell-Jordan 2008; Bogle 1992; Orbe and Kinefuchi 2008). Because the Internet is emerging as a powerful and influential media channel, it seems an essential site for scholarly examination (Plymire 2008). Thus, in line with research that has expanded into online spheres (Brown 2009; Jacobs 2008; Nakamura 2009), it would seem highly pertinent to examine how online discussions between sports fans (re)produce racialized constructions, knowledge, and stereotypes. As the topic of sports is a fluid conversation piece that one can discuss in multiple contexts, the Internet may facilitate people being more open in their disclosures, especially if they feel more secure in voicing what may be extremely problematic views and perspectives that may not get publicly disclosed in face-to-face or less anonymous contexts. And although these comments may be troubling, they nonetheless say a great deal about how racism gets perpetuated.

NOTES

1. In 2008–2009, there were only six minority head coaches in the FBS, compared with the 14 in 2010. Thus, although there is still progress to be made, a dramatic increase has occurred over the past year.
2. The site address for Schlabach's story and the commentary is http://myespn.go.com/s/conversations/show/story/3770769 (accessed April 30, 2015).
3. At the time this essay originally went to press, there were a total of 8,563 postings to the story, with the last posting being made on January 11, 2009. Although the exact reason for the smaller number of postings is unclear, one plausible explanation is that some commentary was deleted by espn.com for inappropriate content.
4. The usage of the terms *blacks* and *whites* reflects the terminology used by audience members in the data set, and as such they were incorporated in the analysis. This is not meant to suggest that these are preferred appellations for expressing one's ethnic or racial identity.
5. Although access to the Internet remains a relative privilege, in the United States its adoption and use has reached unprecedented levels, becoming a widespread and common communication channel.

REFERENCES

Bell-Jordan, K. E. 2008. "Black, White, and a Survivor of *The Real World*: Constructions of Race on Reality TV." *Critical Studies in Media Communication* 25: 353–72.

Berkowitz, S., and S. Wieberg. 2009. "College Football's Top Level Has Dearth of Minority Coaches." *USA Today*, May 11.

Berry, B., and E. Bonilla-Silva. 2008. "'They Should Hire the One with the Best Score': White Sensitivity to Qualification Differences in Affirmative Action Hiring Decisions." *Ethnic and Racial Studies* 31: 215–42.

Billings, A. C. 2004. "Depicting the Quarterback in Black and White: A Content Analysis of College and Professional Football Broadcast Commentary." *Howard Journal of Communications* 15 (4): 201–10.

——. 2008. *Olympic Media: Inside the Biggest Show on Television*. New York: Routledge.

Bogle, D. 1992. *Toms, Coons, Mulattoes, Mammies, and Bucks: An Interpretive History of Blacks in Films*. New York: Continuum.

Bonilla-Silva, E. 2001. *White Supremacy and Racism in the Post-Civil Rights Era*. Boulder CO: Lynne Reinner.

——. 2002. "The Linguistics of Color-Blind Racism: How to Talk about Blacks without Sounding 'Racist.'" *Critical Sociology* 28: 41–64.

——. 2003. *Racism without Racists: Color-Blind Racism and the Persistence of Racial Inequality in the United States*. Lanham MD: Rowman & Littlefield.

Boyatzis, R. 1998. *Transforming Qualitative Information: Thematic Analysis and Code Development*. Thousand Oaks CA: Sage.

Brown, C. 2009. "www.hate.com: White Supremacist Discourse on the Internet and the Construction of Whiteness Ideology." *Howard Journal of Communications* 20: 189–208.

Buffington, D. 2005. "Contesting Race on Sundays: Making Meaning out of the Rise in the Number of Black Quarterbacks." *Sociology of Sport Journal* 21: 19–37.

Butler, B., and M. Sagas. 2008. "Making Room in the Lineup: Newspaper Websites Face Growing Competition for Sports Fans' Attention." *International Journal of Sport Communication* 1: 17–25.

Butterworth, M. L., and S. D. Moskal. 2009. "American Football, Flags, and 'Fun': The Bell Helicopter Armed Forces Bowl and the Rhetorical Production of Militarism." *Communication, Culture & Critique* 2: 411–33.

Carr, L. G. 1997. *Colorblind Racism*. Thousand Oaks CA: Sage.

Clavio, G. 2008. "Demographics and Usage Profiles of Users of College Sports Message Boards." *International Journal of Sport Communication* 1: 434–43.

Cole, C. L. 2008. "Golf, Race, and Rituals of Progress." *Journal of Sport & Social Issues* 32: 119–20.

Crenshaw, K. W. 1997. "Color-Blind Dreams and Racial Nightmares: Reconfiguring Racism in the Post-Civil Rights Era." In *Birth of a Nation'Hood: Gaze, Script and Spectacle in the O. J. Simpson Case*, edited by T. Morrison, 97–168. New York: Random House.

Dart, J. J. 2009. "Blogging the 2006 FIFA World Cup Finals." *Sociology of Sport Journal* 26: 107–26.

Deleuze, G., and F. Guattari. 1987. *A Thousand Plateaus*. Translated by B. Massumi. Minneapolis: University of Minnesota Press. First published 1980.

Douglas, D. D., and K. M. Jamieson. 2006. "A Farewell to Remember: Interrogating the Nancy Lopez Farewell Tour." *Sociology of Sport Journal* 23: 117–41.

Ferriter, M. M. 2009. "'Arguably the Greatest': Sports Fans and Communities at Work on Wikipedia." *Sociology of Sport Journal* 26: 127–54.

Fort, R., Y. H. Lee, and D. Berri. 2008. "Race, Technical Efficiency, and Retention: The Case of NBA Coaches." *International Journal of Sport Finance* 3: 84–97.

Foster, J. D. 2009. "Defending Whiteness Indirectly: A Synthetic Approach to Race Discourse Analysis." *Discourse & Society* 20: 685–703.

Frey, J. H., and D. S. Eitzen. 1991. "Sport and Society." *Annual Review of Sociology* 17: 503–22.

Galily, Y. 2008. "The (Re)shaping of the Israeli Sports Media: The Case of Talk-Back." *International Journal of Sport Communication* 1: 273–85.

Gandy, O. H., Jr., and Z. Li. 2005. "Framing Comparative Risk: A Preliminary Analysis." *Howard Journal of Communications* 16: 71–86.

Gazel, J. 2007. "Walking the Talk: Multiracial Discourses, Realities, and Pedagogy." *American Behavioral Scientist* 51: 532–50.

Gemmell, J. 2007. "Cricket, Race and the 2007 World Cup." *Sport in Society* 10: 1–10.

Glier, R. 2008. "Football and Race Debated at Auburn." *New York Times*, December 18.

Glover, T. D. 2007. "Ugly on the Diamonds: An Examination of White Privilege in Youth Baseball." *Leisure Sciences* 29: 195–208.

Halone, K. K. 2008. "The Structuration of Racialized Sport Organizing." *Journal of Communication Inquiry* 32: 22–42.

———. 2010. "The Institutional(ized) Nature of Identity in and around Sport(s)." In *Examining Identity in Sports Media*, edited by H. L. Hundley and A. C. Billings, 239–62. Thousand Oaks CA: Sage.

Hermes, J. 2005. "Burnt Orange: Television, Football, and the Representation of Ethnicity." *Television & New Media* 6: 49–69.

Hickey, P. 2008. "Gill Leads Turnaround at Buffalo: Former Concordes Quarterback Has Taken Only 3 Years to Transform University Program." *Montreal Gazette*, December 24.

Hughes, G. 2004. "Managing Black Guys: Representation, Corporate Culture, and the NBA." *Sociology of Sport Journal* 21: 163–84.

Hurwitz, J., and M. Peffley. 2005. "Playing the Race Card in the Post-Willie Horton Era: The Impact of Racialized Code Words on Support for Punitive Crime Policy." *Public Opinion Quarterly* 69: 99–112.

Hutchins, B., and D. Rowe. 2009. "From Broadcast Scarcity to Digital Plenitude." *Television & New Media* 10: 354–70.

Jackson, J. F. L. 2008. "Race Segregation across the Academic Workforce: Exploring Factors That May Contribute to the Disparate Representation of African American Men." *American Behavioral Scientist* 51: 1004–29.

Jacobs, M. 2008. "Multiculturalism and Cultural Issues in Online Gaming Communities." *Journal for Cultural Research* 12: 317–34.

Kamphoff, C., and D. Gill. 2008. "Collegiate Athletes' Perceptions of the Coaching Profession." *International Journal of Sports Science and Coaching* 3: 55–72.

Kassing, J. W., and J. Sanderson. 2009. "'You're the Kind of Guy That We All Want for a Drinking Buddy': Expressions of Parasocial Interaction on Floydlandis. com." *Western Journal of Communication* 73: 182–203.

King, C. R. 2006. "On Being a Warrior: Race, Gender and American Indian Imagery in Sport." *International Journal of the History of Sport* 23: 315–30.

Lapchick, R. L. 1986. *Fractured Focus: Sport as a Reflection of Society*. New York: D. C. Heath.

Lemke, T. 2008. "Fantasy's New Face on the Web." *Washington Times*, September 9.

Leonard, D. 2004. "The Next M. J. or the Next O. J.? Kobe Bryant, Race and the Absurdity of Colorblind Rhetoric." *Journal of Sport & Social Issues* 28: 284–313.

Li, W., L. Harrison Jr., and M. Solmon. 2004. "College Students' Implicit Theories of Ability in Sports: Race and Gender Differences." *Journal of Sport Behavior* 27: 291–304.

McCarthy, M. 2005. "Stern Stern on Player Dress Code: Comply or Leave." *USA Today*, October 19.

Mean, L. J., J. W. Kassing, and J. Sanderson. 2010. "The Making of an Epic (American) Hero Fighting for Justice: Commodification, Consumption, and Intertextuality in the Floyd Landis Defense Campaign." *American Behavioral Scientist* 53 (11): 1590–1609.

Mixon, F. G., and L. J. Trevino. 2004. "How Race Affects Dismissals of College Football Coaches." *Journal of Labor Research* 25: 645–56.

Nakamura, L. 2009. "Don't Hate the Player, Hate the Game: The Racialization of Labor in World of Warcraft." *Critical Studies in Media Communication* 26: 128–44.

Nakayama, T. K., and J. N. Martin. 2007. "The White Problem in Intercultural Communication Research and Pedagogy." In *Whiteness, Pedagogy, Performance: Dis/placing Race*, edited by L. M. Cooks and J. Simpson, 111–37. Lanham MD: Lexington Books.

Newhall, K. E., and Buzuvis, E. E. 2008. "(e)Racing Jennifer Harris: Sexuality and Race, Law and Discourse in Harris v. Portland." *Journal of Sport and Social Issues* 32: 345–68.

Newman, J. I. 2007. "Old times Are Not Forgotten: Sport, Identity, and the Confederate Flag in the Dixie South." *Sociology of Sport Journal* 24: 261–82.

O'Brien, E., and K. O. Korgen. 2007. "It's the Message, Not the Messenger: The Declining Significance of Black-White Contrast in a 'Colorblind' Society." *Sociological Inquiry* 77: 356–82.

Orbe, M. P., and E. Kinefuchi. 2008. "Crash under Investigation: Engaging Complications of Complicity, Coherence and Implicature through Critical Analysis." *Critical Studies in Media Communication* 25: 135–56.

Perez-Pena, R. 2007. "The Top Player in the League? It May Be the Sports Reporter." *New York Times*, December 24.

Peter, J., and P. M. Valkenburg. 2007. "Who Looks for Casual Dates on the Internet? A Test of the Compensation and the Recreation Hypothesis." *New Media & Society* 9: 455–74.

Plymire, D. C. 2008. "The Wiki Defense: Contesting the Status of Knowledge in the Floyd Landis Doping Case." *International Journal of Sport Communication* 1: 307–19.

Renzetti, C. M. 2007. "All Things to All People or Nothing for Some: Justice, Diversity, and Democracy in Sociological Societies." *Social Problems* 54: 161–69.

Rhoden, W. C. 2008. "Campaign Needed for Minority Candidates for Football Coach." *New York Times*, February 11.

Ruggiero, T. E., and K. S. Lattin. 2008. "Intercollegiate Female Coaches' Use of Verbally Aggressive Communication toward African American Female Athletes." *Howard Journal of Communications* 19: 105–24.

Sanderson, J. 2008. "'You Are the Type of Person That Children Should Look Up To as a Hero': Parasocial Interaction on 38pitches.com." *International Journal of Sport Communication* 1: 337–60.

Schlabach, M. 2008. "Lobbying for Gill, Alum Barkley Says Auburn Should Have Hired Black Coach." espn.com, December 16. http://sports.espn.go.com/ncf/news/story?id=3770769.

Scott, C. R. 2004. "Benefits and Drawbacks of Anonymous Online Communication: Legal Challenges and Communicative Recommendations." In *Free*

Speech Yearbook. Vol. 41, edited by S. Drucker, 127–41. Washington DC: National Communication Association.

———. 2009. "A Whole-Hearted Effort to Get It Half-Right: Predicting the Future of Communication Technologies." *Journal of Computer-Mediated Communication* 14: 753–57.

Scully, G. W. 1989. *The Business of Major League Baseball*. Chicago: University of Chicago Press.

Simpson, J. L. 2008. "The Color-Blind Double Bind: Whiteness and the (Im)possibility of Dialogue." *Communication Theory* 18: 139–59.

Smith, T. 2009. "Rooney Rule Propelling Steelers, Cards, in Super Season." *New York Daily News*, January 28.

Springwood, C. F. 2006. "Basketball, Zapatistas, and Other Racial Subjects." *Journal of Sport & Social Issues* 30: 364–73.

Staurowsky, E. J. 2007. "'You Know, We Are All Indian': Exploring White Power and Privilege in Reactions to the NCAA Native American Mascot Policy." *Journal of Sport & Social Issues* 31: 61–76.

Steinhorn, L., and B. Diggs-Brown. 2000. *By the Color of Our Skin: The Illusion of Integration and the Reality of Race*. New York: Basic Books.

Thamel, P. 2008. "Auburn Dismisses Tuberville and Set Sights on Leach." *New York Times*, December 4.

van Sterkenburg, J., and A. Knoppers. 2004. "Dominant Discourses about Race/Ethnicity and Gender in Sport Practice and Performance." *International Review for the Sociology of Sport* 39: 301–21.

Wieberg, S., and E. Brady. 2010. "An Uptick in Minority Coaches: Looking at Quality of Work, Not Color of Skin, Is Basis for Increase." *USA Today*, January 6.

Wilson, J. 2005. "NBA's 'No Bling' Dress Code Prompts Racism Accusations." *London Guardian*, October 31.

Wilson, W. 2007. "All Together Now, Click: MLS Soccer Fans in Cyberspace." *Soccer and Society* 8: 381–98.

Wise, M. 2005. "Opinions on the NBA's Dress Code Are Far from Uniform." *Washington Post*, October 23.

Zagacki, K. S., and D. Grano. 2005. "Radio Sports Talk and the Fantasies of Sport." *Critical Studies in Media Communication* 22: 45–63.

21

The LeBron James Decision in the Age of Obama

JAMAL L. RATCHFORD

Times sure have changed. Forty years after critics blasted two athletes' silent protest at the 1968 Olympics—when they flung their tightened black-gloved fists into the Mexico City evening sky in the Black Power salute to call attention to human rights concerns and received a chorus of boos—white journalists, spectators, athletes, and administrators honored Tommie Smith and John Carlos at the Excellence in Sports Performance Yearly (ESPY) Awards.[1] In 2008, the Entertainment Sports Programming Network (ESPN) held their annual gala at the Nokia Theater in Los Angeles. Numerous sports and entertainment dignitaries attended and celebrated the apex of athletic accomplishments. Singer and actor Justin Timberlake entertained the audience and hosted the sports premier award show. The evening is normally a jovial and lighthearted attempt to recapture the best athletic achievements from the calendar year. Timberlake's comedic opening remarks featured song and dance and also brought laughter to the audience at the expense of National Football League (NFL) stars Brett Favre and Eli Manning as well as champion Paul Pierce of the National Basketball Association (NBA).

The awarding of Arthur Ashe Award for Courage, an honor presented to persons who made the most significant humanitarian contribution to sports and society, shifted the playful tone to a serious and reflective remembrance of a historical moment. Actor Samuel L. Jackson and NBA All-Star and two-time Most Valuable Player Steve Nash gave the preliminary remarks and introduced the awardees. Jackson said the silent protest remained fresh in his mind. The year 1968, he recalled, "may have been forty years ago but for many of us, like me, a nineteen-year-old student at Morehouse College at the time, the events were so vivid, so personal that they could have occurred yesterday."[2]

The ceremonies continued with actor Tom Cruise narrating a nine-minute clip that documented events leading up to the silent protest. When the film concluded, Tommie Smith and John Carlos were introduced and received the Arthur Ashe award. The audience erupted and gave a standing ovation. A racially and politically diverse crowd that included auto racer Danica Patrick, NFL all-time great Jerry Rice, and internationally renowned English soccer star David Beckham unanimously rose and cheered the two men. The two men gave another raised fist salute in appreciation of the audience. At the microphone, Smith spoke of sacrifice and Carlos reminded current athletes to use sports as a vehicle for social change. ESPN recognized them three years after San Jose State (SJS), their alma mater, erected a statue in their honor. Indeed, American responses to the silent protest were far different in 2008 than in 1968. After their demonstration in the Estadio Olympico during the 200 meters medal presentation and playing of the American national anthem, writers virulently criticized Smith and Carlos. *Chicago Daily News* sportswriter and later American Broadcasting Company (ABC) play-by-play man Brent Musburger disparaged the protest, saying,

> Smith and Carlos looked like a couple of black skinned storm troopers [Nazis], holding aloft their black gloved hands during the playing of the National Anthem. It's destined to go down as the most unsubtle demonstration in the history of protest. . . . And it insured maximum embarrassment for the country that picked up their room and board bill in Mexico.[3]

In other words, how dare these black athletes rebel against a country that, Tommie Smith said, "treated him like just another nigger off the track?"

How and why was it that Smith and Carlos were banned by the International Olympic Committee (IOC) in 1968 but appreciated in 2008? Have Americans become more racially tolerant of black athletes and the decisions they make? As historian Urla Hill suggested, "Smith and Carlos have transcended their place as villainous traitors to become a sort of brand for gallantry and pluck in the face of inestimable odds." Their action, argues sociologist Douglas Hartmann, diminished their place in American cultural history. In other words, the recognition of Smith and Carlos at the ESPYs alluded to the ways American sports media specifically, and white masses more broadly, determine when and how black protest and self-determination are acceptable in national contexts.[4] The use of the term "self-determination" in this essay differs contextually and thematically from the cultural, psychological, socioeconomic, and political veneration that the term represented in the late 1960s as articulated by Stokely Carmichael and others. Rather, as suggested later in the essay, as the term is used here, the implementation of self-determination by black athletes serves in tandem with what I frame, borrowing from historian and black studies scholar Derrick White, as pragmatic black nationalism—in this case, the broad use of celebrity to engagement with and social responsibility for black communities and underrepresented groups.

Despite infringements, criticisms, and sanctions against them, Smith, Carlos, and a host of other black athletes in the late 1960s extended a tradition of black self-determination in sports that tested the limits of American participatory democracy. In 2008, the recognition of Smith and Carlos at the ESPYs elucidated the ways black self-determination is currently understood in American sports and society. In ways similar to the cooption of the late Martin Luther King Jr., American popular culture historically de-radicalized black protest in myth and memory and repackaged it in ways removed from its original and contextual intentions. On the other hand, perhaps recognition at the ESPYs tacitly provided opportunities for spectators to engage historiography on race and sports in the American experience. This essay will explore the way modern reactions to the silent protest shed light on public interpretations of self-determination by black athletes in the age of Obama—sometimes referred to as the "postracial era."[5]

The Black Athlete and Self-Determination

This essay investigates the dynamics of race and sports from the 1968 silent protest to the 2010 LeBron James decision to leave the Cleveland Cavaliers for the Miami Heat.[6] Although it is contextually removed and symbolically different from the silent protest, I argue that the hour-long LeBron James decision extended a lengthy tradition of self-determination by black athletes. His controversial and divisive decision challenged the normative player-owner-spectator relationship when James asserted control and ownership of his present and future. The James decision also was particularly noteworthy because he is a black athlete. Historically, the agency and opportunities for black athletes has been restricted. In the twentieth century many white critics, both players and officials, would not accept integrated competition and discouraged activism in sports. So, it is plausible to situate reactions to the James decision in a legacy of criticism against black athletes. Although James was not the first free agent to switch teams, his decision on national television disrupted the age-old American sporting tradition of the player and owner relationship when James publicly shaped his own destiny. I end this essay with a brief examination on the ways the James decision overlaps with pragmatic black nationalism and serves as a catalyst for social responsibility and community engagement for black athletes in the age of Obama.

In 1968 white politicians, journalists, and administrators attempted to limit black agency and athletic potential. After Smith's and Carlos's silent protest at the Olympics, many whites were perplexed and flustered. How dare black athletes use a sporting event to express dissent? To them, sports best represented American democracy. Integration of athletics meant national integration. To black athletes, athletic integration, which in some ways was a fiction, only deepened the paradox of American democracy.[7] Reactions to the silent protest accorded with two positions on the legacy of white appropriation of black athletic self-determination. First, to whites that may have disregarded black concerns, integrated sports best represented the possibilities of American greatness. Second, black protest was seen as antithetical to the idea of sports as a nonpolitical space. Furthermore, black activism in sports was defined as un-American. Historically, black athletes were viewed as property rather than autonomous individuals—their sole allegiances were supposed to be for team, sport, or country.

To Cleveland Cavaliers owner Dan Gilbert and most journalists and spectators, James was a traitor who turned his back on the team and city. The demonization of James for his self-determination in opposition to the status quo is a bit ironic, contrasting as it does the American core values of individuality, competition, and the profit motive. Thus, I see parallels between self-determination as a contested issue for black athletes in both James's decision and in Smith's and Carlos's raising of the Black Power salute at the 1968 Olympics.[8]

Concurrent to the legacy of appropriation and criticism against black athletes was a tradition of self-determination that was propelled forward by them. The 140 years prior to the James decision saw a tradition in American sports that privileged the owner over the athlete. In the late nineteenth century, paternalistic owners like sports equipment mogul Albert Spalding (of the then Chicago White Stockings) exerted total control over the team. Simply, if players performed poorly, they were not paid, and in some instances they were fired. Despite those restrictions, black athletes challenged the financial boundaries of white-owned sports.[9] In the 1890s, Isaac Murphy overcame racial discrimination and made fifteen to twenty thousand dollars—ten thousand more than white jockeys.[10] By the early twentieth century, the prevalence of white supremacy prohibited black athletes in the sport. When Olympic champion Jesse Owens challenged United States Olympic Committee member (and Nazi sympathizer) Avery Brundage for increased funds for a post-1936 Olympic Games tour he was shunned, scrapped to make a living, and ran against horses and cars for survival. Even Branch Rickey, the legendary white president and general manager of the Brooklyn Dodgers, instructed Jackie Robinson that baseball needed a black athlete who would not advocate physical violence against racism. Although Robinson became the face of integration in Major League Baseball (MLB) in 1947, numerous journalists, spectators, and owners opposed his inclusion. With the advent of integrated professional sports in the 1950s and 1960s, black athletes began to earn high salaries.[11]

Black Athletes and Civil Rights

On the other hand, numerous collegiate black athletes tapped into sentiment espoused in the Civil Rights movement and agitated for human
equality and freedom. As Stan Wright, a black track and field coach at the
1968 Olympics, said, "It's the morality involved and not the money. . . .
They'd sacrifice to serve."[12] Although Wright was referencing collegiate
athletes, acclaimed black professional athletes in the 1960s and 1970s,
including Bill Russell, Muhammad Ali, Wilma Rudolph, and Curt Flood,
also infused self-determination into their careers. In the 1990s, Michael
Jordan continued a tradition of self-determination and marketed basketball
as a global and profit-based enterprise. In spite of criticisms against him
for leaving one team for another, LeBron James prolonged a tradition of
self-determination by black athletes and in doing so publicized that he
and not others controlled his agency and destiny.

James was not the only black athlete in the so-called "post racial age
of Obama" that tapped into self-determination in American sports. On
June 15, 2004, Rasheed Wallace won his only NBA championship when
the Detroit Pistons defeated the Los Angeles Lakers in five games. For
Wallace, occasionally referred to as "Sheed," the title was only a fraction
of his professional legacy. Drafted fourth by the Washington Bullets in
1995, the four-time All-Star was a six foot, eleven inch forward who could
run the fast break, defend post players, and knock down the outside jump
shot. Indeed, Wallace epitomized a new hybrid breed of NBA big men
who played like guards and looked like centers. He also was passionately
outspoken and infamously earned the title as NBA all-time technical fouls
leader. After a loss by his team at the time, the Portland Trailblazers, his
only response in the postgame press conference to the media was, "Both
teams played hard. . . . Both teams played hard, my man. . . . God bless and
goodnight." The interview later became an internet sensation on YouTube
and it also can be found on numerous *SportsCenter* top-ten reels. However,
all of his commentary was not adored. In 2003, Wallace condemned NBA
commissioner David Stern and his league for treating black players like
slaves on a plantation. He claimed, "They don't know no better, and they

don't know the real business, and they don't see behind the charade. They look at black athletes like we're shit. It's as if we're just going to shut up, sign for the money and do what they tell us."[13] As in the 1960s, reactions by white commissioners, writers, and the general public were not sympathetic. Why? For many whites, one cannot be rich and also perceive the world as racist, so highly paid black athletes like Wallace appear to embody a contradiction that they are ideologically unable to reconcile.[14]

To journalist William Rhoden, author of a book on blacks in athletics, *Forty Million Slaves*, however, Wallace was on to something. Indeed, Wallace, like fellow Tar Heel and NBA star Vince Carter, were African and Afro-American studies majors at the University of North Carolina—a discipline rooted in a 1960s black freedom struggle that espoused academic excellence, cultural grounding, and social responsibility. Wallace understood those principles well before he became a millionaire. Despite the fame of numerous black athletes, Rhoden correctly argues, they still are on the periphery of true power in multibillion-dollar American sports.[15] Racism remains a dynamic phenomenon since institutional racism remains the most salient form of racial discrimination.

Sure, at the 1997 Masters, Fuzzy Zoeller commented about golfer Tiger Woods,

> That little boy is driving well and he's putting well. He's doing everything it takes to win. So, you know what you guys do when he gets in here? You pat him on the back and say congratulations and enjoy it and tell him not to serve fried chicken next year. Got it?[16]

Then Zoeller smiled, snapped his fingers, walked away, turned and added, "Or collard greens or whatever the hell they serve."[17] Or, in 2008, Golf Channel anchor Kelly Tilghman joked with former golf champion Nick Faldo that young players should "lynch him [Tiger Woods] in the back alley."[18] Both instances of appalling racist commentary were criticized by the public and then swiftly pushed aside. Why? In my "Introduction to African-American Studies" class, one of my students commented, "It's not status quo to be racist anymore." To be more precise, it is not status quo to be overtly racist and when necessary keep it behind closed doors—more preferably, systematically interweave it into the status quo. Even if Wallace made mistakes—and he certainly did—the former NBA star was conscious of institutional racism in sports and society. Rhoden, in *Forty Million Dollar Slaves*, situated the intersection of racism and sports in broader historical contexts and discussed that one need not be spat upon, verbally abused, or lynched to understand or experience racism.

The LeBron James Decision

Enter LeBron James. For nearly a year, sportswriters, administrators, fans, and fellow athletes anticipated the 2010 NBA free agency period because it was highlighted by mega-stars, including LeBron James, Dwayne Wade, Chris Bosh, Amar'e Stoudemire, and Dirk Nowitzki. Nearly ten million people watched the hour-long announcement of his decision. It was broadcasted live at the Boys and Girls Club in Greenwich, Connecticut, in front of a studio audience. Chaos ensued when the Akron, Ohio, native left the Cleveland Cavaliers (Cavs) and took his talents to South Beach and the Miami Heat. Cleveland fans cried, shouted at television screens, and burned jerseys. They removed anything connected to James as "the witness" or "king"—as he had been hailed—stripping down signs from Quicken Loans Arena days later. Some journalists charged conspiracy and said Wade, Bosh, and James colluded during and after Team USA won gold in men's basketball at the 2008 Beijing Olympics.[19]

Cavaliers owner Dan Gilbert incited anti-James propaganda. He said the once beloved king and savior of Cleveland basketball had become a "coward narcissist" who turned his back on his hometown. Fans agreed. Some sold lemonade to support Gilbert in opposition to NBA Commissioner Stern when he fined Gilbert one hundred thousand dollars. The company Fathead sold replicas of Benedict Arnold for $17.41, as a play on the 1741 birth date of the so-called first American traitor in the Revolutionary War.[20] One local brewery sold a new beer called "quitness." It was described as a beer that will leave a bitter taste in your mouth. White and black Cavs fans made a parody film on a LeBron James video called, "What should I do?" Hit Comedy Central show *South Park* also mimicked the video in an episode. His decision to leave the Cavs also made spectators and journalists unsympathetic to James, the patriot who spearheaded the return to dominance of USA basketball on the international level. Despite everything that James did "right," his one decision made him the epitome of everything wrong with sports, celebrity, and society. Self-determination was not in style for the American public.

Gilbert certainly had his critics. Some sportswriters pondered the irony in Gilbert—a man who wanted James a day prior but excoriated him when he chose Miami. One certainty is that James rebuilt the Cavs into a nationally and internationally acclaimed franchise. One year prior to the arrival of James as an NBA professional, the Cavs finished with seventeen wins and sixty-five losses. That tied their third worst season in franchise history. After he joined the Cavs, James was billed as the savior of the franchise. As a high school athlete he was regularly promoted by national media and he also set a new trend for ESPN. His St. Vincent–St. Mary High School team was televised nationally often because ESPN wanted to feature James. Thus, James spearheaded nationally televised high school basketball. The Cavs needed a savior and James fit the role.

One supporter of James was the Rev. Jesse Jackson. Jackson understood James's impact on the Cavaliers yet framed his decision to go to the Heat in a slavery context. Jackson declared, "His [Gilbert's] feelings of betrayal personify a slave master mentality. He sees LeBron as a runaway slave. This is an owner-employee relationship between business partners—and LeBron honored his contract."[21] Black journalist Jason Whitlock countered, "Jesse has a constituency, a passionate group of idiots who believe the best way to combat white-wing political bigots such as [Rush] Limbaugh and [Sean] Hannity is with black-wing political bigotry."[22] Clearly, the James decision exposed and deepened the complicated relationship between race and sports.

Public Outcry

The public was outraged. How could Jackson identify race in a seemingly non-racial situation? NBA commissioner Stern, a good friend of Jackson's, crafted his response carefully and politely disagreed with him. Some faulted

Jackson and said his remarks were racist. Jackson was seen as a bigot by those who advocated a colorblind agenda, or, in other words, denied the persistence of racism in the United States.[23] Jackson and other critics of a colorblind framework say it defends white advantages.[24] Some scholars parallel colorblindness to "white habitus," or the process in which whites' segregated lifestyle psychologically leads them to develop positive views about themselves and negative views about racial others.[25] To sympathizers, Gilbert became the misunderstood owner who was wrongly compared to a slave owner because of his condemnation of a former employee who happened to be black.

On the ESPN show *Outside the Lines*, two of the three panelists, Dennis Manoloff and Chris Sheridan, agreed that Jackson was out of line with his comments. Host of the radio program *The Morning Jones* Bomani Jones differed. First, Jones said, the general public misinterpreted Jackson's criticism of Gilbert as calling him a racist. And in actuality, he said, Jackson referred to a "slave master mentality" in which Gilbert's letter assumed ownership of a "less than human piece of property that he lost" to free agency. Second, Jones argued, Gilbert incited public rage by posting his letter on the front page of the Cavaliers website—a ploy cementing the owner's message as the voice of the franchise and instantly putting James's safety at risk; police units later patrolled James's multimillion-dollar house. Manoloff asked, "If LeBron James were white, would Jackson make the same comment?" Jones replied, "A better question is, if the slavery statement was semantically clumsy, then why are we discussing it and not the rest of Jackson's statement[,] ... much of which was accurate." To Jones, the bigger issues were threefold. First, Cavaliers supporters assumed players owe them loyalty. Second, Gilbert's letter incited public rage. Third, when Gilbert posted the letter at the Cavs website, a member organization of the broader NBA family, he cemented his sentiments as the official response of the franchise.

Race, sports, and self-determination continue to be hotly contested issues in American popular culture. During the 2011 ESPN Town Hall Meeting in honor of Martin Luther King Jr., Richard Lapchick cited racial discrepancies in American media. According to *Tides*, in 2010, 94 percent of sports editors were white, 2 percent black, and 4 percent other. Nearly 89 percent of assistant sports editors were white, 4 percent black, and 7 percent other. The trend continued in regard to columnists, reporters, and copy editors, with whites representing 88, 87, and 89 percent, respectively, of those types of media. Out of the five surveys, blacks comprised double-digit features in only one category: 10 percent of columnists. Film director Spike Lee asked about the racial dynamic of athletes and media—and in particular the question, if the majority of players are black and the majority of media is white, then in what ways do the athletes perceive media coverage? His question put the legacy of white media coverage in American sports into the spotlight. Although white spectators, administrators, politicians, and journalists were not monolithic, Lapchick's findings elucidated realities that the livelihoods of black athletes often were constructed by persons that either were ill-concerned or unknowledgeable about the reality faced by black athletes. In other words, media criticism about the self-determination of black athletes was shaped in ways that privileged experiences of white Americans.[26]

Youthful Delusions

Because of the historical legacy of American institutional racism, sports became a central strategy for socioeconomic vitality and success for many African American men at the expense of the pursuit of success in education, public policy, and business. The James decision also tapped into debates on the relationship among race, sports, and society in "postracial America." Historian Steven Riess found that 70 percent of black youth ages 13–18 expected to play professionally in the NBA.[27] The Center for the Study of Sport in Society claimed 66 percent of black men believed their first job would be as professional athletes.[28] However, Professor Earl Smith of Wake Forest University asserted that the odds of black student-athletes becoming professional are twenty thousand to one for basketball and ten thousand to one for football.[29]

Harry Edwards, a sociologist and central figure in the advent of activism in 1960s sports and society, discussed the ways in which race and sports are skewed in American culture. Edwards noted that racial discrimination in American labor inhibited blacks' social mobility and benefitted white Americans over African Americans. Since sports, unlike most other forms of labor available to them, offered monetary wealth, blacks over-pursued sports and viewed them as a means to thrive in American society. By contrast, according to Edwards, whites could fluidly move in and out of sports. For example, when collegiate white athletes in the 1960s fulfilled their eligibility, they could become doctors, lawyers, and politicians. Furthermore, it could be argued that American society valued inclusion of African Americans in sports more than in its broader society. Edwards asserts,

> There is still a disproportionately high emphasis on sport achievement in black society . . . relative to other high-prestige occupational career aspirations. Given what is happening to young black people, who have essentially disconnected from virtually every institutional structure in society, sports may be our last hook and handle.[30]

In the late 1960s, some African American public figures recognized disparities in sports and society and offered suggestions that benefitted black people. Edwards remarked that if "President Nixon can spend his time thinking about baseball and football, I can spend my time thinking about the political interests of black people."[31] Earl Graves, publisher of *Black Enterprise*, said, "In 1979, one out of 4,000 black children go on to participate in professional sports—black children unrealistically aspire for athletic careers as their only means."[32] Tennis Hall of Famer Arthur Ashe wrote a letter to the *New York Times* arguing that "black culture expends too much time, energy and effort raising, praising, and teasing our black children as to the dubious glories of sport. . . . Fill up at the library and speed away to Congress and the Supreme Court, the unions and the business world."[33] In 1978, Tommie Smith said,

> The athletic scene is worse now than it was in 1968. There's too many other acts of survival that one has to go through before he can live in this society. And equality isn't one of them. Being black in this society is very abstract now.[34]

Pragmatic Black Nationalism in the Age of Obama

Since sports remain overemphasized for black communities, it is timely for persons of African descent to reverse this trend for the benefit of the race and nation. Thus, the James decision also gives credence to the necessity of public action for community engagement and pragmatic black nationalism, or enlightened self-interest, for black athletes in the age of Obama. More specifically, in 2011 James donated two million dollars to the Boys and Girls Clubs of America. Clubs in Cleveland, his hometown of Akron, and Elyria, Ohio, received approximately five hundred thousand dollars of that sum. In addition to making the cash contribution, James also worked with Hewlett-Packard and Nike and sponsored a million dollars' worth of computers and supplies for the clubs. All told, James assisted fifty-nine Boys and Girls Clubs across the United States. Executive Director Teresa LeGrair said, "It's not the first thing he had done for this community and there will be many more to come. . . . LeBron loves kids and he's proven that time and time again."[35]

The James decision and his partnership with the Boys and Girls Club promote the continuation of what Derrick White (following Martin Delany, the nineteenth-century black nationalist, abolitionist, journalist, physician, and writer) termed "pragmatic nationalism" in his article on the Institute of the Black World (IBW). White argues that the IBW promoted "pragmatic nationalism," or the belief that "flexible and carefully constructed social, political, and economic goals and strategies designed to improve black communities were more important than ideological pronouncements, conformity, and rigidity."[36] I argue that black athletes can build on concepts espoused by the IBW in the early 1970s and engage pragmatic black nationalism as a framework to promote social responsibility in black communities. Indeed, to quote historian Barbara Ransby, "race is not an ahistorical phenomenon rooted in a shared genetic heritage."[37] Put differently, since black people are a diverse and dynamic group, a pluralistic and pragmatic methodology for community engagement becomes useful for black athletes in the age of Obama.

NFL Hall-of-Famer Jim Brown and Tiger Woods are two examples of the necessity of diverse and inclusive approaches to community engagement by black athletes. In 1988, Brown started the Amer-I-Can Foundation program as a strategy to assist people, especially minorities, in educational pursuits and personal confidence through overall achievement. Since its inception, five hundred thousand students have completed the program. In tandem with this organization, Brown is also an activist and mediator against gang violence. As a former professional athlete who competed during segregation and was on the frontline of community engagement, Brown has been critical of black athletes who fail to serve underrepresented groups publicly or privately. "He'll [Michael Jordan or Tiger Woods] run you over, he'll kick your [butt], but as an individual for social change or any of that kind of [stuff]—terrible, terrible."[38] For Brown, charity differs from social change—Jordan and Woods fail to use their celebrity to engage black communities and underrepresented groups. In addition, Brown said,

> We are the least-respected culture of any in this country. . . . One of the reasons is that we allow ourselves to feed on each other. Black kids kill black kids. We allow neighborhoods to run down. Black fathers are not at home. Education suffers. There's a dilemma, and if we don't do something about the violence, if we don't get some self-esteem, then we're going to have a war zone in every community in this country.[39]

J. A. Adande, journalist for the *Los Angeles Times* and panelist on ESPN program "Around the Horn," questioned Brown's critique of Woods and advocated a pluralistic approach to community engagement on the show. Spike Lee noted that

> Jim Brown comes from a different era[,] . . . a different era of black men, a different era of a black athlete. These were the brothers that had to go through segregation, had to go to different hotels. They faced Jim Crow. The time when a brother could get lynched for just looking at a white woman the wrong way. It was a very different time.[40]

In actuality and since its inception, the Tiger Woods Foundation has assisted ten million underrepresented youth, built a thirty-five-thousand-square-foot learning center, and committed significant funding for the Earl Woods Scholarship Program, and he donates all proceeds from the AT&T National and Chevron World Challenge events to his foundation.

In conclusion, the relationship between black athletes and self-determination remains contested in American culture. The LeBron James decision elucidated the ways institutional racism, white privilege, and colorblind ideas linger as prevalent themes in the intersection of sports and society. In particular, many Americans attempt to define what discrimination is, who experiences it, and when they face it. Additionally, racism and specifically attempts by white spectators, fans, writers, administrators, and politicians to define black self-determination are a subplot in the legacy of American racism. For black athletes, more importantly, the LeBron James decision symbolically represented two shifts. First, the spectacle that surrounded his hour-long special and decision reinforced the empowerment and influence of black athletes in American and global cultures. It demonstrated the power of celebrity then, as a tool for the eradication of institutional racism and promotion of community engagement—two endeavors that must be tackled aggressively and publicly.

Second, the financial contributions by James to the Boys and Girls Clubs reinforced the potential of pragmatic black nationalism—a message that must be publicized and utilized for black and underrepresented communities. The LeBron James decision signaled the impact black athletes could have by spearheading efforts related to social and economic development of black communities. In this capacity James was not alone. Jalen Rose, a former member of the acclaimed University of Michigan basketball team's "Fab Five," donated significant funds to inner-city education in Detroit. Basketball player Dikembe Mutombo started his own foundation, and in 2007, the twenty-nine-million-dollar Biamba Marie Mutombo Hospital opened in Kinshasa, Democratic Republic of the Congo. Basketball player Vince Carter has donated upwards of five million dollars to education and alcohol-abuse rehabilitation in Florida. Basketball player Metta World Peace, formally known as Ron Artest, is a vocal advocate for mental health awareness. In December 2010 on *SportsCenter*, the signature show for ESPN, Artest announced his intentions to donate millions for aid in that area. At the 2012 ESPN Town Hall Meeting in honor of Martin Luther King Jr., Jamelle Hill, one of a handful of black women sports journalists in mainstream American media, stated that black athletes must continue engaging in social responsibility as a primary endeavor.

Historically, numerous African Americans have struggled for socioeconomic empowerment of black communities. In some ways, "the decision" reinforced the importance of self-determination and community engagement as primary concerns for black athletes—with attempts to define the parameters of black self-determination in sports and society only contextually relevant in understanding the dynamism and struggle against American racism. Due to many of the hurdles that black communities in the nation and throughout the diaspora face, I argue that the commitment of black athletes to social responsibility and community building is vital and must be publicized on levels comparable to their athletic and celebrity accomplishments. Black athletes thus become cultivators of the importance of social responsibility in black communities because their influence can provide both direct and indirect motivation to future generations of black youth to engage in their communities positively and actively. The freedom struggle continues, and to paraphrase "Sheed," "just play hard, my man. . . . God bless and goodnight."

NOTES

1. The Protest: On the morning of October 16, 1968, U.S. athlete Tommie Smith won the 200-meter race in a world-record time of 19.83 seconds, with Australia's Peter Norman second with a time of 20.06 seconds, and the United States's John Carlos in third place with a time of 20.10 seconds. After the race was completed, the three went to collect their medals at the podium. The two U.S. athletes received their medals shoeless but wearing black socks, to represent black poverty. Smith wore a black scarf around his neck to represent black pride; Carlos had his tracksuit top unzipped to show solidarity with all blue collar workers in the United States and wore a necklace of beads that, he said, "were for those individuals that were lynched, or killed and that no-one said a prayer for, that were hung and tarred. It was for those thrown off the side of the boats in the middle passage." All three athletes wore Olympic

Project for Human Rights (OPHR) badges after Norman, a critic of Australia's White Australia Policy, expressed empathy with their ideals. Sociologist Harry Edwards, the founder of the OPHR, had urged black athletes to boycott the games; reportedly, the actions of Smith and Carlos on October 16, 1968, were inspired by Edwards's arguments. Both U.S. athletes intended on bringing black gloves to the event, but Carlos forgot his, leaving them in the Olympic Village. It was the Australian, Peter Norman, who suggested Carlos wear Smith's left-handed glove, this being the reason behind him raising his left hand, as opposed to his right, differing from the traditional Black Power salute. When "The Star-Spangled Banner" played, Smith and Carlos delivered the salute with heads bowed, a gesture that became front-page news around the world. As they left the podium they were booed by the crowd. Smith later said, "If I win, I am American, not a black American. But if I did something bad, then they would say I am a Negro. We are black and we are proud of being black. Black America will understand what we did tonight." ("1968: Black Athletes Make Silent Protest," BBC, accessed June 22, 2015, http://news.bbc.co.uk /onthisday/hi/dates/stories/october/17/newsid_3535000/3535348.stm).

2. Samuel L. Jackson's remarks, ESPY Awards, July 16, 2008.

3. Brent Musburger, "Bizarre Protest by Smith, Carlos Tarnishes Medals," *Chicago Daily News*, October 19, 1968. For more see C. D. Jackson and John Carlos, *Why? The Biography of John Carlos* (Los Angeles: Milligan Books, 2000); David Steele and Tommie Smith, *Silent Gesture: The Autobiography of Tommie Smith* (Philadelphia: Temple University Press, 2007); Frank Murphy, *The Last Protest: Lee Evans in Mexico City* (Kansas City: Windsprint Press, 2006); Harry Edwards, *The Revolt of the Black Athlete* (New York: Free Press, 1970); Kevin B. Witherspoon, *Before the Eyes of the World: Mexico and the 1968 Olympic Games* (DeKalb: Northern Illinois Press, 2008); Douglas Hartmann, *Race, Culture, and the Revolt of the Black Athlete: The 1968 Olympic Protests and Their Aftermath* (Chicago: University of Chicago Press, 2004); and Amy Bass, *Not the Triumph but the Struggle: The 1968 Olympics and the Making of the Black Athlete* (Minneapolis: University of Minnesota Press, 2002).

4. For more on self-determination in the Black Power movement see Stokely Carmichael and Ekwueme Michael Thelwell, *Ready for Revolution: The Life and Struggles of Stokely Carmichael* (New York: Scribner, 2003).

5. See Ann Morning, "Toward Sociology of Racial Conceptualization for the 21st Century," *Social Forces* 87 (3): 1167–92; David Hollinger, "Obama, the Instability of Color Lines, and Promises of a Postethnic Future," *Callaloo* 31 (Fall 2008): 1033–37; Ricky Jones, *What's Wrong with Obamamania? Black America, Black*

Leadership, and the Death of Political Imagination (Albany: State University of New York Press, 2008).

6. One notable article on the use of race and sports by historians is Allen Guttmann, "Sport, Politics, and the Engaged Historian," *Journal of Contemporary History*, 38 (July 2003): 363-75.

7. In my dissertation I term the dichotomy of infringements on black freedom in a racially equal space "discriminative integration." More broadly, I investigate the symbiotic relationship between track and field and the twentieth-century black freedom movement. I assert that athletics was one of the first integrated social fields in U.S. history. Despite opportunities for integrated competition in track and field, black athletes confronted racial injustices under conditions that were officially framed as integrationist and racially equal. For more see Jamal Ratchford, "Black Fists and Fool's Gold: The 1968 Black Athletic Revolt Reconsidered," PhD dissertation, Purdue University, West Lafayette IN, 2011.

8. Despite this claim, William Rhoden noted key distinctions on race and sports in post-*Brown v. Board* America. He said integration "weakened the collective resolve of African Americans and spawned a mentality of using blackness as a way to get a piece of the pie without necessarily feeling any reciprocal responsibility to sustain black institutions." See William Rhoden, *Forty Million Dollar Slaves: The Rise, Fall, and Redemption of the Black Athlete* (New York: Crown, 2007), 256; Shaun Powell, *Souled Out? How Blacks Are Winning and Losing in Sports* (Champaign IL: Human Kinetics, 2008); and David Wiggins, "'With All Deliberate Speed': High School Sport, Race, and *Brown v. Board of Education*," *Journal of Sport History* 37 (Fall 2010): 329-46. For a general examination of race and popular culture see James Stewart, *Flight in Search of Vision* (Trenton NJ: Africa World Press, 2004).

9. Elliott J. Gorn and Warren Goldstein, *A Brief History of American Sport* (Chicago: University of Illinois Press, 2004).

10. David Wiggins, *Glory Bound: Black Athletes in a White America* (Syracuse NY: Syracuse University Press, 1997).

11. Richard Stone, "Negro Athletes Push for Better Treatment, Wider Job Opportunity—Black Pros Want Managerial, Top Coaching Slots; College Stars Allege Discrimination—Is a Boycott Any Solution," *Wall Street Journal*, June 19, 1968; "Where Negroes Have 'Struck it Rich,'" *U.S. News & World Report*, December 11, 1967.

12. Bill Jauss, "Remodel: Switch Format or Olympics Will be Destroyed, Says Wright," *Chicago Daily News*, November 2, 1968; Robert Markus, "Sports Trail: Future of Olympics Worries Wright," *Chicago Tribune*, November 14, 1968.

13. Jon Saraceno, "Keeping Score: Despite Wallace's Rant, NBA Remains a Players' League," *USA Today*, December 14, 2003; "Blowing Smoke," *Washington Times*, December 12, 2003. In 2012, Duke coach Mike Krzyzewski said, "We're slaves to what the NBA does with early-entry. If they ever put that in on a two-year basis, you'll see more dominant teams." Unlike Wallace, Coach K., a respected white coach in American sports media, was not criticized for comparing NCAA basketball to slavery. See Jeff Goodman, "Coach K Calls UNC Most Talented Team in Nation," CBS Sports, February 6, 2012, accessed February 7, 2012, http://college-basketball-blog.blogs.cbssports.com/mcc/blogs/entry/26283066/34726709.

14. In the 1960s and due to the advent of lucrative contracts earned by athletes such as Wilt Chamberlain and Hank Aaron, numerous spectators and journalists criticized black athletes who spoke against racism.

15. Rhoden, *Forty Million Dollar Slaves*.

16. "Golfer Says Comments about Woods 'Misconstrued,'" CNN, April 21, 1997.

17. "Golfer Says Comments about Woods 'Misconstrued,'" CNN, April 21, 1997.

18. "Tiger OK with 'Lynch' Joke, Sharpton Isn't: Golf Channel Anchor Tilghman Suspended over Comments about Woods," *Associated Press*, January 9, 2008.

19. J. A. Adande, "King and Co. Guilty Only of Dreaming Big," ESPN, July 11, 2010, accessed June 16, 2015, http://sports.espn.go.com/nba/columns/story?page=lebronissue-100711; Marc Stein, "Sources: No Probe from Cavs, Raptors," ESPN, July 12, 2010, accessed June 16, 2015, http://sports.espn.go.com/nba/news/story?id=5371956; Chris Broussard, "Time for Cavs Owner to Act His Age," ESPN, July 9, 2010, accessed June 16, 2015, http://sports.espn.go.com/nba/columns/story?page=gilbertlbj-100709; Scoop Jackson, "LeBron's Big Move? Been There," ESPN, July 10, 2010, accessed June 16, 2015, http://sports.espn.go.com/espn/commentary/news/story?page=jackson/100710; Tom Withers, "LeBron's Mural Coming Down in Cleveland," Yahoo Sports, accessed July 10, 2010, http://www.utsandiego.com/news/2010/jul/10/lebrons-mural-coming-down-in-cleveland; "LeBron's 'Decision' Watched by Nearly 10M People," Yahoo Sports, July 1, 2010; Tom Withers, "Cavs Owner Defends Stance on LeBron," Yahoo Sports, July 12, 2010, accessed June 16, 2015, http://sports.yahoo.com/nba/news?slug=txgilbertjessejackson.

20. "Fathead Suggests LeBron Is the New Benedict Arnold," *USA Today*, July 9, 2010, accessed February 6, 2012, http://content.usatoday.com/communities/gameon/post/2010/07/lebronjames-fathead-dan-gilbert-benedict-arnold/1.

21. Jason Whitlock, "Jesse Jackson Way Off Base on Lebron," *Fox Sports*, July 12, 2010. Ironically, in 2012, Whitlock was engulfed in his own racialized controversy

when he criticized New York Knicks sensation and first Asian American NBA player Jeremy Lin. Whitlock said, "Some lucky lady in NYC is going to feel a couple inches of pain tonight." See Kelly Dwyer, "Jason Whitlock Apologizes for His Unfunny Jeremy Lin Comment on Twitter," Yahoo Sports, February 13, 2012, accessed February 14, 2012, http://sports.yahoo.com/blogs/nba-ball-dont -lie/jason-whitlock-apologizes-unfunny-jeremy-lin-twitter-145934497.html. See also Eric Adelson, "Floyd Mayweather Hits Jeremy Lin on Race," *The Post Game*, February 13, 2012, accessed February 14, 2012, http://www.thepostgame .com/blog/daily-take/201202/floyd-mayweather-plays-race-cardjeremy-lin.

22. Whitlock, "Jesse Jackson Way Off Base on Lebron."

23. For a reference on "colorblindness" debates see Mary Williams, *Discrimination: Opposing Viewpoints* (San Diego CA: Greenhaven Press, 1997).

24. Ann Ansell, "Casting a Blind Eye: The Ironic Consequences of Color-Blindness in South Africa and the United States," *Critical Sociology* 32 (March 2006): 333–56; Ashley Doane, "What is Racism? Racial Discourse and Racial Politics," *Critical Sociology* 32 (March 2006): 255–74; Eduardo Bonilla-Silva, *Racism without Racists: Color-Blind Racists and the Persistence of Racial Inequality in the United States* (Lanham MD: Rowman and Littlefield, 2003); Eduardo Bonilla-Silva, *White Supremacy and Racism in the Post-Civil Rights Era* (Boulder CO: L. Rienner, 2001); David Brunsma, *Mixed Messages: Multiracial Identities in the "Color-Blind" Era* (Boulder, CO: L. Rienner, 2006).

25. Eduardo Bonilla-Silva, Carla Goar, and David Embrick, "When Whites Flock Together: The Social Psychology of White Habitus," *Critical Sociology* 32 (March 2006): 229–53.

26. For an extensive examination on current issues in race and American sports see TIDES or the Institute for Diversity and Ethics in Sport, http://www.tidesport .org/index.html.

27. Steven A. Riess, "Basketball Career Still An Inner-City Dream but Only Few Achieve Star Status, Financial Rewards," accessed June 15, 2015, http://iipdigital .usembassy.gov/st/english/article/2008/04/20080401120426zjsrednao .8432886.html#axzz3dC4Sjxlg.

28. C. Keith Harrison, "There Is More to Life than Sports: Getting Brothers to Take the Road Less Traveled," accessed June 15, 2015, http://diverseeducation.com /article/8143/.

29. Earl Smith, "The African American Student-Athlete" in *Race and Sport: The Struggle for Equality on and off the Field*, edited by Charles K Ross (Jackson: University of Mississippi, 2004), 121–45. See also Wiggins, "'With All Deliberate Speed.'"

30. See Dave Leonard, "The Decline of the Black Athlete: An Interview with Harry Edwards," *Colorlines* 30 (2000): 20–24, reprinted in *The Unlevel Playing Field: A Documentary History of the African American Experience in Sport*, edited by David K Wiggins and Patrick B. Miller (Urbana: University of Illinois, 2003), 435–41; Wiggins, "'Deliberate Speed,'" 342.

31. "Black Power in Sports: From Protest to Political Analysis," *New York Herald Tribune*, March 15, 1972. See also Harry Edwards, "The Olympic Project for Human Rights: An Assessment Ten Years Later," *The Black Scholar* 10 (March-April 1979): 2–8.

32. Wiggins, *Glory Bound*, 191.

33. Wiggins, "'With All Deliberate Speed,'" 340.

34. Neil Amdur, "Tommie Smith at 34: His Struggle Goes On," *New York Times*, December 24, 1978.

35. Mark Gillespie, "LeBron James' 'Decision' Helps Boys and Girls Clubs in Northeast Ohio," *Cleveland Plain Dealer*, April 27, 2011, accessed February 6, 2012, http://blog.cleveland.com/metro/2011/04/boys_and_girls_clubs_in_northe.html.

36. Derrick White, "'Black World View': The Institute of the Black World's Promotion of Pragmatic Nationalism, 1969–1974," *Journal of African American History* 95 (Summer-Fall 2010): 369–91.

37. Barbara Ransby, "Afrocentrism, Cultural Nationalism, and the Problem with Essentialist Definitions of Race Gender, and Sexuality," in *Dispatches from the Ebony Tower: Intellectuals Confront the African American Experience*, edited by Manning Marable (New York: Columbia University Press, 2000), 218.

38. Gene Wojciechowski, "Jim Brown Won't Back Down on Tiger," espn.com, July 2, 2009, accessed February 6, 2012, http://sports.espn.go.com/espn/columns/story?columnist=wojciechowski_gene&id=4301802.

39. Wojciechowski, "Jim Brown Won't Back Down."

40. J. A. Adande, "No Black or White in Life of Brown," *Los Angeles Times*, April 25, 2002, accessed February 6, 2012, http://articles.latimes.com/2002/apr/25/sports/sp-adande25. Actually, many African Americans did not get involved in activism in the 1950s and 1960s black freedom movement. Rather, as articulated by numerous scholars in the last ten years, African Americans understood, appropriated, and acted on the urgency of "Freedom Now."

SOURCE ACKNOWLEDGMENTS

1. Phillip J. Hutchison, "Framing White Hopes: The Press, Social Drama, and the Era of Jack Johnson, 1908–1915," was originally presented to the history division of the Association for Education in Journalism and Mass Communication national conference, 2011. Reprinted with the permission of Phillip Hutchison.

2. Pamela C. Laucella, "Jesse Owens, a Black Pearl amidst an Ocean of Fury: A Case Study of Press Coverage of the 1936 Berlin Olympic Games," was originally presented to the minorities and communication division of the Association for Education in Journalism and Mass Communication national conference, 2002. Reprinted with the permission of Pamela Laucella.

3. Dominic J. Capeci Jr. and Martha Wilkerson, "Multifarious Hero: Joe Louis, American Society, and Race Relations during World Crisis, 1935–1945," was originally published in the *Journal of Sport History* 10, no. 3 (Winter 1983): 5–25. Reprinted with the permission of the *Journal of Sport History*.

4. Thomas G. Smith, "Outside the Pale: The Exclusion of Blacks from the National Football League, 1934–1946," was originally published in *Journal of Sport History* 15, no. 3 (Winter 1988): 254–90. Reprinted with the permission of *Journal of Sport History*.

5. Chris Lamb and Glen L. Bleske, "Democracy on the Field: The Black Press Takes On White Baseball," was originally published in *Journalism History* 24, no. 2 (Summer 1998): 51–59. Reprinted with the permission of *Journalism History*.

6. Ronald Bishop, "A Nod from Destiny: How Sportswriters for White and African American Newspapers Covered Kenny Washington's Entry into the National Football League," was originally published in *American Journalism* 19, no. 1 (Winter 2002): 81–106. Reprinted with the permission of *American Journalism*.

7. William Simons, "Jackie Robinson and the American Mind: Journalistic Perceptions of the Reintegration of Baseball," was originally published in *Journal of Sport History* 12, no. 1 (Spring 1985): 39–64. Reprinted with the permission of *Journal of Sport History*.

8. Brian Carroll, "'This Is It!' The Public Relations Campaign Waged by Wendell Smith and Jackie Robinson to Cast Robinson's First Season as an Unqualified Success," originally appeared as "'This Is It!' The PR Campaign by Wendell Smith and Jackie Robinson" in *Journalism History*, 37, no. 3 (Fall 2011): 151–62. Reprinted with the permission of *Journalism History*.

9. Charles H. Martin, "Integrating New Year's Day: The Racial Politics of College Bowl Games in the American South," was originally published in *Journal of Sport History* 24, no. 3 (Fall 1997): 358–77. Reprinted with the permission of *Journal of Sport History*.

10. Michael Ezra, "Main Bout, Inc., Black Economic Power, and Professional Boxing: The Canceled Muhammad Ali–Ernie Terrell Fight," originally appeared as "Main Bout, Inc., Black Economic Power, and Professional Boxing: The Cancelled Muhammad Ali/Ernie Terrell Fight" in *Journal of Sport History* 29, no. 3 (Fall 2002): 413–37. Reprinted with the permission of *Journal of Sport History*.

11. Jason Peterson, "A 'Race' for Equality: Print Media Coverage of the 1968 Olympic Protest by Tommie Smith and John Carlos," was originally published in *American Journalism* 26, no. 2 (Spring 2009): 99–121. Reprinted with the permission of *American Journalism*.

12. Reed Smith, "*Sports Illustrated*'s African American Athlete Series as Socially Responsible Journalism," was originally published as "*Sports Illustrated*'s African-American Athlete Series as Socially Responsible Journalism" in *American Journalism* 23, no. 2 (Spring 2006): 45–68. Reprinted with the permission of *American Journalism*.

13. William Gillis, "Rebellion in the Kingdom of Swat: Sportswriters, African American Athletes, and Coverage of Curt Flood's Lawsuit against Major League Baseball," was originally published as "'Rebellion in the Kingdom of Swat': Sportswriters,

African-American Athletes, and Coverage of Curt Flood's Lawsuit against Major League Baseball" in *American Journalism* 26, no. 2 (Spring 2009): 67–97. Reprinted with the permission of *American Journalism*.

14. Maureen Smith, "Chasing Babe Ruth: An Analysis of Newspaper Coverage of Hank Aaron's Pursuit of the Career Home Run Record," was originally presented as "Hank Aaron and Home Runs: An Analysis of Black and White Newspaper Coverage of Aaron's Chase for Babe Ruth's All-Time Home Run Record" by the North American Society for Sport History. Reprinted with the permission of Maureen Smith.

15. Pamela C. Laucella, "Arthur Ashe: An Analysis of Newspaper Journalists' Coverage of *USA Today*'s Outing," was originally presented as "Arthur Ashe: An Analysis of Newspaper Journalists' Coverage of the *USA Today* Outing" to the minorities and communication division of the Association for Education in Journalism and Mass Communication national conference, 2007. Reprinted with the permission of Pamela Laucella.

16. Mary G. McDonald, "Michael Jordan's Family Values: Marketing, Meaning, and Post-Reagan America" was originally published as "Michael Jordan's Family Values: Marketing, Meaning, and Post–Ronald Reagan America" in *Sociology of Sport Journal* 13, no. 4 (December 1996): 344–65. Reprinted with the permission of *Sociology of Sport Journal*.

17. Douglas Hartmann, "Rush Limbaugh, Donovan McNabb, and 'A Little Social Concern': Reflections on the Problems of Whiteness in Contemporary American Sport," was originally published as "Rush Limbaugh, Donovan McNabb, and a Little Social Concern" in *Journal of Sport and Social Issues* 31, no. 1 (February 2007): 45–60. Reprinted with the permission of *Journal of Sport and Social Issues*.

18. Lisa Doris Alexander, "I'm the King of the World: Barry Bonds and the Race for the Record," was originally published as "I'm King of the World? Barry Bonds and the Race for the Record" in *NINE: A Journal of Baseball History and Culture* 17, no. 2 (Spring 2009): 80–89, by permission of the University of Nebraska Press. Copyright 2009 by the University of Nebraska Press.

19. Bryan Carr, "Redemption on the Field: Framing, Narrative, and Race in Media Coverage of Michael Vick," was originally presented to the minorities and communications division of the Association for Education in Journalism and Mass Communication national conference, 2012. Published with the permission of Bryan Carr.

20. Jimmy Sanderson, "Weighing In on the Coaching Decision: Discussing Sports and Race Online," was originally published in *Journal of Language and Social Psychology* 29, no. 3 (September 2010): 301–20. Reprinted with the permission of *Journal of Language and Social Psychology*.

21. Jamal L. Ratchford, "The LeBron James Decision in the Age of Obama," was originally published as "The 1960s Black Athletic Revolt Reconsidered: The LeBron James Decision and Self-Determination in Post-Racial America," in *The Black Scholar* 42, no. 1 (Spring 2012): 49–59. Reprinted with the permission of *The Black Scholar*.

CONTRIBUTORS

LISA DORIS ALEXANDER is an associate professor in the department of Africana Studies at Wayne State University. She is the author of *When Baseball Isn't White, Straight, and Male: The Media and Difference in the National Pastime* (McFarland, 2012). Alexander analyzes issues of race, class, gender, and sexual identity in popular culture, and her work has appeared in *NINE: A Journal of Baseball History and American Culture*; *Journal of Popular Film and Television*; and *Black Ball: A Journal of the Negro Leagues*.

RONALD BISHOP is a professor in the Department of Culture and Communication at Drexel University. He is the author of three books: *More: The Vanishing of Scale in an Over-the-Top Nation* (Baylor University Press, 2011); *When Play Was Play: Why Pick-Up Games Still Matter* (State University of New York Press, 2009); and *Taking on the Pledge of Allegiance* (State University of New York Press, 2007). Bishop's research has been published in *Electronic Journal of Communication*; *Journal of Popular Culture*; *Journal of Sports Media*; *Journal of Communication, Addiction Research, and Theory*; *International Journal of Progressive Education*; and *Journal of Poverty*.

GLEN L. BLESKE is professor emeritus in the Department of Journalism and Public Relations at California State University, Chico, where he has taught since 1994. Bleske and Chris Lamb worked as reporters for the *News-Journal* in Daytona Beach, Florida, where they learned about Jackie Robinson and his first spring training with the Brooklyn Dodgers organization in 1946.

DOMINIC J. CAPECI JR. is a distinguished professor emeritus of history at Missouri State University in Springfield. Capeci and Martha Wilkerson have collaborated in their teaching and their research. They cowrote *Layered Violence: The Race Rioters of 1943* (University of Mississippi Press, 1991) and "The Detroit Rioters of 1943: A Reinterpretation" in *Michigan Historical Review* 16 (Spring 1990).

BRYAN CARR is an assistant professor in the Department of Communication at the University of Wisconsin, Green Bay. His primary field of study is identity and representations of race and gender in mass communications and popular culture. His articles have appeared in *Southwest Mass Communication Journal*; *Public Relations Review*; and *Broadcast Education Association Feedback*.

BRIAN CARROLL is an associate professor of communication and director of the Honors Program at Berry College in Mount Berry, Georgia. He is author of *When to Stop the Cheering? The Black Press, the Black Community, and the Integration of Professional Baseball* (Routledge, 2007).

MICHAEL EZRA is a professor in the Department of American Multicultural Studies at Sonoma State University. He is the author of *Muhammad Ali: The Making of an Icon* (Temple University Press, 2009) and *Civil Rights Movement: People and Perspectives* (ABC-CLIO, 2009) and the editor of *The Economic Civil Rights Movement: African Americans and the Struggle for Economic Power* (Routledge, 2013). He is also the founding editor of the *Journal of Civil and Human Rights*, published by the University of Illinois Press.

WILLIAM GILLIS received his doctoral degree from Indiana University School of Journalism in 2013; his dissertation was titled, "Say No to the Liberal Media: Conservatives and Criticism of the News Media in the 1970s." Gillis currently edits *The American Historian*, a magazine published by the Organization of American Historians in Bloomington, Indiana.

DOUGLAS HARTMANN is a professor in the Department of Sociology at the University of Minnesota. He is the author of *Race, Culture, and the Revolt of the Black Athlete: The 1968 Olympic Protests and Their Aftermath* (University of Chicago Press, 2003). He is completing the book *Midnight Basketball: Race, Risk, and the Ironies of Sport-Based Intervention in Neo-Liberal America*. Hartmann received the Midwest Sociological Society's inaugural Early Career Scholarship Award in 2008. He is cofounder and editor of thesocietypages.org.

PHILLIP J. HUTCHISON is an associate professor in the School of Journalism and Telecommunications at the University of Kentucky. His research focuses on cultural approaches to twentieth-century media history and emphasizes the relationship between news and promotional interests.

CHRIS LAMB is a professor in the Department of Journalism at Indiana University–Purdue University at Indianapolis. He is the author or editor of seven books, including *Blackout: The Untold Story of Jackie Robinson's First Spring Training* (University of Nebraska Press, 2004) and *Conspiracy of Silence: Sportswriters and the Long Campaign to Desegregate Baseball* (University of Nebraska Press, 2012). He is currently working on his third book on the link between the press and the color line in baseball.

PAMELA C. LAUCELLA is an assistant professor in the Department of Journalism at Indiana University–Purdue University at Indianapolis and the academic director of the National Sports Journalism Center at IUPUI. She is the author of *Jesse Owens, the Press, and the 1936 Berlin Olympic Games* (Routledge, forthcoming). Laucella's research investigates sociocultural-historical issues in sports media and specifically the intersections of race and gender.

CHARLES H. MARTIN is a professor in the Department of History at the University of Texas at El Paso. He is the author of two books: *Benching Jim Crow: The Rise and Fall of the Color Line in Southern College Sports, 1890–1980* (University of Illinois, 2010) and *The Angelo Herndon Case and Southern Justice* (Louisiana State University, 1976). He is also the author of numerous articles on sports history, southern history, and African American history.

MARY G. MCDONALD is a professor and the Homer C. Rice Chair in Sports and Society in the School of History, Technology, and Society at the Georgia Institute of Technology. She is a past president of the North American Society for the Sociology of Sport. McDonald has published more than three dozen refereed articles and book chapters. She coedited *Reading Sport: Critical Essays on Power and Representation*, which won a Choice award as a top academic title. She is currently directing the new Sports, Society, and Technology program at Georgia Tech.

JASON PETERSON is an assistant professor in the Department of Communication and Theatre at Charleston Southern University. A former journalist, Peterson is author of *Full Court Press: Mississippi State University and the Battle against the*

Press to Integrate State College Basketball, 1955–1973 (University Press of Mississippi, forthcoming). His work has appeared in *American Journalism*.

JAMAL L. RATCHFORD is an interdisciplinary scholar and historian trained as an African Americanist, in Africana Studies, and as a sport studies specialist. In a forthcoming book (tentatively titled *Raise Your Black Fists: Race, Track and Field, and Protest in the Twentieth Century*) Ratchford asserts that athletics was one of the first integrated social fields in U.S. history and that despite opportunities for integrated competition in track and field, black athletes confronted racial injustices under conditions that were officially framed as integrationist and racially equal.

JIMMY SANDERSON is an assistant professor in the Department of Communication Studies at Clemson University. His research interests center on social media and sports. His research has appeared in *Communication and Sport*; *International Journal of Sport Communication*; and *Mass Communication and Society*. Sanderson is the author of *It's a Whole New Ballgame: How Social Media Is Changing Sports* (Hampton Press, 2011).

WILLIAM SIMONS is a professor and former chair of history at SUNY Oneonta. He is the codirector of the Cooperstown Symposium on Baseball and American Culture, an annual baseball conference, and the editor of an anthology series of the same name. His baseball articles, essays, and reviews have appeared in anthologies, journals, and other media. He is a humanities speaker for the New York Council for the Humanities.

MAUREEN SMITH is a professor in the Department of Kinesiology and Health Science at California State University, Sacramento. She teaches courses in the history of sport and the sociology of sport. She is an active member of the North American Society of Sport History (NASSH), the North American Society for the Sociology of Sport, and the International Society of the History of Physical Education and Sport. She is a past president of NASSH.

REED SMITH is a professor of communications and the multimedia communications coordinator at Georgia Southern University. He previously taught at Ohio University–Zanesville. Before entering higher education Smith worked professionally as an NPR station manager and radio news reporter. His research interests are in broadcast and journalism history.

THOMAS G. SMITH is a professor of the Department of History at Nichols College in Dudley, Massachusetts. His research and writing interests are environmental history and sport history. Smith's most recent book is *Showdown: JFK and the Integration of the Washington Redskins* (Beacon Press, 2011).

MARTHA WILKERSON is professor emeritus of sociology at Missouri State University in Springfield. She and Dominic Capeci have collaborated in their teaching and their research. They cowrote *Layered Violence: The Race Rioters of 1943* (University of Mississippi Press, 1991) and "The Detroit Rioters of 1943: A Reinterpretation" in *Michigan Historical Review* 16 (Spring 1990).

INDEX

Aaron, Hank, 5, 14, 417–33, 522–25, 528, 530

Abdul-Jabbar, Kareem, 336–37, 387

Acquired Immune Deficiency Syndrome (AIDS), 448–57, 459–60, 484–88

Adande, J. A., 595

Afro-American newspapers, 150, 155

Ahern, Jesse, 341

Akron OH, 589, 594

Albert, Frankie, 136

Albom, Mitch, 530

Albuquerque NM, 317

Alexander, Holmes, 394

Alexander, Lisa, 14, 15

Al-Gilmore, Tony, 365

Ali, Muhammad, 2, 4, 5, 10, 12–13, 15, 293–318, 339, 357, 361, 364, 393–96, 402, 473, 538–87

All-American Football Conference, 136–40, 174, 179, 181, 185

Allan, Chris, 348

Allen, Dick, 385, 389

Allen, Neil, 348

Altman, Lawrence, 453, 455

American Association (football), 131

American Broadcasting Company (ABC), 314, 336, 392, 480, 502–3, 527

American Football League, 363

American Negro Press Association, 157, 161, 207

American Professional League (football), 134

Amos 'n' Andy, 247, 256–57

Amsterdam (NY) News, 54, 59–60, 68, 73, 202, 206, 208, 215, 217, 224–25, 245, 311, 418–21, 425–26, 428

Anderson, Dave, 422, 428

Anderson, Ezzerett, 134–35, 139

Anderson, Marian, 92

Angelou, Maya, 88

Arizona Diamondbacks, 524

Arizona State University, 524

Arrington, LaVar, 511

Arsenal Stadium, 314

Artest, Ron, 596

Arum, Bob, 298, 305, 318
Ashe, Arthur, Jr., 5, 15, 385, 395–96, 402, 442–60
Ashe, Arthur, Sr., 447
Ashe, Camera, 450–51, 457–58
Ashe, Jeannie, 450–51, 453, 457–58
Ashe, Mattie, 447
Associated Press, 38, 55, 90, 154–57, 216, 247, 272, 274, 303, 307–8, 316, 335–16, 339–42, 427
Athens (OH) Messenger, 393
Atlanta Braves, 418–20, 422–25, 427–28, 431–32, 556
Atlanta Constitution, 341, 343, 418, 421, 423–24
Atlanta Daily World, 311, 418, 421
Atlanta Falcons, 16, 524
Atlanta GA, 245, 295, 339, 432,
Atlanta Journal, 216, 418, 421
Atlantic City NJ, 126, 333
Atlantic Coast Conference (ACC), 281, 287
Auburn NY, 126
Auburn University, 130, 272, 560, 564–65, 568, 570, 573, 575
Austin, Tracy, 450
Australian Open, 442, 447
Axthelm, Pete, 365

Babb, Jesse, 123
Baer, Buddy, 94, 97–98, 102
Baker, William, 56
Bakke, Bruce, 420
Balter, Sam, 125, 128
Baltimore Afro-American, 202, 218, 243, 311
Baltimore MD, 139, 222
Baltimore Morning Sun, 217
Baltimore Sun, 449
Bankhead, Dan, 252

Bankhead, Tallulah, 95
Barkley, Charles, 560–62, 564–68, 573–75
Barnes, John, 484
Barney, Rex, 253
Barry, Jack, 312
Baseball Hall of Fame, 224, 239, 423
Basie, Count, 424
Bass, Amy, 338
Bass, Bill, 139
Battles, Cliff, 134
Baugh, Sammy, 125
Beach, Rex, 30–31
Beamon, Bob, 372
The Beatles, 332
Beijing, China, 589
Belafonte, Harry, 448
Bell, Bill, 123
Bell, "Cool Papa," 431
Bell, Horace, 127
Bell, Madison, 127, 130
Bell, Marty, 274–75
Belth, Alex, 386
Bennett, Lerone, 19
Bennington (VT) Banner, 393
Bentley, Ben, 303–4
Berkow, Ira, 397, 451, 453
Berlin, Germany, 5, 11, 135,
Berman, Chris, 502–3
Berry, Kathleen, 451
Bethune, Mary MacLeod, 120
Big Eight Conference, 281, 287
Biggio, Craig, 531
Big Ten Conference, 123–24
Bilbo, Theodore, 135
Billingsley, Anna Barrow, 451
Binghamton NY, 136
Bird, Elizabeth, 27
Bird, Larry, 474
Birmingham AL, 247, 282

Bishop, Ron, 12

Black Entertainment Television (BET), 544

Black, Julien, 87–89, 90, 96–97, 104

Black Legion, 89

Blackmun, Harry, 401

Black Power, 587

Blair, Sam, 341, 345–46

Blake, James, 457

Blanchard, Doc, 134

Bleske, Glen, 7, 175, 239–40

Boettcher, Brian, 430

Bonds, Barry, 14–15, 417, 433, 522–28, 530–31

Bonilla-Silva, Eduardo, 506

Border Conference, 278

Bosh, Chris, 589

Bostic, Joe, 8, 9, 150, 241

Boston Braves, 254

Boston Celtics, 372

Boston College, 130, 272

Boston Daily Globe, 335, 341, 346–48

Boston Daily Record, 217, 224, 449

Boston Herald, 210–11

Boston MA, 347

Boston Red Sox, 204, 227, 244, 248

Boston Traveler, 223

Boswell, Tom 512

Boyd, Todd, 535

Boys and Girls Club, 589–94

Brachman, Bob, 342

Bramham, William, 211–21

Brancazio, Peter, 480

Bridges, Jeffrey, 22

Briley, Ron, 392

Brodenheimer, George, 502

Broderick, James, 88

Broeg, Bob, 385, 389, 392, 401, 403–4

Brooklyn College, 480

Brooklyn Dodgers (baseball), 7, 12, 136, 148, 150, 152–53, 159, 161, 170–71, 189, 199–200, 206, 210–11, 213, 215–16, 220, 223, 225–27, 237–38, 241, 243–47, 249–56, 350, 387, 524, 586

Brooklyn Dodgers (football), 139

Brooklyn Eagle, 124, 154, 156, 158, 160–61, 202, 206

Brooklyn NY, 136, 245

Brooks, Pat, 87

Brower, William, 1, 131

Brown, Dorothy, 451

Brown, Jim, 298–300, 311, 318, 368, 385, 396, 430, 595

Brown, John, 139

Brown, Leo, 315

Brown, Prentiss, 99

Brown University, 270

Brown v. Board of Education, 282–83, 287

Brundage, Avery, 586

Bruning, Fred, 449–50

Buffalo Bisons, 139

Burns, Tommy, 1–3, 25–26

Busch, Gussie, 403

Bush, George H. W., 482, 496

Butler, Stephen, 70

Byoir, Carl, 99

Cairo, Georgia, 218, 239

Cambridge MA, 341

Cameron, Lucille, 36–37

Campanella, Roy, 432

Camp Gilbert (AL), 103

Camp Hood (TX), 221

Camp Lee (VA), 104

Canada, 306, 313–14, 316

Cannon, Jimmy, 299, 301, 312, 317, 385, 388–89, 393, 401, 403–4

Canton OH, 134

Capeci, Dominic, Jr., 11

Carey, James, 21–22, 52

Cargo, David, 317

Carlos, John, 5, 13, 17, 332–50, 360, 385–86, 389, 402, 582, 584–86

Carmichael, Stokely, 270, 295, 584

Carnero, Primo, 87, 89, 105

Carpenter, Bob, 248

Carr, Bryan, 16

Carr, Fred, 371

Carrington, Ben, 56, 57

Carroll, Brian, 7, 9

Carroll, Dink, 203

Carter, Richard, 386,

Carter, Vince, 588–89, 596

Casey, Hugh, 245

Catholic World magazine, 57

Caudill, Edward, 56

Cave, Ray, 365

Central Intelligence Agency (CIA), 333

Chafe, William, 135

Chalmers, David, 402

Chamberlain, Carl, 424, 431

Chamberlain, Wilt, 360

Chandler, Albert "Happy," 151, 251

Chaote, Clyde, 303

Chapman, Ben, 247–50, 253, 387

Chargin, Don, 308

Charles, Ray, 430

Charleston (WV) Daily Mail, 40

Charlottesville VA, 273

Chase, William Charles, 68–72

Cheney, Ray, 448

Chevigny, Jack, 118

Chicago American, 13, 242, 299, 301–2

Chicago Bears, 118–20, 129, 133, 183, 523

Chicago Black Hawks, 179

Chicago Bulls, 476, 486

Chicago Cardinals (football), 117–19

Chicago Daily News, 207, 229, 300

Chicago Defender, 3, 119, 150, 156, 158, 161, 209, 227, 418, 420–21, 424–27, 431, 437

Chicago IL, 24, 34, 36–37, 55, 92, 127, 132, 136, 191, 218, 296, 299, 303–5, 309, 312, 315, 317, 357, 390, 427

Chicago Rockets, 124, 139

Chicago Sun-Times, 449

Chicago Tribune, 19, 24, 26, 30, 32, 36, 136, 299, 302, 305, 306, 315, 335, 340, 343, 345, 347, 384, 395–96, 400, 418, 426, 428, 431, 459

Chicago White Stockings, 586

Chizak, Gene, 560, 565, 567, 570, 573

Choynski, Joe, 34

Christian Science Monitor, 276

Christman, Paul, 128

Chuvulo, George, 307–11

Civil Rights Movement, 5–6, 87, 91, 93, 149, 151, 163, 177, 218, 241, 256, 286, 294–95, 336, 357, 358–59, 363, 371, 375, 390, 402, 538, 587

Clark, Bob, 64

Clark, Howard, 502

Clark, Wesley, 502

Clary, Jack, 301

Clemente, Roberto, 427

Clemens, Roger, 531

Clemson University, 130, 272

Cleveland Browns, 138–40, 188, 191

Cleveland Cavaliers, 17, 585–86, 589–91

Cleveland Indians, 204, 353, 524

Cleveland Plain Dealer, 224

Cleveland Press, 217

Clinton, Bill, 402, 450, 454

Clinton, Hillary, 402

Coffee, Raymond, 449

Cohen, Richard, 450, 452

Cole, Cheryl, 474–75

Colgate University, 126

College of the Pacific, 286

Colliers magazine, 60, 255

Collins, Bud, 346–47

Collins, Eddie, 204

Collins, Patricia Hill, 493

Columbia Broadcasting System (CBS), 104, 369, 373, 483, 535

Columbia University, 133

Columbus OH, 132

Comiskey Park, 88

Committee on Fair Employment Practices, 135

Computed Mediated Communication (CMC), 555, 558–60, 573–74

Condon, David, 427

Conn, Billie, 94–95, 102, 107

Conrad, "Tank," 129

Consodine, Bob, 395

Coontz, Stephanie, 491

Cooper, Irving Ben, 388, 400

Copley News Service, 392

Corbett, James J., 29, 34, 38

Cornell University, 125–26

Cosell, Howard, 336, 383, 386, 392, 402, 405

Costas, Bob, 386

Cotton Bowl, 130–31, 269–76, 287

Crenshaw, Kimberle, 509, 528

Crepeau, Richard, 200

Cromwell, Dean, 65

Crosley Field, 251

Crowley, James, 138–39

Cunningham, George, 423

Curtice, Jack, 278

Daddio, Bill, 133

Daily Worker, 76, 246

Daley, Arthur, 162, 345, 385, 388–89, 399, 401, 403

Daley, Richard, 302–5

Dallas Express, 275

Dallas Morning News, 275, 335, 341–42, 345

Dallas TX, 271–75, 277, 287

Dancy, John, 95

Danforth, Ed, 216

Danville IL, 253

Dardenne, Robert, 22

Davidson, Herbert, 153

Davis, Angela, 482

Davis, Benjamin, 92

Davis, Glenn, 134

Davis, Laurel, 479

Davis, Spud, 212

Davis Cup, 447

Daytona Beach Evening Journal, 153, 157

Daytona Beach FL, 148–50, 153, 158, 160–62, 213–22, 244

Daytona Beach Morning Journal, 153, 157

Daytona Beach Sunday News-Journal, 160

Deford, Frank, 362, 368, 370, 371, 375, 455, 458

Deland FL, 161

De Leighbur, Don, 218

Dell, Donald, 458

Democratic National Convention (1968), 357

Dempsey, Jack, 90, 96

Denny, Harry, 474–75

Detroit Free Press, 312

Detroit Lions, 140

Detroit MI, 87–89, 95, 101–3, 135

Detroit News, 202, 214

Detroit Pistons, 587

Detroit Tigers, 390, 524

Detroit Tribune, 223

Dewey, Thomas, 217

Dickerson, Borce, 123

Digby, George, 213

Diggs, Charles, 92, 99

Dillard University, 284

DiMaggio, Joe, 90, 523

DiPasqualle, Paul D., 458

Dixon, Randy, 128, 173
Dorazio, Gus, 94
"Double V" Campaign, 93, 97–98, 104
Douds, Jap, 118
Dove, Bob, 133
Down, Fred, 423
Dozer, Richard, 397
Drew, Howard, 71
Drury, Carl, 90
Drysdale, Cliff, 450
Dubois, W. E. B., 52, 56, 293
Duckett, Alfred, 245, 250
Duke University, 281, 523
Duquesne University, 181, 280
Durden, Douglas 450, 455
Durham Morning Herald, 212
Durslang, Melvin, 172, 389
Duryea, Etta, 36
Dyer, Braven, 180
Dyreson, Mark, 471
Dyson, Michael Eric, 471, 505

Eames, Stan, 393
Easton PA, 267–68
Eaton, Aileen, 308
Ebbets Field, 245, 250, 254
Ebony, 255–56, 366, 488–89, 543
Edmonton, Canada, 307
Edwards, Harry, 332–34, 336, 338, 349,
    367–68, 375, 592–93
Egan, Dave, 217, 224
Eig, Jonathan, 245
Eisen, George, 360, 395
Eitzen, Stanley, 485
Eliot, Ray, 133
El Paso TX, 267–68, 270
El Toro CA, 133–34
Emerling, Ernie, 309
England, 11, 313–14
English, Bill, 279

Entine, Jon, 56, 58
Equal Employment Opportunity Com-
    mission, 312
ESPN, 15, 17, 501–3, 508, 511, 524–27, 535,
    558, 560–61, 582, 587, 590–91, 595–97
ESPN The Magazine, 535, 561
Espy Awards, 582, 584
Evans, Lee, 333, 338
Evert, Chris, 363, 450
Ewell, Barney, 273

Fainaru-Wada, Mark, 526
Faldo, Nick, 588
Falk, David, 477, 481
Favre, Brett, 507, 582
Federal Bureau of Investigation (FBI),
    312
Federal Employment Practices Act, 270
Feller, Bob, 204–5
Fentress, J. Cullen, 181, 183, 186
Fessenden, Doug, 128
Fielder, Prince, 531
Fiske, Jack, 315
Fitzpatrick, Tom, 306
Flaherty, Vincent, 183, 185, 187
Fleet City (CA) Blue Jackets, 133–34
Flood, Curt, 5, 113, 383, 387–405, 587
Flood v. Kuhn, 397
Florence, Italy, 269
Florida State University, 282
Flynn, Jim, 35
Folley, Zora, 316
Football Bowl Subdivision (FBS), 558–
    60, 564–67, 569, 572–73
Ford, Gerald, 55–56
Forde, Pat, 526
Fort Leavenworth (KS), 39
Fort Riley (KS), 104
Fort Worth TX, 124, 308, 526
Fountain, Charles, 56, 58, 74

Foxx, Jimmie, 417
Frank, Clint, 120
Freedom's Journal, 258
Freeman, Michael, 450–51, 455–56, 523
Freemont/Newark (CA) Argus, 393–94
Frey, James, 458
Frick, Ford, 251
Friedman, Buddy, 5
Furillo, Carl, 246

Gaines, Ernest, 80
Gallico, Paul, 9, 76, 387
Garagiola, Joe, 252–53
Gates, Henry Louis, 468
Gault, Prentice, 373
Garvey, Marcus, 13, 90, 293–95
Gee, Sammy, 252
George, Thomas, 51
George, Walter, 135
Georgetown University, 442, 448
George Washington University, 123
Georgia Tech University, 123, 283–84
Germany, 185, 272, 314, 350
Gibson, Althea, 447, 457
Gibson, Bob, 357, 423
Gibson, Josh, 207, 431
Gilbert, Dan, 586, 589–91
Gilbert, Doug, 299
Gill, Turner, 560, 565, 567, 570, 575
Gillam, Horace, 139
Gillis, William, 3
Gingrich, Newt, 490
Gitlin, Todd, 374, 445
Glick, Shav, 192
Glickman, Bernard, 317
Goldstein, Warren, 524
Goldwater, Barry, 256
Goodell, Roger, 16, 535
Goodman, Ellen, 449
Governali, Paul, 133

Graham, Frank, 162
Grange, Red, 124, 128, 132, 122, 136, 183
Granger, Lester, 101
Grant, Bud, 134
Graves, Earl, 593
Great Society, 471
Green Bay Packers, 129, 348, 371, 507
Greenberg, Hank, 96, 398, 417
Greenwich CT, 589
Grier, Bobby, 283–84
Griffey, Ken, Jr., 531
Griffin, Marvin, 283–84
Griffith, Clark, 206–8
Griffith Stadium, 208
Grimsley, Jason, 524
Grimsley, Will, 339–40
Gross, Milt, 312, 397
Groux, Henry, 475
Gumbel, Bryant, 458
Gurden AR, 102
Guterson, David, 364

Haiman, Robert, 454
Halas, George, 120, 122, 129, 131, 181
Hall, Liz, 456
Hall, Stuart, 27
Hanfstaengl, Ernest, 65
Hanley, Dick, 134
Hannity, Sean, 590
Harding, Hallie, 137, 171, 176–77, 175–77,
    179–82, 185–86, 188, 191–93
Hardy, Jim, 190
Harlem Brown Bombers, 179
Harlem NY, 87–88, 118, 256, 341
Harmon, Tom, 128, 190
Harris, Homer, 124
Harris, John, 364
Harris, Othello, 56–57, 473
Hart, Gary, 450
Hartford CT, 316

Hartmann, Douglas, 5, 337–38, 402
Hartsock, John, 21
Harvard University, 62, 273, 334, 337, 342, 586
Hastie, William, 92, 120
Havana, Cuba, 38
Heisman Trophy, 270, 357
Henie, Sonja, 95
Hertz, Douglas, 202
Hicks, Tom, 526
Higby, Kirby, 246–47
Hill, Charles, 190
Hill, Herman, 137, 170–71, 175–77, 179–82, 186, 188, 192–93
Hirshon, Hal, 172
Hitler, Adolf, 52, 55, 57, 61–62, 65, 69–71, 90–91
Hoggard, Dennis, 273–75
Holland, Jerome "Brud," 125–30
Hollywood CA, 89
Holmes, John Haynes, 98
Holmes, Michelle, 257
Holmes, Tommy, 154, 156, 161
Holtzman, Jerome, 244
Homestead Grays, 207
Honolulu Bears, 127
hooks, bell, 471, 474, 483
Hope, Bob, 134
Hopkins, Harry, 126
Hopp, Harry, 133, 136
Horkan, George, 103–4
Horner, Jack, 212
Horton, Willie, 483
Houston Astrodome, 316–16
Houston Astros, 524
Houston TX, 4
Howard, Ryan, 531
Howlett, Michael, 302
Hudson, Rock, 446
Hughes, Langston, 89

Hunt, Richard, 153
Hunter, Bob, 172
Husar, John, 427
Hutchison, Phillip, 10
Hutchison, Ralph, 267–68, 278–79
Hutchinson KS, 101

Illinois State Athletic Commission, 302–5
Indiana University, 123, 183,
Indianapolis Colts, 523
Industrial Revolution, 491
I Never Had It Made (Robinson), 245, 387
International League, 205, 218, 222, 238
International News Service, 202
International Olympic Committee, 334, 337, 342, 584
Iowa State University, 560
Irvin, Michael, 508
Irvin, Monte, 428
Ives-Quinn, 217–18

Jackie Robinson: My Own Story (Robinson), 238, 244
Jackson, C. D., 335
Jackson, Jesse, 430, 590–91
Jackson, Marion, 311
Jackson, Peter, 481
Jackson, Stonewall, 458
Jackson, Tom, 508
Jackson (TN) Sun, 211
Jacksonville FL, 158, 160–62, 309–10
Jacox, Carl, 299
James, Jerome, 348
James, Larry, 338
James, LeBron, 5, 10, 16–17, 582, 585–87, 589–92, 594, 596
Jefferies, James, 3, 5, 10, 19, 24–35, 38, 40
Jefferson, Bernie, 123, 139
Jenkins, Dan, 362

Jersey City NJ, 222
Jessup, Roger, 179
Jet magazine, 543
Johnson, Barbara, 468
Johnson, "Cookie," 488
Johnson, Jack, 1-4, 9-10, 17, 19-40, 87, 90, 200, 222, 387, 482
Johnson, Joe, 161
Johnson, Larry, 404
Johnson, Magic, 446, 451, 456, 474-75, 488
Johnson, Robert Walker, 447
Jones, Bobby, 423
Jones, Bomani, 591
Jones, Chipper, 530
Jones, Edgar "Special Delivery," 133
Jordan, Doloris, 476, 488
Jordan, James, 476, 486-88, 494
Jordan, Jasmine, 494
Jordan, Juanita, 486-89
Jordan, Michael, 5, 10, 16, 457, 468-81, 490, 492-96, 587, 595
Jordan, Vernon, 431
Juzwick, Steve, 133, 136

Kalb, Elliott, 446
Kammen, Michael, 201
Kansas City MO, 38, 308
Katkov, Norman, 56, 59
Kay, Michael, 530
Kelley, William, 200
Kellner, Douglas, 5
Kemp, Ray, 118, 121, 129, 170
Kennedy, Robert F., 333, 402, 447
Kansas City Monarchs, 205-7, 238
Kansas City Royals, 517
Kentucky State University, 129
Keough, Hugh, 32
Kerner, Otto, 299, 302-4
Kerner Commission, 358, 377

Ketchel, Stanley, 38
Kidd Field (UTEP), 277
King, Billie Jean, 450
King, C. Richard, 515
King, Dolly, 139
King, Martin Luther, Jr., 6, 177, 242-43, 295, 333, 336, 357, 402, 430-31, 447, 584, 591, 597
Kinnock, Nile, 128
Kipke, Harry, 122-23
Kipling, Rudyard, 60
Kirkpatrick, Curry, 488
Klibanoff, Hank, 8, 387
Knisley, Michael, 529
Koppett, Leonard, 386, 394-95
Kornheiser, Tony, 451-52, 525
Korr, Charles, 386, 396-97
Koufax, Sandy, 423
Kraenzlein, A. E., 71, 74
Kuechle, Oliver, 347
Kuhn, Bowie, 391, 399, 410, 426-28
Kurlansky, Mark, 338
Kurtz, Howard, 455

Lacy, Sam, 8, 150, 155-56, 218, 241, 243, 425
Lafayette AL, 87
Lafayette College, 267-68, 278-79
LaGuardia, Fiorello H. 102, 202
Lamb, Ralph, 317
Lapchick, Richard, 448, 591-92
Lardner, John, 23, 31
Lash, Don, 63
Lassiter, Matthew, 403-4
Las Vegas, Nevada, 35, 316
Laucella, Pamela, 10, 15
Lawrence, Charles, III, 523
Lawton (OK) Constitution, 393
Laxalt, Paul, 317
Leahy, Frank, 130, 272
Leas, Mary, 426

Lee, Robert E., 458

Lee, Spike, 592, 595

LeGair, Teresa, 594

Lemmens, Tuffy, 134

Levinthal, D. H., 189

Levitt, Ed, 395

Lewis, Alfred Henry, 31

Lewis, Arthur, 425

Lewis, John, 295

Lewis, Wooley, 277

Life magazine, 365–66

Lillard, Joe, 118–19, 121, 129, 170, 186

Limbaugh, Rush, 15, 501–13, 516–17, 590

Lincoln, Abraham, 120, 159, 215

Lindbergh, Charles, 19

Lipper, Bob, 450–52

Lipsitz, George, 516, 527

Lipsyte, Robert, 312–13, 395, 451, 453

Liston, Sonny, 217, 308–9

Literary Digest, 89

Little Rock AR, 364

Locke, Hugh, 283

Lomax, Michael, 338, 359

London, Brian, 314

London, Jack, 1, 25, 26

Long, Earl, 285

Long, Lutz, 68, 70, 73

Look magazine, 159

Los Angeles Bulldogs, 135

Los Angeles CA, 102, 127, 136–37, 154,
     171–73, 178, 184, 189, 192–93, 309,
     315–16, 333, 336, 342

Los Angeles (Cleveland) Rams, 12, 120,
     137, 139, 170–71, 174–76, 178–82, 184–
     87, 189–92

Los Angeles Coliseum, 12, 174–82, 184,
     186, 190–91, 193

Los Angeles Dons, 137, 139, 179, 181

Los Angeles Examiner, 172, 175, 182–83,
     185–87

Los Angeles Lakers, 557, 587

Los Angeles Mustangs, 135

Los Angeles Sentinel, 170–71, 175, 185,
     189–91,

Los Angeles Times, 3, 10, 158, 172–74, 180,
     183–84, 186–87, 192, 311, 335, 342–43,
     346, 348, 384, 389, 397–98, 400, 418,
     420, 422–23, 425–26, 428–30, 432,
     459, 595

Los Angeles Tribune, 137, 170–71, 175, 185,
     189–91

Los Angeles Wildcats, 135

Louis, Joe, 4–5, 8–9, 11, 57, 86–107, 184,
     222, 315, 336, 368, 387–88, 432

Louis, Lily Reese, 87

Louis, Marva (Trotter), 87, 95, 104

Louis, Munrow Barrow, 87

Louisiana State University, 286

Louisville KY, 300, 305–6, 313

Louisville Defender, 311

Lowell (MA) Sun, 396

Loyola University, Los Angeles, 279

Luce, Henry, 362–63

Luckman, Sid, 125

Lule, Jack, 22

Lupica, Mike, 526

Lurie, Jeffrey, 502, 535

Lusted, David, 475

Lynchburg VA, 447

MacCambridge, Michael, 361–62, 364

Mack, Connie, 205

Macleans magazine, 449

MacPhail, Larry, 206, 208

MacPhail, Lee, 252

Maddux, Greg, 531

Madigan, Skip, 134

Madison Square Garden, 90, 98–100,
     307, 316

Maher, Charles, 397–98, 400, 422

Main Bout, Inc, 12–13, 293–300, 302, 305–8
Maines, David, 22
Maine State Athletic Commission, 306
Major League Baseball, 252, 257, 269, 357–58, 366, 390 404
Major League Baseball Players Association, 391, 393, 398
Major League Soccer, 559
Malitz, Michael, 298, 310, 317–18
Manchester, William, 76
Mandela, Nelson, 448
Mandell, Richard, 56, 58–59
Manley, Effa, 207
Mann, Arthur, 255
Mann Act, 4, 23, 37, 39, 87
Manning, Eli, 582
Mantle, Mickey, 417, 419
Mara, Tim, 120, 129
Mara, Wellington, 120
Marantz, Steve, 529
March, Hall, 393
Margolik, David, 386
Maris, Roger, 417, 524
Markus, Robert, 395, 400, 428
Marshall, George Preston, 122, 131, 181,
Marshall, Robert "Rube," 117
Martin, Charles, 12
Marzolf, Marion, 53, 59
Masters golf tournament, 588
Mathews, Eddie, 427
Mathews, Ralph, 135
Matthews, Clarence, 311
Mauermayer, Gisela, 63
Maule, Tex, 362
Maxwell, Dick, 393
May, Elaine Tyler, 491
Mays, Willie, 368, 419
McAfee, George, 134
McAllister, Ray, 450–51, 454, 456

McChesney, Robert, 21
McClain, Denny, 393
McCombs, Maxwell, 444
McCormick, Robert, 24
McCoy, Al, 93
McCoy, Horace, 127
McDonald, Mary, 10
McGowan, Bill, 34
McGowen, Roscoe, 255–56
McGuirk, Bernard, 523
McGwire, Mark, 417, 528–29, 540
McKenzie, Bob, 453–54
McLaurin, Kenneth, 488
McLean, Malcolm S., 101
McLeod, Miles, 34–35
McNabb, Donovan, 15, 501–5, 507, 510, 513–14, 517
Memphis TN, 101
Merchant, Larry, 313, 389
Messner, Michael, 445
Metcalfe, Ralph, 62, 71–72
Mexico City, Mexico, 5, 13, 332–34, 341, 347, 360, 386, 582
Mfume, Kweisi, 517
Miami FL, 136, 138–39, 270–71, 280–81, 308
Miami Heat, 17, 585, 589–90
Miami Herald, 304
Miami Seahawks, 136
Michaels, Al, 513
Michaels, William Benn, 56–57
Michaeux, Louis, 245
Michener, James, 376
Michigan Chronicle, 215, 224–25
Michigan State University, 129
Millander, Lucky, 99
Miller, "Buster," 218
Miller, Dennis, 508
Miller, Margery, 105
Miller, Marvin, 391

Millsaps, Bob, 450

Milwaukee Braves, 348

Milwaukee Brewers, 531

Milwaukee Courier, 418, 421

Milwaukee Journal, 418, 420–21, 428, 432

Milwaukee Journal Sentinel, 335, 347

Milwaukee Sentinel, 418

Milwaukee WI, 101, 308

Minneapolis MN, 308

Minor, George Jr., 399

Minor League baseball, 162, 247, 399

Minshew, Wayne, 425

Mississippi State University, 123

Monroe, Al, 119

Montgomery, Lou, 130–31, 272

Montgomery AL, 295

Montreal, Canada, 150, 152, 154, 160, 201, 222–23, 307, 339

Montreal Gazette, 160, 335, 348

Montreal La Presse, 213

Montreal Royals, 7, 139–48, 150, 153, 157, 159–62, 174–75, 200, 204, 213, 218–22, 238, 244, 247, 255

Morial, Ernest, 286

Morris, Carl, 35

Morris, Glenn, 64–65

Morrisey, Chet, 136

Morrow, Lance, 449

Morse, Margaret, 479

Mosnicka, Paul, 396

Motley, Marion, 132, 134, 138–39, 188–89

Much, Joe, 396

Muhammad, Elijah, 297, 299

Muhammad, Herbert, 297, 299

Muller, Eddie, 308, 310

Munich, Germany, 339–40, 350

Murphy, Isaac, 586

Murphy, Jack, 393

Murray, Jim, 311, 343–44, 386, 389, 397, 399, 401, 423

Musburger, Brett, 13, 334

Musial, Stan, 427

Musto, Tony, 94

Mutombe, Dikembo, 596

Myrdal, Gunnar, 8–10, 148, 201, 225–28

NAACP. *See* National Association for the Advancement of Colored People (NAACP)

Nason, Jerry, 347

Nastase, Ilie, 448

National Anthem, 388, 393

National Association for the Advancement of Colored People (NAACP), 89, 92, 96–98, 101, 124, 285, 431, 447, 502

National Basketball Association (NBA), 360, 468, 474–78, 481, 523, 582, 587, 589–91

National Broadcasting Company, 125, 128

National Collegiate Athletic Association (NCAA), 75, 390, 555, 558

National Football League, 117–19, 121–22, 126–29, 131–35, 137, 139–40, 170–79, 181, 185–88, 190–93

National Football League Hall of Fame, 595

National Press Association, 503

National Urban League, 96, 100–101, 131

Nation of Islam, 293, 295, 297–300, 301, 304, 306, 318, 473

Naughton, W. W., 35–36

Naval Air Station (OR), 277

Negro leagues, 135, 204–6, 208–9, 216, 238, 243–44, 255, 538

Neil, Edward J., 98

Nevada State Athletic Commission, 316–17

Nevers, Ernie, 134
Newark Eagles, 204
Newark NJ, 223, 332, 336
New Deal, 120
Newnham, Blaine, 342, 349–50
New Orleans LA, 270–72, 282, 285–87, 363
New Orleans Times-Picayune, 335, 341
The News (Portsmouth, England), 348
Newson, Moses, 31
Newspaper Enterprise Association, 397–98
Newsweek, 365–66, 384, 455
New Year's Day, 267–71, 274, 282–83, 285
New York Age newspaper, 153, 158, 206, 214, 218
New York Amsterdam News. See *Amsterdam (NY) News*
New York Athletic Club, 333
New York Athletic Commission, 317
New York Brown Bombers, 121
New York Citizen-Call newspaper, 256
New York Daily Mirror, 152, 157–59
New York Daily News, 129–30, 152, 155, 159, 161, 298, 301, 387, 392, 510, 517
New Yorker magazine, 385
New York Giants (baseball), 161, 256
New York Giants (football), 118, 120, 126
New York Herald, 1, 25
New York Herald-Tribune, 60, 152, 299
New York Journal newspaper, 24
New York NY, 4, 55, 90, 92, 101, 125, 136, 150–52, 154–55, 157, 162, 210, 218, 309, 316, 333, 376, 394
New York Post, 217, 256, 313, 388
New York Times, 3, 24, 26, 28, 30, 32, 35–36, 89, 95, 97, 99, 131, 152, 157, 166, 218, 253, 255, 312, 335, 343–45, 347, 384, 388, 394–95, 398–99, 401,

403–4, 418, 420, 422, 425, 428, 430, 444, 449, 450–53, 508, 510, 593
New York Tribune, 60
New York University, 123, 130
New York World-Telegram, 152, 301, 303, 310, 313
New York Yankees (football), 135, 185
Nike, 468, 474, 477–80, 594
Nixon, Richard M., 593
Noah, Yannick, 457–58
Nordwig, Wolfgang, 340
Norfolk VA, 4
Norfolk (VA) Journal and Guide, 158, 160–62, 299
Norman, Peter, 335, 340, 344, 348
North American Newspaper Alliance, 397
Northwestern University, 123–24, 134
Notre Dame University, 130, 133–34, 274
Nova, Lou, 95–97
Novak, Ralph, 397
Novitzki, Dirk, 589
Nunn, Bill, Jr., 396
Nunn, William, 129, 139
Nurmi, Paovo, 68, 70–71, 74

Oakland CA, 342, 389
Oakland Tribune, 335, 342–45, 395
Oats, Bob, 172, 174–75, 182, 186–87
Obama, Barack, 535, 582, 584–85, 594
Ochs, Adolf, 24
Ohio State University, 54–55, 123, 132
Olesker, Michael, 449
Olsen, Jack, 362, 364–65, 367–77
Olympia WA, 34
Olympic Games (1924), 68, 70
Olympic Games (1936), 5, 11, 52–56, 58–70, 74–77, 586
Olympic Games (1968), 5, 13, 17, 332–40, 346–49, 360, 365, 386, 513, 582

Olympic Games (1972), 339, 345, 350
Olympic Games (1980), 339
Olympic Games (1996), 339
Olympic Games (2004), 540
Olympic Games (2008), 589
Olympic Project for Human Rights,
    336–38, 348–50
Omaha Herald, 3
Ontario, Canada, 307
Opportunity magazine, 131
Orange Bowl, 269–71, 274, 277, 280–81
Orlando FL, 158, 282
Orndorff, Beverly, 451, 456
O'Rourke, Charlie, 133–34
O'Shanter, Tom, 101
O'Toole, Andrew, 384
Ottley, Roi, 69, 72–73
Outlar, Jesse, 423, 430
Owens, James Cleveland, 54
Owens, Jesse, 5, 9–11, 52–77, 130, 336,
    340, 368, 586
Owens, Mary Emma, 54

Pacific Athletic Conference, 238
Pacific Coast Conference, 126–28, 190,
    278
Pacific Coast League (baseball), 171,
    173–74
Pacific Coast Professional Football
    League, 134–35
Paddock, Charley, 71
Paige, Satchel, 207, 431
Palmer, Jim, 485
Parker, Dan, 159, 186
Parker, Jack, 64
Parker, Jim, 373
Parrington, Vernon James, 201
Parrott, Harold, 124, 249, 253
Pasadena CA, 218, 270
Pasadena (CA) City College, 126

Pasarell, Charles, 458
Paterno, Joe, 448
Patterson, Floyd, 297, 307–9, 316
Patterson, Robert, 100
Patterson (NJ) Panthers, 124, 136
Pearlman, Jeff, 525
Pegler, Westbrook, 9
Pennock, Herb, 248
Pennsylvania State Athletic Commis-
    sion, 317
Pennsylvania State University, 125, 273–
    76, 280, 557
Pensacola FL, 155
People for the Ethical Treatment of
    Animals (PETA), 535
People magazine, 457
People's Voice newspaper, 9, 150, 153, 158,
    161
Pepe, Phil, 312, 313
Perry, Joe, 139
Peters, Jess, Jr., 396
Peterson, Jason, 13
Philadelphia Daily News, 313
Philadelphia Eagles, 15, 16, 501, 510–12,
    525, 536, 542–43
Philadelphia Evening Bulletin, 220
Philadelphia Inquirer, 205
Philadelphia PA, 247
Philadelphia Phillies, 247–48, 250, 383,
    389–91, 399, 403
Philadelphia Record, 217–18, 220
Philadelphia Tribune, 218, 295
Pierce, Paul, 582
Pigott, Bert, 139
Pittsburgh Courier, 7, 12, 128–30, 136–
    37, 139, 150–51, 154, 156, 157, 160,
    170–73, 175–77, 180, 182, 184–85,
    188–90, 202, 204, 209, 220, 222,
    224, 237–46, 250, 254, 256, 258, 275,
    300, 312, 396

Pittsburgh PA, 94, 102, 251, 300, 306, 317, 427
Pittsburgh Pirates (baseball), 212, 387, 401
Pittsburgh Pirates (football), 118, 121, 170
Pittsburgh Steelers, 120
Plessy v. Ferguson, 2
Plimpton, George, 361-662
Policinski, Gene, 442, 449, 452-54
Pollard, Fritz, 118, 121-22, 124, 130, 181, 270
Polo Grounds, 94, 174
Ponce De Leon, Charles, 21
Portland, Rene, 557
Portland Trailblazers, 587
Potter, Bruce, 450
Povich, Shirley, 151, 340-41, 343, 395, 401
Powell, Adam Clayton, Jr., 104, 311, 312
Powell, C. B., 218
Powers, Jimmy, 129, 152, 159, 186
Poynter Institute for Media Studies, 454
Princeton University, 448
Prothro, Tommy, 366
Putnam, Pat, 304
Pye, Brad, Jr., 179, 428, 430

Quayle, Dan, 491-93
Quicken Loan Arena, 589
Quindlen, Anna, 450, 453

The Race Beat (Roberts and Klibanoff), 8
Rader, Benjamin, 269-70
Raisman, Bob, 510, 555
Randolph, A. Philip, 35, 96, 98
Ransby, Barbara, 594
Ratchford, Jamal, 16-17
Ray, Joseph, 372
Reagan, Ronald, 16, 468-73, 490, 492-94

Reasoner, Harry, 366
Reemes, Jackie, 215 245, 247, 253
Reese, Pee Wee, 245, 247, 253
Reeves, Dan, 174, 192
Reinhart, Bill, 133-34
Remnick, David, 385
Reno NV, 30-33, 35
Rhoden, William C., 380, 386, 404, 449-52, 530, 588-89
Rice, Grantland, 53-54, 58-67, 69, 75-75, 125, 162
Richard, Tex, 90
Richardson, Ken, 396
Richardson, Ruth, 451
Richmond, Milton, 392, 424
Richmond VA, 162, 164, 447, 457
Richmond (VA) Times-Dispatch, 148, 444, 450-54
Rickey, Branch, 12, 136, 151-56, 159, 161, 171, 176, 211, 213, 215, 243-44, 248-49, 251-52, 257, 586
Riess, Steven, 592
Riley, Charles, 54
Ring magazine, 90, 92
Roanoke VA, 4
Robb, Chuck, 451
Roberts, Chambers, 430
Roberts, Eugene, 8, 387
Roberts, Randy, 1-4
Robertson, Lawson, 65
Robertson, Oscar, 368
Robeson, Paul, 118, 126, 130, 181
Robinson, Bill "Bojangles," 89
Robinson, Edward "Albie," 170-71, 175-77, 179-80, 182, 188, 192-93
Robinson, Jackie, 5-7, 12, 14, 103-4, 126-27, 135-36, 138, 148-63, 170-72, 174, 176, 185, 189-90, 192, 199-209, 211-16, 218-24, 237-58, 276, 336-37, 357-58, 387-88, 390, 431-32, 447, 524, 586

Robinson, Mack, 68–69

Robinson, Rachel, 154, 250, 253, 255

Robinson, Sugar Ray, 103

Rochester NY, 223

Rockefeller, Winthrop, 96

Rodriguez, Alex, 529–31

Roediger, Dave, 507

Rome, Jim, 526

Rooney, Art, 118–20, 122, 131, 181

Rooney Rule, 102–4, 120, 135, 242, 557, 570

Roosevelt, Eleanor, 96

Roosevelt, Franklin D., 91–93, 96, 99

Rose, Jalen, 596

Rose Bowl, 128, 134, 139, 269, 271, 277

Rowe, Billy, 154

Roxborough, Charles/John, 87, 89–90, 92, 95–97, 104

Rudolph, Wilma, 587

Russell, Bill, 357, 368, 372, 447, 587

Rustin, Bayard, 395

Rutgers University, 523

Ruth, Babe, 14, 417–26, 428–32, 524

Ryan, Joan, 449

Ryan, Pat, 363

Sanderson, Jimmy, 16

San Diego Gunners, 135

Sanford, J. Curtis, 271

Sanford FL, 155–57

San Francisco CA, 24, 30, 136, 315, 526–27

San Francisco Chronicle, 315

San Francisco Clippers, 134

San Francisco Examiner, 24, 26–27, 31–32, 35, 38, 308, 335, 342

San Francisco 49ers, 139

San Jose Mercury News, 335, 341, 344, 346, 348

San Jose State College, 332, 337, 341, 360

Saturday Evening Post, 256

Saturday Review of Literature, 223

Saunders, John, 530

Savannah GA, 162, 390

Sawyer, Diane, 480

Schiprowski, Claus, 340

Schlabach, Mark, 561

Schlissler, Paul, 119

Schmeling, Max, 87–88, 90–91, 105

Schmidt, Freddie, 250

Schoenwald, Irving, 303

Schramm, Tex, 120, 170

Schudson, Michael, 21–22

Seagren, Bob, 340, 342, 346

Seaver, Tom, 423

Segal, Jonathan, 399

Seibel, John, 526

Selig, Bud, 525

Selma AL, 358

Sequin, Ed, 309

Shafer, Raymond, 317

Sharpton, Al, 502

Shaughnessy, Frank, 219

Shaw, Donald, 444

Sheehan, Joseph, 344

Sheffield, Gary, 524

Sheridan, Chris, 591

Shibe Park (Philadelphia), 248

Short, Bob, 399–400

Showell, Dave, 267–68, 278

Sidat-Singh, Wilmeth, 125–26

Simmons, Don, 124

Simmons, Oze, 124, 129–30

Simon, Abe, 94, 100

Simon, Corey, 512

Simon, Louie, 523

Simons, William, 6, 8, 240

Simpson, O. J., 357, 469, 526

Siragusa, Arthur, 302

Slater, Duke, 117, 129–30, 181

Smith, Bill, 401

Smith, Doug, 442–43, 452–55, 457, 459

Smith, Earl 595

Smith, Jack, 155

Smith, Maureen, 14

Smith, Red, 152, 162, 299, 301, 383, 386, 388–89, 394, 399, 401, 422, 427

Smith, Reed, 14

Smith, Stan, 450, 458

Smith, Ted, 455

Smith, Thomas, 11

Smith, Wendell, 7, 8, 128, 136–37, 139, 150–53, 156, 158–59, 162, 175–76, 185, 188, 190–91, 193, 237–46, 248–58

Smythe, Conn, 307

Snyder, Bob, 137, 175

Snyder, Brad, 386, 391

Snyder, Jimmy "The Greek," 483

Snyder, Thomas, 54

Sokol, Jason, 404

Soldier Field, 129

Solem, Ossie, 123–25

Sosa, Sammy, 417, 531, 540

Southeastern Conference, 376

Southern Christian Leadership Council, 295–96

Southern Methodist University, 127, 130, 271, 273–75

Southwest Conference, 272, 276, 283

Spandler, Art, 389

Spartanburg (SC) Herald-Journal, 211

Spink, J. Taylor, 151, 346

Spivey, Donald, 56, 361–62

Sporting News, 150–52, 156–57, 212–13, 216, 218, 221, 255–56, 359, 384, 387, 389, 390, 394, 398, 449, 529, 535

Sport magazine, 59, 255, 384, 400

Sports Illustrated, 14, 343, 357–77, 384, 390, 398, 538

sportswriters and sportscasters, 1, 5, 7–15, 21, 52–53, 57, 59–62, 65–69, 71, 73–77, 119, 124–37, 139–40, 149–63, 170–93, 200–227, 237–58, 271–72, 275–76, 280–81, 294, 299, 301, 303, 306–8, 310–15, 334–50, 357–77, 383–90, 392–401, 403–5, 417–18, 420–33, 442–56, 458–60, 476, 482–83, 501–3, 506, 508, 510–13, 522–31, 535, 538–43, 545–46, 560–61, 585–85, 587–93, 595–97

Stanford University, 127

Stanky, Eddie, 245–47

Stark, Jason, 528

Stein, Jule, 100

Stephens, Helen, 63, 74

Stern, Bill, 133

Stern, David, 475, 478, 587, 589–90

Stevens, Eddie, 246

Stewart, Bob, 310

St. Louis Argus, 202, 223

St. Louis Browns, 252

St. Louis Cardinals (baseball), 251–52, 383–92, 397, 404–3

St. Louis (Chicago) Cardinals (football), 117–19, 170, 373

St. Louis Globe-Democrat, 208, 213

St. Louis MO, 92, 214, 398

St. Louis Post-Dispatch, 203, 205, 214, 392

St. Louis Star-Times, 207

Stricker, George, 340

Strode, Woody, 126–27, 130, 135–38, 172–75, 177, 179, 183–84, 188, 190–91

Stuart, J. E. B., 458

Student Nonviolent Coordinating Committee, 295–96

Sugar Bowl, 269–72, 274, 277, 282–87

Sullivan, Ed, 90, 128

Sullivan, John L., 38

Sun Bowl, 267–71, 277–79, 281

Susman, Warren, 67

Swanson, Arthur, 302

Sydney, Australia, 1, 25–26

Sydney (Australia) Morning Herald, 335, 348

Syracuse NY, 223

Syracuse (NY) Herald-Journal, 223

Syracuse University, 125, 282, 283, 285–86

Syufy, Ray, 308–9

Tangerine Bowl, 282

Taylor, Randy, 69–71, 73–74

Taylor, Robert, 494

Temple University, 124, 148

Tennis magazine, 443

Terrell, Ernie, 12, 293, 296, 302, 305, 307, 308

Tet Offensive, 357

Texas Rangers, 526

Texas Tech University, 278, 280

Thomas, Clarence, 469

Thomas, Frank, 531

Thome, Jim, 531

Thompson, Daley, 484

Thompson, Hank, 252

Thompson, John, 448

Thorpe, Jim, 245–49, 255

Tilghman, Kelly, 588

Till, Emmitt, 431

Time magazine, 254–56, 361–63, 365, 375, 384, 380, 447

Tolan, Eddie, 69–71, 73–74

Toledo Blue Stockings, 237

Toole, J. Lawrence, 32

Topping, Dan, 129

Toronto, Canada, 307, 317

Tri-City (Paso WA) *Herald*, 396

Triplett, Wallace, 273–74

Troupe, Otis, 121

Truman, Harry S., 268

Tuberville, Tommy, 560

Tuchman, Gaye, 366, 370, 444

Tulane University, 282

Tully, Andrew, 392

Tunney, Jim, 172

Turner, Victor, 27

Tygiel, Jules, 6, 7, 174, 199, 200, 241

Tyson, Mike, 469, 482, 483

Unger, Norman, 424, 429, 431

United Negro College Fund, 375, 449

United Press International, 157, 204–5, 213–14, 223, 303, 312, 346, 392, 424

United States Army, 13, 97–98, 101–3, 221, 225, 300, 306, 385, 447

United States Department of Justice, 312

United States Football League, 136

United States Naval Academy, 123, 273, 282

United States Olympic Committee, 336, 342, 580

United States Supreme Court, 6, 276, 282–83, 285, 383, 393, 398, 401, 593

Universal Negro Improvement Association, 295

University of Buffalo, 282, 560

University of California–Los Angeles (UCLA), 126–30, 134, 137, 170, 172–73, 177, 182–84, 186–87, 189–90, 193, 215, 231, 238, 337, 366

University of Florida, 130, 272, 282

University of Illinois, 4, 132, 134, 176, 183, 185, 189–90

University of Iowa, 123, 128, 132, 281

University of Kentucky, 371

University of Maryland, 125

University of Miami, 271, 274, 280–81

University of Michigan, 54, 122–24, 128, 596

University of Minnesota, 123–24
University of Mississippi, 282, 556
University of Missouri, 128, 281
University of Montana, 128
University of Nebraska, 281
University of Nevada, 134, 139
University of North Carolina, 130, 588
University of Oklahoma, 281, 286
University of Oregon, 118, 276–77
University of Pittsburgh, 130, 133, 283
University of Southern California
    (USC), 127–28, 172, 177, 190–91, 525
University of Texas, 273, 277–79
University of Texas El Paso (Texas Col-
    lege of Mines and Metallurgy, Texas
    Western College), 277–79, 295–96
University of Virginia, 273
Urban League, 431
USA Today, 15, 443, 449, 452–55, 459
U.S. Open, 357, 442, 447
Uvaldo GA, 3

Van Brocklin, Norm, 277
Vandenberg, Wayne, 372
Verducci, Tom, 530
Verdun, Canada, 307
Vick, Michael, 5, 10, 524, 534–41
Vietnam War, 13, 15, 57, 60, 294, 300,
    302–4, 308, 357, 361, 385, 402, 473
Vigdor, Jacob, 517
Virginia Commonwealth University, 455
Virginia Tech University, 534
Volk, Gary, 367, 375

Wade, Dwayne, 589
Wagner, Dick, 431
Wake Forest University, 592
Wales, Henry, 19
Walker, Dixie, 212, 245–46, 249
Walker, Doak, 274–75

Walker, Moses Fleetwood, 237
Wallace, Rasheed, 587–89, 597
Wallace, Windy, 123–24
Walt Disney Corporation, 502
Ward, Arch, 136
Ward, Gene, 298, 314
Ward, Willie, 123
War on Poverty, 471
Warren, Morrison "Dit," 278
Washburn, Patrick, 240, 242
Washington, Booker T., 13, 56, 293, 295
Washington, Ches, 243
Washington, Desiree, 487
Washington, Kenny, 5, 126–30, 134–38,
    238, 170–78, 180–93
Washington Afro-American newspaper,
    14, 155–56, 159, 418, 421, 429
Washington and Jefferson College, 271
Washington DC, 122, 131, 135
Washington Post, 151, 206, 208, 224, 335,
    340, 343, 346–47, 383, 395–96, 399,
    401, 418, 420, 443–44, 449–51, 455, 512
Washington Redskins, 122, 129, 133, 174,
    181, 191, 556
Washington Senators, 206, 208, 349,
    400
Waterfield, Bob, 190, 192
Weaver, Bill, 149, 200, 240–41
Weil, Edgar, 54
Werner, Ludlow, 153
West, Charles, 271
West, Cornel, 481
West Point Academy, 133
West Virginia State College, 243
West Virginia University, 279
White, Derrick, 584, 594
White, Horace, 225
White, Ted, 373
White, Walter, 92, 96–97, 431
Whitlock, Jason, 590

Wickham, DeWayne, 449

Wiggins, David, 200, 218, 239–40, 359–60, 363

Wilbom, Michael, 450–51, 456

Wilder, Douglas, 458

Wilkerson, Martha, 11

Wilkins, Roy, 97, 432

Willard, Jess, 38–39

Williams, Cleveland, 315

Williams, Ed, 130

Williams, Jay "Inky," 118

Williams, Joe, 152, 162, 216

Williams, Lance, 520

Willis, Bill, 132, 138–39, 188, 191

Willkie, Wendell, 92–93, 98

Wilson, Orlando, 302

Wimbledon Championships, 442, 447

Winfrey, Oprah, 544

Winslow, Olivia, 451

Wohlschlaeger, Amadee, 393,

Wojciechowski, Gene, 526, 528–29

Wolfe, Rocky, 118

Woods, Tiger, 588, 595

Woodward, Stanley, 162

Woody, Paul, 454, 456

World Series (baseball), 238, 241, 530

World War II, 8, 53, 86, 93, 99–100, 103–6, 117, 131, 133, 135, 140, 149, 173, 221, 225–26, 228, 241–42, 269, 278, 286, 301, 362, 490–91

Wright, Johnny, 154–55, 157, 160–61

Wright, Stan, 587

Wrigley Field, 254, 390

Yale University, 62, 129, 448

Yardley, Jonathan, 449

Young, Andrew, 458

Young, Claude "Buddy," 132–33, 136, 139, 176–77, 181, 183–85, 187, 189, 193

Young, Dick, 162, 301, 385, 392, 401, 403, 404

Young, Frank "Fay," 150, 156, 311, 367

Young Men's Christian Association (YMCA), 118

Zimmerman, Paul, 172, 183, 342

Zinn, Howard, 201

Zirin, Dave, 526, 531

Zoeller, Fuzzy, 588

Zuppke, Bob, 132

CPSIA information can be obtained
at www.ICGtesting.com
Printed in the USA
FSHW011254010921
84463FS